P9-CDS-902

THE BALTIMORE
PLOT

"He must die, and if necessary we will die together!"

P.

THE BALTIMORE PLOT

The First
Conspiracy to
Assassinate
Abraham
LINCOLN

MICHAEL J. KLINE

WESTHOLME
Yardley

Westholme Publishing, LLC

Eight Harvey Avenue

Yardley, Pennsylvania 19067

Visit our Web site at www.westholmepublishing.com

First Printing: November 2008

10 9 8 7 6 5 4 3 2 1

ISBN: 978-1-59416-071-4

Printed in United States of America

Many years ago, my grandfather, Wesley Seitz Watson, gave me his most cherished possession, Carl Sandburg's *Abraham Lincoln: The War Years,* which eventually started me on this journey. This book is in loving memory of him.

CONTENTS

Maps and Chart

PREFACE

CONSPIRACY. A combination or confederacy between two or more persons formed for the purpose of committing by their joint efforts, some unlawful or criminal act.
—*Black's Law Dictionary*

THIS IS THE STORY OF WHAT HAS BECOME popularly known as the "Baltimore Plot." It is a thrilling story, pieced together from literally thousands of bits of evidence, informed by the letters, diaries, testimony, contemporary newspaper accounts, and other records of eyewitnesses to the events described. These scattered clues, never before tied together to tell the complete tale, have been sifted and arranged, as a lawyer might do in presenting a case to the jury. In this instance, the crime charged is that of conspiracy to assassinate Abraham Lincoln in February 1861.

A word of caution: Those expecting to find a smoking gun in the hands of one of the suspects will be disappointed; no such conclusive proof exists. There is no written agreement among the alleged conspirators, no signed confession. With the exception of the few shadowy characters identified and quoted in the reports of Allan Pinkerton's operatives, none of the alleged conspirators is known to have ever admitted their role in plotting to kill Abraham Lincoln in Baltimore in February 1861. Indeed, no one was ever even charged with the crime.

Our proof, therefore, depends largely on circumstantial evidence, of gluing together what we know with the logical inferences we might draw by examining the alleged conspirators's own words, their habits, their known prejudices, their relationships with other suspected conspirators, and other evidence of wrongdoing tending to show a common scheme. If this book succeeds in convincing the reader that the plot was more than a fanciful rumor, then I have done my job.

Lawyers go to trial with the case they have. It is never as good as the case they wish they had. The available evidence is nearly always incomplete. It is almost never the best evidence. Evidence, other than forensic, comes in two primary forms, both suspect: witnesses and documents. Our case depends on both of these.

Witnesses forget. Memories fade. Being mere mortals, witnesses, like writers, get it wrong, often innocently. Sometimes they lie, even under oath. Within the veins of all people, whether lay witness, expert, or the accused, flow the serums of anti-truth—self-interest, bias, and personal grudges.

The contents of documents are tempting to take as gospel. This is generally a mistake, particularly for newspaper accounts, often sensational stories hurriedly dashed off on the telegraph wires before facts are verified. Some documents, of course, are lost forever or destroyed by those intent on eradicating whatever evidence they contain. Some are illegible. Some are forged. Some, like the witnesses who wrote them, simply record lies or shades of truth colored to the writer's liking.

The same shortcomings are true of the evidence presented here. Worse, by trial standards, it is ancient evidence—over 150 years old for documents recorded at the time—or written years, even decades, after the fact. Because we have no living witnesses, ours is evidence that can be neither tempered if true, nor torched if false, in the fire of cross-examination.

And yet, ours is good evidence, insofar as there is a great volume of it, and much of it is corroborated. Our best evidence was recorded contemporaneously with the events described in the writings of well-informed persons and seemingly credible eyewitnesses. It is evidence written at a time in history when, for the most part, people took pride in what they wrote, wrote well, and verified their facts. They tended, in this author's view, to sign their names to what they wrote with solemnity, as though under oath, to a greater extent than exists today.

It is with this evidence that we hope to better inform, if not conclusively answer, the question of whether or not there was a conspiracy to assassinate President-elect Lincoln in February 1861—the "Baltimore Plot."

The people present during the events described here are our witnesses. Their writings are their testimony. The guiding light of historians serves as our rule of law and voice of reason. You are the judge and the jury. Let the evidence speak for itself, and be decided upon fairly.

Republican campaign banner from the 1860 election. (*Library of Congress*)

CHAPTER ONE

MOTIVE, MEANS, AND OPPORTUNITY

Human action can be modified to some extent, but human nature cannot be changed.—*Abraham Lincoln, Cooper Union Address, February 27, 1860*

I N FEBRUARY 1861, AMERICA WAS DYING. To many, Abraham Lincoln, not slavery, was the cause. A man with virtually no administrative experience, Lincoln had won the presidential election the previous November by garnering a majority of the electoral vote, but less than half of the popular vote. In response, seven states in the Deep South seceded, and more threatened to do so. Also in response, many American cities, North and South, fearing civil war was now inevitable, slid into economic recession.

As if these problems weren't bad enough, Lincoln had another practical, yet very real problem. He needed to get from Springfield, Illinois, to Washington to be inaugurated on March 4. Before his political journey could begin, he had to complete a rail journey of over a thousand miles, cutting through the heart of an anxious America. And on this journey, Lincoln would learn, or at least be led to believe, that there existed in Baltimore a plot to murder him. The information would come from several trusted intelligence sources, including the well-known private detective from Chicago, Allan Pinkerton.

But was there, in February 1861, a conspiracy to assassinate President-elect Lincoln in Baltimore? If so, were secessionist members of President Buchanan's administration, the newly formed Washington Peace Conference, or Congress—men such as the fiery Texas senator Louis T. Wigfall—or even Vice President Breckinridge involved? Might John Wilkes Booth, a Baltimore native, those he knew, Baltimore city officials, or Maryland's slaveholding governor, Thomas Holliday Hicks, have been complicit? Did Lincoln's suspicion of a plot to murder him in Baltimore, whether or not such a plot existed, dictate his war strategy, his cabinet selections, the trust he placed in those around him, or his feelings toward Baltimore and Maryland early on in his administration?

The story that is about to unfold, itself more a journey than a destination, addresses these questions. Let the journey begin.

Years before Abraham Lincoln stepped into Ford's Theatre for the last time on April 14, 1865, he was the target of assassins. Before he left Springfield, bound for the Executive Mansion in February 1861, indeed, even before his election on November 6, 1860, Lincoln was a marked man. As early as October 1860, once the likelihood of his presidency matured to near certainty, Lincoln began receiving vile, sometimes obscene, typically anonymous death threats in telegrams and letters from predominantly Southern posts. Those threats only increased after his election. One chilling dispatch, telegraphed two days after his victory read:

> Illinois and Mississippi Telegraph Company
>
> Nov 8th
>
> From Pensacola Fla
>
> To Abraham Lincoln
>
> You were last night hung in effigy in this city
>
> A Citizen[1]

Lincoln scoffed at such portents. "Why would anyone want to kill me?" he asked rhetorically. With cold, hard, self-deprecating logic Lincoln answered his own question—there would be no point in his enemies killing him, for they might wind up with someone no better and possibly worse.

Assassination was not, after all, the American way. Despotic kings and brutal dictators lost sleep over assassination plots; they had their food tested and their rivals, including family members, jailed or executed. Their paranoia was supported by history and logic. Assassinations of kings and emperors fill the pages of history and the plays of Shakespeare. Monarchs were not the choice of the people. They were not subject to reelection or term limits; they reigned for life or as long as their brutal grip on power choked out would-be successors. George III, for example, ruled the British Empire for sixty years (1760-1820). To end his or any king's reign, his subjects had no choice but to end the king's life or, as America had done, revolt and form a new nation.

American presidents were far different from kings. Unlike kings, presidents represented the people's choice. If that choice should, in the fullness of time, prove itself a bad one, a president might be removed from office for "Treason, Bribery, or other high Crimes and Misdemeanors" through the impeachment process.[2] Even if impeachment was not an option, a poor president, like

Lincoln's predecessor James Buchanan, could hold office for as little as four years. Indeed, no president since Andrew Jackson in 1832 had been reelected, making a single four-year term more the rule than the exception in 1860.

The Founding Fathers' political experiment had thus far proven successful; for eighty years no American president had been impeached or assassinated. For the past two decades, they had been voted out of office, died in office, or, like Buchanan, quietly abdicated by not seeking reelection.

Against this background of history and logic, assassination of even an unpopular United States president would seem an extreme and unnecessary long-term solution to a short-term problem. But assassins are not necessarily logical people. They think in terms of the "glory" of the moment, rather than the ultimate futility of their act. Although no previous American president had been assassinated, none had straddled a divide of discord as deep and wide as that Lincoln sought to bridge in 1860. Many in the South deemed his election illegitimate, receiving as he had less than forty percent of the popular vote. To Southerners, Lincoln was a "sectional" candidate; he was most assuredly not *their* choice. In many Southern states, he had received not a single vote. And although Lincoln's term might end in four years, the impact of that term, if it resulted in the abolition of slavery, or merely arrested its expansion, would reconfigure the social, economic, demographic, and political landscape of America forever.

OF all the threats on Abraham Lincoln's life, none presents with such specificity as to time, place, manner, and persons involved as the Baltimore Plot. There are, however, no courtroom confessions by any Baltimoreans suspected of plotting to kill Abraham Lincoln in February 1861. In fact, the written testimonies from Baltimore and Maryland are in the main flat denials that any such plot ever existed.[3] All eyewitnesses are, of course, long dead; we can use their testimony to support or refute the plot's existence, but the credibility of such witnesses cannot be illuminated under the glare of cross-examination.

Any first-year law student knows that unless there exists either a confession or an eyewitness account of a crime, conviction must be had, if at all, by circumstantial evidence. Such proof often finds its way to the jury through the trinity of evidence popularly known as "Motive, Means, and Opportunity." In a real sense, therefore, it becomes necessary to treat the alleged conspiracy of the Baltimore Plot as a circumstantial evidence case. This requires that we explore the concept of motive. What motive would anyone in Baltimore have had to murder President-elect Lincoln on his way through the city?

Before we explore that and related questions, a brief primer on the legal concepts of criminal intent, or *mens rea,* of the guilty act, or *actus reus*, of the crime of conspiracy, and of evidence of motive is important.

In order to be guilty of a crime, one must be guilty of two things, both proven beyond a reasonable doubt: (1) the criminal intent to commit the crime, or *mens rea*, literally "guilty mind"; and (2) the *actus reus*, the wrongful act of having committed it. The accidental discharge of a firearm that results in the death of an innocent bystander might subject the shooter to civil liability, but not to conviction for the crime of murder; the necessary criminal intent, the "vicious will," is lacking.

A person might come upon a horse tied to a tree and, mistakenly thinking it her own, untie the horse and ride it home. The woman intended to take the horse, committed the wrongful act of stealing it, but as it happens, was mistaken in thinking it was her horse. She too lacks the requisite *mens rea* for criminal culpability.[4]

A man might want to kill Abraham Lincoln, hope for it, wish him dead with all the depravity of a malignant heart, resolve to do it, and fix in his mind how he intends to do it, but unless he takes some legally cognizable step, some action that rises to the level of actually attempting to do it, he likewise cannot be charged with a crime. While he possessed the necessary "guilty mind," he stopped short of committing the "guilty act."[5]

The crime of conspiracy is a special case. The only element of that offense is that two or more persons must *agree* by their joint efforts to commit a crime. Their *mens rea* is proven by the fact they agreed. The *actus reus* is the act of agreement. Thus, for the crime of conspiracy, the proof of *actus reus* and *mens rea* merges into establishing a single fact—an agreement among two or more to commit a crime. The actors need take no steps beyond that. They need not even have the capability to commit the crime. The act of agreeing to do it is enough to be charged. Most importantly, the conspirators need not succeed in actually committing the "target crime," that is, the crime contemplated, which is distinct from the crime of conspiracy. A conspiracy may be a continuing one, in which actors drop in or drop out, and in which the details of the plan change. Conspirators need not know each other or know the parts that other conspirators will play; all that is necessary is for each conspirator to know the purpose of the conspiracy and agree to become a party to a plan to effectuate that purpose.[6] This is because the law recognizes the nefarious nature and implicit danger of conspiracy—that when two or more people agree to do a crime, this raises the likelihood that it will be done successfully. Conspirators support and encourage each other, aid and abet one another, egg each other on, and defend and protect each other and their identities. The facts will show that those suspected of conspiring to murder Lincoln in Baltimore in February 1861 did all of these things.

In life, "motive" is that which incites or stimulates a person or group of persons to act. In law, motive is an inducement that leads or tempts the mind to indulge in a criminal act or gives birth to a criminal purpose.[7]

Simply because a suspect or group of suspects might have had a motive to commit a crime, however, does not mean that the individual or group in fact did so, or even that they could be charged with having done so. A man might have motive to kill his neighbor's dog for keeping him awake all night with incessant barking. But merely because the dog is found dead the next morning, a victim of antifreeze poisoning, does not, of course, mean the man did the deed. There might have been other neighbors, perhaps even the dog's owner, similarly motivated. By the same token, the absence of a rational motive does not necessarily eliminate a suspect. Perhaps the dog killer was a mere passerby, acting on a whim or dare.

And yet, the presence of a motive gives us reason to look. It gives us reason to narrow the field of suspects down from all the people in the world to a manageable subset of those who might have had a reason to kill the dog. We presume that in the main, a killing, whether of a dog or a United States president, is done for a *reason*.

The law is not concerned if the motive that induced the criminal act was based on a faulty premise, although such evidence might help refute that a motive existed. Assume, for example, that the motive for murdering Lincoln in Baltimore was based on the false assumption that Baltimore would then be declared the capital of the new Confederacy and the assassin made its new king. That this motive clearly would have been driven by delusions would not negate the evidence that such a motive existed and might have induced criminal conduct. Taking a real-life example, when a would-be assassin attempts to kill a president hoping to win the admiration of a famous actress, this is still motive to commit murder, though it might also be evidence of insanity.

One final word about motive is in order. Because no one can know for certain what motives course through the mind of a criminal suspect who isn't talking, any effort to prove motive must be viewed from the standpoint that such proof is inherently speculative, based on the logical suppositions drawn from lifeless facts. Moreover, proof of motive is based on certain assumptions, for example, that people tend to act out of self-interest, for personal gain, for protection of property, for security, for status, for honor, for recognition, for acceptance of peers, for sex, for food, for preservation of life, among other motivators. Such assumptions are often, but not always, accurate.

With these caveats and ground rules set, we are now ready to explore whether any persons of Baltimore had motive to kill Abraham Lincoln in February 1861. It is important to understand the historical context of key social and political events leading up to that critical month.

By the time of Abraham Lincoln's election on November 6, 1860, the war of words between North and South had edged to the brink of, and even kicked a few stones into, the seething abyss of bloody conflict. Lincoln wanted desperately to avoid war. He believed that if there was to be a fight, it would not, at least initially, be a fair one. Even though it lacked weapons factories, any significant navy and was vastly outnumbered in terms of white males of military age, the South, in the view of many, including Lincoln, held the decided advantage. The South would have the best military officers; most, including Robert E. Lee, hailed from Virginia. Most of the government's forts in the South, thanks in great part to President Buchanan's paralysis, stood weakly garrisoned. To wage war, the North would need to take it to Southern soil. Defense of one's homeland provides the advantage of knowing the terrain, and those defending a position generally command the upper hand over those attempting to take it.

Lincoln also believed that all human actions were caused by motives and that all motives sprang from self-interest.[8] At the core of self interest motivating the South was the protection of slavery, referred to by Senator Clement C. Clay Jr. of Alabama as "that domestic institution of the South, which is not only the chief source of her prosperity, but the very basis of her social order and State policy."[9] Whether that self-interest took the form of "state's rights" or "anti-abolitionism" or "protection of property," it provided the South with a reason for secession, war, or both. In Lincoln's view, the South had been preparing for war for thirty years prior to his election, "while the Government had taken no steps to resist them."[10]

But while the federal government continued to look the other way, the loud, incessant drumbeat of northern abolitionists had been heard by Southern slave owners for decades. In 1848, hostile feelings of a few in the South toward the Union led Alabama fire-eater William Lowndes Yancey to attempt breaking up the Baltimore Democratic Convention. This effort failed. By 1850-51, the acquisition of territory from Mexico caused even more furor—what would become of people already living in such territories that owned slaves? What would be the status of slaves moved from slaveholding states into the new territories? After all, slaves were considered property, and was it not a fundamental right of property owners to secure for themselves the continued right of enjoyment of their property wherever it might be taken or found? The leaders of the slave power sought to convince their constituency that if slavery could not be expanded into the new territories, it would wither and die in the Old South.[11]

There were reasons for those camped on both sides of the slavery divide to believe that, given the right set of circumstances, one might literally get away with murder to further a pro- or anti-slavery agenda. Consider, for example, the chain of explosive events that began with what is condensed to the phrase "Bleeding Kansas" during the mid-1850s.

Hostilities erupted after passage of the Kansas-Nebraska Act in the spring of 1854. The brainchild of Democrat Stephen Douglas, the act was intended to open the Kansas Territory to railroads connecting the East with the West Coast. For practical reasons, the railroad could not be built until the slavery question was settled in Kansas, through which the tracks would run. Douglas wanted the railroad built, as he wanted his home state of Illinois to serve as its eastern terminus. He therefore needed the Kansas-Nebraska bill to pass in order to pave the way for his railroad.

The law held that Kansas residents could decide for themselves whether to be admitted to the Union as a free or slave state. The slaveholding status of an entire territory, a huge swath of open country, would rest in the hands of a few thousand voters. Pro-slavery "Border Ruffians" from Missouri and anti-slavery northerners from as far away as Massachusetts flocked to Kansas in order to stuff the ballot boxes with their respective votes for or against slavery. But stakes being high, and law enforcement low, vigilantism ruled the Kansas Territory. Free-state men clustered in Lawrence, Kansas, and skirmished with pro-slavery Border Ruffians in 1856. Warrants were issued for the apprehension of the Free Staters, and a federal marshal made a handful of arrests. The Border Ruffians, however, were dissatisfied. On May 21, 1856, they sacked the town of Lawrence, destroying free-state newspaper presses, shelled the Free State Hotel with artillery and, along with the governor's house, burned the town to the ground.

These actions, in turn, led Charles Sumner, the abolitionist senator from Massachusetts, to deliver an impassioned speech entitled "The Crime Against Kansas," in which he derided the "rape of a virgin territory, compelling it to the hateful embrace of slavery." During his speech, Sumner assailed the aging South Carolina senator Andrew P. Butler as a man who had "chosen a mistress who, though ugly to others, is always lovely to him; though polluted in the sight of the world is chaste in his sight—I mean the harlot, Slavery."

Sumner's speech brought violent retribution from Senator Butler's cousin, Congressman Preston Brooks of South Carolina, who beat Senator Sumner nearly to death with a gutta-percha cane on May 22, 1856. Sneaking up from behind while Sumner sat peacefully at his desk in the Senate minding his own business, Brooks inflicted blow after blow, shattering pieces off his cane with each strike, while Sumner, powerful even under vicious assault, nearly wrenched the screwed-down legs of his desk from the Senate floor in a valiant attempt to rise and face his unseen attacker.[12]

The South Carolina congressman felt no remorse for his acts. Brooks declared that he had not intended to kill Sumner; he only wanted to half kill him and watch him live and suffer. He would get his wish. So severely had Brooks injured Sumner that he would not return to the Senate for more than two years, infirm as a shattered teacup glued together in vague recollection of its former self. Brooks would avoid prosecution for attempted murder, but resigned his House seat, only to be reelected by the near unanimous vote of his approving constituents in November 1856. Boasted Brooks, whose friends presented him with fresh new canes to use as he saw fit, "Every Southern man sustains me. The fragments of the stick are begged for as *sacred relics*."[13]

The combination of the pro-slavery raid on Lawrence, Kansas, and the caning of Senator Sumner drove fiery Massachusetts abolitionist John Brown to the brink of insanity. Brown roared that "something must be done to show these barbarians," meaning the pro-slavery element. Late on the evening of May 24, 1856, in what would become known as the Pottawatomie Massacre, an enraged John Brown and his followers dragged several pro-slavery men, including Allen Wilkinson, a member of the Kansas legislature, from their prairie homes and slaughtered them like livestock, cleaving their skulls and slicing off limbs in an act of self-righteous vigilante justice. Incredibly, John Brown would never face a hangman's noose for these murders. His day of judgment would be delayed a few more years.[14]

Iɴ May 1858, the Southern Convention met at Montgomery to discuss the supposed wrongs being perpetrated on the South and the potential formation of an independent sovereign. As early as June 1858, William Yancey wrote to Atlantan J. S. Slaughter, disagreeing that the South could "clean out the Augean stable" simply by overthrowing the democracy, or voting it out of office, as this would only result in "giving place to a greater and hungrier swarm of flies." No, the South had, according to Yancey, but one course:"[I]f we could do as our fathers did, organize committees of safety all over the cotton States, . . . we shall fire the southern heart—instruct the southern mind—give courage to each other, and at the proper moment, by one organized concerted action, we can precipitate the cotton States into a revolution."[15]

Yancey may have done more to elect Lincoln than the Republicans, for he *wanted* Lincoln elected. He was reportedly instrumental in splitting the Democratic ticket in 1860 by helping to put Vice President John C. Breckinridge on the ballot against Douglas. A split Democratic Party all but ensured a Republican victory. With an abolitionist president elected, the South would have its pretext for secession and the cotton states' revolution that Yancey and others of like mind had so desperately wanted for years.

By one informal straw poll, however, there existed anti-secession/pro-Union sentiment in the South by as much as a 2–1 majority, at least in the Border States.[16] In the anxious six weeks following Lincoln's election on

PROGRESSIVE DEMOCRACY—PROSPECT OF A SMASH UP.

Republican candidate Abraham Lincoln and running mate Hannibal Hamlin are shown about to destroy a Democratic Party divided by internal dissension between Stephen A. Douglas and Hershel V. Johnson on the left and John C. Breckinridge and Joseph Lane on the right. (*Library of Congress*)

November 6, 1860, leading up to South Carolina's secession on December 20, several Southern states' leaders, including those in Texas, Mississippi, and Georgia, urged unity on the South's common interests and presentation of common grievances, but counseled restraint on the use of secession as a means to that end.[17]

Pro-Union Southern voices were feeble, however, and ultimately were drowned out by the din and intimidation of the slave power machine and the secessionist leaders that greased its gears. That power base sought to "fire the southern heart," and did so by "coercion, misrepresentation, and intoxication."[18] It leveled incendiary charges at Lincoln—that he intended to wage war on the South, exterminate her institution of slavery,[19] and subjugate her people. A full generation of Southern men of fighting age—ultimately, white males between eighteen and fifty-five years old[20]—was thus primed for war by a handful of slaveholding leaders, spurred all the more by what they perceived as decades of Northerners meddling in their affairs.[21]

Abraham Lincoln's election had been all but guaranteed in the spring of 1860 after the Democratic Party rent itself asunder at its national conventions. Two Democratic presidential candidates emerged, Stephen Douglas representing the Northern faction of the party, and Vice President John C. Breckinridge the Southern, thus fatally dividing the party. A fourth candidate, John Bell, representing the Constitutional Union Party, further complicated matters.

Although he earned less than a majority of the votes, the Democratic split gave Lincoln the most popular votes of the four candidates and a majority of the electoral votes, 180 out of a possible 305 electors appointed.[22] Like other Southern states, many of which cast not one vote for Lincoln, Maryland despised him. In the November elections, of the 92,000 Maryland votes cast, only about 2,296, or 2.5 percent, were for Lincoln.[23] Of the 30,155 votes cast in Baltimore for president, roughly half, 14,950, were for the pro-slavery candidate, John C. Breckinridge. Only 1,084 Baltimore men voted for Lincoln.[24] In several Maryland counties, Lincoln received only one vote; in two counties, he received none at all.[25] One Maryland county, Charles County, so despised Lincoln that it demanded all Republicans who had voted for him—all six of them—to leave the county by January 1, 1861.[26]

Lincoln thought the secessionist leaders would use whatever artifice was necessary to see their cause through, including justifying secession as a Constitutional right, and shielding the traitorous act of disunion by hiding behind the U.S. Constitution. During the height of the war, in a lengthy letter to Erastus Corning, Lincoln wrote of the secessionist scheme:"It undoubtedly was a well pondered reliance with them that in their own unrestricted effort to destroy the Union, Constitution and Law, all together, the Government would in great degree be restrained by the same Constitution and Law, from arresting their progress."[27]

By the time Lincoln's special train left Springfield on February 11, 1861, six Southern states had already seceded and Texas had all but made it official. Like a series of tenpins struck, they teetered, then toppled, one knocking over the other, first South Carolina (December 20, 1860), then Mississippi (January 9, 1861), Florida (January 10, 1861), Alabama (January 11, 1861), Georgia (January 19, 1861), Louisiana (January 26, 1861), and finally Texas (February 1, 1861).[28] Other important slave states, including North Carolina, Tennessee, Virginia, and Maryland, though yet standing with the Union, wobbled precariously.

While Lincoln hoped that war might be avoided, many leaders on both sides of the Mason-Dixon line felt it inevitable—an "irrepressible conflict." As with any war, there were key battlegrounds, both geographically and politically, and the most important at the outset were the City of Washington, Virginia, Maryland—and its "monumental city," Baltimore.

If the secessionists could quickly gain control of the nation's capital, they would achieve a decided psychological, if not military, advantage. Washington could then be declared the capital of the new Confederacy. Foreign governments might view the Confederacy as the legitimate government of the United States, possibly rendering aid, as had occurred during the Revolutionary War, or, at the very least, recognition.[29] People North and South who were then undecided, balanced on the fence dividing Union from secession, might tip to the latter. Popular Northern sentiment might swing to that expressed by Horace Greeley, to "let our wayward sisters go in peace."

The key to leveraging control of Washington was the border state of Maryland. Maryland wrapped its broad arms around Washington's waist, hugging it on three sides, while its backside lay snuggled and washed by a mighty natural barrier—the Potomac. If Maryland seceded, together with Virginia, they would capture, geographically at least, the District of Columbia within the borders of two Confederate states. Indeed, as Maryland's governor Thomas Holliday Hicks warned, Maryland's secession was critical to the cotton states' scheme of capturing Washington—the District of Columbia would revert to Maryland in the event the state seceded.[30] People in Washington feared as much. Wrote Senator William H. Seward's son Frederick, "The people of the District are looking anxiously for the result of the Virginia election. They fear that if Virginia resolves on secession, Maryland will follow; and then Washington will be seized."[31]

In order for Maryland to secede, however, its legislature first needed to assemble for a state convention. This required Governor Hicks to call an extra session of the legislature's twenty-two senators and seventy-four members of the House. On January 3, 1861, commencing the last year of his four-year term, Hicks proclaimed that reassembly of the Maryland legislature was being urged on the pretext that Maryland act as mediator between the North and the South. Those Maryland legislators seeking to convene a special legislative session, however, had no intention of mediation. Their real aim was to force a secession vote in Maryland. Hicks publicly sympathized with the South over the North's supposed flouting of the fugitive slave laws. Hicks was a financially troubled slave owner who wanted to keep his slaves at all cost, having publicly declared that he hoped never to live in a state without slavery.[32] He preferred selling Appleby, his 250-acre farm, "desirable as it is, to selling my negroes to pay my debts."[33] Nonetheless, Hicks steadfastly refused to call a special session of the legislature—he had no desire to see Maryland secede, at least not yet.[34]

On December 21, 1860, the day after South Carolina seceded, the editor of Washington's *National Intelligencer*, James C. Welling, informed Hicks that secession leaders in Washington intended to make Maryland their base of operations. Their motive was to "succeed in hurrying Maryland out of the Union [whereby] they will inaugurate the new 'Southern Confederacy' in the present capital of the U. States. If this can be accomplished before the 4th of next March they will succeed in divesting the North of the seat of Government, and by retaining in their possession the public buildings and the public archives they hope at once to extort from foreign Governments a recognition not only of their *de facto* but also of their *de jure* pretentions."[35]

These early suspicions proved accurate. Twelve of Maryland's twenty-two senators, a razor-thin majority, adopted an address to the governor urging him to call the extra session of the legislature. This, Hicks was firmly disinclined to do; he feared that Maryland's secession spelled civil war on its soil, and that spelled Maryland's destruction and ruin. He addressed the legislature harshly, accusing the secessionist faction of blindly following South Carolina's precipitous lead. Maryland was South Carolina's equal, not its subject; Maryland was its own sovereign, subject to the will of its own people. In concluding his rebuke of the Maryland legislature, Hicks accused the disunion element of scheming to push the state into secession, of preparing a list of Confederate ambassadors to visit other states, of drafting resolutions committing Maryland to disunion, needing only the governor to call the extra session so the "aye" votes of a few dozen men could make secession official.[36]

Despite Hicks's resolve not to let Maryland break from the Union, there were sound reasons in February 1861 to apprehend that the state would secede. In 1860, a joint committee of the two houses of the Maryland legislature, both controlled by the Democrats,[37] adopted resolutions to follow other slave states into secession: "We also respectfully but earnestly desire to assure our brethren of South Carolina, that should the hour ever arrive when the Union must be dissolved, Maryland will cast her lot with her sister states of the South and abide their fortune to the fullest extent."[38]

As a slave state, Maryland was obviously unhappy with Lincoln's election. As the head of the hated "Black Republican" Party, Lincoln was deemed synonymous with abolitionism.[39] Maryland depended to a great extent on slave labor to work its fields. In 1860, slaves comprised well over ten percent of the state's population, valued at no less than $50,000,000.[40] Noted one Maryland historian, "Maryland, as an exposed and frontier slaveholding State, had a larger practical interest in the maintenance of the guarantees of the Constitution in regard to slavery than South Carolina, Georgia, Alabama, and Mississippi put together."[41]

In the prewar sorting of states, Maryland was a coveted jewel both sides wanted desperately to control. Its strategic importance, more than its size, made the state a prized possession to be won and, if necessary, captured. The cotton states wanted Maryland to commit to secession—this would, they believed, cause the District of Columbia to revert to Maryland and would add 120,000 white males of military age to the South's fighting force.[42] The North also urgently wanted to know what it would take to keep Maryland in the Union. If Maryland remained loyal to the Union, so too might other vital Border States, most notably Virginia. In the months prior to Lincoln's inauguration, like eager suitors clamoring for a Southern belle's affections, emissaries from both Northern and Southern states came calling on Maryland's Governor Hicks.[43] Hicks would play hard to get.

On December 18, 1860, Major A. H. Handy, a former Marylander living in Mississippi, was dispatched to Maryland to urge his state's views on Hicks. Handy proclaimed that the reason for his visit was "the crisis in the national affairs of this country, and the danger which imperils the safety and rights of the Southern States by reason of the election of a sectional candidate to the office of President of the United States, and upon a platform of principles destructive of our constitutional rights, which calls for prompt and decisive action for the purpose of protection and future security."[44] Translation: *Lincoln's election dooms slavery; drastic and immediate measures are required to stop him.*

Handy, however, received a mild rebuff from Governor Hicks, who refused to see him officially. In Hicks's view, the Constitution prohibited any "league" between the states without the consent of Congress. Hicks agreed only to an unofficial, albeit lengthy, visit with Handy. Perhaps in an effort to intimidate the coy governor into secession, Handy assured Hicks that Lincoln would never be inaugurated.[45] Before returning to Mississippi, Handy addressed a group at the Maryland Institute Building, in which he exhorted Maryland to immediately leave the Union.[46]

When Mississippi seceded from the Union on January 9, 1861,[47] its governor urgently telegraphed the news to Governor Hicks. The Maryland governor's contemporaneous response provides perhaps the best evidence of his innermost feelings about secession. On the envelope in which the telegram had been delivered, Hicks promptly wrote:"Mississippi has seceded and gone to the devil."[48]

On January 16, 1861, the North came calling on Governor Hicks. Pennsylvania's Governor Curtin sent a delegation including Speaker of the Pennsylvania Senate Robert M. Palmer,[49] a leading Republican member of the Pennsylvania House, and Philadelphian Morton McMichael, the editor of the *North American,* to Maryland. Intent on learning what assistance Hicks might need to sustain himself in the face of secessionist threats, they had come to offer Hicks Pennsylvania's support.[50] The Pennsylvanians congratulated Hicks on the stand he had taken to resist secession thus far.

The Pennsylvania delegation may have spoken to Hicks with the warm, buttery sentiments of a prospective suitor, but Hicks must have suspected that he was being stalked by his powerful, populous northern neighbor. In early January 1861, Pennsylvania's U.S. Senator Simon Cameron, one of Lincoln's rivals for the nomination the previous May, but now gunning for a position in Lincoln's cabinet, boldly challenged the possibility that Maryland might secede and halt Lincoln's progress to Washington: "Sir, the old Keystone has 300,000 fighting men," Cameron boasted. "Should that little craft [Maryland] fall into the hands of pirates, one broadside from the Pennsylvania four-decker will clear the road to Washington. Lincoln *if living* will take the oath of office on the steps of the National Capitol on the 4th of March. My State will guarantee him a safe passage to the White House!"[51]

But Hicks would be neither charmed nor intimidated—he played it down the middle with the Pennsylvania delegation. As he had done with

Mississippi's Handy, Hicks explained to the Pennsylvanians that he could not receive them officially. Hicks's advisors had urged him not to show too much intimacy to Pennsylvania's Governor Curtin. This might be viewed as Hicks's unholy alliance with the "Black Republicans" and weaken the position of conservative Union men in Maryland. Even so, as he had done with Mississippi's emissary, Hicks had a lengthy interview with the Pennsylvania delegation.[52]

In addition to these courting visits, Hicks received other entreaties from governors, legislatures, conventions, and private citizens[53] of other states. That same month, January 1861, New Jersey's Governor Olden wrote Hicks urging him not to succumb to secessionist demands.

Hicks's position in Maryland was, however, most tenuous, and the secessionists' pressure upon him great. If Hicks should yield to that pressure, some believed that Lincoln "could never get to Washington except within a circle of bayonets."[54] Moreover, the secessionists in Maryland had become so embittered over Hicks's pronouncements opposing secession that he feared for his life. Wrote Pennsylvanian Alexander K. McClure to Lincoln concerning Hicks on January 15: "He has been advised that his assassination has been plotted, & is still entertained, in order to throw the government [of Maryland] into the hands of the Speaker of the Senate who is a ranting Secession disunionist."[55]

Thus, by February 1861, Maryland was run by a slave-owning governor with decidedly Southern views regarding Southern states' rights, but whose life was threatened because he held that secession was not the solution, rather, it was a prelude to an even bigger problem—civil war and Maryland's ruin. While Hicks's position on secession might well have been viewed by the Pennsylvania delegation and others in the North as a courageous pro-Union, even pro-Lincoln stand, it was really more of a protect-Maryland-from-death-and-destruction platform—a bunker mentality. But Hicks's views on secession were in reality a nose of wax. Though he now twisted toward Maryland remaining in the Union, Hicks later took a position suggesting that if the people of the Maryland, through special elections, voted to secede, he would not interfere.[56]

One never really knew for certain where Governor Hicks stood. The prevailing, ever changing political winds would be his guide. There is evidence that suspected conspirators in Maryland were angered and frustrated by Hicks's inaction. In fact, the governor's failure to call a special session of the legislature gave Marylanders who favored secession ample motive to take matters into their own hands. No formal legislative ceremony would be necessary to assassinate Abraham Lincoln. And by taking no action to stop Lincoln's assassination, Hicks might not only avoid the need to call the legislature: he might save his own life.

IF Maryland's secession was the lever by which the South might secure Washington for itself and prevent Lincoln's inauguration, Baltimore was the fulcrum. Its railroad depots, including the President Street Station, served by the Philadelphia, Wilmington, and Baltimore Railroad, the Calvert Street Station, served by the Northern Central Railroad, and the Camden Street Station, served by the Baltimore and Ohio Railroad, triangulated to form a major Southern rail hub. Indeed, virtually any trains en route from the North to Washington or other points south were required to funnel through Baltimore.[57]

Governor Thomas Holliday Hicks of Maryland. He preferred selling his farm to selling his slaves in order to pay his debts. (*Library of Congress*)

One of the most efficient means of moving troops in 1861 was by rail—about fifty soldiers could be crammed into a railcar, permitting a train of twenty cars to move a thousand men at a speed of about 30 miles per hour. A mere 38 miles north of Washington, and 98 miles south of Philadelphia, Baltimore was thus a vital travel, and hence, military node. If the rail lines north of Baltimore could be disabled, for example, if the bridges on the Northern Central and the Philadelphia, Wilmington, and Baltimore Railroad lines could be burned or blown apart, this would hinder, if not halt, the progress of Union troops to Washington's defense. It might, for example, force the troops to take more circuitous sea and/or Potomac River routes. Worse, the army might need to resort to far more time-consuming and hazardous marches on foot. In any event, delaying Union troops' arrival in Washington could allow the capital to be seized by Rebel forces.[58] President Buchanan, in the event of conflict during the waning days of his pathetic caretaker presidency, might have declared defeat with the first advance on Washington and sought an immediate truce at any price.

If all this—the secession of Virginia and Maryland, the control of Baltimore's rail hub, and the consequent isolation and possible seizing of Washington—could be accomplished before Lincoln attempted to take the oath of office March 4, 1861, the North might be routed without a fight, its hope vanquished before the first shot pierced mortal flesh, its morale decimated before the first saber swirled the blue smoke of battle. More Southern states, and possibly border slave states, like Kentucky, Missouri, and little Delaware, might, whether by geographic proximity, political gravitation, public furor, or emotional swoon, fall into the lap of the Confederacy. The capital of the remaining United States, now reeling, would need to be moved, possibly to Philadelphia, as General Winfield Scott feared. Lincoln's influence as a "sectional candidate," already questioned by virtue of his having received less than half the popular vote in November,[59] would diminish further still, as he and the Union's political leaders skulked north from Washington.

Of course, the best way to eliminate Lincoln's influence altogether would be to eliminate Lincoln. Removing Lincoln might help further the secessionists' short-term goal of capturing Washington. But Lincoln's demise could do far more. If Lincoln never reached Washington to take the oath, if some fatal misfortune befell him along the way, this might be the final push, his death the final tipping point, to a quick and decisive Confederate victory. Lincoln's assassination, especially if achieved while Buchanan still slept in the White House, might precipitate civil war at a time when the Union was most vulnerable and least prepared to fight it. An angry North might descend on Baltimore and Washington in haste, intent on retribution, but without political backing or sufficient military preparation. As will be shown, there is indeed evidence that some believed, perhaps even hoped, that if Lincoln were killed while passing through its streets, Baltimore would soon have the honor of inaugurating the war's first battle.[60]

Alternatively, if war could be avoided, there would also be an advantage to the South in killing the president-elect. If Lincoln were killed, Hicks and others of like mind might have it both ways—slavery might live, and the Union might be preserved. The death of Lincoln would mean the death of the national Republican Party's undisputed leader. Lincoln's death might herald the end, or at least incapacity, of the fledgling Republican Party itself, along with its abolitionist rhetoric, and might, just might, let the South have its way—at least in a fantastic, fleeting moment of wishful thinking. This and a few hundred Union greenbacks would be all the inducement an overzealous assassin might need to point a gun and pull the trigger.

There is evidence, written in his own hand, that Maryland's governor Thomas Holliday Hicks, while publicly declaring he wanted Maryland to remain in the Union, privately wanted Lincoln dead.

On November 9, 1860, unhappy with the election of an anti-slavery president three days earlier, an election that he admitted to have "done all properly in my power to prevent,"[61] Hicks wrote to his friend Maryland congressman Edwin H. Webster bemoaning Lincoln's victory. Hicks's supporters excuse the letter as either a forgery or nothing more serious than "an imprudent attempt at humor between a governor of a state and an intimate friend."[62] Hicks' detractors, on the other hand, cite the letter as evidence of his wish, even his solicitation, for Lincoln's assassination.

A letter attributed to Governor Hicks in which he suggests that the Maryland militia kill Abraham Lincoln. (*The Huntington Library, San Marino, California*)

Governor Hicks's letter had been written in the context of his temporary inability to supply arms to Webster's company of Maryland militia. After John Brown's vigilante raid on Harpers Ferry in 1859, militias throughout Maryland and other Southern states began arming themselves against future attacks. The Maryland legislature had appropriated $70,000 for Hicks to purchase arms for distribution among the local military companies throughout the state.[63] Hicks's letter, however, suggests that the arms requested by Webster might be used for offensive rather than defensive purposes. In it, Hicks reveals a sinister motive: "Will they [the company to whom arms were to be supplied] be good men to send out to kill Lincoln and his men? If not, I suppose the arms would be better sent South. How does the late election sit with you? 'Tis too bad. Harford nothing to reproach herself for."[64]

As the date approached for Lincoln's special train to leave Springfield on February 11, fears that he might be assassinated before his inauguration or that Washington might be captured escalated, as rumors of ever increasing frequency and reports of ever more specific detail came in.

Samuel Morse Felton, president of the Philadelphia, Wilmington, and Baltimore Railroad, who sought to protect his railroad from Southern sabotage, recalled: "It came to my knowledge in the early part of 1861, first by rumors and then by evidence which I could not doubt, that there was a deep-laid conspiracy to capture Washington, destroy all the avenues leading to it from the North, East, and West, and thus prevent the inauguration of Mr. Lincoln in the Capitol of the country; *and if this plot did not succeed, then to murder him while on his way to the capital.*"[65]

But conflicting intelligence also surfaced. There began to develop some evidence that the secessionists would not, in fact, move on Washington before the inauguration, and that Virginia and Maryland would not, in fact, secede. In early February, after Virginia voted for the moment to remain in the Union, Senator William Seward remarked, "At least the danger of conflict, here or elsewhere, before the 4th of March, has been averted. Time has been gained."[66] But perhaps Seward was being lulled into a false sense of security; perhaps the secessionists's real aim was to supplant one plot—seizing Washington—with another—killing Lincoln while on his way there.

Even before his election, in addition to the anonymous threats against his life he received in letters and telegraph dispatches, Lincoln had begun receiving military intelligence that foretold of plots against him. Wrote Major David Hunter in October 1860 from Fort Leavenworth, Kansas: "On a recent visit to the east, I met a lass of high character, who had been spending part of the summer among her friends and relatives in Virginia. She informed me that a number of young men in Virginia had bound themselves, by oaths the most solemn, to cause your assassination, should you be elected."[67] Lincoln undoubtedly trusted Hunter implicitly, seeking additional intelligence from him. On October 26, 1860, Candidate Lincoln replied to Hunter's October 20 letter, telling him that another informant had reported rumors of army officers at Fort Kearny plotting to desert their post and smuggle the fort's arms south for treasonous ends in the event Lincoln won the election. Giving orders with one hand, while deftly deflecting responsibility for them with the other, Lincoln urged Hunter to dip his toe in the rumor mill's churning waters: "While I think there are many chances to one that this is a hum-bug, it occurs to me that any real movement of this sort in the army would leak out and become known to you. In such case, if it would not be unprofessional, or dishonorable *(of which you are to be the judge)* I shall be much obliged if you will apprize me of it."[68]

That same month, Captain George W. Hazzard warned Lincoln that the army in Washington, with the exception of Colonel Edwin V. Sumner, a cousin of Senator Charles Sumner, the Massachusetts abolitionist, was in the hands of secessionists, mostly Virginians.

Hazzard named names, including General William S. Harney, General Joseph E. Johnston, Lieutenant Colonel Hardie, Colonel John B. Magruder, and Major Pierre Gustave Toutant Beauregard. "All these officers are in intimate relations with secession senators and they are all at Washington."[69]

In December, Hunter again wrote Lincoln, reminding him of suspected Southern plots in 1856 to capture Washington in the event of John C. Frémont's election. The major believed that such plotters now intended "to attempt the same game" with Lincoln. Hunter's big idea: avert the problem by enlisting "Wide Awakes," having a hundred thousand of the political supporters "wend their way quietly to Washington, during the first three days of March . . . taking with them their capes and caps . . . By a *coup-de-main* we could arm them in Washington."[70]

There were, however, others in Washington and elsewhere intent on not letting the capital fall into secessionist hands or allowing the president-elect to be murdered before his inauguration. Chief among them was General Winfield Scott, called from his New York headquarters to Washington in December by President Buchanan. "Old Fuss and Feathers," Scott was an obese, flatulent, tottering old soldier, a Mexican War hero, a Virginian more loyal to country than to the state that sired him. As general in chief of the army, he held the same military position George Washington had. At seventy-five, he was older than the Capitol building, its dome then under construction.

Scott knew that his position was tenuous. At this time, the military force that stood in defense of Washington was laughable, consisting "chiefly of General Scott, his staff and orderlies, and the marine band."[71] He knew not whom to trust among his valued military officers. That some of these men would cast their lot with the enemy, he had no doubt. But who? His own military secretary? (Yes.) Colonel George P. Stone? (No.) Colonel Robert E. Lee? (Of course.)

Plotting and planning occurred on both sides of the Mason-Dixon line in late 1860 and early 1861, with cities, states, politicians, citizens, and military men mapping out strategies, choosing sides, forming, drilling, and arming militias, eyeing territory, and deciding how best to guard or attack it. The nation held its breath.

CHAPTER TWO

ACE OF HEARTS

POPULAR AND HISTORICAL LITERATURE AND FILM have focused on the conflict itself, depicting the Civil War as a bloody, fearsome, regrettable, even noble and romantic conflict within a house divided. Less airtime or attention, perhaps, has been paid to the root cause of that conflict—the institution of slavery.[1] American slavery had been birthed in the breach over two centuries before the war commenced, with the arrival of the first African slaves, brought by a Dutch privateer to Jamestown, Virginia, in 1619, a year before the Pilgrims saw Plymouth Rock.[2] By 1860, that American institution, now 241 years old, had matured into a problem of immense social and economic proportion. Slavery had been a part of the Southern way of life for so long it had become part of its cultural genome.[3] The secession states then owned over three and a half *million* slaves, comprising nearly *forty percent* of their population, and valued at, based on a conservative figure of $500 per slave, no less than $1.75 *billion*.[4]

The historical inertia of slavery made it seem almost as expected and acceptable to Southerners in that era as it is abhorrent and unthinkable to all today. But there were symptoms even during the Continental Congress that the newborn nation harbored a latent, deadly disease. During one debate over how to tax slaves, a South Carolinian complained, "Our slaves being our property, why should they be taxed more than the land, sheep, cattle, horses?" This brought a wry retort from Benjamin Franklin: "Slaves rather weaken than strengthen the State, and there is therefore some difference between them and sheep. Sheep will never make any insurrection."[5] Thomas Jefferson, himself an owner of over a hundred slaves, predicted that the institution of slavery would be "the rock upon which the old Union would split."[6] Although it had not yet completely split, following Lincoln's election, the Union had indeed begun breaking off in sizable, sovereign chunks.

The institution of slavery, the South argued, had been woven into the weft and warp of the Constitution, if not expressly, at least implicitly. At the time of the Constitution's framing in 1789, slavery existed in all of the original states except one. Many of the Founding Fathers were slave owners, including George Washington and Thomas Jefferson. Without actually using the word "slavery," the Constitution had arguably given official approval to it, prescribing representation in Congress for three-fifths of a state's slaves, referred to in the text as "other Persons."[7] The Constitution also arguably formed the bedrock on which the fugitive slave laws had been built, providing that "No Person held to Service or Labour in one State, under the Laws thereof, escaping into another, shall, in Consequence of any Law or Regulation therein, be discharged from such Service or Labour, but shall be delivered up on Claim of the Party to whom such Service or Labour may be due."[8]

Southerners thus argued that the same Constitution that Lincoln claimed to uphold was also the source of their rights and that slaves were, like livestock, less than human and hence property to be owned, enjoyed, and exploited, like a plow horse or a milk cow.[9] What other explanation for the Constitution's prescribing three-fifths of a slave for determining a state's number of Congressional representatives? If slavery was "wrong," the South claimed, then it was a wrong "righted" by nothing short of Constitutional mandate. If there had been sufficient desire to abolish slavery, the Bill of Rights would have been a good place to have done it.

Even sixty years after the Bill of Rights, however, scholars and politicians north and south of the Mason-Dixon slave line knew that a Constitutional amendment abolishing slavery could never pass, requiring as it would ratification by three-fourths, or twenty-five of the nation's thirty-three states.[10] Thus, the very thing that bound the Union together, the Constitution, also bound up within that Union a fundamentally flawed way of life. The nation as a whole could neither live with slavery nor live without it. There was no practical way to unbind the problem. The conflict was irrepressible. The house was divided against itself.

Moreover, the drama had, as the nation sat poised to add Kansas, by now a new free state, and potentially even more free states in the West, risen to a climax. If only new free states joined the Union, the ratio of states supporting freedom to those advocating slavedom might, if the five Border States could be coaxed into freeing their slaves, soon reach the three-fourths needed for a Constitutional amendment abolishing slavery, once the fortieth star was sewn onto the flag. Secession and war were therefore not only inevitable—they were, in the waning days of 1860, imminent.

South Carolina was first to secede. She derided efforts of the North to exert power over the South as equivalent to the oppression of Great Britain over the colonies that had led to the American Revolution. "The government of the United States has become a consolidated government; and the people of the southern states are compelled to meet the very despotism their fathers threw off in the revolution of 1776," went the rallying cry.[11] The argument in favor of secession thus became synonymous with American patriotism: secession was no more treasonous and no less noble than the actions of the revolutionary colonists.

The argument propounded by South Carolina also relied on supposed parallels of unfair taxation. Because the Southern states' representatives comprised a minority in Congress, their numbers were insufficient to protect the South from what it perceived as unjust tariffs on low-priced manufacturing goods imported from Europe, forcing the South to pay more for what it needed, or worse, to buy from the North. The southern states, it was argued, "are taxed by the people of the North *for their benefit*, exactly as the people of Great Britain taxed our ancestors in the British parliament for their benefit."[12]

These arguments, of course, neglect the fact that the original thirteen states recognized that states with large numbers of slaves would have minority representation in Congress. While the South's leaders complained bitterly about the negative impact of minority representation, the slave states seemingly failed to grasp that at least part of this problem was the natural consequence of its own doing—a slave counted as only three-fifths of a person; a free African American, as a citizen, counted as a whole. If the South had been willing to free its substantial slave population, it would have been entitled to many additional congressional representatives.[13] This possible amelioration of the South's "underrepresentation" in Congress was, of course, never considered.[14] It must, therefore, be fairly said that the South had joined the Union with its eyes wide open to its minority representation in Congress. Minority representation was therefore not the real reason for the South's grievances against the North.

The reality was that freeing the slaves would have destroyed the cotton states' economy. The notion that cotton was king stoked the fires of Southern rhetoric. Without slaves, cotton could no longer be king, the king would die or suffer great decline.[15] The South not only wanted King Cotton to rule forever, Dixie taunted the North with its king's supposed might.

Senator Louis T. Wigfall of Texas declared in a long-winded, fiery, arrogant, even threatening speech delivered to the U.S. Senate in two chunks on December 11 and 12, 1860: "I say that cotton is king, and that he waves his sceptre not only over these thirty-three States, but over the Island of Great Britain and over continental Europe, and that there is no crowned head upon that island, or upon the continent, that does not bend the knee in fealty and acknowledge allegiance to that monarch."[16]

Wigfall went on and on, attempting to justify with reason what was undeniably wrong—slavery—by equating it or tying it to things undeniably right—the right to own property, the right to expect legal protections for one's property, the right to employ one's property to useful and economically lucrative service. He blew arrogant, boldly claiming that King Cotton's exports would bestow, in one year, $250 million of imports upon the South, potentially filling her coffers with a war chest of $50-100 million, depending on the war tariff assessed. And then Wigfall grew darkly prophetic and even threatening, declaring, "what tariff we shall adopt, as a war tariff, I expect to discuss in a few months, and in another Chamber."[17]

Louis Trezevant Wigfall was a "tall, powerful looking man with a muscular neck and face," an unapologetic white supremacist, a hot-headed duelist, and a pro-slavery secessionist "fire-eater."[18] He wore his thick, dark hair long, and sprouted a full, bushy beard, and the two conspired to reveal almost nothing of his ears and mouth. But the eyes revealed all. Guarded by heavy lids, they held the penetrating gaze of a man who placed honor atop life's pedestal, a man who would at any slight invoke the *code duello* in order to put honor in its rightful place.

Senator Louis Trezevant Wigfall of Texas. He had a tendency to shoot people who disagreed with him and ran a Confederate recruiting office in Baltimore. (*Library of Congress*)

Prone to drunkenness and debate, at times simultaneously, Wigfall had shot and killed at least one man before. Although the charge of murder against him was ultimately dismissed, Wigfall thereby earned a reputation for violence, as a man with a tendency to "shoot people who disagreed with him."[19]

Despite—or more likely because of—his reputation for violence and fanaticism, forty-three-year-old Louis T. Wigfall found himself elected a United States senator in December 1859. His timing had been perfect; had it not been for John Brown's raid in October 1859, Texas might have shied from the volatile fanatic.[20] But the extremism of John Brown's tactics ushered forth the election of extremist secessionists like Wigfall. Fearful of more John Brown-type raids, the South fought fire with fire-eater.

Though he now hailed from Marshall, Texas, Senator Wigfall was born in South Carolina with a silver spoon in his mouth and the blood of aristocratic entitlement coursing through his veins. The "Trezevant" in Wigfall's name derives from his wealthy maternal great grandfather Daniel Trezevant, a French Huguenot who settled in Charleston in 1695. Here, the Trezevants soon established themselves among South Carolina's "Tidewater aristocracy."[21]

In December 1860 Wigfall was rumored to have devised a desperate plot to avoid civil war by kidnapping President Buchanan.[22] According to the account, once Buchanan turned up missing (or dead), Vice President John C. Breckinridge would assume the presidency. A pro-slavery President Breckinridge might, in the weeks before Lincoln's inauguration, feather the nest of secession. Breckinridge might have rendered already weakly garrisoned Southern forts weaker still and might have evacuated Fort Sumter without a shot, thereby encouraging Buchanan's pro-Southern cabinet appointments, including Secretary of War John B. Floyd, (a Virginian), Secretary of the Interior Jacob Thompson (a Mississippian), and Secretary of the Treasury Philip F. Thomas of Maryland, all of whom would resign within days in protest over Buchanan's attempts to reinforce Fort Sumter, to remain.[23] And, if there indeed existed a plot to kill Lincoln in Baltimore, who better than a pro-slavery interim president of the United States to help see it through?

Even though the alleged Buchanan plot failed or was not carried out, Wigfall continued to play dirty tricks in Washington during the winter of 1861. While yet a U.S. senator, he led prewar Confederate military operations and spied on the Union.

On January 2, 1861, after Buchanan replaced War Secretary Floyd with Joseph Holt, Wigfall sent intelligence and military orders to M. L. Bonham of Charleston: "Holt succeeds Floyd. It means war. Cut off supplies from Anderson and take Sumter soon as possible."[24]

Six days later, on Tuesday, January 8, 1861, Wigfall provided more intelligence to South Carolina's governor F. W. Pickens concerning Union efforts to reinforce Major Robert Anderson's meager seventy-man[25] garrison at Fort Sumter. A steamship, *The Star of the West,* had been chartered to take two hundred recruits from Fort Columbus to Fort Sumter: "The *Star of the West* sailed from New York on Sunday with Government troops and provisions. It is said her destination is Charleston. If so, she may be hourly expected off the harbor of Charleston," warned Wigfall.[26]

The intelligence served its purpose. The next day, when *The Star of the West* attempted to enter Charleston harbor, she took fire from Citadel military college cadets, who shot at the vessel with cannon mounted on Morris Island. Major Anderson, meanwhile, was unaware of *The Star of the West*'s purpose. Orders authorizing his defense of the vessel had failed to reach him. Believing the cadets' cannonade unauthorized, Major Anderson held his fire, to the chagrin of his officers. As if to turn the other cheek, *The Star of the West* turned back; for now, civil war was averted.[27] Equally significant, Wigfall's intelligence likely assisted in preventing Sumter's reinforcement.

Three weeks later, on February 1, 1861, Texas seceded, yet Wigfall remained in Washington. His asserted rationale for retaining his U.S. Senate seat was that Texas had neither officially notified him of the act of secession nor recalled him, and besides, in Wigfall's typically sarcastic view, the secretary of the Senate still called his name, and the U.S. Senate made for "a very respectable public meeting."[28] Wigfall's real motivation for staying where he was not wanted was to frustrate Buchanan's feeble efforts to prevent the Union's wobbling wheels from falling off, to keep tabs on the Republicans, and most importantly, to continue spying and recruiting for the Confederacy.

Wigfall was said to be connected with the armed paramilitary group the National Volunteers, formally known as the "Breckinridge and Lane Club," then drilling in Washington. The National Volunteers were organized in 1860 by William Byrne, a prosperous Baltimore businessman, liquor dealer, notorious gambling-house keeper—and secessionist, to aid pro-slavery presidential candidate Breckinridge.[29] After Lincoln's election, the group's objectives allegedly shifted from promoting Breckinridge's inauguration to preventing Lincoln's. Byrne was also allegedly a member of the Knights of the Golden Circle, or K.G.C., another secret secessionist paramilitary unit. The National Volunteers of Baltimore would play a key role in the plot to assassinate Lincoln. Senator Wigfall knew Byrne well enough to later vouch in a Richmond courtroom for Byrne's "character" as a loyal rebel and, most significantly, as captain of the Baltimore gang that was plotting to kill Lincoln.[30]

As early as February 16, 1861, Wigfall sought, and later received, authorization from Jefferson Davis, president of the Confederate States of America, to recruit a Confederate regiment in Baltimore, where Wigfall maintained a recruiting office.[31]

Why *Baltimore?* And more to the point, how would a senator from Texas have had contacts in Baltimore sufficient to enable him to recruit a Confederate regiment there? And why would he even attempt to raise a Confederate regiment in Baltimore, rather than in his home state of Texas? The short answer is that Wigfall may have been doing more than recruiting Baltimoreans to head south. Lincoln and Northern troops would not be passing through Texas or South Carolina on their way to Washington—they would be passing through Baltimore.

Wigfall's motive for wanting Lincoln, and possibly Vice President-elect Hamlin, out of the way was, perhaps, more well reasoned than any other suspected conspirator's. Wigfall's candidate, Vice President Breckinridge, for whom Wigfall had campaigned the previous fall, carried Texas, but had lost to Lincoln in the national elections. For now, Democrats still controlled the House. Every Justice on the Supreme Court, which had given birth to the infamous *Dred Scott* decision in 1856, was, like Wigfall, a Democrat. But with Republicans Lincoln and Hamlin in office, Democratic control of the government could not last. The Supreme Court's complexion would inevitably change, as one by one aged Democratic justices dropped off, to be replaced by Lincoln Republican appointees. The effect in the Senate would be even more immediate. Once Kansas, a free state, was admitted to the Union, the Senate vote would be deadlocked with thirty-four votes each for the North and the South. Hamlin, the "Black Republican vice president," would break the tie.[32]

Wigfall could not live in a country where his party was in the minority. Where *he* was in the minority. He had but two options: leave the country or change its leadership. If Louis T. Wigfall, an avowed secessionist, was not about to leave the United States Senate even after his state seceded from the Union, he was certainly not going to leave the country, at least not yet. And at least not without a fight.

As bold as they were in threatening war publicly, leaders of the Southern secession movement such as Senator Wigfall were intelligent enough to realize in their private moments that the South had at least one undeniable military weakness—it was vastly outnumbered. By one estimate, the number of white males in the cotton states accounted for but one-tenth of the white males of the country.[33] According to the 1860 census, as of April 27, 1861, the free states held 3,778,000 white males between the ages of eighteen and forty-five, while the cadre of slave states that had seceded through February, Alabama, Florida, Georgia, Mississippi, Louisiana, South Carolina, and Texas, held but 531,000—a lopsided ratio of more than seven to one. By the last year of the war, the Union army would outnumber the Confederate army approximately three to one. Unlike the South's initial reluctance to employ African Americans in the conflict, the North would have fewer qualms doing so. The South's leaders must have known that the same truth at the root of Southern angst—that the South's representation in Congress was seriously outnumbered by virtue of a far more populous North—would, in the long term, ultimately spell destruction and ruin for the South in a long, drawn out military conflict. As John Wilkes Booth once foretold in speaking with his sister Asia, "if the North conquer us it will be by numbers only, not by native grit, not pluck, and not by devotion."[34] But the North could take advantage of its numerical superiority only if was led by a man with the courage and determination to see a bloody conflict through to its inevitable conclusion.

The South's best chance for success, therefore, depended on a quick strike. One with cunning. One like David's surprise slingshot or Brutus's flashing dagger. One that might, though skirting the edges of military etiquette, topple a vast, though divided, house of cards, extracting the one card supporting a massive, but shaky, Union structure. A quick strike leading to sudden victory might result if the South could eliminate the one person with the courage and determination to "put the foot down firmly" if necessary—Abraham Lincoln.

Those who knew him knew that Lincoln was no mere face card; he was the ace of hearts, powerful yet compassionate, a winning combination. He was a leader who rose up in the face of ridicule and acrimony, bolstered by the voice of calm reason and eloquent truth, supported by his carefully constructed words, grounded on his bedrock policies of saving a Union he firmly believed was well worth saving. Even more, it was a Union that *had* to be saved if the Constitution, if the Rule of Law, if the United States' system of government by elected leaders, was to survive.

Lincoln could be forgiven if he took secession personally. The states that had seceded even before he left Springfield had done so in direct response to his having been elected.[35] As the second session of the Thirty-sixth Congress opened on December 3, 1860, Southern senators, unable to even refer to Lincoln by name, nonetheless blamed him for the South's impending secession. North Carolina's Democratic Senator Thomas L. Clingman referred to the president-elect as "a dangerous man" who "declares that it is the purpose of the North to make war upon my section until its social system has been destroyed."[36] Lincoln had never made any such declaration.

Blustered Wigfall, "We simply say that a man who is distasteful to us has been elected, and we choose to consider that as a sufficient ground for leaving the Union, and we intend to leave the Union."[37] Wigfall later said, tauntingly, "You have elected your President, and you can inaugurate him; and we will have neither lot nor part in this matter. . . So far as this Union is concerned, the cold sweat of death is upon it. Your Union is now dead; your Government is now dead. It is to-day but lying in state, surrounded, it is true, by pomp and ceremony."[38]

Democratic Mississippi Senator Jefferson Davis likewise believed Lincoln's election represented the death knell of the Union: "The Election was not the Cause it was but the last feather which you know breaks the Camel's back," he wrote in January 1861.[39]

These pronouncements of Southern leaders can, like dots of suspicion, be connected to present a plausible motive for murder. The South believed that slavery was its right, justified by the Constitution, and that Lincoln represented a serious threat to slavery's continued viability. Lincoln's election therefore provided the pretext needed for the Southern states to secede. If, in response to secession, Lincoln warred upon the South to preserve the Union, both the South's perceived right to secession and its perceived right to slavery's expansion, if not the institution itself, would be threatened.

As the storm clouds of battle loomed, the South's elected and appointed leaders, at both the federal and state level, in the executive, legislative, and judicial branches, and its more established citizens, most of whom were slave owners, many of whom were eloquent, if fiery speakers, and none of whom saw slavery as wrong, in part because the Constitution did not expressly forbid it, used their power, influence, and even tactics of intimidation, to gin up Confederate nationalism, to "fire the Southern heart." They justified slavery under the Constitution. They justified slavery *in spite* of the Constitution.[40] They justified slavery under "State's rights." Most incredibly, these leaders, such as Georgian Alexander H. Stephens, vice president of the Confederacy, actually justified slavery on religious principles. To the racist Stephens, the African race was created inferior to the white race, either "by nature or the curse against Canaan."[41]

Bolstered in their self-righteous views by such absurd convictions, Southern leaders neither saw the South as the source of the problem, nor did they seriously seek a nonviolent solution to it; rather, they blamed those in the North for everything gone wrong. It was the *North,* after all, that had sought to impose its Puritan values on the noble South. It was the *North* that had imposed protective tariffs. It was the *North* that permitted unfair labor in its factories under deplorable conditions that made the South's treatment of slaves, they argued, look humane by comparison. It was the *North* that was failing to enforce the fugitive slave laws and refusing to recognize Maryland slave owner and Supreme Court Chief Justice Roger B. Taney's *Dred Scott* decision. It was the *North* that was trying to expand its values west, into the territories, potentially preventing Southern slave owners from taking their property with them should they choose to move there. Writing of this supposed injustice to a Northern audience in December 1860, Baltimore's "favorite son" John Wilkes Booth declared, "What right have you to exclude southern rights from the teritory because you are the strongest? I have as much right to carry my slave into the teritory as you have to carry your paid servant or your children."[42]

But most importantly, it was the *North* that had elected Lincoln, this sectional candidate, this homely, awkward, backwoods, rumpled, jocular, Black Republican "rail-splitter."

Ultimately, the leaders of the South would succeed in firing the Southern heart, including a vast lower class of citizens whose economic status dwelt closer to that of slave than that of slave owner. Among those whose passions were easily aroused was a fiery Baltimore barber named Cypriano Ferrandini, who plied his trade in the basement of Barnum's Hotel, a secessionist hangout. A Corsican immigrant, Ferrandini owned no slaves and had no more claim to the South, state's rights, or Southern values than a migratory bird. Yet Ferrandini and a carefully picked handful of Baltimore conspirators in league with him were prepared to risk their lives in the name of the Southern cause by murdering President-elect Lincoln on his way through Baltimore.

Why would this "Monumental City," this city of Francis Scott Key, of "The Star-Spangled Banner," of Edgar Allan Poe, of Charles Carroll, the last surviving signer of the Declaration of Independence, of Constitutional signer James McHenry, have sired a band of assassins harboring a motive to murder the president-elect of the United States? Lincoln had not yet taken the oath of office, had made no pronouncements, public or otherwise, of his specific intentions upon assuming the presidential chair with regard to Baltimore or to Maryland or even upon the seceded states. And yet, as the Lincoln Special steamed from state to state, from city to city, on its way to Washington, as the president-elect greeted numerous state and city welcoming committees, as he gave speeches until his piercing voice receded to a hoarse whisper, as he stood without complaint for hours in infernal reception lines, shaking hands until his bony knuckles ached, Baltimore began to emerge as an outlier, a city of questionable—perhaps even sinister—intent.

Ominously, among all the major cities published on the Lincoln Special's itinerary, Baltimore was unique in failing to tender a formal invitation to Lincoln to pay the city a visit while on his way to Washington. Baltimore's mayor George William Brown, an avid pro-slavery secessionist, made no invitation. The Baltimore City Council made no invitation. Neither Maryland's legislature, nor its slave-owning governor Thomas H. Hicks made an invitation.[43] It was as if Baltimore and Maryland's leaders knew that by inviting Lincoln to their house they might draw suspicion on themselves if he was murdered within it. Or perhaps they hoped that if they refrained from sending Lincoln an invitation, he might not come at all.

The only invitations sent to Lincoln from Maryland came from private citizens, generally motivated by the hope of pecuniary gain. One was from the president of the Northern Central Railroad, which was to carry Lincoln from Harrisburg to Baltimore. Another came from the proprietor of the Eutaw House in Baltimore, where the presidential party was to stop.[44] Members of the tiny (one hundred or so) ad hoc Baltimore Republican Committee made a feeble attempt to invite Lincoln to Baltimore, but warned him to keep his head low, advising against making any public display while there. These private, almost secretive, invitations speak volumes. Lincoln was not welcome in Baltimore, and even those few Baltimoreans friendly to him were reluctant to show it. They could be excused for being fearful.

Baltimore had a long history of erupting into mob violence, often in relation to the political process. It had always been an excitable town, one whose passions could be stoked by emotional speeches and enflamed, if not cowed, by mob rule.

For decades prior to 1861, tracing back to the previous century, gangs of thugs had terrorized Baltimore, earning the "City of Orioles," its least flattering nickname—"Mobtown."[45] Such mobs were symptomatic of a once lawless city that lacked the will or the capacity to instill order. To Baltimore mobsters, violence was more than an expression of hatred for anyone who disagreed with their views or got in their way; such violence seemed to be the sadistic sport of a depraved culture that marched to the taunting beat of a malignant heart.[46]

One example from an earlier generation of Mobtown thugs aptly demonstrates the point. In 1812, after President James Madison declared war on England, the Baltimore mob viciously and indiscriminately attacked anyone who opposed the war. In particular, the mob sought to quiet a Baltimore newspaper, the *Federal Republican,* whose antiwar views the mob found repugnant. So indiscriminate was the mob's hatred that it brutalized General Henry "Light Horse Harry" Lee, the father of Robert E. Lee, who had defended the paper's right to publish. A Revolutionary War hero, General Harry Lee had commanded "Lee's Legion" during the Revolution, and in 1799, as a member of Congress, delivered the stirring words eulogizing Washington: "First in war, first in peace, and first in the hearts of his countrymen."[47]

But none of this mattered to the Baltimore mob. Late on the night of July 27 and into the early morning of July 28, 1812, to the sound of a beating drum, the mob marched through the streets of Baltimore harvesting accomplices. The marauding horde trapped General Lee and others, first in the house of Alexander C. Hanson, the editor of the *Federal Republican*, and then in the jail, to which Lee, Hanson, and the others had been taken, ostensibly for their safety. Here, after forcing their way into the prison, the mob tortured and beat its victims senseless, gouging their faces and hands with penknives. While holding them down, the mob pried their victims' eyes open, and dripped hot candle grease into them. One of the thugs tried cutting General Lee's nose from his face, but being an incompetent butcher, missed his mark, inflicting instead a deep, disfiguring nose wound.

Another veteran, General James McCubbin Lingan, would also suffer the mob's hatred that morning. He had survived the Revolutionary War, in which he had fought in the Maryland Line at Long Island, had survived as a prisoner of war at Fort Washington, and then survived the horrors of a British prison ship. But General Lingan would not survive the onslaught of the Baltimore mob. Already beaten, he appealed to his tormentors for mercy. He reminded them that he had fought for their liberties during the Revolution, that he was now elderly, and had a large family dependent on him. But the mob showed no mercy. Even while he stretched out his hands pleading for his life, the Baltimore mob beat General Lingan, stomping on his chest, striking him in rapid succession, one of the attackers complaining "the damned old rascal is hardest dying of them all." General Lingan, Revolutionary War hero, expired on the floor of the Baltimore jail.[48]

The mob threw its victims down the jailhouse steps, where they lay dead or dying in a heap for nearly three hours. General Lee survived, but barely. He never recovered from the attack and was "crippled and disfigured, doomed to invalidism for the remaining six years of his life, wholly dependent on the income of his wife."[49]

A full generation later, Baltimore was still prone to mob violence. A Maryland historian observed that, between 1856 and 1859, "Baltimore had been at the mercy of as brutal and reckless desperadoes as ever defied law and justice in a frontier settlement. Brutal assaults were their daily pastime, and murder was a familiar thing. . . . As for brutal assaults, stabbings and shootings in the open streets, desperate affrays between gangs of ruffians, wanton outrages upon the unoffending participants in picnics and steamboat excursions, they cannot be enumerated. Election days were mere carnivals of unchecked ruffianism."[50] During the 1856 presidential election, "riot, ruffianism and murder reigned supreme; almost the entire body of naturalized citizens was disenfranchised, and thousands of even native-born voters were intimidated from voting."[51] During these elections, eight men were killed in Baltimore and more than two hundred and fifty wounded.

Baltimore had been the site of numerous presidential conventions, some of which, including the most recent Democratic Convention in the summer of 1860, brought heated debate and political discord, if not physical violence. Baltimore was, quite literally, a political battleground.

During this period, Baltimore's murder rate climbed dramatically, thanks to a cadre of turf-battling street thugs, including gangs known as the "Plug Uglies," the "Tub Bloods," the "Rough Skins," and "Black Snakes." These gangs had controlled territories that Lincoln's train—no matter which line he took—would necessarily traverse while passing through Baltimore. In a town rife with political cronyism, some gang members had even won political appointments, and at least one suspected gang member was a Baltimore constable. Such gangs constituted a convenient, ready-made army of assassins. They knew the streets of Baltimore and might be more than willing to kill the president-elect, win some bragging rights, and perhaps earn some pocket change in the process.[52]

Although a new police bill had, by 1860, helped collar Baltimore's mob violence, the beast had by no means been exterminated, and now turned its wrath upon the fledgling Baltimore Republican Party. On April 20, 1860, the Republican State Convention assembled in Baltimore at Rechabite Hall. The group had gathered to select the Maryland delegates to attend the Republican National Convention in Chicago that would nominate Lincoln. The convention was broken up by mob violence, however, and was forced to reassemble in a private house.[53]

A few months later, during the fall 1860 elections, Baltimore thugs demonstrated their hatred to the point of violence upon a small group of Republicans peaceably assembled in that city. On November 3, 1860, two days before the election, Worthington G. Snethen, one of Lincoln's few political supporters in Baltimore, wrote to him of two Republican meetings that had been broken up by violent interference, with tacit approval of the Baltimore police. One of the two meetings, held outside, had culminated in a "Wide Awake" march. Reported Snethen, "Our people behaved nobly in the Wide Awake procession. There were some 300 of them. They walked their whole distance amid showers of eggs, brick-bats, and injurious epithets from the mob."[54] While Snethen hoped the mob's violence might induce Republican sympathy voting at the polls, he worried that such votes could not be cast without further violence.

Most significantly, and potentially predictive of the welcome Baltimore might extend to Lincoln, was the reception the city had given President-elect Buchanan four years earlier. Buchanan, who had not been the city's choice, received abusive treatment as he passed through Baltimore with his niece and nephew on his way to Washington for his inaugural in March 1857. While being conveyed from the depot of the Northern Central Railroad to the City Hotel, "for nearly an hour roughs hooted and hissed him, stoned his carriage, and pelted with brickbats his guard of honor." As a result of the assault, Buchanan lost his appetite, declined dinner, and quickly left Baltimore for Washington. But Baltimore's thugs followed him.

The night of Buchanan's inauguration, a party of Baltimore insurgents clustered at the corner of Pennsylvania Avenue and Sixth Street near the National Hotel and "fired revolvers, terrifying the citizenry."[55] And Baltimore had heaped all this trouble on a Democrat, Buchanan, a man far more concil- iatory to Southern "rights" than the "Black Republican" Lincoln would be.

Critical of Baltimore's hostile treatment of Buchanan, the *New York Tribune,* perhaps facetiously, had proposed "the construction of an air-line rail- way post-route from the North to Washington City, which shall avoid Baltimore."[56] Despite such calls for a railway bypass, by 1861 no such detour had been constructed. If he went by rail to Washington from points north, Lincoln, like Buchanan, would have no choice but to pass through Baltimore.

Baltimore's inclination to hooliganism, mob rule, political violence, and even murder provides what lawyers call "evidence of habit," an established pattern of behavior that can be used to predict future actions. Such habits demonstrate the risk to any unpopular leader passing through Baltimore's streets. Baltimore's violent tendencies do not, however, provide evidence of motive in a particular case of *why* persons in Baltimore would want to murder Lincoln. Uncovering such evidence requires deeper digging.

Of all the major published stops along Lincoln's train route, Baltimore was, other than Washington itself, the only city that held slaves. And it wanted to keep them.[57] Moreover, by 1861, there existed in Baltimore a significant por- tion of the population, by some accounts as many as half its citizens, includ- ing a cross section of the entire strata of urban society, from barroom ruffian to local newspaper editor to city merchant to business executive to high society elite, who favored secession.

Baltimore also harbored a significant underclass of unemployed or underemployed people who were more than willing to blame the Union for their economic woes and whose inclination to street violence was checked, if at all, by a Baltimore police force ruled by secessionists, including its chief of police, possible Confederate spy, future Confederate officer, and future Baltimore mayor George Proctor Kane.

"A tough and determined man," forty-year-old Marshal Kane, a full-bearded, pro-slavery secessionist prone to posing for portraits like Napoleon, with his hand tucked importantly inside his waistcoat, had the stern look of a man unable to take, much less make, a joke.[58] That he had courage and would risk his life to protect the people of Baltimore from themselves, there could be no doubt—as a young colonel in the local militia, Kane had placed himself between citizens of Baltimore and a pair of cannon to prevent them from being fired.

Despite his courage, Marshal Kane had his faults, including a tendency to employ any means necessary to justify any ends to which he was committed. One of those ends was secession. In January 1861, Lincoln received ominous warnings from Captain George Hazzard, the same man who had earlier warned Lincoln about disloyalty among the officer corps, concerning street violence in Baltimore and the inability or unwillingness of Baltimore's Marshal Kane to prevent it.

In his January 1861 letter, Captain Hazzard, who had lived in Baltimore for several years, warned Lincoln about Baltimore in general and Marshal Kane in particular: "I have for many years known Col. George P. Kane, the Chief of the Baltimore police. . . . I am constrained to state that I have but little confidence in Col. Kane's abilities and less in the integrity of his character. Independent of this there are men in that city who, I candidly believe, would glory in being hanged for having stabbed a 'black republican president.'"[59]

In February, as Lincoln's train rolled into one welcoming city after another in the North, into Indianapolis, Cincinnati, Columbus, Pittsburgh, Cleveland, Buffalo, Albany, New York, and Philadelphia, Southern secessionist newspapers such as the *Baltimore Sun* published one embittered account after another of the raucous receptions, the military salutes, the flag-waving parades, the adulation of hundreds of thousands of Northerners for their president-elect. Lincoln's speeches, intended to be neutral on any issues of importance, necessarily contained hints of his agenda that the Southern newspapers seized upon and exploited. The faces of angry Southern readers grew more scarlet by the word.[60]

In 1861, Baltimore was a city in a state of economic flux, if not on the road to fiscal ruin. Many workers were unemployed, businesses were going bankrupt, and by some accounts, people were starving.[61] If Maryland seceded, Baltimore would suddenly occupy an enviable place in the new Confederacy— vital seat of commerce, vital link of the railroads to Washington and points north, south, and west, vital port to the world. Every member of the city's social strata would potentially benefit—economically, politically, and culturally. As Horace Greeley observed:

> Baltimore was a slaveholding city, and the spirit of Slavery was nowhere else more rampant and ferocious. The mercantile and social aristocracy of that city had been sedulously, persistently, plied by the conspirators for disunion with artful suggestions that, in a confederacy composed exclusively of the fifteen Slave States, Baltimore would hold the position that New York enjoys in the Union, being the great ship-building, shipping, importing and commercial emporium, whitening the ocean with her sails, and gemming Maryland with the palaces reared from her ample and ever-expanding profits. That aristocracy had been, for the most part, thoroughly corrupted by these insidious whispers, and so were ready to rush into treason. At the other end of the social scale was the mob—reckless and godless, as mobs are apt to be, especially in slaveholding communities—and ready at all times to do the bidding of the Slave Power.[62]

And so, there arguably existed in Baltimore and in Maryland in February 1861 palpable motives for killing a Republican anti-slavery president-elect: To be rid of Lincoln, the undeniable man of the moment. To glory in being hanged for his murder. To preserve slavedom and possibly the Union in one quick strike. To win the war before it was declared. Perhaps, to save many lives by losing just one. And if that did not work, then to precipitate civil war and Northern disarray. To bring the fight to Baltimore. To simultaneously demoralize the North and fuel the already burning hearts of a fired up Southern populace. To induce secession of Maryland. To capture Washington City. To elevate Baltimore to a position of prominence in the Confederate States of America. To eradicate an inexpedient election result.[63] In short, to have it all, and to have it their way.

BUT what of opportunity? If indeed conspirators lay in wait for Lincoln in Baltimore, their opportunities would be many. They would include the opportunity of advance notice, occasioned by Lincoln's announced passage through the city on a date certain, according to a mapped-out route and itinerary with arrival and departure times dictated to the minute, and published for all the world to see—the perfect recipe for the careful planning of anyone intent on assassination.

The opportunities would also include that of a quarry's overexposure and overexertion—that born of the quaint notion that Abraham Lincoln's riding a train filled with family and friends, including his wife and three young sons, on a twelve-day, nineteen-hundred-mile trip, from Springfield, Illinois, to the City of Washington in the District of Columbia, making frequent stops and changing trains, enduring grueling days, riding in vulnerable, open carriages accompanied by too few bodyguards, making numerous public appearances and long speeches before bone-crushing crowds far too vast, all the while getting too little sleep, was somehow a good idea.

Then too there was the opportunity of serendipity, presented like a bow-tied gift basket. The last leg of this twelve-day marathon was to be run through Baltimore, when both Lincoln and his unofficial bodyguards (there not yet being a Secret Service) would be most travel weary. Worse, this last segment would take them through the most hostile city Lincoln would encounter on the entire trip, a hotbed of secession activity, through its crowded depots and streets, where any number of assassins might lie in wait and escape in anonymity. A sanctuary city for secessionists, even Baltimore's police were secessionist sympathizers; they might feign shock at the crime, but do nothing to stop it or track down those who carried it out.

Despite his political views, of all people, Baltimore's Mayor Brown had the best opportunity, if not the sworn duty, to make Baltimore as safe as humanly possible for the president-elect while passing through. A critical component of any security plan is to *have* a plan. There is no evidence Mayor Brown had one, other than to leave the police protection up to Marshal Kane, who seemed to think little protection was needed, to wait at the Calvert Street Station for the president-elect, and to ride alone with Lincoln upon his arrival in an open, two-seat barouche, with no military escort, over a mile from one train depot to the other, through Baltimore's crowded and famously violent streets.

Noted Horace Greeley, "there was forty times the reason for shooting [Lincoln] in 1860 than there was in '65, and at least forty times as many intent on killing or having him killed."[64]

CHAPTER THREE

THE LINCOLN SPECIAL

Monday, February 11, 1861
Springfield–Indianapolis

ABRAHAM LINCOLN COULD NOT HAVE SCRIPTED a worse beginning to the biggest day of his life. For starters, the morning of February 11, 1861, had dawned cold and gray, and ominous clouds foretold rain, sleet, or snow. Things were no better indoors. At 7:30 a.m., in a hotel room at the five-story Chenery House in Springfield, First Lady-elect Mary Todd Lincoln lay on the floor. Her husband, looking more careworn and rumpled than usual, sat miserably in a chair with his head bowed. His wife was not dead. She was not injured. She was not even ill. Mary Todd Lincoln was merely throwing a tantrum.

And she was threatening to make Abraham Lincoln late for the most important event of his life. He had a train to catch. The train would certainly wait for its most important passenger. But it wasn't just a train that waited for Mr. Lincoln—an entire country, what remained of it, waited for him. In many ways, the troubled states had been waiting years for Lincoln's arrival, like a flock of lost, dispersed, and frightened sheep. The scattered Union could wait no longer.

Concerned over what might be keeping him, Lincoln's friend Hermann Kreismann went to the president-elect's hotel room to investigate. The Lincolns had vacated their handsome two-story frame home in Springfield two days before, commencing the exchange of private quarters and private lives for the public display America expected of its leaders.[1] As Kreismann slowly opened the hotel room door, he saw on Lincoln's face a befuddled look that offered few clues as to why his wife lay prone on the floor. The possible reasons were many. She could not go with him this morning, as she was planning a shopping spree in St. Louis. Washington would see its new first lady wearing the latest styles. Perhaps she wanted her husband to wait until she returned. Or perhaps the superstitious Mary Todd felt the gloom of a raw, gray, dripping February morning held portents of ill fortune, a bad day to begin a new life. Or perhaps she was concerned for her husband's safety and did not want him to make the trip at all. Lincoln had been receiving threats of assassination for weeks.

None of these, however, were the reason Mary Todd Lincoln lay on the floor this morning. Her husband offered the explanation. "Kreismann," the dejected Lincoln confided, "she will not let me go until I promise her an office for one of her friends."[2]

That Mary Todd had resorted to a childish tantrum suggests that Lincoln had at first refused her request. For good reason. He had been besieged with office seekers for weeks, as bold and persistent as they were numerous and rude. Though he would later proclaim malice toward none and charity for all, Lincoln might well have made an exception for office seekers; he found them detestable to a man. "This human struggle and scramble for office, for a way to live without work, will finally test the strength of our institutions," he would later say.[3]

The "scramble for office" had begun shortly after the election, when Lincoln began receiving baskets full of mail, which his secretary John Nicolay opened and read, consigning all the office seekers and most of the others to the purge of the stove.[4] Lincoln suffered everything from oblique, entitlement-laden third-party recommendations for cabinet posts to more humble and direct pleas, such as one for an English servant's position in the White House.[5] And now, even his wife had thrown in with the scourge of office seekers.

Then too had come the unsolicited letters of political friends and others, advising Lincoln on everything from when he should arrive in Washington, to what route he should take to get there, to where he should live while waiting for Buchanan to vacate the Executive Mansion.

But the baskets full of mail arriving for Lincoln also contained numerous other letters far more troubling than those of shameless office seekers and well-meaning, if meddlesome friends and advisors. These letters were hate mail in its truest sense; they taunted Lincoln with threats of assassination. Before leaving Springfield, Lincoln reportedly carried an armful of such letters to a cabinetmaker's shop below his third-floor law office, located in the Tinsley Building at Sixth and Adams Streets, and asked if he might throw them into the stove. The shopkeeper asked Lincoln if he could keep the letters instead, and the president-elect granted the favor.[6]

Representative of the so-called "hot stove" letters was one that simply read:

Abraham Lincoln Esq

Sir

You will be shot on the 4th of March 1861 by a Louisiana Creole.

We are decided and our aim is true.

A young creole.

Beware[7]

Another of the salvaged letters, replete with misspellings and grammatical errors, was more of a warning and a request to be appointed head of Lincoln's security detail than an outright threat:

Lynchburg Va January 18th 1861

Hon Abraham Lincolmn
Springfield Ill.

Dear Sir I have heard several persons in this place say that if you ever did take the President Chair that they would go to washington City expressly to kill you. for your wife and Children sake dont take the Chair if you do you will be murdered by some cowardly scoundrel have you had any application for this post if not I wish you would let me have it—if you take the Chair as the president of the United States but dont you take it. resign. If you don't you will be murdered I write you this as a friend I am a friend of yours please answer this letter so I can know whether I must go to washington City and raise a body of men to guard you.

Yours truly &c

R. A. Hunt.[8]

Letters like these, portents of assassination, must have weighed heavily on Lincoln's mind, notwithstanding his apparent lack of concern about them. And the knowledge that seven states had already seceded on account of his election, thereby bringing the nation to the brink of war, combined with the gloom of leaving his beloved Springfield, made all the worse by the depressing weather, visited a crushing weight of despair on the president-elect this morning. And now there lay Mary Todd, not lightening those burdens, but adding to them. Only after bending to his wife's demands would Lincoln be free to leave on the most important journey of his life. It is easy to assume that he did so; obliging the requests of friends and family was in Lincoln's agreeable nature. In any event, Lincoln ultimately did leave the Chenery House, and Mary Todd did get up off the floor.

By the time Lincoln arrived at the Great Western Railroad depot in Springfield between 7:30 and 8:00 a.m., the weather had not improved.[9] But his spirits would have brightened at what he saw there. In addition to the large contingent that had accompanied him to the depot, nearly a thousand citizens of Springfield had gathered there to see him off.[10] In the waiting room at the depot, a small, one-story brick structure with only slightly more pride than a shanty, Lincoln greeted hundreds of friends and neighbors, affectionately clasping their hands.[11] According to an anonymous embedded reporter for the *New York World*, "the scene at the depot before starting was impressive and touching in the last degree."[12] Journalist Henry Villard echoed these sentiments, as reflected in Lincoln's appearance: "His face was pale, and quivered with emotion so deep as to render him almost unable to utter a single word."[13]

To anyone seeing Lincoln for the first time, his appearance and mannerisms would have seemed odd. His peculiar, awkward gate, walking not heel to toe, but flat-footed. Legs too long for his torso. Eyes too small for his head. Hands and feet too big. But none of these oddities would have seemed peculiar to those waiting to greet the president-elect at the depot this morning. This was Lincoln. These were his people, his friends. These folks knew him well. Only half finished, the hand-shaking ceremony was interrupted by the clang of bells and the chuff of a rushing train.[14] The Lincoln Special had arrived, come to take its most distinguished passenger to Washington.

GETTING from Springfield, Illinois, to Washington by rail in February 1861 was no small challenge, even if one was not the subject of assassination plots. There were no nonstop trains. There was no single railroad that ran the entire way. Indeed, over a dozen regional lines, each independently owned and operated, would need to shuttle the president-elect from one city to the next, changing locomotives and cars at each terminus.

The Great Western Railroad had the honor of carrying the great Westerner himself on the first leg of his trip. Lincoln's train this morning comprised a baggage car and a wooden, flat-roofed passenger coach or saloon, both painted bright yellow and pulled by the wood-burning locomotive *L. M. Wiley*.[15]

The finishes on locomotives of the era were as varied as automotive paint colors and trim are today, but in general, during the time of the Lincoln Special, bright colors, artistic decorations, architectural embellishments, and polished brass combined to create in most engines a machine that was as much a work of industrial art as it was functional. Red, green, and black dominated the painted surfaces, complemented by golden polished brass bells, whistles, cylinder jackets and steam domes. Wheels and cowcatchers were frequently painted red. Smokestacks and smoke boxes were generally black. Scrolls and striping of vermilion and rich gilt lettering often provided decorative impact, and panels painted with eagles, portraits, or other images were not uncommon. Natural wood finishes were also sometimes used for the cab.[16]

Passenger coaches of the era were as utilitarian as school buses and about the same size. They generally carried twelve to twenty functional upholstered seats, with long benches or sofas at either end of the car. A lone stove typically heated the coach, and candles or whale-oil lamps lit the space at night.[17] But the Lincoln Special's coaches were not typical. On this trip, each rail line seemed intent on outdoing its predecessor, fitting out their special coaches like elegant hotels, complete with state-of-the art heating and ventilation systems, tapestry carpets, cut-glass globe candle burners, richly upholstered lounges, armchairs, and scroll-backed reading chairs, fine walnut and ebony center tables, and patriotic decorations in silk and plush lining the walls.[18]

Typically, each railroad maintained its own depot within a given city, separated from the depots of competing lines by a mile or more. Locomotives threw sparks and ash high into the air and were not permitted to pass through the heart of most cities, given the obvious fire hazard they created. This required connecting passengers to either walk or take a carriage from one depot to the next, often through rutted, muddy streets.

Further complicating matters was the problem of rivers. In 1861 there were few railroad bridges spanning the wide rivers that Lincoln's train would need to cross. At Havre de Grace, Maryland, for example, it would be necessary to ferry the train across the mile-wide Susquehanna River. In other places, rail lines hugged the shore of mighty rivers like the Ohio, taking passengers many miles and many hours out of their way until a crossing could be made.

The route Lincoln's train would take to Washington had for weeks been a matter of intense speculation, and the president-elect found he had no shortage of advisors who felt they knew the way he should go, and commentators who thought they knew the way he would go. Wrote journalist Henry Villard, who had spent time with Lincoln in Springfield in the weeks leading up to his departure: "I think Mr. Lincoln's preferences are for a southerly route, via Cincinnati, Wheeling and Baltimore, doubtless to demonstrate how little fear he entertains for his personal safety. But there is a great pressure brought to bear on him in favor of a more northerly one, via Pittsburgh and Harrisburg, and it is most likely that this will be ultimately determined upon. Stoppages will be made by him at all the principal points. He knows that those who elected him are anxious to see how he looks, and hence is willing to gratify this, their excusable curiosity."[19]

Indeed, there had been pressure on Lincoln to take a northerly route, whether for his personal safety, to permit him to solidify his Republican base in the Northeast, or for some imprecise combination of these and other reasons. Some of Lincoln's advisors, however, felt a circuitous northern route would be too exhausting. In a letter dated January 28, for example, Ohio's former governor and newly elected Republican senator Salmon P. Chase wrote Lincoln, saying, "I see that your route to Washington is announced through Buffalo and Albany. Will not this roundabout way involve too much fatigue & exhaustion?" Chase recommended instead that the Lincoln Special pass through Indianapolis, Cincinnati, Columbus, Pittsburgh, Harrisburg, and

Dean Richmond, the locomotive that pulled Lincoln's special train from Buffalo to Rochester, New York, on February 18, 1861. (*Western Reserve Historical Society*)

Baltimore as "the natural, direct & least fatiguing route."[20] But that would have meant skipping all of New York State, Philadelphia, and all of New Jersey.

And even if he took a more direct northern route, Lincoln would almost certainly need to pass through Baltimore on his way to Washington. Lincoln Special passenger Captain George W. Hazzard, well aware of the risks in that city, had advised bypassing Baltimore altogether by taking the Cumberland Valley Railroad from Harrisburg to Hagerstown, Maryland, and then tapping into the Baltimore and Ohio Railroad a few miles west of Harpers Ferry. But while this route might avoid Baltimore, Hazzard conceded that "this plan would be tedious and the crossing of the Potomac more difficult at this season."[21]

No matter how Lincoln and his planners looked at it, there simply was no good way to Washington. The most direct route required passing through potentially unfriendly Southern territory and crossing the Potomac. The most hospitable route, through Northern states, would subject Lincoln, for better or worse, to great public exposure and would be the most time consuming and exhausting. And no matter which route he took, Lincoln likely needed to pass through Baltimore.

Moreover, while the owners of many of the railroad lines that would carry Lincoln were pro-Union, some were not. Chief among the major railroads harboring strong Southern sympathies was the Baltimore and Ohio. The previous winter, not long after John Brown's raid on Harpers Ferry, that line's president,

John Work Garrett, delivered a fiery speech in Baltimore, in which he assured his audience that the B&O was a *Southern* line, with a "disciplined force of 3,500 men" in its employ, constituting "the nucleus of an army" capable of transporting 10,000 troops daily.[22] While it is possible Garrett meant his comments only in the context of defending against future John Brown-type raids, his words suggest a broader, possibly offensive intent—that he was positioning his road and the city of Baltimore for a war he thought was inevitable. Queried Garrett: "During a period when agitation, alarm and uncertainty prevail, is it not right, is it not becoming, that Baltimore should declare her position in 'the irrepressible conflict' threatened and urged by Northern fanaticism?"[23]

Perhaps Lincoln's handlers were wary of Garrett and his road. Lincoln certainly had reason to avoid the line and the territory through which it passed. *New York Tribune* editor Horace Greeley had written to Lincoln in December, warning him "your life is not safe, and it is your simple duty to be very careful of exposing it. I doubt whether you ought to go to Washington via Wheeling and the B. & O. Railroad unless you go with a very strong force."[24]

Even Washington's mayor, James G. Berret, worried about Lincoln's safety in passing over Garrett's road. Ten days earlier Berret had written to Garrett, concerned about rumors that Lincoln's passage to Washington might be interfered with:

> Mayor's Office, Washington
>
> February 1, 1861
>
> Sir: I learn that the President elect, until very recently, contemplated passing over your road from Wheeling to this city, and that, owing to rumored intentions on the part of citizens of Maryland and Virginia to interfere with his travel to our capital, you were induced to make diligent inquiry as to the truth of these threats. If correctly informed, will you do me the favor to state the result of your inquiries touching this matter?
>
> Very respectfully, your obedient servant,
>
> James G. Berret, Mayor.[25]

Three days later, Garrett replied, denouncing the rumors as "the simple inventions of those who are agents in the West for other lines, and are set on interfering with the trade and travel on the shortest route to the seaboard than with any desire to promote the safety and comfort of the President elect." To Garrett's chagrin, plans to take the Lincoln Special over his B&O line through Virginia were abandoned. Instead, Lincoln's planners settled on a circuitous northern route that cut a jagged, bowel-shaped swath through the nation's torso, zigzagging across Illinois, Indiana, Ohio, Pennsylvania, New York, and

New Jersey—the heart of Lincoln's base of supporters. So gerrymandered was the route that Lincoln would pass in and out of Ohio twice and in and out of Pennsylvania three times on the way to Washington. Sour grapes clinging to every word, Garrett complained that Lincoln's safety "would have been perfectly assured from the Ohio River to Washington, had he adhered to his original purpose."[26] Even then, however, Garrett's B&O line could not be avoided entirely; Lincoln would necessarily ride that road on the final—and arguably most dangerous—leg of the journey; the scant 40-mile, hour-and-a-half trip from Baltimore to Washington.

A northern route, although by no means a guarantee of safety, would at least present less risk for the polarizing leader. But passing through Northern territory and major Northern cities might also have some unanticipated consequences. First of all, not all of the Northern cities were pro-Lincoln, New York City chief among them. Indeed, there had been rumors that New York, led by its corrupt mayor, Fernando Wood, might actually secede from the Union in order to protect the city's commercial interests, which might suffer should war break out.

In pro-Lincoln cities, large throngs of adoring, cheering, handkerchief and flag-waving Northerners would certainly make Lincoln feel welcome. But this too had potential consequences. Northern correspondents of Southern, secessionist newspapers, like the *Baltimore Sun*, could report on the multitudes of civilians and military men that greeted Lincoln in every city, and the vigor with which they received their new leader. Such crowds would be a subtle way of sending south the "arithmetic" of Northern support for Lincoln's policies, if not the potential for vast Northern armies. Large Northern displays might also infuriate the South. Many of the cities on Lincoln's route had been visited recently by the Prince of Wales, and in many places Lincoln would even ride in the same coaches and carriages and stay in the same hotels. The symbolism of an American monarch would not be lost on Southerners looking for reasons to confirm their hatred and mistrust of Lincoln. In any event, the route had now been set, the timetables printed, the itinerary published. It was time to board the train.

As Lincoln's friend and bodyguard Ward Hill Lamon recalled, "At precisely five minutes before eight, Mr. Lincoln, preceded by Mr. Wood, emerged from a private room in the depot building, and passed slowly to the car, the people falling back respectfully on either side, and as many as possible shaking his hands. Having reached the train, he ascended the rear platform, and, facing about to the throng which had closed around him, drew himself up to his full height, removed his hat, and stood for several seconds in profound silence. His eye roved sadly over the sea of upturned faces, as if seeking to read in them the sympathy and friendship which he never needed more than then."[27]

Lincoln had not prepared any written remarks for this morning. The press had therefore been given no advance copies of the speech he was about to give. Perhaps Lincoln himself hadn't even known what he would say until the moment arrived. Whether Lincoln had in fact intended to give a farewell speech all along, but only if the moment seemed right, or whether he gave his parting words with no advance preparation whatever is not known. What is known is that the crowd of one thousand Springfield residents insisted on a speech. Abraham Lincoln would not disappoint them. The short address he was about to make ranks among the four or five most memorable speeches Abraham Lincoln would ever give. And it included an oblique reference suggesting that Lincoln knew that his life was in danger.

After removing his hat and asking for silence, from the rear platform of the train, without notes, and from the heart, Lincoln satisfied the demands of the black-umbrella crowd.[28] So somber was the moment it might have seemed as if Lincoln was speaking not at some joyous event, but at his own funeral. His heart was heavy with sorrow and foreboding. It would be reported that "during the speech, Mr. Lincoln betrayed much emotion, and the crowd was affected to tears."[29]

As recorded by Lamon, Lincoln gathered his composure. "At length he began, in a husky voice, and slowly and impressively delivered his farewell to his neighbors:"[30]

> My friends.
>
> No one, not in my situation, can appreciate my feeling of sadness at this parting. To this place, and the kindness of these people, I owe everything. Here I have lived a quarter of a century, and have passed from a young to an old man. Here, my children have been born, and one is buried. I now leave, not knowing when, or whether ever, I may return, with a task before me greater than that which rested upon Washington. Without the assistance of that Divine Being, who ever attended him, I cannot succeed. With that assistance I cannot fail. Trusting in Him, who can go with me, and remain with you and be everywhere for good, let us confidently hope that all will yet be well. To His care commending you, as I hope in your prayers you will commend me, I bid you an affectionate farewell.[31]

Almost immediately, Lincoln's extemporaneous remarks won plaudits as gems of wisdom. One reporter predicted that Lincoln's short little speech "will do more to win the confidence and esteem of the American people for their new chief magistrate, and thus strengthen his administration, than any thing else that has transpired; and will give them assurances that they have been guided by a higher wisdom than their own choice of a man."[32]

After Lincoln concluded his remarks, the small crowd burst into loud applause, interspersed with cries of "we will pray for you."[33]

The anonymous embedded reporter for the *New York World* recounted the departure of the Lincoln Special moments later: "As he entered the car, after a final adieu to Mrs. Lincoln and a few near friends, three cheers were given, every hat in the assemblage was lifted, and the crowd stood silent as the train moved slowly from the depot."[34]

Mary Todd and the two youngest Lincoln sons, Willie and Tad, did not join Lincoln on the train this morning, but his eldest son, seventeen-year-old Robert, did. Robert Todd Lincoln, named for his grandfather Robert Todd, had gotten the best of both parents, and, it seemed, none of their worst. Handsome as a stage actor, even dashing, he looked nothing like his father and seems not to have inherited the heart complications of Marfan syndrome, the disorder some speculate afflicted Lincoln. But Robert had inherited his father's keen intellect, and Lincoln was proud of his son, a freshman at Harvard. Speaking of heart complications, the charming young Bob would break more than a few of them along the Lincoln Special's route in February 1861.

At least one newspaper erroneously reported that Mrs. Lincoln would remain in Springfield until the following week and catch up with her husband in New York.[35] In fact, she had plans to go to St. Louis on a pre-inaugural shopping excursion.[36] In his dispatch of this date, the embedded anonymous reporter for the *New York World* offered an explanation for Mary's change in plans. It had to do with Lincoln's safety, or more to the point, the public's perception of it.

Mary had been induced by a telegram from General Winfield Scott to abandon her earlier plan to follow her husband a week later to Washington.[37] Scott's supposed rationale: Mrs. Lincoln's not being present might be seen as a sign of alarm or weakness, an indication that Lincoln expected trouble on the trip. "So many vapory rumors of contemplated assault upon Mr. Lincoln have been current in Washington for months, that the general may have come at last to regard such a contingency as at least possible," the anonymous reporter wrote.[38] Ironically, General Scott had apparently found the rumors of threats to Lincoln sufficiently credible to recommend that the Lincolns publicly demonstrate no fear of them.

An alternate hypothesis offered is that General Scott felt that Mrs. Lincoln and the boys might in fact provide a measure of protection for her husband—assassins, it was supposed, would be less likely to strike when their victim's family was near.[39]

Whatever the rationale, Mrs. Lincoln resolved that "she would see Mr. Lincoln on to Washington, danger or no danger."[40] She and their two youngest sons, Willie and Tad, planned to join the Lincoln Special in Indianapolis the following morning.[41]

At precisely 8:30 a.m.,[42] and exactly thirty minutes behind schedule, with Lincoln standing in the doorway of the rear car[43] for a last glimpse of Springfield, the journey began. Lincoln rolled slowly away from friends, family, and familiar settings toward a great unknown.

The Great Western's timetable set forth departure times and arrival times for stops. It further ordered that the Special was entitled exclusive access to the road. "This train will be entitled to the road, *and all other trains must be kept out of the way.*" Perhaps reflective of the threats made on Lincoln's life, the time card placed an emphasis on caution: "It is very important that this train should pass over the road in safety, and all employees are expected to render all assistance in their power. *Red is the signal for danger,* but any signal apparently intended to indicate alarm or danger must be reported, the train stopped, and the meaning of it ascertained. Carefulness is particularly enjoined."[44] Perhaps also reflective of perceived danger, J. J. S. Wilson, superintendent of the Illinois-Mississippi (Caton) telegraph lines, with an assistant, carried a portable telegraph transmitter on the train that could be used for emergencies at any point by attachment to the wires.[45]

Lincoln was reportedly somber, even despondent as the train pulled away, headed east, and for much of the ride that morning kept to himself. He might be forgiven this. As reflected in his farewell speech, Lincoln clearly apprehended the possibility that he would never return to Springfield alive. Perhaps in recognition of this possibility, two weeks before, he had begun saying his good-byes, to both the living and the dead. He visited his father Thomas Lincoln's unmarked grave in Coles County. With his penknife, he carved the initials "T. L." on an oak board, before placing the temporary memorial at the head of the plot and giving instructions for a more permanent marker to be erected.[46] In Farmington, he visited Sarah Bush Lincoln, his elderly stepmother who had raised and loved him like a true son.[47] Upon Lincoln's tender parting from her, with tears of grief and worry streaming down her aged cheeks, Sarah "gave him a mother's benediction, expressing fear that his life might be taken by his enemies."[48] Back in Springfield, Hannah Armstrong, an old acquaintance from New Salem, called on Lincoln to pay her respects, conveying her fears that she too would never see him alive again.[49]

On February 10, his last full day in Springfield, Lincoln met with his longtime friend and law partner William H. Herndon. He had an unusual request: to keep the Lincoln and Herndon law firm shingle, "which swung on its rusty hinges at the foot of the stairway," swinging. "Let it hang there undisturbed," he asked, lowering his voice. "Give our clients to understand that the election of a President makes no change in the firm of Lincoln and Herndon. If I live I'm coming back sometime, and then we'll go right on practicing law as if nothing had ever happened."[50]

Locomotives need fuel to keep going, and in the 1860s that meant frequent stops to take on wood or coal for the firebox and water for the boiler. As one noted historian observed, locomotives of the era were "heavy smokers and heavy drinkers."[51] At one of the first stops along the way, journalist Henry Villard of the *New York Herald* telegraphed the following description of the Lincoln Special: "The train is in the charge of L. Tilton, President, and W.C. Whitney, conductor, and moves at the rate of 30 miles an hour. It is driven by a powerful Rogers locomotive, and consists of baggage, smoking and passenger cars. Refreshments for the thirsty are on board. The cheers are always for Lincoln and the Constitution. The President-elect continues reserved and thoughtful, and sits most of the time alone in the private saloon prepared for his special use."

To Abraham Lincoln, a man who clearly wanted some private time to reflect, the rattling, jostling train must have seemed uncomfortably crowded and loud as it rolled across the prairie toward Indiana. For one thing, it seemed as if the entire population had turned out to catch a glimpse of Lincoln's train. Wrote the anonymous *New York World* correspondent, "it has been a continuous carnival; rounds of cheers, salvos of artillery, flags, banners, handkerchiefs, enthusiastic greetings—in short, all the accessories of a grand popular ovation, have been essayed along the line."[52]

Inside the train it was no less raucous and only slightly less crowded. The reports of exactly who accompanied Lincoln when he left Springfield are varied, but the short train, composed of an engine, a wood tender, a baggage car, a "smoking" car, and Lincoln's private saloon, was most definitely full.[53] As many as forty people, including Lincoln's political and social friends,[54] like Illinois governor Richard Yates, family members,[55] including his son Robert, journalists,[56] such as Henry Villard, numerous railroad employees,[57] and his most loyal campaign soldiers, Norman B. Judd, Ward Hill Lamon, Elmer Ellsworth, John Nicolay, and John Hay among them, were on board. Most prominent among Lincoln's supporters, both in size and mirth, was Judge David Davis.

"A most intimate and confidential friend of Lincoln,"[58] forty-five-year-old Judge Davis had also been, along with Judd, one of Lincoln's unofficial campaign managers and closest advisors. But Davis distrusted, if not despised, Judd, whom he never forgave for opposing Lincoln in the 1855 Senate race. An obese man roughly twice Lincoln's 160 pounds, Davis, a Maryland native, was now an Illinois Circuit Court judge. Judge Davis "will probably attract more attention than any other member of the suite, by virtue of his rotund corporation, the inexpressible humor of his broad, good natured countenance, and the roar-like laughter in which he all but constantly indulges. Without the mirthfulness of the Judge, the trip [would be] like a body without a soul,"

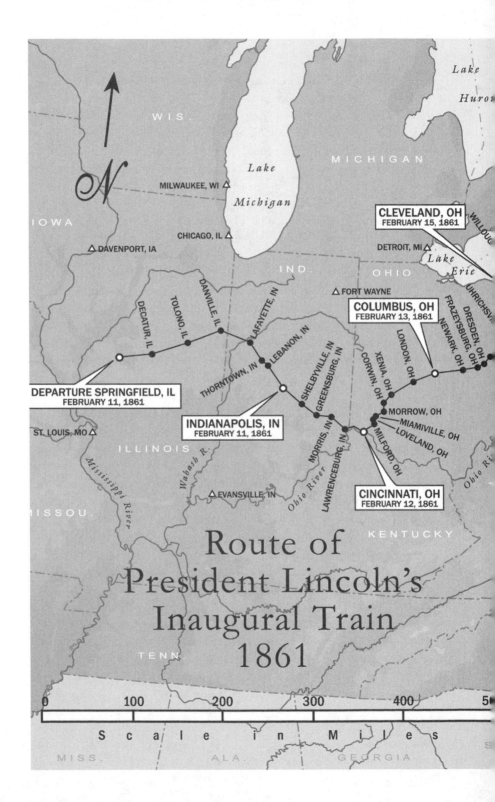

Route of President Lincoln's Inaugural Train 1861

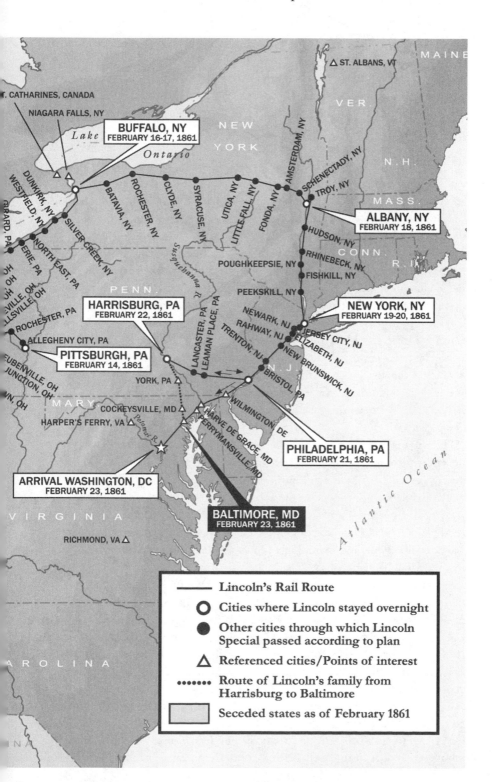

noted one reporter.[59] Judge Davis had reason to be in a particularly good mood on this trip; he hoped that Lincoln, as president, would nominate him to fill a vacancy on the U.S. Supreme Court. Davis's lofty aspirations, however, yet rested on two uncertainties: the Electoral College votes to be tallied ostensibly in Lincoln's favor in Washington on February 13, and Lincoln's living to be inaugurated on March 4.

One man in Lincoln's entourage who drew little attention was his valet, William Johnson. As far as we know, Johnson, described as "a likely mulatto, although not exactly the most prominent," was the only African American to accompany Lincoln from Springfield. Perhaps for this reason, his name does not appear in most published reports of passengers on the train. Variously described as Lincoln's hired servant, porter, and bodyguard, he likely served many roles on behalf of the president-elect, reportedly waiting on Lincoln and his party with "untiring vigilance."[60] Most significantly, Johnson shaved and helped obtain new clothes for his frequently rumpled boss. Despite his tendency to tilt off kilter in terms of dress and grooming, Lincoln would appear as level and plumb as possible, thanks to William Johnson.

There were also plenty of people who had opposed Lincoln along for the ride. The president-elect felt it important to be seen as an inclusive leader, as if to rebut the divisive criticism of him and the polarized political climate that prevailed. Accordingly, a dozen members of the opposition parties, including Breckinridge Democrats and Bell-Everett supporters, were invited and came along.[61]

Newspaper accounts of precisely who all these forty-odd people were are generally incomplete and inaccurate. In one report, for example, Lamon is listed as "Lemon." William Johnson is omitted, while military officers, such as Colonel Edwin Sumner, who would actually join the train later, are included.[62] Indeed, it is unclear if any U.S. Army officers at all were on the train when it left Springfield, although certainly Colonel Sumner, Captain George Hazzard, Captain John Pope, and Major David Hunter would come on board by the following day in Indianapolis.[63]

An Illinois native and member of a wealthy family "widely celebrated for their hospitality and cultural taste,"[64] Major David Hunter, an 1822 West Point graduate, wore his thinning hair like a Roman ruler, combed forward at the temples, as if symbolic of his desire for advancement. His mustache was thin and unruly, a feeble attempt that looked like a stage prop, an imposter stuck to his stern face with horse hoof glue. Hunter, fifty-eight, had seen his contemporaries, including Colonel Sumner and two of his subordinates, promoted over him. He blamed this not on his ability or the fact that he had resigned from the army in 1836, returning in 1841,[65] but on his having been "kept down" as a man loyal to the Republican cause. He charged those advanced ahead of him with being "good Democrats," subservient to that party's politicians.[66] Major Hunter, who had been providing Lincoln with valuable intelligence, wanted a promotion and, now with Lincoln being the president-elect, saw his opportunity.

Lincoln trusted Hunter enough to include him among the small cadre of military officers on his train.[67] His trust was apparently well placed. Before the journey was over, Major Hunter, whom John Hay would later call "the best fighting General in the army,"[68] would demonstrate his mettle, to the point of peril to life and limb.

Judge David Davis. He hoped for an appointment to the Supreme Court in Lincoln's administration. (*Library of Congress*)

Captain John Pope would also join the party. The son of a United States District Court judge, topographical engineer John Pope was born in Illinois. Like Colonel Sumner, Captain Pope was a West Pointer, and he had served with valor in the Mexican War, where, as an officer in his early twenties, he was cited for gallant and meritorious conduct at Monterey and Buena Vista.[69] His most recent topographical efforts included searching in vain for water in the "Staked Plains" on the line of the Pacific Railroad.[70] Now in his late thirties, broad shouldered and barrel-chested, Pope sported a full, brushy beard, which contrasted with his softly flowing hair.

Pope's experience as a topographical engineer might prove invaluable on the Lincoln Special's journey. He could use his skills to divine the topography of the train's route, predicting where trouble might lie in wait—for example, on steep climbs or horseshoe bends that would force the train to slow to a crawl, or at the mouth of narrow rocky mountain passes, where a party of ambushers might hurl boulders or fell trees onto the tracks. Or he might map out all of the steep descents on the route, wherein the rush of gravity would pull the train like a roller coaster into a perilous swoop, during which overheated, primitive car brakes might be unable to stop or even slow the hurtling Lincoln Special, even if no obstruction intended to derail both train and presidential hopes lay in wait at the bottom. Such intelligence would be of obvious value to those intent on protecting the life of the president-elect and his family—if, that is, anyone in the party had thought to use Captain Pope's topographical skills.

Another military man on the train, "an excellent officer and a highly cultivated gentleman," U.S. Army Captain George W. Hazzard had served with General Zachary Taylor's army in Mexico, engaged in almost continual skirmishes with Indians on the Rio Grande after the Mexican War, before serving in Florida and Kansas.[71] A West Point honor graduate of the Class of 1847, and member of the Fourth Artillery, Hazzard deemed himself one of the country's foremost authorities on the army, having studied its organization, laws, tactics, and economic affairs for seventeen years. On November 5, 1860, Hazzard, who was on extended sick leave, invited himself to the presidential party. Confident of Lincoln's election the next day, he wrote: "I have a leave of absence until spring and if in the mean time my professional knowledge (not advice) would be of any service to you it would afford me pleasure to be near your person."[72]

During the previous summer, Hazzard had infiltrated Democratic campaign meetings and conferred with Democratic political insiders to learn what he could about Lincoln's opposition. As early as July, Hazzard began providing political intelligence to Lincoln from Indianapolis. By this time, the Democratic Party had cleaved itself in two, one block supporting Stephen A. Douglas for president, the other backing Vice President John C. Breckinridge. Hazzard closed one dispatch to Lincoln in frothy mockery of the divided Democrats, saying: "much hostility is evinced between the factions and they are as profane as the army of William the 3d. in Flanders. . . . Wishing them confusion and confident of your success, I remain Respectfully yours."[73]

By late October 1860, with state election returns in the North favoring Republican candidates, and Lincoln's election all but certain, Hazzard's intelligence-gathering efforts shifted from political to military. While Lincoln must have found October's political news intoxicating, that month's military portents were sobering. Even more amazing than Hazzard's "dirty tricks" methods of intelligence gathering, and his bypassing proper military/political channels, eschewing General Winfield Scott and President Buchanan by going straight to a private citizen not yet elected president, is the information itself, which was startling. Writing to Lincoln from Cincinnati, Hazzard reported: "I have watched the War Department very closely for the last six months and I have little doubt that Secretary [of War John B.] Floyd is playing into the hands of the secessionists."

As secretary of war, Floyd had the power to order weapons and call for troops and supply each to the government's arsenals and forts. Floyd seized this opportunity. With the silent stealth of a swooping hawk, from the end of 1859 until Floyd's resignation at the end of 1860, his War Department ordered over a hundred thousand muskets transferred from Northern posts to Southern arsenals in Charleston, South Carolina; North Carolina; Augusta, Georgia; Mount Vernon, Alabama; and Baton Rouge, Louisiana.[74] According to Hazzard, these arsenals had received new rifles "drawn from the armory at Springfield Mass. as fast as they could be fabricated." Compounding matters, those arsenals were being weakly guarded, if guarded at all. Some arsenals in Georgia, North Carolina, Alabama, Arkansas, Louisiana, and Harpers Ferry

David Hunter, left, would be seriously injured in the crush of the crowd gathered in Buffalo, New York, to greet Lincoln. John Pope, right, was a decorated Mexican War veteran and topographical engineer before joining Lincoln's entourage. (*Library of Congress*)

were garrisoned by at most fifty men, while others were "totally unprotected and [could] each be captured by a party of twelve men."[75] Floyd bled the federal army dry, removing troops from where they might defend the nation to where they would be of no use—to remote locations, in Texas, New Mexico, Arizona, Oregon, California, and other frontier outposts. From these distant places, it would take the federal government a full year to return them.[76]

Hazzard reported to Lincoln that the Southern forts were equally vulnerable, with forts at Charleston being garrisoned with two companies (108 men), and three immense forts at Pensacola "(the finest harbor on the Gulf)" having an aggregate guard of fifty-four men. Forts at Savannah, Mobile, New Orleans, and most significantly, Baltimore, had no garrisons at all.[77] As Hazzard later observed, "Fort McHenry commands Baltimore and Baltimore is the back door of the National Capital."[78]

As if all this weren't bad enough, the leadership of the army over which Lincoln would be commander-in-chief tilted decidedly South, as Secretary of War Floyd, a Virginian, had feathered his clutch of military commanders with Southerners, most also Virginians. "So long has southern influence and southern patronage controlled our army that I know only one officer of any rank in it who is not an avowed admirer of the peculiar institution," wrote Hazzard. That one officer was Edwin Vose Sumner.[79]

Hazzard's most significant communiqué to Lincoln is his January 1861 dispatch, sent on the eve of the Lincoln Special's departure. In it, Hazzard warned Lincoln of the dangers that awaited him in Baltimore, of Marshal Kane's suspect integrity, and of men in Baltimore who Hazzard believed would "glory in being hanged for having stabbed a 'black republican president.'" He provided intelligence on wealthy influential Baltimore secessionists and offered Lincoln viable alternatives to passing openly through the city.[80] Lincoln would, on his journey, heed some of Hazzard's suggestions, and ignore others. But he would bring Captain Hazzard along for the ride. And Hazzard would, in turn, bring with him on the trip a protector's swords and shields, in the form of a dirk, brass knuckles, and protective eye goggles possibly intended to shield the wearer from an attack of acid tossed in the face.[81]

WHILE Lincoln was the newly elected head of state, he was not in charge of his own train. That distinction fell to the superintendent of arrangements, William S. Wood. Recommended by New York's Thurlow Weed, he was an odd choice, as he was completely unknown to Lincoln. Weeks before, the punctual and fastidious Wood had scouted out the entire route his train would take. He published a "Circular of Instructions" offering "suggestions" regarding matters of security to those on board and to the "Committee of Arrangements" in the host cities receiving Lincoln. Elmer E. Ellsworth, a young friend of Lincoln's, whom he adored like a son, was given top billing in Wood's instructions.

"First: The President elect will under *no circumstances* attempt to pass through any crowd until such arrangements are made as will meet the approval of Col. Ellsworth, who is charged with the responsibility of all matters of this character, and to facilitate this, you will confer a favor by placing Col. Ellsworth in communication with the chief of your escort, immediately upon the arrival of the train."[82]

Young, daring, and handsome, with a neatly trimmed mustache, likely intended to put some age to his otherwise boyish face, and shrouded with long shocks of lustrous hair that hung in ringlets, twenty-three-year-old Elmer E. Ellsworth was, next to Lincoln himself, perhaps the most famous celebrity on the train. He commanded the corps of United States Zouave Cadets of Chicago, a paramilitary unit he had formed. The uniformed Zouaves had performed complicated gymnastic drills to the delight of large audiences throughout Eastern cities, including Baltimore, during the summer of 1860.[83] In an era without professional athletes, Hollywood actors, or MTV, Ellsworth was the equivalent of a knighted rock star, albeit one who, along with his corps of sober cadets, neither smoked nor drank.[84]

Like Lincoln, Colonel Ellsworth's rise to fame had required escaping the gravity of economic hardship. His father's financial woes had prevented his boyhood dream—a cadetship at West Point—from becoming a reality.

Undaunted, young Ellsworth worked hard, studied hard, and moved to Chicago, where he became a patent solicitor, though not yet of age. After being defrauded of his hard-earned savings, Ellsworth turned to the study of law, supporting himself by copying legal papers at night. And yet Ellsworth never lost sight of the dream of military valor, and had organized his Chicago Zouave regiment not for show, but for the defense of Illinois, anticipating the looming "unpleasantness."[85]

Prior to leaving Springfield, Ellsworth had been studying law with Lincoln's partner William Herndon. But he had also been active in campaigning for Lincoln and other Republicans in Illinois, his Zouaves performing in parades and shows at huge Republican rallies.[86] Henry Villard, who visited with Ellsworth prior to the Lincoln Special's departure, found him "very thoroughly posted on military matters and, in my opinion, his love for the military will override his intention to become a lawyer."[87]

Along with Ward Hill Lamon, Ellsworth also represented an important, if unofficial, wing of Lincoln's security detail. On November 6, in Springfield, he and Lamon had escorted Lincoln to the polling place to ensure his safety while he cast his vote.[88]

As to the arrangement of carriages in host cities, William S. Wood's instructions placed Lincoln and Lamon and "One or two members of the Escort of Committee" in the first carriage, Sumner, Hunter, Judd, and Davis in the second carriage, Ellsworth, Hazzard, and Nicolay in the third carriage, and Robert Lincoln and Hay in the fourth carriage with "Two Members of the Escort." The instructions further detailed that "Two carriages will be required to convey Mrs. Lincoln and family and her escort from the cars." The instructions also required for the arrangement of rooms in the numerous hotels in which Lincoln and his suite would stay on the way. His secretaries, Nicolay and Hay, were to be given rooms contiguous to the president-elect, and a private dining room with a table for six or eight persons was to be provided. Almost apologetically, Wood closed his instructions with Victorian decorum: "Trusting, gentlemen, that inasmuch as we have a common purpose in this matter, the safety, comfort and convenience of the President elect, these suggestions will be received in the spirit in which they are offered."[89]

Despite Wood's instructions, not one person traveling with Lincoln was designated to officially take charge of his security detail—to the extent the little ad hoc cluster of friends, officials, and military men on board could fairly be said to constitute a security detail. There was in 1861 no Secret Service, and no special agent in charge. There were many who likely felt, whether by dint of personal connection, such as Lamon and Ellsworth, political proximity, such as Davis and Judd, military rank and combat experience, such as Colonel

Sumner, or some other entitlement, that they held claim to being head of Lincoln's security.

Wood's circular of instructions declared that he was "charged with the safe conduct of the President elect." Indeed, as head of operations for the train, Wood issued printed, sealed, and signed passes to all who could board.[90] But Wood had a train to run and a schedule to meet. He could hardly keep an eye on Lincoln at all times. His personally signed passes made nice mementos but could do nothing to stop people from crushing around the president-elect once he left the train, sat in an open barouche, or got to a hotel thronged with curious onlookers.

Ellsworth was in charge of escorting Lincoln through crowds. Not only was this a ridiculously impossible task, pitting one man against thousands, it was a role that fell far short of complete responsibility for Lincoln's security.

By one account, Colonel Sumner had been sent by General Scott himself to ensure Lincoln's safe passage to Washington. A gray-bearded, unsmiling officer in the First United States Cavalry, sixty-three-year-old Colonel Edwin Vose Sumner had the cavernous scowl and cold, steely eyes of a man who had, perhaps, fought too many battles and seen too much death. He had served on the American frontier, defeating a body of Cheyenne warriors in Kansas in 1857. A decade before that, he had fought with valor under Winfield Scott during the Mexican War, earning a promotion to brevet lieutenant colonel for gallant and meritorious conduct at Cerro Gordo, Mexico, where he was wounded in action while commanding a mounted rifle regiment.[91] Despite his age and battle-hardened body, the colonel maintained his vigor. Noted a reporter for *The Philadelphia Inquirer*, "His figure is as erect as ever, and his faculties, physical and mental, are totally unimpaired—the result of an active, temperate life."[92]

The old soldier firmly believed that secession was treason, not only for the seceded states collectively, but also for the individual citizens of such states. Sumner also worried for Lincoln's safety, writing to Nicolay in January 1861:

> Dear Sir:
> I have received your note of the 4th inst.—
> The political excitement is becoming so intense, that a feeling of personal hostility, and bitterness, is increasing every day.
> I have heard of threats against Mr. Lincoln, and of bets being offered that he would never be inaugurated.—I know very well that he is not the man to live in fear of assassination; but when the safety of the whole country depends upon his life, I would respectfully suggest to him, whether it would not be well to give this matter some attention.—It has occurred to me that if any such attempt should be made, it would most likely be made at Springfield. Mr. Lincolns habit of walking about alone at night,

Elmer E. Ellsworth, left, and Colonel Edwin Vose Sumner, right—the young buck and the old guard. Forty years separated in age, these two stalwart defenders of Lincoln shared an intense desire to see him safely to Washington. (*Library of Congress*)

gives an opportunity to make the attempt, with a good chance of escaping detection.—I would respectfully urge him to carry such arms about him, when walking alone at night, as will make him secure against any crazy fanatics.

I am
very truly yours
E V Sumner
Col USA[93]

Perhaps as a result of this letter, Colonel Sumner was charged by General Winfield Scott to accompany Lincoln safely to Washington in February 1861. Prone to following military etiquette and his superiors' orders, and anxious for the president-elect's safety, Colonel Sumner, the ranking military officer on the Lincoln Special, was determined not to let Lincoln out of his sight or out of his charge during the trip.

But rank without validation is little more than a costume. Unless everyone on board, including those not in the army, recognized Sumner's superior rank and acknowledged his authority, his uniform was little more than a stage prop. And speaking of props, Ward Hill Lamon, who would assume the role of Lincoln's bodyguard, wore on the trip what might be appropriately termed a costume, a personally designed uniform that he had worn as an aide to Illinois governor Richard Yates.[94]

Despite the presence of these well-meaning men, each of whom may have felt he was in charge of Lincoln's security, in reality no one was. This was a serious oversight. It would, as decisions pertaining to Lincoln's safety presented themselves, lead to consequences that from a security standpoint were at once comical, reckless, and potentially deadly.

H ALF a continent away, in Hampden, Maine, Vice President-elect Hannibal Hamlin and his twenty-something wife Ellen were also preparing to leave their home and head to Washington. They planned to catch up with Lincoln in New York City. Mindful of secessionist threats to seize Washington before the inauguration, and of rumors concerning desperate rebel efforts to induce Virginia and Maryland to secede, Hamlin had worried about his wife's safety, and even considered not bringing her with him. But Senator Preston King wrote him reassuringly in early February, detailing General Scott's plans to secure Washington with one thousand regulars, some cavalry, and three batteries of flying artillery "if he can get them." Wrote King teasingly from Washington, "I wish I had a wife—and if I had I should not hesitate to have her with me here."[95]

King's letters, and similar assurances from Lyman Trumbull, the U.S. senator from Illinois, cinched the deal. On February 18, Hamlin's wife would be with him as they rode in a horse-drawn sleigh, escorted by friends and neighbors to Bangor's train station, 5 miles away. If Hamlin's eyes watered that morning, it might have been excused on account of the sting of a bitterly cold Maine winter. Or Hamlin might have been inspired by what he and his wife would see waiting for them at Bangor—a line of sleighs over a mile long, filled with well-wishers gathered to see him off.[96] In a speech with overtones and themes eerily reminiscent of Lincoln's parting words, and perhaps based upon them, Hamlin would also tenderly address his hometown crowd:

> Neighbors and fellow citizens . . . For nearly a third of a century I have resided in your midst, and my highest ambition has been to secure your confidence and good-will. . . . I go to the discharge of official duties which have been conferred on me by a generous people. Relying upon a Divine Providence, I trust that the confidence shall never be betrayed. A man may cheerfully lay his life upon the altar of his country, but he who surrenders his integrity loses self-respect and the respect of others. I know full well that dark clouds are lowering around the political horizon, and that madness rules the hour. . . . Whatever may betide me as a man, or in my official position, I will endeavor through all to stand faithfully by my duty and the right, and I shall hold even my life at the service of my country. Looking to Him in whose hands are the destinies of all nations as well as individuals, and

who has been our safety and our shield in the past, and with a firm and unshaken reliance upon His care and protection, let us look hopefully to the future.[97]

Thus, like Lincoln, Hamlin recognized the darkness of the hour, risks to his country and his life, and the need to rely on divine providence to see him through it all. His decision to bring his wife with him, despite the risks, had been based on his friends' assurances that Washington would be kept secure. If Virginia and Maryland do not secede, King wrote, "then I think there is not the slightest reason to apprehend any disturbance here. It is my opinion that we shall not have any disturbance—here any way."[98] By "here," King was, of course, referring to Washington. Like Lincoln, however, Hamlin would first need to pass through Baltimore in order to get there. And like Lincoln, Hamlin had no way of knowing that trouble also awaited him—and his wife—in Baltimore.

A T 10:00 a.m., as the Lincoln Special chugged across Illinois, passing small towns like Oakley, Cerro Gordo, and Bement, a congressional inquiry, the Select Committee of Five, reconvened in Washington.[99] The Select Committee had been formed in early January at James Buchanan's request, to investigate and report on, among other secessionist schemes, rumors "on the subject of a secret hostile organization, or conspiracy, to seize the capital, &c."[100] In a special message delivered to the committee on January 8, Buchanan summed up his reasons for supporting the committee's investigations: "It is said that serious apprehensions are, to some extent, entertained, in which I do not share, that the peace of this District may be disturbed before the 4th of March next. In any event, it will be my duty to preserve it, and this duty shall be performed. . . . I have often warned my countrymen of the dangers which now surround us. This may be the last time I shall refer to the subject officially. I feel that my duty has been faithfully, though it may be imperfectly performed; and whatever the result may be, I shall carry to my grave the consciousness that I at least meant well for my country."[101] For a man who was clearly out of breath, empanelling the Select Committee of Five seemed like James Buchanan's last gasp.

During the next month, the Select Committee rounded up both accusers and suspects, compelling those from out of town to come to Washington, and had them testify under oath. The witnesses called would range from those loyal to the government, such as General Winfield Scott, to those possibly suspected of complicity in seeking its overthrow, or at least having evidence of such a plot, including Marylanders John R. Tormey of Baltimore and James Hicks of Colesville, both called on January 30,[102] Benjamin Berry of

Colesville, called on January 31, and Maryland's former governor Enoch Lewis Lowe of Frederick, called on February 1.[103] The Select Committee then examined Cypriano Ferrandini on February 5, Otis K. Hillard and another Baltimorean, Philip T. Dawson on February 6,[104] and yet another Baltimore man, Joseph H. Boyd, on February 8.[105] Clearly, the Select Committee of Five had reason to believe that if there was a conspiracy to seize Washington, a number of men from Baltimore and Maryland, some of them prominent, others not, knew something about it.

Thirty-eight-year-old Cypriano Ferrandini was a Corsican immigrant who had lived in Baltimore sixteen years.[106] Allan Pinkerton would describe him as "a fine looking, intelligent appearing person . . . whose eyes fairly glared and glistened."[107] The previous winter, he had served a three-month stint in Mexico in Juarez's army as an infantry captain, before resigning his commission and returning to Baltimore.[108] Variously titled a "barber," a "hair dresser," and the "head barber," he worked in the basement of Barnum's City Hotel, where meetings of the National Volunteers, of which Ferrandini was allegedly a member, also took place. Ferrandini was also reportedly a former Italian military officer and a "captain" of the Knights of the Golden Circle.[109]

A Richmond native and soldier of fortune who proudly displayed the secessionist badge of honor—a "Palmetto Cockade"—on his chest, O. K. Hillard had recently returned to Baltimore after a seven-year absence. Allegedly a scion of Baltimore high society, he also had friends in low places, in particular, at Annette Travis's house of prostitution at Number 70 Davis Street. Hillard was allegedly a member of three secretive societies, the Palmetto Guard, the Knights of the Golden Circle, and, like other suspected conspirators, the National Volunteers.[110]

During his testimony, Ferrandini freely admitted that he was part of a company of "Constitutional Guards" in Baltimore that had been formed "to prevent Northern volunteer companies from passing through the State of Maryland . . . to come here [to Washington] to help the United States troops, or anybody else, to invade the South in any shape whatever."[111] Ferrandini testified that another corps, the National Volunteers, also organized to protect the state of Maryland, had begun drilling just the previous Saturday, February 2. Ferrandini also boldly claimed that he had "heard that the minute-men have fifteen companies" in Baltimore.[112]

Otis K. Hillard claimed during his February 6 testimony that he was not part of any military organization and had no knowledge of any conspiracy to overthrow the government or to harm Lincoln. Most likely, Hillard was lying.

Just six days later, Hillard would admit to a Pinkerton operative that he was indeed part of a conspiracy involving Lincoln and was a member of the National Volunteers.[113] Hillard did concede during his testimony in Washington that the National Volunteers might resist armed troops should they pass through Baltimore en route to Washington. But when asked to identify members of the National Volunteers, he refused to do so. Although the Select Committee might have compelled him to answer, it did not.[114]

Ferrandini and Hillard were permitted to return to Baltimore after giving their testimony. They were never recalled to testify. While they had admitted that Baltimore was arming itself to prevent Northern troops from passing through its streets, they had not yet confessed to any plan to murder Lincoln.

By this morning, February 11, the Select Committee of Five had examined all of its twenty-eight witnesses but one. For at least the past week, they had attempted to secure the testimony of Maryland's elusive governor, Thomas H. Hicks.

As he had done with Northern and Southern suitors clamoring for his state's affections, Hicks would play hard to get with the Select Committee of Five. The committee deemed Hicks's testimony exceedingly important, and on February 6, the committee's chairman, William A. Howard, sent Hicks a letter urging him to appear before them.

The next day, Hicks replied from Annapolis, complaining of overwork, doubting the propriety of his appearing before the committee, "occupying the peculiar position I do," and insisting that he really had nothing new to add to statements already made. "I can do no more than repeat verbal relations made, and written statements," he insisted. Even so, Hicks was smart enough to know he could not simply refuse a congressional committee's request. "Yet, if really thought by yourself and committee very material, I will go to Washington," he offered meekly, before abruptly changing course; Hicks closed his letter wondering if the Select Committee in Washington could come to Annapolis: "Cannot you or some member of your committee run over and see me here?" he asked.[115]

Hicks's reluctance to appear before the Select Committee might be excused on the basis that he was a busy governor of a troubled, even conflicted, border state and had not even the time to take a 30-mile train ride from Annapolis to Washington, down and back the same day. But his reticence might equally have been based on fears that other witnesses had testified about him. Perhaps the real reason Governor Hicks did not want to appear before a congressional investigating committee is that he knew the best, most important, or most suspect witness is often saved for last in an investigation, after previous witnesses have already leaked out bits and pieces of the story, setting the final witness up, either to tie it all together, to knock him down, or to implicate him. Possibly and understandably, not knowing for certain what these prior witnesses had said about him, Hicks did not want to be subjected to rigid cross-examination. Perhaps Governor Hicks, the same man who had in November urged his friend "to send out to kill Lincoln and his men," had a guilty conscience. Perhaps Governor Hicks had something to hide.

Seizing on Hicks's half-baked invitation to come to Annapolis, the committee dispatched its chairman, Howard, and committeeman Lawrence O'Bryan Branch of North Carolina, along with the clerk, to meet with Hicks there. They gave Hicks no advance warning that they were coming. Howard and Branch arrived in Annapolis later that afternoon. They were informed that Governor Hicks was not there.[116]

THE firing in rapid succession of thirty-four guns at sundown, one for each state, announced the 5:00 p.m. on-schedule arrival of the Lincoln Special into Indianapolis on February 11, its first overnight stop.[117] Wood's itinerary had been carefully planned to ensure that Lincoln's train would end each day by arriving at the host city's depot before dark. There were good reasons for this. Traveling by rail during daylight hours and concluding before dusk meant that obstacles on the track could be more easily seen and the engineer given at least a fighting chance to throw the locomotive's massive wheels into reverse to stop the train in time.

The merit of such precautions had been proven earlier this morning, between 9:30 and 10:00 a.m., after the Lincoln Special was a few miles beyond Decatur, Illinois. As the train headed out of town into open prairie, without a pilot engine in front to watch for obstructions, a barricade appeared on the tracks. The Special screeched to an unexpected stop. Well-wishers, not conspirators, had placed a stake-and-rider fence in the way to force the train to a halt so they could see Lincoln, who had not planned to stop there.[118] From here on out, a pilot engine—the railroad equivalent of a king's food taster—would run ahead of the Lincoln Special.

As he emerged from the car in Indianapolis, Lincoln was met on the platform by Indiana governor Oliver P. Morton, who escorted him to an open barouche drawn by four white horses.[119] A grand procession formed, comprising members of both houses of the state legislature, public officers, municipal authorities, military men, and firemen. Reported the press the next day, "Great enthusiasm was manifested along the line of the march. The President elect stood in the carriage acknowledging the welcome of the surrounding masses."[120]

Traveling by day also insured that Lincoln could be seen by his supporters during stops and upon his arrival in host cities. Lincoln had fully intended that he see the people and be seen by them, and he would not disappoint, quipping along the way that he was getting "the better part of the bargain."

But if any conspirators in Baltimore or elsewhere were reading newspaper accounts to gather intelligence of Lincoln's travel habits, or if any Southern spies were shadowing Lincoln, their eyes would have danced with glee at what they saw. They, not Lincoln, were getting the better part of the bargain.

Lincoln rode in host cities not in a closed carriage, but in an open one. He arrived before dark. He did not crouch behind bodyguards in a sitting position, but stood tall in the carriage, bowing to the crowd. He wanted to be seen. His excessive height insured good visibility. A skilled marksman might easily shoot Lincoln where he stood in the carriage and disappear into the crowd before his body crumpled to the seat.

Lincoln's procession ambled to the Bates House, a large, four-story hotel with rows of elongated, closely spaced windows and street level awnings.[121] Once there, after a brief rest, Lincoln again exposed himself to danger. Escorted by Governor Morton, he appeared on a balcony in response to the demands of the crowd that had gathered below, as he would on other occasions during the trip.

Unlike the impromptu emotional speech he had given in Springfield, Lincoln had planned this one and would deliver it with spunk. It was his first speech in a major city on the trip, and he intended to make it count. Accordingly, Lincoln came out of his corner swinging, taking sharp jabs at the seceded states. In a "clear, sonorous voice" that the *World* reporter found "singularly effective and admirable,"[122] Lincoln thanked the citizens for Indiana's support to a "political cause which, I think, is the true and just cause of the whole country and the whole world."[123] He cautioned against the bad-tempered, hot-blooded use of terms like "coercion" and "invasion," words that the South had been using to justify secession and to ridicule attempts by the Union to hold or retake forts in seceded states. "What is the meaning of these words?" Lincoln asked. "Would the marching of an army into South Carolina with hostile intent be an invasion? I think it would. And it would be coercion also if South Carolina was forced to submit. But if the United States should merely hold and retake its own forts, collect its duties, or withhold its mails where they were habitually violated, would any or all of these things be invasion or coercion?" Lincoln let the obvious answer to his own rhetorical question hang in the cool February air. He then criticized those who treated the Union, in terms of family relations, not as a marriage, but a sort of "free-love arrangement, to be maintained by personal attraction." He concluded his short speech, returning to the theme of coercion. He took a poke at South Carolina, asking upon what rightful principle may a state, "being not more than one-fiftieth part of the nation, soil and population, break up the nation, and then coerce the larger division of herself? What mysterious right to play the tyrant is conferred on a district of the country, with its people, by merely calling it a state?"[124]

"Fellow citizens," he closed, "I am not asserting anything. I am merely asking questions for you to consider. And now, allow me to bid you farewell."[125]

Finally, the president-elect, who had taken such pains to say nothing since his election on matters of policy, had said something. True, he had tried to take it all back by claiming he was "not asserting anything." But Lincoln's true intentions were not lost on those who gathered in the bar and parlors of the Bates House that night to disassemble and reconstruct the speech and its meaning. "Although he assured his hearers that his remarks were rather suggestions for their consideration than statements of his policy," the anonymous *World* reporter wrote that night, "none can fail to discern in them the index which points the executive way."[126] Lincoln would defend the Union.

While others crowding the Bates House that evening could indulge in the revelry of the moment, Lincoln was not so lucky. His evening was predictive of what he would experience at other hotels in upcoming host cities: dangerously congested hallways, long reception lines punctuated by hundreds of painful, bone-crushing, arm-wrenching handshakes, and confused dinners of varying quality given late, if at all. Reported one correspondent from the Bates House that night, "the crowd, swaying to and fro, forget all etiquette, each seeming to outdo his elbow companion."[127] It was all enough to drive a man to drink.

Indeed, a nightcap was just what several Illinoisans who would be returning home in the morning likely had in mind. After saying their good-byes and God-speeds to Lincoln, Illinois governor Richard Yates, Orville H. Browning, state auditor Jesse K. Dubois, and O. M. Hatch, among others, hustled Ward Hill Lamon into a private room at the Bates House and locked the door. It would not be surprising if they poured Lamon a drink, although he does not record this. What Lamon does record is that these men "proceeded in the most solemn and impressive manner to instruct me as to my duties as the special guardian of Mr. Lincoln's person during the rest of his journey to Washington."[128]

Thirty-one-year-old Ward Hill Lamon was a pro-slavery Virginian by birth with a reported penchant for heavy drinking. Despite these vices, Lamon would be the closest thing to a personal bodyguard or a Secret Service agent Lincoln would have on the trip from Springfield. Notwithstanding their differing views on slavery and hard liquor, Lincoln and Lamon were good friends, having practiced law together for a time. Lamon had campaigned for Lincoln among delegates from his home state of Virginia at the Chicago convention.[129]

Tall, brusque, and burly, with hollow cheekbones, deep, penetrating eyes, long, flowing dark hair, and a walrus mustache, Lamon traveled well-armed, habitually wearing a brace of pistols he was not shy about using. He also had prior law-enforcement experience, as a Bloomfield, Illinois, prosecutor. The Lincoln Special's circular of instructions required that Lamon be placed in the first carriage with Lincoln at all stops.[130] Despite his tough outward appearance, Lamon doted on Lincoln like a mother hen, worrying constantly for his friend's safety, as if to counter Lincoln's own famous casual disregard for it.

"Now, Lamon," Dubois concluded in a jocular tone, "we entrust the sacred life of Mr. Lincoln to your keeping. If you don't protect it, never return to Illinois for we will murder you on sight." Whether Dubois's threat was serious or not, Lamon took it that way. He would, henceforth, do his best to protect the "sacred life" of Mr. Lincoln.[131]

Indeed, if assassins were going to get to Lincoln on this trip, they would likely have to go through the barrel-chested Ward Hill Lamon to do it.

Ward Hill Lamon. In the days before the Lincoln Special's departure, Lamon worked behind the scenes to secure numerous letters of recommendation to his friend Lincoln for an appointment as Consul to Paris. (*Library of Congress*)

CHAPTER FOUR

THE STOCK BROKER

I N FEBRUARY 1861, THANKS TO THE ELECTION of a "Black Republican" president, Baltimore's burning embers, whether from a new generation of street gangs, from disaffected, unemployed, even starving citizens, or from fire-eating secessionist mouthpieces, were growing hotter from without as well as within. Baltimore was home to a bustling seaport that welcomed ships daily from places like Mobile and Savannah and New Orleans. The city harbored distinctly pro-Southern sympathies and was a sanctuary for secessionists. Almost daily, citizens held secret secession meetings, some of which offered as entertainment the hometown attraction of local firebrands and guest speakers from romantic places like South Carolina and Mississippi. The allure of patriotic causes and independent thinking, taken to the extreme of secession, made such speakers the toast of the city's secessionist elements. Even a stranger, claiming with a measure of credibility to be from the Deep South, would be welcomed and trusted in Baltimore.

At 44 South Street, one such stranger, a man named John H. Hutcheson, prepared to open his doors for business. An early riser who routinely woke at 4:30 a.m. and needed but a few hours of sleep every night, Hutcheson likely had been at his desk long before sunup. Lodging at the Howard House, Hutcheson was new in town, having opened his stockbroker's business just the week before.

Hutcheson's choice of this location for his business was no accident. The building, situated near the docks and tidal basin, was equidistant from the Camden Street and President Street railway stations. This would enable Hutcheson to quickly leave his office and hop aboard the next train out of town, heading south to Washington from the Camden Street Station, or north to Philadelphia from the President Street Station. More importantly, the building at 44 South Street was surrounded by streets and alleys and had an entrance on all four sides.[1] This permitted anyone coming to see Hutcheson to enter and exit by different doors, in the event any particular entrance was being watched. And if anyone had been watching the doors at 44 South Street during February 1861, they would have noticed a brisk traffic in and out. It might have seemed to some that whatever type of operation the stern-looking, cigar-smoking John H. Hutcheson was running, business was good.

But if any observers took more careful notice of Hutcheson or his business, they would have spotted more than a few oddities. It wasn't that his visitors carried closely guarded envelopes or packages or satchels that would have been particularly noteworthy—they might contain stock certificates or currency. And if these persons were also seen carrying weapons, in an era when many people did so, this also would not have raised alarm—they were merely guarding their security instruments. But there was something strange about the clients who paid Hutcheson almost daily visits. They came to his South Street office or his Howard House hotel room at all hours of the day or night. They were constantly riding the trains in and out of Baltimore, generally to points north. And they were only four or five in number and always the same four or five. Most curiously, two of them were women.

Hutcheson had carefully chosen his office location for another important reason. On the same floor in the building at 44 South Street, Baltimore businessman James H. Luckett also had a stockbroker's office. Hutcheson wanted to be close to Luckett, not to trade stock, but to obtain insider information from him.

In fact, John H. Hutcheson was not a stockbroker. The men and women that came to see him were not clients. He was not, in fact, from the Deep South, although he had spent some time there and could make a convincing show of it. Indeed, John H. Hutcheson was not even the man's real name. And the insider information he sought from James H. Luckett had nothing at all to do with gaining hot stock tips.

Hutcheson was seeking information concerning secessionist conspiracies in Baltimore. The stockbroker's business was a mere ruse, and it was a clever one. Few people in Baltimore, a city now in financial straits, had the sort of disposable income needed to purchase stock.[2] Those who did would have already had their own stockbrokers. There was thus little danger that anyone actually interested in buying or selling stock would darken John H. Hutcheson's doors. Even if they did, Hutcheson might scare them away with a demand for a princely retainer or minimum purchase. Hutcheson's real name, of course, was Allan Pinkerton.

Born into poverty on August 25, 1819 in Glasgow, Scotland, Allan Pinkerton had, from an early age, demonstrated an indomitable spirit and a gritty, stubborn determination to persevere. At eight, his father died, and he found himself apprenticing from morning until night for a few coppers a day in a dreary patternmaking shop. By twelve, he was apprenticing for a Glasgow cooper, building strong arms and shoulders swinging a ten-pound hammer all day. But it was not his strength that people found remarkable. A man who had known him as a lad in Glasgow remembered most of all his "searching, cool blue-gray eyes that never left your face when he spoke to you, and the intense drive that animated him."[3]

Slowly, relentlessly, Pinkerton pulled himself from poverty's scrap heap. Branded since birth by loss and hardship, he gravitated to political causes of social equality.[4] He joined the Chartists, a revolutionary agitation movement then gaining traction in Great Britain. But by the winter of 1842, young Pinkerton's name appeared on a list of Chartists for whom king's warrants had been issued. "I had become an outlaw with a price on my head," Pinkerton later recalled.[5] He and his young wife, Joan Carfrae, fled to Canada. A few months later, they were in Chicago, and from there they moved to the small Scots settlement of Dundee, Illinois. It was here, in this small village on the Fox River about 50 miles northeast of Chicago, that Pinkerton resumed his cooper's trade. And it was here, in Dundee, that Allan Pinkerton the cooper would become Allan Pinkerton the detective.

It happened by accident in 1847. Pinkerton, in need of lumber for making barrel staves, boarded a raft barefoot and poled to a little island on the Fox River. While on the island gathering lumber, he happened upon the charred remains of a campfire. Pinkerton knew the island was uninhabited. His suspicions were immediately aroused. He returned to the island late one night, where he waited and watched, hiding in the shore grass. Soon he heard the rhythmic sound of oars chopping at the water and watched as a rowboat moved downriver and came ashore on the island. Several silhouettes got out and started a fire. Pinkerton wasn't sure what they were up to, but clearly the late night campers were not having a picnic. The next day, Pinkerton alerted the sheriff of Kane County. One night soon thereafter, Pinkerton and the sheriff, together with a posse from Dundee, raided the island and arrested a gang of counterfeiters, seizing a bag of bogus dimes and tools used to make them. This fortuitous event led to a modicum of local fame for Pinkerton. More detective opportunities followed, ultimately leading the sheriff to hire him as deputy sheriff of Kane County.[6]

But Pinkerton soon outgrew Dundee and yearned for the big city. When the Cook County sheriff offered him a deputy's position, Pinkerton accepted immediately. He sold his cooperage business, packed all his earthly belongings in a wagon, and moved to Chicago. In 1849, Chicago's mayor appointed Pinkerton as the city's first detective. He gained a reputation as an honest, tough lawman, and in the process made some enemies. Several attempts were made on his life. One night, a would-be assassin fired two high-caliber slugs at Pinkerton's back at such close range his coat caught fire. His life was spared because of his habit of walking with his left hand tucked behind his back,

under his coat. The slugs, reported the
Chicago Daily Democrat Press, "shattered the
bone five inches from the wrist and passed
along the bone to the elbow where they
were cut out by a surgeon together with
pieces of his coat."[7]

In the early 1850s, Pinkerton decided to
form a private detective firm. Together with
a Chicago attorney, he formed the North-
Western Police Agency. Pinkerton's agency
was not the first in the world, or even the
first in the United States.[8] But his timing
and location were nearly perfect. Chicago
was a growing city and an important railroad terminus. Railroads brought big
money, and big money brought big crime.
When Pinkerton formed his agency, local
law enforcement was a fragmented, patch-
work collection of bounty hunters, rural
marshals, small-town sheriffs and part-time
deputies. Police departments in big cities,

Allan Pinkerton photographed at
Antietam during the Civil War. A
staunch abolitionist, Pinkerton
assisted slaves escaping north along
the Underground Railroad in addition to running his detective
agency. (*Library of Congress*)

like Chicago, New York, and Baltimore, were often thinly staffed and subject
to political cronyism and corruption. Moreover, local police could not cross the
county line, and there was no FBI.[9] As a private detective, Pinkerton filled the
growing need for effective law enforcement that could, like the railroads, cross
both county and state lines. His agency quickly grew and prospered.

Pinkerton was a perfectionist and left little to chance. For starters, he hired
only the best detectives. He believed, as if to counter the furtive nature and
scurrilous reputation of spying, that his agents should be "honest . . . bold in
the truth, sleepless in energy and loyal in thought and act."[10] Pinkerton and his
right-hand man, George H. Bangs, trained their agents well. Their Chicago
office often looked like the backstage of a theater, complete with disguises and
other props used to coach inexperienced agents in the art of playing various
roles—riverboat gambler, horsecar driver, or Southern gentleman.[11]

By February 1861, the forty-one-year-old former patternmaker, cooper,
Glasgow outlaw, and deputy sheriff had hit his stride as a nationally known
private investigator. Of broad shoulders and medium height, he was prone to
wearing a low-crowned bowler hat, perhaps to disguise his thinning hair.[12] As
if to alter his appearance, Pinkerton sometimes wore his beard the same as
Lincoln's, without a mustache, albeit long and bushy. At other times, he wore
it full, with lip hair, and neatly trimmed. Narrowly and deeply planted above
high cheekbones defining a broad, serious face were his closely spaced, pene-

trating blue-gray eyes. Although Allan Pinkerton's name was well known by 1861, his distinctive appearance, at least in Baltimore, was not.

Pinkerton had arrived in Baltimore on or about February 3, having left Chicago two days earlier with five of his best operatives.[13] These agents included two women, Hattie Lawton and Kate Warne, and three men, Timothy Webster, Harry W. Davies, and Charles D. C. Williams.[14] Pinkerton and his agents had stopped in Philadelphia along the way to obtain instructions from the man who had hired them, Samuel M. Felton, president of the Philadelphia, Wilmington, and Baltimore Railroad.

The information Pinkerton was to gather for Felton would paint a picture of secessionist plans to disrupt Felton's railroad between Philadelphia and Baltimore. He was to expose the participants of such a plan so their actions might be thwarted and Felton's railroad preserved. As of early February, Pinkerton had no idea that the Marylanders suspected of planning to ruin Felton's railroad had even bigger plans—Lincoln's assassination.

ALLAN PINKERTON and his Chicago operatives were not the only northern detectives who had descended on Baltimore in February 1861 to gather intelligence of suspected rebel plots. In fact, Pinkerton's group had not even been the first to arrive. That distinction belonged to several New York City detectives.

As George W. Walling, New York City's police chief, recalled, "one day, early in January, 1861, Superintendent [John] Kennedy ordered me, by telegraph, to report immediately to headquarters." When Walling arrived, he found that Kennedy had already gone. Walling ultimately caught up with Kennedy at the Cortlandt Street ferry, "deep in consultation with certain officials." Kennedy ordered Walling to "buy two tickets for Washington; you are to go with me. I will explain later."

Walling bought the tickets. Fifteen minutes later, without even having time to pack a change of clothes, he and Kennedy were on the fast express to Washington. During the journey, Kennedy explained the situation to Walling. "He was alarmed at the state of public feeling in Maryland, especially in Baltimore, through which Mr. Lincoln was to pass on his way to Washington to assume office. Riots were feared, and there were sinister rumors of threatened attempts to assassinate the President-elect."[15]

Kennedy also reported that the authorities in Washington, most likely General Winfield Scott, Senator William Seward, and Illinois congressman Elihu B. Washburne, were uneasy. "They had requested that some of the most trustworthy officers of the New York police should be detailed for service in Baltimore to ascertain what grounds there were for such suspicions."[16] Accordingly, Kennedy and Walling dispatched several New York City detectives to Baltimore, under assumed names, to gather intelligence.

There was only one problem with this plan. The "Washington authorities" who had retained the services of Superintendent Kennedy and his men had no idea that Allan Pinkerton and his agents would be shadowing the very same people in the very same places, ultimately in search of the very same information. The Pinkerton and Kennedy detective forces knew nothing about the other's presence in Baltimore. Both groups of operatives would be posing as secessionist sympathizers, running headlong toward the same objective. There was bound to be a collision.

Samuel M. Felton, president of the Philadelphia, Wilmington, and Baltimore Railroad. (*Smithsonian Institution*)

SEVERAL hundred miles north of Baltimore, another host city on the Lincoln Special's route, Albany, New York, eagerly anticipated the president-elect's visit. The widely published itinerary announced that Lincoln would arrive in Albany at 3:00 p.m. on Monday, February 18.[17]

But on the night of February 11, 1861, much of the talk in Albany was not about Lincoln; rather, it concerned a handsome and talented, yet impulsive and accident-prone young actor from Baltimore. He had, that very night, opened at Albany's little New Gayety Theater on Green Street. The young man, not yet twenty-three, was already a veteran of the stage, having launched his acting career at the tender age of seventeen, playing Richmond in *Richard III* at Baltimore's Charles Street Theater.[18] With intense eyes his sister described as "black and brilliant, the white ball is bluish from the excessive darkness of the pupil,"[19] and a voice praised as "melodious, sweet, full and strong,"[20] the dark, fair-skinned, striking young actor had become a favorite of beautiful young women and audiences alike. The previous fall, one fawning actress had written, "as the sunflowers turn upon their stalks to follow the beloved sun, so old or young, our faces smiling, turned to him."[21] A lovestruck Baltimore woman once described the actor's appearance as "like a new blown rose with the morning dew upon it."[22]

On this night, in Albany, a somewhat more mature rose, nearly in full bloom, would play the lead—Romeo—opposite Annie Waite as Juliet. Upon seeing him that night, Albany would confer upon him the title of America's most handsome actor: John Wilkes Booth.[23]

Booth almost certainly knew by the time he took the stage that night that Lincoln would arrive in Albany the following week—how could anyone who read the papers, especially those published in cities along the route, not know? Perhaps he even imagined that the president-elect would take in a show, see the rising young star, and be impressed by his élan, his stage presence, his mastery of Shakespeare. After all, Lincoln was known to be a fan of the Bard. And if Lincoln would not come out to see Booth, then perhaps Booth would go to see him. Booth almost certainly would want to see and hear the president-elect; he had a penchant for putting himself where the action was, even if it meant donning a disguise, missing a performance, and assuming an unpaid role in order to be in the scene.

A little over a year earlier, on November 19, 1859, Booth had abandoned his role on one stage, as a stock actor for the Old Marshall Theatre in Richmond, Virginia, in order to assume another bit part—as a member of the Richmond Grays, a local company of militia. The Grays, professionally uniformed and shouldering knapsacks and muskets, were heading to Charles Town, Virginia. Their mission: to guard John Brown, imprisoned and about to be executed for his infamous and deadly October 16, 1859, raid on Harpers Ferry.

The Grays anticipated the real possibility of seeing action—rumors swirled that hordes of abolitionists might rise up and attempt to rescue John Brown. Always the opportunist, Booth spotted the train parked just steps from the Marshall Theatre on Broad Street that would carry the Grays to the expected seat of battle.[24] Impulsively, he decided to board the train. After being initially refused passage, the young Thespian likely bought or borrowed a uniform and used his acting skills to talk his way onto the baggage car.[25] Booth habitually had trouble telling fact from fiction, however, and later claimed not only to have joined in the hunt for John Brown, but to have participated in his capture and execution. "I may say I helped to hang John Brown," he asserted, adding, "his [Brown's] treason was no more than theirs [abolitionists] for open *force* is *holier* than hidden *craft*. The Lion is more noble than the fox."[26] Years later, he would boast, "When I aided in the capture and execution of John Brown . . . I was proud of my little share in the transaction, for I deemed it my duty and that I was helping our common country to perform an act of justice."[27]

In fact, the boastful young actor played no part in the capture of John Brown, that act having been performed on October 18, 1859 by troops under the command of an able, but as yet largely unknown Virginian—Colonel Robert E. Lee.[28] At best, Booth had, weeks later, assumed the role of a Richmond Gray, possibly playing bit parts as an assistant commissary, quartermaster, or scout.[29] Whatever role he played, the young actor was indeed at the gallows on December 2, 1859, as confirmed by eyewitnesses.[30] Before the hood fell over John Brown's face, the old man stood, one eye scanning the horizon for a last minute rescue by unseen abolitionist hordes he had hoped to inspire, the other eye trained on the noose poised to launch him into eternity.

The horde of abolitionists never came to John Brown's aid—his last view this side of the grave may have been that of treed snipers poised to gun down any would-be saviors.[31] A long, silent moment after the hemp collar was fitted around his grizzled neck, the rope snapped taught, and John Brown swung and kicked his way to a slow, strangulating death. Booth watched it all, standing near Major Thomas J. Jackson, who would later earn his more famous moniker "Stonewall." Booth had come to Charles Town seeking vengeance and a good show. But the young actor may have been surprised that at the climax of the execution, the blood ran from his face, and he actually felt a pang of sorrow and grudging admiration for John Brown. He now regarded the abolitionist as a tragic, even heroic, figure. "He was a brave old man; his heart must have broken when he felt deserted," the actor later confided to his sister.[32] In a perverse way, John Brown's hanging may have inspired Booth, a man already inspired by Shakespeare's tragedies, to aspire to martyrdom.

The young actor would exit the boards of the gallows and return to the boards of the stage, leaving Charles Town and the Richmond Grays soon after Brown's hanging, and rejoining Richmond's Old Marshall Theater on December 5, 1859. He carried with him a cherished souvenir. Lewis Washington, taken hostage by John Brown during the raid, had given the young actor a prized memento—John Brown's spear.[33]

JOHN WILKES BOOTH was born to unwed parents on May 10, 1838, about 20 miles north of Baltimore in Harford County, near Bel Air, Maryland, in a modest farmhouse that had begun as a log cabin. The farm, with a complement of leased slaves, ultimately achieved plantation-like status, complete with the grand-sounding name of Tudor Hall. As a boy on the farm, John Wilkes Booth admired the then popular "Southron" notions of knighthood and chivalry. He practiced the art of "riding the ring," spearing a bracelet-sized target with a lance astride a horse at full gallop.[34]

The ninth of ten illegitimate children[35] born to Junius Brutus Booth and Mary Ann Holmes, "Johnny" spent much of his early life away from the farm, in Baltimore, at his father's home at 62 North Exeter Street. His was a privileged, if sometimes troubled youth. In Baltimore, he would have his first run-in with the law, being briefly arrested for his role in a schoolboy's prank.[36] John Wilkes attended private schools, including a prestigious military academy, St. Timothy's Hall in Catonsville, just a few rail miles west of Baltimore.[37] Here he would mingle with the well-to-do sons of slaveholding families, proudly wear the gray uniform of an artillery cadet, and meet future co-conspirator Samuel Arnold.[38] Booth would have a more serious scrape with authority at St. Timothy's. Following a squabble with school administrators, he joined Sam Arnold and others in stealing guns from the school's offices and setting up a rebel camp, boldly daring school officials to come root them out.[39]

John Wilkes was anything but a quick study in school. "He had to plod, progress slowly step by step," his sister Asia Booth Clarke wrote. Even though the negative was slow to develop, however, the image once formed was unfading; Booth's memory was indeed photographic. As Wilkes told his sister, once he learned something, it became "stamped on the sight of his mind." Asia recalled that "He not only recollected, but saw it, so as to be able to turn to the part of the page immediately."[40]

Acting, extramarital dalliances, impulsiveness of youth, unbridled patriotism, and fanatical politics ran turbulent and deep in J. Wilkes Booth's bloodline. His namesake, former London mayor John Wilkes, to whom he was distantly related, was a radical eighteenth century English politician and reformer.[41] Wilkes supported the colonies' goal of independence from the tyrannical reign of King George III, even serving as the British representative of the Sons of Liberty, a Boston revolutionary society.[42] J. Wilkes Booth's grandfather, Richard Booth, attempted at age twenty to run off to America, intent on joining colonial troops during the American Revolution. His father put a stop to such treason; Richard would remain in England and become a lawyer. But Richard Booth would never forget his dream of becoming an American. In eccentric defiance of father and crown, he insisted in later years that visitors to his quarters on Queen Street in Bloomsbury remove their hats and bow to a portrait of George Washington hung on the wall.

J. Wilkes Booth's father, Junius Brutus Booth—named after Marcus Junius Brutus, the tragic hero and assassin of *Julius Caesar*—would succeed where his father had failed, pursuing his chosen career—acting—and getting to America. Both came at a great price. As a young actor in Brussels, Junius had married Adelaide Delannoy in 1814 after stealing her from her mother, his landlord. As a condition for her consent to the marriage, Adelaide's mother insisted that Junius return to Brussels and give up acting for a more stable career. This, of course would never do; stability would never be a character trait of Junius Brutus Booth. In May 1821, Junius abandoned Adelaide and the son she had borne him, two-year-old Richard Junius, and set off for America. The twenty-four-year-old Junius had in tow a pretty young flower girl, eighteen-year-old Mary Ann Holmes, then pregnant with J. Wilkes's eldest brother, Junius Jr.—the itinerant father's third child (at least) by his third woman.[43] Junius Brutus Booth and Mary Ann landed in Norfolk, Virginia, on June 30, 1821,[44] in the land that would ultimately idolize him as a star of the American stage.

Thirty years later, Junius Brutus would try to make things right, finally divorcing his first wife, Adelaide, and marrying John Wilkes's mother, Mary Ann, in 1851, on the boy's thirteenth birthday.[45] Cognizant of his bastard status, J. Wilkes crudely tattooed the initials "J.W.B." in shaky script on his left hand, perhaps in a pathetic attempt to legitimize himself. Years later, the marks would legitimize not his life, but his death—helping to identify his body.

J. Wilkes Booth's acting career began in earnest in the summer of 1857, when he apprenticed for eight dollars a week at Philadelphia's Arch Street Theater.[46] Wilkes felt he had not yet earned the right to use the Booth name on stage. Or perhaps he wished to become famous in his own right. Either way, he billed himself simply as "J. Wilkes."

Between 1858 and 1860, Booth worked for eleven to twenty dollars a week as a stock actor in Richmond's Marshall

John Wilkes Booth. A glancing dagger wound he received while performing on stage in Albany, New York, allowed Booth to cancel his public appearances at the same time Lincoln's train was traveling across the state. (*Library of Congress*)

Theatre, honing his acting skills, which were at first crude.[47] He continued to bill himself as J. Wilkes, telling an acquaintance that he would not use the Booth name until he had legitimized himself as an actor.[48]

Time and place conspired to feed Booth's appetite for fame and glory. On October 20, 1860, he recited Marcus Antonius's *Julius Caesar* funeral speech on stage in Columbus, Georgia.[49] Southern audiences loved the young Shakespearean; theater attendance swelled when Booth played and shrank when he did not.[50] As he extolled the "noble Brutus," it would have been easy for J. Wilkes to equate the public's adoration for him with the famous words of Marc Antony's funeral oration: "Friends, Romans, countrymen, lend me your ears; I come to bury Caesar, not to praise him." It would also have been a simple matter for the young actor to equate Brutus's murder of Caesar with the nobility, the justice, of the Southern cause. The South was Rome, Lincoln was her oppressive Caesar, and all she needed was a Brutus to free her from the impending tyranny of abolitionism.

By late October 1860, billed as "the talented young Tragedian, Mr. John Wilkes," Booth was playing Pescara in *The Apostate* in Montgomery, Alabama.[51] Here, the air smoldered with the tantalizing smell of secession as the presidential election neared. On November 5, the day before Lincoln's victory, Southern fire-eater William Lowndes Yancey, as well as Georgia senator Robert Toombs and Stephen A. Douglas, all delivered impassioned speeches to a Montgomery audience.[52] Ever the man of the moment, J. Wilkes may have been at the root of the stump, hanging on every incendiary word. On December 1, 1860, Booth concluded his Montgomery run in a "Grand Complimentary Benefit" alongside Maggie Mitchell. For the first time, he would be billed as "Mr. J. Wilkes Booth."[53]

Angered over the election of Lincoln, the "sectional candidate," Booth reportedly joined the Baltimore order of the Knights of the Golden Circle in the fall of 1860[54]—the same secret rebel society to which Baltimoreans and suspected co-conspirators William Byrne, Cypriano Ferrandini, and possibly Otis K. Hillard were key members.[55]

As the air swirled with talk of Southern causes and patriotic glory in the winter of 1860-1861, J. Wilkes Booth must have recalled and been inspired by the legacy of his ancestors, of his grandfather's pining patriotism for America, of being forced to live under the rule of a tyrannical king. Of his father leaving that monarchy behind, striking out boldly for America to become a storyteller—for that is what actors are—and not just any storyteller, but a famous Shakespearean, a tragedian, a teller of tales of tyranny and oppression, of bold moves by bold men, like Richmond and Brutus, to over-throw tyrants in one swift stroke of justice, concentrating the will of the people at the point of a dagger.[56]

Tyranny and oppression must have weighed heavily on Booth's mind that fall and winter. The presidential election had been won not by majority vote, but by the electoral process, a quirk of the Constitution—a scrap of paper the abolitionists appealed to when it suited their fancy and ignored when it did not. The will of the people had not been met, for fewer than forty percent of them had voted for this sectional candidate. And if fewer than half had been for Lincoln, then a majority of Americans were against him.[57] To John Wilkes Booth, tyranny and oppression had a new name—abolitionism—a new king—Lincoln—and the king and his court would be setting out from Springfield in a mock royal coach, drawn by a chuffing iron horse, intent on occupying an illegitimate Black Republican throne.

In December 1860, the itinerant Booth was in Philadelphia, visiting his mother and sister.[58] Perhaps it was during this visit that Booth gave John Brown's spear to his sister Asia, for she did come to possess it.[59]

While in Philadelphia that winter, Booth may well have attended pro-Southern rallies being held in the City of Brotherly Love. He might have eas-ily ridden the flat hundred miles to Baltimore, perhaps running down and back the same day, perhaps staying overnight at Barnum's Hotel. It is certain-ly possible that in late 1860 and early 1861, while Byrne, Ferrandini, Hillard, and others were fomenting hatred of all things North in secret Baltimore conclaves, J. Wilkes Booth was right there with them, reciting passages from *Julius Caesar* to inspire and incite.

Booth's seething hatred of Lincoln, or at least the Republican Party, had clearly begun to stir by then. Evidence penned in Booth's own hand even before the president-elect left Springfield points ominously, if vaguely, to Booth's intent to murder Lincoln.

At the time of Booth's visit to Philadelphia, South Carolina careened toward secession and, on December 20, hit it head on. Philadelphia, a little over a dozen miles north of the slave line, held rallies supporting its Southern neighbors. Possibly moved by one such rally, a "Grand Union assembly" given December 13 at Independence Hall under a banner that read "Concession before Secession," the young actor wrote a lengthy, impassioned lecture, actually more of a political manifesto, in his room, likely between December 22 and 27, 1860.[60] Whether he delivered the speech, which began, "Gentlemen allow me a few words," is not known, though it seems unlikely. But his beliefs, as expressed in that speech and in his later actions, are known.

In his manifesto, Booth pleaded to Philadelphians for his beloved South: "She cannot live, while the republican principals still exist! . . . If . . . abolition principles are not entirely swept away, why we have but smoothed our troubles o're, which in a few years will burst forth with redoubled horror. *Now that we have found the serpent that madens us, we should crush it in its birth.*"[61]

The serpent to be crushed at birth was the newly elected president of the hatchling Republican Party, which Booth derided as synonymous with abolition.

By February 1861, J. Wilkes Booth was earning vast sums, playing to packed houses as a leading man in theaters throughout the North, including some in cities along the Lincoln Special's route. He was emerging not only as a theatrical drawing card, but also as a fanatical, if somewhat closeted, secessionist.[62] He was only twenty-two. But by some standards the bloom of opportunity was fast fading from the rose of fame he had so desperately craved for years. True, he had achieved a measure of notoriety on the stage, but it was an actor's glory only, an ephemeral fame that began fading to black with the footlights' last flicker. But the fame of a conquering hero—of a Richmond, a William Tell, a Brutus—now there was a fame that could endure forever. The patriotic passions of Booth's ancestors, as well as their Shakespearean legacy, coursed through his veins. The stars of fate, of motive, means, and opportunity, were fast aligning.

CHAPTER FIVE

A MESSAGE OF IMPORTANCE

Tuesday, February 12, 1861
Indianapolis–Cincinnati

ABRAHAM LINCOLN'S FIFTY-SECOND BIRTHDAY dawned in Indianapolis as a beautiful springlike day that would be sunny and mild.[1] But with the rising sun also came the rising tide of humanity. Crowds had "besieged" the Bates House until nearly midnight the previous evening.[2] Like predators resuming the hunt, they returned this morning. Reported the *New York Times,* "Immense crowds commenced gathering at the Bates House at daylight, and at 9 o'clock every available space near the hotel was occupied. The crowd in the parlors, reception rooms and halls was equally great."[3]

Everyone, it seemed, wanted a piece of Lincoln. That included Indiana governor Oliver Morton, who called on the president-elect at the Bates House and escorted him and a few other members of the Lincoln entourage to the Governor's Mansion for breakfast.[4] The trade-off of leaving the swarm at the Bates House was that it required Lincoln to endure breakfast with a pack of hungry politicians gnawing at his elbow.

At 10:30, breakfast over, Lincoln and his suite were escorted in carriages to the Union Depot. Here, U.S. Army Captain George W. Hazzard joined the already crowded party.[5] By now, Colonel Sumner, Captain Pope, and Major Hunter had also joined the traveling suite.[6] The schedule called for the Lincoln Special to leave Indianapolis at 11:00 a.m. This would be the latest scheduled departure of the twelve-day trip. The reason for the delay was the need to await the arrival of Mary Todd and the two youngest Lincoln sons. Shortly after Lincoln arrived at the depot, the special train carrying Mrs. Lincoln also arrived, and she was conducted to a car reserved for her and her mini-suite, comprising Tad, Willie, and the boys' nurse.[7]

At just before 11:00 a.m., Lincoln boarded a train of the Indianapolis and Cincinnati Railroad, pulled by the locomotive *Samuel Wiggins,* named for a

Cincinnati banker and Unionist who was a director of the road.[8] Thirty-four stars set in a blue field encircled the balloon stack. Portraits of fourteen presidents and Lincoln grouped around Washington covered the front end of the locomotive. The train now consisted of four freshly varnished coaches decorated with red, white, and blue bunting. Lincoln's coach, the last on the train, included a hand-carved frescoed ceiling, and crimson plush wall covering accented with blue silk studded with silver stars. National flags festooned the doorways.[9] Precisely at 11:00 a.m., the train pulled out, and Lincoln, somberly dressed in a dark suit and long shawl, bowed to shouting spectators.

Only after passing through the outer suburbs of Indianapolis did Lincoln enter his coach. He found his family there waiting for him. His little boys, seven-year-old Tad and ten-year-old Willie, rushed into his outstretched arms.[10] It was the best birthday present a father could ever want. At stops along the way, Tad would ask people if they wanted to see Old Abe, and when the inevitable answer came, the little imp would point to someone other than Lincoln, laughing naughtily. Willie too joined in the pastime.[11]

Whether the Indianapolis and Cincinnati Railroad was on high alert or was merely taking prudent precautions, the road stationed signalmen all along the route to watch for trouble. Reported the press, "every precaution is taken by the Railroad Company to ensure the safety of the train. Flagmen are stationed at every road and crossing, and half way between them; they display the American flag as the signal for 'all right.'"[12] There was, however, real cause for concern.

The Lincoln Special was now heading southeast, toward Cincinnati, a riverboat town that lay just across the Ohio River from slaveholding territory—Kentucky. At Lawrenceburg, a small Indiana border town on the Ohio River, Lincoln alluded to this fact in a brief speech. Cheers erupted as he hoped that everyone in the immense crowd that had gathered to hear him were Union men and friendly with their neighbors across the river. "I suppose," Lincoln remarked pointing to the Kentucky shore, "that you are in favor of doing full justice to all, whether on that side of the river, or on your own."[13]

If one of Lincoln's campaign managers, Norman B. Judd, had seemed aloof, even secretive before the train started this morning, there was good reason. A capable lawyer and a former adversary of Lincoln, Norman B. Judd had opposed Lincoln's senatorial bid in 1855. Having failed in his own efforts to win the Illinois Republican gubernatorial nomination in the spring of 1860, however, the forty-five-year-old stubby-fingered Judd needed to find an alternative political pursuit. He became one of Lincoln's strongest supporters and one of his shrewdest political advisors. On the trip from Springfield, Judd would now serve, in many ways, as Lincoln's unofficial chief of staff.

Next to Lincoln himself, Norman Judd was probably the most well known civilian among the presidential traveling suite. Newspapers described him as a "chunky gentleman of about five feet five inches. He has a broad ruddy face, which shows well from the contrast of his gray hair and flowing beard approaching whiteness. He has a dark blue eye, hooked nose—rather short, and a mouth neither expressive nor forcible. He is evidently a character of much more tact than talent, and is fully impressed with the onus of the mysterious position he occupies in relation to the President elect. The shrewd ones slily say he managed to make Mr. Lincoln believe that he nominated him, and so puts in for a large share of the spoils."[14] Judged a "lawyer of great ability and a most agreeable traveling companion," Judd would be easily recognized on the trip by his unlit cigar, "which all but constantly protrudes from his lips."[15]

While he despised office seekers generally, Lincoln indeed likely felt obligated to confer a share of the office-seeking spoils on Judd. At Lincoln's urging, Judd had maneuvered the Republican National Committee to select Chicago for the 1860 Republican Convention. It was a strategic stroke of genius. The Windy City's newspapers and crowds would tend to favor a native Illinois son over other candidates, like New York's William H. Seward and Pennsylvania's Simon Cameron.[16] Judd, who chaired the Illinois delegation at the convention,[17] brilliantly seated the New York delegates at one end of the convention hall, the Pennsylvania delegates at the other, with Lincoln's supporters dividing them. Lincoln needed Pennsylvania if he was going to win the nomination; if Pennsylvania supported Seward, the Lincoln cause would have been lost. Thus separated by Judd, however, the New York and Pennsylvania delegations would have no opportunity to caucus and form alliances during the balloting.[18] While a house divided against itself might not stand, a convention hall thus divided would stand unanimously for Lincoln.

Judd had spent much of January in Springfield, looking after and polishing his political masterpiece—such as it was—with his trademark unlit cigar clenched between his teeth.[19] The previous May, he had insured that nothing would happen to prevent Lincoln's nomination. In November, he hoped for, then celebrated, Lincoln's election. Now, in February, Judd wanted to make sure nothing would happen to prevent Lincoln's March 4 inauguration. They had come so far. All that remained was to get Lincoln safely to Washington. Everything seemed to be going relatively smoothly in that regard until this morning. Just before the train left Indianapolis, Judd received an unexpected telegram. The intriguing message had been sent from Chicago at 9:10 a.m. by a man named George H. Bangs on behalf of his boss, Allan Pinkerton. The provocative message, uncoded and lacking aliases, read as follows:

N. B. Judd in company with Abraham Lincoln
Indianapolis Ind.

I have a message of importance for you—
Where can it reach you by special Messenger.
Allan Pinkerton.[20]

That Pinkerton should reach out to Judd would not have come as a surprise to him. First, like Pinkerton, Judd was from Chicago, and the two men knew each other well from their days as school chums. Second, Judd was considered to be the "most active and influential member of the suite of the President-elect."[21] If there was anyone traveling with Lincoln best able to convey a message of importance to him, Pinkerton knew it would have been Norman B. Judd. But while the fact of Pinkerton's communication may not have surprised Judd, the communication's content—or lack of it—must have stunned him. What possible message of importance could Pinkerton have? Why not just relay it in the telegram? Why the need for a mysterious special messenger?

Moments after reading Pinkerton's message, Judd fired off a brief reply:

Indianapolis 12 Feby 1861
A Pinkerton
At Columbus the thirteenth—Pittsburg the Fourteenth.
N.B. Judd.[22]

But Judd's telegram would be unnecessary. By the time the telegram arrived at Pinkerton's Chicago headquarters, Allan Pinkerton had already dispatched a special messenger, William H. Scott, intent on catching up with Lincoln's suite, who would attempt to intercept them using the widely published reports of Lincoln's itinerary.[23] Whatever the content of the important message Scott carried, it was clearly too critical to trust to the telegraph wires and could not wait. But if there were any changes in Lincoln's itinerary, there was the risk that Pinkerton's vital message, whatever it was, would not be delivered in time, if at all.

Judd quietly boarded the train after sending his message. He told no one— not Ward Hill Lamon, not the military officers, not even Mr. Lincoln—about the telegram he had received or the one he had just sent.

In Albany, the *Atlas and Argus,* a Democratic newspaper, would have been readily available to John Wilkes Booth. Perhaps Stanwix Hall's management had even brought him a complimentary copy this morning. If Booth read the *Argus* on February 12, however, he would have been disappointed—there were no reviews of the previous night's performance. Worse, the front-page news would have stung him like a slap to the face. Tennessee had voted overwhelmingly for the Union and against secession. Indeed, one county gave 5,700 votes for the Union, only 675 for secession. Then, as if that weren't bad enough, the

Confederacy's own vice president, A. H. Stephens, had made a conciliatory speech in Montgomery in which he asked that "peace, fraternity, and liberal commercial relations with all the world be our motto."[24]

But something else in this morning's paper would have caught Booth's eye. The *Argus* reported that Abraham Lincoln had left Springfield the day before, and gave an account of his farewell address. Lincoln would be in Buffalo Saturday of the present week, where he would remain until Monday morning. Most importantly, the paper confirmed prior reports that Lincoln would arrive in Albany Monday afternoon, February 18, at approximately three o'clock.[25] Booth's engagement would keep him in Albany through the end of next week. He and Lincoln would be in the same city on the same day.

In an editorial, the *Argus* noted that "We trust that Mr. Lincoln's journey to Washington will be marked by good taste and good sense, not only on his part, but also on the part of his friends and the public generally." The opinion emphasized that "all party demonstrations at this time are out of place, and we are glad to see it announced that they are discouraged by Mr. Lincoln." The Democratic newspaper closed, "We doubt not he will receive such attentions, here as are appropriate to the occasion, extended by our citizens and authorities without distinction of party."[26]

Perhaps. But perhaps Booth had other ideas. Except for rehearsals and performances, Booth—and any likeminded Southern sympathizers—would have six full days to prepare for Lincoln's arrival in Albany. Perhaps he could make a show of it.

AT 3:00 p.m. on February 12, once again right on schedule, Lincoln's train arrived to a huge ovation and fantastic pageantry in Cincinnati, at the Ohio and Mississippi Railroad depot at Fifth Street.[27] Reported the newspapers the next day, "The foot of Fifth street was literally blocked with people, and the locomotive was compelled to stop; the crowd was so great that it was impossible to get out of the way. At the depot it was found necessary to bring the military and police forces into requisition to clear the track."[28]

This report would have provided yet additional vital intelligence to the Baltimore plotters: Lincoln's train could literally be stopped in its tracks by a large crowd. This might be done in advance of the train's arrival at the depot, where the police force would be greatest. And if a twenty-ton locomotive could be stopped, an open barouche driven by a team of horses could be even more easily waylaid by a large crowd.

Lincoln was greeted by Cincinnati's mayor, Richard M. Bishop, and welcomed to the city with a few appropriate words. Whereas the barouche that had hauled Lincoln through Indianapolis did so with four white horses, Cincinnati would go one pair better, doing so with six.[29] An eyewitness described the scene: "The day was mild for mid-winter, but the sky was overcast with clouds, emblematic of the gloom that filled the hearts of the unnumbered thousands who thronged the streets and covered the house-tops. Lincoln rode in an open carriage, stand-ing erect with uncovered head, and steadying himself by holding on to a board fastened to the front part of the vehicle. A more uncom-fortable ride than this, over the bouldered streets of Cincinnati, cannot well be imag-ined. . . . Mr. Lincoln bore it with characteris-tic patience. His face was very sad, but he seemed to take a deep interest in every-thing."[30]

Norman B. Judd. Although Judd became a staunch supporter and confidante of Abraham Lincoln, Mary Todd Lincoln did not trust him. (*Picture History*)

Once again, Lincoln repeated the proce-dure he had performed in Indianapolis: ride in an open carriage, through crowded streets, standing erect. One of the reporters traveling with Lincoln, Joseph Howard Jr. of the *New York Times*, offered an apt description of Lincoln to readers who had never seen him:

> Mr. Lincoln stands six feet and four inches high; he has a large head, with a very high, shelving forehead; thick, bushy dark hair; a keen, bright, indeterminable colored eye; a prominent, thin-nostriled nose; a large, well bowed mouth; a round, pretty chin; a first crop of darkish whiskers; a clean, well built neck; more back than chest; a long, lank trunk; limbs of good shape and extreme longitude; arms ditto, with hands and feet symmetrical but naturally large. He wore a black silk hat (plug,) a dress coat, and pants of sombre hue; a turn over collar, and (I presume) other garments, such as usually are found upon gentlemen who enjoy the annual income of at least $25,000. . . . Mr. Lincoln stood up bare-headed, holding on by a conveniently arranged board, and bowed his backbone sore, and his neck stiff, all the way to the hotel.[31]

If they didn't know what Lincoln looked like before, the Baltimore plotters would have little trouble spotting him now.

After two hours of being paraded in this fashion through town, amid a blur of fluttering handkerchiefs, flags, and cheers, Lincoln and his party arrived at the Burnett House at 5:15 p.m. When he entered the hotel, a band played "Hail Columbia" and "The Star-Spangled Banner."[32] This triumphal procession and reception contrasted sharply with Lincoln's first visit to Cincinnati. He had stayed there a few years before, in the summer of 1857, while working as co-counsel on the McCormick reaper case, an important patent dispute. But the trial team, composed of primarily eastern lawyers, would have nothing to do with Lincoln. Believing him a buffoon, the other lawyers on the case shunned him, not permitting him to make oral arguments, not even inviting him to sit at counsel table or walk to court with them. This treatment was due in large part to an arrogant lawyer from Pittsburgh, none other than Edwin McMasters Stanton. "Why did you bring that d—d long armed Ape here," Stanton sneered at one of his co-counsel, "he does not know anything and can do you no good." The snub wounded Lincoln deeply. Upon leaving Cincinnati, he vowed to never come back, telling a hostess, "I have nothing against the city, but things have so happened here as to make it undesirable for me ever to return."[33] Once back in Springfield, Lincoln dejectedly told William Herndon the reason why: he had been "roughly handled by that man Stanton."[34]

What a difference a few years could make. Now in Cincinnati, no one would leave Lincoln alone or even give him room to walk. Now, everyone begged him to speak. Stanton, who had snubbed Lincoln here, soon would be answering to him.

But while there would be no more snubs for Lincoln in Cincinnati, there would be one from just across the river, in his native state of Kentucky. Reported the World's anonymous correspondent, "The mayor of Covington, a Kentucky town into which, from the roof of the Burnet house, an arrow might almost be shot, is one of the disaffected. He declines to wait upon and pay his respects to the President elect, a circumstance of no further consequence than that it saves the presidential hand a violent grip and his arm a tremendous wrench."[35]

In reality, Lincoln was likely wounded by this snub too. He had been born in Kentucky and, now that he was so close to his home state, wanted to cross the river and speak directly to its residents. He had even prepared a speech that appealed to them in Kennedy-esque "Ich bin ein Berliner" fashion: "Gentlemen, I too, am a Kentuckian," Lincoln had written.[36] He sought to explain to Kentuckians why he could not compromise the platform on which he had been elected—roughly translated, no extension of slavery where it did not already exist. To do that would betray the trust of those who had elected him and, if taken to extremes, would ruin the man elected, ruin his party, and ultimately ruin the government itself. Eerily reminiscent of threats on his life, Lincoln closed: "I do not deny the possibility that the people may err in an election; but if they do, the true cure is in the next election; and not in the

treachery of the party elected."[37] But no
invitation from Covington's mayor ever
came. Lincoln did not cross the river. His
Kentucky speech was never given.

In Baltimore, one of Allan Pinkerton's
operatives, under the alias Charles D. C.
Williams and the initials C.D.C.W.,[38] sat
down in Pinkerton's "stockbroker's" office
to write his report for the previous day.
He worried that he was not up to the task
of playing the role of a Southerner and
told Pinkerton so. "I . . . told him that I
was afraid I could not play my part, as I
had come across a Mississippi man who
knew every place. A.P. said there was no
danger, and all I wanted was self confidence."

Williams left the office and went to
Sherwood's Hotel, where he was staying.
He engaged Howell Sherwood, the landlord's brother, in a conversation.
Sherwood typified the sentiment of many
in Baltimore: he wanted peace and the
Union preserved, but failing that, would
side with the South. Sherwood confided
that while he was not a secessionist himself, he had spoken with a friend who had
attended a secret secession meeting in
Baltimore just the week before. The

One of the few known full-length photographs of Abraham Lincoln, taken in
1860 by an unknown photographer.
His unusual height would make him a
tall target while riding in open
barouches. (*Library of Congress*)

morning after that meeting, Sherwood's
friend reported "that if anyone had said there was such a conspiracy in this or
any other City, amongst Christians, he would not have believed it: that last
night he heard the vilest proposition proposed by men, calling themselves
men, that ever was heard of: that they proposed to blow up the Capitol on the
day that the Votes were counted, and then blow up the Custom House, and
Post Office (Baltimore), and what else he dare not tell."[39]

Williams would have known that Sherwood's reference to "the day that the
Votes were counted" meant the following day, February 13, when both Houses
of Congress would convene at the Capitol to count the electoral votes, as
required by the Constitution.

Williams tested the veracity of Sherwood's story, and he confirmed that the conspiracy was real: "Oh my God, it is so," Sherwood insisted. Sherwood reported that one of their number was a "d—d white headed son of a b—, a Lawyer, named Mc—something, who goes every day to Washington, and brings the news to this crowd, and that they hold secret meetings every night." Most significantly, Sherwood reported that he thought one of the places the group held their secret meetings was at Baltimore's Eutaw House.[40]

As of this date, Lincoln had not received any public invitations to visit Baltimore. But he had received a private one. Sent on January 24, it had come from a Mr. R. B. Coleman in the form of a request to stay in Baltimore "for a week or more." There were some curious things about Mr. Coleman's invitation. First, it had not been sent to Lincoln, but to an intermediary, Simeon Draper. Second, it was sent under the heading "Strictly Confidential" and with an injunction that it be kept that way. Third, the invitation almost seemed to have been sent behind the scenes on behalf of Governor Hicks. Wrote Coleman, "Gov Hicks will be here & see him [Lincoln] and it will give Gov Hicks strength to hold out manfully as he has done against the pressure that has been upon him to convene the Legislature." Equally strange, in closing his letter to Draper, Coleman wrote with a slant that almost dared Lincoln to accept his invitation: "this move would show that he is not afraid to stop in a slave state . . . I am sure he would be treated very kindly."[41]

But there was something even more curious, and far more intriguing, about Coleman's invitation. The plea was for Lincoln to stay at the Eutaw House, one of the places in which secret secession meetings were now allegedly being held. If in fact such meetings were taking place there, R. B. Coleman, of all people, should have known about them: he was the proprietor of the Eutaw House.[42]

ANOTHER Pinkerton agent in Baltimore, Harry W. Davies, had, like his colleague Charles D. C. Williams, also learned vital intelligence that day. Davies, whom Pinkerton described as "a young man of fine personal appearance, and of insinuating manners," was of French descent. He had studied to become a Jesuit priest but disliked the vocation and abandoned it. He had traveled extensively and knew several foreign languages. Most importantly, Davies possessed an intimate knowledge of the South, having spent several years in New Orleans and other Southern cities.[43] If there was anyone who could make a convincing show of being from the South and being sympathetic to secession causes, it was Harry W. Davies.

In Baltimore, Davies had taken up with Select Committee of Five witness and suspected conspirator Otis K. Hillard. After a night of carousing in restaurants, billiard rooms, concert saloons, and Annette Travis's house of prostitution at Number 70 Davis Street, and unsuccessfully seeking out suspected co-conspirator Captain Ferrandini at his barbershop under Barnum's Hotel, the two men returned to Davies' room at Hall's boardinghouse on Holliday Street. Hillard, likely drunk, was in a talkative mood when they got there. He talked about Company Number 4 of the National Volunteers drilling that night. He talked about his own company drilling the following night. And then Hillard talked about something most important.

Wrote Davies,

> He then asked me if I had seen a statement of Lincoln's route to Washington City—I replied that I had—Hillard said, "By the By, that reminds me that I must go and see a certain party in the morning the first thing." I asked him what about—He replied "about Lincoln's route, I want to see about the Telegraph in Philadelphia and New York and have some arrangement made about Telegraphing." I remarked, "how do you mean?" Hillard said "Suppose that some of Lincoln's friends would arrange so that the Telegraph messages should be miscarried, we would have some signs to Telegraph by: for instance supposing, that we should Telegraph to a certain point 'all up at 7,' that would mean that Lincoln would be at such a point at 7 o'clock."[44]

Hillard had just revealed that he and other conspirators were aware of Lincoln's route, that they knew it would take the president-elect through New York and Philadelphia, and that they had operatives of their own prepared to shadow Lincoln in at least those two cities. And now the conspirators were in the early stages of developing a cipher system for telegraphing coded messages concerning Lincoln's movements. But most alarming, Hillard had revealed tantalizing clues to Davies that there was a plan having something to do with Lincoln. He would not specify what that plan was. And he would not reveal anything further about it to Davies. "My friend," said Hillard, "I would like to tell you, but I dare not—I wish I could—anything almost I would be willing to do for you, but to tell you that I dare not."[45]

THE night of February 12, 1861, saw John Wilkes Booth switching roles from the previous night, playing one of his favorites, Pescara, in Richard Sheil's 1817 tragedy *The Apostate*. Stage actors of the era, particularly circuit-riding stars like John Wilkes Booth, had to be able to quickly assume new roles with little, if any, time to rehearse. They needed the endurance to travel great distances by rail and coach in search of adoring and hopefully large paying audiences. They had to be versatile— a tragedian in *Hamlet* in a certain city one night, a comedian in *As You Like It* in another city the next.[46]

But this night, during the last act, the flamboyant young actor would injure his co-star, inflicting a minor cut on the head. The scene continued. Later, the audience learned that Booth too had been injured. Booth's acting had been too realistic, but the critics loved it. "His acting was so fearfully real in some of the scenes as to cause a thrilling sensation to pervade the audience, and when at the conclusion of the play, in answer to the repeated calls . . . , it was announced that he had seriously wounded himself, it seemed as though the climax of the TRAGEDY had indeed been reached."[47]

One account of the accident reported that "while engaged in combat with Mr. Leonard, J. W. Booth inflicted a slight cut with his rapier on the head of the former gentleman, and soon after met with a mishap himself, by falling on his dagger, which entered his side, and glancing from the ribs, cut away the muscles for some three inches."[48] By other accounts, the wound was between one and two inches in depth. A Dr. Crouse, who happened to be in the audience, dressed the injury.[49] The wound, a laceration under his right arm, would sideline Booth for six full days, until the evening of February 18—the day of Lincoln's published arrival in Albany.[50] And yet the wound was reported as "not serious in character."[51] Serious or not, the injury provided Booth a convenient excuse for missing performances and likely rehearsals as well. It gave the young actor, a man with seemingly boundless energy, the luxury of time. Time to recuperate. Time to read. Time to study. Time to plan.

THE same night Booth was wounded on stage, in Cincinnati, at the Burnett House, Lincoln hosted a reception in the hotel's large dining room. He stood on a platform about six inches high, surrounded by a cordon of police. Behind Lincoln stood his stalwart military guards: Colonel Ellsworth, Colonel Sumner, and Major Hunter. They waited for the doors to open and the dammed-up tide of humanity to roll in. Finally, Ellsworth roared "Let 'em come." The doors flung open and the crowd gushed in. Lincoln shook their hands for about an hour. Eventually, he was persuaded to get up on a chair and call it a night. He did so, telling the crowd that still waited to pump his arm that while he would by happy to join hands with all of them, the time had come for him to retire. A ring of policemen and friends instantly surrounded him, and only with some difficulty was Lincoln able to force his way through the crowd to his room.[52]

Among the crowd eying Lincoln at the Burnett House that night was a shadowy man whose name likely would have meant little to the president-elect in February 1861. The man was George N. Sanders. A former Kentuckian, now a New York Democratic political operative and left wing radical, Sanders had spent time in Europe the previous decade nurturing a passion for political assassination.[53] During the height of the war, Sanders would become a C.S.A. government contractor and engage in clandestine operations for the Confederacy in Canada. Most intriguing, witnesses would testify they had seen Sanders meeting in the fall of 1864 in Montreal with Confederate officials and none other than John Wilkes Booth. The question becomes, what was George N. Sanders, no fan of Republicans, an avowed advocate of political assassination, and future Booth confidante, doing here in Cincinnati, within reach of Lincoln, on the night of February 12, 1861?

George N. Sanders, an advocate of political assassination, was identified at several stops along Lincoln's trip East. (*Library of Congress*)

The presidential party, meanwhile, settled in for a good night's sleep. As grim as things had seemed yesterday, they had brightened considerably today. The *World's* anonymous correspondent would write this day that "The arrangements here throughout were admirable. Cincinnati has honored herself in her manner of honoring the President. The weather has been delightful."[54]

Abraham Lincoln, worn out from an evening of speech giving and hand shaking, retired to his room in the Burnett House. He found there little Tad, sleeping in a chair fully dressed, having waited up for his father, fighting sleep as long as a seven-year-old's little body might, until sleep prevailed. The president-elect gathered the child in his arms, dressed him for bed, and with the love only a father can know for his son, laid him beside Willie before covering both his precious little boys.[55] Perhaps Lincoln actually felt at peace, if only momentarily. His family was all together for the trip to Washington. Two days down, ten more to go. But tomorrow was bigger than most of them. Tomorrow, in Washington, Lincoln's electoral votes would be counted, and he would be officially, constitutionally, declared elected as president of the United States—at least so he hoped.

CHAPTER SIX

THE ELECTORAL COLLEGE

Wednesday, February 13, 1861
Cincinnati–Columbus

GREETING A CLEAR, CRYSTALLINE BLUE SKY, the sun rose slowly over the Potomac and Washington City. The weather was balmy for February, and the air so calm, so still, that the Union flags hanging over the Capitol lay motionless against their staves.[1] The serenity at the Capitol was misleading, however, and it would not last. Beneath the surface, Washington was anything but calm and soon would be anything but motionless.

By 8:00 a.m., crowds begin climbing Capitol Hill. By 10:00 a.m., amid bright sunshine and springlike temperatures, "the broad, northern sidewalk of Pennsylvania Avenue was thronged with ladies and gentlemen on their way to the Capitol."[2] The crowd anticipated a spectacle and everyone wanted a front-row seat. On this day, Congress was to witness the electoral vote. The security of the vote count was in serious doubt. This is because February 13 had also been the date set for secessionists to seize Washington.[3] The majority of those seeking gallery seats this morning were Southerners.[4] Some expected to witness not only a war of ballots, but one of bullets. Revolution, or at least rumor of it, was in the air.

But if there was to be a war in the Capitol building this morning, it would be a private one. The house divided convened behind closed doors. Only senators, congressman, and those bearing a prized and rare ticket of admission signed by the Speaker of the House or Vice President Breckinridge could gain entry. Everyone else would be turned away by General Scott's guards, "civil but inflexible soldiers," posted at every doorway. Offers of bribes, pleas for mercy, and threatening oaths were equally unavailing.[5]

General Scott had good reason to worry. In early January, a secret meeting of secession leaders had assembled in Washington. They reportedly conspired to commit at least two treasonable acts. First, they resolved that rather than postponing a formal act of secession until after March 4, all the slave states should immediately secede and hold a convention in Montgomery to form a new government. In fact, by February 13, seven slave states had seceded, a new Confederate government, though infantile, had been birthed, and their president elected. Second, these secession leaders resolved that Southern senators and representatives should remain in their seats in Washington as long as possible to "aid the cause of liberty" by "exposing and thwarting measures hostile to the secession movement."[6] This also occurred, with Senator Louis T. Wigfall of Texas remaining in Washington as the Confederacy's most vocal advocate.

There thus occurred, albeit briefly, a singular event in American government: legislative representatives loyal to one sovereign, the Confederacy, retained their offices to another sovereign, the Union, now their sworn enemy. In effect, for several critical weeks, they acted as legislative double agents.

One of the "measures hostile to the secession movement" that the rebels hoped to thwart, it was feared, was the count of Lincoln's electoral vote. Lincoln himself worried over this possibility. "It seems to me the inauguration is not the most dangerous point for us," he wrote Seward on January 3. "Our adversaries have us more clearly at disadvantage, on the second Wednesday of February, when the votes should be officially counted."[7] The reasons for this disadvantage were clear: President Buchanan was weak. The Union was weak. Washington's military security force, though stout in heart, was small in number. Most importantly, the electoral vote count would be presided over by Vice President Breckinridge, the secessionist's candidate in the presidential elections.

Lincoln's hunch was prescient. As the date for the vote count neared, Washington swelled with out-of-towners. "Train after train from the South, the West, and the North poured its volume of passengers into the streets of an already overcrowded city."[8] Thousands of rooms had been rented in Washington by Southerners up until March 4, the objective being, according to Wigfall,[9] "to have our friends on the ground in case of emergency."[10] The "emergency" was apparently the interruption of the vote count and the seizure of the capital and national archives prior to Lincoln's inauguration. Wrote Lucius E. Chittenden, a delegate from Vermont to the Washington Peace Conference, "preparations had been made; armed bodies of men had been enlisted and drilled, and many of them had reported in the city pursuant to orders."[11] Undoubtedly some of these armed men would have come from Baltimore, where, as Otis K. Hillard revealed, the National Volunteers had been drilling. The man allegedly in charge of the coup d'état was Major Benjamin McCulloch of Texas. He had, it is said, surveyed the city of Washington, preparing both for its seizure and consequent repulsion of Northern invaders.[12] Seward had earlier warned Lincoln of this threat. On December 29, he wrote: "A plot is forming to seize the capital on or before the

4th of March, and this too, has its accomplices in the public councils. I could tell you more particularly than I dare write, but you must not imagine that I am giving you suspicions and rumors. Believe me I know what I write. In point of fact, the responsibilities of your Administration must begin before the time arrives. I therefore renew my suggestion of your coming here earlier than you otherwise would—and coming in by surprise—without announcement."[13]

If the rebels planned to seize Washington by stealth, Seward wanted Lincoln to do the same, by seizing it first.

In view of these apprehensions of conspiracies to seize Washington, the federal government's public buildings, including the Capitol, had, the past several weeks, been guarded. Every night, capital police made an examination of the cellars and vaults of the Capitol building, to insure that no explosives had been planted. But not all of Seward's warnings had been heeded. While Lincoln did plan to arrive in Washington a little over a week before March 4, he was not planning to arrive by surprise or without announcement. And while rumors of secessionist's intent to seize the capital had by February 13 largely subsided, they had not gone away. Today, it was reported, "officers of artillery were on duty for the purpose of immediately communicating with Congress, should an attempt be made to attack the capital. The military was ready to advance at a moment's warning."[14]

PINKERTON'S special messenger, William H. Scott, had been lucky. The previous day, Pinkerton's Chicago agency had tried to reach Scott in Lafayette, Indiana, with a telegram conveying the intelligence from Judd's dispatch. This telegram would have confirmed for Scott that Judd would be in Columbus on February 13 and Pittsburgh on February 14.[15] This telegram, however, failed to reach Scott. Without knowing for certain where he might catch up with Lincoln's traveling show and Norman B. Judd, Scott had taken a gamble that they would, as the itinerary announced, arrive and stay in Cincinnati on the twelfth. Scott doggedly trudged into the Burnett House around 2:00 a.m. on the thirteenth.[16]

William H. Scott might have been anyone. He might have been who he claimed, a special messenger for the Pinkerton Agency with an important message for Mr. Judd. Or, he might have been an impostor telling a fabricated story to get close to Lincoln. Despite this, someone in the Burnett House confirmed to Scott that Judd, and therefore Lincoln, was there. Scott learned that Judd had been in bed since 11:00 p.m. He would not be disturbed. Scott could see Judd in the morning before he left at 9:00 a.m.[17]

Scott woke at 7:00, and by 8:00 a.m. managed to gain an audience with Judd. Scott gave him Pinkerton's letter. Judd indicated to Scott that he had been expecting it. He was about to say more, when Scott cut him off. Judd read the dispatch. The information was stunning. The contents of the letter and the circumstances relating to it were too important to discuss even privately. Scott admonished Judd that Pinkerton wanted the letter kept strictly confidential. "That is true," Judd agreed, "and I am very much obliged to you and A. P— for the information."[18]

Although the import of Scott's dispatch survives, the letter itself does not. Perhaps Judd burned it that morning in his hotel room. Perhaps he threw it into the Lincoln Special's firebox as the train departed. In any case, Judd would later recall the two essential points of the message; first, that Pinkerton had reason to believe "there was a plot on foot to murder the President on his passage through [Baltimore]," and second, that Pinkerton would communicate further with Judd as the Lincoln Special progressed eastward.[19]

Judd would take literally Pinkerton's admonition to keep his letter strictly confidential. Whether he did so in order to follow Pinkerton's instructions as precisely as possible, to avoid unnecessarily alarming anyone in the party, or to preserve for himself the inherent power that came with being the sole proprietor of Pinkerton's intelligence is not important. What is important is that Judd would share the information about a brewing plot to assassinate Lincoln in Baltimore with no one—not even with Lincoln.[20]

By 10:00 a.m. on February 13, as Lincoln's train chuffed northeast toward Columbus after leaving Cincinnati, the Select Committee of Five had reassembled in Washington. The committee was preparing to examine its final and most evasive witness, Maryland's governor Thomas H. Hicks.[21] For several reasons, this morning's session would be brief. First of all, each of the five members of the Select Committee was also a member of the House. As such, they needed to be present for the joint session of Congress, gathering at noon to count the electoral votes. Second, Hicks was the committee's only witness today, and he would be their last. The Select Committee was ready to wrap things up. Finally, Hicks's testimony would itself be brief. He had previously advised the committee that he had little information to add, and this morning he would make good on that promise. But it seems that Hicks had fretted over what kind of reception might greet him in Washington. Whether for emotional and physical support or merely to have a trusted and loyal friend on hand, Hicks brought with him fellow Marylander J. Bond Chaplain.[22]

Testifying this morning, Hicks, weary-looking and paunchy, seeming to droop and sag at every opportunity—eyes, mouth, chin, and shoulders—claimed that all of the information he had concerning various anti-Union plots was based not on his own knowledge, but had been derived from personal interviews with "several distinguished gentlemen." Hicks refused to reveal who these gentlemen were. "I would much prefer not to give any names for this reason: it must be apparent to all of you gentlemen that if I bandy names about in this connexion, it may deprive me of sources of information which may be important hereafter."[23] Governor Hicks apparently deemed himself proficient in the art of intelligence gathering.

Despite throwing the Select Committee a few bones about having heard rumors from Baltimore "that the installation of Lincoln and Hamlin would never come off," the issue was not pressed by the committee, and Hicks did not volunteer any specifics. The committee seemed primarily and almost exclusively interested in knowing about threats to Washington. Hicks's testimony was music to the Select Committee's ears, because he played the tune they wanted to hear. Hicks claimed there was no longer any danger to Washington.[24]

> QUESTION. Now, regarding the State of Maryland . . . have you any present belief that there are organizations there disciplined with a view to an attack upon the District of Columbia, the federal property here, or the federal authorities?
>
> ANSWER. I have not although I believe it was decidedly contemplated at one time.[25]

The Associated Press would report that Hicks's "belief that a conspiracy existed in connection with the Federal Capital was, he said, superinduced by private and anonymous letters and newspaper articles, and that such combinations did not exist in Maryland, but in other Southern States. That at the time of his publication, in the beginning of January, he was satisfied that there were existing organizations, having in view an illegal interference with the Federal authorities, and the seizure of public property; but for some time past, whatever may have been the designs of any secret confederations or associations, he was satisfied that such purposes have been abandoned." In view of this and other testimony, reported the AP, "The Special Committee are unanimously of the opinion whatever combinations or intents may have existed at an earlier period, that for the last six weeks there has been no appearance or vestige of an organization with a hostile intent on Washington or the public property therein."[26]

Hicks's reassuring testimony, however, was mere frosting on a cake that had already been iced. By the time Hicks testified, the Select Committee had made up its mind. Its 178-page report had largely been prepared; it would be laid open the following day. In that report, despite conflicting testimony, the committee members concluded that they were "unanimously of the opinion that the evidence produced before them does not prove the existence of a secret organization here or elsewhere hostile to the government, that has for its object, upon its own responsibility, an attack upon the Capitol, or any public property here, or an interruption of any of the functions of the government."[27]

Hicks's testimony affirmed, if it did not contribute to, the unanimity of the Select Committee's opinion. At best, however, Hicks's testimony was not the whole truth; at worst, it was an outright lie.

For starters, the letters he had received were not all anonymous—unless, by "anonymous," Hicks meant that he had snipped off the signatures before showing the letters to suspected conspirator Baltimore Marshal Kane. One of Hicks's warnings had come from a credible source, Washington's *National Intelligencer* editor James C. Welling, who on December 21, 1861, the day after South Carolina seceded, informed Hicks that secessionist leaders in Washington—which almost certainly would have included Louis T. Wigfall—intended to make Maryland their base of operations. Their motive, according to Welling, was to: "succeed in hurrying Maryland out of the Union [whereby] they will inaugurate the new "Southern Confederacy" in the present capital of the U. States. If this can be accomplished before the 4th of next March they will succeed in divesting the North of the seat of Government, and by retaining in their possession the public buildings and the public archives they hope at once to extort from foreign Governments a recognition not only of their *de facto* but also of their *de jure* pretentions."[28]

Admittedly, Welling's December news was stale by February 13. Other intelligence in Hicks's possession on that date, however, was fresh and savory indeed. By the time Hicks testified to the Select Committee of Five that all was well in Maryland, he had received a letter advising just the opposite. That letter had been sent just six days—not six weeks—before, by George Stearns, an employee of the Philadelphia, Wilmington, and Baltimore Railroad. It reported credible evidence of a plot by persons in Baltimore to disrupt the rail line and assassinate Lincoln while on his way to Washington. The letter, found among Hicks's papers, reads:

> Annapolis Feb 7th 1861
> Governor Hicks
>
> Dear Sir
>   On Sunday last a man who said he was from Baltimore called on our Bridge tender at Back River and informed him an attempt would be made by parties from Baltimore and other places to burn the Bridge just before the train should pass, which should have Mr. Lincoln on Board and in the excitement to assassinate him. The man who imparted this information will not give his name. He was an old gentleman very respectable in his appearance. He said he was a friend to the R Road and did not wish to see its property destroyed if it could be protected.
>
> Very Respectfully Your Obt Servant
> George Stearns[29]

In view of such evidence, that there existed a plot among parties from Baltimore to burn railroad bridges and murder Lincoln on his way to Washington, why would Hicks have testified that no combination adverse to the government existed in Maryland? Most significantly, why would he have withheld credible and precise information in his possession of threats to assassinate Lincoln near Baltimore? Hicks made only a vague, obtuse reference to such threats before dismissing them: "Now I have letters going to show that there is a design contemplated to *burn a particular bridge* and to *assassinate particular individuals*. All this is to be done in the State of Maryland. *But I attach no consequence to this information.*"[30]

There are only three possible reasons why Hicks was not more candid with the Select Committee regarding threats to assassinate Lincoln.

First, it is possible that Hicks had not seen the Stearns letter. This seems highly improbable, given that the letter was found among his papers and may be fairly presumed to have been delivered in due course and read upon receipt. And his vague testimony about having letters "going to show that there is a design contemplated to burn a particular bridge and to assassinate particular individuals" is evocative of the Stearns letter.

Second, perhaps Hicks truly believed, the evidence notwithstanding, that there were no secessionist conspiracies in Baltimore or Maryland. This too seems improbable. Hicks was a man who feared his own shadow. He would have taken seriously any threat, whether to himself or to Lincoln. Instead, he downplayed the Lincoln threats, telling the committee, "I have no doubt these things are talked over, but by a set of men who, in my opinion, cannot organize a system that they can carry out. But that the matter is talked over in secret conclave I have no doubt."[31] Incredibly, Hicks's testimony suggests that he knew who the "set of men" were that had been conspiring to blow up railroad bridges and assassinate Lincoln—otherwise how could he have rendered a judgment regarding their ability to carry out the threat? But Hicks did not tell the Select Committee their names and the committee did not press for them.

The third and most likely reason Governor Hicks testified as he had is that he was taking an overly legalistic view of the Select Committee's scope of inquiry—there was no conspiracy in Maryland to seize Washington, only one to kill Lincoln and burn railroad bridges there. Hicks was thus intentionally downplaying the threats, telling half-truths and withholding vital information. In other words, Hicks was covering up. The question is why? Possibly, Hicks had something to hide. He wanted to get on the stage, sing the reassuring notes that the Select Committee wanted to hear, and exit stage left as quickly as possible. There are a number of possible motives or combinations of motives to account for Hicks's behavior, such as not wanting federal troops sent to Maryland, which might lead to his state's destruction, or that Hicks secretly hoped that Washington would fall, or even that he did not want to do anything to prevent the rumored assassination of Abraham Lincoln in Baltimore.

Indeed, the upshot of Hicks's testimony was this: he had offered the Select Committee vague intelligence concerning threats to Lincoln. If Lincoln should be murdered, it could hardly be said that Hicks had never warned Congress. But in failing to provide specifics, including the Stearns letter and the names of his sources, or the "set of men" who were conspiring, Hicks also insured that the committee could not follow up on his leads.

Perhaps it was mere coincidence that Hicks should be in Washington on the same day that the electoral votes were to be counted, the same day that a revolution was to commence. Perhaps, as his friend J. Bond Chaplain wrote, he had decided against returning to Annapolis after testifying and determined to stay in Washington another day, in hopes of "doing good here" for the "Union."[32] Perhaps, on the other hand, if the Union fell and shattered that day, Hicks wanted to be present in order to witness the spectacle and possibly gather up some of the pieces for himself.

As Governor Hicks was concluding his testimony in Washington, the Lincoln Special pulling three coaches and a baggage car continued to steam toward Columbus, Ohio, on this winter morning. Like a candy apple rolled across a long, dirty carpet, the train had gathered more than a few pieces of lint and litter along the way; there were now over a hundred people clinging to the train. These included the press and railroad personnel in the forward car, working staff and local committees in the middle car, and Lincoln's family in the rear coach.[33]

Lincoln stayed in the rear coach, as its platform made a convenient perch from which to speak on brief stops. But there might have been another reason. Here, well over a hundred feet behind the engine, Lincoln and his family would have been more secure, from either a catastrophic locomotive explosion or an obstacle on the road.

Rumors of possible sabotage swirled around the Lincoln Special, such as a published claim that on Monday, February 11, as Lincoln's train was about a mile west of the Indiana state line, an attempt had been made to wreck the train. An employee of the Toledo and Western Railroad claimed that just before 12:30 p.m., when the Lincoln Special tender was running low on fuel, the engineer throttled the engine to a moderate speed in order to stop for wood. As the engine slowed, the engineer noticed an obstruction on the track and quickly brought the locomotive to a stop. Reported the press, *"a machine for putting cars on the track had been fastened upon the rails* in such a manner that if a train run at full speed had struck it, the engine and cars must have been thrown off, and many persons killed. The whole thing was admirably planned—the obstruction so near a station and on a straight track, where it would not be deemed necessary to exercise any great degree of caution."[34]

Another rumor, which would not be revealed until over a week later, claimed that a grenade had been found on board before the train left Cincinnati that morning. Of this latter story, the press would report:

> The Syracuse Journal states that just as the Presidential train was leaving Cincinnati a grenade of the most destructive character was discovered in the car occupied by Mr. Lincoln, his family and personal friends. It was found in a small carpet bag, which had been deposited in a seat of the car by some unknown person. Attention was drawn to it from the fact that no baggage was allowed in the cars. On examination, the grenade concealed in the carpet bag was discovered to be ignited, and so arranged that within fifteen minutes it would have exploded, with a force sufficient to have demolished the car and destroyed the lives of all the persons in it.[35]

Years later, Ward Hill Lamon would debunk both rumors as inventions of the press's fertile imagination.[36] But one report, made more proximate in time to the rumored event, Lamon would not rebut. On February 12, it would be reported from Cincinnati that "a queer looking box was left at the hotel for [Mr. Lincoln] this afternoon, under suspicious circumstances, and given to police."[37]

AT noon, in Washington, the joint session of Congress convened in the Capitol to witness the electoral vote count. Although there were uniformed guards at the entrances to the Capitol, none were visible in the chamber. Indeed, the House seemed to be fortified not by guns and sabers, but by ribbons and lace. Recorded the Illinois congressman Elihu B. Washburne, "beautiful and gorgeously dressed ladies entered the Hall, found their way into the cloak rooms, and many of them occupied the seats of the members, who gallantly surrendered them for the occasion."[38] According to Lucius E. Chittenden, who was in the House gallery, "to one who knew nothing of the hot treason which was seething beneath the quiet exterior of the spectators, the exercises would have appeared to be tame and uninteresting."[39]

But beneath the surface, matters were neither tame nor uninteresting. The chamber was in fact filled with both guns and roses, the latter in plain view, the former out of sight. A friend of Chittenden's who lived in Washington recognized him and took a seat next to him. Chittenden was surprised to see his friend out of uniform. The man was a colonel in a recently formed Washington regiment of pro-Union minutemen.

"I supposed you would be on duty to-day with your regiment," Chittenden queried.

Replied his friend with a smile, "We are *minute* men, you know; that is, we enter a room as private citizens, and come out of it a minute afterwards, a regiment, armed with loaded repeating-rifles. . . . My men are within easy call, and their rifles are not far away."

Chittenden noticed another gentleman, a quiet man, seated near his friend. Apparently, his friend the colonel was not alone. Chittenden had previously noted that two large connecting committee rooms, on the north side of the hall, were cordoned off. He now suspected why. If trouble broke out in the Capitol today, the minutemen would respond. If the colonel's regiment was, as he said, within "easy call," it stood to reason that they were ensconced in the two large committee rooms.[40]

The House was called to order, and a message was ordered to be sent from the House to the Senate, informing the waiting senators that the House was now in session and awaited their presence so that the electoral votes for president and vice president might be opened and counted before the joint session. At twenty minutes after twelve, the Senate was announced. Preceded by Vice President Breckinridge, the senators entered the chamber.[41] Members of the House rose and remained standing while the senators took their seats in a semicircle arranged in front of the clerk's desk. The vice president took his chair. Senator Trumbull and Representative Washburne, both of Illinois, and Representative John Phelps of Missouri, who had been appointed tellers, were shown to their seats at the clerk's desk.[42] Senators Seward, Douglas, and Joseph Lane took center seats in the front row of senators. The absolute silence of the chamber foretold the drama of the ceremony. Reported the *New York Times*, "From the moment the Senators took their seats, and throughout the proceedings, the audience looked on with almost breathless interest and silence, appreciating fully the grave solemnity of the occasion, and the decorum belonging thereto."[43] Vice President Breckinridge rose, "and in tones no louder than those of an ordinary conversation, but which were heard in the most distant corner of the gallery," announced that the joint session of Congress had assembled pursuant to the Constitution to count the electoral votes for president and vice president. Declared Breckinridge: "It is my duty to open the certificates of election in the presence of the two Houses, and I now proceed to the performance of that duty."[44]

One member of the body rose to speak, but Breckinridge interrupted: "Except for questions of order, no motion can be entertained."

The member insisted that his question was one of order. He resented that General Scott had posted armed guards at the Capitol, before a joint session of

Congress no less. "Is the count of the electoral vote to proceed under menace?" The legislator railed. "Should members be required to perform a constitutional duty before the janizaries of Scott were withdrawn from the hall?"

"The point of order is not sustained," Breckinridge stated emphatically. The complainant took his seat.

Breckinridge opened each of the thirty-three envelopes, one by one, handing the electoral ballots of each state to Trumbull and Phelps to be read. The two men complied, reading out the lengthy certificates. Phelps read the returns for those states that had voted for Lincoln; Trumbull read the returns from those that had not.[45] Senator Stephen Douglas, perhaps stinging from the relatively few electoral votes being announced for him, wanted to speed the process, and suggested that reading the formal parts of the remaining certificates be omitted. There was no objection. The announcement of votes proceeded rapidly thereafter, the only interruption coming in the form of mixed expressions of contempt and respect when the vote of South Carolina was declared.

After all the votes were announced, a profound silence followed. The tellers tallied the votes on a sheet of paper, left their seats, and handed the tally up to the vice president. Breckinridge read the result. He rose, and in what must have startled some like a rifle shot, he pierced the utter silence with a rap of his gavel. Then, with the utmost dignity, standing ramrod straight, he declared: "That Abraham Lincoln, of Illinois, having received a majority of the whole number of electoral votes, is duly elected President of the United States for the four years beginning on the fourth day of March, 1861; and Hannibal Hamlin, of Maine, having received a majority of the whole number of electoral votes, is duly elected Vice-President of the United States for the same term."[46]

Although he didn't yet know it, Abraham Lincoln was now officially elected as president of the United States. There came a brief attempt at applause that was quickly hushed.[47] The Senate retired to its chamber. The press would report that those in attendance rose silently and left the chamber in an orderly manner.[48]

Chittenden, however, recalled things differently. Before the door had closed behind the departing senators, a dozen outraged and crestfallen men shot out of their seats and demanded recognition by the speaker. "For a few minutes the tumult was so great that it was impossible to restore order," Chittenden recorded.[49] Lincoln was jeered as a "rail-splitter." Jefferson Davis and South Carolina were cheered. But for the most part, the secessionist element directed its vitriol at General Winfield Scott. He had engineered placing armed men to guard the chamber. He had ensured that the count would be conducted without the presence of mobs of citizens. He had, as a Virginian, sided with the Union, when secessionists had perhaps hoped against hope that he might side with them, or at least not against them. "Superannuated old dotard!"

"Traitor to the state of his birth!" "Coward!" "Free-state pimp!" were only a few of the epithets fired at Scott.

Chittenden thought the packed house "would officiate in a revolution." Amid the din, he glanced around the gallery. The seat of his friend, the colonel, was empty. True to his name, the minute-man and the quiet gentleman Chittenden had noticed nearby had quickly vanished—"where and for what purpose," Chittenden wrote, "I knew only too well."[50]

PUNCTUAL as ever, the Lincoln Special pulled into the Columbus railroad station at 2:00 p.m., right on time. And predictable as ever, Lincoln's adoring hosts again welcomed him with overwhelming crowds, booming cannon, and lusty cheers. He was conveyed under military escort to the

Vice-President John Cabell Breckinridge presided over the electoral vote count that officially made Abraham Lincoln president of the United States. (*Library of Congress*)

Capitol, where Governor William Dennison received him in the executive room.[51] After a brief introduction, Lincoln was escorted to a joint session of the Ohio legislature.

In response to a short welcome from the lieutenant governor, Lincoln made a wordy, somewhat repetitive response. He alluded to the great weight of responsibility that rested upon him, greater than ever rested on Washington. He would look to the American people and to God for assistance. He acknowledged that he had been the subject of ridicule for not speaking plainly about the policies his incoming administration would follow. "I still think I was right," Lincoln declared. "In the varying and repeatedly shifting scenes of the present, without a precedent which could enable us to judge by the past, it has seemed fitting that before speaking upon the difficulties of the country, I should have gained a view of the whole field to be sure, and after all being at liberty to modify and change the course of policy as future events may make a change necessary."[52]

After he spoke to the legislature, Lincoln briefly moved outside and addressed a large crowd from the steps of the capitol. He thanked them for greeting him "without distinction of party," meaning even though many in the crowd had not voted for him, they honored the office he would hold, and the country he would serve, and in so doing, honored themselves. He closed with a vague, almost biblical reference to his impending death. Everyone likely assumed that this was merely an acknowledgment by Lincoln that he was getting older; he had just turned fifty-two. "I am doubly thankful that you have appeared here to give me this greeting. It is not much to me, *for I shall very soon pass away from you*; but we have a large country and a large future before us, and the manifestations of good-will towards the government, and affection for the Union which you may exhibit are of immense value to you and your posterity forever."[53]

At 5:00 p.m., Lincoln was led to Governor Dennison's room in the Ohio State Capitol building, where a Western Union employee handed him a special dispatch from Washington. As newspapers would later report, "When a dispatch announcing the peaceful counting of the electoral vote was received, there was great curiosity to see how he would look and to hear what he would say. When he read it he smiled benignly, and looking up, seeing every one waiting for a word, he quietly put the dispatch in his pocket and said, 'What a beautiful building you have here, Gov. Dennison,' at which the crowd, who were considerably sold, laughed and moved off."[54] The Western Union telegram that the poker-faced Lincoln had casually stuffed into his pocket simply read: "The votes were counted peaceably. You are elected."[55]

THE commotion in the House chamber following the electoral vote count dissipated almost as quickly as it had erupted. Chittenden left the building, hired the first carriage he spotted, and ordered the driver to take him to Willard's Hotel. The avenue in the direction of the Treasury however was choked with a "howling, angry mob" that forced Chittenden to escape through one of the cross streets to F Street, entering the rear entrance of Willard's. A vindictive, drunken crowd ruled the streets of Washington well into the night. They cheered for Jefferson Davis. "There was much street fighting and many arrests by the police, but no revolution." Chittenden credits both Scott and especially Breckinridge for conducting the republic "safely through one of the most imminent perils that ever threatened its existence."[56]

But even Chittenden, a firm critic of secessionist duplicity, had failed to recognize that there might have been a reason behind Breckinridge's dignified counting of the votes, an ulterior motive that lay hidden beneath an exterior show of gallantry, of performing a constitutional duty. And that reason, that motive, had nothing whatever to do with Breckinridge wanting to see Abraham Lincoln assume the presidency.

AT 8:00 p.m., Lincoln and his suite joined Governor Dennison at the Executive Mansion for a fine soirée and dinner reception. Although the event was by invitation only, the governor and his wife had extended those invita-

Abraham Lincoln addressing the joint session of the Ohio legislature. (*Library of Congress*)

tions liberally, and virtually everyone accepted. Accordingly, the Dennison house was not divided that night, but overflowing with guests. The governor, his wife, and their daughters were perfect hosts and lively conversationalists. But it would have been a relatively easy matter to throw a successful party for Lincoln tonight. There was much to celebrate. *New York Times* correspondent Joseph Howard Jr. reported on the reason for the jubilant atmosphere that prevailed: "It is very evident that the news received here this afternoon, concerning the undisturbed counting of the electoral votes at Washington, the Union news from Virginia and Tennessee, and assurances of entire safety at the National Capital from General Scott, have produced a profound and quieting impression upon the friends of Mr. Lincoln, while he is but reassured that his constant judgment in these matters is but good and correct. . . . Mr. Lincoln seemed in better spirits, was less fatigued and uneasy to-night, than he has been at any time since he left Springfield."[57]

But while all this good news would have had a quieting, reassuring effect on Lincoln and his party, it would have precisely the opposite effect on some in Baltimore.

CHAPTER SEVEN

CROSSING THE RIVER

Thursday, Friday, February 14–15, 1861
Columbus–Pittsburgh–Cleveland

MORNING BROKE IN COLUMBUS, greeted by dreary low-hanging clouds and later, a persistent rain that would be described as "pelting."[1] The Lincoln Special today comprised the locomotive *Washington City* and only two passenger coaches and a baggage car. This was to minimize the throngs that had crowded on board at Indianapolis without William S. Wood's permission, but at the railroad's invitation.[2] Security on board the Lincoln Special had, until now, been lax; "hereafter none but those invited by Mr. Woods will be allowed upon the train," one embedded reporter noted with apparent relief.[3] This news would have been important information for the Baltimore conspirators to have. If, for example, they hoped to murder Lincoln by boarding his train with hordes of other pushy, uninvited guests, that plan would no longer work. They would now need Mr. Wood's permission to gain access to the cars. Whether to increase safety or decrease annoyance, the president-elect's people were belatedly, perhaps unwittingly, plugging holes in their leaky security plan. An opportunity had been lost between Springfield and Cincinnati.

A few minutes before 8:00 a.m., the Lincoln Special pulled out of Columbus past a sea of umbrellas covering those who had come to bid him farewell. Running late, Mrs. Lincoln and her two young sons reportedly had to make a dash for the train.[4] Today, they would make an all day run in the rain to Pittsburgh. The gloomy day initially cast a melancholy pall over the Lincoln party. Young Robert Lincoln seemed particularly out of sorts. It is suspected that "Bob O'Link"[5] was pining over a beautiful young woman he had met the previous day in Columbus. Ward Hill Lamon helped lighten the mood by singing songs. Bob Lincoln joined in, and everyone's mood brightened.[6]

But there remained many security gaps that either could not or would not be filled. Lincoln would continue to speak from balconies of hotels, or from the rear platform of the Lincoln Special. He would continue to put himself in vulnerable positions once leaving the train, passing on foot through crushing crowds before seating himself, and sometimes standing, in open barouches drawn through teaming city streets by multitudes of plumed and Union cockaded horses that garishly signaled to all, even if his stovepipe hat did not, that Mr. Lincoln rode behind.[7]

The Lincoln Special cut through the driving Ohio rain, passing through little towns like Newark, Frazeysburg, Dresden, Coshocton, Newcomerstown, and Uhrichsville, where large crowds of men and women waited in the downpour for a glimpse of the train and Lincoln. The party stopped at Cadiz Junction for an elegant lunch provided by the wife of the president of the Steubenville and Indiana Railroad. At 2:30 p.m., the train arrived at Steubenville. Here, the rain took a break, and gave Lincoln another chance to repeat himself to yet another large crowd amid yet another round of cannon fire. Five thousand people had turned out. Lincoln ascended a stage and was welcomed by Judge W. R. Lloyd.[8] Lincoln's words were provocative: "If the majority does not control, the minority must—would that be right? Would that be just or generous? Assuredly not! Though the majority may be wrong, and I will not undertake to say that they were not wrong in electing me, yet we must adhere to the principle that the majority shall rule."[9]

Lincoln appeared to be saying that the majority got to decide who became president, and in so doing got to decide what the Constitution meant. He was, of course, simultaneously wrong and right on both scores. He had not been elected by a majority of the people, but he had been elected by a majority of the electoral vote. He himself could not interpret the Constitution, but he could appoint Supreme Court justices who would interpret it the way he wanted. And the majority might rule, but the minority is protected from the majority's whims by the Constitution's restraints.

As he had done previously, Lincoln reminded everyone that if the majority should determine that they had made a mistake in electing him, they would have another chance in four years. "No great harm can be done by us in that time—in that time there can be nobody hurt. If anything goes wrong, however, and you find you have made a mistake, elect a better man next time. There are plenty of them."

As if on cue, the engine's whistle blew, and Lincoln knew he had to close. He also sensed he had spoken imprudently. While the minority might not be able to rule, they could also not be ignored. If, by "minority," Lincoln meant the disaffected in the Southern states, his words had just disaffected them further. He needed to take those words back, for he still hoped to take the seceded states back. And one vital state that threatened to secede and take other states with it, Virginia, lay just across the river, on the Ohio's opposite shore. Indeed, a large number of Virginians had crossed the river to meet Lincoln in Steubenville.[10] "These points involve the discussion of many questions which I have not time to consider," Lincoln hastily explained. "I merely give them to you for your reflection. I almost regret that I alluded to it at all."[11]

From Steubenville, the Lincoln Special traced the path of the Ohio, the wide river flowing in the opposite direction on its way to join the Mississippi. Running north, turning east at East Liverpool, across the Ohio border, then south at Rochester, Pennsylvania, and on to Allegheny City, the route defined a roundabout horseshoe-shaped path, and the longest distance between the two points of Steubenville and Pittsburgh. The detour was necessary because at that time there was no railroad bridge across the Ohio at any point on its 980-mile course, making a direct route from Steubenville to Pittsburgh impossible.

Pittsburgh eagerly anticipated Lincoln's arrival. Earlier in the day, the "Smoky City" had taken on a campaign, even holiday, atmosphere. Hundreds of people from outlying counties began filling the streets, businesses closed early, and a multitude of newly unfurled flags fluttered in the breeze. At 5:00 p.m., a military and civic procession reached the Federal Street Station in Allegheny City, the modern-day North Side area of Pittsburgh. Soon thereafter, a booming cannon announced the train's approach. The eager crowd watched with anticipation. The gathering, described as "immense and impenetrable," had packed every available space—the depot, both sides of Federal Street, even the suspension bridge that spanned the Allegheny River. But the cannon was premature; by 5:30 p.m., darkness began to fall, and the train had not yet arrived. By 6:00 p.m., a light rain destined to become a heavy shower began falling. And still there was no train. The Lincoln Special was late.

Eventually, it was announced to the crowd that an accident had delayed Lincoln's train. Between Baden and Rochester, a freight train had derailed, blocking the track.[12] The Pittsburgh crowd was assured that Lincoln would be there soon. After another two hours, many lost their patience and left, while thousands of others remained near the depot, seeking shelter under the platforms.[13]

Finally, at 8:00 p.m., nearly three hours late, the puffing engine and ringing bell announced Lincoln's arrival, and moments later his train rolled into a dark, rain-soaked Allegheny City, at the Federal Street Station of the Pittsburgh, Fort Wayne, and Chicago Railroad.[14] The foul weather and lateness of the hour had conspired to threaten Allegheny City and Pittsburgh's unified plans for a grand parade, reception, and speech at the Monongahela House, where it had been announced Lincoln's entourage would spend the night.

Despite being wet and weary, or perhaps because of it, the tenacious crowd besieged the platform, blocking Lincoln's path to the waiting carriages. "It was with great difficulty that the military succeeded in obtaining a passage sufficient to permit the President elect and his suite to get from the cars to the carriages in waiting to convey them to their quarters in Pittsburgh."[15] Once the crowd was finally cleared, Lincoln stepped from the car, accompanied by Allegheny City's mayor Simon Drum. "His appearance set the people wild with excitement, and cries of 'speech,' 'speech,' intermingled with continuous cheering, indicated they were not to be put off without a word or two."[16] After he reached the carriage, Lincoln complied with the crowd's demands. He stood in the rain, alluding to the train's delay and the inclement weather. He could not speak to them tonight, but offered a political rain check to do so the next morning. "When he concluded, cheer after cheer was given for 'Old Abe,' and the procession soon began to move off."[17]

Any early riser buying Friday's *Pittsburgh Gazette* would learn the complete details of Lincoln's plans this morning. First, he would speak at 8:30 from the balcony at the Monongahela House on Smithfield Street. After that, his procession would wind through the city's streets until it reached the Federal Street Depot. From there, the party would board the Lincoln Special and depart for Cleveland at 10:00 a.m.[18]

Once again, the press had published an assassin's playbook, complete with times, places, and directions pointing to multiple opportunities to get near Lincoln. But while navigating arteries narrowed and clogged with the plaque of humanity had been annoying to Lincoln, it had not, to this point, been life threatening. There seemed to be no reason to change the protocol. There had been, after all, no Pittsburgh Plot. No Cincinnati Plot. No Indianapolis Plot. In many ways, the trip was going as planned—Lincoln was being seen, heard, and roundly cheered by adoring thousands, despite saying very little.

At precisely 8:30 a.m., as promised, Lincoln appeared on the balcony at the Monongahela House. An immense crowd gathered on Smithfield Street to hear what he had to say. The hotel too was dangerously packed: "No arrangement for the preservation of order having been made, the Hotel was soon a perfect jam, the aisles, halls, rooms and every spot was soon occupied by the eager populace."[19]

Lincoln acknowledged, as he had done before, that the country was in a "distracted condition" and that naturally people expected him to say something about the subject. "But to touch upon it at all," Lincoln said, "would involve an elaborate discussion of a great many questions and circumstances, would require more time than I can at present command, and would perhaps unnecessarily commit me upon matters which have not yet fully developed themselves."[20]

Then, smiling and pointing south across the Monongahela River, Lincoln argued that "notwithstanding the troubles across the river, *there is really no crisis . . .* except an *artificial one . . .* gotten up at any time by designing politicians." His advice was "to keep cool." If Americans on both sides of the line could only hold their tempers, "the troubles will come to an end, and the question which now distracts the country will be settled just as surely as all other difficulties of like character which have originated in this government have been adjusted."[21]

It was a hopeful, if naïve prognosis. That same day, far "across the river," in Baltimore, Allan Pinkerton and fellow operative Charles D. C. Williams would meet with several suspected Baltimore plotters who would not keep cool. These men were not designing politicians. To them, the crisis was not artificial. And they most certainly could not hold their tempers.

Even the smart shower that fell on Pittsburgh the morning of February 15 had not deterred crowds from lining the streets to see the president-elect off. Soon after delivering his speech, Lincoln and his suite set out for the carriages that would take them from the Monongahela House to the Allegheny depot. At the depot, the crowd was so dense that Lincoln and his party had to squeeze through it, "one by one in Indian file" to reach the platform.[22] Moments later the party boarded the train and pulled away. Lincoln stood on the rear platform and bowed to the crowd until the last house was left in the distance.[23]

For the most part, after leaving Pittsburgh, the dreary day would be relatively uneventful. Lincoln sat by himself for most of the trip, "either reading the paper or absorbed in thought." Mary Lincoln sat with the two little boys, conversing with friends. Robert spent much of the time in the forward car with the reporters.[24] Possibly to break the monotony, Robert Lincoln also sat in driver's seat of the locomotive *Comet,* and managed the controls as the engineer's assistant.[25] At stops in Salineville and Bayard, Ohio, Lincoln bowed, but did not speak, to the large crowds that waited there in the mud and rain.[26] The party moved along.

One notable exception to the otherwise uneventful day occurred when the cortege stopped for a brief, twenty-minute lunch in Alliance, Ohio. Here, the president of the Cleveland and Pittsburgh Railroad, John N. McCullough, hosted a dinner at Sourbeck's Hotel. The press would vote it the best meal of the trip.[27] During the elegant dinner, the Canton Zouaves, whose "strenuous efforts" were needed to clear a passage through the crowd,[28] stood guard in full uniform, and a band played patriotic tunes. At some point, what the press would describe as a "salute" was fired so near the hotel that it shattered windows, including one near where Mrs. Lincoln sat. She was sprayed with glass shards, but unhurt.[29]

As the party left Alliance, Lincoln again yielded to demands for a speech. He explained good-naturedly that he had no time for a long speech and that if he gave one every place he stopped, he would wear himself out and not get to Washington until sometime after the inauguration. "But as I am somewhat interested in the inauguration," Lincoln mused, "I would like to get there a few days before the 4th of March."[30]

IN BALTIMORE, however, it was beginning to seem less likely that Lincoln would get to Washington before the 4th of March. Or that he would get there at all. At around the same time Mary Lincoln was being showered with glass, Allan Pinkerton was holding court with suspected plotter James H. Luckett. Luckett appeared to be exercised over several frustrating developments. For one thing, Governor Hicks had not called a special legislative convention, without which Maryland could not vote to secede. "I tell you my friend," Luckett told Pinkerton, "it will be but a short time until you will find Governor Hicks will have to fly, or he will be hung—He . . . is a traitor to his God and his Country."[31]

Despite Hicks's inaction, the legislature had determined to call its own convention. It would meet the following Monday. Luckett bragged that he had been elected to the convention by the entire vote of his county but two, after advocating Maryland's immediate secession. Luckett claimed that he had told those who had elected him that only men who "would not hesitate if necessary to peril their lives for the rights of Maryland and the Southern Confederacy" should be elected.[32] Luckett was apparently just such a man.

Luckett also seemed aggrieved that Washington had not fallen into secessionist hands two days earlier, thanks to General Scott's precautions. But once Virginia and Maryland seceded, Luckett felt, Washington would revert to their possession. He claimed that Virginia and Maryland could concentrate a hundred thousand men around the Capitol in short order. "Then see where General Scott would be," he gloated.[33]

As they talked, Luckett informed Pinkerton that there was in Baltimore an organization that planned to prevent Northern troops from reaching Washington. Thousands of the city's starving, unemployed workers were being enlisted for the enterprise daily. They were being told that all their suffering came at the hands of Black Republican rule. The paramilitary organization was arming these men, paying them, and poisoning their minds with anti-Lincoln rhetoric. "Those men," said Luckett, "will fight when they believe that Lincoln is the cause of all this misery, aye, and they will fight to the death."

Most significantly, Luckett hinted that Lincoln himself might be a target of the organization. Reported Pinkerton, "Mr. Luckett in reply to a remark of mine about President Lincoln passing through Baltimore said—'He [Lincoln] *may pass through quietly but I doubt it.*'"[34]

Pinkerton took out his wallet. He handed Luckett twenty-five dollars to be used in furthering the patriotic causes of Southern rights. The act must have led Luckett to believe that he could trust Pinkerton even with the most sensitive information. He provided additional details of the plot against Lincoln. The leader was an Italian, Captain Ferrandini. He was prepared to sacrifice his life for the cause and had a plan fixed to prevent Lincoln from passing through Baltimore. The organization of Southern rights men had every confidence that before Lincoln could pass through Baltimore, Ferrandini would kill him. Luckett claimed to be a close friend of Ferrandini's and promised to give Pinkerton's twenty-five dollars to him.

And then Pinkerton hit the jackpot. Luckett offered to introduce him to Ferrandini at Barr's Saloon on South Street later that very night. "This was unexpected to me," Pinkerton wrote, "but I determined to take the chances, and agreed to meet Mr. Luckett at the place named at 7:00 p.m."[35]

Undoubtedly, Pinkerton would have felt the need to put the intelligence he had just learned into the hands of Norman B. Judd for delivery to Lincoln as soon as possible. But there were more than a few problems, some practical, some contractual, in doing so. The last dispatch to Judd had been clumsily delivered, sent by letter mailed to Chicago and then via special messenger hand carried to Cincinnati. This method of communication had taken too long. But attempting to communicate directly with Judd via telegraph was out of the question. The operators in Baltimore could not be trusted with such sensitive information. Pinkerton had a cipher, but Judd did not have the key. He would have to find another way.

Moreover, the confidential information Pinkerton was gathering, though it concerned Lincoln, could not legally be shared with Lincoln. The information belonged to the man that had hired Pinkerton to obtain it, Samuel M. Felton, president of the Philadelphia, Wilmington, and Baltimore Railroad. Pinkerton would need Felton's permission to relay the information to Lincoln.

But first things first. In a few hours Pinkerton, who thus far had been able to convince Luckett that he was a man of Southern sympathies, would be meeting with Captain Ferrandini. "Mr. Hutcheson" would need to be more convincing than ever now.

AMID roaring artillery, the Lincoln Special arrived in Cleveland at 4:20 p.m., twenty minutes behind schedule. The weather was foul. "Mr. Lincoln alighted from the train leaning on the arms of two members of the City Council Committee and proceeded through the station house to the carriage provided for him," noted the Cleveland *Plain Dealer.*[36] Accompanied by military and

Lincoln speaks from a balcony of the Weddell House, Cleveland, to an overflowing crowd. (*Library of Congress*)

fire companies and trade associations, Lincoln's procession marched "amid the wildest enthusiasm" for 2 miles through rain, snow, and deep mud along Cleveland's Euclid Street to the Weddell House.[37] Despite the inclement weather, "a large number of vehicles of all descriptions followed, several ships, fully rigged, and wagon loads of mechanics."[38]

After arriving at Cleveland's Weddell House, Lincoln was again called on to make a speech. From a balcony hung with colored lanterns,[39] he echoed the "artificial crisis" theme that had played well in Pittsburgh. The disaffected, he claimed, had no basis to complain. Their fugitive slaves were being returned now as ever. They had the same Constitution that had protected them for seventy years. They still held American citizenship. "What then, is the matter with them?" Lincoln asked his Northern audience. "Why all this excitement? Why all these complaints? As I said before, the crisis is all artificial; it has no foundation in fact; it was argued up, as the saying is, and cannot, therefore, be argued down. Let it alone and it will go down of itself."[40]

But in Baltimore, at least, the crisis would not go down of itself. At 6:15 p.m., Pinkerton went to supper and after that to Barr's Saloon, where he found Mr. Luckett and several other gentlemen. Luckett invited Pinkerton to have a drink with them and introduced him as "Mr. Hutchinson" to Captain Ferrandini and a Captain William H. H. Turner, clerk of the Baltimore Circuit

Court. Possibly, the men's titles indicated their membership in Baltimore's Constitutional Guards[41] or the Knights of the Golden Circle.[42]

In the 1850s, Cypriano Ferrandini served as a captain in the old Fifth Infantry Regiment of the Maryland National Guard.[43] Early on the morning of October 18, 1859, a "Captain Ferrandini," likely the same man, turned out at the Camden Street train station along with the Lafayette Guards and other armed Baltimore militias, including the Law Greys and the Baltimore and Turner Rifles. The group was intent on proceeding to the "seat of war," that is, Harpers Ferry, whose arsenal had been seized by John Brown and his gang of thirteen white and five black vigilantes on October 16. The raid having been quelled and Brown imprisoned by federal troops under the command of Colonel Robert E. Lee, however, Ferrandini's help was not needed.[44]

But if Lincoln was going to be assassinated in Baltimore, Ferrandini's help would be needed. Luckett's introduction sealed the detective's legitimacy. "He eulogized me very highly as a neighbor of his, and told Ferrandina that I was the gentleman who had given the Twenty five Dollars." Pinkerton's money had talked, and spoken well of him.

The conversation immediately turned to politics. As Pinkerton noted, "Ferrandina who is a fine looking, intelligent appearing person, became very excited. . . . He has lived in the South for many years and is thoroughly imbued with the idea that the South must rule: that they (Southerners) have been outraged in their rights by the election of Lincoln, and freely justified resorting to any means to prevent Lincoln from taking his seat. . . . As he spoke his eyes fairly glistened, and his whole frame quivered, but he was fully conscious of all he was doing."[45]

In Ferrandini's own words, "Murder of any kind is justifiable and right to save the rights of the Southern people." Pinkerton marveled at Ferrandini's almost magical allure: "Even I myself felt the influence of this mans strange power, and wrong though I knew him to be, I felt strangely unable to keep my mind balanced against him."[46]

Just ten days earlier, when he had testified before the Select Committee of Five, Ferrandini had denied that there existed in Baltimore any plans to prevent Lincoln's inauguration or prevent his safe passage through Maryland:

> By the Chairman.
>
> QUESTION. Do you know of the existence of any organization, any military company, or any secret society, or of any understanding among individuals, that has for its object the prevention of the inauguration of Mr. Lincoln on the 4th of March?
>
> ANSWER. No, sir.
>
> QUESTION. Or to prevent his coming through the State of Maryland?

ANSWER. No, sir; none whatever.

QUESTION. But it is simply, as you understand it, to prevent northern volunteer companies from coming through?

ANSWER. A northern invasion; that is about the whole of it.[47]

But now, Ferrandini was not under the glare of a congressional investigating committee. Rather, he was ensconced in the relative comfort and safety of a shadowy Baltimore saloon. It now appeared that Ferrandini's primary and most immediate objective was not, in fact, preventing Northern troops from passing through Maryland. It was preventing Lincoln from doing so.

According to Pinkerton, Ferrandini was willing to become a martyr for his cause: "Ferrandina said that never, never shall Lincoln be President—His life (Ferrandina) was of no consequence—he was willing to give it for Lincoln's— he would sell it for that Abolitionists, and as Orissini[48] had given his life for Italy, so was he (Ferrandina) ready to die for his country, and the rights of the South, and, said Ferrandina, turning to Captain Turner, 'we shall all die together, we shall show the North that we fear them not—every Captain,' said he, 'will on that day prove himself a hero. The first shot fired, the main Traitor (Lincoln) dead, and all Maryland will be with us, and the South shall be free, and the North must then be ours.' 'Mr. Huchins,' said Ferrandina, '*If I alone must do it, I shall—Lincoln shall die in this City.*'"[49]

Captain Ferrandini had just given Pinkerton a lot to think about. Had Pinkerton known about Ferrandini appearing before the Select Committee of Five, he would now have known that Ferrandini's testimony was perjured. Pinkerton would also have realized that Ferrandini's motives for wanting Lincoln dead were complex, if misguided, and included *bravado*—showing the North that the South did not fear it; *honor*—proving himself a hero; *inducement*—encouraging Maryland to secede by using the event as a rallying cry; and most significantly, *implementing a war strategy*—freeing the South by conquering the North.

While Ferrandini, Turner, Luckett, and Pinkerton were talking, two strangers drew near. They appeared to be eavesdropping. Ferrandini said he thought the men were spies. He had a secret meeting to attend that night and was concerned that the two strangers might follow him. Luckett volunteered that he and Mr. Hutchinson would stay behind and, if necessary, prevent the strangers from following Ferrandini. "I assured Ferrandina," Pinkerton reported, "that if they did attempt to follow him we would whip them."[50]

Ferrandini and Turner left Barr's Saloon to attend their secret meeting. Pinkerton wanted to follow them, but was obliged to stay behind with Luckett to watch the strangers. Pinkerton must have suspected that the strangers were government spies. What he did not yet know was that the two men were in all likelihood New York City detectives. By their clumsy gumshoe tactics, they had done more than draw suspicion on themselves. Far worse, they had threatened to blow Pinkerton's entire operation.

CHAPTER EIGHT

HOTEL FOUNTAIN

Saturday, February 16, 1861
Cleveland–Buffalo

THE PREVIOUS NIGHT'S CLOUDS, RAIN, AND SNOW yielded to a bright and sunny winter day. The sky was cloudless. The ground, muddy last night, was frozen this morning.[1] The train left Cleveland at 9:00 a.m. The president-elect's car was "beautifully carpeted, curtained, and upholstered." Once more, at the depot and all along the track a long line of people had assembled.[2]

It would be a grueling day of fits and starts for Lincoln; the Special's eleven scheduled stops included Willoughby, Painesville, Geneva, Ashtabula, and Conneaut, Ohio; Girard, Erie, and North East, Pennsylvania; and Westfield, Dunkirk, and Silver Creek, New York, before a scheduled 4:30 p.m. arrival at Buffalo. On the way between Cleveland and Buffalo, Lincoln encountered two people of note, one old, one young, who would board his train. The first of these was a bespectacled man who bore an uncanny resemblance to Benjamin Franklin, and in 1861 would have been nearly as famous. The man wore a long, white overcoat, its pockets crammed with papers, and an old white Quaker's hat tilted back on his head. He boarded Lincoln's train unexpectedly in Girard, Pennsylvania, just off Lake Erie. He was an outspoken, controversial celebrity. The man had reportedly boarded accidentally, absent-mindedly mistaking the Lincoln Special for the regular train. This seems unlikely, given the need for a pass to board the special train. The man carried a yellow bag boldly proclaiming his name and address "in characters which might be read across Lake Erie."[3] He was Horace Greeley, rabid abolitionist and lecturer, who also owned and edited the *New York Tribune*.

Greeley had arrived in Cleveland two days before. Noted the Cleveland *Plain Dealer* sarcastically, "This drab-coated, white-hatted Philosopher arrived in this city this morning, unannounced by guns, drums or Herald-ry of any kind. The man that made Lincoln President is thus unnoticed, and yet he pines not."[4]

But Greeley would not go unnoticed for long. After boarding the reporter's car of the Lincoln Special, the highly identifiable Greeley was recognized and "captured and marched off in triumph, by Mr. Secretary Nicolay, to the President's car." Here, he met Mrs. Lincoln for the first time.[5] Perhaps to cover his balding pate, Greeley never removed his Quaker's hat; he made no exception for Mrs. L. "We believe," the editor of a rival newspaper crowed, "that politeness is not one of Mr. G's eccentricities."[6] At the next stop, Greeley vanished as suddenly as he had appeared. Reported the *World*, "his arrival and departure were altogether so unexpected, so mysterious, so comical, that they supplied an amusing topic of conversation during the rest of the journey."[7]

The second noteworthy person Lincoln would meet today was not yet famous, but is forever remembered by those who have a fascination with Lincoln's life. It was a young girl. At Westfield, New York, despite being clearly fatigued and hoarse,[8] Lincoln determined to speak briefly. "I am glad to see you; I suppose you are to see me; but I certainly think I have the best of the bargain," Lincoln began, repeating a joke that was becoming as tired as he was. The crowd applauded anyway. "Some three months ago," Lincoln continued, "I received a letter from a young lady here; it was a very pretty letter, and she advised me to let my whiskers grow, as it would improve my appearance; acting partly upon her suggestion, I have done so; and now, if she is here, I would like to see her; I think her name was Miss Barlly."[9]

In response to Lincoln's request for "Miss Barlly," a ripple moved through the crowd, after which an old man leading a young girl of twelve was brought up onto the platform.[10] The old man introduced his beautiful daughter, a blushing lass with black eyes, to the president-elect as Grace Bedell, the girl who had written him. Recalled Ms. Bedell, "I was conveyed to him; he stepped from the cars, extending his hand and saying, 'you see I have let these whiskers grow for you, Grace,' kissed me, shook me cordially by the hand, and was gone.'"[11]

Reported the *World* of Lincoln's greeting: "A beard of several months' growth covers (perhaps adorns) the lower part of his face. The young girl's peachy cheek must have tickled with a stiff whisker, for the growth of which she was herself responsible."[12]

Both the Greeley and Bedell incidents would have revealed another key piece of intelligence to the Baltimore plotters. It had previously been announced that no one except persons holding a pass from the train's manager, William S. Wood, could board the Lincoln Special. Exceptions, however, were clearly being made for some well-wishers, the famous and even the ordinary, provided they had a good story.

Whether he considered this option for getting close to Lincoln or not, in February 1861, the young tragedian John Wilkes Booth would certainly have considered himself famous. He was now a star actor. His name was appearing almost daily in Northern newspapers like the Albany *Atlas and Argus*. Indeed, two days later, just a page behind news of Lincoln's movements, Monday's *Atlas and Argus* would report that J. Wilkes Booth, now recovered from his injury, would appear again that evening, in *The Apostate*.[13] Monday, February 18, 1861, would be one of the first times, but of course not the last, that John Wilkes Booth's and Abraham Lincoln's names would appear together in the same newspaper. As to Booth, "The Tragedian's many friends and admirers, will be glad to learn that he is able once more to appear before them," the *Atlas and Argus* assured its readers.[14]

Abolitionist, Lincoln supporter, and publisher, Horace Greeley, absent-mindedly boarded the Lincoln Special thinking it was a regularly scheduled train. (*Library of Congress*)

During the Civil War, Booth would tell his sister Asia Booth Clarke that his fame opened many doors for him. He had "Grant's pass," allowing him to move freely among Northern armies and behind Union lines, where he aided the Confederacy with his money and medicines that he smuggled. "I have free pass everywhere," he boasted, "my profession, my name, is my passport."[15]

Even Mary Todd Lincoln's sisters would have difficulty securing passes to travel between North and South during the war.[16] But not Booth. If his winning smile and fame could, during the height of the war, open doors that remained shut to almost everyone else, how much easier could he gain a free pass through far less securely guarded doors now? Perhaps even now, at the dawn of his fame, the young star's name could secure a coveted pass from William S. Wood, could open the door to Lincoln's railcar. To his dining parlor. To his hotel room.

Booth's injury from February 12 had presumably left the recuperating actor with five full days with nothing to do before his upcoming February 18 performance, save study lines to a part he already knew, sleep, eat, drink, and possibly consort with his lady friends. A vital young man as ambitious, athletic, and impassioned as Booth must have gone stir crazy sitting on the sidelines, waiting for his wound to heal. Booth was a man of action; he craved it. His injury had bought him some free time, and he would have wanted to fill it. Booth could not act during those five days off the boards. But he could spy.

Since Lincoln's itinerary and schedules were readily available in great detail in newspapers, Booth or other Southern spies might stalk Lincoln, watch his movements, hear his remarks, count the number of bodyguards in his party, observe what security precautions the party used (or failed to use), and report it all by telegraph, possibly in code, to trusted colleagues waiting in Baltimore.

Eerily, one of Samuel Felton's railroad employees, George Stearns—the same man who informed Governor Hicks of a plot to destroy railroad bridges in Maryland and assassinate Lincoln—would report that an anonymous informant from Baltimore had revealed that the Baltimore plotters "had spies following Mr. Lincoln and were in constant communication with these parties in Baltimore giving them information of Mr. Lincoln's movements."[17] One of the suspected Baltimore plotters, Otis K. Hillard, would confirm this, admitting that those intent on killing Lincoln were indeed watching his movements: "they had men on the look out all the time."[18] Perhaps George N. Sanders, the shadowy Confederate operative, former Consul to London, and advocate of political assassination, who had been spotted lurking around Lincoln's hotel in Cincinnati, was one of those spies. Perhaps Baltimore native John Wilkes Booth was another.

Booth might also attempt to rendezvous with other Baltimoreans suspected to be following Lincoln's movements. The most likely point to do this would have been at Buffalo. It was a large city, offering good cover, an opportunity to blend into the crowd. The city on Lake Erie was a day's train ride from Albany, about as far as Booth could venture from his current home base in Albany and be back in time for his February 18 performance. Assuming he felt well enough for the nine-hour ride west from Albany, Booth could take a train to Buffalo as late as Friday, February 15, three days after his accident, scout the Exchange Street Depot, walk the procession route up Exchange and Main Streets, visit the American Hotel where the party would stay,[19] perhaps even talk his way past a blushing maid for a quick inspection of the presidential suite, and be waiting for the presidential party when it arrived on Saturday the sixteenth at 4:30 p.m. He might stalk the president-elect, playing the role of spy on Saturday, perhaps catch him off guard as an assassin on Sunday, and return to the stage as Pescara on Monday. In February 1861, there were no metal detectors, no X-ray machines checking railway passengers for concealed weapons. Booth was an experienced marksman, known to travel with weapons. He had time. He had money. His profession and his name were his passport.

AT 5:00 p.m. the Lincoln Special arrived in Buffalo.[20] At that time, Buffalo was the tenth largest city in the country, with a population of over eighty thousand people.[21] Most of them seemed to have turned out to see Lincoln this evening. The *World's* anonymous correspondent estimated that at least seventy-five thousand people attended the "turbulent ceremonials" intended for the president-elect.[22] At the Exchange Street Depot, a crowd of at least ten thousand waited for Lincoln. Former President Millard Fillmore was among them.

While Fillmore would welcome Lincoln to his city, sit with him in church, and host him at his home, there would likely be undercurrents of tension between the two men. Fillmore knew of Lincoln's opposition to him in the 1856 election, and Lincoln knew of Fillmore's support of Bell and his opposition to the Republicans in the most recent presidential contest. Fillmore had been critical of Republicans for what he perceived as their failure to make reasonable concessions to the South on the slavery issue. He believed the Crittenden Compromise should have been implemented. This plan would have extended the Missouri Compromise line all the way to California, protecting slavery in the federal territories south of the 36°30' line and prohibiting slavery north of that line.[23] Lincoln, of course, was for no compromise that would open any of the territories, whether north or south of some arbitrary line, to slavery.

Despite their differences, Fillmore and Lincoln greeted one another with a hearty handshake as Lincoln emerged from the car. A file of Buffalo police and a local infantry regiment parted the sea of onlookers, forming a narrow crevice through which two presidents, past and future, might pass. But the security detail was insufficient; the surging crowd pressed tightly, perilously, upon Lincoln.[24]

The eloquent, if anonymous reporter for the *New York World* described the mayhem best: "The President himself narrowly escaped unpleasant personal contact with the crowd. An intrepid body-guard, composed partly of soldiers and partly of members of his suite, succeeded, however, in protecting him from maceration, but only at the expense of incurring themselves a pressure to which the hug of Barnum's grizzly bear would have been a tender and fraternal embrace."[25]

Eventually, and likely due in great part to Ward Hill Lamon's brute strength, Lincoln and Fillmore broke through the swaying, shouting surge of humanity in the depot to the relative calm of a waiting carriage. Reported the press, "The President elect was safely got out of the depot only by the desperate efforts of those immediately around him. His party had to struggle with might and main for their lives, and after fighting their way to the open air found some of the carriages already occupied, so that not a few had to make for the hotel afoot as best they could."[26] One of Lincoln's protectors, Major David Hunter, was seriously injured, dislocating his shoulder in the struggle.

The Buffalo incident foretold that Lincoln would need to take extreme precautions when arriving at all the future cities on his itinerary, but particularly in Baltimore. If a joyous, eager, friendly Buffalo crowd could, by its sheer size, overwhelm a police force and infantry regiment intending to protect, what might happen if Lincoln were caught in the teeth of a crowd of the same size, whose opinion of him was at best blurred, at worst openly hostile? Particularly if the police force there were small and ambivalent at best, complicit or invisible at worst?

One way or another, those waiting for Lincoln in Baltimore would have learned of today's debacle in Buffalo. If there were indeed Baltimore plotters following Lincoln's movements, they might have telegraphed home base with news of Buffalo's crushing crowds and the confusion and sense of helplessness with which such a tidal wave of humanity could overwhelm a relatively small presidential party—even one guarded by a military escort. Although there is no evidence he was there, perhaps John Wilkes Booth himself stood in the crush of the Buffalo crowd. But even if Booth was not there, joined by other Baltimore conspirators, news of the event would be reported in the national press the next day and reach Baltimore in plenty of time to make the most it. Confirming and augmenting previous published accounts, the key takeaways of the Buffalo incident to the Baltimore plotters would have been these:

Lincoln acts with casual disregard for his own safety, arriving at crowded depots in broad daylight, and passing on foot and in open carriages through throngs of people. Even a loyal police force and an armed infantry regiment is no match for a pressing crowd of sufficient size. Amid the confusion that results from an ungovernable, swaying, pressing, frantic crowd, an assassin might stab or shoot the president unseen—and escape unnoticed.

THAT afternoon in Baltimore, Allan Pinkerton chose to employ a subtle, yet effective, intelligence-gathering technique: slip quietly among a brood of vipers and, once in their pit, listen to what all the snakes are hissing about—hopefully without getting bitten. Barnum's Hotel was a well-known secessionist hangout. In its basement, Captain Ferrandini, the fiery man Pinkerton had met the evening before, plied his trade as the hotel's head barber. Pinkerton knew if he hung around the lobby or the bar at Barnum's long enough, the place would soon sizzle and pop with valuable conversation.

The man Pinkerton was particularly interested in this afternoon was not Captain Ferrandini, however, but Baltimore's police marshal, George P. Kane. Spotting Kane at Barnum's, Pinkerton listened intently as he spoke to a cluster of presumed secessionists. Pinkerton could not hear everything, but he could hear enough. By this time, it would have been known to Kane and everyone else in Baltimore that one week from today, Lincoln would be passing through town.

Eavesdropping, Pinkerton must have had to struggle to maintain his poker face as he heard just a few tantalizing words. He overheard Marshal Kane indicate that he would not be "giving a Police Escort." Pinkerton could not be sure that Kane was talking about a police escort for Lincoln, but the evidence

Lincoln arrives in Buffalo, New York, to a crushing crowd of supporters. Several in the crowd were seriously injured, including Major David Hunter. (*Library of Congress*)

pointed strongly in that direction. First, Pinkerton knew of no other upcoming event in Baltimore that might need a police escort except for Lincoln's arrival. Second, "from the familiar manner of Marshall Kane and many of the rabid Secessionates, there could be no doubt but that they were aware that Kane was not going to give an Escort."[27] Presumably, the disloyal men Kane was talking to appeared satisfied, even delighted and reassured at what they were hearing from him.

Pinkerton did not yet know of the crushing, unmanageable crowd in Buffalo that had swarmed and pressed dangerously around Lincoln and his suite. But Pinkerton knew that a police escort for Lincoln was necessary in any city, and particularly here, where the threat of an ungovernable Baltimore mob loomed large. And he knew that Marshal Kane knew it too. Wrote Pinkerton in his report, "It was impossible for Marshall Kane not to know that there would be a necessity for an Escort for Mr. Lincoln on his arrival in Baltimore, and, that if with this knowledge Marshall Kane failed to give a Police Escort, then I should from this time out doubt the loyalty of the Baltimore Police."[28]

THAT night in Buffalo, at the American Hotel, his voice raw from constant speaking, his bony hand bruised from interminable hand shaking, Lincoln held yet another levee. He made little bows; he lifted and kissed little girls; he gave little speeches.[29] Across the street from the hotel, a banner hung on the Young Men's Christian Union building. Possibly, the banner had been displayed in response to Lincoln's farewell remarks in Springfield, where he said that without the same divine assistance Washington had received, he could not succeed, but with it he could not fail. The banner simply read: "We Will Pray for You."[30]

It was a good thing he planned on going to church in the morning with President Fillmore. Abraham Lincoln would need all the prayers he could get.

After church, Lincoln spent the remainder of the day recuperating at the American Hotel. Perhaps he read the newspapers, and caught up on some news. He certainly rested his weary body and strained vocal chords.[31]

While Lincoln rested his voice, Jefferson Davis tested his. En route to his February 18 inauguration, Davis reached Montgomery, Alabama, on board his own special train from Jackson, Mississippi, capping a journey that, although shorter than Lincoln's, had also been highlighted by numerous speeches, also made to enthusiastic crowds. But the two men's speeches were, like the sections of the country they represented, polar opposites.

Lincoln had thus far seemed almost deaf and his speeches almost mute to the drumbeat of approaching conflict. This was intentional—he had determined not to say anything definitive on that subject until the inaugural. As a consequence, his speeches would be described as falling like "a wet blanket," as "most ordinary," as "destitute."[32] In contrast, Davis had confronted the brewing conflict head-on during his trip. His oratory had been full of fiery rhetoric and even overt taunts. For example, in Stevenson, Alabama, Davis made grandiose predictions and even terrorist threats to the North: "Your Border States will gladly come into the Southern Confederacy within sixty days, as we will be their only friends. England will recognize us, and a glorious future is before us. The grass will grow in the Northern cities, where the pavements have been worn off by the tread of commerce. We will carry war where it is easy to advance—where food for the sword and torch await our arms in the densely populated cities; and though they [the enemy] may come and spoil our crops, we can raise them as before; while they cannot rear the cities which took years of industry and millions of money to build."[33]

Unlike Lincoln, Davis had no predecessor who currently held power. He could speak freely and passionately, painting wildly on a fresh political canvas. It was in his interests to do so, to add fuel to an already fired Southern heart. But Lincoln was compelled to hold his powder. Buchanan, weak though he was, still occupied the White House. That place would not be Lincoln's until March 4. Lincoln had steadfastly refused to make his case as president until he was in fact president—assuming he got to be president. Still unknown to Lincoln, however, evidence continued to gather against the likelihood of that possibility.

In February 1861, there was no United States Secret Service. No Federal Bureau of Investigation. No Central Intelligence Agency. No well-trained, steel-nerved special federal agents who could be dispatched to dangerous locations in Baltimore or elsewhere to gather intelligence relating to broods of conspirators intent on presidential assassination or governmental overthrow. The art of clandestine operations, to the extent that it was practiced at all, thus fell upon the shoulders of private detectives like Allan Pinkerton, policemen like New York's John Kennedy, and military men like General Winfield Scott—men generally more experienced in dispatching blunt force, delivering cold steel and hot lead upon their adversaries, than the more subtle tradecraft of secretly gathering intelligence from them.

Most remarkably, therefore, and perhaps out of sheer necessity, Union intelligence-gathering responsibilities also fell upon a loose-knit, tight-lipped cadre of civilians, government leaders motivated as much by the instinctual needs of protecting their party and friends as by the more lofty aspirations of duty to country. Into this class fell men like Representatives Elihu Washburne of Illinois, Schuyler Colfax of Indiana and Peace Conference delegate Lucius E. Chittenden of Vermont.

Chittenden had joined forces with a small group of young Republicans who, by early 1861, had formed an "independent committee of safety" in Washington, the aim of which was to gather intelligence of rebel activities. These men constructed a network of operatives throughout the major Northern cities and maintained near real-time communication via the web of the era—the criss-cross weave of telegraph lines that connected all major cities in the country to one another. In a real sense, this independent committee of safety was the antidote to the shadowy conclaves of secessionists and, like them, also operated in secrecy, using passwords and coded messages. Explained Chittenden modestly, "the investigation and exposure of rumors was part of their work."[34]

This afternoon, while Lincoln rested in Buffalo, a duly authenticated messenger "from reliable friends in Baltimore" arrived in Washington to say that they wished two or three members of Chittenden's secretive organization to return with the messenger to Baltimore. The Peace Conference was then in session at Willard's Hotel in Washington but had adjourned the previous day, Saturday the sixteenth, until Monday the eighteenth. The messenger was evasive as to the purpose of the meeting. The matter was too vital to be entrusted to mail, telegraph, or even a written hand-passed note. An explanation would come upon their arrival in Baltimore.[35]

Chittenden, along with a single unnamed associate, took a late train from Washington, stopping at the Relay House, a few miles south of Baltimore. There, a Baltimore friend of Chittenden's boarded the train, stared at him, but passed him without apparent recognition. The train started. A few minutes later, a stranger passed through the aisle of the dimly lit car and stumbled over Chittenden, grasping him by the hand as if to catch his fall. The man apologized. Chittenden felt the stranger press a piece of paper into his hand. He went to the car's dressing room to see what it was. The paper was a note with instructions written on it. In the dim light of the dressing room, Chittenden read the curious note. It said: "Be cautious. At the station follow a driver who will be shouting 'Hotel Fountain,' instead of 'Fountain Hotel.' Enter his carriage. He is reliable and has his directions."[36] Chittenden destroyed the note.

Upon arriving at the Camden Street depot in Baltimore,[37] Chittenden and his associate found the driver shouting "Hotel Fountain."[38] The two men got into the carriage and were driven to a private residence. As both Chittenden and his associate were unfamiliar with Baltimore, they did not know where this place was. A gentlemen waiting for them outside the private residence showed them in and the driver hurried off. Soon afterward, Chittenden and his associate were met by Chittenden's Baltimore friend from the train, the man who had passed by pretending not to know him. They were taken to an upper room of the house. Here, a half dozen Baltimore Republicans were already waiting and were hurriedly introduced to them. According to Chittenden, "no time was wasted."[39]

What Chittenden was about to learn must have stunned him. A man known to Chittenden as a true Republican, whom he would identify only as "Mr. H——,"[40] opened the meeting with an urgent plea, followed by a bombshell: "We want you to help us save Baltimore from disgrace, and President Lincoln from assassination."[41]

Mr. H—— proceeded to explain that their work had been difficult, as they were being watched and shadowed such that they could not leave Baltimore without raising suspicion. This seems credible. Republicans were a scorned superminority in Baltimore; they had been the subject of insults, taunts, and intimidation at a peaceful march the previous October, during which a mob hurled epithets, eggs, and brickbats at them. During the presidential election, they had risked their lives merely by showing up to vote for Lincoln.[42] More recently, they had sent messengers to leading Republicans in Washington, notifying them of a plot against Lincoln's life but had not succeeded in convincing anyone of its existence. Continued a frustrated Mr. H——, "we also learn that Mr. Lincoln declares that he will pursue his journey openly, if he loses his life in consequence. Within ten minutes after the presidential train reaches the Canton station[43] it will be surrounded by a mob of twenty thousand roughs and plug-uglies, from which he will never escape alive. We have every detail of the plot; we know the men who have been hired to kill him; we could lay our hands on them to-night."[44]

Chittenden wanted proof. Mr. H——
offered as evidence that "sporting men"
were giving odds that Lincoln would never
reach Washington alive. More recently, the
bet had been modified to a narrower subset
of possibilities—that he would not pass
through *Maryland* alive. But this was a
gambler's proof only. At good enough odds,
wishful men would bet on almost any future
outcome, no matter how improbable.
Chittenden needed more.

Mr. H—— proceeded to tell Chittenden
that he had a witness. A woman had been
abandoned by her lover, a man who had
been one of the conspirators. This woman
had betrayed the man to them. The man,
having no scruples, then revealed the names
of his associates in the plot. Chittenden was

Lucius E. Chittenden, a Peace
Conference delegate from Vermont,
recorded suspicious activities of the
Baltimore plotters. (*Picture History*)

still not convinced. "You cannot condemn reputable men upon such evidence,"
Chittenden argued.[45]

At this, Mr. H—— ordered the man brought in. Two men entered the
room leading a third man, whom Chittenden regarded, perhaps prejudicially,
as looking the part of a villain. "His square, bull-dog jaws, ferret-like eyes,
furtively looking out from holes under a low brow, covered with a coarse mat
of black hair; a dark face, every line of which was hard, and an impudent swagger in his carriage, sufficiently advertised him." The man spoke with an Italian
accent. He declared that "A bad president was coming in the cars to free the
negroes and drive all the foreigners out of the country." The man claimed that
some "good Americans" wanted Lincoln killed and had employed a man
named Ruscelli, a barber who called himself Orsini, to do the job.[46]

"Ruscelli" seems to be an alias for Captain Ferrandini; he also was a barber
and compared himself to Felice Orsini, an Italian zealot executed for attempting to assassinate Napoleon III. Indeed, Ferrandini had just two days before
told Pinkerton that "as Orissini had given his life for Italy, so was he
(Ferrandina) ready to die for his country, and the rights of the South."[47] This
hired assassin, "Ruscelli," apparently was an experienced murderer; he had
allegedly escaped from Italy after "killing some men who failed to pay their
ransom."[48]

It would have been helpful for Chittenden and his "independent committee of safety" to compare notes with Allan Pinkerton and his operatives. If, for
example, "Ruscelli" was indeed an alias for Ferrandini, this would have been
useful intelligence for Pinkerton to have followed up on. But there was one

1   President Street Station
2   Camden Street Station
3   Calvert Street Station
4   Monument Square/Battle Monument
5   Mount Vernon Place
6   Pinkerton's Headquarters
7   Anna Travis's House of Prostitution
8   Barnum's City Hotel
9   Eutaw House
10 Boyhood home of J. Wilkes Booth,
    62 North Exeter Street
11 Possible positions of National Volunteers
    on February 23, 1861
12 Possible secret meeting location of
    National Volunteers

13 Post Office
14 Holliday Street Theater
15 Guy's Hotel
16 Likely point where Mary Lincoln and sons
    left train
17 Presbyterian Church - site of Constitutional
    Union Convention (Bell-Everett nominated)
18 Front Street Theater - site of first National
    Democratic Convention (Douglas nominated)
19 Howard House - Pinkerton's Baltimore Hotel
20 Fountain Inn
21 Mann's Hotel
22 Howard Athenaeum - location of J. Wilkes
    Booth's first performance
23 John S. Gittings residence - where Mrs.
    Lincoln and sons dined

------- Route Lincoln's carriage would likely have taken per published
        itinerary from Calvert Street Station to Camden Street Station
        (assuming no stop at Eutaw House)

—————— Route of horse-drawn sleeper car from P.W. & B. President Street
        Station to Camden Street Station

BALTIMORE–1861

SCALE IN FEET

minor problem. Neither Pinkerton's nor Chittenden's group knew of the existence of the other. They were gathering intelligence in silos.

The shadowy informant provided Chittenden with a few more tantalizing details of the plot and the plotters. He and his associates were but pawns on a chessboard controlled by much more powerful players. The assassin's employers were "secessionists, pot-house politicians of a low order, with some admixture of men of a better class, some of them in the police."[49] Some of these men, Chittenden was told, "were influential politicians and citizens who had argued themselves into the belief that this was a patriotic work which would prevent greater bloodshed and possible war." These well-heeled conspirators had freely given money to aid in the enterprise, and even purchased a schooner for the assassins to make their escape.[50]

Chittenden's Baltimore friends claimed to have an agent who had joined in the conspiracy and attended all of their secret meetings. Through this unnamed agent, they had learned that the assassination had been rehearsed several times in order to avoid mistakes. Assuming Lincoln's train arrived from Philadelphia at the President Street Station, his car would be uncoupled and drawn along tracks through the city by a team of horses to the Camden Street depot a little over a mile away. Once there, Lincoln's car would be coupled to a locomotive of the B&O Railroad and driven to Washington.

But Lincoln's car would never get to the Camden Street depot. The plan was to tear up the track at the end of a bridge, likely after the horse-drawn car turned left off President Street and headed west onto Pratt Street. There, the car would cross over Jones Falls, now at the head of Pier 6 on the Inner Harbor. The conspirators had likely determined to tear up the track at that point, forcing the car to stop. "When the President's car was stopped at the obstruction the assassins were to follow their leader into the rear of the car, pass rapidly through it, each knifing the president, out at the forward door, through the crowd to a rum shop, at the rear of which lay a schooner, with a tug under steam, which would immediately go down the bay with the schooner in tow. Clearance papers would be provided for the port of Mobile, to which the schooner would as speedily as possible make her way."[51] To add to the confusion, "bombs and hand-grenades, which exploded by concussion, were to be thrown into the cars through the windows."[52]

If, instead of having his car uncoupled and drawn by horses, Lincoln left his car at Canton Street for a carriage, the job would be even easier. The carriage would be blocked at the same location where the track would be torn up, at which point Lincoln would be killed in the open barouche.

Having rehearsed their plot, the assassins had found that the entire plan—halting Lincoln's car or carriage, killing him, and escaping amid the ensuing confusion on the departing schooner—could be accomplished in an astounding five or six minutes.[53]

Rehearsals are necessary not only for successful assassins, but for successful actors as well. Indeed, at least one of the Baltimore plotters was an actor. The men that had called Chittenden to Baltimore that night told him they knew who some of the conspirators were: "We know that they are not all hired assassins. There are men among them who believe they are serving their country. One of them is an actor who recites passages from the tragedy of Julius Cæsar in their conclaves. They are abundantly supplied with money."[54]

How many men might have fit the profile of a secessionist actor, with ties to Baltimore, prone to reciting passages from *Julius Caesar*, who believed the South should be served patriotically, for love, not money, in February 1861? Possibly a few. But we know for certain of at least one—John Wilkes Booth.

Booth knew Shakespeare's plays by rote. He certainly could have called up from *Julius Caesar* any apropos line, anywhere, any time, to impress, inspire, or incite.[55] Indeed, that would have been Booth's style. He had, in October, recited Marcus Antonius's *Julius Caesar* funeral speech on stage in Columbus, Georgia.[56] Then, in December, in his manifesto written while in Philadelphia, Booth made clear his pro-Southern, pro-slavery, anti-black, anti-abolition beliefs.[57] While he was not currently living in Baltimore, he had grown up there and certainly knew the city. He frequently returned to Baltimore between acting engagements; indeed, he would spend the latter part of the following April and most of May there.[58] And he knew and sometimes stayed, at least in later years, at Barnum's Hotel, where Ferrandini worked. Also in later years, Booth would use his money to help the Southern cause and to aid co-conspirators in other Lincoln plots. Most significantly, he had been recuperating since falling on his dagger during his February 12 performance in Albany. He might have rested a day or two, ridden by train day and night for a quick trip to Baltimore, attended a secret conclave or two, and been back in Albany with time to spare before the next evening's performance.

Equally curious, Booth's whereabouts between February 2, when he closed in Rochester, and February 11, when he opened in Albany, are not known.[59] It is certainly possible that he hung around either city for the entire nine-day stretch. It is also certainly possible that he returned to Baltimore during that time—a time when the Select Committee of Five was questioning Baltimore witnesses and the Baltimore plotters' meetings and military drills were just beginning to gel.

With all of this evidence, the question is not so much who could this mysterious actor that recited passages from *Julius Caesar* in the Baltimore plotters' conclaves have been. The better question is, who *else* could it have been—other than John Wilkes Booth?

LINCOLN had survived the halfway point of his journey. Seven days down, six to go. Thus far, the trip could be summed up, as it would be later by the *World's* embedded reporter, in three words—"crowds, cannon, and cheers."[60] But what would the next six days bring? Before him lay many more miles of track and many more throngs of people. People in the Big Cities—New York and Philadelphia—and in the state capitals of New York, New Jersey, and Pennsylvania. And of course, there would be people waiting for Lincoln in Baltimore. They had six more days to prepare for each other.

But first things first. Tomorrow Lincoln and his suite would set out for Albany. John Wilkes Booth would be there when he arrived.

CHAPTER NINE

ACTORS

Monday, February 18, 1861
Buffalo–Albany

Assuming John Wilkes Booth had followed his likely pattern of behavior, he had gone to bed late, woke late, likely hung over, perhaps in the arms of his latest paramour. One of his lovers around this time was the accomplished actress Henrietta Irving. Three weeks before, Booth and Irving had played together in Rochester, in *Romeo and Juliet*, each assuming a title role.[1] Two months from now, on April 26, 1861, Ms. Irving would attempt to murder Booth here in Albany, slashing him with a knife across the face during the heat of a drunken lover's spat, brought on by Wilkes's admission that had no intention of marrying her.[2] He had merely been leading her on—this was another of Booth's patterns of behavior.

As he would be performing tonight, Booth had probably resumed rehearsing with the cast the previous day, Sunday, likely an all day dress rehearsal.[3] Never one to be accused of overworking himself, the rehearsal might have seemed unnecessary to Booth. Perhaps he hadn't even shown up. After all, he was the star, the drawing card. Besides, tonight's role was a part he knew well, Pescara, in *The Apostate*, the same role he had been playing when he suffered the self-inflicted dagger wound the evening of February 12.

Whether he had rehearsed the day before or not, this morning Booth would likely have enjoyed breakfast and read the morning newspapers, scanning their pages for mention of his return to the stage that evening, paying particular attention to any accolades being showered upon him. Today's *Atlas and Argus* would massage the young star's ego. The February 18, 1861, edition reported that Booth was "quite recovered" from his self-inflicted dagger wound and that "The Tragedian's many friends and admirers will be glad to learn that he is able once more to appear before them. The Tragedy of 'The Apostate' has been selected at the repeated request of numerous patrons of the Gayety, and all who are fortunate enough to secure seats for its representation, will obtain a rare dramatic treat."[4]

But as he read the newspapers at Stanwix Hall this morning, Booth would have paid even closer attention to something other than praises being sung for him. Later that very day, Abraham Lincoln and his suite would be arriving here, in Albany. Booth would certainly have anticipated this before, but today's newspapers would have confirmed and punctuated the event.

Although Albany was a Northern city, it was heavily Democratic, and the *Atlas and Argus* was no fan of Lincoln's.[5] Booth would have found a dose of inspiration in reading its pages, a measure of support for believing that even here, in the great white North of upstate New York, many opposed Lincoln, just as many adored the young tragedian. If, just perhaps if, twenty-two-year-old J. Wilkes Booth harbored thoughts of martyrdom, of slaying a tyrant, there would be no better opportunity for him to act out those thoughts than later today. Lincoln and his suite would arrive in Albany at yet another over-crowded train station, for yet another head-jostling, bone-crushing, mad rush through a landslide of citizens, to be spit out and deposited in yet another open barouche, conveying the readily identifiable Lincoln and his suite slow-ly through the city's streets, pulled by easily spotted plumed fine horses.

If Booth had entertained notions of murdering Lincoln before this, those notions would now have been aroused to the point of imagining, of contem-plating fantastically how it might be done, perhaps even carrying him to the very brink of excited planning. He would have considered the opportunities and the options. The opportunities were almost too many, and at first they would have seemed almost too easy. Booth would have known from previous newspaper accounts how ridiculously simple it was to get close to Lincoln. For example, there had been numerous, mostly humorous reports of men eager to measure their height next to the lanky rail-splitter. Most, although not all, had gone away being bested by a president-elect who seemed all too eager to go back to back with anyone and everyone. Booth too might have considered such a possibility for putting himself within striking distance of Lincoln. But swagger and strut as he might, the bow-legged little bantam rooster Booth, at five feet eight inches tall, would have been laughed at, perhaps even shoved off the platform before he could go heel to heel with the six-foot-four Lincoln. No, Booth would not use that ploy to get close to the president-elect. But there would have been plenty of other tantalizing opportunities.

The Saturday edition of the *Atlas and Argus* had laid out a minute-by-minute timetable of Lincoln's arrivals and departures. The fine print reported that Lincoln's train would stop at the Broadway crossing when it arrived in Albany at 2:30 p.m, where he would be formally received by the mayor and common council, before being escorted by the Twenty-Fifth Regiment to the capitol. Upon reaching the capitol, Edwin D. Morgan, New York's governor,

would formally introduce and welcome him outside. He would then be escorted into the assembly chamber for a reception by a joint session of the legislature. After these formalities, he would proceed to the executive chamber,
where he would have a brief reception, and "where all, indiscriminately, will
have an opportunity to greet him." If "all, indiscriminately" might meet
Lincoln, how much easier would it be for a rising star to be introduced to him?

After the reception in the executive chamber, Lincoln would be taken to
the Governor's Mansion, to be his guest for the night. Then, on Tuesday,
February 19, at 9:00 a.m., Lincoln would hold a ladies' reception in the parlors of the Delavan House. Previous editions had reported Lincoln's train
would leave Albany at 10:00 a.m.[6]

Albany's newspapers would have provided J. Wilkes Booth, or anyone else
for that matter, with an overwhelming number of choices for getting dangerously close to Lincoln. Most importantly, none of these options, except possibly being present as Lincoln left the Executive Mansion, would require Booth
to miss that night's performance. Each option provided its own golden opportunity. The option most appealing to Booth, however, would have been the
ladies' reception the next morning at the Delavan. Booth, of all people, would
have been attracted to a ladies' reception, with or without Lincoln being there.
Perhaps, if he had read Saturday's paper, he ticked off that option as the best
one for getting close to the president-elect.

But in Monday's newspaper, Booth would have immediately noticed that
there had been a change in plans from those reported Saturday. Lincoln would
still be arriving in Albany today, but his itinerary had curiously been
rearranged: The ladies' reception had apparently been rescheduled and would
no longer take place Tuesday morning at the Delavan but at Congress Hall
that night, *after dinner*, when Booth would be performing at the Gayety
Theater. His most promising opportunity had just been taken off the table.
And yet, where the door to one opportunity had abruptly closed, a loud knock
beckoned at another. Lincoln would not be having dinner at the Executive
Mansion, apparently, but instead would be having a private dinner at the
Delavan House, a five-story block-shaped building that had all the external
charm of a textile mill but was, on the inside, Albany's finest hotel. Most sig-
nificantly, the Delavan was but a city block north of Booth's hotel, Stanwix
Hall, on Broadway, near the train station and the Hudson River.

What were Booth's options? Perhaps Lincoln would be staying in a suite
on an upper floor. Booth might rent a room on a floor below Lincoln. A log
from a roaring fire might roll carelessly across the hearth and onto the carpet,
igniting the drapes. Within minutes the fire might spread to the floor above.
But fires were unpredictable. There was no telling where they might spread
and how fast. Lincoln might escape unscathed, while innocents burned alive.
And there was no honor in arson.

Perhaps an explosive device, an infernal machine of some sort, a hand grenade, tossed casually into Lincoln's suite, might do the job. But one could not simply walk into the local hardware store and purchase a hand grenade. That required access to a military arsenal.

Other options might have casually crossed Booth's active mind. He might take a shot at the tall tyrant as he emerged from the train. Or while he rode in the carriage. This was one of the options the Baltimore plotters had selected. Booth was handy with firearms, a crack shot. Even as a schoolboy of fourteen, he could, along with his St. Timothy's Hall chums, handle a five-chamber Colt revolver with such skill that he could "kill a rabbit running, and about once in three times a partridge flying."[7] Lincoln made for a much larger, slower moving target. Certainly, a man who could hit a rabbit running or a partridge flying could easily dispatch a six-foot-four-inch sitting duck.

Or Booth might choose the Brutus-Pescara option. Ironically, the words of the fiendish, hate-filled Pescara, whom he would play that night, may have coursed through his mind:

What if I rush,
And with a blow strike life from out his heart?[8]

Yes, he might lunge at Lincoln with a dagger while the vile Black Republican stood shaking hands in any number of reception lines that welcomed all who had the patience to wait their turn, none of whom would be searched for concealed weapons. There would be such a reception tonight at Congress Hall. But this option too would not work; Booth would have recalled that he was to reopen tonight as Pescara in *The Apostate*. The doors would open at 7:00 p.m.; the show would start at 7:30.

Each option, though offering a promising initial path, seemed destined to the dead end of failure. Whether the course chosen was an arson's flame, a hand grenade, a flashing dagger, or a pistol shot, each would require that Booth be physically and temporally proximate to the president-elect, that he take careful aim, in the case of a pistol, likely with no opportunity for a second shot, or that he have sufficient room and arm strength to maneuver and thrust a knife in an arcing death blow.

Unlike in Baltimore, there would be no secessionist police here in Albany to look the other way, no gang of accomplices to get up a diversionary row. Unlike in Baltimore, where there would be no loyal Union troops to escort Lincoln, here, in Albany, the entire Twenty-fifth Regiment, under arms, would clear his path with gleaming bayonets and oil-polished gunstocks. Even if he might succeed, both in getting close to the president-elect and in hitting his mark, Booth's capture would be almost certain. On top of all this, there was another, more serious problem. Booth's bone-deep dagger wound suffered the week before had not, despite the newspaper's exaggerations, yet fully healed. He was right-handed, and the wound prevented full use of his right arm. In fact, for tonight's show, he would need to perform Pescara's fencing scene left-handed, with his right arm tied to his side. He would, in all likelihood, be unable to strike a death blow with a knife or even aim a pistol with his shooting hand with any steadiness, confidence, or accuracy.

Booth may well have imagined the swift justice, the primitive retribution an angry Northern mob might visit on one who murdered Lincoln before their eyes. Amid hisses and hooting they might lynch him on the spot, that very day, tethered by the neck to a stiff, frozen rope strung from a rafter in the depot, launching him into eternity backwards off the tail end of a buggy-whipped horse. They would watch him drop. Watch him swing until he stopped kicking. Cut him down. Lop off his head. Hoist it on a pike.

At this point in his young life, Booth likely was not yet ready to perform an assassination in public and thereby become a martyr. The war had not yet begun. The South had not yet been vanquished. The cause was not yet ripe. But even now, in the cold, gray dawn of the Civil War, Booth despised Lincoln enough to wish him dead. There might still be a way. It was a quiet method, one more fitting for an act to save the Union from being rent asunder by the Black Republican abolitionist threat than a violent means struck to slake the thirst of vengeance. From his firsthand knowledge of the many murders performed by Shakespeare's players, Booth, of all people, would have known of one method in particular that might be performed by even a one-armed man, with stealth, in total concealment, with near certain success, and with virtually no way of being found out.

Poisoning. Indeed, in the weeks prior to leaving Springfield, Lincoln had received ominous warnings that he might be poisoned. Wrote one man from Cincinnati in January, "The midnight or noonday assassin may be in wait for you. There may be corrupt men who would be willing [to] destroy many lives to reach your plate with poison. 'Watch.'" That same month, another man wrote poetically from Pennsylvania, "You Sir be careful at the Kings table what meat and drink you take there might be poison in the ink. Your life and health are precious."[9] Joshua Allen, after visiting Lincoln in his temporary office in Springfield, wrote his mother on January 26, saying, "he has got stacks of preserved fruit and all sorts of trash which he is daily receiving from various parts of the South, sent him as presents. He had several packages opened and examined by medical men who found them all to be poisoned."[10]

If Booth was thinking of poisoning Lincoln now, in February 1861, it would not be the last time such thoughts would cross his mind. In 1864, while spinning off his oil interests in Pennsylvania, Booth would, with a diamond from a ring or stickpin, etch the following bizarre and chilling graffiti on a windowpane in his hotel room at the McHenry House: "Abe Lincoln, departed this life August 13, 1864, by the effects of poison."[11]

During the war, Booth would demonstrate a knack for obtaining and smuggling drugs. All it would take then, as now, was a little pluck, a few connections, and money. Indeed, the resourceful Booth would, during the height of the Civil War, smuggle high grade quinine South, hidden in horse collars, destined for Confederate wounded.[12] If he was able to secure and deliver large quantities of quinine to scores of soldiers behind enemy lines during the war, could he not now, in 1861, with just the right story, just the right amount of coin, secure a single lethal dose of poison and administer it to just one man?

Booth had been treated by a physician just a few days earlier after suffering his dagger wound. He might have had access to a physician's office, a physician's tools, and, most important, a physician's medicines, which, if used in just the right dose, in just the right combination, might bring on sudden death. Perhaps he was feeling great pain this morning. Certainly he could make a convincing show of it. He would need to see the doctor again. He must perform tonight, with his trademark vigor and realism. The audience must not see him wince. Perhaps the pain was so great that he could not sleep. Perhaps the doctor might prescribe a sleeping potion that, if administered in a large enough dose, would kill. But why bother with medicine at all, when the real purpose could be fulfilled with poison rather than medicine? Strychnine, arsenic, and prussic acid were well known poisons that a doctor might have had access to.[13] Perhaps he might bypass the doctor altogether. Perhaps he might convincingly tell the management of his hotel that his room was infested with rats and request poison.

Booth would have known that there would be at least two opportunities to poison Lincoln while in Albany. Tonight at dinner. Tomorrow at breakfast. He would need to verify where Lincoln would take his meal tonight. In his suite at the Delavan House? In one of the parlors? But what if he succeeded? What then? Should he flee? If so, where?

Booth had been off the boards since the performance on February 12. He would thus have had plenty of time to plot out not only how he might dispose of Lincoln in Albany, but also how he might make his escape—if he chose to escape. He might have been tempted to flee south, into the arms of the growing Confederacy, perhaps back to Richmond or even Montgomery. But getting to the South from upstate New York would have presented monumental challenges. Taking a train from Albany to points south would require, as the Lincoln Special's itinerary publicly documented, taking numerous rail lines and changing trains in a host of cities and towns, any one of which might be on high alert for a fleeing Lincoln assassin. Even if he was not recognized as the assassin, Booth's sudden and unexpected disappearance from Albany and his previously announced stage appearances, commensurate with Lincoln's murder, might be noticed by the authorities and would likely arouse suspicion.

If Booth was planning to end Lincoln's reign before it began and get away with it, he would likely have considered leaving the country as one possible means of escape, and, to do so by the most direct route, heading straight north some 300 miles for Montreal. Such a route would offer the protection of natural barriers, of snowy mountains, isolated rural towns, frozen rivers and lakes. And he might find safe haven in Montreal, the city that would soon be so infested with Confederate spies and sympathizers that it would become known as "Little Richmond." There, he might blend in, wait things out for a spell, and possibly sail for Europe, for London or France, if things got too hot.

Or perhaps he might take the risk of riding the train five hours south to New York City. The reward would be that once there, he could stay with his brother Edwin. And if Edwin would not provide him safe haven, there were plenty of secessionist sympathizers in New York City, starting with Mayor Fernando Wood. There was even talk that Mayor Wood was attempting to build support for New York itself to secede, to form a free city.[14] Indeed, there were rumors of Manhattan Island, Long Island, and Staten Island seceding from the Union and forming a new country to be named "Tri-Insula."[15] New York might thus offer sanctuary for a secessionist fugitive on the run. But if New York would not have him, even now, in winter, her port brimmed with sailing ships heading to England and points south, to a new life free from tyranny. Perhaps he could make his escape aboard the same ship, the *Huntsville,* on which he had arrived in New York two months earlier, back to Savannah, to a hero's welcome as the Brutus of the Confederacy. Indeed, the local papers were reporting that the *Huntsville* had that very week been caught attempting to smuggle arms and ammunition south from New York.[16] Certainly, if it was still in port, her captain would welcome a Southern sympathizer like J. Wilkes Booth.

But first things first. If Booth was going to poison Lincoln in Albany in the next twenty-four hours, he would need to know more about where and when the president-elect would be eating. He would need to know what foods he would be likely to eat, and with whom he would dine. Almost by definition, however, there would be collateral damage if poison was placed in food being passed around. Lincoln's children might ingest the poison. Booth had nothing against them and would not likely have wanted the little boys killed if it could be avoided. He might have once again considered the Apothecary's words from *Romeo and Juliet*: "Put this in any liquid thing you will." Tonight at dinner, the children would not be drinking the wine.

İn Baltimore, Lucius E. Chittenden was up early. Indeed, he had not slept. The consultation with his Republican friends in Baltimore had lasted well into the night. Their intent had been to convince Chittenden and his associate that the Baltimore Plot to murder Lincoln was both a real and present danger. They hoped Chittenden would convince others in Washington who might be able to do something about the threats to Lincoln's life.

Chittenden's associate confirmed that he was satisfied that the risk was real and that he believed he could satisfy General Scott as well. Chittenden and his associate boarded the early morning train to Washington. After reaching the capital, recalled Chittenden, "in the gray of the morning we drove to the house of Elihu B. Washburne, called him from his bed, and in a few words summed up our night's experience, with the statement that we had come for his assistance in precautionary measures."[17]

Washburne's response stunned Chittenden. Washburne claimed he already knew of the Baltimore Plot. "He said that we might put aside our anxiety; that he knew positively that Mr. Lincoln had determined to follow the advice of his friends, and would reach Washington without risk." Washburne revealed that he, William Seward, and General Scott had become convinced that precautions would be needed to protect Lincoln's life, and that "none but those who had charge of the President's journey should know by what route or at what time he would pass through Baltimore."[18]

Everything seemed to be under control. Except for one thing. As of February 18, 1861, Abraham Lincoln had not yet determined to follow the advice of his friends. Indeed, he had not yet received any advice from them. Lincoln did not yet know that a well-formed plot to murder him had been hatched in Baltimore. No one had told him.

HAVING been woken at 4:00 a.m., a grumpy Lincoln party had left Buffalo less than two hours later. "What peculiar exigence of time tables may have led Mr. Superintendent Wood to indicate 5 A.M. as the hour up which to start from Buffalo," wrote the *New York World's* special correspondent later that day, "I do not know. I only know that Mr. Wood did indicate that hour, and that that relentlessly executive person, like time, tide and rent day, waits for no man."[19]

Wood's fastidious attention to time and schedules, particularly on this day, was understandable. One published schedule had them leaving Buffalo at 5:48 a.m., arriving in Albany at 2:20 p.m.[20] Today the Lincoln Special, initially pulled by the locomotive *Dean Richmond*, would make the longest one-day journey of the trip, crossing the entire 300-mile width of upstate New York from Buffalo to Albany at breakneck speeds sometimes exceeding 50 miles per hour, with frequent stops along the way, including Schenectady, where the president-elect's arrival would again be greeted by "crowds, cannon, and cheers."[21]

In Albany, the day was cloudy and seasonably cold, the thermometer hovering at just above freezing. A light wind blew chilled Canadian air out of the northwest.[22] At 2:25 p.m., right on time, after the longest day of the trip in terms of miles covered, the Lincoln Special, now pulled by the brightly decorated locomotive *Erastus Corning, Jr.,* replete with fluttering American flags, squealed to a stop at Albany's Broadway Street crossing.[23] The *Atlas and Argus* described the scene:

> A platform had been erected by the Central Railroad Company, for the accommodation of the party, and the space was kept clear by the Police. When the train came in sight, the engine gaily decked with flags, loud shouts were sent up by the crowd, which numbered some thousands. The locomotive drawing the special train was . . . a new and handsome one. Only two carriages were attached, and they were completely filled. Some delay occurred, the military not having reached the ground in time, and the people gave vent to their impatience by repeated cries of "Come out on the platform," "Get off the cars!" "Show us the Rail Splitter" "Trot out Old Abe!" and the like. At last the music of the military was heard, and the 25th Regiment . . . marched on the ground and took up their station, clearing the platform and opening a pathway for the President elect and his party to the carriages.[24]

Lincoln's party had apparently learned its lesson from the chaos that had prevailed when they arrived at the depot in Buffalo just two days before. Seeing the mob on the platform outside their cars today, they waited patiently for the military escort to clear their path.

The crowd erupted in applause when they saw the president-elect descend from the car to the platform, and he bowed appreciatively. Albany's Democratic mayor, George H. Thacher, extended a brief, yet respectful welcome that might have served as a model greeting for any heavily Democratic city welcoming a Republican president-elect. Said the mayor, "We trust that you will accept the welcome we offer, not simply as a tribute of respect to the high office you are called to fill, but as a testimony of the good will of our citizens without distinction of party, and as an expression of their appreciation of our eminent personal worth, and their confidence in your patriotism."

Lincoln's reply, though terse, was equally respectful. Perhaps in a veiled stab at humor, he referred to the "two or three courses through which I shall have to go" that evening as an excuse for not delivering any extended remarks. In fact, three state dinners had been prepared for the president-elect; one waited for him at Congress Hall, prepared by General Mitchell, another was being thrown at the Delavan House, courtesy of the Joint Reception Committee, and a third, prepared "in the Russian style," awaited him at the Executive

Mansion, thanks to Governor Morgan. "It was not known up to the hour of dinner which of the three Mr. Lincoln would partake of," wrote the *Atlas and Argus*.[25]

This uncertainty would have frustrated any plans for poisoning Lincoln at dinner tonight. Indeed, a controversy had been brewing all of the previous week in Albany between Governor Morgan (a founder of the banking house) and state senators, assemblymen, and various committees, over who would have the honor of being the first to welcome and then host Lincoln. As things turned out, Mayor Thacher would do the initial meet and greet. Contrary to what the newspaper reported that day about Lincoln dining at the Delavan House with the Joint Reception Committee, Governor Morgan would host Lincoln for dinner at the Executive Mansion. It is said that Morgan wanted Lincoln all to himself to gain insider information concerning whether or not there would be war, so that he could then consult with his cousin and partner in their brokerage business about whether to hold or, in the case of war being imminent, sell their Missouri bonds.[26]

After the brief exchange with Mayor Thacher, Lincoln stepped into the first of five elegant, open barouches provided for him and the suite, each drawn by four bay horses. A man in the crowd had been eyeing Lincoln, watching for an opportunity to get close to him. As he pushed his way near Lincoln's carriage, the man attracted the attention of the Albany police. He resisted their efforts to stop him. This determined man, "being more or less influenced by liquor, was present on the arrival of Mr. Lincoln, . . . and persisted in crowding upon the carriage which that distinguished citizen occupied." Whether deemed harmless, because of his inebriated state, or due to an ineffective police presence, the man succeeded in getting close enough to Lincoln to shoot him dead. Instead, the drunk heartily shook Lincoln's hand, seemingly intent on keeping the president-elect all to himself. Finally, the police intervened and carted the inebriate, a man named Fennessey, off to jail.[27]

The incident would have demonstrated to all present in Albany that day, and those reading the account in the next day's newspapers, a critical truth: it was ridiculously easy to get dangerously close to Lincoln. All it took was the three "P's" of any daring enterprise—patience, perseverance, and pluck. One might feign drunkenness or insanity to repel both the crowd and the police. The vignette would also have confirmed for the Baltimore plotters that local police could indeed be distracted from attending to Lincoln by a simple diversion, such as a staged fight. Which is exactly what the Baltimore plotters determined to do.

Fennessey having been dispatched, Lincoln's procession headed north on Broadway and then turned left onto State Street toward the Capitol, "the whole route being crowded with citizens."[28] Might Booth have been among the thousands of citizens crowding the Albany depot or lining its streets that afternoon? There is no conclusive evidence that he was. There is likewise no conclusive proof that he was not. No diaries, letters, or newspaper accounts survive to pinpoint Booth's precise location on the afternoon of February 18, 1861. But he was most certainly in Albany that day. And both common sense and the known habits of Booth conspire to suggest that he was there when Lincoln arrived, waiting—and watching.

Even if Booth was expected at rehearsals this afternoon, he had in the past shirked his theatrical responsibilities in favor of appearing at the footlights of an even bigger stage. Besides, Lincoln's procession, moving down Broadway and onto State Street, would take the president-elect less than a few hundred paces from the Gayety Theater.[29] Even assuming rehearsals were going on and Booth was there for them, the din of the crowd lining Broadway and State Streets would, in all likelihood, have caused everyone to stop whatever they were doing and look, or even run, outside.

If Booth stood among the crowd that day, the scene then playing would not have been to his liking. This crowd was actually *cheering* for Lincoln. They adored him. Perhaps his brief exchange with the Gayety Theater's treasurer on the morning of his arrival in Albany a week before resonated in Booth's ears now:

"Is not this a democratic city?" Booth had asked indignantly after being warned to throttle his secessionist tongue while in Albany.

"Democratic? Yes; but disunion, no!" had been the unwelcome response.[30]

Most significantly, if John Wilkes Booth stood amid the throng of applauding, waving, huzzahing Albany citizens that afternoon, he would have instantly realized that he could not act alone against such overwhelming numbers of Lincoln supporters. Even if he could inch close, as the drunk had done, and fire off a clear, fatal shot, he could never escape from this crowd, let alone from the gang of military men—including New York's Twenty-fifth Regiment under arms—huddled around Lincoln. Perhaps even then, Booth realized he would need help.

If Booth had let wild thoughts of assassinating Lincoln roam unchecked through the wilderness of his mind, or if he had tracked those thoughts to the early planning stages, he would indeed have lamented his lost opportunity. John Wilkes Booth did not suffer fools lightly or accept his own failures gracefully. Whether it was frustration occasioned by his wound, or whether he was angered by Lincoln's presence in the same city and regretted a lost opportunity, Booth would clearly be exercised about something the night of February 18, 1861. Despite the dagger injury that forced him to tie his right arm to his side and fence with his left, during Monday night's performance, Booth would fence "like a demon."[31]

INSIDE the old capitol building, a relatively small and poorly ventilated space, Lincoln was escorted to the executive chamber, where various state dignitaries and legislative committees waited for him. Lincoln was introduced to Governor Morgan, chairman of the Republican National Committee, who shook his hand a long while, as if afraid to lose possession of the man over whom he had been wrangling with his rivals for control all week. Moments later, Governor Morgan and Lincoln emerged from the capitol, and the throng erupted in "a perfect roar of applause." The excited crowd pressed forward, ignoring the efforts of the police and soldiers to hold them back.

Lincoln gazed in wonder at the immense crowd that had jammed into the park and hung in the trees. He turned to Governor Morgan, saying, "Do you think we can make these people hear us?" Governor Morgan said nothing, merely shaking his head "no." He made a feeble gesture to quiet the crowd, a sweeping wave of his hat, but to no avail. So intense was the press of the crowd that several panes of glass in the capitol building were shattered. Amid the din, and in an era without microphones, Governor Morgan welcomed Lincoln with a short speech that was a "mere dumb-show, except to those in the immediate vicinity of the speakers."[32]

Lincoln thanked Governor Morgan for his state's hospitality and for the invitation to pass through the capital. "I am notified by your Governor that this reception is given without distinction of party, and I accept it the more gladly because it is so. Almost all men in this country, and in any country where freedom of thought is tolerated, attach themselves to political parties. It is but ordinary charity to attribute this to the fact that in so attaching himself to the party which his judgment prefers, the citizen believes he thereby promotes the best interest of the whole country. But when an election is passed, it is altogether befitting a free people, that, until the next election, they should be as one people."[33]

Lincoln concluded his short speech by appealing to the preeminence of Constitution and Union over any party. After bowing to "loud and repeated cheers," Lincoln retired to the assembly chamber, which was packed to the rafters—most of those in the galleries and lower lobbies were women. When he entered, the entire assembly rose and applauded.[34]

Quite possibly, as he clung to and hovered around Lincoln, Governor Morgan carried in his pocket a letter from the Baltimore Republican Committee addressed to him for delivery to the president-elect. The letter, written from Baltimore by William G. Snethen and dated February 15, 1861, was about as uninviting an invitation as one might make. It read:

> Dear Sir—
> On consultation with some of our leading Republican friends, it has been deemed inadvisable, in the present state of things, to

attempt any organized public display on our part, as
Republicans, on the occasion of your approach to and passage
through Baltimore, on your way to the Capitol, however gratify-
ing it would be to our feelings to do so. But it has been proposed,
that, as many of the gallant little band who voted for you in this
City, as may choose to do so, shall meet you, as your political
friends, in their individual capacity, either in Philadelphia or
Harrisburg, according to the route you may take, and accompany you thence to Baltimore, and on to Washington. We further
propose to have at the depot, a sufficient number of open
barouches with four horses each, for yourself and suite, to convey
you and them to your the Hotel, should you decide to stop in
Baltimore, and thence to the Washington depot, or if not, from
one depot to the other.

It is possible, that the Mayor and councils may take action,
and give you a formal reception, in which case, they will, of
course, provide the necessary conveyances and escort, but as yet,
we have had no intimations of the kind. The City authorities are
all opposed to us, and some of them are even hostile.[35]

The contrast between Albany and Baltimore, and between their states'
respective approaches to Lincoln's arrival, is stark indeed. New York's
Governor Morgan had written Lincoln on January 19, weeks before his itinerary was set, inviting him to Albany: "I most cordially invite you to the
Capital, and tender to you the hospitalities of the State, and of my house and
respectfully urge you to arrange to spend at least one day in Albany."[36]

Several weeks later, as the president-elect's train approached New York,
Governor Morgan sent a committee of state dignitaries 300 miles west to meet
Mr. Lincoln in Buffalo, to greet him at the first major city upon entering the
state. That committee had begun arriving in Buffalo February 14, two days
before Lincoln, to smooth the path for their distinguished guest's arrival in
Albany.[37]

In contrast, Maryland's Governor Hicks did nothing and would do nothing. He would send no committees ahead to welcome Lincoln at the Maryland
line. Hicks made no plans to meet the president-elect in Baltimore, or for that
matter, anywhere in Maryland. He never even tendered an invitation for
Lincoln to come see him privately at his farm, Appleby, near Annapolis, or to
visit him at the Executive Mansion. Even the investigatory congressional
Select Committee of Five had been accorded that honor.

And the contrast between the two cities could not be chalked up to
Lincoln's popularity in Albany versus Baltimore. Then, as now, Albany was a
heavily Democratic city. Lincoln was not their candidate. And yet Albany,

unlike Baltimore, had been able to suppress partisan animosity and welcome a Republican president-elect with open arms.

AT the President Street Station in Baltimore, a slim twenty-eight-year-old woman with chestnut-colored hair boarded the 5:16 p.m. train for New York. She carried vital intelligence in the form of letters addressed to Norman B. Judd and Edward S. Sanford, President of the American Telegraph Company.[38] In this era women were generally deemed fit for but a few professions, including secretary, teacher, and nurse, among other professions less noble. But this young woman was a detective.

Five years earlier, on an afternoon in 1856, Allan Pinkerton sat in his office, "pondering deeply over some matters," when his secretary informed him of a young woman visitor who wanted to see him about a job. Pinkerton likely assumed that the young woman he rose to greet was applying for a secretarial position. She was, as Pinkerton described her, "above the medium height, slender, graceful in her movements and perfectly self-possessed in her manner." She was "captivating"—the word Pinkerton used to describe the twenty-three-year-old.[39]

Pinkerton offered her a seat. He studied her face. "Her features, although not what would be called handsome, were of a decidedly intellectual cast. Her eyes were very attractive, being dark blue, filled with fire. She had a broad, honest face, which would cause one in distress instinctively to select her as a confidante, in whom to confide in time of sorrow, or from whom to seek consolation."[40]

The young woman introduced herself "in a very pleasant tone" to Pinkerton. She was Mrs. Kate Warne. No, she was not married. She was a widow. No, she did not seek a secretarial job. She wanted to be a detective.[41]

There were, however, no female detectives in 1856. The male-only private eye profession was itself relatively new, with Pinkerton having started his agency just a few years earlier.[42] Now seated, Pinkerton, who had never considered the possibility of a female detective before, leaned back in his chair and asked Mrs. Warne how a woman detective might help his agency.

Warne obviously had pluck, courage of conviction, and the power of persuasion. She assured Pinkerton that she could "go and worm out secrets in many places to which it was impossible for male detectives to gain access."[43] She impressed Pinkerton as having given the matter a great deal of thought and provided him with compelling reasons why she could be of great service. Pinkerton had to think it over. No one had ever heard of a female private detective before. He asked Mrs. Warne to call the next day.[44]

There may not have been female private detectives as of 1856, but women had, of course, been spies before. The role Pinkerton might assign to Warne

President Street Station, Baltimore. Passengers from Philadelphia and New York arrived at this station and would have to travel to Camden Station over a mile away to connect to trains heading to Washington and other points south. (*Library of Congress*)

could more closely assume that of female spy. Pinkerton believed he lived in a progressive era, in a progressive country. He decided to give the idea a try, "feeling that Mrs. Warne was a splendid subject with whom to begin." When she came to his office at the appointed time, he offered her a job and they entered into an agreement; shortly thereafter Warne was assigned her first case. Pinkerton would not be disappointed: "She succeeded far beyond my utmost expectations, and I soon found her an invaluable acquisition to my force."[45]

Two years later, in 1858, Pinkerton employed Warne during the Maroney case, which involved a $40,000 robbery of the Adams Express Company in Mobile, Alabama. In that case, Warne gathered intelligence by befriending the wife of the suspect, Nathan Maroney, using the assumed name of "Madam Imbert." In ways relevant to this story, she also learned the customs of Southern culture and became steeped in its dialect. From the very outset of the case, Warne impressed Pinkerton with her positive attitude. "Kate Warne felt sure she was going to win. She always felt so and I never knew her to be beaten."[46]

With Kate Warne's help, Pinkerton solved the Maroney case, recovering all of the money except $400. The case catapulted Pinkerton onto the national detective scene; he changed the name of his agency from Pinkerton's North-Western Police Agency to Pinkerton's National Detective Agency.[47] While Pinkerton certainly did not invent spying, he was perfecting the technique of the undercover agent, and Kate Warne was becoming a key operative in his clandestine operations. Two years later, in 1860, Warne moved into management at Pinkerton's agency, supervising a small group of women operatives, and acting as their dormitory keeper in Chicago.[48]

By now, Pinkerton and his operatives had obtained a great deal of valuable, even startling, information. He had independently confirmed William Stearns's intelligence—there was in fact a plot to assassinate Lincoln in or near Baltimore. Stearns, an employee of the Philadelphia, Wilmington, and Baltimore Railroad reported, "I felt very solicitous for the safety of Mr. Lincoln; but there was a delicacy with me in relation to the matter, in regard to the action to be taken, inasmuch as the programme of the route of Mr. Lincoln to Washington was published as via [the] Northern Central Railroad, from Harrisburg to Baltimore, and that road was considered, to some extent, as a competing road to our road from North to South."[49] In other words, Stearns could not communicate his intelligence directly to Lincoln because it might be viewed as a self-promoting attempt to divert the Lincoln Special from the Northern Central to the PW&B, a competing railroad of which Stearns was an employee. No such suspicion would attend the communication if it came from Pinkerton. Because Judd was "a personal friend" of Mr. Lincoln, Pinkerton had decided to communicate the particulars of the plot to him. The letters Kate Warne carried with her to New York contained that communication.

Hopefully, Lincoln and his suite would arrive safely in New York City tomorrow to receive them.[50]

CHAPTER TEN

THE VAST AND SILENT CROWD

Tuesday, February 19, 1861
Albany to New York City

A BRAHAM LINCOLN WAS OUT OF SORTS THIS MORNING. "Owing to the unusual fatigue sustained on Monday night, Mr. Lincoln felt far from well, when at 7 o'clock . . . he was called to rise."[1] His illness would not be attributed to poisoning, but to overexertion. The demands of the trip were clearly taking their toll. At 7:30 a.m. Mayor Thacher and other Albany dignitaries accompanied Lincoln in waiting carriages to the depot, and by 7:45 a.m., the train was on its way.

Lincoln's early departure from Albany likely had nothing at all to do with giving would-be assassins the slip. There were at least two other reasons for the suite to shake Albany's snow off their boots and make an early exit. For starters, their visit had been marred by the tug-of-war between Governor Edwin D. Morgan and members of his legislature for the honor of entertaining Lincoln during his stay. So divisive had been the squabbling that when Mr. and Mrs. Lincoln and their party left Albany, they reportedly resolved never to return.[2]

But there was another, more practical reason for leaving two hours ahead of schedule this morning. An early thaw had caused the frozen Hudson River to hurl massive blocks of ice downstream, destroying the State Street bridge and severely damaging the Hamilton and Columbia Street bridges. The planned route to New York for the Lincoln Special was no longer viable. As a result, Lincoln's train was forced to make a two-hour detour. It headed north, first on the Albany and Vermont Railroad, crossed the Mohawk River, and then at Waterford Junction, switched to the tracks of the Rensselaer and Saratoga line, where it turned south, recrossed the Mohawk River, and then crossed the Hudson over the only bridge spanning it, at Green Island. The party made its first stop in Troy, where a host of fifteen thousand Trojans greeted Lincoln with deafening cheers inside the brand new depot.[3] On a platform surrounded by the Troy City Guards, Lincoln spoke briefly, thanking the people for the reception and alluding to his weariness: "I have neither strength nor time to make any extended remarks."[4] The party entered the waiting cars of the Hudson River Railroad, which would carry them south to New York City.

This morning, the Lincoln Special was pulled by the locomotive *Union,* decorated with flags and "looking as gay as a bride."[5] The *Union* was brand new and one of the road's first coal-burning engines. The coach in which Lincoln rode was the most elegant of the day. Its exterior was deep orange, highlighted with dark brown and black ornamentation and highly varnished. The car's sides were draped with red, white, and blue silk, and national flags were suspended at each end. The interior featured plush crimson walls, decorated with blue silk panels studded with silver stars. The center of the coach featured a long ebony table, accompanied by numerous and varied chairs, including lounges, parlor chairs, armchairs, and reading chairs, all in black walnut and upholstered in blue mazarine cloth. The car also included patented heaters and ventilators and four wax-candle chandeliers with cut-glass globes. In effect, the coach was a luxury hotel parlor on wheels.[6]

The line to New York was a model of railroad security. Every employee of the road was used to station flagmen and track guards within signaling distance of each other. A wood-burning engine, *Young America*, ran ahead of the *Union* as its pilot. Ice-skaters plying the frozen Hudson with flags waved and cheered as the Special sped by.[7]

The train arrived at Poughkeepsie at 12:25 p.m., where the party was greeted by yet more throngs of adoring well-wishers. Mrs. Lincoln was presented in the car with a rare winter treat, a large basket of flowers. The crowd recognized her and begged her to come to the window. She complied and raised the window to greet them.

"Where are the children. Show us the children," a loud voice pleaded.

Mary Todd called Robert to the window, and the crowd cheered.

"Have you any more on board!" someone shouted.

"Yes," Mary replied, "here's another."

A reporter for the *New York Times* reported the scene: "She attempted to bring a tough, rugged little fellow, about eight years of age, into sight. But the young representative of the House of Lincoln proved refractory, and the more his mother endeavored to pull him up before the window the more stubbornly he persisted in throwing himself down on the floor of the car, laughing at the fun, but refusing to receive the proffered honor of a reception. So his mother at last was constrained to give up the attempt to exhibit 'the pet of the family.'"[8]

At this point, the engine was changed, the *Union* yielding the track to the *Constitution*. A platform had been erected for Lincoln, but the train had not pulled up far enough for the car to reach it. Because the engine had been uncoupled, "a crowd of men rushed to the cars and pushed them to the platform." When Lincoln came out to speak, he echoed a familiar theme: in the recent election, there had been winners and losers. Some were satisfied with the outcome, others were not. But whether Americans were happy or disaffected, Lincoln reasoned, they should not sink the ship merely because it was caught in a storm; rather, they should give the vessel of liberty a chance to run "through the tempest in safety."[9] The Union was the ship. Lincoln was her captain. He was appealing to her crew, Americans North and South, not to mutiny. Lincoln the captain would soon use the same analogy of a ship in peril when appealing to a larger crew of more uncertain loyalty—in New York City.

WHILE men in New York State were conspiring to help Lincoln by pushing his train to the platform in Poughkeepsie, men in Maryland and Baltimore were conspiring to halt it in its tracks. In the small town of Perrymansville, about 25 miles north of Baltimore on the Bush River,[10] Pinkerton's best agent, Timothy Webster, continued gathering information from suspected plotters and informants.

Timothy Webster had emigrated from Sussex County, England, to Princeton, New Jersey, with his parents as a boy of twelve. At thirty-two, he cast aside his machinist's trade to become a policeman. At the 1853 World's Crystal Palace Exposition in New York City, he would meet Allan Pinkerton. A man with a keen eye for talent, Pinkerton immediately saw in Webster the makings of a fine detective and hired him.[11]

The former New York City policeman was, by 1861, one of Pinkerton's most skilled operatives. The James Bond of his era, he had sparkling blue eyes, expressive and large,[12] wavy hair, and a handsome beard. The totality of his confident expression read: "Catch me if you can, but if you succeed, beware." Pinkerton described Webster as "a man of forty; good-looking, tall, broad-shouldered, of great physical strength and endurance, skilled in all athletic sports, a good shot, strong-willed, and absolutely fearless. His face indicated a character of firmness and amiability, of innate force and gentle feeling, of frankness and resolution; a thoughtful, self-contained man of an appearance at once to attract attention."[13]

After playing a game of "Ten-pins" with a "Captain Keen"[14] and four or five others at around 1:45 p.m. on the afternoon of February 19, Webster went to dinner with men he knew only as "Springer" and "Taylor."[15] Lincoln's arrival in Baltimore was but four days away. Webster reported that Springer and Taylor bickered over the route Lincoln's train would take. Springer believed that Lincoln would come over Felton's Philadelphia, Wilmington, and Baltimore road. Taylor disagreed, claiming that Lincoln's route would be over the Northern Central road. The disagreement was in some ways understandable—the more direct route would be for Lincoln to take the PW&B line from Philadelphia to Baltimore. But as of this date, Lincoln's published itinerary had him leaving Philadelphia on February 22, traveling to Harrisburg, and then to Baltimore at 12:30 p.m. the next day via the Northern Central's line.[16] It was vital for the plotters to know by which route Lincoln would approach Baltimore if they hoped to either halt the Lincoln Special, throw it from its tracks, or kill him at the depot—the two lines approached Baltimore from different directions and terminated in the city at different stations, over a mile apart. Whether by dumb luck or design, the uncertainty over Lincoln's route to Baltimore would have frustrated the plotters' planning. They could place assassins in two separate locations, but would thereby diminish their combined effectiveness and likelihood of success by half.

Taylor continued, telling Webster that Lincoln had better not attempt to take any military over "this Road [the PW&B]," because if he did "that Boat would never make another [trip][17] across the River."[18] Taylor was likely referring to sinking the *Maryland,* a steamer used to ferry trains across the wide Susquehanna River at Havre de Grace.

Later that afternoon, Webster and Springer left for Aberdeen, but had to turn back because of bad roads. On their way back to Perrymansville, Springer talked some more about Lincoln, saying that when Lincoln arrived in Baltimore, "they would try to get him out to speak, and if he did come out, he (Springer) would not be surprised if they killed him; that there was in Baltimore about One Thousand men well organized, and ready for anything."[19] Webster then asked Springer if the leaders were good men. Springer replied that they had the very best men in Baltimore and that nearly all of the Customs House officers were in the organization.

Springer's admission corroborates other evidence. First, it indicates either that the plotters were reading newspaper accounts of Lincoln's tendency to yield to repeated calls to leave the cars to speak, or they had been receiving telegraphed intelligence of this fact. Second, Springer's comment about Customs House officers supports other evidence of Baltimore government employees being involved in the plot. The night of February 15, when he met Captain Ferrandini, Pinkerton had also met conspirator Captain William H. H. Turner, clerk of the Baltimore Circuit Court.[20]

Webster pressed Springer for more information about the identity of the Customs House officers but was unsuccessful. "I could not learn from him any of their names."[21]

As Timothy Webster worked his informants in Maryland, Pinkerton operative Kate Warne, operating under the alias "Mrs. Barley," waited patiently, if exhausted, at the Astor House in New York City. On Pinkerton's orders, Warne had left Baltimore the previous evening, February 18, on the 5:16 train for New York by way of Philadelphia. She rode all night, arriving in New York at 4:00 a.m. on February 19. After haggling for a room at the Astor House, she went to bed but could not sleep.[22]

She had in her possession important letters, including one addressed to Norman B. Judd, given to her the previous afternoon in Baltimore by Pinkerton. These letters contained alarming news. They could not be trusted to the mails or the telegraph. Only personal delivery by a Pinkerton agent to a trusted Lincoln friend would do. But as she waited for Judd to arrive in New York so that she could hand-deliver the vital information to him, Kate Warne did not yet know what

One of Pinkerton's best agents, Timothy Webster would be given the most daring missions while investigating the Baltimore Plot, and later, spying for the Union. (*Harper's Weekly*)

those on board the Lincoln Special certainly did—that Norman B. Judd, master architect of the House of Abraham, was now not with them.

A man could set his watch by the comings and goings of the Lincoln Special. At 3:00 p.m., precisely on time, the train, pulled by the brand new coal-burning locomotive *Constitution,* rolled into New York City at the Hudson River Railroad's just completed Thirtieth Street Station.[23] Lincoln had been pensive while in the private car, not participating in the political conversations of those on board. Journalist Henry Villard, also on the train, along with Chicago delegate Martin J. Townsend and New York Republican political operative Thurlow Weed, attributed Lincoln's lack of interest to his being "unwell and fatigued." Villard described Lincoln this way: "Towering above all, with his face and forehead furrowed by a thousand wrinkles, his hair unkempt, his new whiskers looking as if not yet naturalized, his clothes illy arranged, Mr. Lincoln sat toward the rear of the saloon car."[24]

For a metropolis situated firmly in the North, New York, or at least some of its leaders, tilted decidedly toward the South. The merchants and money-men of New York feared that a civil war would bring them financial ruin. Ever since Lincoln's election, their businesses faltered and their stock market swooned. They desperately wanted compromise, and eyed an uncompromising Lincoln warily. But at least some of them also saw a good opportunity to make a quick, if treasonous, buck. Even now, New York's harbor brimmed with ships, some intent on smuggling guns and ammunition south.

As recently as January, Mayor Fernando Wood had advocated the secession of New York City, saying it would have the "united support of the Southern States."[25] Lincoln could blame the secession that had already occurred in the Deep South on precipitous, hot-headed action by slaveholding leaders in the cotton states. But if New York City, a vital Northern commercial city in a free state, abandoned the Union ship, then would any Northern city or any Northern state be safe?

But there were other, more personal reasons Lincoln might have been pensive before his arrival in New York City. Many of the masses that he saw gathered outside grimy hovels and clothesline-bedecked row houses were there not so much because they supported him, but rather because they simply had nothing better to do. Indeed, many watching him now were idle, unemployed, even starving workmen. Lincoln was a curiosity that could be seen free of charge. He might have been seen as the reason for their suffering.

All winter, as Southern presses fired Southern hearts, a faction in the New York City press had been feeding empty Northern heads and stomachs with bitter notions that all of their troubles were Lincoln's fault. By remaining mum on his intended policies, the argument went, Lincoln had permitted doubts to fester, infecting businesses with uncertainty and workers with unemployment. Noted the *New York Times* in an editorial critical of such Lincoln bashing:

> Mischief-makers have been feverishly busy all Winter in exaggerating the popular suffering, in aggravating the popular temper, and in impressing upon the masses a conviction that the responsibility for their woes rests mediately upon the triumph of the Republican Party, but directly upon Mr. Lincoln, for not announcing the programme of his Administration, and so giving peace to the country. Acts of outrage and violence have been counseled and justified. Mob-law has had its advocates, and the South has been taught to expect, that the Winter could not pass without an uprising of the many-headed, and the plunder and destruction of the opulent classes.[26]

Perhaps, thanks to a hostile media, at least one outlet of which, the *New York Daily News,* was owned by the notoriously corrupt Mayor Wood,[27] New York had a mob of its own intent on venting its frustrations on Lincoln.

Lincoln's train squealed to a halt. Sensing her husband's inner turmoil as much as his external disarray, Mrs. Lincoln smoothed his coarse, unkempt chestnut-colored hair and planted a warm, tender kiss on his wrinkled cheek before he left the car. Supported by Judge Davis and Colonel Sumner, a weary Lincoln passed through the gleaming new Thirtieth Street Station, festooned with patriotic flags, and emerged from the building. Lincoln was met not by

New York's Mayor Fernando Wood, but by New York Police Superintendent John Kennedy. Mayor Wood's absence was telling. At most of the other overnight stops Lincoln had visited thus far, the city's mayor or the state's governor had greeted him, either at the depot or at the hotel. In New York, Lincoln was being welcomed by the superintendent of police.

Kennedy escorted Lincoln "amid cheers and waving handkerchiefs," to an open barouche, the same one in which the Prince of Wales had ridden several weeks before, drawn by a team of six stately black horses.[28] Kennedy had done everything in his power to instill order in New York, both at the depot and along the procession route: "None were admitted [to the depot] but those who had tickets. The police were stationed in force within and without, and in Thirtieth-street confined a swaying, compact crowd of men, women, and children within the limits of the sidewalks. The carriage-way was kept clear."[29]

Lincoln's cortege, comprising a train of thirty-five carriages, was headed by a mounted squad of New York's finest, who led a platoon on foot that extended across the street. Another platoon of police on foot and a second squad of mounted New York police bracketed the procession at the rear. Perhaps the heavy police presence tamped down the crowd's enthusiasm. Ominously, the *Herald* would report only a "faint cheer" for Lincoln as he entered the carriage.[30]

The caravan rolled east on Thirtieth Street to Ninth Avenue, then south to Twenty-third, turning left and heading east again. Despite Lincoln's uncertain place in New York, and the city's uncertain place in the Union, the Great Metropolis displayed smatterings of patriotism. "The ships in the harbor, particularly those of the London, Liverpool, and Havre lines, were handsomely decorated with bunting, and the Stars and Stripes waved from many flag poles on the New York, Brooklyn, and New Jersey sides of the river."[31] Between Seventh and Eighth Avenues a banner spanned Twenty-third Street and read: "Fear not, Abraham, I am thy shield, and thy exceeding great reward."[32] Other banners, however, were less sanguine. One hung by a merchant at the store of Isador Bernhard and Son pleaded with Lincoln: "Welcome, Abraham Lincoln, we beg for compromise."[33]

The slow moving cavalcade continued east to Fifth Avenue, where it turned right and headed south until it finally arrived at the Astor House at Broadway and Vesey Street around 4:00 p.m.[34]

The route from the station to the Astor House was three and a half miles long. Thirteen hundred metropolitan police, on average fifteen feet apart, lined the route. Nearly fifty police officers guarded the Astor House itself, and two hundred men from the Sixteenth Precinct kept the street in front of the hotel clear—spectators were forced to stand on the opposite side of the street facing the hotel. Compared with every other city Lincoln had visited thus far, New York had proven itself a model of security.

Walt Whitman, watching the procession from his perch atop the roof of an omnibus parked nearby, wrote of Lincoln's arrival at the Astor House:

> I shall not easily forget the first time I ever saw Abraham Lincoln. . . . It was rather a pleasant afternoon in New York city. . . . I saw him on Broadway. . . . The broad spaces, sidewalks, and streets in the neighborhood, and for some distance, were crowded with solid masses of people, many thousands. The omnibuses and other vehicles had all been turn'd off, leaving an unusual hush in that busy part of the city. . . . A tall figure stepp'd out of the center of these barouches, paus'd leisurely on the sidewalk, look'd up at the granite walls and looming architecture of the grand old hotel—then, after a relieving stretch of arms and legs, turn'd round for over a minute to slowly and good-humoredly scan the appearance of the vast and silent crowds. . . . He look'd with curiosity upon that immense sea of faces, and the sea of faces return'd the look with similar curiosity. In both there was a dash of comedy, almost farce, such as Shakspere puts in his blackest tragedies.[35]

"Vast and silent crowds" likened to Shakespeare's blackest tragedies. One of the largest masses of humanity ever gathered in New York City, by some estimates a quarter of a million people, apparently stood in an eerie hush. No less a Lincoln chronicler than Carl Sandburg interpreted the silence as "having a touch of the sinister."[36] Where were the rousing cheers of towns previously visited? Where were the brass bands? Where were the brightly uniformed military escorts and booming salutes?

Perhaps many in the crowd really did blame Lincoln for their economic woes, or at least worried that he would in the future drive them to financial ruin; they wanted to see what the ogre looked like. Or perhaps the crowd's stillness was reflective of the fact Lincoln's arrival on Broadway was but the opening act on opening night. The audience had turned out in huge numbers to witness the spectacle, but the drama had yet to unfold, the players had yet to earn their acclaim. Indeed, some in the crowd were already disappointed by the performance they saw unfolding. Observing Lincoln, preacher and writer Dr. S. Irenæus Prime witnessed: "As the carriage in which he sat passed slowly by me on the Fifth avenue, he was looking weary, sad, feeble, and faint. My disappointment was excessive; so great, indeed as to be almost overwhelming. He did not look to me to be the man for the hour."[37]

But for better or worse, Lincoln was the man of the hour. The stage was set. The performance was in motion. Pinkerton operative Kate Warne, who had waited all day at the Astor House, was also there to witness it. According to

Warne, "At 4:00 p.m. the President and Suite arrived at the Astor House. Lincoln looked very pale, and fatigued. He was standing in his carriage bowing when I first saw him. From the carriage he went direct into the House, and soon after appeared on the Balcony, from where he made a short speech, but there was such a noise, it was impossible to hear what he said."[38] Even if they were not cheering wildly, a quarter of a million curiosity-seeking people could still drown out a single voice.

Almost exactly one year earlier, on February 27, 1860, Lincoln had spoken in New York to a much smaller, much more receptive audience. On that date, he addressed the Young Men's Republican Union, a group committed to preventing New York's own William Seward from winning the nomination. Their rationale: as an antislavery Easterner, Seward could not carry the political water for the whole country. An antislavery Westerner like Lincoln, it was argued, could win in both the West and the East. History had proven them right. The speech Lincoln gave that evening was his famed Cooper Union address. So inspiring was the speech that *New York Tribune* editor Horace Greeley wrote: "The tones, the gestures, the kindling eye, and mirth-provoking look defy the reporter's skill. . . . No man ever before made such an impression on his first appeal to a New York audience."[39]

Perhaps as he scrambled through a second-story window and perched atop the Romanesque coping above the doorway to the Astor House, Lincoln recalled that day in New York a year before. He had walked down this same Broadway, and stepped into famed photographer Mathew Brady's temporary studio to pose for what would become his most celebrated campaign image, before giving what would become his most lauded campaign speech.[40] Then, as now, New York wanted to hear him speak. But as he stood before this New York audience a year later, Lincoln would make not nearly the same impression, in part because he no longer looked the same man, in part because he could not be heard, and in part because he had much less to say. A year before, he appeared clean-shaven, as stout and determined as he would ever look, and spoke with vitality. Now, he appeared bearded and bony, pale and fatigued, and spoke in a hoarse whisper. Then, he had given a rousing address some 7,000 words in length. Now, his words were inaudible and few, and they fell from the ledge on which he balanced precariously—both literally and figuratively—with no more power than a fistful of tiny pebbles dropped to the street:

> Fellow Citizens—I have stepped before you merely in compliance with what appeared to be your wish, and with no purpose of making a speech. In fact, I do not propose making a speech this afternoon. I could not be heard by any but a very small fraction of you at best; but what is still worse than that is, that I have

nothing just now to say worth your hearing. (Loud applause) I beg you to believe that I do not now refuse to address you through any disposition to disoblige you, but the contrary. But at the same time I beg of you to excuse me for the present.[41]

During the flutter of applause that followed, the president-elect retreated to his suite at the Astor House. Lincoln's decision to stay there had been made more or less by default—none of the other hotelkeepers in New York supported him. Accordingly, the previous December, Vice President-elect Hamlin had urged Lincoln to stay at the Astor House if his journey to Washington should take him through New York City. Lincoln complied with Hamlin's request.

Security inside the hotel was tight. Only those visitors with sufficient rank of privilege—aldermen, councilmen, and the like, were admitted. While the press derided the overwhelming police presence, Lincoln praised it. "Mr. Lincoln frequently expressed his admiration of the excellent police arrangements of the day, and desired that Mr. Kennedy, the Superintendent of Police, should be brought in person, that he might be complimented as he deserved."[42]

Per his wishes, Alderman Charles G. Cornell brought Superintendent Kennedy before the president-elect. Lincoln complimented Kennedy on the superb police protection. Kennedy replied modestly that he was merely doing his duty. "Well," said Lincoln, "a man ought to be thanked when he does his duty right well."[43]

Lincoln may, however, have been thanking Kennedy for more than doing his duty "right well" in New York. It is not clear if Lincoln then knew that Kennedy had, during the previous month, been sending his best New York City detectives to Baltimore to investigate conspiracies there. Earlier letters, however, suggest that Lincoln likely did know of Kennedy's Baltimore operation.[44] If so, Lincoln might have been excused for pulling Kennedy aside for a confidential update on the reports from Baltimore.

Standing with his back to a crackling fire, Lincoln continued to shake hands with members of the city council and others who had ridden in the procession. One of those who had gained admission drew an interesting response from Mr. Lincoln:

> To one of those introduced, Mr. Lincoln said: "Haven't I seen you somewhere with a set of Shakespearian pictures?"
>
> "No Sir," was the reply.
>
> "Then," said Mr. Lincoln good-naturedly, "I must give it up."[45]

History is left to wonder at the identity of the individual whom Lincoln apparently mistook for a Shakespearean actor that afternoon in New York—

and where he might have seen him before.

IT had not been a good day for Norman B. Judd. When the Lincoln Special left Albany at 7:45 on the morning of Tuesday February 19, Judd was not on board. Perhaps he had overslept. Perhaps he had been confused about the earlier departure time, the itinerary previously having scheduled the train to leave Albany at 10:00 a.m. For whatever reason, Judd had missed the Special and had to take a regularly scheduled train to New York, arriving three or four hours after the rest of his party.

Abraham Lincoln addresses the New York crowd from above the doorway to the Astor House hotel. It would later be reported that two or three of the Baltimore plotters were shadowing Lincoln in New York City. (*Library of Congress*)

As soon as Judd arrived at the Astor House, a servant came to his room. A lady in another room in the hotel wished to see him. Judd was obviously intrigued. Captain John Pope, a fellow Illinoisan, was in Judd's room at the time. Excusing himself and taking one of his trademark cigars with him, Judd followed the servant to one of the upper rooms of the hotel, sometime after 6:30 p.m. "Upon entering," Judd recalled, "I found a lady seated at a table with some papers before her." The woman rose as Judd entered, and said, "Mr. Judd, I presume."

"Yes, madam," Judd replied. The woman handed him a letter. It was from Allan Pinkerton. She said Pinkerton did not trust the mail with a letter of such importance.[46]

Norman Judd habitually strode about with an unlit cigar protruding from his lips. He may have been trying to cut back or quit. In any event, now that he had another letter from Allan Pinkerton in his hands, he felt the need to light up. He had received his first dispatch from Pinkerton in Cincinnati, the letter indicating vaguely, and perhaps in Judd's mind improbably, that a plot to assassinate Lincoln in Baltimore had been uncovered. Pinkerton had indicated that further communications would come as the party headed east. Judd kept this intelligence to himself. Then, in Buffalo, Judd had received a second brief and vague Pinkerton note, saying that "the evidence was accumulating." Judd kept that intelligence to himself as well.[47] Now, Judd knew without being told that this third communication from Pinkerton would be the most revealing of all. After asking the young woman if he could light his cigar, Judd sat down to read Pinkerton's latest dispatch. The letter introduced the woman as Kate Warne, chief of Pinkerton's female detective corps. She had been sent to arrange for a personal interview between Judd and Pinkerton.[48]

Whatever additional specific information the letter contained, history fails to tell us. Its contents, however, staggered Judd. Warne reported that after reading the letter, Judd asked a "great many questions, which I did not answer."[49] Rather, Warne told him that she could not talk to him about the business at hand but would take any message he might have for Pinkerton. Judd, who thus far had held his tongue about the Baltimore Plot, ostensibly "to avoid causing any anxiety on the part of Mr. Lincoln, or any of the party,"[50] now wanted to sing. "He said he was much alarmed and would like to show the letter I had given him to some of the party, and also consult the New York Police about it." Warne told Judd that would never do. "I advised him to do no such thing, but keep cool, and see Mr. P———."[51]

Clearly flustered, Judd asked Warne what he should do. She advised that she would be leaving in the morning for Baltimore and would have Pinkerton advise him by letter and telegraph. But that option would cost precious time and was unacceptable to Judd. He asked if Pinkerton might come to New York instead. Warne said it would be impossible for Pinkerton to arrive in New York in time to see Judd there.[52]

At just that moment, Edward S. Sanford, President of the American Telegraph Company, came into the room, and Warne introduced him to Judd. Sanford handed Judd another note, this one also from Pinkerton, relating to the same matter. Pinkerton had anticipated how difficult it might be for Mrs. Warne to obtain an interview with Judd, and so had given her a note to hand to Sanford, also asking him to arrange for a meeting with Warne and Judd.[53] After reading Sanford's note, Judd said it was "all right." Sanford offered Judd any assistance he might require, including the use of his telegraph lines for any message he might need to send. But the only people Judd was interested in conveying messages to were right here in this hotel. He had vital information and wanted desperately to tell someone right away, Kate Warne's admonitions notwithstanding. Judd left, promising Warne he would see her again later that night.[54]

"Now," Sanford asked once Judd had gone, "what is the trouble?"

Warne replied that she had come to deliver letters to him and Judd from Pinkerton and would take any message he might have for Pinkerton back to him. In other words, her role was merely that of a courier of confidential messages. But Sanford suspected Warne knew more than she let on. He wanted to know what it was. "I replied that [there] was no reason why I should tell him all I knew, and that I had no more to say."

Unmoved, Sanford persisted. "Barley," he said, using one of Warne's several aliases, "there is something more, and if you will only tell me how you are situated, and what you are doing at Baltimore I can better judge how to act."

The stalwart Kate Warne repeated, "Mr. Sanford, I have nothing more to say." Sanford grew irritated.

"He appeared quite dissatisfied, and said he supposed I had 'roped' so many, [that] I thought I could not be 'roped' myself. I replied that it was as easy to 'rope' me as any one else, but that just now I really had nothing to say. Mr. Sanford laughed at this, and said that I was a strange woman. He seemed good natured again, and asked my advice about writing a Dispatch to A. P——, and sending Burns to Baltimore."[57]

Edward S. Sanford, President of the American Telegraph Company.

Sanford wanted to send his agent George H. Burns to Baltimore as an assistant to Pinkerton. Sanford intended for Burns to take full control of the telegraph wires from Baltimore. Burns could, in effect, black out all of Baltimore by jamming communications to or from anywhere or, more importantly, intercept telegraphic communications to or from anywhere, creating the functional equivalent of a citywide wiretap. If anyone had the unquestioned authority to implement such a plan, it was the president of the American Telegraph Company.

Before leaving her room, in an apparent effort to satisfy his curiosity, Sanford again goaded Warne, telling her he suspected that she and Pinkerton were frightened. Reported Warne, "I suppose he thought now that I would tell him all I knew, but I said nothing, only that we were not frightened and what was more I had never known A. P—— to be frightened."[55]

After some idle banter, Sanford finally left Warne's room. "He was very friendly and staid until after 10 o'clock, when he bade me good night and left."[56]

Shortly after Sanford left, Warne received a telegram from Pinkerton. Although the hour was late, Pinkerton's latest dispatch, though vague, contained new intelligence so startling it caused Kate Warne to urgently send once more for Norman Judd.

After receiving her message, Judd immediately came to Warne's room. She showed him Pinkerton's most recent telegram: "Tell Judd I meant all I said, and that to-day they offer Ten for one, and Twenty for two."[57]

Pinkerton, then posing as a stockbroker in Baltimore, was not referring to stock swaps or harmless betting odds at the horse track. Pinkerton's oblique reference was to the odds being offered by bookmakers in Baltimore that Lincoln would not pass through that city alive.[58] If Judd was troubled before, he was sick with worry now. He wanted desperately to sound the alarm. Clearly panicked by Pinkerton's latest dispatch, Judd said he wanted to show it to Vice President-elect Hamlin and implored Warne to meet with Hamlin. Warne refused. The hour was late. She could tell Hamlin no more than she had told Judd. In any event, Hamlin would not arrive in New York until tomorrow afternoon; she was returning in the morning to Baltimore.[59]

Although Judd was the man deemed to have more influence over Lincoln than anyone else in the suite, he concluded not to immediately warn Lincoln directly of what he had learned from Pinkerton's letters and telegrams. Rather, Judd preferred to wait another day to tell Hamlin. Possibly Judd feared that without Pinkerton's or Hamlin's support, he would be unable to convince Lincoln that the danger was real and his route needed to be altered.[60]

Judd urged Warne to have Pinkerton come to Philadelphia for a meeting there when the Lincoln party arrived on Thursday, February 21, and to advise what course should be taken. Warne promised to do what she could.[61] In devising this plan, which now included withholding vital intelligence from Lincoln for two more days, Judd was taking a few dangerous gambles. First, that he would actually be able to connect with Pinkerton in Philadelphia. Second, that the Baltimore plotters intended to strike in Baltimore rather than any other place. And third, that Lincoln would prefer not to be informed at this time about intelligence pertaining to threats on his life.

In Baltimore that same evening, while Timothy Webster gathered intelligence and braved the rutted roads in Perrymansville, while Kate Warne conferred with Norman Judd and Edward Sanford at the Astor House, and while Lincoln dined in ignorant bliss before retiring, Pinkerton agent Harry W. Davies continued to befriend and beguile suspected conspirator Otis K. Hillard. Hillard had come to Davies' room, bringing him a pair of "worked slippers" as a gift. After presenting Davies with the slippers, Hillard inquired, "You look sober—what is the matter with you?"

"I am thinking," Davies answered, "about what a d—d pretty tumult this country is in—I have had all kinds of bad thoughts shoot through my mind—you know you cannot prevent a man from thinking."

"Of course not," Hillard agreed, "what have you been thinking about?"

Davies told Hillard that he was thinking that a man could immortalize himself by taking a knife and plunging it into Lincoln's heart, but that it would be impossible to find a man with the pluck to do it. "It is not," Davies lamented to Hillard, "as it was in the time of Brutus and Caesar—there is not the courage now that was then."

Hillard disagreed. "There are men who would do it!"

"I will give Five Hundred Dollars to see the man who will do it," Davies offered.

"Give me an article of agreement that you will give my Mother Five Hundred Dollars, and I will kill Lincoln between here and Havre-de-Grace," Hillard said.[62] Then, paraphrasing Brutus's justification to the citizens of Rome for his murder of Caesar, Hillard exclaimed, "Not that I love Lincoln less, but my Country more!"[63]

Hillard then added, "Five Hundred dollars would help my Mother, but it would do me no good, because I would expect to die—and I would say so soon as it was done—Here gentlemen take me—I am the man who done the deed." Then, Hillard boasted, "If our Company[64] would draw lots to see who would kill Lincoln, and the lot should fall on me, I would do it willingly."

Having left Davies' room while conversing, the two men went to a private upstairs dining room at Mann's Restaurant.[65] There, they resumed their conversation. Hillard had been spooked ever since being called to testify before the Select Committee of Five, and he was growing suspicious, even paranoid of people around him.

"Ever since I went to Washington," Hillard said, in reference to his testimony, "I am very careful in what I say—there are Government spies here all the time, even now, do you see that old man at the other end of the Room? This is the first time I have noticed him—just as likely as not he is a government spy—there is no telling—and may be before this he has my name down and what I have said."[66]

Hillard went on to explain that he and the other members of the National Volunteers were now forced to be much more cautious than they had been previously. They knew not whom they could trust. It wasn't that Hillard didn't trust Davies, it was that he had taken an oath not to reveal any details of his organization's plans to anyone.

> Do not think my friend that it is a want of confidence in you that makes me so cautious, it is because I have to be. I do not remember to have spoken to a person out of our Company, and the first thing I knew I was at Washington before that Committee—*We have taken a solemn oath, which is to obey the orders of our Captain, without asking any questions, and in no case, or under any circumstances reveal any orders received by us, or entrusted to us, or anything that is confidential*, for instance I was called to Washington City before the Committee—I must not divulge *the object nor the nature of our organization, but evade and if necessary decline to answer their questions*.[67]

Indeed, Hillard had been evasive when he testified before the Select Committee of Five two weeks earlier, on February 6, 1861. Even under threat of being recalled to testify, he declined to answer questions seeking the names of persons belonging to the National Volunteers in Baltimore.[68]

By the Chairman:

QUESTION. Are you connected with any military organization?

ANSWER. I am not. [Clearly, based on his admissions to Davies, Hillard was connected with the National Volunteers.]

QUESTION. Do you know of the existence anywhere of any organization, secret or open, that has for its object . . . or that contemplates any interruption of the operations of the government in any respect, as, for instance, the inauguration?

ANSWER. There is an organization in Baltimore city now, having no such purpose as that that I know of; but it is to prevent what is termed Wide-awakes, or any armed body of men, from coming on to Baltimore with Mr. Lincoln. Mr. Lincoln will not be interrupted as a citizen alone, but with an armed body of men would be. . . .

QUESTION. You stated that their main purpose was to prevent armed bodies of men coming here with Mr. Lincoln?

ANSWER. To the best of my knowledge and belief, that is it.

QUESTION. Who is at the head of that organization?

ANSWER. I do not know who is at the head of it. I expect there are fifty heads of it.

Question. That is, the heads of the different companies who compose it?

ANSWER. I suppose so; I presume every captain of every company has something to say in the matter. I do not know that they have elected a general-in-chief yet.

QUESTION. Can you mention any of these heads of companies?

ANSWER. I had rather not answer that question. I will answer any question concerning myself, but I should dislike to answer the other.

QUESTION. Have they adopted any name?

ANSWER. I think it is the National Volunteers.

QUESTION. Do you know any of the men that are connected with it?

ANSWER. I think I do.

QUESTION. Are there any men in Baltimore that you ever heard say that they were connected with it?

ANSWER. Yes sir.

QUESTION. What are their names?

ANSWER. I would rather not answer that question.

QUESTION. I suspect that is the very question we want answered.

ANSWER. I do not think I ought to compromise my friends. I will answer anything in connexion with myself individually; and if you will mention some name, and ask me if I know it to be one connected with the organization, I will tell you; but I do not think I should tell you the names I know. It is a very delicate matter, and I do not know what the consequences would be to myself.

At this point in the testimony, a debate ensued among the members of the Select Committee on matters of procedure and the extent to which Hillard might be compelled to testify. Hillard repeated his earlier answer; that he owed it to his friends not to reveal their names. In reality, he feared for his personal safety if he revealed them. In the ensuing questioning Hillard, perhaps without realizing it, implicated Cypriano Ferrandini as one of the members of the National Volunteers when he offered that, "I think you had one of that organization before you yesterday. . . Mr. Ferrandini."[69] The day before Hillard's testimony, Ferrandini had testified knowingly about the National Volunteers without clearly admitting that he was a member.[70]

Pinkerton operative Davies, like the Select Committee of Five, wanted to know what the primary object of the National Volunteers was now. As he had done before the Select Committee, Hillard replied evasively: "It was first organized to prevent the passage of Lincoln with the troops through Baltimore, but our plans are changed every day, as matters change, and what its object will be from day to day, I do not know, nor can I tell. All we have to do is to obey the orders of our Captain, and whatever he commands we are required to do. Rest assured I have all confidence in you, and what I can and dare tell you I am willing to do it—I cannot come out and tell you all—I cannot compromise my honor."[71]

CHAPTER ELEVEN

FACTS AND PHANTOMS

Wednesday, Thursday, February 20–21, 1861
New York City–Philadelphia

NEW YORK METROPOLITAN POLICE Superintendent John A. Kennedy was already mindful of the threats awaiting Lincoln in Baltimore. Several of his detectives were there, on the ground, investigating assassination rumors. But Baltimore was three days away. New York was here and now. And although Kennedy did not know it, Allan Pinkerton would soon come to possess evidence suggesting that some of the plotters were operating here, out of New York City.

On this date, the following cryptic dispatch was sent from New York to Baltimore. Somehow, possibly through the efforts of "C.D.C.W.,"[1] or Charles D. C. Williams, a Pinkerton operative who was shadowing suspected conspirators at Sherwood's Hotel, the message would fall into Pinkerton's hands:

> St Nicholas Hotel N.Y. Feby 20th
>
> Saul Thompson
> Sherwoods Hotel
> Baltimore
>
> One of you will go to Cockeysville on North Central Road and advise by telegraph how things are thereabouts.
>
> Wm Alexander[2]

What could this vague message mean? For one thing, that the message was vague suggested that the sender and recipient were attempting, without the use of codes, to be discreet. Furthermore, the dispatch suggested that the plotters were eyeing Cockeysville, Maryland. Lincoln's train was scheduled to leave Harrisburg on the Northern Central Railroad in just three days. Cockeysville was a small town located along that line about 14 miles north of Baltimore and about 20 miles west of Bel Air, where Pinkerton knew infantry to be drilling.[3] Bel Air, Maryland, was about midway between Cockeysville and Havre de Grace, a town on the Philadelphia, Wilmington, and Baltimore road. Local militia might be quickly dispatched, at a moment's notice, from Bel Air to either place, once the plotters had confirmed which road Lincoln was taking to Baltimore. Bel Air is also interesting for another reason—it is the location of Tudor Hall, the boyhood farm of John Wilkes Booth.

The telegram could also be interpreted to mean that one of the Baltimore plotters was a man named Saul Thompson and that he was staying at Sherwood's Hotel in Baltimore with at least one other plotter. Perhaps the plotters were to go to Cockeysville to make ready, to rendezvous with the military companies from Bel Air, and to plan an attack on Lincoln's train in the event he came by that route. Finally, the cryptic message suggested that the plotter's operations were being directed from New York.

Indeed, there had been previous rumors of a New York connection to the National Volunteers in Baltimore.[4] One of the suspected plotters, Otis K. Hillard, had lived in New York for several years, where he had been a member of the Seventh Regiment of the New York National Guards.[5] Perhaps Hillard was now in communication with his old chums in New York; he had previously told Pinkerton operative Harry Davies he wanted to make arrangements for telegraphing ciphered messages regarding Lincoln's movements in Philadelphia and New York.[6] And in the coming days it would be reported that "two or three of the conspirators were in New York . . . watching the course of events while the President-elect was there."[7]

That night, in Baltimore, Charles D. C. Williams, wrote his report for the day. Williams's report was brief, but interesting. By now, Williams had penetrated the inner circle of the National Volunteers, having become a member of "Company A," complete with a certificate of membership. Upon returning to Sherwood's Hotel from Gerry's Saloon earlier that evening, Williams wrote that he and a fellow National Volunteer, a Baltimore man known only by the name Sherrington, had made conversation with two gentlemen, one claiming to be an Englishman recently from Alabama, calling himself "Thompson," and his friend, a businessman calling himself "Davis." That night, Williams and Sherrington went to the Melodion Concert Hall with Thompson and Davis. Thompson spent much time talking about a nice little farm he owned in Iowa. Williams, trying to draw Thompson out, stated that he also owned land in Iowa, but that he would never live in a Northern state. Echoing the popular sentiments of many in Baltimore, Thompson claimed that he was for the South but hoped that the Union would be preserved. Something about Thompson and Davis did not ring true to Sherrington. "[T]here was something peculiar about their movements that Sherrington did not like,"

Williams recalled.[8] Sherrington warned Williams to be careful of the two men, "for he . . . suspected that they were not 'all right.'"[9]

In all likelihood, "Thompson" was the same man identified as "Saul Thompson" in the dispatch written this day from New York for delivery to Sherwood's Hotel in Baltimore. But who on earth was William Alexander, the man who had written the dispatch from New York's St. Nicholas Hotel? And who was the other man with Thompson, the man calling himself "Davis?"

If any of the plotters were in New York watching Lincoln, they were presumably reading the newspapers that reported his schedule for the day. He would be at a reception in City Hall at 11:00 a.m. Later, he would visit Barnum's Museum. And this evening, the *Times* reported, "Mrs. Abraham Lincoln, accompanied by the President elect and *suite,* will attend the opera."[10]

Whether he was merely being overly prudent or he also had intelligence of suspected trouble in New York, Superintendent Kennedy was clearly doing all he could to keep his city—and Lincoln—as secure as possible. This morning, as Lincoln prepared to meet with New York's pro-secession mayor, Fernando Wood, "two carriages were provided for the Presidential party, who were forthwith hurried through the gaping crowd, amid the most enthusiastic cheering, to the entrance to City Hall, whence through the excellence of the Police arrangements of Mr. Kennedy, an unobstructed passage was afforded to the Governor's Room."[11]

As Lincoln made his way inside City Hall, the crowd waiting on the stairs erupted in shouts that "reverberat[ed] through the building like a miniature thunder storm."[12] Holding his hat in his hands, Lincoln advanced to where Mayor Wood stood waiting, behind George Washington's writing desk, near a statue of the great general, and in front of a portrait of Governor Seward.[13] It was as if Mayor Wood, a man long suspected of duplicity and corruption, needed the support and protection of bigger men not present in order to confront the bigger man who was.

Standing erect and emotionless, the sartorial mayor, wearing a tightly buttoned black coat and a bushy white mustache, addressed the president-elect as "Mr. Lincoln."[14] Nearly a full day after Lincoln's arrival, in a voice described for a moment as "slightly tremulous," Wood welcomed Lincoln to New York on "behalf of the Corporation." He dove right in, reminding Lincoln of what he already knew: that a grave responsibility rested on his shoulders. That the country had shattered into brittle pieces, and that it would take an "elevated comprehension" of the whole to put those pieces back together. And then Wood told Lincoln why the nation's troubles really mattered to New York: the city's—and therefore Mayor Wood's—pecuniary interests were at stake. "If I refer to this topic, Sir, it is because New-York is deeply interested. . . . All her material interests are paralyzed. Her commercial greatness is endangered. . . . [W]e fear that if the Union dies, the present supremacy of New-York may perish with it."[15]

To Wood's veiled stab at Lincoln's ability to comprehend the magnitude of the problems he faced, Lincoln, speaking in a voice still not recovered from a severe cold,[16] responded with a characteristically self-deprecating retort: "As to my wisdom in conducting affairs so as to tend to the preservation of the Union, I fear too great confidence may have been placed in me. I am sure I bring a heart devoted to the work." Lincoln assured everyone that saving the foundering Union from sinking, if possible, was of paramount importance to him:

> There is nothing that could ever bring me to consent—willingly consent—to the destruction of this Union, (in which not only the great city of New-York, but the whole country has acquired its greatness,) unless it would be that thing for which the Union itself was made. I understand the ship is made for the carrying and preservation of the cargo, and so long as the ship is safe with the cargo it shall not be abandoned. This Union shall never be abandoned unless the possibility of its existence shall cease to exist, without the necessity of throwing passengers and cargo overboard. So long, then, as it is possible that that the prosperity and liberties of this people can be preserved within this Union, it shall be my purpose at all times to preserve it.[17]

Lincoln saw something even more important than the all-important objective of saving the Union: saving her passengers—American citizens—and saving their precious cargo—their liberty, freedom, and prosperity—and thereby saving America and American ideals. These would not be jettisoned merely to save an empty craft. The people of New York, of Tri-Insula, of all the states that had seceded, could jump ship if they chose in an effort to save themselves, but Lincoln appeared to be saying he would not permit them to disperse, to swim away or tread water separate and apart from the crew that remained. The Union was one ship populated by one crew. Either the Union would be saved with all its passengers and cargo intact, or the passengers and cargo—all of them—would need to find a new ship. Lincoln would neither see the cargo and crew jettisoned and broken up, nor would he see the Union's crew go down with the ship.

Irenæus Prime, who had been overwhelmingly disappointed by Lincoln's "weary, sad, feeble, and faint" appearance upon arriving in New York the previous day, was converted upon hearing Lincoln's reply. "I was with him and others in the Governor's Room in the City Hall, when the Mayor of the city made an official address. Mr. Lincoln's reply was so modest, firm, patriotic, and pertinent, that my fears of the day before began to subside, and I saw in this new man a promise of great things to come."[18]

After the brief meeting with Mayor Wood, Lincoln stood in the Governor's Room preparing to shake hands with thousands of New Yorkers who had lined up outside. Kennedy's police formed to receive the anticipated onrush.

As the doors opened, an "avalanche" of people thundered into the room, funneling between lines of police, at a rate of three thousand per hour, or about one per second. With Norman Judd and Ward Hill Lamon standing to his right, and Mayor Wood to his left, Lincoln greeted all manner of humanity. One exchange typified Lincoln's good humor:

"I have been told I look like you," remarked a tall, weason-faced individual, the color of mud on his boots, indicating New Jersey as his residence.

"You do look like me, that's certain," responded Mr. Lincoln, "the fact is settled that you are a handsome man."[19]

Lincoln continued to shake hands until about 1:00 p.m., when the doors were closed. He then appeared on the balcony at City Hall and made a very brief farewell.

The beauty of speaking in parables, whether one is a president-elect or a prophet, is that they can be interpreted in a variety of ways. Fortunately for Lincoln, his parable about preserving the Union ship, its passengers, and cargo had apparently been interpreted, as reported in the *Times* the next day, as meaning he would not coerce the seceded states back into the fold, but rather would attempt to restore the Union by peaceful means. Perhaps Wood interpreted Lincoln's remarks the same way; in any event, "the parting of the Mayor with Mr. Lincoln was most friendly and cordial."[20]

Later that afternoon, Lincoln was waited on by Mr. Knox, a New York hatter, and presented with one of his hats, in which was inscribed "Abraham Lincoln." Within the hour, news of the gift had spread to Mr. Leary, another hatter whose shop was in the basement of the Astor House. Leary requested Lincoln's hat size so that he too might offer the president-elect one of his hats as a gift. After trying on several of Leary's hats for size, Lincoln sent down the Knox hat as the one providing the best fit. Soon thereafter, the Knox hat was returned to Lincoln, along with one of "Leary's best!" When asked which of the two hats he preferred, Lincoln, ever the politician, gave a nonpartisan response: "They mutually surpass each other," he quipped.[21]

Lincoln might laugh about the hats now. He had no way of knowing that in a few days, one of these gifts, a "Kossuth hat," would play a critical role in confronting the dangers that awaited him in Baltimore.

AT 6:00 p.m., dinner was served in Lincoln's private dining room at the Astor House to a party of ten. Their train having arrived in New York just over an hour before, Hannibal Hamlin and his wife Ellen joined Mr. and Mrs. Lincoln in the private suite. Upon seeing her arrive at the Astor House, one reporter described Mrs. Hamlin as "about twenty-five years of age, smaller, and not so full in form as Mrs. Lincoln. She has a mild blue eye, rather sharp features, but a gentle expression of face. Having but just arrived from the cars, she was still in her black traveling-dress."[22]

The mood at the Lincoln-Hamlin dinner was celebratory. Things were going well. For once, the Lincolns could enjoy a quiet, private, even extravagant dinner with a few friends, saved from the hordes of local welcoming committees and party dignitaries.

Furthermore, the police arrangements in New York had been stellar and had, like tonight's dinner, also given Lincoln breathing room. If every city from here on out followed New York's lead regarding crowd control, the rest of the trip would proceed without incident.

New York Metropolitan Police Superintendent John A. Kennedy. Lincoln would congratulate him for providing ample protection in New York City. At the time, Kennedy's best detectives were also shadowing suspected plotters in Baltimore. (*Library of Congress*)

Moreover, Lincoln and Hamlin were together now. They could cement and celebrate their political partnership. From here on out, they might appear together, at dinners, at depots, on platforms, in carriages, and tonight, at the opera.[23] Their personal unity and spirited reunion would symbolize their hope for national unity and their optimism for a national re-Union.

Lincoln, who had so often appeared somber on the journey, was in bright spirits tonight. Wrote Hamlin's biographer, "The President-elect was genial and unaffectedly glad to welcome his associate and wife; Mrs. Lincoln was brilliant, and an exceedingly pleasant hour was passed at the table. Mr. and Mrs. Hamlin were charmed with Mr. Lincoln's kindness of manner and perfect simplicity of nature."[24] Lincoln recounted for the Hamlins the rousing patriotic receptions he had received since leaving Springfield and listened intently as Hamlin echoed similar experiences. Thus far, all signs pointed to patriotic support for the Union.[25] Indeed, the next day it would be reported that even in the Deep South, Arkansas had followed Tennessee's lead and determined not to secede.[26] Missouri, a border state, had voted by a large majority against holding a secession convention.[27] Things were looking brighter everywhere.

The party enjoyed their dinner at a round table patriotically decorated with a mounded centerpiece of red roses, white camellias, and violets, set in a bed of yellow pansies and green ferns trimmed with ribbon. The menu, as reported the next day in the *New York Herald,* included several courses, delicacies like fillet of chicken with truffle sauce, Shrewsbury oysters baked in the shell, roast stuffed quail, trays of delectable French pastries, and ice cream.[28]

Lincoln's personable and unassuming nature revealed itself as he confronted the oysters. "He looked at them with a half-doubting, half-smiling look and said, as if he had never eaten such a dish before, 'Well, I don't know that I can manage these things, but I guess I can learn.'"[29]

ARRIVING in Washington City on the morning of February 21, 1861, New York City detective David S. Bookstaver called on Colonel Charles P. Stone, a recent recruit to General Winfield Scott's staff. Detective Bookstaver had, at the request of his boss, Police Superintendent John A. Kennedy, been stationed in Baltimore the past few weeks, working under cover as a music agent.[30] In this role, Bookstaver could rub elbows with a more refined grade of Baltimore society than Pinkerton's men. In his undercover capacity, "Bookstaver gave particular attention to the sayings and doings of the better class of citizens and strangers who frequent music, variety, and book stores."[31] Colonel Stone had requested that Kennedy's men report their intelligence to him in person because he did not believe he could trust the mails.[32]

Three weeks before, however, Colonel Stone seemed less inclined to believe the walls had eyes and ears. Indeed, he had testified to the Select Committee of Five that he had only "very vague" information that he did not "consider as entirely reliable" of threats to prevent Lincoln's inauguration. Some of Stone's information came to him at that time secondhand, not from reliable police investigators, but a Washington newspaperman named Mr. [Simon P.] Hanscom.[33]

This morning, however, Colonel Stone would receive stunning news that was much more reliable—information from a credible New York City detective. Bookstaver reported that he had heard men in Baltimore declare they wanted to kill Lincoln.

Stone listened intently as Bookstaver conveyed the details, which he jotted down on a memorandum later that same day.

According to Colonel Stone, Bookstaver's

> information was entirely corroborative of that already in our possession; and at the time of making my morning report to the General-in-Chief, I communicated that. General Scott had received from other sources urgent warnings also, and he stated to me that it was almost a certainty that Mr. Lincoln could not pass Baltimore alive by the train on the day fixed. "But," said the General, "while you know this, we cannot convince these gentlemen that Mr. Lincoln is not coming to Washington to be inaugurated as quietly as any previous President."[34]

The information already in General Scott's and Colonel Stone's possession included dozens, perhaps even hundreds of letters, many unsigned, warning of a more general Southern conspiracy and of vague assassination threats. The largest percentage of these warnings came from Virginia, but many also came from Maryland, and some from Baltimore. One such letter, revealed by General Scott during his testimony before the Select Committee of Five, is representative. In it, the writer acknowledged Scott's efforts to organize forces to prevent an attack on the capital before March 4.

> But you can hardly be fully acquainted with the magnitude of the danger, and the extent of the preparations to prevent Mr. Lincoln's inauguration. A secret society exists through all the southern States, bound together by solemn obligations to prevent it at all hazards, even to the extent of causing his assassination before taking the oath of office. . . . The society to which I refer embraces not a few men sworn to support the Constitution and laws of the United States; men high in public life; some holding office at this time under the general government. Its numbers are already very great. Not a few of its members are in Washington. You meet them daily. Several are members of Congress. Treason is all around you, I fear to a far greater extent than you are aware. . . . If your preparations are not of a nature to render an attack hopeless, it will certainly be made towards the last of February.[35]

The pieces were coming together. New, credible, corroborating intelligence of a Baltimore Plot to assassinate Lincoln had now come, not from outdated, anonymous letters or thirdhand, sensational newspaper stories. It had come from an eyewitness—and a New York City detective at that.

Colonel Stone recommended to General Scott that Lincoln be officially warned and that he take the train that evening from Philadelphia, reaching Washington early the next day. "Mr. Lincoln's personal dignity would revolt at the idea of changing the programme of his journey on account of danger to his life," responded Scott. Stone cautioned that

> it appeared to me that Mr. Lincoln's personal dignity was of small account in comparison with the destruction, or, at least, dangerous disorganization of the United States Government, which would be the inevitable result of his death by violence in Baltimore; that in a few days more the term of Mr. Buchanan would end, and there would (in the case of Mr. Lincoln's death) be no elected President to assume the office; that the Northern cities would, on learning of the violent death of the President-

elect, pour masses of excited people upon Baltimore, which would be destroyed, and we should find ourselves in the worst civil war, with the Government utterly unprepared for it.

General Scott, after asking me how the details could be arranged in so short a time, and receiving my suggestion that Mr. Lincoln should be advised quietly to take the evening train, . . . directed me to seek Mr. W. H. Seward, to whom he wrote a few lines, which he handed me.[36]

By now, it was 10:00 a.m. Colonel Stone hurried to William Seward's house, only to learn that he had already left for the Capitol building. Finding him there after noon, Stone handed Seward General Scott's note. Seward listened attentively to what Colonel Stone had to report and asked him to write down his information and suggestions. Stone did so. Taking the report that Colonel Stone had just written, William H. Seward hastily left.[37]

There now existed reliable, firsthand intelligence of an imminent threat to assassinate President-elect Lincoln in Baltimore. But could that information be securely delivered in time and with sufficient urgency to induce the headstrong Lincoln to alter his course? Although Seward felt he should go to Philadelphia and press the case with Lincoln personally, he believed "peculiar sensitivities" compelled him to remain in Washington in attendance "at the Senate at this crisis."[38] He would therefore need to send someone else as his envoy, someone he could trust completely, someone who could credibly speak for him, someone he could entrust with his very life if necessary.

William H. Seward had just the man in mind.

In Philadelphia, a windy and cool, but bright day dawned;[39] already the streets teemed with excitement, as the City of Brotherly Love made hasty last-minute preparations to welcome the president-elect and his party.[40] Just six days before, Lincoln had accepted Philadelphia's invitation, and the city had precious little time remaining to make grand preparations.

Having been telegraphed by Edward S. Sanford, Norman Judd, and Kate Warne with a request to meet Judd in Philadelphia upon the arrival of Lincoln's party, Allan Pinkerton was also in Philadelphia on the morning of Thursday, February 21.[41] Pinkerton met his client, Samuel Felton, at 9:10 a.m. at the La Pierre House, located on Broad Street at the northwest corner of Sansom, and strolled with him to the depot of Felton's Philadelphia, Wilmington, and Baltimore Railroad. It should be remembered that Pinkerton and his operatives had not sought evidence of an assassination plot when they first arrived in Baltimore. Their mission had been to ferret out suspected secessionist plans to disable Felton's railroad. Pinkerton was now armed with the various reports of Kate Warne, Timothy Webster, Charles D. C. Williams, and Harry W. Davies, as well as the intelligence that he, posing as "Mr. Hutcheson," had gathered. Whether the plotters had the means or the courage to actually carry out their plan was a subject open to debate; but the intent was there, as were the intricate moving parts of a carefully devised plan, which Pinkerton found "much better conceived than the one which finally succeeded four years after in destroying Mr. Lincoln's life."[42] Pinkerton deemed it his duty to convey the information, which he had tested and found reliable, to Felton. Felton, however, had apparently heard rumors of a plot to assassinate Lincoln even before he hired Pinkerton.[43]

In January 1861, Felton had received a visit from a prominent social reformer, Dorothea Dix. She had come to his office with alarming news. As Felton recalled years later:

> Miss Dix, the Philanthropist, came into my office on a Saturday afternoon. I had known her for some years as one engaged in alleviating the suffering of the afflicted. Her occupation in building hospitals had brought her into contact with the prominent men South. She had become familiar with the structure of Southern society, and also with the working of its political machinery. She stated to me that she had an important communication to make to me personally.
>
> I listened attentively to what she had to say for more than an hour. . . . The sum of it was, that there was then an extensive and organized conspiracy through the South to seize upon Washington, with its archives and records, and then declare the Southern Confederacy de facto the Government of the United States. At the same time they were to cut off all means of communication between Washington and the North, East, and West, and thus prevent the transportation of troops to wrest the Capital from the hands of the insurgents. Mr. Lincoln's inauguration was thus to be prevented, or his life was to fall a sacrifice. In fact, she said, troops were then drilling on the line of our own road, the Washington and Annapolis line, and other lines of the railroad. The men drilled were to obey the commands of their leaders, and the leaders were banded together to capture Washington.[44]

While walking with Felton, Pinkerton reported what he and his operatives had learned, conceding that while the information gleaned was imperfect, he had "no doubt but that there would be an attempt to assassinate Mr. Lincoln and his Suite" in Baltimore. Pinkerton did not believe the organization was either large or wholly committed, but felt there were at best ten or fifteen men reckless enough to attempt assassination. Pinkerton cited Otis K. Hillard as an example and urged that even a few such men, united in common purpose in a large crowd, could, in concert with a Baltimore mob, do much harm.[45]

Pinkerton also conveyed to Felton his suspicions concerning Marshal Kane and the substance of the oblique conversation he had overheard at Barnum's Hotel the previous Saturday afternoon, when Kane had denounced the idea of "giving a Police Escort."[46]

Pinkerton need not have worked hard to convince Samuel Felton of Kane's suspected disloyalty. Felton had, weeks before arrived at the same conclusion.[47] And, although Pinkerton likely did not know it yet, Kane had, consistent with the statement Pinkerton overheard, written a corroborative letter to the mayor of Washington several weeks before, stating virtually the same thing concerning there being no need for armed protection for Mr. Lincoln. The people of Baltimore were, in Kane's words, "a conservative and law-abiding people. They hope and believe, and mean to act upon that belief, that the day for mobs and riots in their midst has passed, never to return. . . . The President-elect will need no armed escort in passing through or sojourning within the limits of this city or State, and, in my view, the provision of any such at this time would be ill-judged."[48]

Kane's letter continued, pressing the absurdity of the thought of any harm coming to Lincoln in Baltimore, even though his predecessor, Buchanan, had endured real threats in Baltimore while en route to his inauguration in March 1857:

> The insult offered to President Buchanan in the streets of this city on the eve of his inauguration, to which reference has been made as the ground for apprehending a similar indignity to the President-elect, it is well known, was the act of two or three members of one of the fanatical clubs of his political opponents which at that time infested our city, but which have long since been numbered among the things that were.[49]

Kane's statement about "fanatical clubs" no longer existing in Baltimore was patently false. As of February 12, Pinkerton's operatives had infiltrated and, as of February 20, in the case of Charles Williams, even become members of one of the "fanatical clubs" in Baltimore, the National Volunteers. This suggests either that Kane had no knowledge of the Knights of the Golden Circle or the National Volunteers (an improbability, given that it was his job to know and that he claimed such organizations could not exist without his knowledge) or he *did* know of such organizations and was lying to the mayor of Washington.

As they walked and talked, Felton agreed with Pinkerton that Lincoln was in peril. In fact, Felton had already mentioned the existence of danger to Morton McMichael, editor of the *Philadelphia North American*. Felton instructed McMichael not to mention the subject to anyone except Mr. Judd.[50] Felton and Pinkerton parted at 11:15 a.m., Pinkerton agreeing to meet him, Judd, and McMichael that evening and suggest "the absolute necessity" for a change in Lincoln's travel plans. Pinkerton then returned to the St. Louis Hotel, where he directed Kate Warne, who had joined him in Philadelphia, to remain. He might need her assistance.[51]

It would have been well for the Pinkerton-Felton-Judd contingent to trade notes with the Kennedy-Bookstaver-Stone-Scott-Seward investigative group. Each had, almost simultaneously, gathered compelling evidence of a conspiracy to assassinate Lincoln in Baltimore, and each wanted desperately to communicate this information to the president-elect. Working as a unit would not only permit the exchange of vital intelligence; it would also present a more forceful case to Lincoln. Unfortunately, neither group yet had any idea of the existence of the other. They were busy building, even guarding, their own silos of intelligence.

As Pinkerton was voicing his suspicions regarding Baltimore's Marshal Kane to Samuel Felton, the good marshal was busy as well. One would presume that the man in charge of preserving order in a town known for its mob violence would be at his post, rounding up suspected gang leaders and making preparations for insuring the president-elect's safe passage through his city in two days. But the marshal was not in Baltimore today. He was in Washington.

Kane had gone to Washington "on business of a purely private nature," paying a "friendly visit" to friends of Lincoln, "with whom I had been for many years on kind and intimate relations."[52] One of the Lincoln friends Kane visited was Thomas Corwin.[53] Kane later alleged that he advised Corwin and the other Lincoln friends that there were plans among the Baltimore Republican Committee, "a few hundred men, particularly obnoxious to the people and public sentiment of Baltimore, [who] had determined to avail themselves of the opportunity to use Mr. Lincoln, and to accompany him in procession from the depot to his hotel."[54] The purpose of Kane's visit to Lincoln's friends in Washington was to remonstrate against such a procession. Although Kane assured Corwin and the others that Lincoln would be treated with respect, the same could not be said for the Republican Committee, who would likely be pelted with eggs, if not otherwise mistreated.[55] A Republican procession would, in Kane's view, tend to "place the people of Baltimore in a false position, as neither they nor the citizens of Maryland sympathized with Mr. Lincoln's political views."[56]

But there was one more thing that an escort of a few hundred loyal Republican Baltimore men might do that Marshal Kane did not reference—they might, should the need arise, render aid to a Republican president-elect under attack. They would certainly complicate a plan to surround and isolate Lincoln in his carriage while driving from one Baltimore depot to the other. A few hundred Republican men might, as an escort, create a buffer around Lincoln, absorbing the stones, brickbats, and bullets meant for him.

IN Philadelphia, Allan Pinkerton had a busy day ahead of him, and time was growing short. In less than forty-eight hours, the president-elect was scheduled to arrive in Baltimore. This, Pinkerton had already determined, could not stand. The program would need to be changed. But how? Pinkerton knew he needed to find a discreet way of communicating the sensitive information he possessed to the president-elect. He needed to do it with enough urgency to demonstrate the seriousness of the risks Lincoln faced, but without alarming the rest of the suite and potentially causing a panic or a leak of information. Assuming he succeeded in meeting with Lincoln, or at least with Judd, he would need to convince Lincoln to change his program. And of course there were Mary Todd and the three young Lincolns to consider. What to do about them?

Pinkerton would need to have a plan already worked out. The plan would require numerous interconnected working parts, all of which needed to be layered with utmost secrecy. Every solution to one problem seemed to raise several new obstacles to be overcome.

First, Lincoln would need to take a different train. He was expected in Baltimore at midday on Saturday, February 23. He would need to go earlier, passing through Baltimore when no one expected him, before the time the suspected conspirators were anticipating him. If he went later the same day, the conspirators, already assembled for a noon arrival, might merely wait him out. A night train would be best, both because a darkened train would make recognition less likely and because fewer people would be milling about the depots in Baltimore in the middle of the night.

But going on a different train presented its own problems. Taking another special train might itself attract attention, even if one could be arranged. Taking a regularly scheduled train would, in turn, require some means of concealing the president-elect from the general public and potential conspirators. Even then, the highly identifiable Lincoln might be recognized.

Lincoln's dress, looks, and mannerisms, by any standard, were unique. At six feet, four inches tall, he towered a full head above most men of the era, and with his stovepipe hat appeared even taller. His clothes were generally rumpled, and when he wore store-bought suits, his sleeves and pant legs were often too short. His striking face—with its sharp cheekbones, sunken gray-blue eyes, sloped forehead, bushy eyebrows, large jutting ears, and raisin-sized mole on his right cheek—was immediately recognizable and unforgettable.

Beyond his unique height, face, and dress, Lincoln had other notable traits. His hands and feet were huge—he wore a size 10 glove and a size 16 1/2 shoe.[57] And his long feet contributed to his peculiar gate. Yet, as one who knew him well, Ward Hill Lamon recalled, "his gait was not altogether awkward, and there was a manifest physical power in his step."[58]

Such were the peculiar looks and mannerisms of Abraham Lincoln. Even with his newly sprouted beard and without his trademark stovepipe hat, trying to disguise Lincoln would be like trying to disguise a loping giraffe.

In addition to arranging for a different train and possibly a disguise, precautions would need to be taken to insure that if the suspected plotters in Baltimore had spies on the ground stalking Lincoln in Philadelphia, Harrisburg, and other places, they would not be able to send word to their accomplices of a change in Lincoln's program. Otherwise, the conspirators too might alter their plans. Despite Pinkerton's best efforts at concealment, it had to be anticipated that his plan might be found out. But cutting the telegraph lines would also create problems. A telegraph blackout would mean no communications along any train route Lincoln might take. There would be no warning of oncoming trains until, perhaps, it was too late. Even with the telegraph, head-on collisions of trains were not unheard of.[59]

And there was one more significant consideration. The president-elect was traveling with a suite of thirty-five friends and relatives, not even counting the numerous and intrusive welcoming committees that boarded the Lincoln Special at every state line and many of the larger cities. Too many people were too near Lincoln for him to make a clean break without attracting attention or raising unwanted questions. Moreover, to work, the plan depended on secrecy and rendering Lincoln as invisible as possible on his journey through Baltimore. That meant no hordes of reporters, friends, family, and the infernal welcoming committees. Ideally, it meant no one at all accompanying the president-elect save one or two trusted bodyguards. This raised an important decision point. Should the president-elect be armed with weapons to protect himself?

Perhaps many or all of these problems haunted Pinkerton's active mind as he arrived at Number 413 Prune (now, Locust) Street, Philadelphia, at 2:30 p.m. on February 21, intent on meeting George H. Burns, a confidential agent of Edward S. Sanford.[60] But at this moment, none of these concerns was more critical than this: To discreetly communicate with the president-elect Pinkerton's suspicions of the plot, his plan to thwart it, and most importantly, to convince the trusting Lincoln of the need for evasive action.

In his meeting with Burns, Pinkerton set in motion his plans. Pinkerton asked George Burns to hurry to Philadelphia's Kensington Depot and wait for the Lincoln Special, expected at around 3:00 p.m. Burns was to meet Morton McMichael, editor of the *Philadelphia North American* who had joined the Lincoln Special's party on its way from New York to Philadelphia, and pass along an important message to him at the first opportunity. If he was unable to see McMichael, Burns was to get to Judd however he could and arrange a meeting with Pinkerton and Felton as soon as possible. Pinkerton was particular about the meeting place. The Continental Hotel would be too crowded. Pinkerton feared he might be recognized there. Pinkerton also did not trust meeting Judd at the Girard House or the La Pierre House; too many Southerners were staying there. He advised Burns that his room at the St. Louis Hotel would be the best and safest place to meet.[61]

AT 4:00 p.m., booming cannon announced the Lincoln Special's arrival at Philadelphia. The late winter afternoon had turned quite cold, and gray clouds threatened snow.[62] As had occurred at other stops, vast masses of people had gathered at the depot for a chance to see Lincoln, along with "squads of police in their soldierly uniforms." A band played patriotic tunes while they waited. As one local paper recounted, "on the arrival of the train the confusion within the depot enclosure was great, and the noise and cheering outside was equally great."[63]

Like New York and Baltimore, Philadelphia in February 1861 was in the economic doldrums. Reportedly, thirty percent of its workforce was idle.[64] Although Philadelphia was a free city in a free state, the City of Brotherly Love sat a mere 16 miles north of the slave line and the neighboring state of Delaware. Plenty of Philadelphia residents sympathized with their Southern brethren and feared that the current secession troubles would drive their already faltering economy even deeper south.[65] Just two months earlier, on December 13, the city held a rally, a "Grand Union Meeting," at which speakers, including Philadelphia's mayor Alexander Henry and prominent lawyer Theodore L. Cuyler, urged conciliation with the South. Criticizing abolitionists, Mayor Henry declared: "The misplaced teachings of the pulpit, the unwise rhapsodies of the lecture room, the exciting appeals of the press on the subject of slavery, must be frowned down by a just and law-abiding people."[66]

Visiting his mother and sister in Philadelphia at the time, John Wilkes Booth may have attended the rally. Something, perhaps Philadelphia's rally combined with South Carolina's secession a few days later, certainly aroused his passions. For it was here, in Philadelphia, in December of 1860, that Booth sat down to write his lengthy manifesto that foretold of things to come. "I wish to speak," Booth told his imaginary audience, "not for the sake of being looked at, ~~and~~ ^or^ talked about. But to vindicate myself in the steps I intend to take."[67] What steps did Booth intend to take? His manifesto does not specify. But in that document, Booth exhorted his imagined audience that now was the time to save the South from Republican rule. And now, the man deemed synonymous with those Republican principles was in Philadelphia.

Lincoln rode with Judd in an open barouche, conspicuously pulled by four plumed horses, escorted by mounted police and the Pennsylvania Dragoons, while a hundred thousand onlookers watched.[68] The route taken by the procession through Philadelphia to the Continental Hotel was about 4 miles, and "throughout the whole way the streets, windows, and balconies were crowded."[69] A linear formation of policemen linked arms to form a human chain to cordon off the street and dam up the crowd surge. Despite its proximity to the South, despite its economic hardship, Philadelphia welcomed Lincoln's arrival like the Second Coming. Huge flags and banners bearing patriotic mottos, some thirty feet by fifty, snapped in the breeze. Firehouse bells rang. Bands played. It would be difficult, according to one reporter, "to attempt to describe the crowd, the enthusiasm of the populace, the cheering, the tumult, and the general gratulation which attended the progress of the President elect from the Kensington depot to the Continental."[70]

But while he gloried in the moment, Lincoln still had no idea that beneath the surface of all this Union triumph lay possible rebel treachery. Newspaper reports reveal that literally dozens of men from Virginia, Maryland, and Baltimore had been checking into Philadelphia hotels all week, including the Continental, where Lincoln would be staying.[71] At least one such individual stands out. His name appears in both the February 19 and February 21 editions of the *Philadelphia Inquirer.* On both occasions he is listed as having checked into the Continental Hotel, most likely the day before. His name is given as George Sanders. His address is given as Baltimore.[72]

The intriguing question becomes, could this man be the same George N. Sanders, the radical Democratic operative, political crony under both the Pierce and Buchanan administrations,[73] and outspoken advocate of political assassinations, who had been spotted lurking around Lincoln's hotel in Cincinnati? If so, what was he doing here, staying at Lincoln's hotel in Philadelphia? Was George N. Sanders shadowing Lincoln? Had he recently been urging Lincoln's assassination in Baltimore?

While riding in the carriage en route to the Continental Hotel with Lincoln, Norman Judd observed a young man walking briskly on the outside of the line of policemen. Unbeknownst to Judd, the young man had already been arrested by the police several times before, attempting to break through the line. Near the corner of Broad and Walnut Streets, the young man elbowed his way through the line of policemen with such force that he nearly upset two of them. He hurried to the side of the carriage with something in his hand.

DESPITE his fears of meeting Judd at the La Pierre House, Pinkerton met Samuel Felton there at 5:00 p.m. The two men discussed the likelihood of being able to convince Lincoln to change his route. Pinkerton knew such a recommendation would need to be handled delicately. But Pinkerton was absolutely convinced of imminent danger to Lincoln if he took the published route. He would at least warn the president-elect of that danger and let him and his advisors, armed with the full body of intelligence Pinkerton had gathered, determine whether or not to alter the route.[74] Felton could hardly disagree. In fact, he advocated a change to his road, the Philadelphia, Wilmington, and Baltimore line, and that Lincoln move tonight rather than tomorrow. Felton was firmly convinced, both from Pinkerton's reports and from other sources of information he had received,[75] that there would be bloodshed if Lincoln passed through Baltimore openly by the planned route.

Interestingly, while they talked at the La Pierre House, Felton also reported to Pinkerton that earlier in the day he had received a curious telegram from Vice President-elect Hannibal Hamlin. Hamlin was seeking a special car for himself on Friday's noon train from Philadelphia to Baltimore. The timing of Hamlin's request to Felton for a special car is intriguing. Two days earlier, on Tuesday evening, when Norman B. Judd met with Pinkerton agent Kate Warne in her room at the Astor House in New York, Judd wanted Warne to meet with Hamlin and share her intelligence. Warne had refused to do this.[76] After Warne's rebuff, might Judd have taken the information he then possessed concerning the Baltimore Plot to Hamlin? If he did so, Judd does not mention it in his account, recorded by William Herndon in an 1866 interview.[77] But the timing of Hamlin's unusual request suggests something of this nature may have occurred. From a security perspective, it made logical sense. Lincoln and Hamlin should not travel together. Even *without* the threat of an assassination plot in Baltimore, the remote possibility of accidental death of both men, whether by train wreck, hotel fire, carriage accident, crowd trample, or otherwise, could be avoided by separating them. But *with* such an assassination threat extant, keeping Number One and Number Two separate made all the more sense.

Hamlin's request for a special car, however, presented a dilemma for Pinkerton and Felton. Felton feared that Hamlin's dispatch might leak into the news of the Associated Press, who paid for access to telegraphs, and complicate a change of route for Lincoln.[78] If Felton complied with Hamlin's request, this too might become known and questions would then likely be asked of Felton by the voracious press about why Mr. Hamlin needed to separate from Lincoln and order a special car.

The risk of a leak to the Associated Press was easily solved. Pinkerton determined to have George Burns, whose arrival he expected at any moment, telegraph Mr. Sanford at the American Telegraph Company in New York to prevent the Hamlin dispatch from appearing in the Associated Press news.

As to dealing with Hamlin's request for a special car, Pinkerton told Felton "that in view of this move of Mr. Hamlin I thought it would be advisable for us to meet Mr. Judd as early as possible and lay the whole matter before him."[79]

Just then, Pinkerton heard the sound of music approaching the La Pierre House.[80] Pinkerton went outside and just as he reached Walnut Street, he saw a determined young man break through the mass of people and policemen surrounding Lincoln's procession. It was the same man who had been stopped several times previously by the police. He was not an assassin, but George Burns, the very man Pinkerton needed to see. In his hand, Burns held a slip of paper,

Worried about their safety, Vice-President Hannibal Hamlin and his wife left the Lincoln Special and passed through Baltimore a day earlier than planned. (*Library of Congress*)

which he passed to Judd. The paper cryptically read: "St. Louis Hotel, ask for J. H. Hutchinson."[81]

A few minutes later, Burns picked his way through the dense crowd and met up with Pinkerton. He advised Pinkerton that the meeting with Judd had been arranged for 7:30 p.m. in Pinkerton's room in the St. Louis Hotel. This would be too late. In order to meet with Judd, advise Judd of the need to change Lincoln's plans, convince Lincoln of that need, make hasty travel arrangements, and then get Lincoln on the eleven o'clock train that night to Baltimore, they needed to meet with Judd immediately. Pinkerton instructed Burns to once again hack his way through the crowd and get to Judd to arrange an earlier meeting. "How Mr. Burns was to get through the crowd and overtake the carriage I could not see," said Pinkerton, "nor how he would again break the ranks of the Police I could not tell. But he left me and with superhuman strength I saw him go through the crowd like nothing, and bursting through the ranks of the Police again reach the carriage." A few minutes later, Burns returned, with the happy news that Judd would see Pinkerton immediately at the St. Louis Hotel.[82]

If, while riding in the carriage with Judd, Lincoln took notice of Burns, his note, or his request to Judd for a meeting with "Mr. Hutcheson," history fails to record it. If Lincoln did take notice, both Burns's and Judd's behavior must have struck him as curious.

Burns and Pinkerton returned to the La Pierre House and called on Samuel Felton, who agreed to join them immediately at the St. Louis Hotel. Pinkerton also requested that Burns telegraph Mr. Sanford at the American Telegraph Company in order to prevent the Associated Press from publishing the news of Vice President-elect Hamlin's intent to take a special car on Friday's noon train to Baltimore. Back in his room, Number 21, at the St. Louis Hotel, Pinkerton lit a fire and waited for Felton to arrive, which he soon did, followed about 6:45 p.m. by Norman Judd.[83]

Finally, after nearly two weeks of trading cryptic telegrams and meeting with tight-lipped female operatives, Norman Judd could hear firsthand the whole story from Allan Pinkerton himself.

Pinkerton introduced Judd, "Mr. Lincoln's intimate friend,"[84] to Samuel M. Felton. "We lost no time in making known to [Judd] all the facts which had come to our knowledge in reference to the conspiracy," Felton later reported.[85]

Judd knew Pinkerton and vouched for his ability, honesty, and integrity. He said that he knew Pinkerton well enough to know that he would not exaggerate the facts. He requested that Pinkerton summarize his various reports.[86]

As a good lawyer might present an opening argument, Pinkerton laid out the salient facts, colored with his professional opinion, which, when filtered through the lens of deductive reasoning, presented a compelling case. The case, as pleaded by Pinkerton and echoed by Felton, was this:

—That in Perrymansville, a town on the line of Felton's Philadelphia, Wilmington, and Baltimore Railroad, rangers pretending to be Union men had been drilling, with their real purpose being to destroy the road's bridges and march on Washington.[87]

—That infantry troops had assembled at Bel Air, a small town near Cockeysville, which was on the Northern Central Railroad line—the published route for Lincoln's passage from Harrisburg to Baltimore.

—That there existed in Baltimore a class of extremists such as Otis K. Hillard, whose "every sympathy" was with the South, who were as fervent in their radical cause as John Brown had been in his, and who would, Pinkerton believed, consider it an honor to become martyrs for that cause.

—That such men had bound themselves with solemn oaths in secret societies such as the National Volunteers.

—That Hillard had sworn he "would do whatever his Captain called upon him to do, without asking a why or a wherefore."

—That these men were determined, in Pinkerton's view, that Lincoln should not pass through Baltimore alive.

—That, in Pinkerton's opinion, it would not require many such men to accomplish their purpose and, indeed, a small band of resolute men might be more effective than a large group, as they could act in concert. (Consider how easily George Burns reached Lincoln's carriage.)

—That the Baltimore plotters had spoken of using fire balls and hand grenades.

—That Pinkerton suspected the Baltimore police were disloyal, that Lincoln's cortege would enjoy no police protection in Baltimore.[88]

—That even with a loyal police force in Buffalo, Major Hunter had been seriously injured by a crowd that intended no injury.

—That a prime opportunity for assassination would present itself if Lincoln were hemmed in by a crowd and unable to move, in which case even a few men determined to take his life, even at loss of their own, might be effective.

—That Lincoln's assassination would mean war.

—That now was not the time for war, since at present there was no effective government, there could be none before Lincoln's inauguration, and Lincoln was powerless before his inauguration.[89]

Pinkerton punctuated the threats to Lincoln with the reality that the president-elect had little in the way of an effective security detail. He told Judd that "nameless and unknown as I was, I could stand a better chance for my life than did Mr. Lincoln, as I at least had some of my own men with me who would die in their boots before I should be injured."[90]

It would have been known to the Baltimore plotters, thanks to newspaper accounts, that Lincoln tended to ride in the rearward car.[91] If they intended to attack the train, that would be where they would likely initiate the assault. Pinkerton, however, did not believe the danger to Lincoln was as significant while on the train as it would be while he passed, open and vulnerable, in a carriage through the streets of Baltimore the mile and a quarter between the Calvert Street Station of the Northern Central Railroad and the Camden Street Station of the B&O's Washington Branch Railroad. "I . . . said to Mr. Judd that I did not believe it was possible he (Lincoln) or his personal friends could pass through Baltimore in that style alive."[92]

Pinkerton asked Judd if any arrangements had been made in Baltimore for a patriotic welcoming reception for Lincoln, as had been made that day in Philadelphia and every other major city along the Lincoln Special's route thus far. Judd's ominous answer spoke volumes. He did not know of any such arrangements in Baltimore.[93]

However, while in Albany, Lincoln had received a letter from Worthington G. Snethen, a Baltimore Republican. Snethen's Albany dispatch warned against any organized public celebration upon his arrival in Baltimore. Instead, Snethen offered to meet Lincoln in Philadelphia or Harrisburg with "as many of the gallant little band who voted for you in this City, as may choose to do so . . . as your political friends, in their individual capacity." From Philadelphia or Harrisburg, they would escort Lincoln to Baltimore, where, at the depot, would be a number of open barouches with four horses each. The carriages would take the president-elect and his suite either to their hotel, should they decide to stop in Baltimore, or if not, to the Washington depot. Snethen's Albany note further indicated that Baltimore's mayor George W. Brown and his city council might give Lincoln a formal reception, in which case they would provide the necessary conveyances and escort, but he had no news of this yet. Concluded a seemingly helpless Snethen, "[t]he [Baltimore] City authorities are all opposed to us, and some of them are even hostile."[94]

Now, a week after Snethen's Albany letter, and less than forty-eight hours before Lincoln's published arrival in Baltimore, there still were no definite arrangements for his reception there, whether from the "gallant little band" of Baltimore Republicans, from Mayor Brown or his city council, or even from Maryland governor Thomas H. Hicks.[95]

Pinkerton next asked Judd if he knew William S. Wood, the superintendent in charge of the Lincoln Special these past ten days. Judd revealed the astounding truth that neither he nor Lincoln had any idea who Mr. Wood was.[96] From a security standpoint, William S. Wood arguably held the single most important job on the Lincoln Special. Like many others, including the suspected plotters in Baltimore, he of course knew the Special's published times of departure and arrival at every depot in every city—indeed, Wood set those times and therefore knew them before anyone else. And Superintendent Wood could give, or refuse to give, boarding passes to whomever he chose.[97] He had the power to expedite or delay the Lincoln Special's departure or arrival times.[98] He could, within reason, dictate who rode in what cars and possibly who rode with Lincoln in his carriage. As superintendent, he would likely have known, or been able to readily learn, all the most intimate aspects of the Lincoln Special's party and program, including the hotels where the suite would stay; what room numbers each person would occupy; how to send, receive, and possibly intercept telegrams from almost anywhere to or from almost anyone in the party; who would be in the various welcoming committees; and what routes the carriages would take through each of the cities where the party stopped. Pinkerton's suspicious mind now likely added Superintendent Wood to his growing list of persons to watch—and to keep in the dark.

Having listened to Pinkerton's summary of the evidence, with which Felton concurred, Judd agreed Lincoln was in grave danger if he attempted to pass through Baltimore according to the published program. As Judd later reported, "From their representations I became satisfied that a well-matured and organized plot did exist to kill Lincoln in Baltimore; and I then saw that something must be done."[99]

Judd claimed that he had, up to now, kept Pinkerton's information, including the letters received from him in Cincinnati, Buffalo, and New York, secret from everyone, including Lincoln. But he could no longer maintain secrecy. Judd now needed to advise Lincoln. He wanted Pinkerton's and Felton's advice. Said Felton, "I most earnestly advised [Judd] that Mr. Lincoln should go to Washington that night in the sleeping-car. Mr. Judd fully entered into the plan, and said he would urge Mr. Lincoln to adopt it."[100]

Judd was convinced of the need for a change from the published route and had no doubt whatsoever that Pinkerton's information was accurate, "the manner in which it was obtained stamping it as reliable."[101] But Judd did doubt that he would be able to convince Lincoln to change his route.[102] "Mr. Judd said that Mr. Lincoln's confidence in the people was unbounded, and that he did not fear any violent outbreak; that he hoped by his management and conciliatory measures to bring the secessionists back to their allegiance."[103] After a long discussion, Judd therefore asked Pinkerton to go with him to the Continental Hotel to meet Mr. Lincoln and present the evidence to him in person.[104] Despite Pinkerton's earlier misgivings about being recognized at the crowded Continental Hotel, he consented.

It was now 9:00 p.m. Judd had been meeting with Pinkerton and Felton for over two hours. It had already been a long day for all of them, but it was far from over. If they were to get Lincoln on the 11:00 p.m. train from Philadelphia to Baltimore they would need to act fast.

Pinkerton and Judd left together for the Continental Hotel, parting company with Felton. Pinkerton agreed to see Felton later and give him Lincoln's decision at the La Pierre House.[105] That meeting with Felton would never take place.

THAT night in Philadelphia, the city threw a party. "The weather was fair, the air bracing, and the moon and stars shone brightly." Bands played patriotic tunes. People cheered. A man impersonating Lincoln appeared on the balcony at the Continental Hotel, waving his arms and shouting as if making a speech. The people groaned. At ten o'clock, brilliant fireworks lit up the night sky. One pyrotechnical display blazed with letters of silver fire, "Welcome Abraham Lincoln. The Whole Union."[106]

Earlier that afternoon, a young man intent on finding Abraham Lincoln had hurriedly boarded a train bound for Philadelphia. In fact, the young man had left in such haste that he neglected to find out at which of Philadelphia's numerous hotels Lincoln was staying. He learned from newspapers and conversations with passengers on the train that Lincoln and his party would be at the Continental Hotel tonight, "where he would be serenaded."[107] Several hours later, under the brightly shining stars and moon, the young man's train, "a tedious one," brought him into Philadelphia. Although the young man had never met Lincoln before, his name was the only passport he would need to gain an audience. He arrived at the Continental Hotel sometime later and recorded the scene:

> Within, the halls and stairways were packed, and the brilliantly lighted parlors were filled with ladies and gentlemen who had come to "pay their respects." A buzz of animated conversation pervaded the throng, and, in its centre, presentations to the President-elect appeared to be going on. . . . I turned into a room near the head of the stairway, which had been pointed out as that of Mr. Robert Lincoln. He was surrounded by a group of young friends. On my introducing myself, he met and greeted me with courteous warmth, and then called to Colonel Ward H. Lamon, who was passing, and introduced us to each other. Colonel Lamon, taking me by the arm, proposed at once to go back into the parlor to present me to Mr. Lincoln. On my telling him that I wanted my interview to be as private and to attract as little attention as possible, the Colonel laughed and said:
>
> "Then I think I had better take you to his bedroom. If you don't mind waiting there, you'll be sure to meet him, for he has got to go there some time to-night; and it is the only place I know of where he will be likely to be alone."
>
> This was the very opportunity I desired. Thanking the Colonel, I sat and waited for an hour or more in the quiet room that was in such contrast with the bustle outside.[108]

At the time, Lamon's courtesy of letting the young man into Lincoln's bedroom to wait for him likely went by without a second thought, particularly under the fuzzy glow of a party atmosphere. With over 150 years of hindsight and several presidential assassinations and near misses under the American belt, however, Lamon's move now appears downright reckless. Neither Robert Todd Lincoln nor Ward Hill Lamon, to whom the president-elect's "sacred life" had been entrusted just the week previous, had ever met this young man before. And yet, here he was, an essentially unvetted man, waiting alone, in the dark stillness of the president-elect's bedroom. This was the very opportunity he desired. No matter who the young man claimed to be, he might have been anyone.

By the time Pinkerton and Judd got within a block of the Continental Hotel, "the crowd was one dense mass of people"[109] that filled Chestnut Street. "[E]very square inch of ground was occupied by them as Mr. Lincoln was holding a reception at the Continental, and it was with the utmost difficulty that we were able to get into the building."[110] Pinkerton led Judd around the corner one block south, to Sansom Street, where they entered the Continental through the rear servant's door.[111] Pinkerton told Judd he would join him soon, as he had a brief errand to run. Thirty minutes later, Pinkerton returned to the Continental. Pinkerton's words best describe the scene:

> The interior of the house was as densely crowded as was the outside and I found that all were "getting up stairs." When I reached the last of the stairs I found that Mr. Lincoln was in a balcony at the head of the first landing, bowing to the people as they passed up the stairs. There was no way for me to get up but go into the jam and go up with the human tide, so I went in— but such a jam. In due time however I reached the head of the stairs where I found the Halls about as much crowded as they were below. The people were kept moving in a steady stream around through a double file of Police to the stairway on Tenth Street and thus out. I managed to get outside of the file of Police and soon found Mr. Judd's room where I found him waiting for me. Judd said that as soon as Mr. Lincoln got through with receiving the people on the Balcony he (Judd) would send for him [Lincoln] to come to his room.[112]

While they waited in Judd's room, located on the same floor as the ladies' parlor,[113] Pinkerton sent a note by a hotel waiter, calling for one of Edward S. Sanford's agents, either George H. Burns or Henry Sanford[114], at the Girard House. This was the errand Pinkerton had attempted thirty minutes before, only to be turned back by a crushing tide of people. The waiter must have had better luck reaching the Girard House than Pinkerton, for soon after Henry Sanford arrived in Judd's room.

There came a request that must have at first struck everyone in the room as curious. Pinkerton asked that Henry Sanford's Adams Express Company double the number of messengers on each of its runs between Philadelphia and Baltimore and between Harrisburg and Baltimore. The Adams Express

Company delivered packages, parcels, freight, bank notes, gold and silver coin, and so on, much like UPS or Wells Fargo might do today, except by rail, rather than jet or armored truck.[115] Pinkerton explained his rationale: if there was an attempt made on Lincoln's life, professional thieves might see an opportunity to plunder and join the attacking party.[116] In other words, Lincoln's murder might create a diversion for robbing the Adams Express, or vice versa.

Henry Sanford agreed to have the messengers doubled. But Pinkerton had one more odd request. No mention of the reason for doubling the messengers should be made to Samuel Shoemaker, the Adams Express manager in Baltimore.[117] As Pinkerton explained, "not that I doubted the Honesty or Loyalty of Mr. Shoemaker, but that I feared his discretion."[118] The very people Pinkerton needed to implement his plans could not know the reasons why.

Time marched on. It was now becoming increasingly clear that the events of the day, the crushing crowds, and the relentless clock, had all conspired to make it impossible to get Lincoln on the 11 o'clock train. Even before the plan could be implemented, it would need to be amended. At around 10:15 p.m., having learned that Lincoln had retired, Pinkerton set out to see the president-elect in his room. He carried a note from Judd asking Lincoln to come to Judd's room as soon as convenient on important business. Pinkerton asked Colonel Elmer E. Ellsworth, who, Pinkerton reported, was "officiating as Equery in waiting,"[119] to deliver the note to Lincoln. Ellsworth would have none of it and refused. Ellsworth did, however, accompany Pinkerton back to Judd's room. Judd immediately ordered Ellsworth to deliver the note to Lincoln. This time, Ellsworth complied.[120]

Roughly ten minutes after Ellsworth delivered the note, Lincoln entered Judd's room.[121] Pinkerton, Henry Sanford, and possibly John Nicolay were also there.[122] Judd had withheld from Lincoln the information he was receiving from Pinkerton for over a week. He would now deliver it, with plenty of backup.

CHAPTER TWELVE

THE BALTIMORE PLOT

The evening of February 21, 1861
Philadelphia

NOW INSIDE JUDD'S ROOM, JUDD INTRODUCED Lincoln to Pinkerton, who noticed that Lincoln "was rather exhausted from the fatigues of travel and receptions." Pinkerton next introduced the president-elect to Henry Sanford. Sanford then left the room.[1] Judd reported that "Lincoln liked Pinkerton—had the utmost confidence in him as a gentleman, and a man of sagacity."[2] Lincoln "at once" remembered Pinkerton.[3] They had spun in similar orbits in recent years, and their paths had crossed before. Both were from Illinois. Both had done work for the railroads. Pinkerton caught violent train robbers, while, as legal counsel for the Illinois Central Railroad from 1853 to 1859, Lincoln had dealt with a more civil variety of thieves.[4] In the process he had come into periodic contact with Pinkerton's detective agency.[5] Both Lincoln and Pinkerton despised slavery, although Pinkerton was more extreme in his views. Pinkerton considered John Brown "a greater man than Napoleon ever dared to be, and as great a man as Washington."[6] He aided not only the visible railroads, but those underground as well, assisting runaway slaves on their passage to freedom.

Judd initiated the discussion,[7] briefly detailing to Lincoln the background information. He explained that Pinkerton had gone to Baltimore initially to gather intelligence on behalf of the Philadelphia, Wilmington, and Baltimore Railroad, intending to protect that company from suspected secessionist plans to vandalize it. But while operating undercover among the secessionists, Pinkerton had discovered that certain individuals intended to murder Mr. Lincoln while he was passing through Baltimore.[8] He, Pinkerton, and Felton had all concluded that the prudent course was for Lincoln to go to Washington tonight, in a sleeping car of Felton's line. "But," Judd added, "the proofs that have now been laid before you cannot be published." That would expose

Pinkerton's operatives still on the ground in Maryland and Baltimore and potentially cost them their lives. One man in particular, Timothy Webster, was especially vulnerable. He was at that moment serving in a rebel cavalry company drilling in Perrymansville, Maryland. Judd also cautioned Lincoln, "If you follow the course suggested—of proceeding to Washington to-night— you will necessarily be subjected to the scoffs and disapproval of your friends, who cannot be made to believe in the existence of so desperate a plot."[9]

According to Pinkerton, "Whilst Mr. Judd was talking, Mr. Lincoln listened very attentively, but did not say a word, nor did his countenance which I had watched very closely, show any emotion. He appeared thoughtful and serious, but decidedly firm."[10] Judd then asked Pinkerton to go over the outline he had previously given, detailing individuals such as Cypriano Ferrandini, Otis K. Hillard and James Luckett, and to provide his opinion concerning the probability that these men would attempt assassination. Pinkerton complied, recounting the statement he overheard the previous Saturday night at Barnum's Hotel, made by Baltimore's marshal George Kane, that he would provide "no police escort," which Pinkerton surmised to refer to Lincoln's passage through Baltimore.

Pinkerton further reported the bravado of Ferrandini and Hillard, who claimed they were prepared to sacrifice themselves for the good of their country, that is, the Southern states, in order to rid that country of a "tyrant," Mr. Lincoln. Pinkerton conceded that there were likely only fifteen to twenty men with enough courage to attempt assassination. Pinkerton described Hillard, as a fair example: "a young man of good family, character and reputation—honorable, gallant and chivalrous, but thoroughly devoted to Southern rights, and who looked upon the North as being aggressors upon the rights of that section and upon every Northern man as an Abolitionist, and he (Mr. Lincoln) as the embodiment of all those evils, in whose death the South would be largely the gainers."[11]

Pinkerton advised Lincoln that there would be a very large crowd waiting for him in Baltimore, reminded him of the dangers of large crowds, recalling the events in Buffalo. He predicted, however, that things would be "infinitely worse" in Baltimore, where there was an economic depression, people were out of work, the crowd would be large and easily agitated, and the police would either not show or be disloyal and ineffective if they did show. Pinkerton further warned of the opportunity for the assassins: they would know from the published route the exact time of the Lincoln Special's arrival, shortly after noon, at Baltimore's Calvert Street depot, whereupon the party would be required to pass, at a snail's pace, a mile and a quarter through congested streets in an open carriage to the next depot. Under such conditions, Pinkerton said, it would be simple for any assassin to blend into the crowd, wait for his opportunity, and shoot or stab the president-elect.[12]

Indeed, the ease with which anyone wishing to get within close range of Lincoln while he was being conveyed in an open carriage had that very afternoon been amply demonstrated, when Judd had been handed a note by George Burns, who had broken through protective lines of Philadelphia policemen with much less persistence than one bent on assassination would have exhibited.[13]

During Pinkerton's discussion, Lincoln listened attentively, asking the occasional question, subjecting Pinkerton to "a thorough cross-examination."[14] There came but one interruption. At some point while Pinkerton spoke, Ward Hill Lamon entered the room, acknowledged Pinkerton, and handed Lincoln a note, then left immediately.[15] Pinkerton seemed irritated, not necessarily at the interruption, but that his presence in the room had been leaked to Lamon: "Mr. Lamon recognized me, but I am positive he could not have known me had he not been informed by some one that I was with the President Elect."[16] A sleuth like Pinkerton should have been able to deduce how Lamon had learned of his presence. There was but one man not in Judd's room who knew that Pinkerton was then meeting the president-elect. He had been guarding the door to Lincoln's room and had refused Pinkerton's first request to pass: Colonel Elmer Ellsworth.

Lincoln listened attentively the entire time as Judd and Pinkerton spoke. There were reportedly three possible plans whereby the conspirators intended to attack the president-elect. According to one plan, at some point south of the Maryland line, the Lincoln Special was to be thrown from the track and sent cascading down a steep embankment. The advantage of this plan, in the minds of the conspirators, was its straightforward execution. Its primary disadvantage was that in killing the president-elect, a large number of innocent lives, including Lincoln's wife and children, might be needlessly lost. Even secessionists who favored putting Lincoln out of the way might blanch at the notion of murdering innocent women and children in the process—this would do little to win public opinion in favor of secession or rebellion.

A second plan reportedly involved the use of some "infernal machine"—a hand grenade—to blow up the car in which Lincoln was riding. Objections to this plan were that the "infernal machine" might kill both predator as well as prey—and possibly innocent bystanders—and that it might not function properly.

The third option was deemed most favored by the conspirators and most feasible. According to this plan, "a large and organized crowd of roughs" would surround Lincoln's carriage in Baltimore as he was being conveyed from one depot to the next. They would

> cheer lustily and demonstrate in lively ways their delight at the
> condescension of the distinguished guest, as he bowed gracious-

ly to them or possibly extended his dexter hand for a friendly shake. At a convenient opportunity the keen stiletto would be buried in the heart of the President elect, and aided by his fellows, the assassin, slipping into the surrounding mass of brother conspirators, would avoid recognition or detection, while the end would be accomplished and the fate of the country sealed.

The name of the instigators, the role of the subordinates, the sum paid for the attempt, and the amount to be paid in case of success, with certain other data, were given with such accuracy of detail, as to satisfy Mr. Lincoln of the propriety of immediate consultation with his friends.[17]

Although this news was disturbing, if not terrifying, the president-elect received it courageously. During the entire discussion, "Mr. Lincoln was cool, calm and collected."[18]

After presenting the facts to Lincoln, Pinkerton concluded his assessment of the dire situation by offering Lincoln his professional judgment—he believed that "if Mr. Lincoln adhered to the published programe of his route to Washington that an assault of some kind would be made upon his person with a view to taking his life."[19]

Lincoln asked Judd and Pinkerton what course they recommended.[20] Pinkerton informed the president-elect that there was a train leaving Philadelphia for Washington tonight—the 11:00 p.m. train. He urged Lincoln to take it with him.[21] In this way, Lincoln could avoid the conspirators, who would not be expecting him to travel through Baltimore tonight. There was little time to think. It was around 10:30. It would take a mad, desperate rush to push and pull Lincoln through the packed house, seat him in a carriage, and pick his way through Philadelphia's gridlocked streets at Ninth and Chestnut to the PW&B depot on Broad and Prime Streets some sixteen blocks away in time to catch the eleven o'clock train.[22]

Lincoln remained quiet, even pensive, for a few minutes. He was thinking about Pinkerton's proposed plan: "He [Pinkerton] urged me to go right through with him to Washington that night. I didn't like that," Lincoln recalled. "I had made engagements to visit Harrisburg, and go from there to Baltimore, and I resolved to do so. I could not believe that there was a plot to murder me."[23]

Sensing Lincoln's reluctance, Judd broke the silence: was there anything more they might say that would induce Lincoln to leave that night on a train bound for Washington? Lincoln replied that he "appreciated these suggestions" and that he "could stand anything that was necessary."

But then, rising from his seat,[24] he said, firmly: "No, I cannot consent to this. I shall hoist the flag on Independence Hall tomorrow morning . . . and go to Harrisburg to-morrow, then I . . . have fulfilled all my engagements, and if you . . . think there is positive danger in my attempting to go through Baltimore openly according to the published programe—if you can arrange any way to carry out your views, I shall endeavor to get away quietly from the people at Harrisburg to-morrow evening and shall place myself in your [hands]."[25]

However, Lincoln left a door open: "I told [Judd] that if I should meet at Harrisburg, as I had at other places, a delegation to go with me to the next place [Baltimore], I should feel safe, and go on."[26]

Lincoln's tone was firm. His words were unmistakable. He would not go to Washington tonight; neither Pinkerton nor Judd saw any point in pressing the issue further. Judd then said to Lincoln, "We will then complete the arrangements, and I will tell you in detail on tomorrow in the cars between Philadelphia and Harrisburg."[27]

Pinkerton asked Lincoln if any arrangement had been made in Baltimore with the public officials for a reception there, and he said he did not know of any. He also said that he had not heard from a "single individual in that City" (Baltimore); he had left the details of making such arrangements for receptions in host cities to Mr. Wood. Suspicion once more seemed to turn to the Lincoln Special's superintendent, William S. Wood. Pinkerton asked Lincoln who Wood was. Lincoln replied that he knew "nothing" of Wood, that he had been recommended by Mr. Seward, and that Lincoln had acquiesced—"an evidence of the confiding and innocent feeling of the man."[28] The president-elect now also seemed wary of the Lincoln Special's superintendent. Instead of a warm invitation from Baltimore had come rumors of a plot to murder him there. Recalled Pinkerton, "Mr. Lincoln said that Mr. Wood should not know anything in regard to our movements."[29]

Judd asked Pinkerton how best to implement leaving from Harrisburg the following evening. Pinkerton felt that if Lincoln could slip away around dusk, they might take him on a special train on the Pennsylvania Railroad from Harrisburg to Philadelphia, arriving in time to connect with the Philadelphia, Wilmington, and Baltimore train headed to Baltimore from Philadelphia. By securing seats on the sleeping car, they might avoid being seen in Baltimore, as the sleeper would be drawn by horses through Baltimore from one depot to the other, avoiding the need to leave the car.

After some discussion, this nascent plan was agreed to. Pinkerton promised to handle the details of arranging for the special train from Harrisburg and advised Lincoln that no one save Judd and Pinkerton should know about the new arrangement. But Lincoln could not agree to that level of secrecy. The excitable Mrs. Lincoln would obviously need to know. Once she was told of the plan, it was likely that she would insist that Lamon go with Lincoln. Other than these two, Lincoln agreed that no one else should know.[30] This gratified Pinkerton. Secrecy was key to his plan's success. Pinkerton vowed that if the secret was kept, that he, Pinkerton, would answer for Lincoln's safety with his life.[31]

Lincoln left Judd's room around 11:00 p.m., "without any apparent agitation,"[32] once again injecting himself into the dense and persistent crowd that still huddled around the door in the hallway outside.[33] Once he fought his way through them, the clearly fatigued Lincoln would have liked, at last, to fall into bed, even if it was a bed too short for him to stretch out in. But he knew better. Lamon's note, handed to him in Judd's room, likely told him there was yet one more important meeting to attend to before there could be any rest for the weary. A young man was waiting for Mr. Lincoln in his bedroom.

At around 11:00 p.m., after having "waited for an hour or more in the quiet room that was in such contrast with the bustle outside," the un-vetted young man who had seemed so desperate to see Lincoln received a visit from Colonel Lamon. Fortunately for Lincoln, the young man was who he claimed to be— Frederick Seward, William Seward's thirty-year old son. The elder Seward had handpicked his son earlier that day in Washington for the vital mission of relaying General Scott's intelligence to Lincoln. Together, Lamon and Seward met Lincoln, who was then coming down the hallway, working his way through the crowds back to his room. Seward recorded his first impression of Lincoln: "I had never before seen him; but the campaign portraits had made his face quite familiar. I could not but notice how accurately they had copied his features, and how totally they had omitted his careworn look, and his pleasant, kindly smile." Lincoln and Seward made their way back to Lincoln's room. "After a few words of friendly greeting, with inquiries about my father and matters in Washington, he sat down by the table under the gaslight to peruse the letter I had brought."[34]

The information young Seward had brought Lincoln actually comprised three letters. The first was from William H. Seward to Lincoln, the second was from General Scott to Seward, and the third was the memorandum of Colonel Charles P. Stone, written earlier that day after his meeting with Detective Bookstaver. The letters contained news that should have troubled Lincoln. Curiously, Seward saw, they did not seem to faze him in the slightest. Although the letter's contents "were of a somewhat startling nature, he made no exclamation, and I saw no sign of surprise in his face."[35] The first of the three letters Lincoln now perused so coolly read as follows:

Washington, February 21 [1861]

My dear Sir

My son goes express to you— He will show you a report made by our detective to General Scott—and by him communicated to

me this morning—I deem it so important as to dispatch my son
to meet you wherever he may find you.

I concur with General Scott in thinking it best for you to
reconsider your arrangement. No one here but Genl. Scott,
myself, & the bearer are aware of this communication.

I should have gone with it myself but for the peculiar sensi-
tiveness about my attendance at the Senate at this crisis. . . .
Very truly yours,

William H. Seward[36]

The second note was a letter of introduction for Colonel Stone to Senator
Seward written in large, bold, jagged letters by Winfield Scott's shaky hand:

My dear Sir:
Please receive my friend, Colonel Stone, chief of Genl.
Weightman's staff, & a distinguished young officer with me in
Mexico. He has an important communication to make.
Yrs. truly

Winfield Scott.

Feb. 21, 1861.[37]

But it was the third note that was the most stunning. It had been written
earlier that morning after Colonel Stone caught up with William Seward at
the Capitol. There, Colonel Stone had written, at Senator Seward's request,
this "closing piece of information" now in Lincoln's hands.[38] It read:

Feb 21st/61

A New York detective officer who has been on duty in
Baltimore for three weeks past reports this morning to Col Stone
that there is serious danger of violence to and the assassination of
Mr Lincoln in his passage through that city should the time of
that passage be known—He states that there are banded rowdies
holding secret meetings, and that he has heard threats of mob-
bing and violence, and has himself heard men declare that if Mr
Lincoln was to be assassinated they would like to be the men—
He states further that it is only within the past few days that he
has considered there was any danger, but now he deems it imminent—He deems the danger one which the authorities & people
in Balt. Cannot guard against—(over)

Lincoln turned Colonel Stone's report over and continued reading on the
obverse side of the page:

All risk might be easily avoided by a change in the travelling arrangements which would bring the Mr Lincoln and a portion of his party through Baltimore by a night train without previous notice—[39]

After reading the reports carefully through, Lincoln held the papers up to the gaslight and deliberately read them through a second time. He had to be sure. Then, after brief reflection, he looked up at Fred Seward, and asked: "Did you hear anything about the way this information was obtained? Do you know anything about how they got it?"

"No," Seward said, he had known nothing of the information until that very day, when his father called for him.

Lincoln continued his cross-examination. "Your father and General Scott do not say who they think are concerned in it. Do you think they know?"

On that point, Fred Seward likewise could give no additional information, except that it was his impression that his father's knowledge was limited to what Colonel Charles P. Stone, "in whose statements he had implicit confidence," had communicated to him.

"Did you hear any names mentioned?" Lincoln wanted to know. "Did you, for instance, ever hear anything said about such a name as Pinkerton?"

No, Seward replied; he had heard no such name in connection with the matter. In fact, he had heard no names at all except for General Scott and Colonel Stone. Lincoln

thought for a moment, and then said:

"I may as well tell you why I ask. There were stories or rumors some time ago, before I left home, about people who were intending to do me a mischief. I never attached much importance to them—never wanted to believe any such thing. So I never would do anything about them in the way of taking precautions and the like. Some of my friends, though, thought differently—Judd and others; and without my knowledge they employed a detective to look into the matter. It seems he has occasionally reported what he found; and only to-day, since we arrived at this house, he brought this story, or something similar to it, about an attempt on my life in the confusion and hurly-burly of the reception at Baltimore."

"Surely, Mr. Lincoln," said [Seward], "that is a strange corroboration of the news I bring you."

He smiled and shook his head.

"That is exactly why I was asking you about the names. If different persons, not knowing of each other's work, have been pur-

suing separate clues that led to the
same result, why, then it shows there
may be something in it; but if this is
only one story, filtered through two
channels, and reaching me in two
ways, then that doesn't make it any
stronger. Don't you see?"[40]

To young Seward, Lincoln's logic was
"unanswerable." Seward asserted his strong
belief that the two investigations,
Pinkerton's and Bookstaver's, had been conducted independently of one another. This
corroboration convinced Lincoln that the
Baltimore Plot was real. As Lincoln would
later report to historian Benson J. Lossing
during his interview on the subject, once he
concluded that General Scott and William
Seward had acted independently of
Pinkerton, "I now believe such a plot to be
in existence."[41]

Frederick Seward, son of Senator
William Seward, provided Lincoln
with intelligence from New York
City detectives that corroborated
Pinkerton's reports. (*Library of
Congress*)

Seward urged the president-elect to change the hour of his passage through
Baltimore and his train, to avoid all risk. The two men discussed the subject
a little longer, after which Lincoln rose, saying, "well, we haven't got to decide
it to-night anyway, and I see it is getting late." The compassionate Lincoln
could see that his reluctance to heed the warning concerned Fred Seward. He
said kindly, "You need not think I will not consider it well. I shall think it
over carefully, and try to decide it right; and I will let you know in the morning."[42] Lincoln went to bed. Those planning for his safety, however, would be
up all night.

ALLAN PINKERTON had much work to do. The impression Lincoln had left
was that *if* Pinkerton and Judd continued to believe the danger in Baltimore
was real, and *if* Pinkerton and Judd could devise a plan to avoid that suspected danger, and *if* there was no Baltimore reception committee waiting for him
in Harrisburg tomorrow, then he, Lincoln, would endeavor to slip away quietly the following evening and place his life in Pinkerton's and Judd's hands.[43]
Clearly, Pinkerton was not going to change his mind regarding the danger in
Baltimore. He had spent too much time, put too many agents at risk, and
developed too much corroborated evidence of a conspiracy. Even had he known
of Marshal Kane's seemingly spurious claim that "the day for mobs and riots

in their midst has passed, never to return,"[44] Pinkerton's own evidence would have told him to disregard it. No, in Pinkerton's mind, the danger in Baltimore was both clear and present.

For Pinkerton's plan to work, it would be necessary to involve the Pennsylvania Railroad. While that line expected to convey Lincoln's cortege from Philadelphia to Harrisburg the next morning, they were not planning on a return trip; Lincoln's party was scheduled to go straight from Harrisburg to Baltimore the morning of Saturday, February 23, on the Northern Central Railroad's line.[45]

Although the hour was late, Pinkerton took a carriage to the Spruce Street residence of his friend Colonel Thomas Scott, vice president of the Pennsylvania Railroad.[46] But Scott was not home; he was already in Harrisburg. Undaunted, Pinkerton then took a carriage to Chestnut Street, where he hoped to find George C. "Charles" Franciscus, division superintendent of the Pennsylvania Railroad. But Franciscus had gone to the Continental Hotel, the place from which Pinkerton had just come. Back to the Continental went Pinkerton. But Franciscus was not at the Continental Hotel either; upon inquiry, Pinkerton learned that Franciscus had left the hotel and gone home just before Pinkerton's arrival. It was now midnight, and Pinkerton had just blown a full hour tracking Scott and Franciscus.[47] He must have felt like he was chasing his tail. He persisted nonetheless.

In later years, the logo that advertised Allan Pinkerton's National Detective Agency depicted a single, attractive, wide-open eye that bore the motto "We Never Sleep."[48] In Allan Pinkerton's case, the motto was almost literally true. The man was tireless and reportedly slept no more than a few hours a night.

Just after midnight on February 22, Pinkerton once again set out in search of G. C. Franciscus of the Pennsylvania Railroad. Before leaving the Continental, Pinkerton had called on Judd, asking him to remain until he returned.[49]

When he arrived at Franciscus's house on Chestnut Street for the second time, Pinkerton was again informed that Franciscus was not at home. He likely had never come home after leaving the Continental Hotel. Rather, he had sent word to his family that he had gone to his office in West Philadelphia. Pinkerton took a twenty-block carriage ride to Franciscus's office at 3300 Market Street.[50] He must have sighed with relief when he arrived.[51] Franciscus was there. In all likelihood, he was making last-minute preparations for his railroad's turn to carry Lincoln; the trip to Harrisburg was but a few hours away.

Pinkerton knew Franciscus to be "a true and loyal man" and therefore had no qualms about telling him what he needed.[52] At Pinkerton's request, Franciscus accompanied Pinkerton back to Judd's room at the Continental

The Continental Hotel, Philadelphia, where Lincoln stayed during his visit to the city. It is reported that Democratic political operative and future member of the Confederacy's "Canadian Cabinet," George N. Sanders, was also staying here at the same time. (*Library of Congress*)

Hotel. While in the carriage on their way, Pinkerton told Franciscus what he needed and why: there was in Baltimore a plot to murder Lincoln if he followed his published program; Pinkerton needed a special train to bring Mr. Lincoln from Harrisburg, around dusk, to Philadelphia that evening, in time to take the 11:00 p.m. train to Baltimore.[53] Franciscus advised Pinkerton that this request presented a practical, but not insurmountable, problem.

The Pennsylvania Railroad already had three special trains scheduled to be on the road that evening, carrying citizens and soldiers. But Franciscus assured Pinkerton that, if necessary, a special train for Lincoln could be arranged.[54] Lincoln's special train could be the last to leave Harrisburg. The other special trains from Harrisburg to Philadelphia could be sidetracked along the way and delayed to arrive in Philadelphia after Lincoln's had continued on its journey south.[55]

When Pinkerton and Franciscus got to Judd's room in the Continental, Henry Sanford was also there. The four men, Pinkerton, Judd, Franciscus, and Sanford, huddled in Judd's room, "where every supposed possible contingency was discussed and rediscussed," until around 4:30 a.m.[56] At last, they had devised a brilliant, if extremely complex plan. To work, their stratagem would need to be carefully constructed and perfectly implemented; the plan had more moving parts than a William Mason wood-burning locomotive, and was no less elegant.[57]

The basic elements of the arrangement were these: The president-elect would fulfill his scheduled programs in Philadelphia and Harrisburg for Friday, February 22. After the reception at Harrisburg that evening, and preferably as soon after dark as possible, around 6:00 p.m.,[58] a special train, waiting about a half mile from the Harrisburg depot, comprising a baggage car and one passenger car, would carry Lincoln back to Philadelphia. The special train from Harrisburg would be under the control of G. C. Franciscus and Enoch Lewis, general superintendent of the Pennsylvania Railroad.[59] All other traffic on the track between Harrisburg and Philadelphia would be cleared or sidetracked from 5:30 p.m. until Lincoln's special train had passed, bringing the president-elect to the Pennsylvania Railroad's West Philadelphia depot at Thirty-second and Market Streets by about 10:30 p.m.[60] There, Pinkerton would be waiting with a carriage to take Lincoln to the depot of the Philadelphia, Wilmington, and Baltimore Railroad at Broad Street and Prime (now Washington Avenue). Felton would detain, if necessary, his railroad's eleven o'clock train bound for Baltimore until Lincoln's arrival. Kate Warne would, by then, have obtained berths on the train's sleeping car, and Lincoln, represented as an invalid, would be ushered aboard. Henry Sanford, meanwhile, would ensure that no telegraphic messages could pass from Harrisburg to Baltimore or anywhere else from six o'clock that evening until Lincoln's safe arrival in Washington was verified. Only the Pennsylvania Railroad's lines from Harrisburg would remain open to permit safe running of the trains.[61]

Although the basic elements are easily reported, they had been crafted with careful planning and attention to detail. Judd reported, "I was up nearly all night, getting these arrangements made, which none of our party as yet knew about, although they saw that something was *up*."[62]

CHAPTER THIRTEEN

PINKERTON'S PLAN

Friday morning, February 22, 1861
Philadelphia–Harrisburg

ONE OF THE REASONS LINCOLN HAD REFUSED TO LEAVE for Washington City the previous night was that he had promised to raise a flag at Independence Hall this morning to commemorate Washington's Birthday. Noted one reporter, "At the rising of the sun, crowds of people streamed from all parts of the city towards the State House, and very soon every inch of ground was occupied, a vast number of ladies being present."[1] Embedded *New York Times* reporter Joseph Howard Jr. described the throng of humanity braving the cold for a chance to see Lincoln:

> Gathered around the Independence Hall were, at the least calculation, thirty thousand people. They had come, many of them, from a distance. Hard-fisted farmers, whose votes helped swell the tide which swept, irresistibly, the Republican Party into power; greasy mechanics, sneered at by snobbish South Carolina, but recognized by their fellow freemen as the very foundation of the temple of Liberty; milkmen from their rounds; young clerks, dry goods and otherwise, on their way from lonely bedrooms to dreary stores and shops; students with badge and pipe; Quakers with broad brims and knowing eyes; old men unshaven, but happy; thousands of intelligent, thinking, voting, middle-aged men, and other thousands of that peculiar look found only in cities—a knowing, cunning look—had taken the trouble to rise at an unusual hour of the day, on a cold, bleak, but bracing morning, that they might witness the performance of a deed, the solemn beauty of which cannot be well overestimated.[2]

In a dramatic scene, Abraham Lincoln arrived amid this cross section of America in a carriage drawn by four white horses, escorted by Scott's legion resplendent in their uniforms punctuated by white Sam Bowie belts and white gun slings, bearing the tattered flag they had carried victoriously in Mexico twelve years earlier.[3] Little Tad Lincoln rode with his daddy in the carriage.

A massive wooden platform, nearly six feet off the ground, sufficient to hold dozens of standing dignitaries, had been erected in front of Independence Hall.[4] Lincoln left the carriage at the door to the Hall and, with his head uncovered, went inside, "his face betraying the emotion with which he stood in that historic room."[5]

Once inside, Lincoln received a warm welcome from Theodore Cuyler,[6] a prominent Philadelphia lawyer and president of the Select Council. He was the same man who, just two months before, had spoken at the "Grand Union" rally on a stand also erected at Independence Hall. During that speech, which was either heard or later read by John Wilkes Booth, Cuyler expressed his view that the Constitution was a pledge, a bargain the thirteen original states had struck in order to obtain the "inestimable benefits of good government," in exchange for compromise and concession—code words for turning a blind eye to the institution of slavery. He urged Philadelphians to honor that pledge, to make concessions with the South, and faulted "fanaticism" and "misguided philanthropy"—code words for abolitionism—for the present crisis.[7]

Now, two months later, Cuyler reminded Lincoln, almost patronizingly, that here the Declaration of Independence was signed, and not far away the Constitution was framed. The legacy of the Founding Fathers, whose portraits gazed down upon them now, "is worthy to be preserved by every *concession* short of eternal principle itself."[8]

Cloaked in patriotic rhetoric, Cuyler had used the term "concession." This code word for compromising on the slavery question must not have been lost on Lincoln. "In a low tone, hardly audible,"[9] Lincoln responded to Cuyler:

> Mr. Cuyler:—I am filled with deep emotion at finding myself standing here in the place where were collected together the wisdom, the patriotism, the devotion to principle, from which sprang the institutions under which we live. You have kindly suggested to me that in my hands is the task of restoring peace to our distracted country. I can say in return, sir, that all the political sentiments I entertain have been drawn, so far as I have been able to draw them, from the sentiments which originated, and were given to the world from this hall in which we stand. I have never had a feeling politically that did not spring from the sentiments embodied in the Declaration of Independence. (Great cheering.) I have often pondered over the dangers which were

incurred by the men who assembled here and adopted that
Declaration of Independence—I have pondered over the toils
that were endured by the officers and soldiers of the army, who
achieved that Independence. (Applause.) I have often inquired of
myself, what great principle or idea it was that kept this
Confederacy so long together. It was not the mere matter of the
separation of the colonies from the mother land; but something
in that Declaration giving liberty, not alone to the people of this
country, but hope to the world for all future time. (Great
applause.) It was that which gave promise that in due time the
weights should be lifted from the shoulders of all men, and that
all should have an equal chance. (Cheers.) This is the sentiment
embodied in that Declaration of Independence.[10]

Lincoln's stirring retort to Cuyler carried its own coded message. The
Declaration of Independence held "that *all* should have an equal chance." In
emphasizing the word "all," Lincoln's interpretation of what it meant to be
created equal, as had the Declaration itself, drew no distinctions and made no
exceptions, whether for race, religion, age, or perhaps, "in due time," even for
gender.

"Now, my friends," Lincoln closed,

can this country be saved upon that basis? If it can, I will consider myself one of the happiest men in the world if I can help to
save it. If it can't be saved upon that principle, it will be truly
awful. *But, if this country cannot be saved without giving up that principle—I was about to say I would rather be assassinated on this spot
than surrender it.*—(Applause.)

Now, in my view of the present aspect of affairs, there is no
need of bloodshed and war. There is no necessity for it. I am not
in favor of such a course, and I may say in advance, there will be
no blood shed unless it be forced upon the Government. The
Government will not use force unless force is used against it.
(Prolonged applause and cries of "That's the proper sentiment.")

My friends, this is wholly an unprepared speech. I did not
expect to be called upon to say a word when I came here—I supposed I was merely to do something towards raising a flag. I may,
therefore, have said something indiscreet. [Cries of "No, no."] *I
have said nothing but what I am willing to live by, and, in the pleasure of Almighty God, die by.*[11]

It had been announced that Lincoln would raise the flag at sunrise.[12]
Assuming punctuality, at around quarter to seven, the party moved outside to

the wooden platform erected in front of Independence Hall for the ceremony. "On Mr. Lincoln's appearance on the platform he was hailed with outbursts of applause from the surrounding multitude."[13] Many in the crowd held their own flags or wore them in breast pockets. Ever since South Carolina had torn down Old Glory in December, replacing her with the sickle moon and palmetto tree, people in the North displayed the American flag in the manner of a home crowd showing its colors at a packed stadium. "The flag began to appear at every window, in every buttonhole."[14]

Before Lincoln raised the new, thirty-four-star flag, now including a star for Kansas, admitted into the Union on January 29, 1861, the president-elect gave a brief speech, alluding to the original flag and its thirteen stars, which had multiplied, as the nation had multiplied, in people and prosperity.[15] "The future," he said, amid cheers and great applause, "is in the hands of the people. It is on such an occasion as this that we can reason together, reaffirm our devotion to the country and the principles of the Declaration of Independence. Let us make up our mind, that when we do put a new star upon our banner, it shall be a fixed one, never to be dimmed by the horrors of war, but brightened by the contentment and prosperity of peace. Let us go on to extend the area of our usefulness, add star upon star, until their light shall shine upon five hundred millions of a free and happy people."[16]

As the Reverend Dr. Henry Steele Clark gave a brief prayer, many, including Lincoln, uncovered their heads. The only known surviving photographs of Lincoln during his journey to Washington were taken at this moment; a blurry Lincoln appears bareheaded, holding his stovepipe hat in his hands, while Clark says the prayer. Little Tad Lincoln, who had not doffed his hat, is seen resting his arm on the platform, watching Scott's legion below.[17]

Everyone left the platform except for Lincoln and a few dignitaries. The flag, which had been folded "man-o-war style," was readied. A signal gun fired, breaking the silence of the solemn gathering. "Mr. Lincoln then threw off his overcoat in an offhand, easy manner, the backwoodian style of which caused many good-natured remarks."[18] Lincoln, his expression "serene and confident," grasped the halyards, extended his long arms, and "hand over hand," raised the new flag over Independence Hall. As it rose, the flag gradually unfolded itself.[19] "A stiff breeze caught the folded bunting and threw it out boldly to the winds."[20] The crowd roared its approval as a band struck up "The Star-Spangled Banner." A cannon boomed, signaling that the ceremony was over.[21]

ALLAN PINKERTON had no time to watch flag-raising ceremonies. Early that morning, even before Lincoln's carriage had rolled up to Independence Hall, Pinkerton drove to the St. Louis Hotel. It was still early, and in the predawn

The only known photographs of Abraham Lincoln during his journey to Washington were taken in Philadelphia at the flag raising ceremony at Independence Hall on Washington's Birthday, February 22, 1861. Lincoln is standing bare-headed, hat in hand, in the center of the photograph. His son, Tad, standing above the last star on the right, is looking down at Scott's legion in their white Sam Bowie belts. (*Free Library of Philadelphia*)

gloaming Pinkerton observed the rapidly assembling horde of Philadelphians, eager to witness the president-elect raise the flag at sunrise. Pinkerton washed, changed his clothes, and at 6:00 a.m., while Lincoln was arriving at Independence Hall, went to meet George R. Dunn, of Newark, New Jersey,[22] on Chestnut Street near Third.[23] Dunn was an agent for Harnden's Express Company. Pinkerton had a vital, secret mission for him. Pinkerton wanted Dunn to go to Baltimore on the 8:00 a.m. train and see operative Harry W. Davies (alias "A.F.C." in the Pinkerton reports) and retrieve the dispatches that his agents had prepared since Pinkerton had left Baltimore. These reports probably included Davies' February 19 documentation of Otis K. Hillard's important statement that members of his National Volunteers organization "have taken a solemn oath. . . . to prevent the passage of Lincoln with the troops through Baltimore"[24] and Charles D. C. Williams's February 20 report that identified William Byrne as the president of the National Volunteers and most likely the plotters' "Captain."[25]

Pinkerton gave Dunn a key to his 44 South Street stockbroker's office in Baltimore and a letter to Davies introducing Dunn as "fully reliable." The letter instructed Davies to send the written reports and any oral reports he might deem necessary for Pinkerton back with Dunn, who was to return to Philadelphia on the 5:15 p.m. train. Once back in Philadelphia, Dunn was to meet "Mrs. Cherry" (another alias for Kate Warne) in the ladies' room at the Philadelphia, Wilmington, and Baltimore depot.[26] There, Dunn was to give Warne all the reports, written and oral, obtained in Baltimore and to watch for Pinkerton, who would arrive a few minutes after the scheduled departure time of the trains.

Pinkerton had one more task for Dunn—arguably one of the most critical to his plan's success. At the Philadelphia depot, Dunn was to procure for Warne tickets for the most important anonymous passenger any sleeper car would ever carry—Abraham Lincoln.[27]

At 8:10 a.m. Pinkerton went to Judd's room at the Continental Hotel. Pinkerton needed to see Judd before the presidential cortege left for Harrisburg, to ensure that Lincoln would follow the plan, in which case Pinkerton would complete the arrangements. But Judd was not in his room.[28]

Judd was at that moment likely meeting with Lincoln. Judd later recalled that around eight o'clock that morning, Lincoln had sent for him to come to his room, where he found Frederick W. Seward with the president-elect. "Mr. Lincoln said to me that Mr. Seward had been sent from Washington by his father to warn him of danger in passing through Baltimore, and to urge him to come directly to Washington."[29] That Senator William H. Seward had, from an entirely independent source, arrived at the same conclusions as Pinkerton reinforced Judd's views of the necessity for carrying out Pinkerton's plan. "I told Mr. Seward," Judd recalled, "that he could say to his father that all had been arranged, and that so far as human foresight could predict, Mr. Lincoln would be in Washington at six a.m. the next day, that he understood the absolute necessity for secrecy in the matter."[30]

Finding Judd's room at the Continental empty, Pinkerton sent Lamon to locate him. A few moments later, Judd came into the room. He confirmed that Pinkerton's plan was satisfactory, that he should complete the arrangements as planned, and that he could count on meeting Mr. Lincoln later that evening at the West Philadelphia depot. Judd told Pinkerton that he had thought the matter over and had concluded that despite the calamity that Lincoln's evasive maneuver would cause throughout the country, it was the only feasible course; Judd would take full responsibility for it. Pinkerton reassured Judd, telling him that he fully believed his recommended course "was the only one to save the country from Bloodshed at the present time."[31] There is no indication that Judd advised Pinkerton of Senator Seward's independently obtained information.

At some point that morning, Ward Hill Lamon also caught up with Fred Seward. Recalled Seward, "Shortly after breakfast Colonel Lamon met me in the hall, and, taking me aside, said that Mr. Lincoln had concluded to do as he had been advised. He would change his plan so as to pass through Baltimore at a different hour than that announced."[32]

Despite the interchange between Judd and Seward, between Judd and Pinkerton, and between Seward and Lamon, the suggestion that Lincoln had decided to follow a plan to pass through Baltimore at a different time than that published was premature and possibly incorrect. Neither Judd, nor Pinkerton, nor Seward record that Lincoln actually approved the plan this morning. Indeed, the previous night, Lincoln had indicated that if a Baltimore delegation was in Harrisburg to greet him, he would feel safe and go on to Baltimore with them according to the published program. In fact, unbeknownst to Pinkerton, Judd, Seward, or even Lincoln, a Baltimore delegation was, at that very moment, finalizing plans to meet up with Lincoln later this day in Harrisburg.

FOLLOWING Pinkerton's orders, George H. Burns, confidential agent of E. S. Sanford, president of the American Telegraph Company, began to set in motion the vital task of jamming telegraphic communications to Baltimore. At the American Telegraph Company's Philadelphia offices, located at 105 South Third Street,[33] W. P. Westervelt, superintendent of that office, introduced Burns to H. E. Thayer, the office's manager. The importance of Burns's task, and the level of trust he placed in those charged with carrying it out, cannot be overstated. There were in 1861 no telephones, no Internet, no e-mail, and regular mail was slow. Those who controlled the telegraph lines and the offices from which dispatches were sent and received therefore controlled rapid communications—period. Pinkerton had preached secrecy and involving as few others as possible, and even then on a strict need-to-know basis. But it was now necessary to bring several men at the American Telegraph office in Philadelphia under Pinkerton's tent. It is possible, if not likely, that one or more of these men had not voted for Lincoln and were not particularly happy with his having been elected. Worse, if even one of them was a closet secessionist (not an unlikely possibility), he might derail all of Pinkerton's careful planning, secretly telegraphing news of Lincoln's altered route to a fellow secessionist in Baltimore, news that could be quickly passed into the hands of the conspirators.

In what must have felt like a blind leap of faith, Burns advised H. E. Thayer, a man whom he had never met, of the suspected Baltimore Plot, of the plan to thwart it by sending Mr. Lincoln on a special train that night from Harrisburg, and of the need to prevent telegraphic news of the president-elect's early departure from reaching Baltimore. Thayer was told of the need to cut the telegraph wires from Harrisburg to Baltimore. Thayer, as office manager, was not the man to climb telegraph poles. Burns wanted to know if Thayer had "a trusty man" to do the job. Thayer replied that he did. The man was Andrew Wynne, his lineman.[34]

There was, however, one minor problem with this plan. The telegraph office in Harrisburg did not belong to the American Telegraph Company. It belonged to a rival company, owned and operated by the Northern Central Railroad.[35] Unless employees of that company were also to be brought into Pinkerton's plan, its lines would need to be cut by Andrew Wynne. But Mr. Wynne was a trustworthy man; he could not be expected to sabotage private property, another company's lines, without adequate justification.

Thayer sent orders to Wynne, instructing him to stand by for important duty to be performed within the hour. Thayer asked Wynne if he had any objections with fixing the lines of another company to prevent communications from passing over them. According to Wynne, "I answered that I would not in some cases." Thayer then let Wynne in on the secret. Mr. Lincoln's life was in great danger. Thayer needed a reliable man to cut the wires between Harrisburg and Baltimore. Under these circumstances, would Wynne consent to fix the wires? "I replied," Wynn recalled, "under that circumstance I would."[36] Thayer ordered Wynne to take the next train for Harrisburg with W. P. Westervelt. This was likely the noon train.[37]

Thayer had yet another important task. The telegraph lines into and out of Philadelphia would *not* be cut. Pinkerton had wanted someone to "mind the store," to remain in the telegraph company's operating room in Philadelphia and watch for any important dispatches coming or going from there. Thayer promised Burns that he would remain on duty throughout the night, until Mr. Lincoln arrived safely in Washington. He would ensure that no messages passed from Harrisburg to Baltimore through Philadelphia. Just as important, he would receive and deliver to the St. Louis Hotel any dispatches that might come for "J. H. Hutchinson."[38] At this point, Thayer had no clue that J. H. Hutchinson was Pinkerton's alias—Thayer had not been fully ushered into Camp Pinkerton.[39]

Thus, on Pinkerton's orders, George H. Burns placed in the hands of two men he did not know, H. E. Thayer and Andrew Wynne, the critical tasks of disabling communications from Harrisburg, of preventing dispatches from getting to Baltimore by way of Philadelphia, and of reporting to Pinkerton any messages that might come to Philadelphia addressed to J. H. Hutchinson.

Aτ around 8:30 a.m., Lincoln, seated in an open carriage drawn by "four noble greys"[40] and enveloped by mounted police, left the Continental Hotel, still thronged with people, for the Pennsylvania Railroad's West Philadelphia depot at Thirty-second and Market Streets. The carriage, which also carried Colonel Sumner, Judd, and Philadelphia Common Councilman William P. Hacker, retraced the route Pinkerton had most likely taken the night before, heading west on Walnut and then north on Twenty-third Street to Market.[41]

Philadelphia had apparently learned an important lesson on crowd control following the complete breakdown of order at the Continental Hotel the night before, in which a rude and vulgar crowd jammed every conceivable space and corridor, making ingress and egress from the hotel as painful and dangerous as attempting to walk among a herd of cattle crushing and stomping through a narrow pass. But this morning, thanks to the Philadelphia police, there was order, and despite the crowds gathered along the carriage route and at the depot, the police ensured ample space for the presidential suite to pass comfortably onto the train.[42]

Mr. Lincoln's family accompanied him and entered what the press dubbed "The Prince of Wales' car."[43] Lincoln was introduced to the train's engineer, Philadelphian Edward R. Black, with whom he exchanged pleasantries and a hand shake, before handing Black a cigar as he boarded the train. "Could I only have foreseen what was to occur in the next few years," wrote Black almost forty years later, "I think that cigar, instead of being smoked, would have been kept as a precious and hallowed remembrance."[44] Engineer Black did not know it yet, but he would, that very night, be called upon to make the most important and daring run of his career.

At 9:30 a.m., as Lincoln stood on the rear platform of the last car and bowed, a salute was fired, the crowd cheered, and the Lincoln Special headed on to Harrisburg, pulled by the Pennsylvania Railroad's smartly decorated, flag and evergreen festooned, coal-burning locomotive number 161, recently completed at the company's Altoona works.[45] In addition to the luggage car, which carried refreshments for the passengers, the locomotive pulled one ordinary coach, number 29, into which the insufferable committeemen had been sequestered, and one special coach, number 160, that was divided into compartments offering a welcome measure of solitude for Lincoln, his family, and friends.[46]

The Lincoln Special, pulled by its new smokeless, sparkless engine, traversed the westerly route from Philadelphia to Harrisburg, traveling roughly parallel to the section of U.S. Route 30 now known as the "Lincoln Highway."[47] Rolling into small towns like Downingtown and Coatesville and Parkesburg and Leaman Place,[48] the Special intermittently cut through fertile fields of black loam, some perhaps already bristling with the neat, emerald green rows of winter wheat, bowing in the wind.

Security precautions for the Special belied the quaint towns and the serenity of the rolling countryside through which it passed. Flagmen stood watch at one-mile intervals along the route. Spare locomotives waited in reserve, one at Parkesburg and another in Lancaster.[49] A telegraph operator, perhaps one of George Burns's men from the American Telegraph Company, was on board, ready "with apparatus to make a connection with wires in case of accident."[50] There is evidence that both Burns and a pole climber were expected aboard the Lincoln Special.[51] Several other men who were aware of the plot and the plan to avoid it also rode the train with Lincoln from Philadelphia to Harrisburg, including Enoch Lewis, general superintendent of the Pennsylvania Railroad, and G. C. Franciscus, its division superintendent.[52]

Abraham Lincoln, however, did not look out the window at the rolling farmland as the train sped west. He was tired, exhausted in fact, having gone to bed late and endured a fitful night's rest made even more uncomfortable by the noisy crowd jammed into the Continental Hotel, and he had risen early to raise the flag at Independence Hall. The rigors of the long train ride from Springfield, combined with the overwhelming demands of the crowds, his family, his friends, and now, apparently, his would-be assassins, pressed down upon him without letup. Lincoln consulted William Wood's relentless timetable and saw a gap. A single, solitary, wonderful hour-long gap between the Lincoln Special's screeching, jaw-rattling, bone-jarring starts and stops. Lincoln used the time wisely. He took a nap.

As soon as he could get a moment with Lincoln, Norman B. Judd held a private audience in which he detailed the complex plan to smuggle the president-elect into Washington. Others in the presidential party had become curious, if not suspicious, of Judd's private meetings with Lincoln, of which there had been at least three during the previous twelve hours—one late the night before in Judd's room at the Continental Hotel, one this morning, around eight o'clock, at the hotel before the party left, and now this private discussion on the train en route to Harrisburg. Judd believed that Lamon, Nicolay, and Ellsworth all knew something was up, but thus far had remained discreet, asking no questions. But Judd strained under the weight of maintaining closely guarded secrets; he alone in the presidential party had known of the plot and of Pinkerton's movements; indeed, he had known for nearly two weeks. It was time for others in Lincoln's party to know, people close to him. Judd suggested to Lincoln that the gentlemen of his party, those who had ridden with him from Springfield, who had known him and befriended him and supported him and protected him, not only deserved an explanation; prudence dictated that they be advised and consulted on a matter of such vital importance. Perhaps Judd, who had earlier volunteered to bear all the consequences for the planned move, now wanted others to share in that responsibility. Lincoln consented. It was therefore arranged that after the reception at the State House in Harrisburg, and before dinner at the Jones House, the entire matter—the suspected plot and the plan to thwart it—would be laid before Lincoln's inner circle. "I reckon they will laugh at us, Judd," Lincoln lamented, "but you had better get them together."[53]

The matter now decided, Judd changed his seat on the train. John G. Nicolay joined him and asked, "Judd, there is something *up,* what is it, if it is proper that I should know?"

"Geo[rge]," Judd replied, "there is no necessity for your knowing [and] one man can keep a matter better than two."[54]

But several others on the train were already in on the secret. Lamon seemed to be, based on Seward's account. And Franciscus was as well. As Franciscus recalled, "after we had left West Philadelphia, with Mr. Lincoln and party, Mr. Judd said to me: 'Mr. Frederick Seward arrived from Washington, bringing a note from his father and Gen. Scott, the contents of which have decided Mr. Lincoln, and the trip will be made as arranged by Mr. Pinkerton last night.'"[55]

It now seemed that Lincoln had made up his mind to travel through Baltimore rather than risk stopping. But if he had, it was without consulting most of the members of his suite, including stalwart military advisors and an excitable wife. If indeed Lincoln had made up his mind, at least some of these people might try to change it.

THE LINCOLN SPECIAL continued on its four-hour journey to Harrisburg. The *New York Times* correspondent on board, Joseph Howard Jr., summed up the trip from Philadelphia to Harrisburg this way: "I shall not weary you with a description of our journey hither. Short-hand would express it thus: — crowds—enthusiasm—little speech—little bow—kissed little girl—God-blessed old man—recognized old friend—much affected."[56]

All along the way, and especially at Lancaster, the embedded and anonymous *New York World's* special correspondent found the crowds to be more curious than enthusiastic. "Even at Harrisburg," he wrote later that day, "not one man in a hundred cheered."[57]

Small wonder. This was Buchanan territory; Lancaster was the hometown of the lame-duck president. Ensconced in Washington, Buchanan was doing his best to keep the seat of the presidential chair warm, but little to shelter the country from the coming storm. A Democrat, he had been excoriated in the Northern press. Lincoln, the Republican, was advertised as the anti-Buchanan. It was only natural that the Lancaster citizenry might take a dim view of Lincoln, the man destined to supplant their native son. And yet, when Mr. Lincoln's train chuffed into Lancaster, an "immense crowd" greeted the president-elect. A thirty-four-gun salute, one for each of the nation's states, fired from the town's locomotive works. The Lincoln Special stopped in front of the Cadwell House. Despite being "so unwell he could hardly be persuaded to show himself,"[58] Mr. Lincoln climbed the stairs to the house's balcony and from that vantage good-humoredly addressed the Lancaster throng that, hungry for a speech, had spilled onto East Chestnut Street below him:[59]

> Ladies and gentlemen of old Lancaster: I appear not to make a speech. I have not time to make a speech at length, and not strength to make them on every occasion, and worse than all I have none to make. I come before you to see and be seen, and as regards the ladies I have the best of the bargain, but as to the gentlemen, I cannot say as much. There is plenty of matter to speak about in these times, but it is well known that the more a man speaks the less he is understood,—the more he says one thing his adversaries contend he meant something else. I shall soon have occasion to speak officially, and then I will endeavor to put my thoughts just as plain as I can express myself,—true to the Constitution and Union of all the States, and to the perpetual liberty of all the people. Until I so speak, there is no need to enter upon details. In conclusion, I greet you most heartily, and bid you an affectionate farewell.[60]

WHILE the Lincoln Special ran west toward Harrisburg, Allan Pinkerton remained in Philadelphia. After his meeting with Judd, Pinkerton headed on to the La Pierre House to provide his employer, the railroad's president S. M. Felton, a full report of the detailed arrangements made the previous evening. Pinkerton had planned to meet Felton the previous night, but circumstances had made that impossible.

In some ways, Pinkerton must have felt relieved to be temporarily rid of Lincoln and his party for a few hours, to be free of the self-important military men and the nosy reporters and the dozens of other political and social moths determined to encircle the great Republican flame. In other ways, however, Pinkerton must have agonized that the main object of his detective efforts, Lincoln, was well beyond the gravitational pull of his protective forces.

Even worse, Lincoln was now about to be passed along a three-railroad, 250-mile, night-run relay. The first leg, run by the Pennsylvania Railroad, would carry Lincoln the 110 miles from Harrisburg back to Philadelphia. The second leg, served by the Philadelphia, Wilmington, and Baltimore Railroad, would run him the 103 miles from Philadelphia to Baltimore. The final leg, at 40 miles, was the shortest, but in many ways also the most critical—the Baltimore and Ohio Railroad would take the president-elect from one potentially hostile environment—Baltimore—to another—the City of Washington—through a part of Maryland reportedly brimming with secessionists intent on throwing trains from tracks, burning bridges, and seizing Washington. To a certain extent, Felton had been able to protect his own road, the section between Philadelphia and Baltimore, from such plots; he had no control, however, over the 40-mile stretch of track joining Baltimore to Washington.

While Felton felt more confident with the Pennsylvania Railroad, he had reasons to be wary of the B&O. It was well known that John Work Garrett, president of the B&O Railroad, had, the previous winter, declared his railroad to be a "Southern line" and asked rhetorically was it not right that "Baltimore should declare her position in 'the irrepressible conflict' threatened and urged by Northern fanaticism."[61] By 1861, however, Garrett had mellowed some-what in his views. Garrett's road had been losing business, as rail shippers from the West believed sending goods through Maryland and Baltimore presented too great a risk. By February 1, 1861, Garrett's business had fallen off so badly that he took bold measures, declaring the B&O safe from any "warlike dan-gers," and guaranteeing that his road would indemnify shippers against all losses incurred, whether from "political or military causes."[62] For John Work Garrett, the idealistic pull of patriotism had yielded to the more practical pull of the purse.

Notwithstanding Garrett's guarantees made three weeks earlier, Felton did not believe it would be safe to trust the B&O with Lincoln's secret travel plans for this evening.[63] And if Felton couldn't trust the superintendent of the B&O Railroad, how then could he entrust any of its employees? No, this Hobson's choice, between forcing Lincoln to stay over in Baltimore should the connec-tion with the B&O train be missed, and bringing the B&O Railroad into the plan, needed to be avoided at all cost. It was up to the Pennsylvania Railroad to get Lincoln from Harrisburg to Philadelphia in time for the night train to Baltimore to meet the scheduled B&O connection to Washington. Franciscus had to give his assurance that his train would not be late. But first, Pinkerton needed to find Franciscus.

Franciscus had, unbeknownst to Pinkerton, boarded the Lincoln Special, now on its way to Harrisburg. Alternative planning was now necessary. Pinkerton went to Felton's office and had a "very long interview" with him concerning the situation.[64] The men needed to devise a plan to delay the train of the B&O Railroad until the arrival of Felton's train from Philadelphia, in the event that Franciscus's Pennsylvania Railroad failed to get Lincoln to Philadelphia on time, or Felton's Philadelphia, Wilmington, and Baltimore Railroad failed to bring him to Baltimore on time.

Felton had an idea. He could send for William Stearns, master machinist of his railroad, and his brother George Stearns. These men could be trusted completely. Indeed, in January, George Stearns had been the first person to inform Felton of intelligence alleging designs of three-hundred persons from in and around Baltimore intent on burning the railroad's Back River Bridge, halting the Lincoln Special at a point between that bridge and Stemmer's Run, and putting Lincoln out of the way.[65] This intelligence had induced Felton to organize an armed force of about two hundred men, who were regularly trained by drillmasters, to guard his road.[66]

Now, Felton believed that William Stearns could be sent to Baltimore to see the superintendent of the B&O and ask that he hold his night train for Washington. Stearns could claim that his train from Philadelphia was carrying important government dispatches for delivery in the nation's capital. But if the B&O Railroad superintendent could not be trusted with the facts concerning Mr. Lincoln's passage on his train this evening, why could he be entrusted with secretly delivering "important" government—Union—dispatches to Washington on that very same train? Pinkerton and Felton perceived this risk, however, and they determined how to manage it. George Stearns would wait in Wilmington, Delaware, some 30 miles down the line from Philadelphia, for Lincoln's train to pass through. If it was behind time, George Stearns would telegraph his brother William, waiting in Baltimore, as "it was deemed unsafe to do so from Philadelphia."[67] Only if the train was running late by the time it reached Wilmington would William Stearns notify the B&O superintendent of the "important government dispatches" and the need to delay the train on the B&O's Washington branch. If, however, the train reached Wilmington on schedule, then "nothing need be said to the Superintendent of the Baltimore and Ohio Rail Road."[68] The decision was made to dispatch William Stearns to Baltimore that afternoon.

DESPITE receiving no reply to their invitation, the Republican Committee of Baltimore, led by Worthington G. Snethen, decided to meet Lincoln in Harrisburg on February 22, and accompany him back to their city. Snethen claimed that the previous night, Thursday, the Baltimore Republicans had determined that the Baltimore City Council would not make any effort to welcome the president-elect. Baltimore's mayor, George William Brown, had previously advised the Baltimore Republican Committee that he did not believe the City Council would take any action, but that he, Mayor Brown, would be present in his official capacity to receive Mr. Lincoln at the depot and to accompany him personally, in a private two-seat carriage. The Republican Committee also decided to take no part in conveying Lincoln through the streets of Baltimore—that would only add fuel to the fires of hatred already smoldering there. Unlike all of the other major cities and many of the smaller ones that the Lincoln Special had visited during the past eleven days, there would be no formal procession whatever for Mr. Lincoln in Baltimore.[69]

Whether Lincoln received Snethen's original invitation, we may never know, but it stands to reason that if Governor Morgan had gotten Snethen's invitation, he would have passed it on to Lincoln or someone in his party. As late as February 21, however, while they caucused at the Continental Hotel in Philadelphia, Lincoln confided in Pinkerton that he had not heard from "a single individual" in Baltimore regarding a welcoming reception from that city and further that Wood had not advised him of any such reception.[70] The fact that Lincoln never responded is evidence that he never saw the invitation.[71] But the letter resides in the Lincoln Papers at the Library of Congress with a handwritten annotation "Reception in Balt." faintly scrawled on the envelope—evidence that Lincoln's handlers received it.[72]

Even so, earlier this morning, Snethen had telegraphed William S. Wood, the Lincoln Special's superintendent, informing him of the Baltimore Republican's travel plans. They would leave Baltimore on the 6:00 p.m. train and arrive in Harrisburg later that evening. Snethen sent another telegram about an hour before leaving Baltimore. Mr. Wood received these telegrams.[73] But if Wood informed Lincoln, Judd, Lamon, Nicolay, Hay, or any of Lincoln's other advisors of these telegrams from Baltimore, they do not report it. It seems likely that Wood would have advised someone in Lincoln's party of the Baltimore Republican's travel plans. Apparently, someone was determined to keep this information from Lincoln. Assuming Lincoln did receive Snethen's original invitation, the fact that Lincoln's party never replied to it suggests that matters had gotten so hectic that Lincoln's arrangers dropped the ball and failed to reply, an oversight. Or, because the invitation also sought travel specifics, Lincoln's party may have deemed it more prudent to ignore the invitation and avoid the need to provide such details; in short, Lincoln's staff did not trust the Baltimore Republicans with such information.

As far as the Baltimore Republicans and everyone else knew, however, based on published accounts, Lincoln would be arriving in Harrisburg as scheduled.[74] Lincoln would visit the Pennsylvania legislature in Harrisburg on the afternoon of February 22, spend the night there, and then take a special train over the Northern Central Railroad to Baltimore, arriving Saturday, February 23, around one o'clock in the afternoon. Once in Baltimore, Lincoln and his party would dine at the Eutaw House and then proceed to Washington that same afternoon.[75] Relying on this published itinerary, Snethen and seven fellow Baltimore Republican Committeemen—Judge William L. Marshall, Chairman of the Committee of 100, Leopold Blumenberg, James E. Bishop, William E. Gleeson, William E. Beale, Judge Joseph M. Palmer, of Frederick City, and Francis S. Corkran—departed Baltimore's Calvert Street Station at 6:00 p.m. on the Northern Central, bound for Harrisburg.[76] They would be joined on their arrival in Harrisburg by William Gunnison and William E. Coale.[77] One is left to wonder, given Lincoln's statement that if a delegation from Baltimore was waiting for him in Harrisburg he would feel safe and go on, how the course of history might have been changed if the Baltimore Republicans had left for Harrisburg a few hours earlier.

Like the Baltimore Republican Committee, the Northern Central Railroad also had every reason to believe that its line would be taking the president-elect to Washington from Harrisburg. By Friday, Colonel John Sterrett Gittings and James C. Clark, president and superintendent, respectively, of the Northern Central, were also in Harrisburg, preparing the special train for Lincoln's party. Clark brought with him several master mechanics from Baltimore machine shops. "On Friday night these men went to work and took the celebrated locomotive *John H. Done* apart, examined and tested every part of the machinery, and so far as mechanical skill could suggest, provided against the possibility of an accident."[78] So careful was the Northern Central in its planning that even after having taken *John H. Done* apart piece by piece, duplicate pieces were placed on board the train, along with all the hardware and tools necessary for making any possible repairs that might prove necessary for the locomotive.

But as the Lincoln Special rolled from Philadelphia toward Harrisburg, neither the Baltimore Republican Committeemen nor the Baltimore contingent of the Northern Central Railroad had any inkling of Lincoln's new travel plans. All of their careful preparation and planning would prove as pointless and deflating as lavish wedding arrangements made for an eager bride whose groom had already determined not to appear for the ceremony.

CHAPTER FOURTEEN

THE KOSSUTH HAT

Friday, February 22, 1861
Harrisburg

As the city of Harrisburg awaited Lincoln's arrival on the morning of February 22, a letter was being written and posted in Baltimore by an anonymous "lady" intent on warning Lincoln:

> Dear Sir
>
> I think it my duty to inform you that I was advised last night by a gentleman that there existed in Baltimore, a league of ten persons, who had sworn that you should never pass through that city alive—This may be but one of the thousand threats against you that have emanated from some paltry Southerners, but you should know it that your friends may be watchful while you are in the place as it was asserted positively to be the fact. God defend and bless you—The prayers of many go with you.
>
> A Lady.
>
> Friday Morning
> 11 1/2 A.M.[1]

The "league of ten persons" sounds eerily reminiscent of the "Fifteen or Twenty men" that Pinkerton had estimated were prepared to murder Lincoln.[2] Even the "lady's" language, describing plotters "who had sworn that [Lincoln] should never pass through [Baltimore] alive," closely tracks the intelligence gathered by Pinkerton.[3] Written as it possibly was the day before Lincoln's scheduled arrival in Baltimore, however, the writer must have known how unlikely it was that her posted, not telegraphed, warning would reach the president-elect in time.[4]

A swarm of soldiers met the Lincoln Special upon its arrival in Harrisburg at 1:30 p.m. To the anonymous *World* correspondent, there appeared to be as many men in uniform as those without. "The corps of Zouaves elicited special attention. Colonel Ellsworth was in his glory to-day," he wrote.[5]

There had been compelling reasons for Lincoln to travel four hours out of his way to visit Harrisburg, Pennsylvania. During the fall 1860 elections, it was believed that unless the Republican state ticket carried Pennsylvania in October, Lincoln would fail to be elected in November. Noted Alexander McClure, a Republican Pennsylvania politico, "Pennsylvania was thus accepted as the key to Republican success, and Lincoln naturally watched the struggle with intense interest."[6] So critical was Pennsylvania to Lincoln that the previous summer he had dispatched Judge Davis and Leonard Swett to the state to check on the Republican Party's organization there. The Republican ticket did carry Pennsylvania in October. Andrew G. Curtin was elected governor. And Lincoln was elected president. He was literally going out of his way this morning to say thanks.

Lincoln must have been impressed, perhaps inspired, by the patriotic display as his eyes scanned the crowd of War of 1812 veterans, soldiers, Zouaves, and more than fifty military companies and various clubs, including the Sons of Malta, Masons, firemen, and Odd Fellows. But if anyone in the crowd had taken the time to study Lincoln's face, they might well have found him searching, perhaps desperately so, for something more than a cheering throng.

Until now, Lincoln's itinerary had been dictated by "the invitation, arrangement, direction, and responsibility, of legislatures, governors of States, and municipal authorities of towns and cities."[7] Accordingly, at every overnight stopping point along the route thus far, the Lincoln Special had been greeted by a delegation from the next city or state on the route. But no invitation had come from Maryland, from its legislature, from Governor Hicks, from Baltimore's mayor, or from its municipal authorities by the time Lincoln reached Philadelphia.[8] Even so, Lincoln had held out an almost desperate hope of seeing here, in Harrisburg, a delegation from Baltimore or Maryland.[9]

It seems likely that citizens of Maryland and Baltimore were there, not to greet, but to watch. Baltimore was but a short, three-hour train ride from Harrisburg on the Northern Central's line. Maryland and the Mason-Dixon line were but 40 miles to the south. One newspaper reporter in Harrisburg this afternoon noted that "the city is crowded today with strangers."[10]

The president-elect proceeded to the Jones House in a carriage "drawn by six stately grey horses." The *World* reporter noted that, "Mr. Lincoln was so unwell he could hardly be persuaded to show himself."[11] Indeed, when the train had stopped at Leaman Place, Lincoln spoke only briefly to the crowd assembled there on plea of being too unwell to address them at any length.[12]

At the Jones House, Governor Curtin welcomed Lincoln on the portico, alluding to the challenges that lay ahead for him—of the need to restore peace, prosperity, and healing to a restless, anxious, festering country. Speaking from the hotel balcony to a reportedly unruly crowd of five thousand, Lincoln acknowledged Curtin's remarks and the "weight of great responsibility" that awaited him in Washington.[13] He questioned his own strength to bear that burden alone and prophetically called upon the strength of the Pennsylvania masses before him to insure his success. Most significantly, he expressed his hope that war might be avoided.

> While I have been proud to see to-day the finest military array, I think, that I have ever seen, allow me to say in regard to those men that they give hope of what may be done when war is inevitable. But, at the same time, allow me to express the hope that in the shedding of blood, their services may never be need-ed, especially in the shedding of fraternal blood. It shall be my endeavor to preserve the peace of this country so far as it can pos-sibly be done, consistently with the maintenance of the institu-tions of the country. With my consent, or without my great dis-pleasure, this country shall never witness the shedding of one drop of blood in fraternal strife. And now, my fellow-citizens, as I have made many speeches, will you allow me to bid you farewell?[14]

After greeting guests in his hotel suite, Lincoln was escorted three blocks north to the State Capitol, where at 2:30 p.m., the president–elect entered the hall filled with the combined Pennsylvania General Assembly. Here, Lincoln spoke for at least the sixth time today.[15]

By now Lincoln knew, thanks to the meetings the previous night with Pinkerton, Judd, and Frederick Seward, of the suspected plot to assassinate him. His private meeting with Judd on the train from Philadelphia this morn-ing had detailed the actions then underway by Pinkerton's men, by Felton's men, by E. S. Sanford's men, and others to thwart the plot in order that he might survive the trip through Baltimore.[16] Lincoln also knew by now that no delegation from Baltimore had met him in Harrisburg. What Lincoln seems not to have known is that a Baltimore delegation had, that very morning, telegraphed William S. Wood to inform him of their plans to arrive in Harrisburg later that night.

The speech Lincoln had just given at the Jones House and the one he was about to give to the Pennsylvania House of Representatives differed in tenor from that made in Trenton just the day before, in which he had indicated it might be necessary to "put the foot down firmly." Today, Lincoln presented arguably the most conciliatory, pacifistic sentiments of the trip. His speeches in Harrisburg seemed to signal to those who meant to harm him that he meant no harm to them. Echoing sentiments expressed at the Jones House, Lincoln closed out his brief remarks to the Pennsylvania legislature. These would be the last words Lincoln would speak publicly on this journey:

> It is not with any pleasure that I contemplate the possibility that a necessity may arise in this country for the use of the military arm. [Applause.] While I am exceedingly gratified to see the manifestation upon your streets of your military force here, and exceedingly gratified at your promise here to use that force upon a proper emergency, . . . I desire to repeat, in order to preclude any possible misconstruction, that I do most sincerely hope that we shall have no use for them—[loud applause]—that shed fraternal blood. I promise that, (in so far as I may have wisdom to direct,) if so painful a result shall in any wise be brought about, it shall be through no fault of mine. [Cheers.][17]

At about 3:00 p.m., after the reception at the Pennsylvania State House of Representatives, Lincoln and his party returned to the Jones House, "where the party . . . was fairly mobbed" by a crowd.[18] In the carriage on the way back to the hotel, Lincoln confided in Governor Curtin. A conspiracy had been discovered to assassinate him while on his way through Baltimore the next day. He informed Curtin matter-of-factly that he had been advised by his friends to go to Washington by way of Philadelphia, as privately as possible. Reported Curtin, "He seemed pained and surprised that a design to take his life existed, and although much concerned for his personal safety as well as for the peace of the country, he was very calm, and neither in his conversation or manner exhibited alarm or fear."[19]

But an unforeseen event at the Jones House would strike Lincoln with both alarm and fear. It was here at the Jones House that, by most accounts, young Robert Todd Lincoln had famously misplaced his father's only draft of the inaugural address, a masterpiece the president-elect had prayed over for weeks before leaving Springfield.[20] Only four precious copies of the speech had been printed on foolscap paper and kept in perfect secrecy. Although Lincoln reportedly kept notes and speeches tucked inside his stovepipe hat, the four printed copies of the inaugural speech had gotten special treatment—Lincoln stuffed them into his gripsack, "a little old-fashioned black oil-cloth carpetbag," which he carefully locked up.[21] He had entrusted the grip, which reportedly also contained "a large bundle of letters and other papers of indispensable utility,"[22] to Robert, who, like most seventeen-year-olds, likely had things on his mind other than heeding his father's instructions.

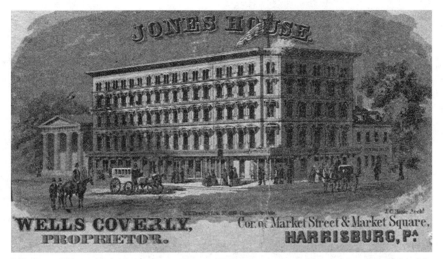

The Jones House, Harrisburg, Pennsylvania. By some accounts, Lincoln temporarily lost his only copy of the inaugural address while staying here. (*Historical Society of Dauphin County*)

After Lincoln returned to the Jones House, he had time to remember the grip. Robert, however, could not be found. A furious search ensued, but Robert was reportedly off with "the boys." Finally, Robert was located and then subjected to his father's grueling cross-examination. As Lincoln recounted, after washing up, "I asked Bob where the message was, and was taken aback by his confession." With "bored and wounded virtue," Robert explained that in the excitement caused by the enthusiastic reception, arriving at the hotel with no room yet ready for him, and unaware of the speech inside, he *may* have given the gripsack to a hotel waiter or clerk.

"And what did the clerk do with it?" Lincoln queried.

"It is on the floor behind the counter."[23]

"My heart went up into my mouth," recalled Lincoln.[24] Furious, he lost his generally cool temper and by some accounts scolded his son. "I had never seen Mr. Lincoln so much annoyed, so much perplexed, and for the time so angry," Lamon later recalled. Lincoln "seldom manifested a spirit of anger toward his children,— this was the nearest approach to it I had ever witnessed."[25] Lincoln set off to find the grip in the hotel's storage area. "I started down-stairs, where I was told that if a waiter had taken the gripsack I should probably find it in the baggage room," Lincoln recalled.[26]

Almost immediately, the normally good-natured Lincoln regretted his treatment of Robert. "I guess I have lost my certificate of moral character, written by myself," Lincoln lamented to Lamon. "Bob has lost my gripsack containing my inaugural address. I want you to help me find it." But even amid regrets and foreboding, Lincoln grasped the humor of the moment: "I feel a good deal as the old member of the Methodist church did when he lost his wife at the camp meeting, and went up to an old elder of the church and asked him if he could tell him where abouts in hell his wife was. In fact, I am in a worse fix than my Methodist friend, for if it were nothing but a wife missing, mine would be sure to pop up serenely somewhere. That address may be a loss to more than one husband in this country, but I shall be the greatest sufferer."[27]

Lamon recalled that "Lincoln was in despair" over losing the address. He had labored on it for weeks, had it nearly complete, and now with but ten days remaining until the great speech was to be given, "not even a trace of the notes was preserved from which it had been prepared."[28]

But it wasn't merely that the gripsack and inaugural address were lost that concerned Lincoln; to the contrary, perhaps his greatest fear was that the speech might be found—by the wrong people. The draft and the private letters also in the gripsack, "whose exhibition might turn the world of politics upside down,"[29] might be seized and devoured by a voracious press. Only three weeks earlier, the editor of the *Louisville Journal*, a leading Whig newspaper Lincoln had read in his youth, had written him requesting an advance copy of the inaugural. Politely, but noncommittally, Lincoln replied, "I have the document blocked out; but in the now rapidly shifting scenes, I shall have to hold it subject to revision up to near the time of delivery. So soon as it shall take what I can regard as its final shape, I shall remember, if I can, to send you a copy."[30]

The real reason, of course, that Lincoln would not send the *Louisville Journal* or any other newspaper an advance copy of his inaugural address is the same reason he had spoken so benignly this entire trip; the great egg was still incubating. It would not hatch until March 4. Lincoln had taken such care since being elected, and most noticeably on this trip, to make a point of holding his tongue on matters of presidential substance until he could speak as President Lincoln and "as near right as possible."[31] He would have been mortified to find his inaugural speech prematurely printed on the front page of tomorrow morning's papers.

Now, on a frantic quest for the grip, Lincoln determinedly strode to the hotel baggage room. "Going there I saw a large pile of gripsacks and other baggage."[32] One lanky stride of his long legs "swung him across the clerk's desk, and he fell upon the small mountain of luggage accumulated behind it." Lincoln yanked a grip that looked like his from the pile and pulled a little key from his pocket. "My key fitted it, but on opening there was nothing inside but a few paper collars and a flask of whiskey."[33] Lamon recalled the grip also containing a soiled shirt, a pack of cards, and that the bottle of whiskey was nearly full. Clearly, the grip did not belong to the teetotaler Lincoln. "In spite of his perplexity, the ludicrous mistake overcame Mr. Lincoln's gravity, and we both laughed heartily, much to the amusement of bystanders."[34]

A comedic needle-in-the-haystack search ensued, as Lincoln and Lamon continued to rummage through the pile of identical-looking black gripsacks. "Bystanders craned their necks, and the horrified clerk stood open-mouthed." After a brief, but frenzied search, Lincoln found his gripsack. To his great relief, the blessed inaugural address lay inside, untouched.[35]

Later, Lincoln would be able to joke about the incident, creating as it did an opportunity for yet another of his apt stories. He told of a man who had saved $1,500. But the bank in which he had deposited the money failed, and the man received only $150 of his original deposit. He deposited this $150 into a second bank, which also failed, returning but $15. As the man looked pitifully at what remained of his $1,500, he said, "Now, darn you, I've got you reduced to a portable shape, so I'll put you in my pocket."[36] Lincoln did the same with his inaugural address.[37]

LATER, that evening at the Jones House, Judd summoned together Judge David Davis, Colonel Edwin Sumner, Captain John Pope, Major David Hunter, Ward Hill Lamon, and John Nicolay.[38] George Hazzard and Elmer Ellsworth were apparently unavailable at the time, and possibly with Lincoln's boys. The group gathered in a private parlor. Perhaps Lincoln was waiting for them there; he would join the meeting, but say little. "The conversation was earnest and prolonged, and carried on in whispers, inaudible even to the few persons who were privileged to remain."[39] In hushed tones, Judd revealed to the startled group the suspected Baltimore conspiracy and how it was uncovered. "It was a great surprise to all of us," Lamon recounted.[40] Judd then revealed the plan that he, Pinkerton, and Felton had devised to thwart the conspirators: Send Mr. Lincoln secretly on a midnight train from Philadelphia to Washington tonight. "There was a diversity of opinion and some warm discussion, and I was subjected to a very rigid cross examination," Judd wrote.[41]

Colonel Sumner uttered the first military assessment of the plan: "That proceeding," he said, "will be a damned piece of cowardice."

Judd was unmoved. "I replied to this pointed hit, by saying that that view of the case had already been presented to Mr. Lincoln."

Retorted the Mexican War veteran Sumner, "I'll get a squad of Cavalry Sir, and *cut* our way to Washington, Sir."

"Probably," replied Judd sarcastically, "before that day comes the inauguration day will have passed; it is important that Mr. Lincoln should be in Washington that day."[42]

Captain Pope favored Judd's plan.[43] Judge Davis, however, seemed skeptical. Expressing no opinion on the proposed course of action, Davis peppered Judd with questions.[44] In Judd's view, because Davis was a native Marylander, he wanted to protect his home state from the stigma that would attach if the plan were carried out. Reported Judd, "finally, after insinuations of doubt on his part, both of the facts and wisdom of my plan," Judge Davis turned to the man of the moment and asked, "well, Lincoln, you have heard the whole story, what do you think about it yourself?"[45]

Lincoln, who thus far had remained silent, must have been observing both Judd and Davis with a critical eye. Davis was oil to Judd's water—he never forgave Judd for contributing to Lincoln's defeat in the 1855 U.S. Senate race.[46] Clearly, Judd had been keeping secrets from Lincoln on this trip. Whose counsel could Lincoln trust among his two closest advisors, Davis or Judd, when the two were such bitter rivals? To go with Judd's plan meant to perhaps avoid risk but to sacrifice honor. To follow Davis's implied course and Sumner's express one would preserve honor but perhaps sacrifice life.

"I've thought the matter over fully," Lincoln replied calmly, "and reckon I had better do as Judd says. The facts come from two different and reliable sources, and I don't consider it right to disregard both."[47]

"That settles it," Judge Davis said, with a touch of bitterness. The plan would be a slight on Maryland. Worse, it was Judd's plan. And if all this weren't bad enough, it had been hatched under the wings of private detectives, a business Davis loathed.[48]

The party thus determined that Lincoln should leave that night. It does not appear that the *World's* anonymous reporter was in on the decision—his dispatch on this date makes only oblique mention of changed arrangements and indicates, erroneously, that Lincoln, "completely exhausted," had retired to his room by 8:00 p.m. The reporter does indicate that "The route to Baltimore was not determined till this evening, as it was debated whether or not Mr. Lincoln should ride from depot to depot or go by a route which avoided a change of cars."[49]

Curiously, a member of the party had already devised the actual course Lincoln decided upon long before Pinkerton, Felton, and Judd—all of whom would, to a greater or lesser degree, lay claim to it. In his neatly penned letter written to Lincoln in January 1861, Captain George W. Hazzard had not only warned the president-elect of the dangers of passing openly through Baltimore, but provided several alternatives for avoiding the risk, including the following option, virtually identical to that ultimately seized upon by Pinkerton and others early in the morning of February 22:

> Passing through Baltimore incognito
>
> This could be accomplished
>
> 1st By leaving Philadelphia privately and unannounced with a very few friends (not more than five) at 10 oclock 50 minutes at night and taking the sleeping car all the way through to

Washington, by which means you would avoid the exposure at the crossing of the Susquehanna and the transhipment at Baltimore. You would arrive in Washington at 5 o'clock 48 minutes in the morning. A false mustache, an old slouched hat and a long cloak or overcoat for concealment could be provided, by a friend, while in N.Y. City, No trunks or other articles having marks should be taken. Leaving the hotel at Philada would be the greatest difficulty.[50]

It is worth speculating whether Judd, Pinkerton, and Felton arrived at a similar plan by coincidence or whether had they been coached by Hazzard— or even by Lincoln himself.

The question of Lincoln's passing unannounced through Baltimore being settled, it now became necessary to determine who among the group would accompany the president-elect to Washington. Judd reported that previous discussions had concluded that but one man should leave Harrisburg with Mr. Lincoln. But who?

Colonel Sumner was the most senior officer. That fact alone should have put him on the short list. But Sumner was in his sixties. With no armies to command, he would have only his aging body and such weapons as he might carry to protect Lincoln. Colonel Ellsworth should also have merited serious consideration. His loyalty and courage were beyond question. And his Zouaves had performed in Baltimore the previous August; he would therefore have had some familiarity with the city's streets.[51] But that fact and Ellsworth's fame also made it more likely he would be recognized either on the night train or in the Monumental City. Major Hunter, the man itching for a promotion and who had proposed arming a hundred thousand "Wide Awakes" in caps and capes to defend Washington, would certainly have been eager to be the chosen one. But Major Hunter's arm still hung in a sling from the injury suffered in the crush at Buffalo; he could do little to protect Lincoln tonight.[52]

Judd announced that Ward Hill Lamon would be the one to go with Lincoln.[53] His reasons for choosing Lamon over Sumner and the others were likely these: First, Lamon was a Southerner, a Virginian, and had the Southern dialect and appearance. Should it prove necessary to talk their way out of a jam south of the slave line, Lamon could credibly do it. No one would suspect that a Southerner had Mr. Lincoln in his charge. Second, Lamon habitually carried a brace of two revolvers in his belt, so boldly displayed that Judd had no doubt they would be effectively used if necessary. Third, Colonel Sumner, Major Hunter, and the other military men might be recognized, particularly wearing their uniforms. Lamon, however, in street clothes, would not be recognized.[54] Fourth, according to Nicolay, Lamon "was a man of extraordinary size and Herculean strength." In Columbus, Lamon had impressively demonstrated his physical prowess by holding back a surging crowd.[55] Finally, as one of Lincoln's closest and most trusted friends, Lamon was likely the least objectionable person, one that Judd perhaps hoped would provide a soothing balm for the wounded egos of those not chosen, literally left behind, as it were, with the women and children.[56]

But bruised feelings were not to be avoided by Lamon's selection over others. As Lincoln recounted, both Colonel Sumner and Major Hunter wished to accompany him. Lincoln said no. "You are known and your presence might betray me," he told them. He would take Lamon, whom no one knew. "Sumner and Hunter felt hurt," Lincoln recalled in classic understatement.[57]

Indeed, Colonel Sumner objected bitterly to Lamon's selection, violently exclaiming, "*I* have undertaken to see Mr. Lincoln to Washington!"[58] Sumner's affront is understandable; he was the ranking military officer in the group. In an era without a Secret Service, without a special agent in charge to decide without debate who goes where and does what in the name of presidential security, everyone wanted to take charge, but no one really could. The whole affair, the entire "damned piece of cowardice" had been against Sumner's judgment, both as a military officer and as a man. But the ill-advised plan having been decided upon, Sumner was determined that *he* would take charge of its execution. He would play the role assigned to him. "One thing I want distinctly understood," Sumner insisted, "that *I'm* going to Washington with the President. Such were my orders from General Scott, and I'm going to carry them out."[59]

The party tried to convince Colonel Sumner that every additional person added risk of Mr. Lincoln being discovered, "but the spirit of the gallant old soldier was up, and debate was useless."[60] According to Judd, "we all tried to reason him out of it, but made no impression at all and I was then sorry I told him anything about it. In fact, I am sorry I told anybody."[61]

And so, in the critical moment when unanimity of plan and purpose were most needed among Lincoln's protectors, there existed instead disharmony and discord. Judd insisted on the plan—"his plan"—and now regretted having told the others about it. Colonel Sumner objected to the plan, and with bullheaded stubbornness intended to modify it to his liking. The other military men, like Sumner, felt hurt and snubbed, if not betrayed. Judge Davis doubted and resented the plan. Perhaps, as the party broke around four o'clock that afternoon,[62] Lincoln too harbored a few doubts, both about the plan and the men he had chosen to advise and protect him.

And yet, in that moment of dissention, Lincoln began to emerge as a leader. After patiently listening to the disparate views of his trusted advisors, both civilian and military, he took a decisive step through the brambles of outward disagreement and inner conflict, as he would necessarily do throughout his presidency. The ultimate decision had been his all along. Lincoln had made what likely for him was the more difficult choice. In a room full of courageous military men, the more popular course for Lincoln would have been to stick with the program, to ride into Baltimore without fear, to prepare for and face whatever assaults awaited him there, as the head of his family, his party, and his nation. But instead, with full apprehension of the loss of face he would endure from his military comrades, the ridicule he would suffer at the hands of his detractors, and with the knowledge that he would need to leave his wife and young sons behind in Harrisburg, Lincoln chose the unpopular course— that of stealth, of dishonor, of deception, of apparent weakness.

When viewed in these terms, Lincoln chose the more difficult path for the greater good, as leaders often must. Whether his decision was right or wrong, it was a trait of Lincoln's that once his mind was made up, it was made up.[63] He had determined to follow Judd's plan. He would go through Baltimore tonight. Assuming something could be done to restrain Colonel Sumner, only Ward Hill Lamon would accompany him. There would be no turning back now.

NICOLAY and Hay referred to her as the "hell-cat." Her temper was the talk of Springfield. But love is blind; one man's hell is another's heaven, and to Abraham Lincoln, Mary Todd was the cat's meow.

Mary had been born into a prominent, if overly populous, Lexington, Kentucky, family. As a young woman, she moved to Illinois to live with her older sister Elizabeth, who had married the wealthy son of the state's former governor, Ninian Wirt Edwards.[64] In Springfield, Mary Todd quickly became the talk of the town. Upon their first meeting at a festive dance party, the gangly, love-struck Lincoln blurted out to the bright-eyed, vivacious Mary Todd, "I want to dance with you in the worst way." Tittered the twenty-something Mary to her cousin later that evening, "he certainly did."[65]

The dark side of Mary's spirited, chirpy nature was a high-strung temperament that made her prone to emotional outbursts and panic attacks. She was known in Springfield to mercilessly berate both husband and help, reportedly bonking the former on the nose with a stick of firewood during one or more episodes of his inattention.[66]

But she was fiercely loyal to Lincoln, and he to her. She staunchly supported him in the face of critics, on one occasion rebutting an unfavorable comparison to Stephen Douglas with a proud retort: "Mr. Lincoln may not be as handsome a figure . . . but the people are perhaps not aware that his heart is as large as his arms are long."[67]

By some accounts, Mary's presence on the Lincoln Special had been arranged by General Winfield Scott, who had urged her to abandon earlier plans to follow her husband to Washington a week later. Scott's supposed rationale: Mrs. Lincoln's absence might be seen as a sign of alarm or weakness, an indication that Lincoln expected trouble on the trip.[68] An alternate and more likely hypothesis offered is that General Scott felt that Mrs. Lincoln and the boys might, ironically, provide a measure of protection for the president-elect—assassins would, it was supposed, be less likely to strike when their victim's family was near.[69]

In early January, Mrs. Lincoln had received a painting on canvas from South Carolina, depicting Mr. Lincoln, tarred and feathered, feet chained, with a rope around his neck. Despite such sinister taunts, and her friends' warnings of newspaper rumors of suspected attacks on the president-elect while on his way to the capital, Mrs. Lincoln had courageously resolved that "she would see Mr. Lincoln on to Washington, danger or no danger."[70]

But now, it would be impossible for Mary Todd to see her husband on to Washington. Unbeknownst to her, plans had just been made by men she either did not know or did not trust to take Mr. Lincoln from her. One thing remained to be done by these men that quite possibly evoked even more fear than the thought of conveying the president-elect alone, in the dark, through Baltimore's famously violent streets. There would likely be no volunteers for this mission. Some poor, courageous soul would have to reveal the plan to Mrs. Lincoln.

A_T the same time the Lincoln Special had arrived in Harrisburg, Vice President-elect Hamlin was on a train bound for Baltimore. Hamlin's experience there would be a tense one, and possibly foreshadow what Lincoln might encounter—assuming Lincoln adhered to Pinkerton's plan.

Hamlin, it will be recalled, had telegraphed Samuel Felton from New York on February 21, asking for passage to Baltimore on a special car on the next day's noon train from Philadelphia. Pinkerton had seen to it that no details of Hamlin's altered travel arrangements would be leaked through the telegraph offices, lest such news "complicate any change of route which Mr. Lincoln might deem advisable." The American Telegraph Company had agreed to suppress any such communications.[71]

But Pinkerton's efforts to keep Hamlin's travel plans secret would fail. News of Hamlin's early departure must have passed—whether from a telegraph operator in New York, from someone making Hamlin's travel arrangements, from one of the political leaders riding with him or otherwise, we may never know. We do know that on Thursday, February 21, 1861, the *New York Times* reported that "Mr. Hamlin will remain here until to-morrow, when he will continue his journey to Washington."[72] This news was unexpected. It had been supposed that Hamlin would leave on the morning of February 21 with Lincoln.[73]

But when the Lincoln Special pulled out of New York, Hamlin was not on board. Rather, he stayed behind and spent the rest of the day in the Empire City. "Against his inclinations," reported his grandson-biographer vaguely, "Mr. Hamlin was forced to modify his plans in a slight measure for prudential reasons."[74]

Hamlin and his wife left New York the following morning, February 22, at seven o'clock, accompanied by a portion of the Maine congressional delegation and several other men who acted as a traveling escort.[75] He boarded the Jersey ferryboat *John P. Jackson,* the same gaily decorated craft Lincoln had ridden the previous day. In Jersey City, Hamlin and his traveling suite of New Englanders boarded a special train provided by the New Jersey Railroad, the same one Lincoln had used the day before.[76]

Upon arriving in Philadelphia, Felton honored Hamlin's request to ride in a special sleeper car coupled to the regular noon train.[77] As Hamlin's train headed south, "one or two demonstrations were made at Chester [Pennsylvania] and Wilmington, Delaware, but Mr. Hamlin did not appear or speak."[78]

No evidence has been found that Felton or anyone else arranged for any personal protection for Hamlin and his wife while passing through Baltimore—other than hiding them in the sleeper car. The New York Metropolitan Police had accompanied Hamlin only as far as Newark. Pinkerton's operatives and assistants, a dozen or so men and women, were already stretched thin, playing parts the spymaster had scripted for them in Philadelphia and Harrisburg and Baltimore and places in between.[79] In all likelihood, the Hamlins would need to pass through Baltimore fending for themselves, protected only by a handful of New England politicians and one or two friends.

As his train rolled into Baltimore, Mr. Hamlin and his wife lay quietly in their sleeping berths, behind closed curtains. Perhaps Felton had urged them to do so in order to reduce the risk of being identified. Hamlin's biographer picks up the story:

> The station was filled with rough characters, and the temper of the crowd was unmistakably hostile to the Union. There were oaths heard that "no damned Abolitionist like Lincoln or Hamlin should enter the White House," and the mob seemed capable of carrying out its threats. The ruffians were there to watch the trains for Mr. Lincoln, and a horde of them rushed through Mr. Hamlin's car. Some of them even brushed aside the curtains of his compartments, and stared at him, but failing to recognize the Vice-President-elect, the uncleanly creatures took themselves away, leaving an atmosphere of profanity and whiskey behind them.[80]

It is possible that the inebriated Baltimore roughs were intent on murdering Hamlin and, as his biographer reports, merely failed to recognize him. This leads to an obvious question—why would the Baltimore roughs not have recognized Hamlin? Both Lincoln's and Hamlin's likenesses had been widely published during the presidential campaign. If the Baltimore mob was hunting Hamlin, presumably they would have had some idea of what their prey looked like. Perhaps it was growing dark and the sleeper car was too dimly lit for Hamlin to be recognized. But there might have been another reason. Hamlin might have worn a disguise while passing through Baltimore— indeed, Lincoln would wear one, his defenders' denials notwithstanding, later this very night.

It also seems plausible that the Baltimore roughs were not looking for Hamlin, but that they were already hunting for Lincoln. Perhaps they had been tipped off. Perhaps they knew Lincoln had changed his route, and had determined to come through Baltimore earlier than published, hidden behind curtains in a sleeping berth. What other explanation for the roughs who "were there to watch the trains for Mr. Lincoln" rudely pulling aside Hamlin's curtains?

After reaching the President Street Station in Baltimore, Hamlin needed to get to the Camden Street Station, over a mile away. He would not have wanted to risk being recognized by leaving the sleeper for a carriage. In all likelihood, therefore, his car was uncoupled at President Street and slowly drawn by a plodding team of horses through the congested bustle of Pratt Street, past the Inner Harbor, toward the Camden Street depot. While this course would be more secure than riding in an open barouche, it would still have left the vice president-elect vulnerable to attack. For the next fifteen or twenty minutes, while he lay quietly in his berth, Hamlin would be separated from Baltimore's roving street hordes by nothing more impenetrable than a car door and a hanging wall of curtains.

CREDIT and blame are but two sides of the same coin. Along with taking all the glorious credit for devising and advocating the Lincoln evacuation plan would thus have fallen the least pleasant of its obligations—accepting the blame from those who would inevitably find the plan foolhardy. Chief among these detractors was Mrs. Lincoln. Although Lincoln himself likely informed Mary Todd of his altered course, what was in all probability a thankless task— reassuring her that the plan was both necessary and sound—likely fell on Norman B. Judd's shoulders. Evidence of this comes from one account that notes Judd's absence from the dinner table at the Jones House, where Mr. Lincoln and his party dined with Governor Curtin around five o'clock. As one of Lincoln's closest advisors, Judd would have been expected to be present with the others discussing the secret arrangements at dinner. Judd, however, reportedly "was not a guest, as he was giving personal attention to Mrs. Lincoln, who was much disturbed by the suggestion to separate the President from her . . . she narrowly escaped attracting attention to the movements which required the utmost secrecy."[81]

Put more bluntly, Mrs. Lincoln was pitching a fit. Judd was reportedly trying to keep her quiet, so as not to blow the cover story. This reaction and result is hardly surprising. Mrs. Lincoln was notoriously high strung. News of a plot to kill her husband held portents of a bad dream coming true. After rumors of threats on her husband's life reached her ears in Springfield, she had resolved to "see Mr. Lincoln on to Washington, danger or no danger."[82] And now she, like Colonel Sumner, was being denied that resolution by, of all people, Norman B. Judd.

A worse balm for comforting and assuring a wounded spirit could never have been chosen; Mary Todd Lincoln despised and mistrusted Norman B. Judd. In January, when Judd's name began circulating as a possible cabinet appointee, Mary bypassed her husband and wrote confidentially to Judge David Davis, beseeching him, for the good of the country and her husband's reputation, to urge Lincoln to dispatch any thoughts of appointing Judd to a Cabinet post. "*Judd* would cause trouble & dissatisfaction, & if Wall Street testifies correctly, his business transactions, have not always borne inspection," she wrote, concluding, "It is strange how little delicacy those Chicago men have."[83] And now, she was expected to believe Judd, to separate from her husband on account of Judd, to entrust the life of her husband to Judd, whom she did not trust, according to a plan purportedly hatched by this very same man.

But Mrs. Lincoln's anxiety attack might equally be attributed to a realization that others now influenced her husband's will and actions. She was, quite literally, losing control. But she would not give in without a fight. Her demands that night to accompany Lincoln through Baltimore reportedly became so "unmanageable" that she would ultimately be locked in her room at the Jones House by some of Lincoln's men.[84]

During dinner, meanwhile, the party continued its discussions of the alleged conspiracy. "The admonitions received from General Scott and Senator Seward were made known to Governor Curtin at the table, and the question of a change of route was discussed for some time by every one with the single exception of Lincoln." According to Alexander K. McClure, a member of the Pennsylvania delegation, Lincoln remained silent until compelled to speak. When he did speak, Lincoln uncharacteristically voiced second thoughts about going through with the plan. "What would the nation think of its President stealing into the Capital like a thief in the night?" Lincoln reportedly asked the group. Curtin and the others advised Lincoln that the decision was not his to make. His friends would bear the cross of ridicule and scorn by deciding the matter for him—or at least that is what the world would be told.[85] Lincoln could play the part of the ambivalent, yet courageous leader, acceding to the wishes, if not the demands, of his friends and advisors. He would follow the plan—for their sake.

Just before sunset,[86] at about 5:45 p.m., Judd, presumably having left Mrs. Lincoln locked in her room, strolled into the dining room, where he saw Lincoln still sitting at the table. Among those at dinner, in addition to Lincoln, were Colonel Sumner, Ward Hill Lamon, David Davis, Lincoln's brother-in-law, Dr. William S. Wallace, and the Pennsylvanians—Governor Curtin, Thomas A. Scott of the Pennsylvania Railroad, Secretary of the Commonwealth Eli Slifer, Attorney General Samuel A. Purviance, Alexander L. Russell, and Alexander McClure.[87]

A few moments after Judd arrived in the dining room, a closed carriage, driven by G. C. Franciscus of the Pennsylvania Railroad, pulled up to the side door of the hotel at the Second Street entrance.[88] As he arrived, Franciscus observed Lincoln dining "with a large company" that made it difficult for him to leave without attracting attention.[89] Meanwhile, Colonel Sumner, still determined to accompany the president-elect to Washington, had been keeping a "strict watch" over Lincoln. Perhaps on cue, either Nicolay or Lamon called Lincoln from the dinner table. Judd noticed Colonel Sumner, resplendent in his blue and gold uniform, vigilantly observe Lincoln, who was dining hastily, as he rose from the table, excusing himself on plea of fatigue.[90] Mr. Lincoln, wearing his dress coat, retired to his room.[91] It was here that Lincoln likely said his last good-byes to Mary Todd and possibly to his sons. We are left to imagine their parting—tears, pleas to reconsider, tender embraces, brave reassurances that all would be well, and hopeful if uncertain promises to reunite tomorrow in Washington all seem fitting to the anxious occasion and the somber mood.

When Judd next saw him, Lincoln had changed out of his dinner suit and into his traveling clothes. He wore a bobtail overcoat he had worn all winter, with a soft hat sticking out of his pocket, and a shawl draped over his arm.[92] The overcoat resembled a sailor's pea jacket. The hat, described as a "Kossuth" hat, one with a low crown and a brim, "was a felt hat such as were in common use at the time."[93] Lamon confirms this description: "As Mr. Lincoln's dress on this occasion has been much discussed, it may be as well to state that he wore a soft, light felt hat, drawn down over his face when it seemed necessary or convenient, and a shawl thrown over his shoulders, and pulled up to assist in disguising his features when passing to and from the carriage."[94]

Governor Curtin and Lincoln strode quickly to the hotel's side door and the waiting carriage. Lamon followed. In a low tone, Judd instructed Lamon: "As soon as Mr. Lincoln is in the carriage, drive off. The crowd must not be allowed to identify him."[95]

As Lamon got to the side door, Governor Curtin halted him and asked if he was well armed. Lamon, the same man who yearned to be appointed to the refined and elegant position of Consul to Paris,[96] "at once uncovered a small arsenal of deadly weapons, showing that he was literally armed to the teeth. In addition to a pair of heavy revolvers, he had a slung-shot and brass knuckles and a huge knife nestled under his vest."[97] By another account, Lamon would have needed at least six arms to wield all the weapons on his person, which reportedly included "a brace of fine pistols, a huge bowie knife, a blackjack, a pair of brass knuckles, and a hickory cudgel."[98]

The heavily armed Lamon led the way. Following Lamon and taking Governor Curtin by the arm, Lincoln exited the hotel's side door, and stepped outside into the twilight, down the steps and across the pavement to the waiting carriage. Colonel Sumner, still determined not to be left out, followed closely behind Lincoln.[99]

Lincoln later recalled the effectiveness of his disguise as he exited the Jones House: "In New York some friend had given me a new beaver hat in a box, and in it had placed a soft wool hat. I had never worn one of the latter in my life. I had this box in my room. Having informed a very few friends that I had with me, and putting the soft hat in my pocket, I walked out of the house at a back door, bareheaded, without exciting any special curiosity. Then I put on the soft hat and joined my friends without being recognized by strangers, for I was not the same man."[100]

By now a raucous crowd of thousands had gathered around the Jones House, eager to see the president-elect. This, of course, presented a problem. Suspicions would be aroused if Lincoln were seen leaving the hotel.[101] As Governor Curtin stepped outside the Jones House, he called in a loud voice for the driver to take the carriage to the Executive Mansion.[102] "Few saw him depart, and these were assured that he had gone to Gov. Curtin's residence to rest."[103] Curtin's announcement would hopefully misdirect anyone who had recognized Lincoln to believe that he was headed to the governor's house. But the loud announcement might equally have drawn the unwanted attention of those not previously recognizing Lincoln and signaled that he was in the carriage with the governor. Had there been time, or had they thought of it, Lincoln's protectors might have provided a second closed carriage as a decoy to convey presidential and gubernatorial doubles to the Executive Mansion. Instead, they used the real Lincoln and the real Governor Curtin and relied on the combined elements of misdirection, speed of action, and cover of approaching darkness to fool the crowd.

As Lincoln and Curtin stepped into the closed carriage, Colonel Sumner followed, still intent on joining the president-elect. Judd put his hand gently on Sumner's shoulder, saying, "One moment, Colonel,"[104] thereby halting and distracting the grizzled officer momentarily. "He turned around to see what was wanted, and before I had time to explain the carriage was off," trailing four plumed horses galloping down the street.[105] "A madder man," Judd said, referring to Sumner, "you never saw."[106] "I never got such a scoring in all my life—I was fearful he would assault me."[107]

Small wonder. As the carriage faded into the twilight, Sumner felt his pride fade along with it. He had failed to carry out Winfield Scott's orders. Worse, he had been made the fool by one he likely saw as a doughy, conniving, political hack.

Judd used diplomacy in an attempt to pacify Sumner: "When we get to Washington Mr. Lincoln shall determine what apology is due to you."[108]

Meanwhile, Lincoln's carriage careened southeast on Second Street. Contrary to Curtin's orders, the carriage did not stop at the Executive Mansion but raced right on by.[109] The mansion was awash with spectators as Lincoln's carriage hurried past. Curtin later wrote, "The halls, stairways and pavements in front of the house were much crowded, and no doubt the impression prevailed that Mr. Lincoln was going to the Executive Mansion with me."[110] Of course, he was not. Lincoln's carriage continued south, past Chestnut, to where the tracks of the Pennsylvania Railroad crossed the street.[111]

As Lincoln's carriage hurried on down Second Street, a few hundred feet to the right, the wide Susquehanna River drained lazily in parallel to the southeast. Here, the river was shallow and rocky, dotted with brushy little islands. The long-legged Lincoln, stepping stone to shoal, might almost cross it without getting his bony knees wet. But later tonight, he would need to cross the same river at a deeper spot, Havre de Grace, Maryland, where the Susquehanna spilled into the northern neck of the Chesapeake. There, Lincoln's railcar would—if all went well—leave the tracks and be ferried across on a steamer. There was much to be done, however, between Harrisburg and Havre de Grace.

ANDREW WYNNE, an accomplished pole climber for the American Telegraph Company, had arrived in Harrisburg earlier that day, having reportedly taken the noon train from Philadelphia.[112] The orders from his manager, H. E. Thayer, were simple enough. Wynne was to fix the wires of another telegraph company in Harrisburg to prevent any messages from being sent to Baltimore. Wynne and the American Telegraph Company's Superintendent, W. P. Westervelt, met up with George Burns after arriving in Harrisburg. The trio proceeded to the office of the rival telegraph company and, perhaps trying not to appear suspicious, traced the wires they would need to cut from there through the city. To avoid detection, they walked to a remote spot about 2 miles south of town. At around 6:00 p.m.,[113] as a cloak of darkness fell, Wynne strapped his knife-pointed climbing irons to his boots, crawled insect-like up one of the wooden telegraph poles, and went to work.[114] Westervelt and Burns likely acted as lookouts. Perhaps they had even invented a cover story. They were repairmen fixing some lines that were down.

At the top of the pole, Wynne disabled the lines by connecting fine copper ground wires to the lines passing between Harrisburg and Baltimore. He connected a ground wire to each of the two lines and hid the grounding wires, attaching them to the back of the pole to ground them.[115] Electronic impulses to and from Harrisburg and Baltimore would now be shunted harmlessly into the earth. Though disruptive, the disabled lines would hopefully not attract suspicion from the telegraph operator in Harrisburg. Particularly in winter, telegraph lines went down all the time for any number of reasons— downed trees, high winds, clinging ice, heavy snow. Sabotage would not have been high on the list of possible causes.

After disabling the lines, Wynne and the others walked the 2 miles back into town, to the telegraph office. Wynne needed to test his work, so he asked the operator to send a message to Baltimore. Wynne's heart likely quickened at the operator's reply; he could not send the message. All communications to and from Harrisburg had been cut off. A sense of relief must have washed over Andrew Wynne; he had done his job well. Most importantly, he had not been caught doing it.[116] Moreover, for at least two reasons, his timing had been perfect. First, it was now dark. The break in the lines could be anywhere along the 90-mile stretch between Harrisburg and Baltimore. There would be no way of finding it until daylight and no point in looking for it now.

Second, and perhaps more importantly, Wynn had managed to disable the lines to Baltimore just as Lincoln was leaving Harrisburg. Even if spies from Baltimore had been watching Lincoln's movements, even if they had managed to see him hurry out of the Jones House, or race past the Executive Mansion, even if they could follow the carriage and watch Lincoln board a waiting train heading toward Philadelphia over the Pennsylvania Railroad's line, they could give none of the conspirators in Baltimore the "all up" signal. Assuming Lincoln was being watched, and that those watching him were not prepared to kill him here, the best Lincoln's stalkers might do at this point would be to follow his train to Philadelphia on one of the regular night trains headed there.

As Lincoln was leaving the Jones House, Pennsylvania Railroad fireman Daniel E. Garman of Lebanon, Pennsylvania, saw the first of several unusual sights he would see tonight—engineer Edward Black running toward him down the track. Garman was tending to the Pennsylvania Railroad's engine number 161. He had oiled her up, lit her headlamp, and turned up a hot, glowing fire in her firebox.[117] Under the dim light of the setting sun and rising moon, the iron horse chuffed eagerly, ready to run. Only moments before, a "very much excited" Pennsylvania Railroad division superintendent, G. C. "Charles" Franciscus, had paid Garman an impromptu visit. Without explanation, Franciscus ordered Garman to look after the engine and make her ready to run, while he went for engineer Ed Black. Without question, Garman did what Franciscus asked.

As he saw Ed Black running toward him, Garman would have surmised that Franciscus had gone to the United States Hotel, where Black was staying, and ordered Black to the engine. What Garman would not have known is that Franciscus then doubled back to the Jones House to pick up Lincoln and Lamon. The winded engineer mounted the cab and asked Garman if she was oiled up. Garman replied that everything was ready. The two men backed the engine up to the depot and coupled her to a lone regular coach, car 29. They ran the short train below town, about one mile southeast of the Harrisburg Station, then located at Fifth and Market, to Front Street crossing, near Hanna Street.[118] Here they waited. By now, dusk had fallen.

Garman and Black would not need to wait long. After about a minute, Garman saw four plumed horses and a closed cab dash up along side the waiting train. Franciscus, Enoch Lewis, general superintendent, and Ward Hill Lamon stepped out of the coach.[119] A tall solitary figure, last from the carriage and unrecognized by Garman, "quietly alighted, walked down the track to the car, went to the saloon and lay down."[120]

The accounts of who joined Lincoln and Lamon in the coach vary, but at least Franciscus and Lewis likely were among them.[121] As soon as all were aboard, the signal was given to Ed Black, "and after a quiet but fervent 'Goodbye and God protect you!'" the engineer pulled out, vectoring Mr. Lincoln east, toward Philadelphia.[122] According to Garman, "the gong rang and we did some lively running."[123]

The Lincoln Special was on its way once more, with but six or eight passengers on board, fewer than it had carried the entire trip, and only two—Lincoln and Lamon—who had seen every mile of it. Perhaps, as he lay in the dark, quiet solitude of the saloon, Lincoln now questioned everything. His decision to run for president. His decision to leave his law practice, his beloved Springfield, and the warmth of family and friends cultivated over a lifetime there. His decision to make this hasty retreat, without his wife and sons. But second thoughts were of no moment now. He had run for president and was the president-elect. He had left Springfield and was going to Washington. If assassins awaited him in Baltimore, it was his duty, as the elected head of the nation, to beat them at their own cunning, secretive game. To hell with them and to hell with what others might think. He would be president—or die trying.

Back in Washington, Congressman Elihu B. Washburne and Senator William Seward had no way of knowing for certain Lincoln's travel plans— their telegraph lines were also down. They knew young Fred Seward had been dispatched to Philadelphia the previous evening to deliver the intelligence of the Baltimore Plot from General Scott and Colonel Stone that they, in turn, had gathered from the New York City detectives. Thanks to young Seward, they had reason to believe that Lincoln had received and would heed those warnings. Despite the lack of confirmation from Lincoln himself, they expected Lincoln to arrive late that afternoon on the regular noon train from Philadelphia.

Earlier that afternoon, Senator Seward had met Washburne at the latter's seat in the House of Representatives.[124] Seward advised Washburne that he had received no new information from his son or from anyone else concerning Lincoln's movements. Further, Seward informed Washburne that the telegraph lines had all been cut, and he therefore could receive no news. Obviously, an anxious Seward could dispatch no queries either.

Seward told Washburne that he thought it "very probable" that Lincoln would arrive in Washington on the regular train from Philadelphia and suggested that he and Washburne wait at the depot to meet the president-elect. Although Seward had received no information from his son detailing Lincoln's movements, he had received from Fred Seward a coded message sent from Philadelphia, indicating that Lincoln had determined to change his travel plans. As Fred Seward recorded, after having met with Lincoln in Philadelphia, "I hastened to the telegraph office and sent my father a word previously agreed upon, upon receiving which, he would understand that his advice had been taken."[125]

Not knowing which train Lincoln would take, but assuming it would be coming from Philadelphia, William Seward and Elihu Washburne were accordingly at the Washington depot in time for the regular afternoon train. Seward and Washburne were the functional equivalent of the Baltimore Republicans who had gone to Harrisburg that afternoon to greet Lincoln: hopeful, anxious, expectant, eager—and critically uninformed. And, just like the Baltimore Republicans who would later arrive in Harrisburg to find no Mr. Lincoln, Seward and Washburne would be similarly crestfallen. Wrote Washburne, "We were promptly on hand; the train arrived in time, and with strained eyes we watched the descent of the passengers. But there was no Mr. Lincoln among them; though his arrival was by no means certain, yet we were much disappointed."[126]

Although Washburne and Seward did not find Lincoln, they did meet his vice president-elect, Hannibal Hamlin, that night at the Washington depot.[127] After their brush with the vulgar and inebriated roughs, Hamlin and his wife had made it through Baltimore without further incident. Hamlin likely told Washburne and Seward about his tense passage through Baltimore, about the unruly mob that had swarmed the cars spouting anti-Lincoln epithets and apparently hunting for him. Lincoln could expect more of the same, only worse. But Hamlin's intelligence would have been useless. Even if they could have sent a telegraphic warning, Washburne and Seward did not, at this hour, know how to reach Lincoln.

That they did not know and could not find out about Lincoln's travels must have been maddening to Washburne and Seward, two Lincoln friends who had taken upon themselves the role of safeguarding the president-elect. They could learn no information concerning his whereabouts, his travel plans, whether he was alive or dead. Although it was useless to speculate, it would have been only human nature to do so, coloring in the empty spaces with all manner of dark, dreadful imaginings and unpleasant outcomes. "Sad, disappointed, and under the empire of conflicting emotions," said Washburne, "we separated to go to our respective homes, but agreeing to be at the depot on the arrival of the New York train the next morning before daylight, hoping either to meet the President or get some information as to his movements."[128]

Seward and Washburne had no way of knowing for certain at this point that Lincoln, in fact, intended to be on that early morning train. And Lincoln, Lamon, and Pinkerton had no way of knowing that Seward and Washburne intended to be at the Washington depot to meet them.

In Philadelphia meanwhile, Allan Pinkerton was, to a certain extent, an anxious victim of his own devices. It was after dark, and still he had received no confirmation of Lincoln's departure from Harrisburg. Lincoln should have left by now. Pinkerton should have received word by now.

Pinkerton certainly could have accompanied the president-elect from Philadelphia to Harrisburg this morning. Had he done so, he could have insured that his plan, to get Lincoln on a special train as darkness fell on Harrisburg, would be carried out. Instead, he had to rely on others, including pole climbers like Andrew Wynne, railroad men, like G. C. Franciscus, and politicians, like Norman B. Judd to execute the plan. None of these men were experienced in the art of spycraft, of conducting clandestine operations, and most importantly, of the need to keep the spymaster informed—none had seen fit to advise Pinkerton of Mr. Lincoln's travel status.

There had been too much important work for Pinkerton to do in Philadelphia that day, however, to spend precious time following Lincoln to Harrisburg and back. It was here Lincoln hopefully would land later tonight, and from here he would need to be dispatched on Samuel M. Felton's regular night train to Baltimore, the continuation of the night train from New York.

Earlier that afternoon, around 3:30 p.m., Pinkerton reported, "I left Mr. Felton and returned to the St. Louis Hotel and after getting dinner went to M. B's room."[129] "M. B." was Pinkerton's shorthand for "Mrs. Barley," one of his aliases for Kate Warne, "Mrs. Cherry" being another. Pinkerton gave the following instructions to Warne: She was to leave the hotel around 9:20 p.m. She was to hire a private carriage. She was to drive to the Philadelphia, Wilmington, and Baltimore Railroad station and meet George Dunn, who was expected to arrive from Baltimore at 9:50 p.m. She would have Dunn purchase three tickets to Washington. She would secure four double sleeping berths on the train, in the rear portion of the sleeping car. She would ask Dunn to be certain the rear door of the sleeping car, normally locked, would be open, so Pinkerton and Lincoln could enter unobserved through the back of the car.

After leaving Warne's room this evening, Pinkerton went to the telegraph and express

Senator William Seward, former governor of New York. Seward warned Lincoln of the Baltimore Plot in February 1861, and would himself narrowly escape an assassination attempt by Booth conspirator Lewis Powell on April 14, 1865. (*Library of Congress*)

offices to see if he had received any dispatches. Pinkerton hoped for a message concerning the whereabouts of "Nuts," his unflattering code word for Lincoln. He found no such message, however. This greatly troubled Pinkerton. Lincoln's train certainly should have left Harrisburg by now. An anxious Allan Pinkerton returned to the St. Louis Hotel. There he remained, "in a State of suspense."[130]

CHAPTER FIFTEEN

NIGHT TRAIN

Friday night, February 22, 1861
Harrisburg–Philadelphia–Wilmington

THE ENGINEER AND FIREMAN DRIVING the Lincoln Special out of Harrisburg had several hurdles to contend with. First, they needed to get to Philadelphia's 30th Street Station in time for Lincoln to catch the regular 10:50 p.m. train to Baltimore. "I was told," Engineer Black recalled, "to make no stops (and when obliged to take on water, to do so at the most secluded places I could, to keep a sharp look out) and to arrive at 30th Street, West Philadelphia by 10 o'clock *sure.*"[1]

Trains of the Lincoln Special's era could achieve speeds of about 30 to 40 miles per hour.[2] The distance between Harrisburg and Philadelphia was roughly 110 miles. Getting Lincoln to Philadelphia by 10:00 p.m. was thus theoretically quite possible, assuming his train had left Harrisburg around 6:00 p.m. Practically speaking, however, getting Lincoln to Philadelphia by 10:00 p.m. presented a significant challenge.

Even assuming the train made a smooth run without incident, the trip would necessarily include stops every 25 miles or so to fill the engine's hot, thirsty boiler with copious amounts of water. Furthermore, the run was at night—the first time on the entire 1,900 mile journey the Lincoln Special would be traveling in darkness. Night travel had its obvious safety challenges.[3] Broken rails, misaligned switches, and washed out bridges were common threats even for trains whose passengers were not the target of assassins.[4] If an obstruction lay on the track, it might not be seen by the engineer in time to stop, particularly with the engine barreling down the track at full throttle. Tonight, there had been no time to employ a pilot engine to run interference in front of the Special, as had occurred previously on the trip. Even if there had been time, the mere existence of a pilot engine might have signaled the special nature of the train and its very important passenger. Likewise, there had been no time to dispatch hundreds of signalmen with lanterns between Harrisburg and Philadelphia, and their presence, like that of a pilot engine, would also have marked the special nature of the train. Moreover, the tracks back to Philadelphia would be crowded with other trains carrying Philadelphians home after spending the day with Lincoln in Harrisburg. The risk of a railroad traffic jam—or worse, a train wreck—loomed large.

This latter problem was easily solved, but at some expense. All trains on the Pennsylvania Central Railroad's tracks between Harrisburg and Philadelphia would be sidetracked until Lincoln's Special passed. Enduring the nineteenth-century equivalent of being stuck for hours on a grounded plane, no doubt more than a few waylaid passengers grumbled, even if they had been given some plausible explanation for the delay.

The problem of night travel would be at least partially solved by lighting the engine's headlamp. Headlamps were a relatively new innovation to railroading, having come into general use around the mid-1850s. Tonight, in all likelihood, the Pennsylvania Railroad's engine number 161 employed a square or box lamp with a silver-plated parabolic reflector that could direct a straight, powerful, oil-fired beam of light a thousand feet down the track.[5] But the headlamp could not see around corners. And at 40 miles per hour, the locomotive would cover a thousand feet in about seventeen seconds. Even with the headlight showing the way, running in the dark at top speed, the engineer would necessarily be taking a risk that he might not see an obstacle on the track in time to bring his twenty-ton locomotive to a stop.

Although the headlamp of the engine pulling Lincoln's train was lit, the lamps of his coach were not.[6] This precaution would make it less likely that the president-elect might be recognized, for example, when the train stopped for water, or whizzed past the curious passengers stuck on sidetracked trains. Thus, the handful of passengers in Lincoln's coach would have sat through the three- or four-hour trip in darkness. They could not read or play cards. Lincoln could not edit his precious inaugural address. Perhaps he used the idle time to catch some much-needed sleep. Or perhaps he told a few appropriate yarns.

But despite having no coach lamps to light their car, astronomical fortune prevailed for the Lincoln Special tonight. On the evening of February 22, 1861, the moon was virtually full, "waxing gibbous," with 92 percent of its visible disk illuminated. The moon would have provided a welcome source of illumination, both to the train's engineer and his passengers.[7]

The asserted reason for tonight's special train was to convey Pennsylvania Railroad executives G. C. Franciscus and Enoch Lewis to Philadelphia.[8] Both of these men knew Lincoln was in the special car with them. But when the train left Harrisburg, it is not clear if its engineer Ed Black knew. Clearly, however, fireman Dan Garman did not know. The failure to invest Garman with the same knowledge of others on the train would nearly cost the very secret that they had so jealously guarded.[9]

When the train stopped at "Lemonplace"[10] to take on water, Garman connected the hose and watered the iron horse. While he waited, curiosity overcame Garman, and he peeked into the saloon's car door. In the dimness of the unlit coach, illuminated only by the gibbous moon, he saw Lincoln. Although Lincoln had his back turned, Garman recognized the president-elect. "I knew him because he was so much taller than the rest of the inmates." The excited Garman cried out to Ed Black, "the rail-splitter is on the train!" This brought Superintendent G. C. Franciscus running to the door, and a stern, hushed warning to Garman not to mention that the president was on board. Garman got the message. "You bet I kept quiet then."[11]

When the train started up again, Garman turned to the engineer and asked, "Ed, what's up?"

Edward R. Black, the same man Lincoln had handed a cigar in Philadelphia earlier that day, replied, "I don't know, but just keep the engine hot."[12]

Garman did as he was told, and kept the engine's coal-burning furnace full of fire. "[I]f ever I got a fast ride, I did that night," Garman recalled. "We ran so fast, that when I got a shovel full of coal to put in the furnace, I would be laying on the foot board rolling in the coal instead of getting it in the furnace, but with all that I kept up steam."[13]

En route, Lincoln remained in the saloon the entire time.[14] At Downingtown, the train again stopped to take on water. As the train filled its belly, all the passengers but one got out and filled theirs. "At this place [Downingtown] all the gentlemen excepting Mr. Lincoln got out of the car for lunch [a light meal, in ninteenth-century usage]." For Lincoln, it would be meager fare. "A cup of tea and a roll was taken to him in the car."[15]

The train started up again, racing east to Philadelphia. "I have often wondered," engineer Ed Black recalled, "what the people thought of that short train whizzing through the night. A case of life and death perhaps, and so it was."[16]

AFTER dropping Lincoln off at the train on the outskirts of Harrisburg, Pennsylvania Governor Andrew Curtin had returned to the Executive Mansion. As Curtin recalled, "To avoid inquiries I remained in the house when repeated calls were made by persons who supposed [Mr. Lincoln] was there."[17] The misdirection had worked. If any of the Baltimore plotters had been shadowing Lincoln in Harrisburg this evening, they would now have been led to believe he was still there, with Governor Curtin, in the Executive Mansion. But if any of the Baltimore plotters had been shadowing members of the press rather than Lincoln, they might have been able to learn the truth.

Between 10:30 and 11:00 p.m., members of Lincoln's traveling suite who were not in on the plan, including the reporters for the *New York Times*, *New York Herald*, and *New York World*, were growing suspicious.[18] The president-elect was to have attended a levee hosted by Governor Curtin this evening. By some accounts circulating around Harrisburg that night, he had gone to the Executive Mansion around 6:00 p.m. But Lincoln had not been seen returning to the Jones House. Indeed, other accounts had Lincoln retiring to his room at 8:00 p.m., on the plea of fatigue.[19] This was unusual. Not that Lincoln was not fatigued—the entire trip had been a marathon that was running the man into the ground. But it was unusual that he should decline a previously accepted engagement, fatigued or not. Those who were not privy to the truth, whether at the Executive Mansion or at the Jones House, would naturally have wondered, "Where is Lincoln?" And the newspapermen, including the anonymous reporter for the *New York World*, would have wondered the loudest. All had a deadline to meet but little story to tell.

By several accounts, however, two newspaper reporters traveling with the presidential suite succeeded in gaining access to the real story in Harrisburg the night of February 22. By one account, Joseph Howard, of the *Times*, and Simon P. Hanscom, the reporter for the *New York Herald*,[20] complained when Mr. Lincoln and Governor Curtin failed to appear for the banquet thrown in Lincoln's honor. The reporters had been traveling on the Lincoln Special and reporting faithfully on its exploits for days and must have felt that they had earned the right to know where the president-elect was. And it seems that someone in the presidential suite agreed. Or perhaps there was concern that, with the suspicions of two crack reporters having been raised, it would be better to tell them the truth on the condition that they sit on the story, rather than risk having them learn the truth on their own with no preconditions on their use of the information.

In any event, security risks notwithstanding, someone reportedly decided to let the two newspapermen in on the secret. It would arguably do no harm now. Lincoln was already well on his way. The telegraph lines were cut. The reporters could write salacious stories to their heart's content, but without access to telegraph lines, there would be no way to send them. Besides, it would be far better for Lincoln's handlers to stuff the pillow into the shape they wanted than to let those twin monsters lurking under the bed, Rumor and Gossip, have their way with the story.

The newspapermen were quietly pulled aside to a private room where they were told the astonishing news: the president-elect was no longer in Harrisburg; he was now on his way to Washington. As Howard reported things, "The information had been given under an injunction of secrecy. . . . We were bound by honor not to attempt to use it until the morning, and did not."[21]

But by other accounts, the reporters were bound to secrecy not by honor, but under lock and key and at gunpoint. Indeed, according to this version of the story, they were prevented from running to the telegraph office to report what every fiber of their being must have ached to tell the world. In exchange for having been treated to an exclusive story, the reporters would be precluded from publishing the news until the next morning. To insure they honored the agreement, they were placed under house arrest.[22] Years later, the *Times* would confirm this version of the story, reporting that an officer entered the room of its correspondent Joseph Howard Jr. at the Jones House, informing him of Lincoln's altered course. The officer, however, would not permit the correspondent to leave his room until morning.[23]

By the time he dispatched his report of the day's events from Harrisburg on Saturday morning, Howard of the *New York Times* knew the truth—that Lincoln was no longer there. But if Howard did know, his initial report from Harrisburg would not betray Lincoln. Indeed, his story dated Saturday morning, February 23, 1861, would publish disinformation concerning Lincoln's whereabouts the previous evening and be vague, even cautiously optimistic, about his location that morning: "Mr. Lincoln being physically prostrated by hard labor, did not give the anticipated reception, but like a prudent man went to bed early. We anticipate an exciting time to-day, and praying that it may prove an agreeable excitement, having a prosperous termination, I close."[24]

HAVING waited nearly two hours at the St. Louis Hotel in Philadelphia for word of Lincoln's departure from Harrisburg, Allan Pinkerton could wait no longer. At around 8:30 p.m., he went to the telegraph office and wired the following dispatch to Harrisburg:

> Geo. H. Burns
> Harrisburg
>
> Where is Nuts
>
> J. H. Hutcheson.[25]

While the Northern Central's telegraph lines between Harrisburg and Baltimore had been cut, Pinkerton's plan called for maintaining at least one open line between Harrisburg and Philadelphia and posting a trusted operative, H. E. Thayer, in Philadelphia to monitor all communications, particularly any messages received for "J. H. Hutcheson."[26]

The anxious minutes ticked by as Pinkerton waited for a response from George Burns. By 9:00 p.m., however, Pinkerton still had gotten no reply.

Earlier that morning, Pinkerton had received a telegram from Henry Sanford who stated that "I think we may safely rely that Harrisburg will be isolated completely." Having still not heard anything from George Burns a full thirty minutes after sending him an urgent telegram, perhaps Pinkerton wondered if Henry Sanford's men had done the job of telegraphically isolating Harrisburg just a little too effectively.

Finally at 9:15 p.m., Pinkerton got the news he had so desperately hoped for, a telegram from George H. Burns,[27] indicating that the movements Pinkerton had been directing for the past twenty-four hours were being played to perfection.

> Harrisburg Feb'y 22 1861
>
> J. H. Hutcheson
> St. Louis Hotel Philadelphia.
>
> Nuts left at six—Everything as you directed—all is right.
>
> (Signed) Geo. H. Burns.[28]

Pinkerton, likely relieved, but having no time to celebrate, immediately hired a carriage for Kate Warne and rode with her from the St. Louis Hotel to the corner of Tenth and Chestnut Streets. If Lincoln had left Harrisburg at 6:00 p.m., his train would be arriving in West Philadelphia within the next hour or so; Pinkerton was expecting him around 10:30 p.m. Pinkerton exited the carriage and sent Warne on to the PW&B depot, thirteen blocks south at Broad and Prime Streets. Near the Girard House, Pinkerton hired a second carriage, with a closed cab, and ordered the driver to West Philadelphia, to the Pennsylvania Railroad's depot some twenty blocks away. Unlike an open barouche, the closed cab would offer Pinkerton and Lincoln modest protection, both from the chilly night air and from being recognized.[29]

H. F. Kenney, an employee of the railroad, met Pinkerton at the Pennsylvania depot around 10:00 p.m., and joined him at the carriage, where they waited in the shadows for the short, special train from Harrisburg. They would not need to wait long. But Pinkerton and Kenney apparently had no idea if Lincoln would arrive wearing the same clothes, donning the same stovepipe hat he had doffed this morning at the flag-raising ceremony at Independence Hall, or whether he might be wearing a disguise. If the latter, they appear to have had no advance notice what that disguise might be.[30] It was dark. But they knew Lincoln would be traveling with G. C. Franciscus. If they could spot Franciscus, they'd easily spot Lincoln, no matter how he was dressed. He'd be the tall one.

Pinkerton describes the scene as he waited at the West Philadelphia depot: "I stood with the carriage a few rods west of the Stairs leading from the Street to Mr. Franciscus Office, and was soon joined by Mr. Kinsey [Kenney]. About three minutes past ten, Mr. Lincoln accompanied by W. H. Lamon,

Superintendant Lewis, and assistant Superintendant Franciscus arrived. I met them on the steps. Mr. Lincoln wore a brown Kossuth Hat, and an overcoat thrown loosely over his shoulders."[31] Lincoln thanked Lewis and Franciscus for their kindness, and a grateful Pinkerton promised to send them a telegraph the next morning.[32]

Assuming that they had left Harrisburg at 6:00 p.m., Garman and Black had made great time, given the need to stop at least two or three times to take on water. The two men were rewarded for bringing Mr. Lincoln quickly and safely to Philadelphia. As Garman recalled, "as soon as we stopped, the super-inten[den]t came up to us and handed us two ten dollar gold pieces with the President's compliments, one for the engineer & one for me. So we can say that we got the first money in protecting the President."[33]

The problem now facing Pinkerton, however, was that Lincoln had arrived in Philadelphia a half hour earlier than expected. Pinkerton had instructed Franciscus to get Lincoln to the West Philadelphia depot at around 10:30 p.m.[34] Thanks to Garman shoveling coal into the furnace so furiously that he was rolling in it, and thanks to Black having successfully carried out his instructions to arrive in West Philadelphia "by ten o'clock *sure*," Lincoln was here early. In some ways, it was a nice problem to have, clearly better than the alternative of arriving too late to catch the night train to Baltimore. But Lincoln's early arrival was a problem nonetheless. The regular train to Baltimore was not scheduled to leave until 10:50 p.m., and Pinkerton had made arrangements with S. M. Felton to have its departure delayed a few minutes beyond that. The PW&B Railroad depot in South Philadelphia, at Broad and Prime Streets, was only about 3 miles away, about a fifteen- or twenty-minute carriage ride.

Even as he watched Lincoln step into the closed carriage, Pinkerton must have fretted over what to do with the president-elect to chew up the clock for the next hour. They could not just wait at the West Philadelphia depot or arrive early at the PW&B depot—spies might be stationed at both places. And the telegraph lines between Philadelphia and Baltimore had not been disabled. Even if no conspirators lurked in the shadows at the depots, a stationary closed carriage might attract attention, if only from curious passengers wondering why this particular coach was not for hire. Moreover, Pinkerton couldn't take Lincoln back to the St. Louis Hotel and wait in his room there; Pinkerton hadn't planned on returning to the hotel and had likely settled up and checked out. Besides, even in disguise and under the dimness of the hotel lobby's gas lamps, Lincoln might still be recognized.

Darkness had been Lincoln's ally since leaving Harrisburg, when he needed to escape the throng at the Jones House and beat the clock. Now, darkness would again be the ally with which he would kill time.

)   Pinkerton directed Kenney "to get on the box with the Driver and con-
sume the time by driving Northward in search of some imaginary person, so
that we should not arrive at the Depot until about 11:00 p.m."[35] The carriage
driver would not know the real reason for driving aimlessly about
Philadelphia—and likely did not care, as long as he was compensated for his
time.

Pinkerton took his seat in the carriage with Lincoln and Lamon, and
Kenney climbed up and sat beside the driver, directing him first down Market
Street. Driving "rapidly off without attracting the least attention,"[36] the carriage headed east, crossing the Schuylkill River via the covered bridge to
Nineteenth. Here, the carriage should have turned south in order to head to
the PW&B depot. Instead, Kenney directed the coach three blocks north, to
Vine Street, then east to Seventeenth, where Kenney finally ordered the driver to turn south, proceeding toward the depot slowly, "as if on the lookout for
someone."[37]

While Kenney and the driver wiled away time in this fashion, Lincoln
recounted for Pinkerton what had transpired since they parted company the
night before, of his meeting with Fred Seward, and this evening's events in
Harrisburg. Under any circumstances, Lincoln was a great storyteller. Tonight,
however, he would have been in his glory. His story was real, it involved the
storyteller himself, accompanied by the nodding assent of an eyewitness—
Ward Hill Lamon—and was being told, in essence, in amended form to its
author—Allan Pinkerton. But in all likelihood, Allan Pinkerton, the man
who had worked so tirelessly to develop, to implement, and to maintain secrecy over the plan now being set in motion, grew more anxious by the word.
While he would have been most interested in Lincoln's side of the story, he
most certainly would not have enjoyed what he was about to hear. Contrary to
Burns's telegram, not everything had gone off precisely as Pinkerton had
directed. Equally troubling, Pinkerton was about to learn that his intelligence
from Baltimore may have underestimated the magnitude of the threat waiting
there.

AT approximately 9:50 p.m., George R. Dunn arrived in Philadelphia, having taken the 5:15 p.m. train from Baltimore. He proceeded to the PW&B
depot, where Pinkerton had told him he would find Kate Warne. Dunn knew
the woman operative by sight, and by the alias "Mrs. Cherry." Dunn met
Warne as planned, in the ladies' lounge. In some ways, Warne's was the most
critical part of the plan—she needed to insure that there would be a very private place for a very public person on the regular train to Baltimore.

Dunn gave Warne both oral and written reports from Baltimore as
instructed by Pinkerton.[38] Dunn then left and bought tickets for sleeping car

berths to Washington—one for Pinkerton, one for Warne, and one for an "invalid friend."[39] Shortly after purchasing the tickets, Dunn walked through the waiting train and into the sleeper. Something did not feel right.

As Dunn recalled: "On the front platform & inside the front door of the Sleeping Car, I noticed a small party of men, who from their quiet talk, vigilant appearance and watchfulness, seemed to be on the alert, for Somebody or Something—this feature was not at all satisfactory to me. Knowing the public feeling, I felt very sure that it boded no good to my expected party."[40] Dunn, "turning the matter over" in his mind, felt that, under the circumstances, the rear berths would be best for Lincoln's party and immediately concluded they must enter the sleeper through the rear door.[41] In this way, Lincoln might avoid passing by the watchful men at the front of the car. He could, in theory, be safely tucked behind a curtained berth without ever being seen.

There were several problems to overcome. While tickets could be purchased for the sleeper car, individual berths could not be reserved. Lincoln would be arriving late as it was and would need to take whatever berth—if any—remained. Also, the rear entrance to sleeper cars was typically locked— as this one was. Were it otherwise, stowaways could sneak aboard by slipping through the back door. In some ways, that is exactly what Lincoln was—a stowaway who needed to sneak aboard the sleeper unnoticed.

Dunn went searching for the key to the rear door. He found that a man named Knox held the key. Knox, however, refused Dunn's request for it. Dunn persisted, explaining with the perfect ruse why he needed the key—"for the accommodation of an invalid, who would arrive late, and did not desire to be carried through the narrow passage way of the crowded car." Apparently moved by this explanation, Knox gave Dunn the key.

Dunn returned to Kate Warne in the ladies' room of the depot and told her what he had done regarding the key to the rear door. She seemed satisfied and asked to be shown to the berth of the sleeper. Dunn escorted Warne through the crowd at the front of the sleeper and toward the rear, which convinced her that Dunn's decision to have Lincoln pass through the rear door was "very correct." As Dunn recalled, "so soon as the lady was comfortably fixed, I slipped quietly out of the back door, locking it after me, and kept a good lookout."[42]

While Dunn watched for Pinkerton at the rear door, it became Kate Warne's job to save the sleeping berths. This proved more difficult than saving a pew of seats for a family in church. As Warne reported: "I found it almost impossible to save the Berths to-gether. This sleeping car was conducted differently from any I ever saw before—they gave no Tickets, and any person could take a Berth where they pleased. I gave the Conductor half a dollar to keep my berths, and by standing right by myself we manage[d] to keep them."[43]

As they continued to ride through the dark streets of Philadelphia "in search of some imaginary person," Lincoln told Pinkerton about Fred Seward coming to see him the night before, bearing letters from his father, Senator William Seward, and General Scott, stating substantially the same intelligence of a plot to assassinate him as Pinkerton had uncovered, "but much stronger: that about Fifteen Thousand men were organized to prevent his passage through Baltimore, and that arrangements were made by these parties to blow up the Rail Road track, fire the Train &c."[44]

This news would have been startling and even incredible to Pinkerton. His operatives had discovered only a small group of suspected Baltimore plotters intent on murdering Lincoln. Seward's intelligence, however, as relayed by Lincoln, revealed that about *fifteen thousand men* were organized to prevent Lincoln's passage through Baltimore.[45] Pinkerton, Lamon, and Kate Warne would have trouble enough providing safe passage for Lincoln through a gauntlet of a dozen or so suspected assassins. But *fifteen thousand?* If Seward's intelligence was accurate, Baltimore had amassed an army sufficient to man its three railroad depots with a brigade of five thousand assassins each. Hopefully, putting Lincoln on a night train through Baltimore nine hours before he was expected, in disguise, hidden behind curtains on a sleeper car, under the ruse that he was an invalid, with three armed guards, would get him through. It had better. It was too late now for Pinkerton to devise any other plan.

While their carriage continued to kill time ambling through the narrow streets of Philadelphia, Lamon offered Lincoln a revolver and a bowie knife to carry with him through Baltimore. Pinkerton protested immediately, saying he "would not for the world have it said that Mr. Lincoln had to enter the National Capitol Armed."[46]

Lincoln agreed. He said he wanted no arms. He said he had no fear. He felt confident Pinkerton's plan would work.

"Mr. Lincoln was cool, calm, and self possessed—firm and determined in his bearing. He evinced no sign of fear or distrust, and throughout the entire night was quite self possessed."[47]

The carriage carrying Lincoln, Lamon, Pinkerton, and H. F. Kenney continued slowly in the shadow of red-bricked eighteenth-century row houses, heading south on Seventeenth Street, crossing Chestnut Street, then Walnut, passing Rittenhouse Square, across Spruce, Pine, Lombard, and South Streets.

Intelligence received from Baltimore by PW&B Railroad employee George Stearns weeks before revealed that the conspirators intent on assassinating the president-elect had been stalking him. Such persons "had spies following Mr. Lincoln and were in constant communication with . . . parties in Baltimore giving them information on Mr. Lincoln's movements."[48] If perchance any such spies had followed Lincoln this evening, they would have seen his carriage slow as it neared the PW&B station. They would have seen one of the

occupants of the carriage, a man carrying a package, jump out a block shy of
the depot. They would have seen "Package Man" stand in the shadows, watching as Lincoln's carriage moved on. They might at first have concluded that
the man was unrelated to Lincoln's party, just another fare, splitting the cost
of the ride. But if unrelated, why did the man continue to watch the carriage
from which he had just alighted, then walk in the same direction the carriage
took, following it toward the depot?

After dropping off the man with the package, Lincoln's carriage proceeded
quietly up Carpenter Street, the cross street nearest the depot, "so that its
occupants might alight in the shadow of the yard fence there."[49] Pinkerton,
Lincoln, and Lamon left the carriage in a dark spot a short distance from the
depot. Leaning heavily on Pinkerton's arm, and "stooping a considerable for
the purpose of disguising his height," Lincoln headed into the depot, led by
Pinkerton. Lamon followed behind. The three men walked briskly through
the train station.[50]

For the first time on this journey, Abraham Lincoln, the man who had
countless times risen up to his full height, whether to stand erect in an open
carriage, to give an impromptu speech, or to go back-to-back in a measuring
contest, now shrunk from his height, stooping, he likely felt, beneath more
than just his stature. "What would the nation think of its President stealing
into the Capital like a thief in the night?" Lincoln had reportedly wondered
aloud earlier tonight in Harrisburg. Perhaps now to himself, he wondered it
still.

As Lincoln emerged from the other side of the depot, he passed between
the train's conductor, John Litzenberg, and a police officer standing at the
door. Would they know him? Unlike other cities that had not yet seen the new
Lincoln with his crop of freshly sprouted whiskers, Philadelphia had seen plenty of him that morning and the previous day. Perhaps the police officer was
one of the several hundred links that had stood in the long blue chain of arm-
locked or mounted policemen holding back the crush of humanity as Lincoln's
carriage passed through the crowded streets the day before and again this
morning.

Seeing, but apparently not recognizing the late-arriving Lincoln intent on
boarding the night train, Conductor Litzenberg remarked, "well, old fellow, it
is lucky for you that our president detained the train . . . or you would have
been left."[51] Perhaps Lincoln's heart jumped upon hearing that "our president"
had detained the train, before realizing the conductor meant the railroad's, not
the country's president. Perhaps Lincoln replied; perhaps he merely nodded in
a motion barely noticed beneath the soft felt hat pulled low over his eyes and
behind the muffler wrapped around his throat. Perhaps he felt a pang of guilty
deception, blended with the syrupy satisfaction of knowing that he had just
passed completely unrecognized between the two men, close enough to touch

them. Pinkerton too must have felt a sense of pride in hearing that, as scripted, the train had been held for them and seeing that Lincoln, stooped and cloaked, was unrecognizable. Pinkerton's plan was working.

George Dunn, still waiting for Pinkerton by the rear door to the sleeping car, saw Lincoln emerge from the depot. Dunn recalled Lincoln wearing an ordinary sack overcoat, a Kossuth hat, and a muffler around his throat, carrying a traveling bag—likely the same grip Robert had lost—in his hand. Lincoln, accompanied by Pinkerton, was being followed by another man, whom Dunn did not recognize.[52] There was no time for questions. Dunn "quickly caught Mr. Pinkerton's eye," unlocked the rear door to the sleeping car and led him, Lincoln, and the burly man he did not know, into the car. No one appeared to notice them. "In less time it takes to write this," Dunn recalled, "all . . . were safely housed, and locked in the rear end of the car."[53]

Once inside the sleeping car, the party was met by Kate Warne. She showed Pinkerton the rear berths she had struggled, and then bribed, the conductor to hold. Pinkerton introduced Mrs. Warne to Mr. Lincoln. Lincoln then crawled into his sleeping birth and drew the curtains. Dunn left the car.[54]

Meanwhile, the man who had jumped out of Lincoln's carriage carrying a package had remained in the shadows a short distance from the depot. There he stood until he saw Pinkerton and Lincoln get out and walk into the station.[55] Once he was certain Lincoln had boarded the sleeping car, he strode quickly to the huffing engine, where he delivered the package to its conductor, John Litzenberg. Unlike the late arriving, stooped passenger he had seen moments before, Litzenberg recognized the man with the package—indeed, the conductor had been holding the train for him.

The man with the package was H. F. Kenney. Earlier that afternoon, in Felton's office, Pinkerton and Felton had instructed Kenney to have Litzenberg, who was unaware of Pinkerton's plan, hold the train until Litzenberg should receive from Kenney's hands an "important parcel." Kenney was to inform Litzenberg that Mr. Felton wanted this parcel delivered to E. J. Allen at Willard's Hotel in Washington.[56] Felton had addressed the parcel "in a fair, round hand,"[57] attached a great seal to it, marked it as very important, and endorsed his name on it. He gave the package to Kenney, along with a note to Litzenberg not to start his train until he received the all-important parcel from Kenney, "as this package *must* go through to Washington on *tonight's train*."[58]

Now, as planned, Kenney gave Litzenberg the package and the order to start the train. "It was at once put in motion, the time being 10:55 p.m., five minutes after the regular time for starting," and only about three minutes after Lincoln's party had boarded.[59]

As his train left the station, Conductor Litzenberg must have indulged his imagination with visions of what vital contents the heavy package might contain. Litzenberg had no idea, however, that the most important package of all rested not in his hands, but cramped at the back of the sleeping car, behind a curtain covering the last section of berths. As Mr. Lincoln lay in the sleeping car, Kate Warne recalled "He talked very friendly for some time." She added, however, that "Mr. Lincoln is very homely, and so very tall that he could not lay straight in his berth."[60]

For the first time since leaving Springfield eleven days earlier, Lincoln was no longer riding on a special train. The train, being a regular, was open to anyone able to procure a ticket. There would be no military escort. There would be no gang of friends. These facts and the possibility of Lincoln's altered travel plans being leaked to outsiders like Fred Seward, combined to create a tense situation for Pinkerton. Fred Seward had this morning telegraphed his father, Senator William Seward, suggesting that his urgent messages, including the letter from General Scott, had convinced the president-elect to "arrive in Washington at a different hour than that announced." Indeed, young Seward's message had induced his father and Congressman Washburne to wait for Lincoln at the Washington depot earlier in the afternoon, only to leave disappointed.[61]

If the Baltimore plotters had somehow learned that Lincoln would be on tonight's regular train from Philadelphia to Washington, or even if they merely suspected as much, for example, by intercepting and deciphering Fred Seward's communication to his father, there was nothing that Allan Pinkerton or Kate Warne or even the burly Ward Hill Lamon could do to prevent them from boarding this train, even armed as they were to the teeth.

Indeed, unbeknownst to Pinkerton, Warne, or Lamon, just a few berths away in Lincoln's sleeping car lay a man who, like Pinkerton, was also eager to reach Baltimore. Like Pinkerton, the man was also interested in Lincoln's movements. Most likely, he was one of the furtive, watchful men that George Dunn and Kate Warne had observed lurking around the front of the sleeping car moments before. Like Pinkerton and Lamon, this man was also heavily armed.

At approximately 11:00 p.m., as Lincoln's night train was leaving Philadelphia, the "gallant little band" of Baltimore Republicans, with Worthington G. Snethen at the lead, finally arrived in Harrisburg without knowing what to expect.[62] The committee immediately called on Lincoln at the Jones House. They must have been tired; their journey from Baltimore had taken five hours, and it was late.

After being told Lincoln was unavailable, Snethen sought out "Commissariat" Wood. Wood confirmed to Snethen that he had received his two telegrams. Although Lincoln was indisposed this evening, Wood promised Snethen that his Baltimore committee would see the president-elect the next morning, and that they could accompany him on the train to Baltimore.[63]

Those in Lincoln's party who did not know Lincoln had already left Harrisburg, the Baltimore Republicans chief among them, went to bed believing that they, and Lincoln, would be taking the Northern Central Railroad directly to Baltimore the next day. But for much of the evening, the route the party would take remained in doubt. The anonymous correspondent for the *New York World*, who was either not in on the secret or intentionally sending disinformation, wrote in his dispatch: "The route to Baltimore to-morrow was not determined till this evening, as it was debated whether or not Mr. Lincoln should ride from depot to depot or go by a route which avoided a change of cars."[64]

"Riding from depot to depot" meant taking the Northern Central route direct from Harrisburg and riding in a carriage in Baltimore from the Calvert Street Station to the Camden Street Station.[65] Going "by a route which avoided a change of cars" meant going to Baltimore via Philadelphia on S. M. Felton's road, which permitted the cars at the President Street depot to be uncoupled from the locomotive and drawn by horses along tracks in the streets to the Camden Street depot, avoiding the need to change cars. This was the same route Lincoln was taking.

Clearly, this indecision had been precipitated by fears of what awaited them in Baltimore. Wrote the *World's* anonymous correspondent: "The party call Baltimore an infested district, and doubted what to do. Finally it was arranged to leave here at 9 o'clock, arriving at Baltimore and Washington at different hours than were before arranged. They go by direct route from here, and ride through Baltimore, dining, by invitation of Mr. Coleman, at the Eutaw house."[66]

This dispatch, under the anonymous byline "From our Special Correspondent," would be published the next day in the *New York World*.[67] Any Baltimore plotters reading the news would have blanched at seeing their city referred to as "an infested district." Upon reading this report, however, they would have been led to believe, erroneously, that Lincoln would indeed plan to ride in a carriage through Baltimore and dine at the Eutaw House tomorrow afternoon.

AT around midnight, some 20 to 30 miles southwest of Philadelphia, Lincoln's night train approached the half-moon arc scribed by the border of northern Delaware, and Lincoln crossed the slave line for the first time on his journey. Pinkerton, a staunch abolitionist who had assisted runaway slaves heading north to freedom on the Underground Railroad, should have appreciated the irony—he was now using the rails to smuggle the nation's new leader south, into slave territory.[68]

As the locomotive's drive wheels reversed and the train slowed at the Wilmington station, a brakeman on board took special interest. As the train screeched to a stop, the man noted the time of its arrival. Lincoln's friends had disabled the telegraph lines between Harrisburg and Baltimore. They had, however, left the lines between Wilmington and Baltimore untouched. Whether the brakeman on board was watching the clock or eyeing his pocket watch, he knew his objective. If Lincoln's train was running late, he was to telegraph that intelligence to another man, one with whom he had conspired, who now waited in Baltimore. If, on the other hand, the train was running on time, no telegraph would be sent, and his colleague would know to expect Lincoln's train in Baltimore on schedule. The man checked the time. And then he made an important decision. He needed to send an urgent telegram to Baltimore.

Lincoln's train, which had left Philadelphia five or ten minutes late, had indeed arrived late in Wilmington, causing George Stearns to telegraph his brother William in Baltimore. Now it was William Stearns's time to act. His boss, Samuel Felton instructed him

> to say to the people of the Washington Branch road that I had an important package I was getting ready for the eleven P.M., train; that it was necessary I should have this package delivered in Washington early the next morning without fail; that I was straining every nerve to get it ready by eleven o'clock, but, in case I did not succeed, I should delay the train until it was ready,— probably not more than half an hour; and I wished, as a personal favor, that the Washington train should await the coming of ours from Philadelphia before leaving. This request was willingly complied with by the managers of the Washington Branch; and the man whom I had sent to Baltimore so informed me by telegraph cipher.[69]

But Felton's "personal favor," requested of the B&O in Baltimore, must have raised suspicions. What contents could this "important package" contain that justified holding an entire train of weary, impatient, paying passengers even for half an hour?

The "important package" was now in the hands of the train's conductor, John Litzenberg. As his train once again rolled south, Conductor Litzenberg approached his brakeman, George Stearns. Litzenberg had a probing question that must have frozen Stearns in his tracks. "George," Litzenberg asked, "I thought you and I were old friends; and why did you not tell me we had Old Abe on board?"[70]

For weeks, rumors had swirled that those intending to murder Lincoln in Baltimore had been stalking him, likely to gather information about how Lincoln was guarded, how many there were, and how they were armed, a reality that must have passed through George Stearns's mind the moment his conductor correctly identified their precious cargo. Ironically, however, stalking Lincoln was not necessary. For two cents—the price of the *Philadelphia Inquirer*—such intelligence was within the easy grasp of anyone plotting to kill Lincoln. A gang of assassins in Baltimore would have known from published reports that when Lincoln arrived in Baltimore with no military escort to greet him, they would face a small band of no more than seven armed men. Some of whom, like Edwin Sumner and George Hazzard, were indeed battle tested, but others, such as the youthful, yet forcefully protective Elmer Ellsworth, likely were not. The plotters would have known that David Hunter was likely out of commission due to his dislocated shoulder suffered in Buffalo, possibly reducing the security detail to six. They would have known that while Sumner was a courageous military veteran, he was aging fast. They would have known of the Herculean efforts of these men, most prominently Ward Hill Lamon, in stemming the tide of crushing humanity that had pressed dangerously upon Lincoln at the numerous train depots along the route. And if the assassins had done their homework, they would have known that in addition to having at least one man designated as the trigger man for killing Lincoln, they would need at least one man to run interference with each of these seven military men who would almost certainly be willing to lay down their lives in defense of the president-elect. This meant that the Baltimore plotters would require a total of at least eight men—one to kill Lincoln and seven to run interference.

Whether by coincidence or design, there is some evidence that those masterminding the Baltimore Plot knew that they would need precisely eight men to carry out their objective. The Baltimore plotters' plan can be reconstructed from Pinkerton's reports, derived in turn from shadowy sources, from sensational newspaper stories, and even from folklore and legend. Piecing these bits of often vague and sometimes contradictory information together, the blurry outline of a plan that had reportedly been hatched and nurtured for about the past three weeks emerges. To the extent the plan needed money— whether to hire assassins, to induce them with a success bonus, to purchase weapons, to buy police complicity, or to hire schooners for escape—the blood money was reportedly provided by wealthy Baltimoreans and others, but their names have never been identified. To the extent the plan needed assassins, they were allegedly chosen from a select group of around twenty men. By one popular story, a secret conclave of these men, including two of Pinkerton's operatives, Timothy Webster and Harry W. Davies, a.k.a. "A.F.C." a.k.a. "Joseph

Howard," gathered on the evening of February 18 in a solemn ceremony. Under oath, in a darkened room in Baltimore, they would choose lots placed in a box.[71] Behind closed doors and with heavy quilts covering the windows, they were told that one among them would draw a red ballot. He would tell no one. He could choose his weapon, whether the bullet or the blade. He would be honor bound to carry out his mission. Like a firing squad in which all the rifles but one contained live rounds, no one would know for certain who the assassin would be. But unlike the firing squad, the assassin would know.

As the legend goes, the twenty men, their pledge of secrecy having been given with their hands on the ballot box and on Captain Ferrandini's stiletto, drew their ballots. They each left the darkened room. Under a street lamp, a hotel gas lamp, or by the glow of a hearth, they read their fate, the luck of the draw, as dictated by the color of their ballot, red or white. Anyone that night seeing he had drawn a red ballot would have believed that he alone had been chosen. But he had been deceived. The plot was too vital to be entrusted to one bullet, to one blade, or to one lone assassin. As the legend goes, there was not one red ballot among the group of twenty that night. There were *eight*. And if the legend is true, tonight the leaders of the Baltimore Plot believed eight anxious men prepared to immortalize themselves—each without knowing that seven other men prepared to do the same.[72]

But if the legend is true, the Baltimore Plot leadership had not only outsmarted the eight assassins, they had been outsmarted themselves. Reportedly, after Webster and Davies, ballots in hand, left the conclave, they returned "by devious byways to the Pinkerton headquarters, entering about the same time." Each drew out his ballot. They were both red. The Baltimore Plot leadership, believing they had just inaugurated eight assassins, had unknowingly reduced their number to six.[73] But even six assassins are more than enough. Indeed, one lone assassin might be enough to kill Abraham Lincoln in Baltimore.

CHAPTER SIXTEEN

AN UNEXPECTED ARRIVAL

Saturday morning, February 23, 1861
Baltimore–Washington

IT HAD BEEN A STROKE OF GENIUS to put Lincoln in the last sleeping car. From here, only one door, the front entrance, would need to be watched while the train rolled south. Lincoln's regular night train would have to make up to thirty scheduled stops on its four-and-a-half-hour jaunt from Philadelphia to Baltimore. There were no air brakes in this era, no air hoses running from one control to multiple breaking mechanisms on the car wheels. Individual brakemen needed to man every platform, both fore and aft of each car, and manually apply braking levers to halt the train as smoothly as possible while the engineer reversed the locomotive's drive wheels. The front of Lincoln's sleeping car was most likely manned by one of Felton's trusted men, George Stearns, for this purpose. But the rear platform of the last car needed no brakeman. From this vantage, Pinkerton could therefore maintain a sharp lookout without being observed or suspected.[1] And while the train paused at its many stops, Pinkerton and/or Lamon could guard the rear door with their brace of weapons, ready to warn any who might try to enter of the sick and presumably contagious man who lay within. Even if, as Kate Warne suspected, there were men on the sleeper car who were not "all right," they would have a difficult time identifying Lincoln. At best, the car was dimly lit by a few flickering candles. It would have been difficult to recognize Lincoln even were he not wearing a disguise and shrouded by curtains drawn across his berth.

For Lincoln and his party, it must have been a long and lonely hundred miles between Philadelphia and Baltimore that night. But no more so than at the crossing over the mile-wide Susquehanna River from the northeastern shore to Havre de Grace on the southwestern bank. Pinkerton knew it was here, while crossing the river, that Lincoln was most vulnerable. For it was here that

Lincoln's railcar would need to be rolled onto a steamer and be ferried across the same river he had ridden beside in Harrisburg several hours earlier.

Allan Pinkerton could not have slept even had he wanted to. He was on duty. Moreover, he had reason to believe the Baltimore plotters might attempt to assassinate Lincoln by throwing his train from the track, by sinking the ferry at Havre de Grace, or by destroying one of the bridges north of Baltimore over which the train would pass. Aware of the possiblity of sabotage, Pinkerton had just about enough operatives stationed in and around Baltimore to post one before each crossing. Their job would be to signal Pinkerton with a flashing light ostensibly in time for Pinkerton to warn the conductor if there were trouble. As Pinkerton recalled:

> In order to prevent the possibility of accident, I had arranged with my men a series of signals along the road. It was barely possible that the work of destroying the railroad might be attempted by some reckless individuals, or that a suspicion of our movements might be entertained by the conspirators, and therefore, the utmost caution must be observed.
>
> As the train approached Havre de Grace, I went to the rear platform of the car, and as the train passed on a bright light flashed suddenly upon my gaze and was as quickly extinguished, and then I knew that thus far all was well.[2]

Upon returning to the car, Lincoln remarked to Pinkerton, "We are at Havre de Grace, we are getting along very well. I think we are on time."[3] Pinkerton observed that while Lincoln did not sleep, he was nonetheless calm throughout the night. "I cannot realize how any man situated as he was could have shown more calmness or firmness than he did during the whole trip," Pinkerton recalled.[4]

The train continued on, the ferry safely making it across the Susquehanna. From Havre de Grace all the way to Baltimore, Pinkerton observed a flashing signal light before every bridge crossing; "their rays carried the comforting assurance 'All's Well!'"[5]

All was indeed well at the river crossings. This was good news. But by posting his operatives at these remote bridges north of Baltimore, Pinkerton had taken a calculated risk. Guarding against one danger had left another unattended. Stationing Pinkerton's men at the bridges tonight made it impossible for them to shadow the suspected conspirators in Baltimore.

IN Baltimore at around 3:30 a.m., Abraham Lincoln's train from Philadelphia, laden with weary, unsuspecting passengers, a suspicious conductor with an important, mysterious package, gun-toting, knife-wielding agents and bodyguards, and the president-elect of the United States, rolled unceremoniously into the President Street Station. Here, William Stearns entered the sleeper car, and before replacing his brother George at the brake,[6] whispered something into Pinkerton's ear.[7] As Pinkerton recalled: "We reached Baltimore at about half-past three o'clock in the morning, and as the train rumbled into the depot an officer of the road entered the car and whispered in my ear the welcome words 'All's Well!'"[8]

Less than twelve hours before the city had been far from all right, overrun with hordes of roving Baltimore roughs; but the mob had gone, back to their familiar haunts, their back alleys, their saloons, their houses of prostitution, perhaps under the impression that Lincoln was sticking to the published itinerary and would leaving Harrisburg the next morning for Baltimore, arriving at the Calvert Street Station at half past noon. They would have plenty of time to return and secure a good spot, either near the tracks, or near the depot where Lincoln would pass in an open barouche

In all their wildest imaginings, the conspirators must not have expected that Abraham Lincoln, the man who had thus far traveled only in broad daylight, who had stopped at every major city along the Lincoln Special's route to speak to large crowds, and often rode standing and exposed in open carriages, would slip through Baltimore under cover of darkness, without his family and friends, wearing a disguise. Such, however, was the brilliance of Pinkerton's plan. Whatever the Baltimore plotters believed, and wherever they were at 3:30 on the morning of February 23, 1861, they were not at the President Street Station waiting for Lincoln.

After Lincoln's train came to a stop, Kate Warne left the car and got into a carriage for her hotel.[9] Her mission now was to take Baltimore's pulse, to diagnose "what the feelings of the people were in the city."[10] The party was now down to three, Pinkerton, Lamon, and Lincoln. Their train to Washington would not leave for another forty-five minutes. Their sleeping car was uncoupled from the train. From here, the car would be drawn by a team of horses from the President Street Station to the Washington Station (also known as the Camden Street Station) a little over a mile away.[11] An eerie silence met the now vulnerable party.

"The city was in profound repose as we passed through," Pinkerton recalled. "Darkness and silence reigned over all." As Ward Hill Lamon recalled, "the passengers, tucked away on their narrow shelves, dozed on as peacefully as if Mr. Lincoln had never been born."[12]

Lincoln's horse-drawn car headed north on President Street, four blocks to Pratt Street. During the day, Pratt Street was a crowded boulevard passing along the heads of the docks and the waterfront of the Inner Harbor. Now, at 3:30 a.m., Pratt Street lay quiet, but for the gentle clop of horses pulling Lincoln's sleeper and the rhythmic lapping of the harbor off the left side of the car.

Lincoln's rail car now turned south on Howard Street. Here, it drew near the Camden Street Station, a wide, three-story brick structure dotted with numerous windows that gave the institutional appearance of a school building or a hospital. If William Stearns had been successful—his "package" not arousing suspicion—the regularly scheduled B&O train to Washington would be waiting, idling in the station. The horse-drawn sleeping car would then be coupled to the train with the cold clank of metal, the engine would heave forward, and the train would lurch toward Washington, where it was scheduled to arrive at dawn; that is, assuming no Baltimore plotters were waiting for him at the Camden Street Station.

IN Harrisburg, members of Lincoln's party were up early, if they had slept at all. Recalled one witness, "It was a long, weary night of fretful anxiety to the dozen or more in Harrisburg who had knowledge of the sudden departure of Lincoln. No one attempted to sleep. All felt that the fate of the nation hung on the safe progress of Lincoln to Washington without detection on his journey."[13]

The telegraph wires between Harrisburg and Baltimore that Andrew Wynne had disconnected the night before would be reconnected later this morning. By the time that happened, Lincoln would either have made it through Baltimore, or he would not. Either way, reconnecting the lines now could do nothing to help the Baltimore plotters, any more than it could harm Lincoln. At the Jones House, "anxious watchers" and "a wife whose sobbing heart could not be controlled"[14] waited for but a few telegraphed words—that Abraham Lincoln had arrived safely in Washington. The newspaper reporters in Harrisburg also eagerly awaited the news. They had been up early, editing salacious news stories of Lincoln's daring escape. They could not telegraph their sensational dispatches until news of Lincoln's safe arrival in Washington was confirmed.

But the Lincoln party in Harrisburg was not the only group anxiously awaiting news from Washington. In Philadelphia, G. C. Franciscus and Enoch Lewis, executives of the Pennsylvania Railroad who had accompanied Lincoln from Harrisburg to Philadelphia the night before, also waited. Also in Philadelphia, Samuel Felton of the Philadelphia, Wilmington, and Baltimore Railroad that had provided Lincoln's sleeper car, waited, as did H. E. Thayer, manager of the American Telegraph Company's Philadelphia office. In New York, Edward S. Sanford, general superintendent of the American Telegraph Company waited. And in Chicago, George H. Bangs, superintendent of Pinkerton's detective agency, waited for news that all was well in Washington—and that all was well with his boss.

Thomas Nast's fanciful illustration of Lincoln—the tallest figure in the center—secretly arriving at Camden Station, Baltimore. In reality, Lincoln's sleeper car was drawn by horses to the station so that Lincoln could remain hidden. (*Museum of Fine Arts, Boston*)

It was 6:00 a.m. If all had gone well, Abraham Lincoln and Allan Pinkerton should have arrived in Washington by now. All around the country, anxious eyes watched and waited for idle telegraph instruments to start twitching.

AT around 6:00 a.m. on February 23, 1861, in Washington, Congressman Elihu B. Washburne trembled with foreboding as he stood alone, hidden behind a pillar at the old Washington depot. Washburne had plenty of cause to fret. Of all people, he knew well the threats that awaited Lincoln not only in Baltimore, but also in the nation's capital this morning. As a sitting Republican congressman from Illinois, he had stationed himself in Washington months before as a sort of congressional scout for his friend Lincoln, as a member of the unofficial "independent committee of safety" that he and a small band of other young Republican leaders, including Lucius E. Chittenden, had loosely cobbled together. For months, through frequent letters, written more in the nature of confidential, rumor-laden dispatches than personal greetings, Washburne had advised his state's favorite son of the swirling political winds in the nation's capital.

Just two days before, at around 11:30 on the evening of February 21, 1861, three men armed with bowie knives ambushed a young Republican representative from New York, Charles H. Van Wyck, and attempted to assassinate him. While he walked alone on Capitol Hill, a stout assailant rushed the thirty-six-year-old congressman from behind, lunging at him with a knife. Van Wyck turned to face his attacker as the weapon pierced his outer clothing. Miraculously, Van Wyck's life was spared, thanks to a thick memorandum book and a copy of the *Globe* newspaper tucked inside the breast pocket of his frock coat. The second-term congressman reacted quickly, knocking the assailant down, only to be attacked by a second man, who also lunged at him with a bowie knife. Van Wyck parried the blow, sustaining a severe gash to his left palm in the process. Maintaining his presence of mind, Van Wyck drew a revolver and fired at the first assassin. He was then struck with a severe blow on the head by a third assailant, whereupon he fell to the ground unconscious. When he came to moments later, Van Wyck saw two men carrying off the apparently gunshot-wounded first assailant.[15] Van Wyck survived the attack, but his wound was serious. Four days after the ambush, it would be reported that "Mr. Van Wyck's condition is unimproved. His injuries are internal, and he is troubled with frequent fits of vomiting."[16]

The object of the Van Wyck attack was not robbery—nothing had been taken from him. More likely, this was an attempted assassination of an outspoken critic of slavery who, during the last session of Congress, had railed against the institution, citing instances of slave burning. After giving the speech, Van Wyck, like Lincoln, had begun receiving letters threatening his life.[17]

Ironically, it would be reported that "some skilful detective officers, of Baltimore, are on the track of the assassins, and it is strongly intimated that three other members [of Congress] have been picked out for similar attempts."[18] If Pinkerton's suspicions about the Baltimore police were accurate, the three would-be Van Wyke assassins would have little to fear.

If Washburne had considered this recent attack on Van Wyck and the suspected similar threats to other members of Congress, considered the brutal, nearly fatal caning of the Republican senator Charles Sumner by South Carolinian Preston Brooks on the floor of the Senate a few years before, and considered the swirling Lincoln assassination threats, he could be excused for crouching behind a pillar at the train depot. Not only would a Washburne sighting this morning potentially foretell Lincoln's arrival; these days in Washington, it was practically open season on Republicans or anyone else loyal to the Union or critical of slavery.

Against this background of intimidation and violence, Washburne waited anxiously in the dim and dingy Washington train depot for two Republican titans—Lincoln and Seward—to show. Lincoln yet lived, or so he hoped, and Washington was yet the nation's—or at least the *Union's*—capital.

But something was wrong. Senator Seward, with whom Washburne had waited for Lincoln at the depot the evening before, was to have been here this morning, to join Washburne in renewed hopes of meeting the president-elect. But Seward was nowhere to be seen. Perhaps Washburne worried over the future secretary of state's safety as well as Lincoln's. "I was on hand in season," wrote Washburne, "but to my great disappointment Governor Seward did not appear. I planted myself behind one of the great pillars in the old Washington and Baltimore depot, where I could see and not be observed. Presently the train came rumbling in on time. It was a moment of great anxiety to me."[19]

Washburne scanned the hordes of unfamiliar faces exiting the arriving Baltimore train in hopes of seeing but one familiar face, that of his good friend Lincoln. But like Seward, Lincoln was nowhere to be seen. "I stood behind the pillar awaiting the arrival of the train. When it came to a stop I watched with fear and trembling to see the passengers descend. I saw every car emptied, and there was no Mr. Lincoln."[20]

Congressman Elihu Washburne. This Lincoln confidante kept his friend informed of rumors swirling in Washington. (*Library of Congress*)

Seeing the last passengers leave the cars with no Abraham Lincoln among them, Congressman Washburne believed the president-elect was not on board. Moreover, Senator Seward had failed to show. A dejected, disconsolate Elihu B. Washburne prepared to leave the station.

After watching every car empty without Mr. Lincoln, "I was well-nigh in despair," recalled Washburne many years later, "and when about to leave I saw slowly emerge from the last sleeping car three persons." Washburne looked closely. Could it be? "I could not mistake the long, lank form of Mr. Lincoln, and my heart bounded with joy and gratitude. He had on a soft low-crowned hat, a muffler around his neck, and a short bob-tailed overcoat. Any one who knew him at that time could not have failed to recognize him at once, but, I must confess, he looked more like a well-to-do farmer from one of the back towns of Jo Daviess County[21] coming to Washington to see the city, take out his land warrant and get the patent for his farm, than the President of the United States. . . . The only persons that accompanied Mr. Lincoln were Pinkerton, the well-known detective . . . and Ward H. Lamon."[22]

FOR the first time on this godforsaken journey, Abraham Lincoln could arrive at a host city's train depot, exit the train, stroll through the station like a normal human being, and go to his hotel without being put on display like a circus attraction. No handshaking. No speech giving. No crushing crowds. No parades. Lincoln must have relished walking through the depot unrecognized and unnoticed, simply to be left alone, ignored like any other passenger. Except that Abraham Lincoln was not like any other passenger. And he had not arrived unrecognized or unnoticed.

Pinkerton, meanwhile, had gotten Lincoln safely to Washington, but now what? Despite all the days, even weeks, of intelligence gathering and careful planning, there exists no evidence that Pinkerton had thought through the critical endgame of precisely how he would safely transport the president-elect from the old Washington and Baltimore train depot of the B&O Railroad, situated at the corner of New Jersey Avenue and C Street,[23] just north of the Capitol, to Willard's Hotel at Fourteenth Street and Pennsylvania Avenue, roughly a mile away. Perhaps they would walk through the rutted, unpaved streets. Lincoln wouldn't have minded that; in fact, he would have welcomed the chance to stretch his long legs and breathe in the crisp winter air of a promising new day, as the rising sun nudged him from behind. But Lincoln was still incognito. If Pinkerton had admonished Lincoln to stoop over, as he had done in Philadelphia eight hours earlier in order to disguise his almost freakish height, this would have made the option of walking to Willard's impractical. Besides, it would not do for the president of the United States to shuffle like an invalid, stooped over, for a twelve-block slog down Pennsylvania Avenue. It might not be safe, and it would definitely not be dignified. In all likelihood, Pinkerton merely planned to hire a carriage and drive Lincoln as rapidly and anonymously as possible to Willard's.

As he escorted Lincoln through the long, dark, dingy depot, watching the shadows and everything that had eyes, Pinkerton observed a man he knew—William Stearns, master mechanic of Felton's Philadelphia, Wilmington, and Baltimore Railroad, silently pass close by. Two and a half hours before, Stearns had boarded the train in Baltimore and whispered to Pinkerton that "all was right."[24] But the vigilant detective saw something now that did *not* look all right. "A gentleman looked very sharp at Mr. Lincoln who was on my right, and as we passed him he caught hold of Mr. Lincoln saying 'Abe you can't play that on me.'"[25] The gesture and remark might have come from friend or foe alike. Taking no chances, Pinkerton was quick to respond.

"I hit the gentleman a punch with my elbow as he was close to me, staggering him back, but he recovered himself, and again took hold of Mr. Lincoln remarking that he knew him. I was beginning to think that we were discovered, and that we *might* have to fight, and drew back clenching my fist, and raising it to take the gentleman a blow, when Mr. Lincoln took hold of my arm saying 'Don't strike him Allan, don't strike him—that is my friend Washburne—don't you know him?'"[26]

Pinkerton, who had just created a minor incident, ironically cautioned Washburne as they walked through the depot "not to do or say aught which would attract the attention of the passengers."[27] As if elbowing a United States congressman in the gut and "staggering him back" would not have attracted the attention of the passengers.

The four men, Lincoln, Lamon, Pinkerton, and Washburne walked out of the depot and stepped into a hack.[28] They ordered the driver to take them to Willard's Hotel.[29] Now free of the passengers in the depot and able to speak more freely, Pinkerton apologized to Washburne for punching him at the depot, explaining that he did not know him. Washburne "expressed himself satisfied" to Pinkerton, "saying that he ought to have been more cautious."[30]

As the carriage hurried on, an eerie sight emerged in the predawn gloaming. There on the Hill stood the hulking, unfinished dome of the Capitol building, surrounded by scaffolding and derricks and hoists and cranes. The irony must not have been lost on Lincoln. Did his arrival in Washington herald the beginning of a new era or portend the death of an old one? Was his presidency to usher in the Union's reconstruction or to witness its continued deconstruction, state by state, brick by brick, from pillar to post?

While they rode, Washburne explained that he had been waiting for Mr. Lincoln this morning as a result of a telegram received from Fred Seward the day before and that Governor Seward was also to have been at the depot. This information must have startled Pinkerton. He knew from Lincoln's admission last night in Philadelphia that Fred Seward had been advised that the president-elect would change his route, but not this. If Fred Seward, his father, and Washburne all knew, who else might know? Pinkerton had been meticulous in sending his telegraphic dispatches in the crude, yet effective code he had devised, but Fred Seward had not likely done so. What if young Seward's dispatch regarding Lincoln's movements had been intercepted? Might assassins be waiting for Lincoln at Willard's this very moment, with revolvers and bowie knives tucked under their belts? And now, even though Lincoln was incognito, he rode in a carriage with Congressman Washburne, a man not in disguise and a known Lincoln supporter. Discovery of Washburne in Lincoln's carriage might announce Lincoln as surely as a king's coachman heralds the arrival of the monarch himself. Even the brief ride along Washington's unpaved streets must have been tense, as Pinkerton contemplated his next move for quietly depositing Lincoln into Willard's Hotel, unobserved and, hopefully, unscathed.

Following orders he must have found curious, the hack driver suddenly drew back on the reigns and halted the carriage short of Willard's Hotel, near Fourteenth Street. Mr. Lincoln, Congressman Washburne, and Pinkerton got out and began walking. The hack driver was ordered to drive the carriage ahead to Willard's main entrance. Ward Hill Lamon was the coachman's only remaining passenger.[31]

Entering Willard's main entrance, Lamon could scout about the hotel for evidence of assassins waiting to ambush the president-elect. If he saw any suspicious persons lurking about inside the hotel or around the entrances, he could hurry back to warn Pinkerton and Lincoln. If, on the other hand, all was well at the hotel, Lamon could seek out Henry Willard and excitedly utter the first whispered news that Mr. Lincoln had arrived in Washington. The two of them could hurry to meet the president-elect, but not at the main entrance on Pennsylvania Avenue, the entrance Northerners typically used. And the Union's new president would certainly not have entered Willard's through the doors on F Street—that was the entrance through which Southerners came and went. Rather, the president-elect of the United States would approach his temporary quarters in the nation's capital on foot, wearing a disguise, entering by stealth, through Willard's Fourteenth Street entrance—the ladies' entrance.[32]

When Lincoln, Washburne and Pinkerton arrived at the Fourteenth Street entrance, Lamon and Henry Willard were indeed there to greet them. There were no crouching assassins, but there were also no celebrity-seeking hordes choking the entrances, halls, and staircases. Thankfully, for the first time on this journey, Mr. Lincoln could enter a hotel peacefully, known to only a handful of people, without calls for speeches or receptions or handshaking, each painful in its own right.

Recounted Washburne, "we drove rapidly to Willard's Hotel, entering on Fourteenth Street, before it was fairly daylight. The porter showed us into the little receiving room at the head of the stairs, and at my direction went to the office to have Mr. Lincoln assigned a room."

Lincoln was assigned parlor number 6. Located on the second floor just over the main entrance, parlor 6 was the finest suite at Willard's. The elegantly furnished room would offer the president-elect both comfort and a commanding view of Pennsylvania Avenue. For Lincoln, the White House was, both literally and figuratively, just steps away.[33]

Although Willard's was expecting Lincoln and his party later today, they were not expecting him this morning. Accordingly, when the president-elect showed up, parlor 6 was not ready for him. New York businessman and Peace Conference delegate William E. Dodge had to be "hastily evicted" to make way for Lincoln.[34] Dodge and Lincoln didn't yet know it, but their paths would cross again later today.

While Lincoln waited in the receiving room, "Governor Seward hurriedly entered, much out of breath and somewhat chagrined to think he had not been up in season to be at the depot on the arrival of the train."[35]

Thus, Seward, the former governor of New York and now a U.S. senator, had not been missing from the depot because he was in any danger; he had merely overslept.[36] Washburne describes the scene as Lincoln greeted the embarrassed

Seward: "The meeting of those two great men under the extraordinary circumstances which surrounded them was full of emotion and thankfulness."[37]

Lincoln explained to Seward that he had come to Washington unannounced in view of Pinkerton's intelligence regarding the Baltimore plotters. Seward could not have been more understanding.

"Governor Seward said that he and General Scott fully approved of the step . . . and that he (Seward) had in his possession conclusive evidence showing that there was a large organization in Baltimore to prevent the passage of Mr. Lincoln through that City, and he felt confident that Mr. Lincoln could not have come through in any other manner without blood-shed."[38]

It was this intelligence of a "large organization," Seward explained, that had caused him to consult with General Scott and send his son Fred to Philadelphia Thursday afternoon in order to urge Mr. Lincoln to alter his travel plans. Perhaps hoping to relieve Lincoln of any embarrassment, Seward claimed that if Lincoln had not taken evasive steps, in all probability General Scott would have sent troops to Baltimore later today to receive and escort the president-elect safely to Washington.[39] Perhaps Lincoln, thinking of his wife and young sons, privately wished General Scott would yet send troops to Baltimore in order to escort them in safety. But no. Colonel Sumner and Ellsworth and other brave men were with them. All would be well.

Pinkerton, meanwhile, queried Seward's intelligence of a "large organization" in Baltimore harboring designs to prevent Lincoln from passing through the city. He advised Seward of the information he had, of the handful of rabble that he and his operatives had been working in and around Baltimore for the past several weeks, but that he had no intelligence of a "large organization" in Baltimore. But Seward was unshakable. "The Governor reiterated that he had conclusive evidence of this."[40]

Lincoln "expressed himself rather tired," without specifying whether he meant from the twelve-day trip, the all-night journey, or the wearisome conversation regarding the suspected Baltimore plotters.[41] The party then left Lincoln at Willard's and went to Seward's house where they continued the discussions of the dangers in Baltimore.

Perhaps Pinkerton recounted to Seward and Washburne that while Lincoln waited quietly behind his curtained berth for the train to leave Baltimore, the tense minutes had been lightened by an amusing incident. The B&O's night watchman had begun pounding on the side of a wooden building near Lincoln's sleeping car. "Captain, it's four o'clock!" the night watchman yelled repeatedly. Inside the wooden building, the railroad's ticket agent appeared to be asleep, immune to the watchman's incessant pounding and shouting. "This he kept up for about twenty minutes without any change in time," Pinkerton recalled, "and many funny remarks were made by the passengers at the Watchman's time being always the same. Mr. Lincoln appeared to enjoy it very much and made several witty remarks showing that he was as full of fun as ever."[42] Indeed, Lincoln was so "full of fun" that he told jokes as they waited. But he did so quietly, Pinkerton recalled, "so that no one heard it but Mr. Lamon and myself."[43]

Pinkerton and Lamon left Seward's house and returned to the Willard's Hotel, where Pinkerton registered under the name E. J. Allen of New York. For whatever reason, Pinkerton did not immediately send word to those anxiously waiting for news of Lincoln's safe arrival in Washington. Instead, he took a bath and had breakfast.[44] After cleaning up and eating, Pinkerton prepared and sent at least five telegrams, including one addressed to Norman Judd in Harrisburg. In understated tones, each dispatch conveyed essentially the same message: Lincoln was safe in Washington.[45]

After Lincoln left Harrisburg, Thomas A. Scott, vice president of the Pennsylvania Railroad had reportedly spent the night pacing back and forth between the Jones House and the Pennsylvania Railroad's depot. "At last the eastern horizon was purpled with the promise of day. Scott. . . was soon gladdened by an unsigned dispatch from Washington, saying, 'Plums delivered Nuts safely.' He whirled his hat high in the little telegraph office as he shouted, 'Lincoln's in Washington,' and we rushed to the Jones House and hurried a messenger to the Executive Mansion to spread the glad tidings that Lincoln had safely made his midnight journey to the Capital."[46]

Among those waiting in Harrisburg for news of Lincoln's travel status, Mary Lincoln would have been one of the first to learn that he had arrived safely in Washington. Worthington G. Snethen, on the other hand, appears to have been one of the last.

As of 8:00 a.m., Snethen and his Baltimore Republican Committee of Escort still expected to be presented to Mr. Lincoln. Snethen unsuccessfully attempted to locate William S. Wood, whom he understood would do the presenting. Writing to Lincoln, an embittered Snethen later complained that "I failed to find Mr. Wood, but sent up to your room a card bearing the names of the Committee, to which the answer was sent, that you would see us in a few moments."[47] Based on these assurances, the excited Baltimore committee waited at the Jones House to be introduced to Lincoln. "While waiting in the ladies' parlor, a gentleman announced to the crowd, that you had left for Washington the previous evening."[48]

By several accounts, Elmer Ellsworth is credited with sharing this news. "Mr. Lincoln is not in Harrisburg," Ellsworth advised the committee. "He left this place last night, and is now safe in Washington."[49] On hearing this, the long-faced Baltimore committee retreated to the depot where they could return to Baltimore on the special train, scheduled to leave at 9:00 a.m. They would, however, face difficulty attempting to board.

Reported the *Baltimore Exchange:*

> About fifteen minutes of nine o'clock, the Express train took position on the siding. There were but few persons present, the crowd still lingered in and around the Jones House. The Baltimore committee, who were not yet assured that they would be allowed seats in the train, came to the cars looking troubled and dubious. Some of them now expressed the belief that the President had really gone before; whilst others clung to the belief that it was a ruse. The doubt could not last much longer, and while they were engaged in discussing the matter, cheers in the streets announced that the Presidential party was on its way to the depot.—In a short time the carriages made their appearance, and it was evident that the President was not with the party. There were Mrs. Lincoln, the two little Lincolns, and 'Bob'. . . , but the President elect was nowhere to be seen. The committee looked crest-fallen, and immediately became solicitous about their passage home. With but little trouble they gained admission to the cars, and in a few minutes the train was on its way.[50]

Snethen clearly felt unappreciated, if not betrayed. His little band of Republicans had endured, during a Wide Awake procession in Baltimore the previous October, "showers of eggs, brick-bats and injurious epithets from the mob." He was one of Lincoln's precious few political friends in that city. He had written Lincoln extensively during the previous months, reporting on the political climate in Baltimore and making cabinet recommendations. Snethen felt that Lincoln owed him better treatment.

When Snethen finally caught up with Lincoln's proxy, William S. Wood, that morning, he let the man have it.

"This was a shameful way to treat men who had risked their lives to vote for Lincoln," Snethen complained bitterly, "it would have been perfectly safe for Lincoln to have walked through the city. The movement was a blunder . . . a state was never so insulted before."[51]

In the same sentence that Snethen spewed entitlement for having risked his life to vote for Lincoln, he made indignant, even ironic projections that the very man voted for amid such violence would somehow now have been perfectly safe walking the streets of Baltimore. Wood explained that the plan to smuggle Lincoln through Baltimore was not his. Indeed, Wood had not been consulted about it. Wood assured Snethen that he had "every confidence in the Baltimoreans, and intended to trust himself and Mr. Lincoln's family among them."[52]

As William S. Wood began spinning his version of the story, the press began printing theirs. At around the same time that the Baltimore Republicans were being told that Lincoln had already gone, the newspapermen, now freed from their unofficial gag order, were telegraphically zapping their early morning dispatches to their respective newspapers. What follows is one of the first newspaper stories to hit the wires, as reported by special correspondent Joseph Howard Jr. of the *New York Times*. The story would soon be picked up by newspapers all over the country:

HIGHLY IMPORTANT NEWS.

Secret Departure of the President Elect

From Harrisburgh.

Alleged Plot for His Assassination.

UNEXPECTED ARRIVAL IN WASHINGTON.

Surprise of the Harrisburgh People, and Indignation of the Baltimoreans.

Special Dispatch to the New-York Times.

HARRISBURGH, Saturday, Feb. 23—8 A.M.

Abraham Lincoln, the President Elect of the United States, is safe in the capital of the nation. By the admirable arrangement of Gen. Scott, the country has been spared the lasting disgrace, which would have been fastened indelibly upon it had Mr. Lincoln been murdered upon his journey thither, as he would have been had he followed the programme as announced in papers, and gone by the Northern Central Railroad to Baltimore.

On Thursday night, after he had retired, Mr. Lincoln was aroused and informed that a stranger desired to see him on a matter of life and death. He declined to admit him unless he gave his name, which he at once did, and such prestige did the name carry that while Mr. Lincoln was yet disrobed he granted an interview to the caller.

A prolonged conversation elicited the fact that an organized body of men had determined that Mr. Lincoln should not be inaugurated, and that he should never leave the City of Baltimore alive, if, indeed, he ever entered it.

The list of the names of the conspirators presented a most astonishing array of persons high in Southern confidence, and some whose fame is not to this country alone.

Statesmen laid the plan, bankers endorsed it, and adventurers were to carry it into effect. As they understood Mr. Lincoln was to leave Harrisburgh at 9 o'clock this morning by special train, [and] the idea was, if possible, to throw the cars from the road at some point where they could rush down a steep embankment and destroy in a moment the lives of all on board. In case of the failure of this project, their plan was to surround the carriage on the way from depot to depot in Baltimore, and assassinate him with dagger or pistol shot.

So authentic was the source from which the information was obtained that Mr. Lincoln, after counselling with his friends, was compelled to make arrangements which would enable him to subvert the plans of his enemies.

Greatly to the annoyance of the thousands who desired to call on him last night, he declined giving a reception. The final council was held at 8 o'clock.

Mr. Lincoln did not want to yield, and Col. Sumner actually cried with indignation; but Mrs. Lincoln, seconded by Mr. Judd and Mr. Lincoln's original informant, insisted upon it, and at nine o'clock Mr. Lincoln left on a special train. He wore a Scotch plaid cap and a very long military cloak, so that he was entirely unrecognizable. Accompanied by Superintendent Lewis and one friend, he started, while all the town, with the exception of Mrs. Lincoln, Col. Sumner, Mr. Judd and two reporters, who were sworn to secresy, supposed him to be asleep.

The telegraph wires were put beyond reach of any one who might desire to use them.

At 1 o'clock the fact was whispered from one to another, and it soon became the theme of most excited conversation. Many thought it a very injudicious move, while others regarded it as a stroke of great merit.

The special train leaves with the original party at 9 o'clock, and we trust it will reach Baltimore in safety.[53]

The story's account of Lincoln in a "Scotch plaid cap and a very long military cloak" would form the basis for political cartoons that soon mocked Lincoln, depicting him as a coward and a buffoon. One, published in *Vanity Fair,* showed a bony-kneed caricature of Lincoln wearing a Scottish kilt, doing a dance dubbed "The MacLincoln Harrisburg Highland Fling." Another, also in *Vanity Fair*, depicted Lincoln as a long, lank form, his face hidden, capped with a ribboned tam-o-shanter, and draped from head to foot in a military cloak. This sketch bore a caption that simultaneously introduced and derided Lincoln: "The New President of the United States."[54]

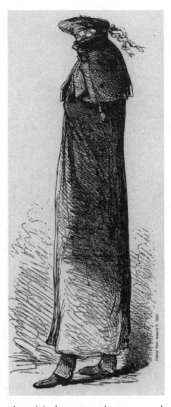

IN slipping quietly through Baltimore, Lincoln had merely bypassed one humming hornet's nest of secession to arrive at another. For starters, the Peace Conference was then in session in the very same hotel where Lincoln now rested. Among its delegates were more than a few secessionists, including at least two on a growing list of men who would ultimately draw suspicion of being complicit with the Baltimore Plot conspirators—James A. Seddon and Waldo Porter Johnson. They were now just steps away from Lincoln.

Other nearby Washington hotels were also brimming with secessionists, many of whom had packed the capital city hoping to witness not an inauguration, but a revolution.

And while many of Washington's secession leaders, including Jefferson Davis, had left the capital for their recently seceded home states and newly formed Confederacy, others, most notably Senator Louis T. Wigfall of Texas, had not. Wigfall had not only been feeding military intelligence to his Confederate brethren, he had allegedly plotted to kidnap President Buchanan just weeks before. Moreover, Wigfall, an oft-inebriated and hotheaded duelist, had "a willingness to shoot people who disagreed with him."[55] Never one to shrink from debate, Lincoln most certainly would disagree with the fire-eating Wigfall should they come face-to-face.

A satirical cartoon that appeared in *Vanity Fair*. Cartoons such as this, based on *New York Times* correspondent Joseph Howard Jr.'s inaccurate and sensational reporting, would plague Lincoln for weeks, branding him a coward or a buffoon.

CHAPTER SEVENTEEN

THE PEACE CONFERENCE

Saturday, February 23, 1861
Washington; Harrisburg–Baltimore

ALTHOUGH HE HAD GOTTEN ABRAHAM LINCOLN safely to Washington, Allan Pinkerton's work was far from over. True, as Pinkerton's telegraphic dispatches had reported, everything was indeed "all right"— for now. But the Baltimore plotters had been made fools of. Pinkerton had to anticipate that they might react with the same vindictive dispatch that had sent hundreds of Baltimore vigilantes to Harpers Ferry just hours after John Brown's raid.[1] They might regroup. They might gather more plotters and devise a new plan. They might board the next train for Washington, seeking vengeance, as they had done after President Buchanan had fled Baltimore's wrath four years earlier.

Pinkerton's success had thus far derived from good luck, good planning, and good execution—a confluence of daring, clandestine intelligence gathering, conspiratorial tongues loosened by strong, free liquor, self-destructive bravado, and misplaced trust, and most important, a counterterrorism plan orchestrated to near perfection.

To run smoothly, all of the intricate gears and works of Pinkerton's security operation had depended upon one vital component—the tightly wound mainspring of secrecy. But now, when Pinkerton needed secrecy more than ever, that critical component was about to snap. Just as liquor had loosened the conspirators' lips, that same vice now threatened one of Lincoln's allies.

After returning to Willard's with Pinkerton, Ward Hill Lamon, prone to imbibing, had gone to the bar. The combined effects of too little sleep, too much excitement, and too much alcohol were predictable. In the very same hotel where Pinkerton had registered under an assumed name, where Lincoln rested in private, and where Peace Conference delegates squabbled and plotted behind closed doors, Ward Hill Lamon was out in the open. He was in a celebratory and talkative mood.

Allan Pinkerton knew that the news of Lincoln's arrival in Washington would leak eventually, but he wished to keep the story bottled up as long as possible. And even when the story did break, Pinkerton was adamant that his name not be associated with the enterprise. He had Lincoln's assurances in this regard. But Ward Hill Lamon had other ideas.

After sending his telegraphic messages confirming Lincoln's arrival, Pinkerton met with Lamon at Willard's. Lamon was "very much excited" about Lincoln's arrival in Washington and wanted to telegraph the story to Charles Wilson of the *Evening Journal* in Chicago.[2] Pinkerton would have none of it. Lincoln's arrival was yet to be considered a secret, he argued. The story should be made public only after Lincoln and his advisors approved and even then should play out carefully, with the precise, tightly controlled spin they wanted put to it. If the story was cast in the wrong light, Lincoln might be seen as a coward, a timid leader afraid to face his opponents, or worse, one who sends his wife and young children to do the job. For now, Pinkerton implored, they must say nothing publicly.

Lamon, however, was determined to talk. "All I could say to Mr. Lamon. . . ," Pinkerton wrote that day, "appeared to be futile—regardless of all consequences he was determined to make a 'Splurge' and have his name figure largely in it."

Lamon reasoned that Governor Seward had endorsed Lincoln's change of plans, and therefore there could be no harm in telling the tale. "He talked so foolishly that I lost patience with him and set him down in my own mind as a brainless egotistical fool—and I still think so," Pinkerton scrawled in his report that day.[3]

Obviously hot over his disagreement with Lamon, Pinkerton left Willard's and walked up Pennsylvania Avenue. When he returned about an hour later, he saw Lamon in the hall near the hotel desk, talking with a Washington correspondent for the *New York Herald,* Simon P. Hanscom. "I could plainly see that Lamon had been drinking," Pinkerton wrote. He watched as Hanscom continued to pump Lamon for information, while Lamon's elbow continued to bend. The same ploy Pinkerton and his operatives had used so effectively to bleed information from the Baltimore plotters was now being used against him. Most troubling, Pinkerton noticed Hanscom staring at him. It was all the detective could take. Pinkerton motioned Lamon toward him and angrily accused him of blowing his cover.

Lamon did not deny that Hanscom knew who Pinkerton was.

"I suppose you have told him," Pinkerton retorted.

"Yes," Lamon admitted, but only after Hanscom had assured Lamon that he already knew Pinkerton.

"I got quite angry," Pinkerton wrote, "and *swore some* and told Lamon that Hanscomb did not know me, but had taken that method to draw it out of him."

Pinkerton warned Lamon that he would "at once see Mr. Lincoln and insist upon his (Lincoln) making Lamon hold his tongue. Mr. Lamon was very much excited at this, and begged that I should not do this, and that he would at once see Hanscomb and have him keep my name out of the paper. Lamon left me and returned and took a seat by Hanscomb."[4]

Willard's Hotel where delegates to the 1861 Peace Conference stayed. Lincoln, Pinkerton, and Washburne would enter the hotel through the ladies' entrance along the hotel's 14th Street side, shown above. (*Library of Congress*)

Lamon had strong reasons for wanting both that his name "figure prominently" in Lincoln's safe arrival and that he not get crosswise, especially now, with his friend Lincoln. Lamon had, at least since early February, been pulling out all the stops, urging countless friends to write letters on his behalf, to induce Lincoln to appoint him to a plum government job—as Consul to Paris.[5]

Ironically, Pinkerton seemed angrier about his name being published than about Lamon's premature, even reckless conduct, spreading intelligence of Lincoln's secret arrival in Washington to the press. But there was good reason for the detective's outrage. If Pinkerton's name became associated with foiling the plot, his cover as "Mr. Hutcheson" or "E. J. Allen" might be blown. His fellow operatives, with whom he had been seen in Baltimore, might be exposed. His life and that of fellow agents like Kate Warne and Timothy Webster would be jeopardized.[6]

But there was an even deeper reason for Pinkerton's anger. He planned to return to Baltimore later today, to receive updated reports and continue his investigation. The story of Lincoln's midnight ride would undoubtedly soon fill every major newspaper in the country—including those published in Baltimore—with sensational stories. To a large extent, the damage had already been done. Even if Pinkerton's name could be kept out of the newspapers, Lincoln's would not. And hungry reporters like Hanscom would spin the story to their liking. The Baltimore plotters would know that they had been betrayed. They might look for the spies who had worked them, to exact vengeance. Worst of all, they might drive their planning more deeply underground, where even Pinkerton's capable operatives could not root it out.

Lamon's conduct had been foolish and enraged Pinkerton. They didn't know it then, but Lamon's casual chattiness, and Pinkerton's harsh and unwavering criticism of it, would set the two men against each other for the rest of their lives.

By 10:00 a.m. on February 23, 1861, Willard's Hotel, a humming hive of political activity for weeks, was even more abuzz with excitement. Rumors of Lincoln's early, unannounced arrival, at first a flurry of unsubstantiated whispers, were becoming more persistent and credible. And yet, as they took their seats on tightly packed chairs beneath the globed chandeliers in the concert hall that morning, most of the Southern members of the Peace Conference had thus far been kept in the dark. That was about to change. The unexpected report that Lincoln had arrived early in Washington would fall like a sledgehammer on the Southern delegates in attendance. Lucius E. Chittenden observed firsthand the manner in which they would receive the news and their stunned reaction to it. His account provides startling evidence that pro-slavery members of the Peace Conference were not only shocked and dismayed by Lincoln's safe arrival; they had actually expected him to die in Baltimore later that day.

Although Chittenden published his account many years later, he had witnessed the events, people, and discussions about which he wrote firsthand and at close range. His is the written testimony of a man so trusted in his ability to report events accurately that he was given the responsibility of recording the Peace Conference debates, including the eloquent and sometimes fiery words spewing from the lips of Southern and Northern delegates alike. Chittenden's stunning testimony of the events that he witnessed at the Peace Conference at ten o'clock on the morning of February 23, 1861, is as follows:

> There were a few Republicans whose faces shone as they greeted each other, when they met at the opening of the Conference that day. They were in the secret of Mr. Lincoln's arrival. Members were not particular about the position of their seats, and mine then happened to be between one occupied by Mr. Seddon and that of Waldo P. Johnson, an impulsive Secessionist, afterwards a Confederate general, who then, in part, represented Missouri. The body-servant of whom Mr. Seddon was then proprietor was a man scarcely darker than himself, his equal in deportment, his superior in figure and carriage. This chattel [slave] had made himself a favorite by his civil and respectful manner, and by general consent was the only person, not a member or officer, who had the entrée to the sessions of the Conference.

As soon as the meeting was called to order, this servant approached his master and handed him a scrap of paper, apparently torn from an envelope. Mr. Seddon glanced at it, and passed it before me to Mr. Johnson, so near to my face that, without closing my eyes, I could not avoid reading it. The words written upon it were *Lincoln is in this hotel!*

The Missourian [Waldo P. Johnson] was startled as by a shock of electricity. He must have forgotten himself completely, for he instantly exclaimed, *"How the devil did he get through Baltimore?"* With a look of utter contempt for the indiscretion of the impulsive trans-Mississippian, the Virginian [Seddon] growled, *"What would prevent his passing through Baltimore?"*

There was no reply, but the occurrence left the impression on one mind that the preparations to receive Mr. Lincoln in Baltimore were known to some who were neither Italian assassins nor Baltimore Plug-Uglies. Mr. Johnson was not the only delegate surprised by the announcement of Mr. Lincoln's presence in Washington. As the news circulated in whispers through the hall, members gathered in groups to discuss it, and were too much absorbed to hear the repeated calls of the chairman to order. No event of the Conference . . . produced so much excitement.[7]

Forty-three-year-old Waldo P. Johnson was a narrow-eyed, stern-looking, bushy bearded secessionist. Johnson hailed from Missouri, a border state that, like Maryland and Virginia, was torn between remaining with the Union and keeping her slaves.[8] Johnson's résumé prior to 1861 reveals a respectable career punctuated by military, legal, and government service. He had served as a member of the First Missouri Regiment of Mounted Volunteers during the Mexican War, then later as a Missouri state representative, circuit attorney, and circuit judge, before being elected as a Missouri Democrat to the U.S. Senate. His Senate term would begin on March 17, 1861, only to be cut short on January 10, 1862, when that body would expel him for disloyalty to the Union. The government's suspicions regarding Johnson's loyalty were well founded; he would soon serve as a Confederate lieutenant colonel in the Fourth Missouri Infantry.[9]

Like Baltimore Plot suspect Otis K. Hillard, on at least one occasion during the Peace Conference, Johnson paraphrased Brutus's famous line uttered to justify assassination: "We Missourians love the Union, but we have fully arrived at the conclusion that the time has come when something must be done to prevent our entire separation. We have hitherto remained silent. We came here to preserve the Union. *Not that we love the Union less, but we love our rights more.* We love our rights more than the Union, our property, or our lives."[10]

While this utterance falls far short of advocating Lincoln's assassination, its timing, made just two days before Lincoln's announced passage through Baltimore, and its similarity to other Brutus-like utterances made around the same time by other Baltimore conspirators lead one to ponder whether Mr. Johnson may have been present at Baltimore assassination conclaves.

Johnson's remark this morning, *"How the devil did he get through Baltimore?"* only adds to the intrigue. The question might have seemed curious, but not necessarily suspicious, to those seated nearby, those who had no advance knowledge of the suspected Baltimore conspiracy and had not yet seen the newspaper accounts that would, in the coming days, tell the startling tale. But Johnson's reaction, and Seddon's icy response to it, must have frozen Chittenden to his seat. Less than a week earlier, on February 17, Chittenden had made his secretive run to Baltimore, cloaked in darkness and intrigue. He had met with Republican friends there and heard firsthand the accounts of the Baltimore assassination plot from one who had withdrawn from the conspiracy. He had reported the story to Elihu B. Washburne and had felt assured that evasive action would be taken, as it apparently had been.

Then, just two days later, Chittenden had witnessed the heated debate between James A. Seddon of Virginia and Lot M. Morrill of Maine that had nearly reduced the Peace Conference to a barroom brawl. According to Chittenden, the forty-six-year-old Seddon "was the most conspicuous and active member of his delegation. . . . He was the most powerful debater of the Conference, skilful, adroit, cunning."[11] During the conference, Seddon struck a sepulchral pro-slavery chord that resonated with his brethren of the South. Morrill, described as the least likely man to engage in verbal or physical combat, finally confronted Seddon directly: "The true question here is, 'What will Virginia do? . . . She to-day holds the keys of peace or war. . . . She undertakes to dictate the terms upon which the Union is to be preserved. What will satisfy her?"[12] Morrill demanded to know.

According to Seddon, Virginia would forcibly resist the Union if it took military action against the states that had seceded so far. Seddon then flipped the debate, asking Morrill about Lincoln's intended policies (which Lincoln had carefully sidestepped in his speeches on the journey thus far). In so doing, Seddon betrayed his motive for wanting Lincoln out of the way. Seddon anticipated that Lincoln's intended policies would run counter to Virginia's "unchangeable" purpose to resist coercion, that Lincoln would use force against the seceded states. "And now," Seddon began, "having answered the gentleman [Senator Morrill] frankly, as he desired, I wish to ask him a question, and I wish also an explicit and frank answer. My question is this: Is it the purpose or is it the policy of the incoming administration to attempt to execute the laws of the United States in the seceded States by an armed force? The answer to this question involves information of the utmost importance to my

State and others whose interests are involved with hers."[13] In referring to states other than Virginia "whose interests are involved with hers," Seddon meant Maryland, as well as other border states such as Missouri and other slave states like North Carolina that had yet to secede. It had been generally believed that if Virginia seceded, Maryland would follow. In fact, according to Baltimore's Marshal Kane, Maryland would wait for the action of Virginia, and "when Virginia seceded through a convention, Maryland would secede by gravitation."[14] The fiery Seddon had seemed a little too eager to know the plans of Lincoln's incoming administration.

Peace Conference delegate James A. Seddon of Virginia. He would become the Confederate Secretary of War. (*Library of Congress*)

And now, here Chittenden was, stuck between Seddon and Johnson, two secessionists who had come to Washington ostensibly to broker peace and avoid civil war, but who now appeared to be part of, or at least aware of, the same Baltimore conspiracy, one that implicated not only the thugs of Baltimore, but also Southern leaders, including members of the Peace Conference itself. If there was a Baltimore conspiracy to kill Lincoln, it now appeared to reach well beyond the backrooms, bars, and brothels of the Oriole City and into the glimmering, lofty concert hall of Willard's—the very same hotel where Lincoln now slept.

Chittenden's account is indeed startling, even more so once the remarkable, if scant evidence he provides is closely scrutinized. Someone at Willard's that morning had gathered intelligence of Lincoln's early arrival, had written the note, and passed it to Seddon's servant for urgent delivery inside the closed concert hall.

That a note was written at all is significant evidence of a conspiracy. It can be assumed that Seddon's servant did not write the note. As a slave, he likely could neither read nor write—it was unlawful in Southern states to teach even such basics to slaves. In any event, there was no need for Seddon's servant to hand his master a note even if he could have written it. The servant could have delivered the important message far more quickly in a low whisper. No, someone else, someone with authority, had instructed the dutiful servant to take the urgent message into the closed-door session and hand it immediately to his master. Whoever wrote the note likely was not a Peace Conference delegate.

Otherwise, the message, too, could have been conveyed to Seddon in person. Only delegates, however, with the exception of Seddon's servant, could gain access to the Peace Conference sessions.

The author of the Seddon note may never be known. From Chittenden's account, however, it may be fairly inferred that whoever wrote it, like Seddon and Johnson, was not merely startled that Lincoln had arrived at Willard's Hotel that morning, but perhaps also expected him to die in Baltimore.

That the author of this note chose Seddon as the person to whom it was to be delivered provides further evidence of a conspiracy. True, delivering the note to Seddon's servant made Seddon the most likely person to receive it. Why, however, of all the delegates in attendance at the Peace Conference, was James Seddon unique in being the only one to have his body servant permitted in the hall?[15]

One possible reason is that Seddon needed to remain in constant communication with the world outside these cloistered debates, to be able to receive—and send—dispatches without delay, indeed, without ever leaving the conference. This and the pointed question Seddon had asked Morrill, demanding to know the Lincoln administration's plans, suggest that Seddon was possibly at the heart of intelligence-gathering operations among his Southern Peace Conference brethren. Even his wife Sarah thought his being a Peace Conference delegate might give him an advantage in his efforts to hasten Virginia out of the Union through a secession convention. She believed he might gain "an insight into the views & purposes of other States [and] . . . greatly increase his usefulness as a member of the Convention while urging the rights of his State & Section."[16]

If Seddon was gathering intelligence at the Peace Conference, and if he had foreknowledge of the Baltimore Plot, he would have wanted to be among the first to know if the plot succeeded. Perhaps Seddon had expected to receive a far different note that morning. Indeed, if Seddon and others of his ilk were expecting Lincoln to die in Baltimore, they would almost certainly have wanted to know as soon as it happened; such a monumental political coup would have required quick and decisive action. Assassination of a president-elect had no precedent in America. Who would then take the oath? Vice President-elect Hamlin? Not necessarily. The Constitution provided for the vice president to replace the *president* upon his removal from office or his death, resignation, or inability to discharge the duties of the office.[17] But as of February 23, 1861, Lincoln was not yet the president and Hamlin was not yet the vice president. Neither had yet taken the oath of office. The Constitution seemed not to anticipate the possibility that a president-elect might die before being sworn in.

Perhaps Seddon and others might have argued that if a president-elect dies before taking the oath, the presidential candidate having the next highest number of electoral votes or controlling the majority of remaining electoral votes should assume the presidency. That person would be the pro-slavery Democratic vice president, John C. Breckinridge of Kentucky. Such an argument is positively Wigfallian in its diabolical logic. Texas senator Louis T. Wigfall, it will be recalled, had allegedly proposed kidnapping President Buchanan the previous December, in order that Vice President Breckinridge might assume the presidency, even if only for a few short months. And both Wigfall and other Baltimore Plot suspects, most notably William Byrne, were rabid Breckinridge supporters.[18]

There is arguably, however, no constitutional support for this outcome, either under the theory that Breckinridge had the second highest number of electoral votes or that he had a majority of the electoral votes excluding Lincoln's. With Lincoln dead, no living candidate would have had a majority of votes of the 303 "Electors appointed" for the 1860 presidential elections, as required by the Constitution.

The Twelfth Amendment would likely have decided the outcome, not by electoral votes, but by a vote in the House. That amendment, enacted in 1804, provides that if no person has a majority of the whole number of electors appointed, then the House of Representatives selects the president by ballot from the top three candidates—with Lincoln excluded, that would have meant Breckinridge, Bell, and Douglas.[19] The North's numerical advantage would have been diluted, however, as each of the states could cast but one vote. This too might have resulted in a Breckinridge election for president, from a largely pro-Democrat House and Senate, respectively, but with South Carolina, Mississippi, Florida, Alabama, Georgia, and Louisiana already seceded, and Texas was poised to do so, this seems doubtful. In any case, the point is that with Lincoln out of the way, the question of who would assume the presidency floated on choppy, even untested constitutional waters. Resolving such a constitutional crisis would in all events have further distracted an already flailing federal government. The ensuing muddy political slurry would have been consistent with the South's headstrong, self-destructive purpose—to ruin what it could not rule.

Throughout the morning, the Peace Conference continued with debates and speeches, including a lengthy and patriotic address by former president John Tyler passionately urging that the Union be restored. But the delegates were clearly inattentive. Whether news of Lincoln's arrival had spread via the clique of Republicans in the know, leaked under the conference's closed doors thanks to Lamon's indiscreet boasting to the press, or through the continued passing of Seddon's mysterious note, the entire room quickly became distracted by the breaking news. "The attempt to go on with the debate was unavailing. The fact of the arrival of the President-elect was quickly known to every one. Members were not in a condition of mind to make speeches or to listen to them," Chittenden recalled.[20]

When a formal announcement of Lincoln's early arrival was finally delivered to the Peace Conference as one body, it came neither from Seddon, nor Chittenden, nor even President Tyler, but from Lincoln's fellow Illinoisan, Democrat Stephen T. Logan.

At the time he recorded the event, Chittenden wrote benignly that Logan's motion to call on Lincoln was "agreed to unanimously."[21] Years later, however, Chittenden gave a fuller, less respectful account of what happened after the announcement of Lincoln's arrival:

> There was a hurried consultation among the Republicans, which resulted in a motion by Mr. Logan, one of the delegates from Mr. Lincoln's state, that the president of the Conference wait upon the President-elect and inform him that the Conference would be pleased to visit him in a body at such time as would suit his convenience. This motion was fiercely opposed. Waste of precious time was the open ground of opposition. There were cries of "No! no! Vote it down!" "Lay it on the table!" with exclamations, in undertone, of "Rail-splitter!" "Ignoramus!" "Vulgar clown!" etc. Again President Tyler interfered to prevent the making of a disreputable record. He declared that "the proposal was eminently proper; that the office, and not the individual, was to be considered; that he hoped that no Southern member would decline to treat the incoming President with the same respect and attention already extended to the present incumbent of that honorable and exalted office." The appropriate observations suppressed the opposition; the motion of Mr. Logan was unanimously adopted, and the Conference, having resolved upon an evening session, adjourned.[22]

It takes but little effort to imagine an embittered James A. Seddon, crumpled note clutched in his hand, storming out of the room as the session adjourned, in search of what had gone wrong in Baltimore—and what might yet be done to correct the error.

SHORTLY before 9:00 a.m. in Harrisburg, on February 23, as the now Lincoln-less Special took its place on the siding, the party stepped out of the Jones House, into waiting carriages, and rode them to the train. It must have been a somber, almost funeral-like procession. Noted one reporter, "very few people were out. There were no cheers, but denunciations of Mr. Lincoln's secret departure were deep and unanimous."[23]

At 9:00 a.m. as scheduled, the presidential train pulled out, bound for Baltimore on the Northern Central's line. For the first time on the traveling suite's 1,900-mile journey, Lincoln was not with the rest of the party. Of the original presidential suite slated to be aboard the train, all except Lincoln, Ward Hill Lamon, and Norman B. Judd were now on board. Lamon, of course, had accompanied Lincoln the night before. But what of Judd? It would later be reported that Judd "preferred taking the early morning route to Baltimore via Philadelphia."[24] "I came on to Philadelphia," according to Judd, "by the first train to get the news and to be within telegraphic reach and do anything necessary, for, of course, I could not be certain what might happen."[25] That he had abandoned the rest of the Lincoln party suggests that Judd perceived the danger in Baltimore to be quite real.

Judd would not have been the only one to anticipate a hostile reception in Baltimore. Noted one reporter on board as the train left Harrisburg, "all the party are on the train, though but few think we shall reach Washington without accidents. Colonel Ellsworth expects the train will be mobbed at Baltimore."[26]

At York, Pennsylvania, the train's first stop, five thousand people had gathered around the depot to see Lincoln, still unaware of his absence. There arose a "general cry of dissatisfaction" when William S. Wood announced from the rear of the car that Lincoln was already in Washington, having been "compelled" to change his route. With Lincoln gone, his heir apparent, the Prince of Rails, would stand in for him. "Robert Lincoln . . . was standing by and was introduced, and the crowd good naturedly cheered as we passed on."[27] Young Robert Todd Lincoln had, throughout the trip, avoided at every turn making public displays, repeatedly refusing to speak to crowds, even declining in Cincinnati to speak at a banquet thrown in his honor. But now with his father gone, Robert found his voice.

At 11:40 a.m., the train crossed the Maryland line, passing from the land of the free into the home of the slave. "At every house along the road the people were out gazing anxiously at the train that was *supposed* to carry 'Old Abe.'" But as the train crossed the Mason-Dixon line, Robert spontaneously led the passengers in a stirring rendition of "The Star-Spangled Banner."[28] Singing the patriotic tune was both an appropriate and an ironic choice. The words had been penned by a Baltimorean, Francis Scott Key.

As the train plowed through Maryland, rumors of hand grenades and burned-out bridges and torn-up tracks plagued the passenger's thoughts.

IN Baltimore a "vast crowd," not yet aware Lincoln was already in Washington, had gathered at the Northern Central's Calvert Street depot by 10:00 a.m., a full two and a half hours before his published arrival time. The crowd, described as "ill-tempered," had come to secure a good spot to witness the president-elect's appearance and whatever events might follow it. A large contingent of Marshal Kane's police force was also reportedly present. Whether the police were there to preserve the peace or merely make a show of force to an unruly crowd was yet to play out. At approximately ten o'clock, there came an announcement that Lincoln had already passed through Baltimore. The news "fell like a thunder clap" on the waiting throng.[29]

As had occurred in Harrisburg, many in the Baltimore crowd did not believe the report, calling it a hoax.[30] Suspected conspirator Otis K. Hillard was among the doubters. By 11:00 a.m., Hillard was waiting in Pinkerton operative Harry W. Davies' hotel room. When Davies returned from breakfast, he found Hillard there, in an agitated state. "He was very much excited on account of a rumor that Lincoln had passed through Baltimore incog. early in the morning."[31] It would be just like the Black Republican cowards to pull a stunt like that. But Hillard told Davies that he did not believe the rumor. In any case, it did not matter. The National Volunteers and Hillard had been given orders to be in position at the Calvert Street depot at 12:30 that afternoon.[32] Hillard would follow his orders.

As the Lincoln-less Special entered Baltimore on time, it was raining hard. Every person on board, except, perhaps for the little Lincolns, had heard various reports of crouching assassins that would be waiting for the president-elect. But word had been wired all over the country, including to Baltimore, that Lincoln was now in Washington. Surely, over six hours after his arrival, even the Baltimore plotters must have heard this news by now. The object of their hatred now gone, so too, it was hoped, the conspirators had gone. But the object of Baltimore's hatred had not entirely disappeared. The Baltimore Republicans were still on the train. And, unbeknownst to those on board, the Baltimore conspirators did not believe Lincoln was really in Washington. They were "under the impression that the rumor was a sell" and remained in their positions.[33]

Indeed, despite the heavy rain, one of the largest crowds ever assembled at the Calvert Street Station had clogged the streets around the depot.[34] As the train approached, their excitement and anticipation grew. Would Lincoln be on board? Shouts, groans, hoots, and hisses rang out as the train squealed to a halt. "On arrival of the train at the *depôt,* some ruffians shouted for old Jeff. Davis and the Southern Republic."[35]

New York Times correspondent Joseph Howard Jr., who was riding on the train, reported the scene as he saw it:

> It was well that Mr. Lincoln went as he did—there is no doubt about it. The City Authorities [of Baltimore] declined to extend him an invitation to visit the city, although the Mayor had made up his mind to receive him at the dépôt and ride with him to the Eutaw House, and many of the police were disaffected, although the Marshal says he would have taken him through in

Thomas Nast's sketch of the Baltimore Crowd waiting for Lincoln at the Calvert Street depot. (*Library of Congress*)

entire safety. The scene that occurred when the car . . . reached the Baltimore dépôt, showed plainly what undoubtedly would have happened had Mr. Lincoln been of the party. A vast crowd—a multitude in fact—had gathered in and about the premises. It was evident that they considered the announcement of Mr. Lincoln's presence in Washington a mere ruse, for, thrusting their heads in at the windows, they shouted—"Trot him out," "Let's have him," "Come out, Old Abe," "We'll give you hell," "You bloody Black Republicans"—and other equally polite but more profane ejaculations. Some rude fellows entered the private apartment in which Mrs. Lincoln was sitting . . . but were promptly turned out by Mr. Hay, who locked the door. As the parties composing the suite, and the various correspondents, issued from the car, there was an expression of rude vulgarity and disregard of personal comfort that I have never seen equaled. Without thinking of the consequences to us, the crowd rolled in upon us like vast tidal waves, and bore us with irresistible force against the side of the car. To go either way was a physical impossibility. If we had been in the crowd, we could have moved with or through them; but as it was we were compelled to stand still, and sustain, as well as we were able, the terrible rush of an excited, rude and thoughtless populace. Oaths, obscenity, disgusting epithets and unpleasant gesticulations, were the order of the day, and had it not been for a lucky accident, I have no reason to disbelieve that the buttons of my vest would have been found, upon a post mortem examination, to be fastening me securely to the yellow painted side of an Eaton & Gilbert car. After half an hour's experience of this sort of thing, . . . a huge omnibus that chanced to be in the yard was chartered by Mr. Wood.[36]

A special correspondent for the *Philadelphia Inquirer* offered a similar account of the scene as the train arrived in Baltimore:

The imperfect arrangements of the railroad company were here brought to a climax when the train stopped. Over ten thousand people were in and around the depot. The officers (either of the railroad or police) whose duty it was to have kept the mob back, were negligent or unable to be of service. The members of the suite were therefore, jostled and tossed to and fro, utterly without protection. Many of them, finding it impossible to remain with their friends, escaped in such manner as they could, and secured private carriages. It is astonishing that those who managed, or pretended to manage, the depot arrangements should have been so ignorant or incompetent as to have allowed the crowd to enter the space necessary for exit from the cars. This was the most trying ordeal which the party were forced to undergo during the entire trip. To add to the unfortunate position, it was raining quite hard.

The crowd surged and pressed, and as one after another of the suite emerged as best he could from the cars, the shouts and yells became almost deafening. One gentleman was taken for the President elect, and narrowly escaped injury through the anxiety and curiosity of those assembled.[37] Others were forced over a platform several feet in height, and others jammed against the sides of the cars. The cry of "pickpocket" was raised, and provoked a rush, and if possible, additional confusion. And amid this noise, bustle, mob and excitement, the visitors were ushered into the Calvert Street Station of the Northern Central Railway at Baltimore.[38]

By another account, the Baltimore Republicans were the target of insults from the mob. "On the arrival of the cars and the appearance on the platform of the Baltimore Republican committee, they were received with groans and hootings. A rush was made at William E. Beale and Francis S. Corkran [a tall man who some thought resembled Lincoln],[39] but they were protected by the police, and neither of them were injured further than knocking their hats over their eyes. . . . One fellow in the crowd at Calvert station, who was known as a violent Republican, had his hat knocked off a dozen times by the rowdies."[40] Still another reporter noted that "there were many reckless boys and dissolute young men in the crowd, who had eggs and other missiles in their pockets, which, as is presumed, they designed throwing at somebody."[41]

In all likelihood, these "dissolute young men" in the crowd were conspirators to the Baltimore Plot. Pinkerton had anticipated that when Lincoln arrived, the plotters would get up a diversionary row to lure Marshal Kane's police away from "protecting" the presidential suite. Throwing eggs or other missiles would have been one such way to create such a diversion. But the dissolute young men held their fire. They watched as, one by one, passengers disembarked from the cars. The rumor was true after all. Lincoln was not among them.

But Abraham was apparently not the only Lincoln missing when the presidential train arrived at the Calvert Street Station. By some accounts, when the train pulled in, the crowd was "gaping for a sight of" Mrs. Lincoln and her three sons. They would be disappointed: the Lincolns were not on board.

Mrs. Lincoln and her sons had left the cars at the Charles Street intersection, nearly a mile north of the seething mass waiting for the train at the Calvert Street Station.[42] While the *Times* account vaguely suggests that Mary Lincoln and her sons arrived with the rest of the suite at the Calvert Street Station,[43] other accounts reveal that they had disembarked earlier, possibly to avoid the crowd gathered there; possibly to avoid anticipated danger. Reported the *Philadelphia Inquirer,* "at the city limits the family of Mr. Lincoln left the train and took carriages that had been in readiness."[44] Another account likewise confirms that Mrs. Lincoln and her family left the train before arriving at the crowded depot: "Mrs. Lincoln and her three sons proceeded to the residence of Col. John S. Gittings, president of the Northern Central railway, at Mount Vernon Square, having accepted an invitation tendered to them on their way to this city, so as to relieve them from the crowd and excitement. They left the cars, we learn, at the junction of Charles-street, where Mr. Gittings's carriage was in waiting for them, and were in a few minutes enjoying the quiet of his spacious mansion, while crowds were gaping for a sight of them at the depot."[45] Colonel Sumner and Judge Davis reportedly accompanied Mrs. Lincoln to the Gittings residence. Even so, a noisy mob greeted Mary Lincoln and her party when they arrived there, the crowd voicing its disappointment at the president-elect's failure to appear. "Yells and catcalls, mingled with hurrahs for the Confederacy, followed Mrs. Lincoln as she entered the [Gittings] house."[46]

But during their midday meal, Mrs. Lincoln reportedly voiced disapproval for the course of action urged upon her husband by his advisors. "She said that she had advised Mr. Lincoln not to depart from the route which he had first intended to take, and was the more satisfied of the folly of the movement when she had witnessed the extraordinary care and caution which had been taken by the officers of the railroad for the safe transit of the party to Baltimore."[47]

While Sumner, Davis, Mrs. Lincoln, and her sons dined in Mount Vernon Square, the other members of the party were treated to a fine dinner hosted by R. B. Coleman at the Eutaw House, located on the northwest corner of Baltimore and Eutaw Streets. Coleman, it will be recalled, had previously invited Lincoln to stay at his house in order to show the world his "manliness," that he had no fear of Baltimore or Maryland. Now, just the opposite had transpired.

No doubt, the topic of conversation at the Eutaw House included the mob that had just greeted this portion of the party when they arrived at the Calvert Street Station. Having left the train early, Mrs. Lincoln would not yet have known of this rowdy reception. Once they were finished eating, Mrs. Lincoln and her family would again need to pile into a carriage and ride through Baltimore's crowded streets to yet another depot, the Camden Street Station— over twenty blocks away.

IN Washington, Lincoln wasted no time flexing his political muscle. At 11:00 a.m., without yet knowing the status of his wife and children, he proceeded with William Seward to the White House, where he called unexpectedly on President Buchanan. "The interview was merely one of courtesy, and not for business. Mr. Buchanan received Mr. Lincoln very cordially."[48] At the time of Lincoln's arrival, Buchanan was holding court with members of his cabinet. He immediately halted the meeting and went to his private reception room, where Seward introduced the president to Lincoln. Buchanan's greatest concern was how the people from his home state had treated Lincoln. "Mr. Buchanan was anxious to know if Mr. Lincoln had a satisfactory reception in Harrisburg, to which the latter responded that it was very enthusiastic on the part of the people, and exceedingly satisfactory to him."[49] After the meeting Lincoln returned to his hotel.

Allan Pinkerton had remained at Willard's, and about 2:00 p.m. he sent his calling card, signed "E. J. Allen," to Lincoln's room. Pinkerton was preparing to leave for Baltimore and wished to see the president-elect before he did so. Lincoln immediately sent Pinkerton a reply and invited him up to parlor number 6. When Pinkerton arrived there, he found Lincoln's suite packed with congressmen, William Seward, and several others. Unknown is whether

Pinkerton advised Lincoln of Lamon's indiscretion with Simon Hanscom earlier that
morning.

What is known is that Lincoln pulled
Pinkerton aside to an adjoining room. "[He]
thanked me very kindly for the service I had
rendered him, saying that [he] fully appreciated them &c., &c., and requesting me to
call upon him every time I came to
Washington, and let him know when he
could be of any service to me."[50] Lincoln
inquired how long Pinkerton expected to be
in Baltimore. Pinkerton said he would
remain there until the inauguration; the
implication being that the danger to Lincoln
from Baltimore was not over. Lincoln understood. He instructed Pinkerton that he
should communicate directly to him or to
Judd any additional intelligence he might
gather in Baltimore. Pinkerton had just
been promoted. He was no longer working

Mary Todd Lincoln, photographed
about the time of Lincoln's first
inauguration. She vowed to see her
husband on to Washington, "danger
or no danger." (*Library of Congress*)

merely for the president of the PW&B Railroad; he was now the de facto personal agent of the president-elect of the United States. He and Lincoln shook
hands, as if to seal the pact. Pinkerton then took the 3:10 p.m. train for
Baltimore. The intelligence he would gather there would be the most explosive yet.[51]

CHAPTER EIGHTEEN

THE PALMETTO COCKADE

Saturday, February 23, 1861
Baltimore, Washington, and Albany

AS COLD RAIN PELTED BALTIMORE ON February 23, 1861, at around 5:00 p.m., Pinkerton returned to the Camden Street Station, where inbound trains from Washington deposited their passengers and where he had been with Lincoln about thirteen hours before. This time conspirator James H. Luckett was there waiting on the platform. Luckett was the stockbroker who worked in a neighboring office in the same building as Pinkerton and had introduced him to fellow conspirators Cypriano Ferrandini and William H. H. Turner. But by 5:00 p.m. on February 23, 1861, it had become painfully clear to Luckett, Turner, Ferrandini, Hillard, and everyone else involved in the conspiracy that their bold plan had failed. Indeed, it never had a chance. Lincoln's suite had arrived from Harrisburg, just as it was supposed to, at the Northern Central's Calvert Street Station around 12:30 that afternoon. But the target was not among them. Somehow, Lincoln had been warned. Rather than face his enemies, Lincoln had eluded them by sneaking through Baltimore like a skulking coward. Luckett knew that someone had betrayed them. He was determined to find out who it was.

And now, here was "Mr. Hutcheson" back in Baltimore, fresh from Washington, where Lincoln had just landed safely. Mr. Hutcheson, who had not been in the office today, last night, or indeed all day on Thursday, February 21, or Friday, February 22. As he saw Pinkerton at the depot, Luckett may have begun lining up the dots of suspicion that marked a path of betrayal straight to Mr. Hutcheson:

> —Mr. Hutcheson learns of the plan to murder Lincoln in Luckett's presence on or about February 15.

—Mr. Hutcheson leaves Baltimore on February 19 or 20 and is away from the office the rest of the week.

—Lincoln eludes Baltimore, either late at night on February 22, or early on the morning of February 23, and is now in Washington.

—Mr. Hutcheson, absent for at least the past three days, now returns to Baltimore from Washington.

Yes, perhaps as he saw "Mr. Hutcheson" arriving at the depot this evening, James H. Luckett should have begun connecting these dots. Remarkably, however, he did not. It seems not to have dawned on Luckett that this man Hutcheson, whom he had known less than a month, who seemed so secretive in his movements and perhaps a little too free with his money, might have had anything to do with Lincoln's evasive maneuvers. Indeed, rather than being suspicious, Luckett seemed happy to see Pinkerton. Most amazingly, Luckett continued to share intelligence with him.

"I arrived in Baltimore about 5:00 p.m.," Pinkerton wrote later that day, "and in the Depot met Mr. Luckett. He was very glad to see me, and took me [to] one side and told me about the d——ble manner in which Lincoln passed through Baltimore."[1]

In a flowing torrent of angry words that must have sounded to Pinkerton like sweet confirmation of his every suspicion, Luckett revealed all. His was a startling admission, complete with curses that Pinkerton felt compelled to censor from his written report, a report that would be admissible against Luckett in any court in the country as a statement against interest, an exception to the heresay rule. As recorded by Pinkerton, Luckett gave the following remarkable testimony:

> He said that he was collecting money for the friends in Baltimore, and they would yet make the attempt to assassinate Lincoln; that if it had not been for d——d spies somewhere, Lincoln never could have passed through Baltimore; that the men were all ready to have done the job, and were in their places, and would have murdered the d——d Abolitionist had it not been that they were cheated. He said that Captain Ferrandina [Ferrandini] had had about Twenty picked men with good revolvers and Knives: that their calculation was to get up a row in the crowd with rotten eggs, and brick-bats, and that while the Police (some of whom understood the game) would be attending to this, that Captain Ferrandina and his men should attack the carriage with Lincoln and shoot every one in it, and trust to mix-

ing up in the crowd to make their escape—but that if any of the members were taken, the others were to rescue him at all cost, and at all hazard.[2]

The diversionary aspects of Luckett's story would within days be confirmed by both the Northern and Southern press. As the Baltimore correspondent for the *Philadelphia Inquirer* reported, among the immense horde that had swarmed the Calvert Street Station, "there were many reckless boys and dissolute young men in the crowd, who had eggs and other missiles in their pockets, which, as is presumed, they designed throwing at somebody."[3]

Another anecdote, originally printed in the *Macon* (Ga.) *Telegraph,* and later reported by the *New York Times* corroborates this:

> THE RECEPTION MR. LINCOLN ESCAPED IN BALTIMORE
> A correspondent of the *Macon* (Ga.) *Telegraph*, writing from Baltimore, states that Mr. Lincoln would have been egged beyond the shadow of a doubt had he passed through that city according to the programme. The writer speaks of his own knowledge, for he was in the crowd at the dépôt, heard the threats of those composing it, saw the eggs, and, what is more to the purpose, had nasal proof of their bad quality as they were prematurely crushed in the swaying crowd.[4]

Humorous, even mocking as the *Macon* reporter's story seems on the surface, the report confirms evidence of a conspiracy, since the *Macon* correspondent saw more than one perpetrator and heard their threats. He saw, and even smelled, the rotten eggs the conspirators held. Luckett too had been specific that eggs were to be thrown and that they were to be rotten. Even more revealing, is that the egg throwers held their fire, at least as to the ammunition not crushed prematurely in the swaying crowd. Why go to the trouble of finding rotten eggs, saving them, attempting to keep them from being crushed, and then abandon the opportunity to throw them and other missiles, even if the primary target is absent? Why not fling a volley at the hated Baltimore Republicans who were also on the train?

The inescapable conclusion is that those intending to throw the eggs and other missiles were more than mere hooligans with an indiscriminate desire to cause a scene. Indeed, they had a specific purpose—to "get up a row" by pelting the party with eggs and brick-bats, to create a diversion to distract attention so others in on the plot could kill Lincoln. But with Lincoln missing, so was their specific purpose. There would be no point now in throwing the eggs, risking the ire of the police. Indeed, the diversion to their diversion, that which would ultimately distract attention from their egg-throwing row—Lincoln's assassination—would not happen. This is why the conspirators held their fire or merely dropped their eggs and other missiles to the paving stones. The *Macon* newspaper correspondent's eyewitness account corroborates Luckett's chilling revelation.

Luckett's remarkable statement to Pinkerton on the evening of February 23, 1861 did far more, however, than merely confirm that there existed in Baltimore a well-organized conspiracy to attack Lincoln. Indeed, Luckett's statement demonstrates that the plotters had gone a critical step beyond conspiring to assassinate the president-elect. Luckett's admission, recorded by the hearer within hours of being spoken, serves as credible proof that the conspiracy had matured to the very brink of *attempted* assassination. The participants had taken active steps to carry out their purpose. They had gone beyond conspiring and planning. "About Twenty picked men with good revolvers and Knives" were "in their places." The conspirators had hand-picked the assassins for the job. These men were poised to act. Some of the police were in on the plot. At least some fights were started and the police diverted to quell them.[5] Although eyewitnesses may not have seen the guns and knives and the malignant hearts of those intending to act, they could smell the rotting eggs with which they had intended to enhance their diversion. All the conspirators lacked was the source of their hatred, Lincoln, who had eluded them—for now.

But perhaps the most stunning aspect of Luckett's admission was his revelation that the *"friends* in Baltimore . . . would yet make the attempt to assassinate Lincoln." Moreover, Lincoln was no longer the conspirator's only target but also "the d——d spies who had betrayed them."[6]

Perhaps Luckett eyed Pinkerton warily, looking for some sign of fear or weakness. He would see none. With remarkable coolness and presence of mind, Pinkerton agreed wholeheartedly with Luckett that the spies should be detected and even offered him ten dollars to assist in the enterprise. At first, Luckett refused the offer, saying Pinkerton had given enough money already. The two men split the difference. "I finally allowed him to return me Five dollars," Pinkerton reported.[7]

Pinkerton left Luckett and went to his office, where he found his other operatives and received their reports.[8] He then went to the post office for his mail. Pinkerton lingered there for about an hour and did what detectives do—observe, listen, and blend in. The scene was near bedlam. "The whole people were in an excited state. The Hall of the Post Office was crowded full with gentlemen and all sorts of rumors were afloat. I mixed in with them and of all the excitement I ever did see it was there—everybody appeared to be swearing mad, and no end to the imprecations which were poured out on Lincoln and the unknown Spies."[9]

Perhaps Pinkerton smiled inwardly at the ruse he had pulled. However, he must have also felt the anxious, stabbing pangs of dread. At any moment, from around a corner, from beneath a shadow, from behind a lamppost, might emerge an assassin whose bullet was no longer destined for Lincoln, but for him. Indeed, as he stood in the post office listening to the angry scraps of gossip, it must have seemed to Pinkerton that the entire populace of Baltimore had been in on the conspiracy. Pinkerton intended that he and his operatives remain in Baltimore. Now, they would need to be even more cautious and more secretive than ever.

JAMES H. LUCKETT was not the only angry conspirator in Baltimore on the evening of February 23. Otis K. Hillard, the brooding, alcoholic, whore-mongering scion of Baltimore high society, felt equally betrayed. He must have wondered if something he had said to someone he had trusted had been the source of the leak. If so who? There would have been at least two likely suspects. One was Anna Hughes, Hillard's "woman" at Annette Travis's house of prostitution.[10] The other was Pinkerton operative Harry W. Davies, who had grown as close as a brother to Hillard, if not closer. The two men had, over the past few weeks, become almost inseparable. Davies shared more than a few drinks with Hillard, more than a few meals, more than a few hours—indeed they frequently slept in the same room. They walked Baltimore's streets together, attended Catholic vespers together, and in the "somebody's got to do it" category, visited Annette Travis's bordello together.

As a member of the National Volunteers, Hillard had orders to be in position at the Calvert Street Station today at 12:30 p.m.—the published time of Lincoln's arrival from Harrisburg. Even after hearing rumors that Lincoln was already in Washington, Hillard intended to be in position at the depot at the appointed time to carry out his mission. His role was critical. Indeed, Hillard claimed that he was to have the first shot at Lincoln. Perhaps needing emotional support, or intending to test his friend's loyalty to the cause, Hillard wanted Davies to be there with him.

Davies accompanied Hillard to Mann's restaurant, where they ate a quick lunch, and then walked to the Calvert Street Station. Echoing newspaper accounts, Davies reported that the streets were thronged with ten or fifteen thousand people. As they walked, all along the way Hillard stopped and spoke with large numbers of fellow members of the National Volunteers. "The Street on each side of the hill from the top down was crowded with men, standing close side by side, probably two thousand or more, and were supposed to be members of the National Volunteers—there were also large numbers around Monument Square," Davies reported later that day.[11]

Hillard explained to Davies why so many National Volunteers were in position at Monument Square. In the event the efforts to murder Lincoln at the depot should fail, they could rush en-mass upon his carriage as it made its way up Calvert Street and passed the square on its way to Eutaw House, where

Calvert Street Station, Baltimore. The building was torn down in 1950 and the site is now the home of the Baltimore *Sun*. One rumor had snipers positioned in the station's prominent towers for a shot at Lincoln. (*Maryland Historical Society*)

it had been reported Lincoln would dine. The Volunteers could surround it, and assassinate the president-elect—they reasoned that with such a dense crowd around the carriage, it would be impossible for any outsider to tell who did the deed."[12]

The point of the spear, however, was at the depot—Hillard's position. Hillard confided in Davies that "from his position he would have the first shot."[13] The plan had been finally agreed to just the night before, at a secret meeting of the National Volunteer Committee. This group, the inner circle of the several-thousand-man National Volunteers, comprised just fifty-four members.[14] As Hillard took up his position at the depot, waiting for Lincoln's arrival, his excitement must have swelled with anticipation. His senses might have become more acute, putting him in the killer's zone. His brain instinctively would have filtered out all of the extraneous crowd noise, the smell of rotten eggs, the thousands of swaying people, permitting him to concentrate on things that mattered. Perhaps, as the train pulled into the Calvert Street Station, Hillard nervously fingered his weapon, possibly a fine revolver, hidden under his coat. He was the one. He was to have the first shot at Lincoln.

Unbeknownst to Hillard, however, he was not the only one. Reportedly, at least five other men likewise believed they were to have the first shot at Lincoln. They too might proudly be wearing palmetto cockades on their chests, anxiously feeling for their weapons as Lincoln's train pulled in.

ALTHOUGH Davies' account fails to identify any of the National Volunteers other than Hillard crowding Baltimore's streets that day, from other accounts the names of at least a few of the rebel organization's members are known. William Byrne was one of its leaders. Robert E. Hasletz was a member. Cornelius Boyle belonged to the Washington branch of the group. Less readily identifiable members include a Mr. Bradford, one of the officers in the National Volunteers, "a man about 45 or 50 years of age: about 6 feet high," having "the appearance of a gentleman,"[15] a "Mr. Hack," and a "Captain Sherrington."[16] Hillard would later identify Captain Samuel McAleby from the Custom House, and a Captain Thomas —— (last name unknown), a Lexington Street restaurant owner.[17]

Two New York City detectives, Eli De Voe and Thomas Sampson, operating under the aliases "Davis" and "Thompson," respectively, had, like Pinkerton's operatives, also infiltrated the inner ranks of the Baltimore paramilitary crowd. Years later, Sampson recalled that the organization they joined had been called the "Southern Volunteers." Possibly, this paramilitary company was part of the similarly named "National Volunteers." Sampson described his experience with the unit as follows: "De Voe and I became members of a military company that met regularly in a kind of barracks. Our presiding officer and military instructor was a Texan, Captain Hays by name, and a picturesque Texan he was, with great flashing eyes and long floating hair, topped with a huge white sombrero. We had no muskets, but that was nothing to the inventive Texan. He put us through the manual of arms with laths. Sometimes there was a squad of forty men at drill."[18]

If out-of-town operatives like Pinkerton and his agents, and Sampson and De Voe could use aliases, it stands to reason that at least some of the rebel leaders of secret organizations in Baltimore might likewise have used assumed names. If the generic sounding "Captain Hays" was not the man's real name, who might fit the description of a secessionist with ties to Baltimore, who hailed from Texas, who had the ability to improvise, who had flashing eyes and long hair, and sufficient military experience and leadership qualities to drill raw recruits?

At least one man fits this rather distinct profile. He was none other than the senator from Texas—Louis T. Wigfall. Wigfall had served as a lieutenant of volunteers in the Seminole War in Florida in 1835.[19] He is suspected of being the head of the Breckinridge and Lane organization that had morphed into the National Volunteers in Baltimore and other cities. Although the precise date is not known, Wigfall would, around this time, open a rebel recruiting office in Baltimore. Wigfall's trademark look was his long hair and penetrating gaze—to some, he had the roving eye of a pirate. It would have been a simple matter for Wigfall to regularly take the brief, 40-mile train ride north from Washington. And, like J. Wilkes Booth, Wigfall had an impulsive, militant streak and a habit of improvising to put himself where the action was. Indeed, less than two months later, brandishing a cutlass with a white handkerchief tied to its point, Wigfall would, without authorization and with cannonade bursting all around him, command a rowboat to Fort Sumter engulfed in flames, in order to urge Major Anderson to surrender. Might the flamboyant Louis T. Wigfall, disguised beneath a white sombrero and going by the moniker "Captain Hays," have been among the crowd in Baltimore that afternoon, intent on inspiring, even leading, the National Volunteers to murder Lincoln?

Let us return to a conspirator that we know for certain stood at Baltimore's Calvert Street depot waiting for Lincoln with the intent to kill him on February 23, 1861—Otis K. Hillard. That day, Hillard wore on the outside of his vest "in full view" a palmetto cockade, the secessionist's highly identifiable campaign button and badge of honor. One version comprised a circular, pleated blue ribbon rosette with a brass button of the Palmetto Guard, the South Carolina volunteer militia, mounted in its center. Another version was a handmade, three- or four-inch-long palmetto tree, of the same style that to this day decorates the South Carolina flag, woven of saw grass, palm fronds, or basket wicking.[20] No matter what version Hillard wore, the cockade would have been readily identifiable and would have marked him as a secessionist and an anti-Lincoln man. This fact in itself is telling. One might think that a would-be Lincoln assassin, rather than attempting to stand out in a crowd by proudly declaring his secessionist sympathies, would try to blend in to avoid detection and later identification. But there might have been a counterintuitive reason for Hillard, and any of the other hand-picked assassins, *not* to want to blend in that day. Indeed, Hillard and the other conspirators may have wanted to stand out.

If the Baltimore police were, as Luckett claimed, in on the conspiracy, they would have needed to make a show of at least attempting to preserve order, while simultaneously permitting the assassination to take place. If, as Hillard claimed, there was to have been a rush at Lincoln's carriage, and the few police present were in on the plot, they might have focused their half-hearted blocking efforts on those *not* wearing palmetto cockades. Indeed, Hillard corroborated Luckett's admission, confessing to Davies, "it was so arranged, or was so understood by him, that the Police were not to interfere only sufficient to make it appear that they were endeavoring to do their duty. Hillard added 'All that heavy Police Force that went down there (to the Depot), they all went into the Station House, and even if they had interfered what could they have done? We had four thousand of the Volunteers at and about the Depot besides what were at Monument Square, and if you did not see Marshall Kane around, He knows his business.'"[21]

Here, we have stunning testimony of one suspect, Otis K. Hillard, implicating another, Marshal Kane, corroborating the admission of a third, James Luckett. In the coming days, Kane's name would figure prominently in sensational newspaper accounts of the plot, inducing him to write a florid rebuttal to the scandalous allegations being leveled against him. But Hillard's comment provides contemporaneous, firsthand evidence that Marshal Kane, the one person in Baltimore most responsible for securing order and preventing violence on the Lincoln cortege, was nowhere to be found at the most critical moment and in the most critical place—when the train supposed to be carrying Lincoln arrived at the Calvert Street Station. "If you did not see Marshall Kane around, He knows his business." This almost innocuous statement, more supposition than admission, also provides evidence of conspiracy; that Hillard, like Kane, knew Kane's "business"—to provide little or no protection for Lincoln in Baltimore.

IN Washington, at around 9:00 p.m., on the evening of February 23, a solitary figure stood in the corner of a dim, gaslit parlor at Willard's awaiting callers. For once, no crushing hordes of eager curiosity seekers pressed around him. No long lines waited to shake his hand, a particularly good thing, given how swollen and sore it had become as a consequence twelve days of arm-wrenching receptions.[22] No welcoming committees or office-seekers clamored for his attention. Not one bodyguard, not even the fiercely loyal Ward Hill Lamon, attended to him. Indeed, the presence of bodyguards would have been most unseemly. Soon, the parlor would be filled with the nation's last best hope for peace—the dignified, respected, stalwart, if aging and sometimes combative members of the Peace Conference. Though he stood alone, Abraham Lincoln was ready for them.

Earlier that afternoon, Lucius E. Chittenden, the Vermont delegate, had called on Lincoln to share some intelligence with him. He wanted to give Lincoln advance warning. Three distinct species roamed with the herd of Peace Conference delegates that would be sniffing about tonight: those who would greet Lincoln out of respect; those who would merely come to satisfy their curiosity; and those whose sole purpose would be to jeer and ridicule the president-elect. Chittenden knew how spiteful and cunning this latter breed was. Their claws and fangs, like their minds, were indeed sharp. Chittenden believed that Lincoln needed preparation and coaching to receive them and emerge unscathed.

"As I entered his apartment," Chittenden recalled,

> a tall, stooping figure, upon which his clothing hung loosely and ungracefully, advanced to meet me. His kindly eyes looked out

from under a cavernous, projecting brow, with a curiously mingled expression of sadness and humor. His limbs were long, and
at first sight ungainly. But in the cordial grasp of his large hands,
the cheery tones of his pleasant voice, the heartiness of his welcome, in the air and presence of the great-hearted man, there was
an ascendancy which caused me to forget my errand, and to comprehend why it was that Abraham Lincoln won from all classes
and conditions of men a love that "was wonderful, passing the
love of women."[23]

Lincoln knew that he had a winning way with people, and he intended to
use it to his advantage this evening. He explained to Chittenden how pleased
he was to have an opportunity to meet such a diverse body as the Peace
Conference delegates. He was particularly interested in meeting those who
most opposed him—Democratic delegates from the slave states. He had been
portrayed unfairly, "as an evil spirit, a goblin, the implacable enemy of
Southern men and women." Even now, less than twenty-four hours after elud-
ing the gauntlet of suspected assassins in Baltimore, Lincoln held out an idealistic hope that once his adversaries got to know him, even the raging tempers of the most vociferous secessionist fire-eaters might be quenched.

As Chittenden basked in the confident aura of Lincoln's presence and his
warm conciliatory glow of optimism, he quickly came to realize that this was
not a hapless neophyte in need of a life coach. True, he was a newcomer, or at
best a latecomer, to Washington. And his arrival had been less than dignified.
Abraham Lincoln had not, however, just fallen off the turnip wagon. He had
regrouped, regained his composure, and was ready, indeed eager, to take on the
worst snapping and snarling political hyenas that might encircle him this
evening. "I left him," Chittenden wrote, "having said nothing I had intended
to, with a conviction that he would require no guardian."[24]

At 9:00 p.m., the appointed time, Lincoln stood alone to receive the Peace
Conference members. According to Chittenden, no one had been deputed to
introduce Lincoln to the delegates. The Vermonter therefore assumed the role,
taking up a position beside the president-elect.[25] From this vantage,
Chittenden could not only introduce the delegates to Lincoln, he could eaves-
drop on what each had to say.

In "straggling groups" the delegates made their way into the drawing
room, as if part of a museum tour group interested in observing the rare,
homely, prairie curiosity known as Lincoln. Initially, the reception was cordial.
In an unstudied manner, Lincoln greeted each member with respect and kindness, often showering accolades on the delegates being introduced, particularly those from the slave states. The museum curiosity was trying to win his
audience over.

"You are a smaller man than I supposed—I mean in person: every one is acquainted with the greatness of your intellect," Lincoln said in greeting Virginian William C. Rives. "It is, indeed, pleasant to meet one who has so honorably represented his country in Congress and abroad." To Kentuckian James B. Clay, he gushed, "your name is all the endorsement you require. . . . From my boyhood the name of Henry Clay has been an inspiration to me." Patriotically, he asked of F. K. Zollicoffer, "does liberty still thrive in the mountains of Tennessee?"[26]

There was, however, at least one event that would mar the gathering, and James A. Seddon would figure prominently in it. Seddon and fellow Virginians William C. Rives and George W. Summers had clustered around Lincoln like a pack of wolves cornering their prey. In response to one of Lincoln's complimentary remarks, Rives demurred, saying he could do little to save the Union from the dark clouds that threatened it. Instead, Rives warned Lincoln, "everything now depends upon you."

"I cannot agree to that," Lincoln responded, holding his ground. "My course is as plain as a turnpike road. It is marked out by the Constitution. I am in no doubt which way to go. Suppose now we all stop discussing and try the experiment of obedience to the Constitution and the laws. Don't you think it would work?"

Summers seemed to agree that Lincoln's suggested course could work. "If the Constitution is your light, I will follow it with you, and the people of the South will go with us."

The conversation was turning a bit too conciliatory for Seddon. He needed to veer the ship away from the safe harbor guarded by a constitutional lighthouse back into the open, choppy waters of rancorous bipartisan debate. Chittenden recorded the exchange.

"It is not of your professions we complain," Seddon barked at Lincoln, "it is of your sins of omission—of your failure to enforce the laws—to suppress your John Browns and your Garrisons, who preach insurrection and make war upon our property!"

"I believe John Brown was hung and Mr. Garrison imprisoned," Lincoln replied dryly. "You cannot justly charge the North with disobedience to statutes or with failing to enforce them. You have made some which were very offensive, but they have been enforced, notwithstanding."

"You do not enforce the laws," Seddon growled. "You refuse to execute the statute for the return of fugitive slaves. Your leading men openly declare that they will not assist the marshals to capture or return slaves."

"You are wrong in your facts again," Lincoln calmly responded. He was putting on a debate clinic now. "Your slaves have been returned, yes, from the shadow of Faneuil Hall in the heart of Boston. Our people do not like the work, I know. They will do what the law commands, but they will not volunteer to act as tip-staves or bum-bailiffs. The instinct is natural to the race. Is it not true of the South? Would you join in the pursuit of a fugitive slave if you could avoid it? Is such the work of gentlemen?"

Seddon had no response. He abruptly changed the subject, diving into even more desperate waters: "Your press is incendiary!" He bellowed. "It advocates servile insurrection, and advises our slaves to cut their masters' throats. You do not suppress your newspapers. You encourage their violence."

"I beg your pardon, Mr. Seddon," Lincoln replied. "I intend no offense, but I will not suffer such a statement to pass unchallenged, because it is not true. No Northern newspaper, not the most ultra, has advocated a slave insurrection or advised the slaves to cut their masters' throats. A gentleman of your intelligence should not make such assertions. We do maintain the freedom of the press—we deem it necessary to a

Abraham Lincoln photographed by Mathew Brady on the day of his arrival in Washington. Lincoln's right hand is positioned behind the chair arm, perhaps to hide its swollenness. (*Library of Congress*)

free government. Are we peculiar in that respect? Is not the same doctrine held in the South?"[27]

If Seddon had a response, history does not record it. The Virginia delegation moved along. Most significant in this exchange is what Seddon did *not* say. There is no record that he, or any other delegate for that matter, inquired of Lincoln about the abrupt change in plans in avoiding Baltimore and arriving early and unannounced in Washington this morning and missing the receptions planned for him in both cities. Although most of the sensational newspaper accounts of the Baltimore Plot had yet to be published, certainly rumors of it would have been swirling by now. And besides, it would seem only natural for Seddon and the other delegates to ask what had induced Lincoln to change his travel plans, to scrap the published program for his arrival in Washington. Perhaps inquiry was made, but Chittenden merely fails to report it. Perhaps the delegates refrained from making inquiry out of respect for Lincoln, anticipating his chagrin at giving Baltimore the slip and being sensitive about, even regretting, the undignified move. But James

Seddon was clearly not above poking his slaveholding thumbs in Lincoln's eyes. Of all people, as a man who had just accused Lincoln of complicity in failing to enforce fugitive slave laws and inciting murderous slave insurrections, Seddon would not have missed an opportunity to also accuse the president-elect of cowardice in sneaking through Baltimore—unless he knew in advance of the plot and wanted to avoid the subject, lest suspicion turn to him.

The delegation from New York greeted Lincoln next. If Lincoln expected a Northern delegation to offer a respite from the sort of heated debate just proffered by the Virginian Seddon, he was sadly mistaken. A fifty-five-year-old mutton-chopped New York City dry goods merchant, William Earle Dodge, now set his sights on the president-elect. Dodge was upset with Lincoln, and not merely because he had been hastily evicted from parlor number 6 earlier in the day to make way for him. Co-founder of the New York City-based mercantile exchange Phelps Dodge and Company, Dodge worried for both his city's and his own personal interests. His company traded American-made products to England in exchange for copper, iron, tin, and other metals.[28] If the nation were suddenly plunged into war, Dodge's business might suffer. Brazenly, in a voice loud enough to be heard by everyone in the parlor, Dodge confronted Lincoln, reminding him how anxious the country was. The entire nation waited expectantly for Lincoln's inaugural address, like the birth of a long overdue child. Dodge's real anxiety, however, was pecuniary in nature: "It is for you, sir," Dodge blustered, "to say whether the whole nation shall be plunged into bankruptcy; whether grass shall grow in the streets of our commercial cities."

Lincoln was unfazed. "With a merry twinkle in his eye," he replied that if such matters were truly up to him, the grass would grow only in the fields and meadows.

"Then you will yield to the just demands of the South," Dodge persisted. "You will leave her to control her own institutions. You will admit slave states into the Union on the same conditions as free states. You will not go to war on account of slavery!"

Chittenden recalled that "a sad but stern expression swept over Mr. Lincoln's face." Without raising his voice to Dodge's level, Lincoln's measured and steadfast response, evocative of the dangers he had just traversed in Baltimore, but mindful of those that yet threatened his life, was classic:

> I do not know that I understand your meaning, Mr. Dodge, nor do I know what my acts or my opinions may be in the future, beyond this. *If I shall ever come to the great office of President of the United States*, I shall take an oath. I shall swear that I will faithfully execute the office of President of the United States, of all the United States, and that I will, to the best of my ability, pre-

serve, protect, and defend the Constitution of the United States. This is a great and solemn duty. With the support of the people and the assistance of the Almighty I shall undertake to perform it. I have full faith that I shall perform it. It is not the Constitution as I would like to have it, but as it *is*, that is to be defended. The Constitution will not be preserved and defended until it is enforced and obeyed in every part of every one of the United States. It must be so respected, obeyed, enforced, and defended, let the grass grow where it may.[29]

Dodge was left speechless. The New York delegation moved along.

A delegate from New Jersey next approached Lincoln and asked whether the North should make concessions to the South in order to avoid civil war. As an example, the delegate wondered whether territories might authorize slavery when admitted to the Union. Replied Lincoln,

"It will be time to consider that question when it arises . . . . Now we have other questions which we must decide. In a choice of evils, war may not always be the worst. Still I would do all in my power to avert it, except to neglect a Constitutional duty."[30]

The faces of the Republicans beamed with "surprised satisfaction." The more ardent Southern delegates left the room, "discouraged and depressed."[31] With good reason. They had expected in Lincoln a buffoon and a coward. Instead they found an eloquent statesman, a constitutional adherent, an intelligent, independent, strong, and charismatic leader.

"He has been both misjudged and misunderstood by the Southern people," Virginian William Rives lamented afterwards. "They have looked upon him as an ignorant, self-willed man, incapable of independent judgment, full of prejudices, willing to be used as a tool by more able men. This is all wrong. He will be the head of his administration, and he will do his own thinking. . . . His will not be a weak administration."[32]

Assuming Lincoln lived to install his administration. If any of the delegates in the room that night, whether Southern slaveholders or Northerners who supported them, had conspired to assassinate Lincoln in Baltimore, they would have had more reason than ever to dispense with him now. If they had paid attention to his words, they would have known. Lincoln was a force to be taken seriously. "In a choice of evils, war may not always be the worst." Those were his words, and they foretold his intent. Lincoln had, in essence, confirmed what Senator Morrill had said in response to James Seddon's cross-examination four days earlier. Secession, whether on account of slavery, any other reason, or no reason at all, was contrary to the Constitution, the supreme law of the land. Enforcing that law, by war if necessary, was an option that clearly remained on Lincoln's table.

In Baltimore, Pinkerton operative Harry W. Davies continued to work suspected conspirator Otis K. Hillard. The two men went to Annette Travis's house of prostitution, where Hillard consorted with his favorite, Anna Hughes, and consumed enough wine to be "quite merry" by the time the two men left, around 11:30 p.m. Hillard, who had been evasive with Davies earlier in the evening, became talkative once the alcohol kicked in. When the two men returned to their hotel room, Hillard reported that the National Volunteers would be having another meeting on Monday evening, February 25. Hillard also claimed that a man in Baltimore had pledged five thousand dollars to any man who could kill Lincoln. When Davies asked the man's name, Hillard refused to tell. But as the men continued talking into the wee hours, Hillard admitted that a liquor dealer in Baltimore named Charles Meyers had that very day given the National Volunteers five thousand dollars. This was a vast sum of money in 1861. Presumably, it was blood money. Although the National Volunteers had claimed to be merely a political organization formed to voice opposition to the pro-Lincoln Wide Awakes, there were no longer any political contests. The election was over. The electoral vote count had been tallied. All that remained to make the National Volunteers' defeat utter and complete was Lincoln's inauguration. Five thousand dollars would have been more than enough money to induce an assassin, even one whose Southern heart had not been fired, into action.

The conspirators' target had landed in Washington. So too their objective had now shifted from Baltimore to the nation's capital, a short train ride away. Hillard told Davies that by Monday, February 25, there would be fifty men in Washington. Presumably, some or all of them would be members of the National Volunteers of Baltimore. They would be looking for another chance to kill Lincoln.[33]

And this very night, February 23, 1861, a "morose and sullen" John Wilkes Booth would end his run at Albany's Gayety Theater to rave reviews. He would cancel his engagement for the following week, on a plea that his dagger wound had not yet healed. This seems quite odd, given newspaper reports five days earlier that Booth had "quite recovered."[34] He would not open again in Albany until March 4—the date of Lincoln's inauguration.

Since early this morning, the sensational story had been flashed across the wires all over the country: Lincoln had passed through Baltimore in disguise to avoid assassination, and was now safely in Washington. Perhaps Booth thought nothing of it. Subsequent events, however, suggest that Lincoln's cunning and evasive strategy of slipping through Baltimore infuriated him. Years later, Booth's sister Asia Booth Clarke recalled his suspicious behavior during the war: "Wilkes came frequently to me at Philadelphia. . . . Wilkes knew that he could come and go at our house unquestioned and unobserved. He often slept in his clothes on the couch downstairs, having on his long riding boots. Strange men called at late hours, some whose voices I knew, but who would not answer to their names; and others who were perfect strangers to me; they never came farther than the inner sill, and spoke in whispers."[35]

During one of these secretive visits, J. Wilkes revealed to Asia what he thought of Lincoln's night ride through Baltimore. Booth had become agitated by the thought that a reelected Lincoln might make himself king. He "whispered fiercely" to her, "that Sectional Candidate should never have been President, the votes were *doubled* to seat him, he was smuggled through Maryland to the White House. Maryland is true to the core—every mother's son. Look at the cannon on the heights of Baltimore. It needed just that to keep her quiet."[36]

Perhaps this week Booth had been staying in touch with colleagues, other secessionist sympathizers in Baltimore. Pinkerton later claimed that the conspirators had indeed developed a cipher to communicate with one another.[37] Whether via ciphered telegrams secretly delivered to his room at Stanwix Hall or through coded personal ads placed in Northern newspapers next to advertisements for hair restoratives or pills claiming to cure everything from constipation to epilepsy, it is possible Booth knew or would soon know the same intelligence Hillard had just shared with Davies—that the very next week, the Baltimore plotters would make a renewed attempt on Lincoln's life in Washington. Whether that fact, rather than his injury, was the real reason Booth sought to be released from his acting engagements is not known. What is known is this: for the next nine days, John Wilkes Booth would be off the boards, with time on his hands and money in his pockets.

CHAPTER NINETEEN

A SHIRT-TAIL PLOT

February 24–March 1, 1861
Baltimore and Washington

ONCE WORD OF THE BALTIMORE PLOT became public, those on all sides of the story saw the need to cast the facts in a light that shone most favorably on their self-interest or cause célèbre. Marshal Kane sought to put his own spin on the story, arguing that ample police protection in Baltimore would have been provided for Lincoln and that the Baltimore Republicans were to blame for any perceived threats. The Baltimore Republicans, having been insulted at home, snubbed in Harrisburg, and ridiculed by the press, lashed out with indignation as they sought a soothing balm for their wounded pride. The press, both North and South, had great fun depicting the president-elect at best as a man prone to wearing ridiculous disguises, at worst, as a shrinking coward.

Marshal Kane, who had seen his name in print in stories implicating his involvement with the Baltimore plotters, published a stern rebuttal in the *Baltimore American*. It read in part:

> I did not recommend that the President elect should avoid passing openly through Baltimore, nor did I, for one moment, contemplate such a contingency. Indeed, I made no recommendation whatever in the premises, but confined my remarks to the expression of an opinion that such an escort or appendage [the Baltimore Republicans] as the one which rumor had indicated, would, in my judgment, be ill advised, and subject that appendage to an expression of public dissatisfaction which might, and doubtless would, have been construed into a premeditated discourtesy by the people of Baltimore to the President elect.[1]

Worthington G. Snethen, by now aware that the Baltimore Republicans were being blamed for Lincoln's flight through their city, wrote a scathing letter to Lincoln. Snethen vehemently denied that the Baltimore Republicans had planned to make any ostentatious show. The Committee of 100 were merely to have been present at the depot to receive Lincoln "in a body, without the formality of introduction."[2] Further, Snethen supported claims that ample police protection would have been provided. Amazingly, Snethen ignored the rowdy reception the presidential suite had endured on arriving in Baltimore and shifted blame by suggesting it had been *Lincoln's* responsibility to request police protection there:

> Carriages were to be provided for the accommodation of the whole Presidential party, which were in charge of Major D. H. McPhail. Mayor Brown had assured Judge Marshall and myself . . . that he should be present in his official capacity, to receive you, and to accompany you alone, in a private two seat carriage. . . . There was to be no procession whatever. A strong force of police was to be present at the Depot, on your arrival, to prevent the pressure of the crowd around the carriages, when they should drive off under the protection of the Mayor. The disembarkation was to be effected within the enclosure of the Depot, in the presence of the Committee of 100, and such other citizens as chose to be present. No request was made by any of your friends for the presence of the Police.[3]

The press, meanwhile, had for once something far more salacious to chew on than bland, dry speeches and ineffective, if saucy Peace Conference ruminations. The president-elect of the United States, wearing a disguise, accompanied by armed detectives, on board a regular night sleeper car, had eluded Baltimore under cover of darkness. These facts were incontrovertible. But the reasons, whether real or imagined for these undeniable facts, were fluid and offered an opportunity for exposition. The press was all too willing to comply. Northern newspapers tended to support Lincoln's move. Wrote the *New York Times* in an editorial, "We have not the slightest doubt that the project of assassinating Mr. Lincoln has been seriously canvassed by very many persons in different sections of the country,—nor that plans have been laid for its accomplishment. In regard to the recent alleged conspiracy, we have no doubt of its existence."[4]

Embedded *New York Times* reporter Joseph Howard Jr. offered a compelling, if totally fabricated, reason for the president-elect's early arrival in Washington: Governor Seward and other prominent Republican members of the Peace Conference needed Lincoln in the capital several hours earlier than expected so that "he might confer with the Convention on points of vital interest to the country."[5]

Another account implied that Lincoln had simply had enough "canons and crowds" and wanted to avoid both the chance of turmoil, as had occurred, for example, in Buffalo, and "be relieved of all further demonstrations, of which his journey had already been amply full."[6]

Another Northern correspondent, reporting from Washington, stated simply, "Mr. Lincoln is in no way responsible for the change in route in coming to this city. He acted under official communication from General Scott, and the advice of prudent friends, who possessed important information."[7]

Even Southern newspapers could not deny that Lincoln had averted possible danger in Baltimore. Still, the Baltimore Republicans were blamed as the spark that would have ignited trouble. To the brethren of New Orleans, the Baltimore correspondent of the *Picayune* confided: "We are very well satisfied that Mr. Lincoln assumed the responsibility of giving us the slip. . . . It is altogether possible some of his Republican friends in our city, had they appeared conspicuously in any parade or procession, might have been roughly handled, and had an affray commenced in this way, with an ungovernable populace of thousands assembled together, none can foretell the consequences."[8]

As might be expected, however, most Southern newspapers and Baltimore correspondents saw things a bit differently than their Northern counterparts and were most scathing in their treatment of Lincoln. They wholeheartedly dismissed the theory that there had been a Baltimore Plot, scoffed at claims that Lincoln's course of action was necessary or well meaning, and claimed that ample police protection would have made the president-elect's passage through Maryland and Baltimore perfectly safe.[9]

The *Baltimore Sun* was perhaps the most caustic in its criticism of the president-elect, declaring him not only a coward, but a lunatic made dangerous to the entire nation by his ascension to power and his access to the government's war machine:

> Had we any respect for Mr. Lincoln, official or personal, as a man, or as President-elect of the United States, his career and speeches on his way to the seat of government would have cruelly impaired it; but the final escapade by which he reached the capital would have utterly demolished it, and overwhelmed us with mortification. As it is, no sentiment of respect of whatever sort with regard to the man suffers violence on our part, at any thing he may do. . . . We do not believe the Presidency can ever be more degraded by any of his successors, than it has been by him, even before his inauguration; and so, for aught we care, he may go to the full extent of his wretched comicalities. We have only

too much cause to fear that such a man, and such advisers as he has, may prove capable of infinitely more mischief than folly when invested with power. A lunatic is only dangerous when armed and turned loose; but only imagine a lunatic invested with authority over a sane people and armed with weapons of offense and defence. What sort of a fate can we anticipate for a people so situated? And when we reflect that fanaticism is infested with like fears, suspicions, impulses, follies, flights of daring and *flights* of cowardice common to lunacy itself, and to which it is akin, what sort of a future can we anticipate under the presidency of Abraham Lincoln?[10]

Predictably, the citizens of Baltimore were indignant that Lincoln would pull such a stunt on them. Having gotten safely through Baltimore's streets hours before his announced arrival, there had been no attack upon him, which of course made it quite easy for Baltimoreans, having no access to Pinkerton's or Seward's contrary intelligence, to claim that there would *not* have been any attack on him. Claimed the Baltimore correspondent for the *Philadelphia Inquirer,* "The assertions, as telegraphed to the New York journals, that a diabolical plot existed to assassinate [Lincoln] are probably exaggerations. Nothing of the kind was known or thought of generally. On the contrary, had such a design been suspected, the whole military, with the official aid of corporation, and all good citizens would have turned out for the protection of the future Chief Magistrate."[11]

The same story in the *Inquirer* reported that Marshal Kane "and four hundred policemen, were at the railroad station, and determined to protect the President at the hazard of their lives, but the Wide Awakes could not be guarantied against harm." The story then contradicted its earlier claim that no harm was intended for Lincoln: "There were many reckless boys and dissolute young men in the crowd, who had eggs and other missiles in their pockets, which, as is presumed, they designed throwing at somebody."[12]

In an unusual twist, the story laid all the credit (or blame) for Lincoln's decision to change his plans on none other than Governor Hicks: "Governor Hicks requested Gen. Scott and Mr. Seward to persuade Mr. Lincoln to pass incognito through Baltimore, to avoid the possibility of danger. This they did by special messenger."[13] Hicks "indignantly denied" this charge days later, insisting "that no dangers whatever threatened Lincoln in Baltimore."[14]

Criticism of Lincoln's secret passage did not confine itself to Baltimore correspondents for Northern newspapers and the Southern press. In Albany, the Democratic *Atlas and Argus* wrote scathingly of Lincoln's trip through Baltimore. Its headlines screamed, "Terrible Conspiracy to Assassinate Abraham Lincoln: Or a Prodigious Hoax. Flight of Mr. Lincoln from

Harrisburgh in Disguise. His Unexpected Arrival at Washington. Great Indignation at Baltimore."[15] In an editorial entitled "Lincoln's Panic and Flight," the newspaper not only accused Lincoln of cowardice, but incredibly argued that it would have been better for him to risk, even confront, assassination in Baltimore than sneak through as he had: "It strikes us that a truly brave man, in Mr. Lincoln's position, would have scorned such a skulking from such a rumor of danger, and would have faced it even at the peril of his life, trusting to the chivalry of the people along the route for his defense."[16]

In an article entitled "The Shirt-Tail Plot," the *Atlas and Argus,* quoting Chicago mayor Long John Wentworth, blamed the affair on an unnamed "Chicago Detective" who had made up the entire story merely to "get up a case" for private gain. "Knowing what we do about this private detective system, had we known in advance that there was a Chicago detective going on to Baltimore, we could have sworn that he would get up an assassination case. One was gotten up; and it has redounded, like all these cases, to the credit of no one of the parties concerned."[17]

A critical editorial in the *New York World* howled, "We don't believe it. . . . But even if it were true how unfortunately was Mr. Lincoln advised! . . . Had he known that there were murderers lying in wait for his life in Maryland, he should have refused the shelter of car or of carriage, and mounting a horse, like a man, have called his friends around him, and he would have ridden into Washington with an escort of thousands, and the conqueror of millions of loyal hearts."[18]

But the criticism that perhaps stung Lincoln most came from one of his strongest allies, Horace Greeley. "Mr. Greeley says that Mr. Lincoln ought to have come through by daylight, if one-hundred guns had been pointed at him," reported the *New York Times.*[19]

IF certain factions were publicly less than complimentary of Lincoln's flight through Baltimore, private correspondence tended to be more understanding and even encouraging. On the day Lincoln arrived in Washington, William Louis Schley, a Baltimore man, wrote Lincoln about the dangers he might have experienced had he passed openly through his city, and to urge his continued caution:

> Private
> Balt. City.
> Feb. 23. 1861.
> Hon. A. Lincoln
> Prest. Of the U States.

Dear Sir.

You will pardon my note, not having a personal acquaintance, but I deem it due to you and myself, to explain a matter in which I am interested. . . . A vast crowd was present at the Depot to see you arrive, this morning, but at "Ten" you may judge the disappointment at the announcement of your "passage" through unseen unnoticed and unknown — it fell like a thunder clap upon the community — was denied as a "hoax" —&c. until the truth was made beyond a doubt—A large "police force" was present to preserve the peace, besides your many friends to resist attack — which I now declare was meditated and determined— By your course you have saved bloodshed and a mob. . . . I have thus explained and am rejoiced to know of your safe arrival in the "Capitol." I desire and request, most respectfully, that my note will be kept private and unknown, relying upon the fact and truth that it was done simply, from the best motive and desire of my heart, as an advisory measure and caution & to enforce upon you caution—I hope to see you before many days, face to face— I remain

Respectfully Your Obt. &c.

Wm Louis Schley[20]

Those who would seek political favors from the Lincoln administration likewise admired the dress of a ruler who, in other's eyes, was an emperor with no clothes. One such admirer, Bronson Murray of the American Telegraph Company in New York, apparently hoped to cash in on government contracts. Writing to Ward Hill Lamon, Murray said of Lincoln, "His passage thro' Balt. is regarded here as wise by the prudent men and as timid by the heedless. I approve it."[21]

Writing condescendingly of Lincoln in her famous diary, even Mary Boykin Chesnut, the wife of the former South Carolina senator James Chesnut Jr., noted that some prominent Southerners privately believed that Lincoln had been wise to avoid Baltimore: "Brewster says Lincoln passed through Baltimore, disguised and at night—and that he did well—for just now Baltimore is dangerous ground. He says he hears from all quarters that the vulgarity of Lincoln, his wife, and his son is beyond credence—a thing you must see before you can believe it. Sen. Stephen Douglas told Mr. C that Lincoln was awfully clever and that he had found him a heavy handful."[22] But Mary Chesnut was clearly no fan of Lincoln's. Two days after his arrival in Washington, she had written: "Then came that ogre Lincoln and rampant Black Republicanism."[23]

The ogre Lincoln, meanwhile, seemed content to go on with his new life in Washington as if nothing had happened or would have happened in Baltimore. At the time, he made no public excuse and provided no public explanation for the remarkable event. He met with heads of state, heads of the military, and most importantly, continued polishing what ultimately he hoped to give as his side of a far bigger story than the Baltimore Plot—his inaugural address. It seems Lincoln's public response to questions being raised about the plot was "no comment."

Publicly, people and the press hooted and howled at the absurdity of the "shirt-tail plot." The *New York World* went so far to name, and essentially blame, Allan Pinkerton for the whole thing, potentially blowing his carefully crafted cover.[24] Privately, however, both the suspected plotters and Pinkerton's agents, who still believed in its existence, knew the game was not yet up. There were both historical and current reasons to suspect that the Baltimore plotters had followed, or soon would follow, Lincoln to Washington.

Thugs from Baltimore had, four years earlier, stalked James Buchanan to Washington, and the night of Buchanan's inauguration in March 1857, they clustered at the corner of Pennsylvania Avenue and Sixth Street near the National Hotel—J. Wilkes Booth's future hangout—and "fired revolvers, terrifying the citizenry."[25]

There was now good reason to believe history would repeat itself. On the evening of February 23, after Lincoln's safe arrival in Washington had been confirmed, Otis K. Hillard walked with Pinkerton operative Harry W. Davies through the streets of Baltimore. Hillard showed Davies where a secret committee of the National Volunteers was then meeting, at Democratic Headquarters on Fayette Street, near Barnum's Hotel. "[A]s Hillard and I passed the building I stopped and listened a moment, but could distinguish nothing that was said. There seemed to be a great deal of bustle and noise in the room, which is in the third story, some one was speaking at the time and at intervals there was clapping of hands and stamping of feet," Davies noted in his daily report. "I should not be surprised if the National Volunteers marched to Washington, between this and the second day of March," Hillard had earlier remarked.[26]

Later, after a night of drinking and whoring, Hillard reinforced everything he had said earlier in the day. Having failed to kill Lincoln in their city, it was becoming clear to Davies that the Baltimore plotters would attempt to do so in the nation's capital. "From what I could gather from him," Davies reported, "Washington City appeared to now be the principal point for action by those in the plot to take Lincoln's life."[27]

The next evening, in Davies' hotel room, Hillard confirmed this. "I asked Hillard if the National Volunteer Committee had come to any understanding as to what course they were going to pursue. He said they had, and from what had been intimated to him they would make a descent on Washington City; that they had received three thousand Dollars more—making Eight thousand in all—with which to purchase Arms, and that they (the Volunteers) would make a pretty hard fight; that there were two thousand Federal Troops in Washington, but said he 'we can easily clean them out.'" Hillard remarked that he was confident that before three days should pass, the National Volunteers' numbers would swell to ten thousand men. Recounted Davies, "he seems to have great faith in their success—appeared in good spirits."[28]

"Passage through Baltimore," by A. J. Volck. (*New York Public Library*)

ALLAN PINKERTON and his Chicago operatives were of course not the only detectives that had descended on Baltimore in February 1861 to gather intelligence that ultimately led to the suspicion of a Lincoln assassination plot. In fact, Pinkerton's group had not even been the first to arrive. John A. Kennedy, superintendent of the New York Metropolitan Police, had previously ordered his chief of police to detail two of his brightest detectives in Baltimore to gather intelligence on a suspected conspiracy to seize Washington and determine how Maryland was to be "precipitated out of the Union."[29] Acting on Kennedy's orders, New York police chief George W. Walling selected the men for the job. "I carefully considered the selection of proper detectives for this delicate affair, and after anxious thought I chose Messrs. Sampson and De Voe. They were instructed to go to Baltimore, look over the ground and ingratiate themselves with the disaffected persons. In other words, to use their own discretion and find out all they could."[30]

In Baltimore, Thomas Sampson and Eli De Voe, using the aliases "Thompson" and "Davis," stayed at the Fountain Inn, "and for some weeks had a good time."[31] There were several similarities between Pinkerton's agents and Kennedy's detectives. Posing as Southern sympathizers, as Pinkerton and his operatives had, Sampson claimed to be from Augusta, and De Voe from

Mobile, where he had lived for some time. "We were well supplied with money, very swaggering and loud-mouthed, and soon made friends with a certain class of Southerners whose talk was 'fight to kill,'" Sampson recalled.[32] As had Pinkerton's operatives, Sampson and De Voe worked their way into the confidence of suspected conspirators and became members of the "Southern Volunteers." But here, their luck ran out. Whereas Pinkerton and his agents were able to maintain the trust of the conspirators they shadowed, Sampson and De Voe came under suspicion. At least part of the blame could be laid on De Voe's wife.

"[S]uddenly I discovered that we were suspected," Sampson recalled.

> It was no laughing matter. The "Volunteers" were loud in their threats against traitors. The desperadoes of the company were in the majority. All carried revolvers, and De Voe and I stood a first-rate chance of being killed on sight. There was even a detail whose duty it was to "do away" with suspected persons.
>
> I do not know how the intimation of danger came to me, but I was positive that we were watched. I had been asked searching questions as to the identity of "Davis" (De Voe). His wife had been indiscreet enough to write him a letter, addressed in his assumed name, and bearing the New York post-mark. It had been in some way seen by one of the "Volunteers." Now a letter from the North for "Davis" did not dove-tail with "Davis's" account of himself. I may here remark that to act an imaginary story or identity straightly is one of the most difficult bits of work a detective has to do.[33]

Sampson was asked many questions about the letter and made an explanation that "was not at all complimentary to the good Mrs. De Voe," but was nonetheless grudgingly accepted by the inquisitors—for the time being. But Sampson and De Voe now knew they had to flee. "I thought it was time to go, and we went," Sampson recalled.

Hurriedly, the men disguised themselves as best they could. Sampson exchanged his fur-trimmed cap for a slouch hat, apparently the disguise of choice for those fleeing Baltimore. Sampson and De Voe left town and headed to Washington. "I cannot understand why we were not murdered in Baltimore, unless, perhaps the conspirators thought something more was to be had by letting us go on to Washington," Sampson wrote years later.[34]

In Washington, Sampson and De Voe registered at Willard's under their Baltimore aliases. This was a clear blunder. Anyone scanning the hotel registry would now know they were here. "As I wrote I noticed the peculiar scrawl of Horace Greeley and remarked to De Voe that we were in good company. We went to our rooms and talked matters over. We made up our minds that we were in a bad box. How much did we know of these 'Southern Volunteers'? They numbered many hundreds, perhaps thousands, and we were acquainted with but a few. We felt certain that they were on the watch for us."[35]

Indeed, they were. Pinkerton's men had also determined that Sampson and De Voe were spies. On February 25, Pinkerton operative Charles D. C. Williams reported a description of the two men. "From Williams report and description of Thompson and Davis who had been stopping at Sherwood's Hotel, I infered that they were Detectives from the Metropolitan Force, New York, and that Thompson was "Sampson," and Davis probably Captain Walling, but I was very positive that Thompson was Tom Sampson," Pinkerton wrote. "Williams said that Sherrington and others suspected those men of being Government Spies, and that they would be anihilated in Washington if opportunity offered."[36]

Now in Washington, opportunity would offer. Quickly growing bored cooped up in their room at Willard's, Sampson and De Voe decided to go back downstairs. But when they approached the main hall, they were frozen in their tracks. As Sampson recalled, "there, sure enough, we recognized several of our genial friends, the 'Southern Volunteers,' who were critically examining the hotel register. I watched them breathlessly. When Mr. Greeley's signature was reached they stopped at that for an instant. Then one of them ran his finger down the column and stopped again while he read our assumed names. I cursed my stupidity in not having thought to change my alias. The man turned and whispered to his associates, and they all went slowly out."[37]

Sampson and De Voe inched down the stairs. "I knew we were watched," Sampson recalled. "Some of the party might be outside." Sampson felt that their only chance to avoid being spotted was to blend in with the crowd in the hall. But he knew it would not be long before they were recognized.

"When we entered the hall, De Voe leaned on the cigar-stand, and I cast my eyes toward the billiard-room. I don't want to disguise matters; I was afraid, and cudgelling my brains how to get out of the mess we were in. I did not move for a few instants, when a man in a long overcoat lounged along and got his back directly toward me. Then he suddenly spoke to me—in a very low tone—so that I could just hear his words."

"For God's sake, Tom, come out of this," the man in the long overcoat whispered. The mysterious interloper, whom Sampson did not recognize, but who clearly knew Sampson, motioned furtively to follow. Sampson, packing a self-cocking pistol he was determined to use if necessary, did follow the stranger, who had a heavy cap drawn over his eyes and his coat collar turned up to his nose. Once outside, near the gas lamps, Sampson could no longer stand the suspense. He swung the man around with one hand, gripping his pistol with the other. "The violence of this movement flung open his coat and shifted his cap, so that his face was revealed." Recognition slowly dawned on Sampson.[38]

The man was neither a Baltimore plotter nor a stranger; he was Timothy Webster, one of Pinkerton's best operatives. Tom Sampson had known Webster from years before, when he was one of George Walling's New York City police officers. Indeed, Webster had been one of Sampson's best friends. "He had been on the force with us in former years and I knew him to be a man of exceptional honesty and courage," Sampson recalled.[39] Webster quickly explained, "it is to save you from death that I have followed you. Your life is not worth a cent. I swear to you there are twenty men after you this very instant. Even now I expect we are being watched. I may not be suspected, for I am with them, but they shan't kill my old friend if I can help it. But you clear out of this just as fast as you can, Tom; it is more serious than you think. The chances are you will not get through safely unless you use every precaution. Quickness of movement is everything now."

Sampson protested, saying he couldn't leave without De Voe, who was still back at Willard's.

"He will have to take care of himself," Webster implored. "You're a dead man if you go back after him." This latter point Webster emphasized by imploring Sampson, "Tom, it's so close a shave that at this moment if there's anything you'd like to say to your wife you'd better say it to me for her."[40]

Despite the clear risks, Sampson insisted on going back for De Voe. The two men returned to Willard's. On the way there, Webster revealed his mission. As Sampson recalled, "Tim told me briefly that he was in detective work himself and had been affiliated with the most desperate branch of the Secession party; that he was one of the leading spirits, and that it was his special duty to kill De Voe and me on sight."

After entering Willard's through a back door and smuggling De Voe out of the hotel, the party set out on foot. Webster convinced the two men that they would be murdered if they attempted to leave from the Washington railroad depot. "You will have to walk around Washington some 15 miles and take the train there," he told them. "I will start with you and put you on the track. It is your only chance of escape, for every other exit is guarded."[41]

Webster led the men out of Washington. They found a barn, where Sampson and De Voe would stay for the night. Perhaps they now felt they could rest easy. From here, they could walk to an outlying station and take the first train for Baltimore the next day. Webster then left the two men.

Ironically, however, Sampson and De Voe's ineptitude may have shielded Pinkerton—even though his name was now publicly connected with the investigation—from suspicion. The plotters would not likely have suspected two detective agencies working independently of each other. But they still suspected Sampson and De Voe. And they still wanted Lincoln dead. A gang of desperate, armed men from Baltimore was lurking about Willard's Hotel, scanning guest registries, intent on shooting suspected Northern spies. Such men would almost certainly have known that Lincoln slept in that very hotel. If they were prepared to shoot spies on sight, it stands to reason that they would be prepared to do the same to a hated Black Republican president-elect.

At the same time Pinkerton was asking his client, Samuel M. Felton, if he should remain in Baltimore until the inauguration, Texas senator Louis T. Wigfall was asking his boss, Confederate president Jefferson Davis, if he should remain in Washington after Lincoln was sworn in. Writing from the U.S. Senate Chamber on February 25, Wigfall provided Davis with intelligence on his efforts, apparently urged by Davis, to seduce U.S. military officers and others into the Confederacy and his prediction that the Border States would secede: "Capt. Humphreys can not under any circumstances join us. The others are doubting & ask time. Johnson says that he will leave the moment he has reasonable ground for believing Virginia will withdraw. He wishes to wait at least till the peace congress adjourns.[42] I pressed the matter as far as I could & Mason joined in it. Maj. Lee has a large property in Maryland which puts a clog on him. I believe you will get all; if not all, most in a short time. They have entertained the proposition & that is some thing. They realize the necessity of having an immediate organization of the Army in the Confederate States for the protection of the border states when they go out."[43]

In referring to "Johnson" wishing to remain "at least till the peace congress adjourns," Wigfall possibly was referring to Missourian Waldo P. Johnson, a Peace Conference delegate, the same man who, upon learning of Lincoln's surprise arrival in Washington, blurted out "how the devil did he get through Baltimore?" If so, Johnson and Wigfall appear to be connected to one another by more than a common party, common beliefs, and a common brief, but an overlapping period of disloyal service in the United States senate.[44]

Wigfall closed his letter to Davis by asking for instructions that are most remarkable, considering Wigfall was, at this time, yet a sitting United States senator: "Write at once if you wish me to remain after the 4 March. If it is necessary to make arrangements for soldiers or ships it may be necessary for me to stay till the purpose is accomplished. I am willing to do any thing or go any where or perform any Service you may require."[45]

Three days later, writing in her diary, Mary Chesnut had this to say about Wigfall: "I asked Brewster how his friend Wigfall liked being left alone with the Black Republicans. He replied: 'Wigfall chafes at the restraints of civil life. He likes to be where he can be as rude as he pleases, and he is indulging himself now to the fullest extent, apparently."[46]

AFTER they awoke in the barn the morning following their narrow escape from Washington, Sampson and De Voe made their way to the outlying station and prepared to board the first train to Baltimore. As Sampson and De Voe stepped into the car, they were stunned to see that three of the Southern Volunteers, men they had drilled with, were on board. Things only got worse. Three more Volunteers boarded, entering from another car. Sampson and De Voe had been spotted. "They knew we were in the car," Sampson recalled. "One of them, with a grin, pointed his thumb backward toward us. We were in the rear end. They were deliberating what to do and how to do it. Then they all sat down. Evidently they were going to wait till we got out at Baltimore, when history would know De Voe and me no more."[47]

Sampson had an idea. "We were going at a rapid rate, but it was certain death to stay on that train; there was a chance for life if we jumped. We sauntered out on the platform, closed the door, and took the leap. De Voe fell with a yell, he had sprained his ankle badly. I was much cut and bruised, but not seriously hurt. The train sped on. We had escaped."

Or so they thought. The two fugitives made their way on foot to the outskirts of Baltimore, Sampson helping the injured De Voe to walk. They hired a horsecar, and Sampson helped De Voe climb aboard.

"But where should that confounded car pull up but exactly in front of our old drill-room. 'Car stops here!' sung out the conductor. Of all places in the world what a terminus! We had to alight. I reconnoitred the house. I dreaded to see the flashing eyes, the floating hair, the huge sombrero of our Texan teacher."

But for once, good fortune smiled on Sampson and De Voe. Neither the Texan nor the Volunteers were lurking about. The two men hired a hack, drove to the President Street Station, and caught a train north. "Our troubles were over," Sampson remembered.[48]

But in Baltimore, in Maryland, and in Washington, the troubles were still not over.

HAVING left Sampson and De Voe the night before, on February 25, Timothy Webster caught the 7:40 a.m. train out of Washington bound for Baltimore. He arrived at Pinkerton's office at 10:30 a.m. and reported on Sampson and De Voe's escape. Before leaving Washington, Webster had called on Norman B. Judd at Willard's Hotel. Reported Pinkerton, "Judd was very much pleased to see T. W. and laughed very heartily at the New York Detectives being discovered."[49] Webster spent the afternoon of February 26 taking the pulse of the people in Baltimore. Everywhere he went, the talk was the same—Lincoln would have been shot had he come through the city according to the program. Webster went to Springer's Store and made small talk with a man named

Forward over a glass of beer. "Whilst we were drinking he told me that the boys felt might sore about Lincoln's giving them the slip: that if Lincoln had gone through when he was expected, he would have been shot, and then Baltimore would have been the battle-field, but now he thought Charleston would be."[50]

Later that afternoon, on Pinkerton's orders, Webster went to the White Beer Saloon, where he took a seat and called for another glass of beer. About half an hour later, Pinkerton operative Charles D. C. Williams came in with a man named Sherrington and introduced the man to Webster. As the three men drank, Webster prodded Sherrington.

"I said I thought Baltimore was going to be the battle-field, but old Abe had got safe to Washington. Sherrington replied 'By G—d, he would not if the boys had got their eyes on him, that they would have shot him, for they had everything ready to do it with, and that if we would go up the street he would show us the kind of tools the boys carried here.'"

Webster and Williams followed Sherrington to a store on Baltimore Street, where he instructed the clerk to show them some pistols. Taking one of the pistols, Webster went into a back room and tried it and found it of high quality. "Sherrington said that those were the kind the boys carried."

The men then went to another saloon, got another drink, and then went to Sherrington's where they had some oysters and another drink. Men were still talking about shooting Lincoln. "Some said that they did not believe Lincoln would have been hurt, and others again said that they knew a d—d sight better, for they were acquainted with men who belonged to the Organization who were ready for anything, and would just as leave shoot Lincoln as they would a rat."[51]

In Washington, meanwhile, Pinkerton operative Harry Davies was also keeping busy. He and suspected conspirator Otis K. Hillard had checked into a room at the National Hotel. Hillard and other members of the National Volunteers had come to Washington, just as Hillard had claimed they would.

As Davies and Hillard walked through the streets of Washington, they came upon a man known to Hillard. After greeting the man, Hillard told him, "I have come to see *Old Abe.*"

"Well, Old Abe had a quick trip through Baltimore," the man replied.

"Yes, and it was well for him that he went through as quick as he did," Hillard remarked.

The three men continued walking. Hillard's friend, seeing someone he recognized, pointed and said, "There stands Jim Burns,[52] commander of the National Volunteers." Hillard would later explain to Davies that Burns was one of the leaders of the National Volunteers.

Hillard's friend left. Hillard then purchased a Baltimore paper. In it was a notice for Company Number 9 of the National Volunteers to meet in

Baltimore to elect officers. Hillard explained to Davies that the notice was in fact a "blind" and that there was no need for electing officers, rather, the notice alerted all the members of the National Volunteers to assemble at their respective quarters.

That night, Hillard and Davies went to Odd Fellow's Hall to hear the New Orleans Minstrels. Upon leaving the show, Hillard saw another man that he knew. He spoke briefly with the man, "but without looking at him, and almost in a whisper." Whoever the man was, Hillard never revealed.[53]

Is it possible that one of the National Volunteers that Hillard knew on the street that day was John Wilkes Booth? There is no way of proving such a hypothesis; Booth's whereabouts the week of February 24, 1861, are not definitively known. The Albany *Atlas and Argus* would report on March 2 that "The admirers of the legitimate drama will be pleased to learn that this talented and favorite actor has been re-engaged by the management of the Gayety Theater. Mr. Booth has been sojourning in Albany since last Saturday [February 23], having been released from other engagements elsewhere, that he might fully recover from his recent injuries."[54]

Unless Booth's wound had become infected or his strength had been sapped by it, we are left to wonder why, after returning to the stage "quite recovered" six days after the accident for a six-night run, he would now need eight full days "sojourning in Albany" in order to recover further.

For the most part this week, however, those who favored secession in Washington seemed to by lying low. As Chittenden recalled, "from Monday, the 25th of February, to Monday, the 4th of March, a kind of paralysis appeared to have fallen upon the disunionists. They did almost nothing to attract public attention."[55] This was only natural. If the Baltimore plotters intended to take a shot at Lincoln in Washington, their best opportunity, both for the kill and the public spectacle, would be on March 4, when he would be out in the open, standing on the raised platform now being constructed on the east steps of the Capitol, poised to deliver his inaugural address.

DESPITE Pinkerton's outrage over being named in newspaper accounts of the plot, he was apparently receiving mail at the post office in Baltimore addressed to him under his real name. Possibly, these letters had been sent to him in Chicago and were being forwarded in packages addressed to "J. H. Hutcheson." One such letter reached Pinkerton in Baltimore on February 28. It had been sent from John A. Kennedy, superintendent of New York Metropolitan Police, on February 26, suggesting that it came straight to Baltimore from New York, and had not been sent to Chicago. Kennedy's letter is curious for several reasons. First, it was addressed to "A. Pinkerton." Second, the letter indicates that Kennedy had not previously known that

Pinkerton was in Baltimore. "Had I been apprised of it I could have seen you on my return. I left Washington yesterday afternoon at 3. o' clock and came through by the Owl, and find yours on my desk this morning." Kennedy had been in Washington February 25. Indeed, John A. Kennedy had ridden on the same night train from Philadelphia early on the morning of February 23 that had carried Lincoln to Washington. It was he who was the heavily armed man that lay in a berth in Lincoln's sleeper car that night. Unaware of Lincoln's night ride, Kennedy was following up on reports from Sampson and De Voe and heading to Washington to personally warn authorities, likely General Scott, that Lincoln would require protection in coming through Maryland later that morning.[56] Third, and most interesting, Kennedy's letter indicated that he had received and was responding to an earlier communication from Pinkerton. Pinkerton's dispatch, which has not been found, apparently made a request of Kennedy. "I shall at once have search made for the man and things you named, and inform you of the result," Kennedy assured Pinkerton.[57]

Who was this man and what things had Pinkerton named? That Pinkerton had sent his request to Kennedy suggests that the man was in New York. Perhaps the man Pinkerton sought was the "William Alexander" who had sent the telegraph dispatch to Saul Thompson.

Kennedy closed his letter stating that "the field of operation is now transferred to the Capital. Whatever is done remote from there will be limited to raising funds and the collection of material, so that I have withdrawn my Corps Observation from your present vicinity—But for that reason I shall be happy to receive any suggestion from you that may require attention from my hands."[58]

Although Kennedy had "withdrawn" his hastily retreating detectives from Baltimore by February 26, Allan Pinkerton had not. By March 1, Pinkerton operative Harry W. Davies was back in Baltimore with his conspiratorial sidekick, Otis K. Hillard. Today, Davies ate both breakfast and dinner at Mann's Restaurant. At around 1:30 p.m., after Davies returned to his room, Hillard joined him.[59]

"Some Detectives have got in with the National Volunteers," Hillard reported to Davies. Perhaps he was looking for a sign of Davies' involvement. "Did you read," Hillard continued, "where they (the Detectives) said that every man of the National Volunteers had to take an oath to kill Lincoln if they could?"

Davies played dumb, remarking that he had not read the story. In any event, he feigned disbelief that such a story could be true. But Hillard assured him that the story was true. "He said that they (the Volunteers) *had taken such an Oath,* and added 'I need not do it because I have withdrawn, but I can exercise my own pleasure about it.'—and that 'the members are bound to kill Lincoln yet, if the oppertunity presented itself.'"

Hillard then remarked that the secret committee of the National Volunteers would be holding a meeting that very night. The two men parted company around 4:30, when Davies went to Pinkerton's South Street office for further instructions. The inauguration was just three days away. Pinkerton wanted Davies to be in Washington to witness it.

When Davies returned to his room at six o'clock that night, he found Hillard there waiting for him. "He was very anxious for me to go in the evening with him and visit his sister, a married lady about 40 years old, whose name I do not recollect."

Quite possibly, the "sister" was a setup, a ruse designed to bring Davies to a location where National Volunteers would be lying in wait, ready to squeeze, and if necessary, bludgeon information out of him. He and Hillard had, for the past few weeks been virtually inseparable, going to dinner together, going to saloons together, going to the whorehouse together, even going to vespers together. But tonight, uncharacteristically, Davies would politely decline a seemingly innocent invitation to join his heavy-drinking informant at his sister's. "I excused myself on the plea of indisposition, for the reason that I did not consider that my business called me there," Davies reported.[60]

Hillard and Davies remained in Davies' room the balance of the evening. They continued to talk. "Hillard remarked that the *New York Herald* said that may be Lincoln would not be inaugurated *yet*."[61] Davies, perhaps to draw Hillard out, confided that he was planning to go to Washington for the inauguration.

In the last surviving entry of a Pinkerton operative connected with the Baltimore Plot, Davies closed out his report:

"Hillard said that he was determined to go to Washington with me on Monday: that he was bound to see Lincoln Inaugerated—He drinks as much as usual."[62]

CHAPTER TWENTY

INAUGURATION DAY

Monday, March 4, 1861
Washington

THE DAY DAWNED WITH DARK HEAVY CLOUDS threatening rain. Dust dev-
ils kicked up by strong and chilling northwest winds whipped through
Washington's unpaved streets this morning, but the few paltry showers that
would fall were insufficient to quell them.[1]

Inside Willard's Hotel, Abraham Lincoln prepared to give his biggest
speech, on this, the biggest day of his life. In delivering Lincoln safely to
Washington, Allan Pinkerton had delivered more than a man, more than a
president-elect; he had delivered an ideal. That ideal, in essence, held that in
the American secular realm, Constitution and Union trumped all else, and did
so in perpetuity. Lincoln had expanded on that basic principle until it assumed
the form of the vital and eagerly awaited message he was about to deliver—
the inaugural address. The address, the subject of intense speculation for
weeks, the subject of a paper chase when it was feared lost, and the subject of
revision upon revision, both by the author and those whose judgment he trusted, was finally ready for delivery. And the American people were more than
ready to hear it. No advance copies had been given to the press, and none
would be passed out until after the words were spoken.[2]

The night before, Lincoln's son Robert had copied portions of the address
that were then finished. Lincoln knew the Senate was having an all-night session; some parts of his inaugural might require amendment depending on any
late action the Senate might take.[3] Lincoln made a few last-minute changes to
the document, putting the finishing touches on the lyrical and moving final
paragraph originally proposed by William Seward. He met briefly with
Seward for one final consultation. And then, for the rest of the morning,
Abraham Lincoln cloistered himself, closing his door on family, friends, advisors, and the rest of the world.[4]

By now, Lincoln almost certainly would have known of Allan Pinkerton's latest intelligence from Baltimore, including claims by suspected conspirator Otis K. Hillard that another attempt would be made on his life in Washington. Eight thousand dollars had been raised for the plotters to purchase arms, and ten thousand National Volunteers were to descend on Washington, every last one of them having sworn an oath to kill Lincoln if given the chance.

Even if Lincoln had not heard Pinkerton's reports, similar, less specific predictions had made their way into the press. In a dispatch written on March 3, the *Philadelphia Inquirer* vaguely reported that "there are rumors afloat of difficulties tomorrow, but they cannot be traced to any particular source. Yet no preparation will be neglected. The West Point company of Sappers and Miners are to march directly in front of the carriage, and a large number of picked men, in citizen's dress, will be near Mr. Lincoln all day."[5] The *New York Times* noted grimly, "strange to say heavy bets are pending on the question of [Mr. Lincoln's] safety through tomorrow's exercises, and great anxiety is felt at Head-quarters concerning certain unpublished designs." Lincoln, however, exhibited no fear or alarm. "He says, 'I am here to take what is my right, and I shall take it. I anticipate no trouble, but should it come I am prepared to meet it.'"[6]

OUTSIDE Lincoln's room, crowds had been gathering in and around Willard's Hotel since early morning. By 9:00 a.m., "the halls were one perfect jam."[7] Many among the horde were shameless office seekers. "Western office-hunters, who have never been so far from home before, push wildly about, eyes and mouths wide open."[8]

Beyond the hotel, Washington had resumed the holiday atmosphere that had permeated the capital's streets all week, with moneyed tourists besieged by pickpockets, organ-grinders, and puppet shows.[9] "From early dawn the drum and fife could be heard in every quarter of the city, and the streets were thronged with the volunteer soldiery, hastening to their respective rendezvous."[10]

Pennsylvania Avenue was ablaze with the national colors. American flags nearly as numerous as people flew all along the length of the wide thoroughfare from the Executive Mansion to the Capitol.[11] The banner hung from public buildings, private homes, and across the avenue.[12] In keeping with the holiday tone, all public buildings, schools, and businesses were closed.[13] Even the saloons had been shut down, on orders from General Scott.[14]

Fresh hordes of people, many from out of town, had been gathering all morning. Indeed, many had been up all night. Unable to find a room at any of Washington's overcrowded hotels, they carried their carpetbags in weary search of a good spot from which to watch the procession.[15] Observed one reporter, "every window, balcony and door step on the route of the procession, are crowded with spectators, and upon every block of marble and timber, or heap of building material, people are clustered like bees."[16] Noted another, "every available spot was early taken possession of by the anxious crowd. The trees upon the corners were as full of small boys as an apple tree in a fruit-bearing season."[17] A large special police force, wearing "conspicuous badges" and aided by cables that had been stretched on either side of the carriageway along Pennsylvania Avenue, were distributed along the line of procession to keep the passage clear for Lincoln's carriage.[18] By some accounts, as many as one hundred thousand people would eventually congregate at the east front of the Capitol in hopes of hearing Lincoln's inaugural address.[19]

Among this crowd, undoubtedly many from Baltimore were on hand. Indeed, to accommodate the large Baltimore influx, it had been announced that the B&O Railroad would, this morning, run extra, hourly trains to Washington.[20] It is possible suspected Baltimore plotters, such as Otis K. Hillard, Cypriano Ferrandini, James Luckett, or William Byrne, were milling about among the crowd. Ominously, as if a portent of the "ten thousand" National Volunteers of Baltimore that were predicted to descend on Washington, this morning's *New York Times* reported the rumored presence the previous evening of Baltimore's "Plug Uglies" in the capital: "There is some apprehension felt concerning the possible action of a large gang of 'Plug-Uglies' who are here from Baltimore. . . . It is generally rumored to-night that a large body of men has arrived here from Baltimore and Virginia, part of whom are Secessionists, and a portion Union men—some seven hundred in all. It is not believed that any very formidable organization is here as a distinct body, but the authorities have kept a very close look-out, and are advised that most of the worst characters of Baltimore and some places in Virginia have left for Washington, and would all be present Monday morning."[21]

W HILE many Americans both North and South were unhappy that Abraham Lincoln was to be inaugurated today, almost none were sad to see President Buchanan depart.

"The sun, thank God, has risen upon the last day of the administration of James Buchanan," wrote the anonymous reporter for the *New York World*. "He sits in the White House, with the chalice of power upturned, making wry faces at the unspeakable bitterness of its dregs."[22]

The *Atlanta Southern Confederacy* saw things a bit differently and put a taunting spin on Buchanan's departure:

THE LAST PRESIDENT OF THE UNITED STATES OF AMERICA
The term of four years, commencing the 4th of March, 1857, for which James Buchanan ("The Old Public Functionary") expired today; and with his term has expired the last president of the United States of America.

An imbecile official is succeeded by a stupid Rail Splitter of Illinois, elevated to position by Aggrarianism and Fanaticism, resulting in the overthrow of the best Government that ever existed.[23]

At around noon, "The Old Public Functionary," feeble and pale, left the White House for the last time as president to gather up his successor at Willard's Hotel.[24] Symbolic of his beleaguered administration, Buchanan arrived moments later, bareheaded and all alone, in a simple, open carriage, at the hotel's Fourteenth Street entrance. Here he got out and entered the building. By now, the weather had changed for the better. The wind had shifted around to the north, driving off the clouds that had earlier threatened rain and giving rise to bright sunshine and clear blue sky.[25]

Soon came cries of "hats off," followed by Lincoln and Buchanan, arm in arm.[26] Given the circumstances under which one man was leaving and the other entering the White House, it must have been difficult to discern which man leaned on the other for support.

By the time Lincoln and Buchanan emerged, their procession had been waiting on Pennsylvania Avenue at least an hour. At 9:00 a.m., Major B. B. French, marshal in chief and head of the parade, had taken his place of honor in front of City Hall, where he was joined by his aides and assistants. Each marshal wore white rosettes and different colored scarves—orange for French and his aides; blue for other marshals, and pink for assistant marshals. Forming behind the chief marshal and his aides was a squadron of U.S. dragoons, volunteers of the District, the full Marine Corps Band, and various other light infantry volunteers. "The streets echoed with the inspiring music of the drums and fifes of the companies, marching about to display their new uniforms. Marshals galloped madly about, as Marshals always do, and verdant special policemen, with red badges, seemed very uncertain what their duties were."[27]

At 11:00 a.m., Chief Marshal French ordered "Forward, march!" and the procession moved down Louisiana Avenue to Pennsylvania Avenue to Willard's Hotel, where it took up its position and waited patiently for Lincoln.[28]

Writing in her diary today, Mary Chesnut sneered at Lincoln's perceived cowardice, which she apparently believed had kept him cloistered in his room at Willard's since arriving in Washington: "[The] New York Herald says,

President James Buchanan and Abraham Lincoln riding to Lincoln's first inauguration. The military guard around Lincoln was reportedly so densely packed that a bullet could never have reached him. (*Library of Congress*)

'Lincoln's carriage is not bombproof, so he does not drive out.'"[29] But Lincoln had no choice other than to drive out now. He and Buchanan entered their carriage, and the procession began its mile-long march down Pennsylvania Avenue to the Capitol. The time was around one o'clock.

At the same time Lincoln's carriage and procession were leaving Willard's, Lucius E. Chittenden was also heading for the Capitol. He was en route to a station where arrangements had been made for invited guests to pass through the crowd to their seats on the inaugural platform. "As my carriage drove rapidly down F Street, . . . I heard the volume of cheers roll down the avenue *pari passu* with the procession. I learned afterwards that the tall form of Mr. Lincoln was exposed during the whole distance, so that a shot from a concealed assassin from any one of the thousand windows would have ended his career."[30]

But no shots were fired. No bombs were exploded. No battalions of National Volunteers stormed Lincoln's carriage. No team of would-be assassins, clutching red ballots, charged the carriage, pistol or stiletto or grenade in hand. No plug-uglies hurled so much as an insult, let alone an egg or a brickbat, at Lincoln. Not only was Lincoln a moving target, he was a well guarded one—both he and Washington City were being protected with far greater planning and infinitely more firepower than at any time on his journey from Springfield. Lincoln's carriage was surrounded by an engineer corps of sappers and miners from the regular army, who had formed a hollow square, with Lincoln's carriage at its center. The carriage was followed by several companies of uniformed volunteers. In all, Lincoln's procession reportedly comprised nearly twenty well-drilled, uniformed military companies and two thousand men, many on horseback.[31] A gang of twenty hand-picked assassins would have had no chance of breaking through, even if the sights of a formidable, uniformed, well-drilled military procession and the sounds of drums, fifes, marching feet, and clopping horses did not dishearten and dissuade them.

One observer noted that "owing to the denseness of the military enclosure" a shot could never have hit Lincoln, while the *Philadelphia Inquirer* reported:

> On Fifteenth street Companies F and H of the Flying Artillery, under Col. Brooks, were drawn up, the cannon covering the Treasury. The 4th Artillery Company had their arms stacked upon the sidewalk at the corner of G and Fifteenth streets. From the windows of the Treasury building the bright epaulettes of United States troops were gleaming. At the Market House a company of Artillery were stationed, with arms stacked, and cannon ready for service. At the City Hall, Patent Office, Post Office and all public buildings, the Artillery had unlimbered their cannon, and at every turn bayonets were bristling. From the house tops at the corners, squads of riflemen were stationed, thus the whole city was under command of the military. Scouts rode around the city continually, and the city presented every appearance of martial law, as if an enemy were looked for every minute from some unknown quarter. Preparations to receive them could not be better made.[32]

The man in charge of these preparations, "Old Fuss and Feathers" Winfield Scott, had arranged to receive reports every fifteen minutes from various points throughout the city and planned to use his dispersed military to quell any uprising from any quarter.[33] "Generals Scott and Wool stood at their respective batteries, which were unlimbered, matches lighted, cartridges prepared."[34] But the most striking indication that General Scott anticipated trouble today was neither reported in the press, nor would have been readily apparent to the crowd or any Baltimore plotters embedded within it. Colonel Stone had hidden squads of snipers on the rooftops of houses offering the best view of Pennsylvania Avenue. Their orders were clear: "to watch the windows on the opposite side, and to fire upon them in case any attempt should be made to fire from those windows on the Presidential carriage." More snipers squatted behind windows on the wings the Capitol itself, their keen eyes trained on the inauguration platform.[35]

That Abraham Lincoln could traverse
Pennsylvania Avenue unmolested says less,
therefore, about the absence of a plot to
assassinate him in Washington than about
the absence of the sort of golden opportunity that Baltimore had afforded the suspected plotters nine days before. At around
1:15 p.m., the military procession entered
the Capitol grounds, "marching by the
flank, in double ranks, and forming a line
clear across the space, about one hundred
feet in front of the Capitol, and as long as
that immense pile. They thus formed a
hedge, and between them and the Capitol
was a dense mass of humanity, the somber
hats of the men relieved by the gay bon-
nets and parasols of the ladies."36

General Winfield Scott at the time of
Lincoln's inauguration. (*Library of
Congress*)

Meanwhile, the procession's marshal in
chief, Major B. B. French, had entered the
Senate Chamber through a private
entrance, ushering in the outgoing and the
incoming presidents of the United States.
They had entered the Capitol through a
secure, covered passageway on the north side of the building. A company of
United States Cavalry, Lincoln's mounted guard, and police officers took up
positions on either side of the carriageway, guarding the enclosed passageway
through which Lincoln and his party entered the north wing of the Capitol,
passing over a temporary planked walkway. "Mr. Buchanan and Mr. Lincoln
entered, arm in arm, the former pale, sad, nervous; the latter's face slightly
flushed, with compressed lips."37

Led by the marshal of the District of Columbia and the justices of the
Supreme Court in their robes, Lincoln and Buchanan left the Capitol for the
podium, erected on the east steps. The Marine band struck up "Hail
Columbia." At around 1:30 p.m., Lincoln's longtime Springfield friend
Edward D. Baker, recently elected Republican senator of Oregon, introduced
the president-elect. Lincoln walked "deliberately and composedly" across the
podium to a small table beneath a wooden canopy. He bowed deeply. Now
wearing his reading glasses, he placed the inaugural address on the small table,
keeping the papers from being lost to the dust-filled winds by laying his cane
atop them.38 "On Mr. Lincoln advancing to the stand, he was cheered, but not
very loudly," some newspapers reported. "Unfolding his manuscript, in a loud,
clear voice, he read his address."39

"Mr. Lincoln's voice was remarkably clear and penetrating, his manner deliberate and impressive, so that I think fully 30,000 persons heard him throughout," noted a reporter for the *New York Tribune*. "The ten thousand threats that he should be assassinated before he should take the oath did not impel him to make a gesture implying fear or haste, and he stood forth a conspicuous mark for the villains who had threatened to shoot him as he read."[40]

Might Senator Louis T. Wigfall, the fire-eater with a tendency to shoot people who disagreed with him, have been one such villain? Might he, even now, have felt the cool handle of a revolver tucked inside his waistcoat as he stood apart, "perched up on one side, hanging on by the railing, surrounding the statue of Columbus and an Indian girl . . . witnessing the pageant"?[41] Four years later, on March 4, 1865, an embittered young man, John Wilkes Booth, would be here, at Lincoln's second inaugural, also standing by a railing overlooking the president while he delivered his second inaugural address. "What an excellent chance I had to kill the President, if I had wished, on inauguration day!" Booth later lamented to fellow Baltimore actor Samuel Knapp Chester, striking the table at a tavern in New York City where the two men sat. Booth claimed he had been as near Lincoln as he was to Chester.[42] But today, March 4, 1861, Booth was nowhere near Lincoln. Indeed, he was not even in Washington. Whether Booth had ever left Albany the previous week is not known, although he clearly had the opportunity to do so. On this day, he was most certainly in Albany, preparing to again take the stage tonight. John Wilkes Booth's most famous theatrical performance was yet four years away.

In the end, Lincoln's first inaugural address was about damage control. The nation was already fractured, wounded, and anxious, in need of mending, healing, and a reassuring balm. His message would attempt to address these needs by expanding on themes he had hinted at during the long, winding route from Springfield: that the Constitution was supreme; that secession was wrongheaded and unnecessary; that he was beholden to the American people, "my rightful masters."[43] He urged all who would listen to give the Constitution, to give the Union, and ultimately to give peace, a chance.

Lincoln's ordinary voice, as Chittenden recalled, "was pitched in a high and not unmusical key. Without effort it was heard at an unusual distance. Persons at the most distant margins of the audience said that every word he spoke was distinctly audible to them."[44] But in the end, those listening to Lincoln today would hear only the words they wished to hear and be deaf to those they did not.

Indeed, if the *Atlanta Southern Confederacy* was to be believed, Lincoln's inaugural address had cleverly concealed his true thoughts, and had essentially declared war on the South: "A very few words will do for this document. It is a medley of ignorance, sanctimonious cant and tender footed bullyism. . . . It is all out now—the late Union was intended to be, by the majority which has clutched its powers, a consolidated majority despotism. . . . If secession stood in need of an apology, if a revolution carrying us through fire and blood was to be justified, here we have the apology and the unanswerable defense . . . there is absolutely nothing in this school boy production except the threat of coercion. There will, then, as they must have it, be war."[45]

But where the *Southern Confederacy* saw threats of coercion, Northern Democrat Stephen Douglas saw none. In fact, Lincoln's longtime rival seemed much in agreement as he listened to the speech. "Mr. Douglas, who stood by the right of the railing, was apparently satisfied, as he exclaimed, *sotto voce,* 'Good,' 'That's so,' 'No coercion,' and 'Good again.'" Douglas remained complimentary soon afterward. "He does not mean coercion; he says nothing about retaking the forts, or Federal property—he's all right." And yet, upon further reflection, the Illinois Democrat became less sanguine. "Well, I hardly know what he means. Every point in the address is susceptible of a double construction; but I think he does not mean coercion."[46]

As Lincoln delivered his address, ex-president James Buchanan, who "was probably sleepy and tired," had spent the entire time "looking as straight as he could at the toe of his right boot." When questioned afterward about Lincoln's speech, Buchanan abdicated giving a clear answer, but "with a wretched and suspicious leer" also hinted that it held double meanings: "I cannot say what he means until I read his Inaugural; I cannot understand the secret meaning of the document, which has been simply read in my hearing."[47]

In the end, Lincoln's address stood on solid, unassailable logic as a basis for urging reconciliation—the Constitution, both those portions that people liked and those they disliked, had to be enforced. To the extent that some felt his message conveyed a double meaning and did so with sleight of hand, it was because he was attempting to quench a smoldering fire with both subtle compromise and subtle warning, not fan the flames of extremists at either end of the political spectrum with harsh rhetoric. That meant delicately giving a constitutional right with one hand, while firmly grasping a constitutional requirement with the other.

In the delicate giving category, Lincoln sought to allay Southerner's fears that he would interfere with their "property, . . . their peace, and personal security."[48] He sought to assure them that all laws, including the repugnant fugitive slave laws, would be enforced—until repealed by Congress or held unconstitutional. "The clause I now read," Lincoln said, "is as plainly written in the Constitution as any other of its provisions: 'No person held to service or labor in one State, under the laws thereof, escaping into another, shall, in consequence of any law or regulation therein, be discharged from such service or labor, but shall be delivered up on claim of the party to whom such service or labor may be due.'"

"It is scarcely questioned," Lincoln continued, "that this provision was intended by those who made it, for the reclaiming of what we call fugitive slaves; and the intention of the law-giver is the law. All members of Congress swear their support to the whole Constitution—to this provision as much as any other."[49]

Southerners and Northern Democrats who sympathized with them, such as Douglas, almost certainly were nodding their heads in agreement. So far so good. But now that he had conceded an express constitutional right, it was time for Lincoln to assert an implied constitutional requirement—that the Union was perpetual and secession was illegal. It wasn't exactly a quid pro quo in a legal sense, but more of a sauce for the goose, sauce for the gander, in a logical sense.

"I hold, that in contemplation of universal law, and of the Constitution, the Union of these States is perpetual. Perpetuity is implied, if not expressed, in the fundamental law of all national governments. It is safe to assert that no government proper, ever had a provision in its organic law for its own termination. Continue to execute all the express provisions of our national Constitution, and the Union will endure forever—it being impossible to destroy it, except by some action not provided for in the instrument itself."[50]

As if advocating a case in court, Lincoln flawlessly presented the legal arguments that supported his views. If the Union was a mere contract, could it be rescinded by less than all the parties that had made it? Was there not precedent for the notion that the Union was perpetual? Lincoln pointed out that the Union was in fact older than the Constitution, formed by the Articles of Association in 1774, continued by the Declaration of Independence in 1776, and expressly made perpetual by the original thirteen states through the Articles of Confederation in 1778. One of the declared objects of establishing the Constitution, he argued, "was '*to form a more perfect union.*'" If that same Constitution could serve as a basis for tearing the Union apart, Lincoln reasoned, then "the Union is *less* perfect than before the Constitution, having lost the vital element of perpetuity."[51]

Having established the facts, Lincoln presented his legal case:

> It follows from these views that no State, upon its own mere motion, can lawfully get out of the Union, —that resolves and ordinances to that effect are legally void; and that acts of violence, within any State or States, against the authority of the United States, are insurrectionary or revolutionary, according to circumstances.
>
> I therefore consider that, in view of the Constitution and the laws, the Union is unbroken; and, to the extent of my ability, I

Abraham Lincoln delivering his first inaugural address on a wooden platform erected on the steps of the partially completed Capitol building, March 4, 1861. Reportedly, after General Scott learned of threats to blow up the platform, Colonel Stone stationed guards beneath it, preventing access. (*Library of Congress*)

shall take care, as the Constitution itself expressly enjoins upon me, that the laws of the Union be faithfully executed in all the States. . . . I trust this will not be regarded as a menace, but only as the declared purpose of the Union that it will constitutionally defend, and maintain itself.[52]

Expressions like these were more than Senator Wigfall could bear. Later that day, Wigfall would send an urgent dispatch to Governor Pickens of South Carolina: "Do not permit any attack on Sumter without authority of Government of Confederate States. This is all important. Inaugural means war. There is strong ground for belief that re-enforcements will be speedily sent. Be vigilant."[53]

But had Wigfall and others listened to Lincoln's inaugural more carefully, they would have heard him say that he did not want war and in fact was looking for a solution to avoid it: "In doing this [enforcing the laws] there needs to be no bloodshed or violence; and there shall be none, unless it be forced upon the national authority. The power confided to me, will be used to hold, occupy, and possess the property, and places belonging to the government, and to collect the duties and imposts; but beyond what may be necessary for these objects, there will be no invasion—no using of force against, or among the people anywhere."[54]

In declaring "inaugural means war," Senator Wigfall was interpreting Lincoln as saying he would use his power to reinforce Fort Sumter and retake other government property in the seceded states. This Wigfall and other Confederate leaders could not abide. Although Fort Sumter was built with Union funds, on a man-made island of granite imported from New England, it now "belonged" to the seceded state of South Carolina. Wigfall's Confederacy would not permit Lincoln to reinforce or retake that fort or any other. The fuse of war had been lit.

It was, perhaps, extremists like Wigfall about whom Lincoln next spoke. "That there are persons in one section, or another who seek to destroy the Union at all events, and are glad for any pretext to do it, I will neither affirm or deny; but if here be such, I need address no word to them. To those, however, who really love the Union, may I not speak?"[55]

At this point, Lincoln moved from presenting legal arguments to making an impassioned plea to independent-thinking Americans. He appealed to reason—why should the Union be broken up when no constitutional rights had been denied anyone? Why should the "desperate step" of secession be employed, replacing what he perceived as a minor, even illusory problem with a far greater problem all too real?

The issue of secession had defined Lincoln's presidency even before he had taken the oath of office, and the theme of secession naturally dominated his inaugural address as he prepared to take that oath. He reminded America that on any issue not expressly delineated by the Constitution, there will always be majority and minority views tending to divide the nation. But the answer to resolving such divisiveness is not secession. If it were, then those holding the minority view could break away ad infinitum, ultimately leading to anarchy and despotism. "If a minority, in such case, will secede rather than acquiesce, they make a precedent which, in turn, will divide and ruin them; for a minority of their own will secede from them, whenever a majority refuses to be controlled by such minority."[56]

Every person, no matter his or her race, sex, age, religion, or other classification, will, throughout his or her life, adhere, at least occasionally, to a minority view on important constitutional issues of the day. These issues, like the times and the people that live through them, are in constant flux. Of necessity, for a government to endure despite the ebb and flow of popular opinion, the majority of the moment must rule, but be held in check by an unswerving Constitution, designed to protect the rights of minority and majority alike. "Plainly, the central idea of secession," as Lincoln saw it, "is the essence of anarchy. A majority, held in restraint by constitutional checks, and limitations, and always changing easily, with deliberate changes of popular opinions and sentiments, is the only true sovereign of a free people."[57]

Lincoln knew such reasoning was preaching to the choir for his Northern audience; he had no need to convince them. He also knew such reasoning would not pull the fire-eaters, men like Wigfall, James Seddon, and Jefferson Davis, from the furnace of secession. In all likelihood, Lincoln was appealing to the non-slaveholders of the seceded South—a majority of the minority. This hit the Southern leadership where it was most vulnerable. The South, ruled by a relatively small slaveholding class, was in essence a minority of states governed by a super minority of aristocratic slaveholding elite; less than one sixth of Southerners actually owned slaves.[58] Perhaps Lincoln was subtly urging the Southern majority to overthrow the antebellum elites, rather than join those elites in their self-aggrandizing effort to break from the Union. Regardless, Lincoln was telling the world that he would not permit the Union, designed for the benefit of all, to be broken for the benefit of a tiny class of the privileged few.

Having declared the act of secession unlawful, in fact void and therefore a meaningless act, Lincoln next turned his sights on the Supreme Court, including the Marylander, Chief Justice Taney. The trembling, ashen relic would administer the oath to Lincoln as he had to a six of his predecessors dating back to Martin van Buren in 1837.[59] Justice Taney had also penned the wildly unpopular and racist *Dred Scott* decision. A critic of that opinion, Lincoln conceded that the Supreme Court's decisions remained binding on the parties to the particular case, and that such decisions are entitled to "very high respect and consideration" by all other departments of the government in parallel cases. But he also reminded the all-Democratic, pro-slavery Court that its role was not judicial activism, usurping its power, limited to deciding a particular case between litigants involved in a particular controversy, for broader, political purposes. In words that ring as clear and true today as they did then, Lincoln declared that "the candid citizen must confess that if the policy of the government, upon vital questions, affecting the whole people, is to be irrevocably fixed by decisions of the Supreme Court, the instant they are made, in ordinary litigation between parties, in personal actions, the people will have ceased, to be their own rulers, having, to that extent, practically resigned their government, into the hands of that eminent tribunal."[60]

Lincoln now began his closing arguments. Deriving all of his authority from the people who had elected him, Lincoln had no power to dictate terms for separation of the states under current law or the Constitution. He alluded to the possibility of constitutional amendments as a means of allaying the present troubles, and of putting faith and reliance in the American people and the Almighty. Both would take time and require patience—the antidote to those who had hurried and would hurry in "hot haste" to hustle their states out of the Union to the brink of war. And it was to them, the disaffected, that Lincoln now addressed his most stirring, and ultimately his most damning, closing argument:

> In your hands, my dissatisfied fellow countrymen, and not in mine, is the momentous issue of civil war. The government will not assail you. You can have no conflict, without being yourselves the aggressors. You have no oath registered in Heaven to destroy the government, while I shall have the most solemn one to "preserve, protect and defend" it.
>
> I am loath to close. We are not enemies, but friends. We must not be enemies. Though passion may have strained, it must not break our bonds of affection. The mystic chords of memory, stretching from every battle-field, and patriot grave, to every living heart and hearthstone, all over this broad land, will yet swell the chorus of the Union, when again touched, as surely they will be, by the better angels of our nature.[61]

LINCOLN had made it through Baltimore. He had survived the trip, survived the inaugural, and would survive to take the oath of office. But his wish that the Union would survive unmolested and be peaceably restored was only a dream, soon to be broken. Within a few weeks, the war would begin with the bombardment of Fort Sumter; Senator Louis T. Wigfall would be there to accept the surrender. Also within a few weeks, Lincoln would attempt to bring Union troops through Baltimore to Washington's defense; an angry, violent, and murderous Baltimore mob would be there to prevent it.

But today, at least, Lincoln could dream of reconciliation, of fraternity, of binding old wounds and of quenching newly fired hearts. And yet, even as Lincoln spoke, even as he dreamed of peace, Senator Wigfall, according to one witness, stood listening to the inaugural address in utter defiance: "I must not forget to mention the presence of a Mephistopheles in the person of Senator Wigfall, of Texas, who stood with folded arms leaning against the doorway of the Capitol, looking down upon the crowd and the ceremony with a contemptuous air, which sufficiently indicated his opinion of the whole performance. To him the Southern Confederacy was already an accomplished fact. He lived to see it the saddest of fictions."[62]

CHAPTER TWENTY-ONE

DEFENSE AND PROSECUTION

THERE ARE, OF COURSE, NO LIVING WITNESSES to the events that together tell the tale of the Baltimore Plot. With the exception of Pinkerton's reports, there are no recorded confessions. And yet, nearly 150 years later, disproving the plot's existence is no easier than proving it. There remain tantalizing clues that cut both ways. These clues include exculpatory evidence, that tending to cast reasonable doubt; evidence of document forgery, of admissions that the plot was a fabrication, of pro-Union conduct by those who stand accused, of bias on the part of the accusers. And there is likewise evidence a prosecutor would seize upon, of similar crimes committed by the accused, of inconsistent statements, of cognizance of guilt, of flight from possible prosecution, for example.

The most compelling evidence against the existence of the Baltimore Plot, and that most often cited by those arguing against it, is that Baltimore plotters were never put on trial for conspiring to assassinate Lincoln. No criminal charges were ever filed against any of them for the crime. They were never arrested. Indeed, no effort to round them up was ever made. The question is, why not?

The Lincoln administration would, in the months following Lincoln's escape through Baltimore, suspend the writ of habeas corpus, place Baltimore under martial law, arrest members of the Maryland legislature on suspicion of conspiring to pass an act of secession, and fill the nation's military prisons with hundreds of suspected disloyal citizens, often without charges.[1] Yet the administration did not round up, try, and convict all of those suspected of complicity in the Baltimore Plot.

It wasn't as if the suspected conspirators were hard to find. Many of their names and addresses, thanks to Pinkerton's work, were known.[2]

A case in point is Cypriano Ferrandini. How difficult would it have been to dispatch a detail of soldiers from Washington or even from Fort McHenry to arrest the barber while he stropped razors in the basement of Barnum's City Hotel?[3]

And what of Richmond native Otis K. Hillard? He had, like Ferrandini, also been summoned to appear before the Select Committee of Five, and so his Baltimore address was known. Indeed, Pinkerton operative Harry W. Davies had essentially become the suspected conspirator's roommate.

One of the most obvious suspected conspirators to arrest, and perhaps the easiest to locate and identify, would have been James H. Luckett. The stock-broker had shared office space with Pinkerton at 44 South Street in Baltimore. Yet Luckett too was never arrested for his role in the alleged conspiracy.

Pinkerton, in fact, took pains to insure that Luckett's name should be kept confidential in later years. On August 5, 1866, Pinkerton wrote William Herndon, who had requested access to Pinkerton's records relating to the Baltimore Plot while gathering research for his works on Lincoln. Pinkerton acquiesced, but on condition that certain pieces of information contained in the records be kept "strictly confidential." Luckett's name was one such piece of confidential information. Pinkerton reminded Herndon of his pledge "that the name of the Broker who occupied rooms adjoining mine in Baltimore should be omitted, as although he was undoubtedly a rebel at heart, yet he is a man of not much means; he has lost considerable during the war, and the publication of his name might tend to his serious injury in business. I depre-cate this in any publications coming from my records."[4]

Was Pinkerton really that concerned about Luckett's finances or was his real fear that once exposed, Luckett might be given a reason and an opportu-nity to rebut Pinkerton's allegations?

The government also failed to follow up on a lead from Major William E. Doster, Provost Marshal of the military district of Washington City from March 1862 to March 1863, whose duties included "guarding the person of the President."[5] Doster once received a letter claiming that an unidentified man who was to have assassinated Lincoln on his way through Baltimore was then living in Ohio. The informant, also in Ohio, offered to reveal the man's identity on certain conditions. After consulting with a "Major Allen," Doster returned the letter and the matter ended there. "Major Allen, head of my detective bureau, then told me that Pinkerton had discovered the plot at Baltimore and had warned the President of it, at the Continental Hotel, Philadelphia. I returned the letter and heard no more of it."[6]

"Major E. J. Allen" was the alias Allan Pinkerton used while gathering intelligence for General George B. McClellan in the field from July 1861 to March 1862.[7] Was the "Major Allen" that Doster was referring to Allan Pinkerton, as one historian suggests?[8] If so, the burning question becomes: why would Pinkerton, the man who knew more about the Baltimore Plot sus-pects than anyone alive, and the man then having at his disposal a network of spies, including several who had worked with him in uncovering the Baltimore Plot, not have followed up on Doster's lead?

Only two reasons seem logical. First, perhaps the tip was regarded as an obvious hoax, the informant seeking some reward for hollow intelligence. As established by the testimony before the Select Committee of Five, Washington in 1861 was a constant swirl of rumors and sensational stories of intrigue and treachery, some credible, others not.[9] Perhaps Doster's letter was regarded as just one more vaporous rumor. In any event, with a war going on and vital current military intelligence to gather, Pinkerton had no time to track down stale leads in Ohio. He had more pressing work elsewhere, and spent some of his early intelligence-gathering efforts for McClellan in Kentucky, Tennessee, and Mississippi.[10]

But if Doster's "Major Allen" and Pinkerton were one and the same man, then there is a second possible reason for the lack of follow-up, far more troubling than the first.

Perhaps the "Baltimore Plot" was itself a hoax. If so, Pinkerton would have known that following up on any letter that claimed to have intelligence relating to the plot would merely layer one vacuous and pointless effort on top of another. It would be the equivalent of the boy who had cried wolf happening upon a stranger claiming to have seen his "wolf," and urging the boy to capture it.

As to any excuse that Pinkerton and his operatives could not take the time to track down leads in Ohio, consider this: Pinkerton's first wartime secret service office, set up to assist George McClellan, was headquartered in downtown Cincinnati.[11]

THE government's failure to put the Baltimore plotters on trial could be argued to cast reasonable doubt that the crime of conspiracy was committed. However, one of the most likely reasons that the Baltimore plotters were never put on trial is that the Sixth Amendment would have required them to be tried in Baltimore. That amendment reads: "In all criminal prosecutions, the accused shall enjoy the right to a speedy and public trial, by an impartial jury of the State and district wherein the crime shall have been committed, which district shall have been previously ascertained by law, and to be informed of the nature and cause of the accusation."[12]

Putting the plotters on trial in Baltimore in 1861, however, would have inflamed an already smoldering local populace at the worst possible time—when keeping Maryland in the Union was critical to maintaining Washington as the seat of government. So important was the border state to Lincoln that he gave Marylander Montgomery Blair a coveted cabinet position, as postmaster general. For a time, this gesture seemed to quiet Maryland.[13] Pursuing the

Baltimore plotters would likely have undone whatever goodwill Lincoln had earned in Maryland from the Blair appointment.

Besides, in view of the public sentiment in Baltimore in 1861, any effort to convict Baltimoreans of a conspiracy to assassinate Lincoln would likely have been futile. The administration recognized this futility even two years later, when the issue of putting Marshal Kane on trial for a different crime of treason reached Attorney General Edward Bates's office. In writing to William Price, U.S. district attorney for Baltimore about Marshal Kane, Bates noted, "I am not prepared for an exact answer to your letter of the 5th about the case of George P. Kane. Serious doubts are entertained here whether you could at this time safely go to trial in any treason case in Baltimore by reason of the supposed popular feeling and judicial bias."[14] If the Lincoln administration could not safely go to trial in Baltimore in early 1863, it most certainly could not have done so in early 1861.

But perhaps the primary reason the Baltimore plotters were never put on trial, and as a practical matter could not have been put on trial, is that the Sixth Amendment also requires that the accused "shall enjoy the right . . . to be confronted with the witnesses against him."[15]

The primary witnesses against the Baltimore plotters were Pinkerton and his operatives, including Timothy Webster, Kate Warne, and all the rest. But Pinkerton would never have sacrificed the identities, and possibly even the lives, of his agents by exposing them to a public trial.[16] Indeed, soon after the Baltimore Plot investigation concluded, Pinkerton had his agents performing clandestine operations on behalf of the Lincoln administration in Baltimore and Richmond; within weeks of Lincoln's inauguration, Sumter fell and the War of the Rebellion had begun. Allegedly, many of the Baltimore conspirators fled from Baltimore to the warm embrace of the Confederacy. Webster, to maintain his cover, fled with them to Richmond, where influential persons vouched for his loyalty to the rebel cause. Reportedly, Webster's connection with the Baltimore Plot conspirators "was the chief, almost the sole, means of accomplishing this result," and Webster became a trusted emissary of the Confederate War Department in Richmond.[17] By October 1861, Webster was operating undercover as a courier between Baltimore and Richmond.[18] Putting the suspected Baltimore plotters on trial, assuming they could have been captured, might well have caused an important source of Pinkerton's military intelligence to dry up and may even have sacrificed Webster as a vital Union agent.[19]

But there were also sound, practical reasons for not pursuing the suspects criminally that have nothing to do with the alleged plotters' innocence, the futility of putting Baltimoreans on trial for treason in Baltimore, or protecting government spies and sources of information. For starters, many, indeed most, of the Baltimore plotters would not have been known. When testifying before the Select Committee of Five, Hillard claimed Baltimore was home to six thousand National Volunteers. When he spotted two thousand or more of the National Volunteers on the morning of February 23, Hillard admitted to Pinkerton operative Harry W. Davies that they were in on the plot.[20] It would have been impossible to identify all, or even most of them, and even if the National Volunteers could have all been identified, it would be impossible to put a gang of several thousand thugs on trial.[21]

Of the handful of suspected conspirators that might have been identified, some, as a practical matter, could not have been put on trial for the simple reason that they could not be found—many likely had fled to join the Confederacy in the weeks and months following Lincoln's passage through Baltimore. On February 28, 1861, New York Police Superintendent John A. Kennedy advised Marshal Kane that large numbers of Southern Volunteers—the group his detectives had been shadowing—had left Baltimore for points South. "Since Wednesday of last week, up to Tuesday of this week, three hundred and twenty-seven of these men have left your city, in squads, for service at the South, and I am advised that about two hundred more will leave during the present week. It has not appeared to me necessary to stop this movement, else I should have notified you of it before. The parties are represented to me as being desperadoes of the worst kind, and whose departure from any community is the only good act they can perform."[22]

Chief among the suspected plotters identified by Pinkerton's agents that fled Baltimore in the spring of 1861 was William Byrne. Byrne, it will be recalled, was President of the Baltimore National Volunteers. In November 1860, he was appointed to carry the state of Maryland's electoral votes—for John C. Breckinridge—from Annapolis to Washington.[23] Byrne had organized the National Volunteers in the fall of 1860, ostensibly as a Democratic political organization to aid pro-slavery presidential candidate Breckinridge. After Lincoln's election, the group's objectives allegedly shifted from securing Breckinridge's inauguration to preventing Lincoln's.[24]

On February 20, 1861, Pinkerton agent Charles D. C. Williams received a certificate of membership in Company A of the National Volunteers under signature of Robert E. Hasletz and William Byrne, its president.[25] Eleven days earlier, Baltimorean Joseph H. Boyd had testified to the Select Committee of Five that the National Volunteers had been formed the previous summer as a Democratic political organization to support the candidacy of John C. Breckinridge.[26] It seems curious that the group, under Byrne's leadership, should continue meeting and begin drilling—reportedly in secret—three months after that candidacy was lost.

Early in 1862, William Byrne was put on trial for operating a gambling house in Richmond. Such crime bears little resemblance to the Baltimore Plot.

But Byrne's chief witness for the defense was none other than former Texas senator Louis T. Wigfall.

Wigfall, the "champion of the South," was expelled from the U.S. Senate on March 23, 1861.[27] He promptly left Washington, and one week later was in Charleston, South Carolina, another place from which he had been exiled years before. On April 10, Wigfall sent Jefferson Davis the following telegram at Montgomery:

> Charleston, 10 April, 1861.
>
> No one doubts that Lincoln intends War. The delay on his part is only to complete his preparations. All here is ready on our side. Our delay therefore is to his advantage, and our disadvantage. Let us take Fort Sumter, before we have to fight the fleet and the Fort. General Beauregard will not act without your order. Let me suggest to you to send the order to him to begin the attack as soon as he is ready. Virginia is excited by the preparations and a bold stroke on our side will complete her purposes. Policy and Prudence are urgent upon us to begin at once. Let me urge the order to attack most seriously upon you.
>
> L. T. Wigfall.[28]

Three days later Wigfall, the same man who had reportedly been appealing to Northern senators for a "peaceful solution" was warring on Fort Sumter as a Confederate colonel, ordering a vanquished Major Anderson to surrender unconditionally after alighting from a rowboat with a white cambric handkerchief dangling from his sword.[29]

Later, Wigfall briefly served as an aide to Jefferson Davis before serving as a brigadier general in command of the Texas Brigade of the Army of Northern Virginia, later John Bell Hood's Texas Brigade. But by February 1862, Wigfall had resigned his commission to take a seat in the Confederate Congress. It was likely in this capacity that he testified at the trial of William Byrne.

As a witness at Byrne's trial, Wigfall swore under oath that Byrne was the ringleader of the plot to assassinate Lincoln in Baltimore in February 1861. His testimony served, in essence, as character evidence that Byrne was "all right," that "he is one of us." A contemporaneous newspaper gives the following account of Wigfall's involvement in William Byrne's trial.

> The Plot at Baltimore Against President Lincoln's Life. A correspondent of the *New York Evening Post*, who dates from Baltimore, March 27 [1862], tells the following story:
>
> For a long time it was believed that an Italian barber of this city was the Orsini who undertook to slay President Lincoln on his

journey to the capital in February, 1861, and it is possible he was one of the plotters; but it has come out on a recent trial of a man named Byrne, in Richmond, that he was the captain of the band that was to take the life of Mr. Lincoln. This Byrne used to be a notorious gambler of Baltimore, and emigrated to Richmond shortly after the 19th of April, of bloody memory. He was recently arrested in Jeff. Davis's capital on a charge of keeping a gambling house and of disloyalty to the chief traitor's pretended government. Wigfall testified to Byrne's loyalty to the rebel cause, and gave in evidence that Byrne was the captain of the gang who were to kill Mr. Lincoln, and upon this evidence, it appears, he was let go. Of course, to be guilty of such an intended crime is a mantle large enough to cover up all other sins against society and the divine law.[30]

Such evidence not only implicates Byrne, it of course implicates Wigfall. In order to have any credibility, Wigfall's testimony about Byrne's role in the Baltimore Plot almost certainly would have been based on firsthand knowledge. This strongly suggests that he and Byrne were acquaintances. Both had been active the previous fall in the Breckinridge campaign. As early as February 16, 1861, Wigfall sought, and later received, authorization from C.S.A. president Jefferson Davis to recruit a Confederate regiment in Baltimore, where Wigfall maintained a recruiting office, which he reportedly frequented.[31] When on March 16, 1861, three officers of the National Volunteers sought induction into the Confederate army, they wrote to Senator Wigfall for assistance.[32]

Wigfall's sworn testimony carries great weight. Such an admission does more to convict Byrne, implicate Wigfall, and verify the existence of the Baltimore Plot than anything Pinkerton might have reported.

THERE is other evidence to consider from some of those closest to the president. In his 1872 Lincoln biography, Lamon wrote that "Mr. Lincoln soon learned to regret the midnight ride. His friends reproached him, his enemies taunted him. He was convinced that he had committed a grave mistake in yielding to the solicitations of a professional spy and of friends too easily alarmed. He saw that he had fled from a danger purely imaginary, and felt the shame and mortification natural to a brave man under such circumstances. But he was not disposed to take all the responsibility to himself, and frequently upbraided the writer for having aided and assisted him to demean himself at the very moment in all his life when his behavior should have exhibited the utmost dignity and composure."[33]

In the same work, without referring to him by name, Lamon bashed Pinkerton and ultimately concluded that there was no Baltimore Plot. "Being intensely ambitious to shine in the professional way, and something of a politician besides, it struck him [Pinkerton] that it would be a particularly fine thing to discover a dreadful plot to assassinate the President elect; and he discovered it accordingly."[34]

But Lamon felt that getting "conspirators" to talk and brag under the influence of alcohol about supposed plans to kill Lincoln was, given the situation in Baltimore at the time, like leading lambs to slaughter—you get them unwittingly to go where you want, but their participation can hardly be considered acquiescence in the conclusion:

> Baltimore was seething with political excitement; numerous strangers from the far South crowded its hotels and boarding houses; great numbers of mechanics and laborers out of employment encumbered the streets; and everywhere politicians, merchants, mechanics, laborers, and loafers were engaged in heated discussions about the anticipated war, and the probability of Northern troops being marched through Maryland to slaughter and pillage beyond the Potomac. It would seem like an easy thing to beguile a few individuals of this angry and excited multitude into the expression of some criminal desire.[35]

Lamon berated not only Pinkerton's methods, but also the reports written by his agents: "These documents are neither edifying nor useful: they prove nothing but the baseness of the vocation which gave them their existence."

Most damaging, Lamon, a man arguably in one of the best positions to know, concluded that no Baltimore Plot conspiracy ever existed:

> For ten years the author implicitly believed in the reality of the atrocious plot which these spies were supposed to have detected and thwarted; and for ten years he had pleased himself with the reflection that he also had done something to defeat the bloody purpose of the assassins. It was a conviction which could scarcely have been overthrown by evidence less powerful than the detective's weak and contradictory account of his own case. In that account there is literally nothing to sustain the accusation, and much to rebut it. It is perfectly manifest that there was no conspiracy, —no conspiracy of a hundred, of fifty, of twenty; no definite purpose in the heart of even one man to murder Mr. Lincoln at Baltimore.[36]

But all of this evidence must be considered in context. Pinkerton's reprimand of Lamon for leaking his name to the press at Willard's on the morning of February 23, 1861 obviously caused Lamon to hold a grudge; several years later, he refused to answer Pinkerton's repeated requests for a statement verifying his role in thwarting the Baltimore Plot.[37] Later still, Lamon gained access to Pinkerton's February 23, 1861 report, in which the detective recounted the name-leaking episode, referring to Lamon as "a brainless egotistical fool." Lamon became so enraged by the report that he wrote in the margins of the manuscript, *"This is an infamous lie from beginning to end.* This Detective, Allen [*sic*] Pinkerton was angry with me because I would not take sides with him, and make a publication in his favor when he and Kenedy [*sic*], the New York detective had the difficulty as to which of them the credit of saving Lincoln's life was due from the public. Ward H. Lamon."[38]

It thus appears that Lamon's claim in his book *Life of Abraham Lincoln*— ghostwritten by Chauncey F. Black—that there was no Baltimore Plot, that Pinkerton sought only to "shine in the professional way," and that his operative's reports "prove nothing," was motivated more by personal animus toward Pinkerton and a vindictive desire to discredit the detective than by personal knowledge of the true facts. In any event, in Lamon's later book, *Recollections of Abraham Lincoln,* edited by his daughter, the Baltimore Plot is neither expressly credited nor dismissed as a fabrication.[39]

Pinkerton's account of evidence of a Baltimore Plot was corroborated contemporaneously by the independent efforts of the New York City detective David S. Bookstaver. On February 20, 1861, Bookstaver uncovered in Baltimore information of such importance that he hopped on the next train for Washington. Upon arriving there early the next morning, he reported to Colonel Charles P. Stone details of threats to assassinate Lincoln that had been made in secretly held meetings Baltimore.[40]

None of this evidence points to a man intent on making up stories in order to gain the sort of publicity that would permit him to "shine in the professional way;" to the contrary, Pinkerton repeatedly demonstrated an overriding desire to avoid the public eye and keep secret the identities of his agents. Indeed, soon after thwarting the plot an obviously angry Pinkerton wrote to his former employer, Samuel M. Felton, all but accusing the railroad executive of leaking confidential information related to the investigation to the press: "I have the pledge of President Lincoln and all to whom it was entrusted, that it [the Baltimore Plot] should forever be treated as strictly confidential. Whoever furnished this information should be known. . . . If it is at all possible to find out who the writer is, I would very much like to know it."[41]

Pinkerton's fear for the safety of his operatives and his desire that their names should be kept secret would soon prove well founded. One of his best operatives used to uncover evidence of the Baltimore Plot would soon be hanged as a spy in Richmond, one of the first such executions of the Civil War.

IT is true that Lincoln claimed that he did not believe he would have been assassinated in Baltimore. In speaking to his friend Isaac N. Arnold years afterwards, Lincoln at first suggested that he never believed in the viability of the Baltimore Plot: "I did not then, nor do I now believe I should have been assassinated had I gone through Baltimore as first contemplated," Lincoln told Arnold.[42] Lincoln was privy to all of the intelligence Pinkerton and Kennedy had gathered during their clandestine operations in Baltimore. While he may not have read the individual reports, he had spoken directly with Pinkerton, Warne, Judd, Seward, General Scott, and others close to the investigation. He was an accomplished lawyer, skilled in the art of cross-examination and gauging witness credibility. Lincoln's belief that he would not have been assassinated in Baltimore necessarily derives, at least in part, from his "interrogation" of these "witnesses."

Lincoln's subjective beliefs, however, are immaterial to whether the conspiracy existed. A conspiracy arises the moment two or more persons enter into an agreement to commit a crime. That the "target crime," the ultimate objective of the conspiracy, is never carried out, never attempted, or has no real chance of success is irrelevant. Thus, the fact Lincoln did not believe he would be assassinated in Baltimore is also irrelevant. He also did not believe he would be assassinated in Ford's Theatre.

In any event, Lincoln ultimately did come to believe that a plot to assassinate him had been hatched in Baltimore. In his December 1864 interview with Bensen J. Lossing and Isaac N. Arnold, Lincoln professed his conviction that the Baltimore Plot was real. During the interview, Lincoln recalled his meeting with Pinkerton and Judd in Philadelphia the night of February 21, 1861, during which the suspected plot was first revealed to him. Lincoln was not persuaded by this initial report. "I could not believe that there was a plot to murder me. I made arrangements, however, with Mr. Judd for my return to Philadelphia the next night, if I should be convinced that there was danger in going through Baltimore."

Lincoln became convinced once Fred Seward showed up moments later. Lincoln, a lawyer well versed in the probative value of corroborative evidence, found persuasive Seward's independent account of a plot in Baltimore that echoed Pinkerton's report. "When I was making my way back to my room, through crowds of people," Lincoln recalled, "I met Frederick Seward. We went to my room together, when he told me that he had been sent, at the instance of his father and General Scott, to inform me that their detectives in Baltimore had discovered a plot there to assassinate me. They knew nothing of Pinkerton's movements. I now believed such a plot to be in existence."[43]

Lincoln was clearly embarrassed and humiliated by the public outcry over his less than dignified passage through Baltimore and unheralded arrival in Washington. He would have wanted the Baltimore Plot story to die as quickly as possible. Pursuing the plotters and bringing them to trial would only have further battered Lincoln's already bruised image; ironically, perhaps the administration felt best to treat the plot as mere rumors that Lincoln did not fear but rather heeded to allay the alarmist concerns of well-meaning friends.

Whether and to what extent the Baltimore mob intended to act with violence against Lincoln on February 23, 1861, can never be known for certain. The mob was never given the opportunity to show how it would have behaved. The object of the mob's anticipated hatred—Lincoln—had eluded it. According to a Baltimore correspondent for the *New York Tribune*, the crowd that had gathered in Baltimore on the morning of February 23, 1861, was immense, reportedly "one of the largest ever gathered in the Monumental City. Franklin street, Center street, North street, and in the neighborhood of Battle Monument, was one dense mass of human beings."[44] This report supports Pinkerton operative Harry W. Davies' account. While walking on the morning of February 23 from Mann's Hotel, located at the corner of Baltimore and North, to the Calvert Street Station, he and Hillard encountered "large numbers" of National Volunteers, some of whom Hillard stopped and spoke with. "I would here mention," Davies reported, "that along the streets and around the Depot were congregated some ten or fifteen thousand people."[45]

Why, one might ask, would a city that had cast but 1,083 votes for Lincoln, only 4.5 percent of the total Baltimore vote,[46] turn out in such large numbers to see him? Certainly not to cheer him on to Washington. Almost certainly not to hear him speak—there had been no indication he would make a speech;[47] to the contrary, the *Baltimore Exchange* that morning declared that it hoped Lincoln would be given no opportunity to speak.[48]

A chilling indication of how the Baltimore mob might have acted had Lincoln tried to run its gauntlet can be drawn from how the mob actually did act just a few weeks later, when President Lincoln called for Union volunteers to defend Washington. Despite Marshal Kane's earlier remarks that "the day for mobs and riots. . . has passed, never to return," the mob would rise again and disprove his assurances.

On April 15, 1861, three days after a solitary boom rang out across Charleston Harbor as a Confederate shell exploded over Fort Sumter to signal the start of Civil War, President Lincoln called for 75,000 Union volunteers to defend Washington. To get there, they would need to take the same route he had taken—through Baltimore.

On the evening of April 18, a "States Rights Convention," was held in Baltimore's Taylor Building. A billiard and drinking saloon, the Taylor was a three-story brown freestone, located at 66 Fayette Street near Calvert Street and Barnum's Hotel.[49] This was likely the same building that suspected plotter Otis K. Hillard had pointed out to Pinkerton operative Harry W. Davies on the evening of February 23, 1861, as the secret meeting place of the National Volunteers. Reported Davies, "The National Volunteers, so Hillard said, have a meeting this evening, and showed me the place where the secret Committee met—which is on Fayette Street near Barnum's Hotel, Democratic Headquarters."[50] One of the witnesses before the Select Committee of Five, Joseph H. Boyd, testified that the National Volunteers held their meetings "on Fayette street, in the neighborhood of Battle Monument, just a few doors from Calvert street."[51]

The effect of the "States Rights Convention" held in the Taylor Building that evening was the unanimous adoption of resolutions made on the motion of Ross Winans, a wealthy and influential Baltimore businessman, philanthropist, inventor, locomotive manufacturer—and secessionist member of the Maryland legislature. Others in attendance at the convention were A. C. Robinson, its chairman, and G. Harlan Williams and Albert Ritchie, its secretaries. The names of the others in attendance are not known and were apparently kept secret.[52] The adopted resolutions stated that Lincoln's call for troops meant civil war and that the convention protested in the name of the people of Maryland against garrisoning Southern forts with militia drawn from free states or quartering free state militias anywhere in the slave states. The resolutions decried massing large bodies of militia from the free states in Washington as "a standing menace to the state of Maryland, and an insult to her loyalty and good faith." The resolutions closed with ominous-sounding propaganda, vowing "to repel, if need be, any invader who may come to establish a military despotism over us."[53] Winans would, on Marshal Kane's orders a few weeks later, fabricate 2,000 pikes with which to arm Baltimore against the North.[54]

Such pronouncements, cast in the form of official-sounding resolutions unanimously adopted by Baltimore's leading citizens at a patriotically-titled "States Rights Convention" would be more than enough authorization to incite a Baltimore mob to violence, even treason.

The next day, on the morning of April 19, 1861, the National Volunteers Association organized a rally at Monument Square, led by T. Parkin Scott, a prominent Baltimore attorney and Maryland state delegate,[55] Fiery speeches ridiculed Lincoln and urged Baltimoreans to follow Virginia's lead, by pushing for Maryland's secession.[56] The National Volunteers didn't know it yet, but even as they were massing at Monument Square and ginning up secessionist bravado, federal troops were on their way to Baltimore.

At around 10:30 on the morning of April 19, 1861, a train of thirty-five cars on Samuel M. Felton's Philadelphia, Wilmington, and Baltimore Railroad arrived at the President Street Station without warning. The cars carried the Sixth Massachusetts Regiment, seven hundred fully armed, smartly uniformed, and well-organized troops. At the other extreme, the train also carried a ragtag group of unarmed Pennsylvanians in civilian dress, ten companies of the Twenty-sixth and Twenty-seventh Infantry known as the "Washington Brigade."[57] These troops, among the first to respond to Lincoln's call for 75,000, expected trouble in Baltimore. After leaving Philadelphia, the troops had received the following order: "The regiment will march through Baltimore in columns of sections, arms at will. You will undoubtedly be insulted, abused, and perhaps assaulted, to which you must pay no attention whatever, but march with your faces square to the front, and pay no attention to the mob, even if they throw stones, bricks, or other missiles; but if you are fired upon, and any of you are hit, your officers will order you to fire. Do not fire into any promiscuous crowds, but select any man whom you may see aiming at you, and be sure you drop him."[58]

But instead of marching through Baltimore, the cars carrying the troops were uncoupled from the engine and, according to custom, drawn by a team of four horses through the streets—just as Lincoln's night coach had been in the early morning hours of February 23, 1861. A few cars, carrying the first seven companies of the Massachusetts Sixth Regiment, got through to the Camden Street Station in this fashion before the Baltimore mob began to notice—and then began to act. The angry crowd pelted the cars with stones and bricks. Soon, the mob gathered more rioters, who swarmed Camden Street Station, Pratt Street, and President Street Station. Obstructions were quickly thrown on the tracks—loads of sand, paving stones, anchors, anything the enraged citizens of Baltimore could lay hands on to stop the flow of troops. Barricades were placed on Pratt Street, at the bridge crossing at Jones Falls, and the intersection of Gay Street. Marshal Kane, meanwhile, was able to muster out only about fifty policemen at the Camden Street Station.[59]

Thanks to the mob and the obstructions on the tracks, it was now impossible to move the remaining troops still at the President Street Station by horse-drawn railcar to the Camden Street Station. (The question must be asked—if the Baltimore mob could so quickly assemble and so readily prevent hundreds of young, armed soldiers—whose arrival had not been anticipated—from passing through its streets in massive, horse-drawn railcars, how much easier would it have been for the mob to assemble and halt the anticipated progression of Abraham Lincoln, sitting unarmed and unguarded in an open, two-seat barouche?)

The remaining Union troops still at President Street Station had three alternatives. They could board a northbound train and retreat to Philadelphia. They could stay where they were and hope the raging Baltimore mob would suddenly turn peaceful. Or they could proceed on foot to the Camden Street

Station, roughly a mile and a quarter away. For volunteer soldiers answering their president's call to defend Washington and their country, there could be but one option. For despised Union troops running the gauntlet of an inflamed Baltimore mob, there could be but one result.

The Union troops began to march. They braved taunts, a continual hail of rocks and bricks and bottles, and the sounds of gunshots being fired into the air. The Sixth Massachusetts Regiment, ordered to the "double quick," picked up their pace in a desperate attempt to get through more quickly. This action enraged the mob. Wrote one eyewitness, "the mob became so frenzied that they bared their bosoms daring the troops to shoot. Some cried out . . . don't be afraid, down with Yankee hirelings."[60]

Who fired the first shot is not known. What is known is that the Baltimore mob began shooting at the troops, in some cases from sniper's positions, including from the upper veranda of the Maltby Hotel. Upon seeing one of their comrades fall dead in the street, the Massachusetts volunteers, following their orders, returned fire into the crowd. So dense was the mob that the soldiers could barely raise their muskets.

Eventually, the troops reached the Camden Street Station, where they boarded a train and left Baltimore around 12:30 p.m. Even then, the mob was unrelenting and moved out ahead of the train, attempting to prevent it from leaving by throwing obstacles across the tracks. "A dense crowd ran down the platform and out the rail road track toward the Spring Gardens, until the track for a mile was black with an excited rushing mass."[61]

Baltimore had not won the distinction some of its residents likely had hoped for, of being the first battleground of the civil war.[62] But its mob had won the distinction of claiming the first battle casualties of the war. By the time the dust had cleared, four volunteers of the Massachusetts Sixth and six from the unarmed Pennsylvania brigade lay dead in the street, along with eleven Baltimoreans.[63]

GEORGE P. KANE'S defenders against his involvement in any antigovernment plots point to his gallant conduct in protecting Union troops as they marched through the Baltimore mob's hailstorm of rocks and lead on April 19, 1861. Indeed, Marshal Kane acted bravely, along with Mayor Brown and a small contingent of Kane's police force in an apparent attempt to restrain the mob. Kane and his men placed themselves with drawn revolvers in a line at the rear of the troops and in front of the mob between Light and Charles Street, and threatened to shoot anyone who attempted to pass through.[64] But the small number of police reinforce the supposition that a similar lack of sufficient police protection would have awaited Lincoln back in February.

"The Lexington of 1861," a lithograph of the Baltimore riot of April 19, 1861. (*Library of Congress*)

But as if to confirm the suspicions of Pinkerton and others about Baltimore's disloyal police force, within hours of his gallant conduct, Marshal Kane would participate in outright treason, plotting to burn railroad bridges to prevent further passage of troops, sending telegrams calling for military reinforcements from western Maryland and Virginia to repel Union troops intent on passing through the state, and collecting arms and ammunition with which to equip a small army of Baltimore volunteers he planned to lead. Marshal Kane intended to do far more than defend Baltimore from the potentially violent consequences of Union troops passing through the city. He intended to take the fight to the Union troops with an all-out offensive.

On the evening of April 19, Marshal Kane dispatched a telegram to Colonel Bradley T. Johnson of the Frederick Mounted Dragoons of the Maryland Militia urgently asking him to send troops to Baltimore. The telegram and Johnson's call to arms appeared in the following handbill published the next morning:

LATEST NEWS.

MARYLANDERS AROUSE!

Frederick, Saturday, 7 a.m.

At 12 o'clock last night I received the following dispatch from Marshal Kane, of Baltimore, by telegraph, to the Junction, and expressed to Frederick:

"Thank you for your offer. Bring your men by the first train, and we will arrange with the railroad afterward. Streets red with Maryland blood!

"Send expresses over the mountains and valleys of Maryland and Virginia for the riflemen to come without delay. Fresh hordes will be down upon us to-morrow (the 20th.) We will fight them, and whip them or die."

Geo. P. Kane

All men who will go with me will report themselves as soon as possible, providing themselves with such arms and accoutrements as they can. Double barreled shot guns and buck shot are efficient. They will assemble after reporting themselves at 10 1/2 o'clock, so as to go down in the 11 1/2 o'clock train.

Bradley T. Johnson[65]

As a result of the violence of April 19, and possibly at Marshal Kane's urging, Baltimore Mayor George Brown also issued a public call to arms, in which he said: "All citizens having arms suitable for the defense of the city, and which they are willing to contribute for the purpose, are requested to deposit them at the office of the marshal of police."[66]

By Saturday, April 20, 1861, the city of Baltimore had raised an army of more than 15,000 men, with about three-fourths of them armed with muskets, shotguns, and pistols, many by Marshal Kane's ad hoc armory. They were placed under the command of Colonel Isaac R. Trimble. Mayor Brown claimed that Trimble's small army was "enrolled temporarily" and not for war, but for the defense of the city, presumably from a fresh onslaught of Union soldiers intending to pass through Baltimore on the way to Washington.[67] But the Union soldiers who had previously passed through Baltimore had been ordered not to fire their weapons unless fired upon. Indeed, many were unarmed. They were not intending to war upon Baltimore, but to defend Washington. Under such circumstances, how does arming 15,000 men for the "defense of the city" from federal troops heading to Washington not amount to an act of war, treason, or both?

If the number of men in Kane's and Trimble's army—15,000—sounds familiar, it is precisely the same number that William Seward and General Scott's intelligence had gathered as the size of the force suspected of massing in Baltimore just two months before to prevent Lincoln's passage through the city.[68] Did Baltimore, as Seward suspected, have an army of 15,000 men organized and ready to strike at Lincoln on his way to Washington, or is the number a mere coincidence? We may never know. But we do know that

Marshal Kane was actively preparing *for* war, as opposed to preparing for the *prevention* of war, by April 21, 1861.

Baltimore's Marshal of Police, George Proctor Kane. His conduct on April 19, 1861 would land him in prison. Once released he would conduct special operations for the Confederacy.

Wrote Helen M. Linscott to Lincoln in 1864: "I arrived in Baltimore on the 14th of March 1861, and remained there several weeks I was there at the time of the *riot*, and was personally acquainted with Marshall Kane. It was on Sunday April 21st that Kane was making preparations to march out and attack the Federal troops that were encamped in a wheat-field a few miles from the city— that I entered the room where his ammunition was stored, and wet as many procussion caps, rifles powder &c. as I could conveniently reach."[69]

On April 24, 1861, Frank A. Bond, Captain of the United Rifles, a secessionist outfit stationed at Annapolis Junction, sent the following telegram to Marshal Kane: "I have acted on your advice but am disappointed about the troops from Balto., who were to come here. The Northern troops are still in Annapolis and those from Washington have left here. I am informed by a messenger from Prince Georges that five thousand (5000) Virginians are near Bradensburg but don't believe it possible. Send me some word or advice."[70]

From this, we can surmise that Marshal Kane had been advising Captain Bond on military matters, including that troops from Baltimore could be expected in Annapolis Junction, presumably to engage federal troops. Perhaps thanks to Helen Linscott's efforts in spoiling their powder and cartridges, Marshal Kane's troops from Baltimore never arrived at Annapolis Junction.

Against the backdrop of Marshal Kane's actions taken immediately following the Baltimore riots, it might be argued that his efforts to quell the mob violence on April 19 were the equivalent of a military order to cease fire, withdraw, and await reinforcements. It might also be argued that while Kane's actions to halt the mob on April 19 undoubtedly saved many Union lives, those actions also saved the lives of many Baltimore insurgents and potentially averted an all-out Union offensive against Baltimore.

On June 27, 1861, Marshal Kane was arrested at his home by Union troops and removed to Fort McHenry. Worthington G. Snethen, despite any hard feelings, continued to provide intelligence to the government. Writing two days later, on June 29, to Winfield Scott, he provided a report on the cache of weapons seized from Marshal Kane's police headquarters and further evidence against Kane and others, including Mayor Brown:

> I sent you a list, yesterday, of the arms and munitions found in the office of the late Marshal of Police, Geo. P. Kane. Last night, a further depot of 800 stand of arms was discovered at Jackson Hall in the 8th Ward. In reference to the arms found in the Marshal's office, it is obvious, that the Commissioners Howard, Getchell, Davis and Hincks and Mayor Brown, must have been cognizant of their secret deposit there. Kane actually informed Cadwallader, that he had surrendered *all* the arms in possession of the city! More than half of them are stolen property, stolen from the 6th Mass. Regiment. So that the late Police Board and its Marshal, and the Mayor too, have demonstrated that they are traitors, rebels, conspirators, murderers and liars, by their acts and deeds. I repeat, that justice and the future peace of the city demand the arrest of the four Police Commissioners.[71]

Possibly on the strength of Snethen's testimony, the Baltimore police commissioners were arrested on July 1, 1861.[72] Mayor Brown too would be arrested, confined to Fort Lafayette on September 26, 1861.[73]

In June 1868, an article appeared in *Harper's New Monthly Magazine* entitled "The Baltimore Plot to Assassinate Abraham Lincoln." According to a Maryland historian, in this article "unwarrantable liberties were taken with Colonel Kane's name and character."[74] That the article should have outraged Marshal Kane is not surprising. The article quotes an unnamed conspirator "Captain T——" (likely Turner)[75] as telling Pinkerton that "I have seen Colonel Kane, Chief of Police, and he is all right, and in one week from to-day the North shall want a new President, for Lincoln will be dead."[76] While the article bears the sheen of sensationalism, it is in many respects a remarkably accurate reflection of the Pinkerton reports, to which the *Harper's* author had access for writing the story. For example, the article accurately quotes Kane's statement, overhead by Pinkerton, that Lincoln would receive "no police escort."

But what likely most stirred Kane's ire was the article's statement that Kane was to have been an active participant in the assassination: "It was known among the leaders [of the conspiracy] that George P. Kane, the Marshal of Police . . . would detail but a small police force to attend the arrival and nominally clear and protect a passage for Mr. Lincoln and his suite, and that that small force would be sympathizers with the secessionists. When the train should enter the depot, and Mr. Lincoln should attempt to pass through the narrow passage leading to the street, some roughs were to raise a row on the outside, and all the police were to rush away to quell the disturbance. At this moment, the police being withdrawn, Mr. Lincoln would find himself in a dense, excited, and hostile crowd, hustled and jammed, and then the fatal blow was to be struck."[77]

In rebutting the *Harper's* accusations, Marshal Kane's letter of June 21, 1868, to the *Baltimore Sunday Telegram* indeed sheds some interesting light on at least a revisionist history of how he—and Baltimore—planned to receive Lincoln on February 23, 1861. First, Kane's letter blames Lincoln's people for failing to provide "definitive" notice of his arrival time in Baltimore until "a few days in advance of his coming." But Lincoln's itinerary, complete with his plans to arrive in Baltimore at 12:30 on February 23 and leave at 3:00 p.m. that same day, had been published at least as early as February 13, 1861, ten days before.[78] How can Lincoln be fairly criticized for failing to provide any more "definitive" notice of his arrival in a city that had utterly failed to provide any "definitive" invitation to receive him?

Second, Kane blames the Baltimore Republicans, "the very scum of the city," for not doing the honor of receiving Lincoln. And yet, it was George P. Kane who had gone to Washington to urge Lincoln's friends *not* to allow the Baltimore Republicans to march with Lincoln, for fear that it would create a disturbance by inflaming the Baltimore crowd. A few days later, Kane argued that Snethen's Baltimore Republicans would have been the cause of any problems Lincoln might experience in Baltimore. Then seven years later, Kane blamed the same group for having failed to make adequate plans to greet Lincoln in Baltimore. Kane's later argument is not only inaccurate; it is inconsistent and therefore lacks credibility.

Kane wrote in his June 1868 letter that he could not accept an invitation from Mrs. Lincoln to call on her after arriving in Baltimore because a "sudden and severe indisposition prevented me from doing so." Kane failed to mention that the "sudden and severe indisposition" likely involved several fights that had broken out at the Calvert Street depot. This corroborates Pinkerton's suspicions that a diversionary row had been planned to distract the police. A gang of roughs also gathered at the Camden Street Station and began threatening Lincoln's party as they prepared to leave Baltimore. Given that the Baltimore police cleared these roughs out "in mighty short order"[79] meant their attention from Mary Lincoln's suite had been distracted, even if momentarily; it seems the diversionary row Pinkerton had anticipated at the Calvert Street Station to distract Marshal Kane and his police had been staged at the Camden Street Station instead by roughs that were unaware Lincoln was not with the party.

Apparently it was Marshal Kane's plan to have Lincoln and his family disembark from the train at Charles Street before reaching the Calvert Street Station.[80] While Kane's purpose might well have been to free Abraham

Lincoln from annoyance and offer him a pleasing view of the city while en route to Mount Vernon Square, the move would also have tended to isolate Lincoln. And Marshal Kane makes no mention of how many policemen, if any, were with him to guard Mr. Lincoln during the roughly half-mile carriage ride from the Charles Street crossing to Mount Vernon Square prior to dining at the Gittings mansion, or what security arrangements had been made to convey him from the Gittings home to the Camden Street Station after dinner.

If Marshal Kane had planned to greet Lincoln in carriages at the Charles Street crossing, why then was Baltimore's mayor waiting for Lincoln at the same time in a two-seat carriage at the Calvert Street Station?

Mayor Brown admits that he was ready and waiting to receive Lincoln at the Calvert Street Station on February 23, 1861. As Brown stated twenty-six years later, "I, as Mayor of the city, accompanied by the Police Commissioners and supported by a strong force of police, was at the Calvert-street station on Saturday morning, February 23d, at half-past eleven o'clock, the appointed time of arrival, ready to receive with due respect the incoming President. An open carriage was in waiting, in which I was to have the honor of escorting Mr. Lincoln through the city to the Washington station, and of sharing in any danger which he might encounter. It is hardly necessary to say that I apprehended none."[81]

It is true that no direct evidence ties Mayor Brown to any of the Baltimore plotters' suspected plans. Why, however, would Mayor Brown be waiting for Lincoln in an open two-seat barouche at the Calvert Street Station when Marshal Kane had planned to meet him nearly a mile north, at the Charles Street crossing? Perhaps Mayor Brown was unaware of Marshal Kane's plan or vice versa. This seems unlikely, given that Brown was the mayor and was accompanied by a "strong force" of Marshal Kane's police and the police commissioners. What seems more likely is that both Kane and Brown knew of the other's plans to meet Lincoln. Marshal Kane might have informed the president-elect upon his arrival at the Charles Street crossing that he had two options: he could hop off the train early for a leisurely private carriage ride to dine in relative solitude at the Gittings mansion—with the old men, women, and children. Or, he could continue on the train, as would other members of the suite, to the Calvert Street Station, where Baltimore's mayor was waiting to officially receive him. Since leaving Springfield, Lincoln had never missed an opportunity to "see and be seen" by vast crowds, often while separated from his family. Might Marshal Kane's true objective—and possibly Mayor Brown's—have been to beguile Lincoln into separating from his family, thereby exposing him to assassination, while sparing his wife and children both from danger and from witnessing the horrific event?[82]

It is true that Mayor George Brown acted with valor in attempting to protect the Massachusetts troops from the seething Baltimore mob during the riot of April 19, 1861.[83] It is also true, however, that later the same day, a large secessionist crowd enthusiastically cheered Mayor Brown's fire-eating rhetoric that, "The civic authorities would take full measure for the protection of the city against the recurrence of today's occurence. . . . The people of the North will soon . . . know that it is the height of folly for one portion of the country to attempt to subjugate the other. The South can never be coerced, never, never, never!"[84]

Later that same day, Mayor Brown would make good on his promise to prevent additional Northern troops from passing through Baltimore.

LATE on April 19, Marshal Kane received a communication from William Prescott Smith, of the B&O Railroad, passing on a dispatch Smith had received from the Pennsylvania Railroad warning of more troops heading south, and "that it was impossible to prevent these troops from going through Baltimore." Fearful that additional Union troops would be sent to Washington through Maryland, at around midnight, Mayor Brown, Marshal Kane, Brown's brother J. Cumming Brown, and Maryland's former Governor Enoch Lewis Lowe met with Governor Hicks in Mayor Brown's home, where Hicks was then a guest, having retreated from the Baltimore hotel at which he was then staying, apparently out of fear for his life. Hicks was apparently feeling so unnerved that the conference had to be held in his bedroom.[85] Brown and Kane sought Hicks's authorization to set fire to a half-dozen railroad bridges north of Baltimore, in order to prevent additional Union troops from passing over the Northern Central and the Philadelphia, Wilmington, and Baltimore lines to Washington. The bloody riots of Baltimore's mob earlier that day were fresh in their minds. Brown and Kane, as well as other city leaders, anticipated that a continuous influx of Union troops to Baltimore, overrun by an angry mob that its police force could not or would not control, would lead inexorably to more violence.

Brown and Kane's rationale for appealing to the governor was, in effect, that they did not have authority beyond Baltimore's city limits.[86] The bridges that had been targeted for destruction were 15 or 20 miles north of Baltimore, and hence beyond Brown's and Kane's jurisdiction. Only Maryland's governor could sanction the Baltimorean's proposed action.

Hicks seemed, to those making the request, to be persuaded by the arguments in favor of bridge burning. Most telling, Hicks abdicated his authority, stating that Mayor Brown "could do as he pleased."[87] But Brown was not seeking tacit permission in the form of Hicks's offer to look the other way, to wash his hands of the responsibility like some Pontius Pilate. Mayor Brown was seeking an order to act or, at the very least, the governor's express consent—his agreement to engage in the plan. Mayor Brown was a lawyer who well knew the elements of conspiracy. If he and others were ultimately to be charged with conspiring to torch bridges, Brown wanted Governor Hicks in on it. The Union government might not think twice about arresting a pro-secession Baltimore mayor and police chief, but the apparently pro-Union governor of a state as vital as Maryland? Surely, Brown must have figured, the governor's sanction would demonstrate to Washington the legitimacy of the act and save them all. This midnight meeting is the most damning piece of evidence against Governor Thomas Hicks suggesting a common anti-Union scheme consistent with the Baltimore Plot.

Mayor Brown later swore that Hicks authorized the destruction of the railroad bridges. Several eyewitnesses back this up, including fellow alleged Baltimore conspirator Marshal Kane, as well as Brown's brother and former Governor Lowe.[88] Stated Mayor Brown: "Governor Hicks was first consulted and urged to give his consent, for we desired that he should share with us the responsibility of taking this grave step. This consent he distinctly gave in my presence and in the presence of several others, and although there was an attempt afterward to deny the fact that he so consented, there can be no doubt whatever about the matter. He was in my house at the time, where, on my invitation, he had taken refuge, thinking that he was in some personal danger at the hotel where he was staying."[89]

Brown and Kane clearly believed, Hicks's later denials notwithstanding, that the governor had given his affirmative authorization to act. Within an hour or so of the meeting with Hicks, under command of future Confederate general Isaac R. Trimble, two parties left Baltimore, one comprising a squad of police accompanied by one company of the Baltimore City Guard under the command of Captain J. G. Johannes, on the Northern Central line, and the other a posse of police officers with one company of the Baltimore City Guard under the command of Marshal Kane, on the Philadelphia, Baltimore, and Wilmington Railroad. "Each squad was equipped with picks, axes, crowbars and a good supply of turpentine."[90] Soon, telegraph lines were cut and the bridges north of Baltimore on the Philadelphia, Wilmington, and Baltimore and on the Northern Central Railroad lines were ablaze. Like Nero who fiddled while Rome burned, Hicks did nothing, while railroad bridges so vital to his state and to his nation—the Union he had so ardently claimed to love—literally went up in smoke.

Governor Hicks weakly denied that he had consented to the destruction of the railroad bridges. Hicks put the following spin on his role in the bridge-burning conspiracy, admitting that he had said, "that the Mayor could act as he pleased—and that I had no power to interfere with his designs. If this be consent to the destruction of the bridges, then I consented. If this be complicity in an unlawful act, then I was accessory."[91]

This admission by Hicks is an astounding one for a governor to make. At best, it demonstrates a total abdication of responsibility. At worst, no matter whether his role in the conspiracy is termed inaction, tacit consent, or active participation, Hicks conferred state authority where previously there was none. How is it that Maryland's governor was powerless to interfere with the designs of Baltimore's mayor and Baltimore's police marshal to burn bridges in the Maryland countryside many miles north of Baltimore, particularly when Hicks's authority extended statewide and Brown's and Kane's ended at the Baltimore city limits?

Hicks's admission also demonstrates that he had prior knowledge of Mayor Brown and Marshal Kane's plans to commit treason, and yet he did nothing to stop them. Hicks thereby became a co-conspirator in a plot to burn no less than six commercially and militarily vital railroad bridges and thereby interfere with the efforts of the United States government to

Baltimore Mayor George William Brown denied any plot to murder Lincoln. Yet he never sent an invitation to visit the city, and waited for Lincoln in an open, two-seat barouche that would have exposed the president-elect during a long, slow carriage ride through a city clogged with National Volunteers.

defend Washington at a most critical time. Such actions would also isolate both Baltimore and Washington from being provided with food, mail, and other essentials from points north. The bridge burners even cut the telegraph lines, rendering Baltimore totally isolated. And what of the reckless nature of the act? What precautions would be taken to ensure that night trains, whether military or civilian, unable to see the twisted tracks and gaping abysses left by the bridge burners, would be warned in time to prevent loss of life? We are not told of what, if any, precautions were taken in this regard.

It is true that Baltimore was in a highly excited state the evening of April 19, 1861, and that the passage of additional Northern troops through Baltimore would likely have led to more bloodshed. But Governor Hicks's authorization to burn bridges heaps one wrong atop another. A governor in control of his state, a governor who was truly pro-Union, a governor of courage, would at least have tried to quell a riotous populous and prevent the destruction of such vital communication, commercial, and military links as telegraph lines and railroad bridges.

It might be asked, how does this alleged crime of Governor Hicks, of conspiracy to burn railroad bridges in April, have any relevance to the allegation that he conspired with those plotting Lincoln's murder in February? The answer lies in the nature of commonality of scheme and of using the pattern of behavior embedded in one crime to show motive and intent to commit another. Indeed, Pinkerton recounted the Baltimore plotter's nearly identical plan following Lincoln's assassination: "as soon as the deed had been accomplished in Baltimore, the news was to be telegraphed along the line of the road, and immediately upon the reception of this intelligence the telegraph wires were to be cut, the railroad bridges destroyed and the tracks torn up, in order to prevent for some time any information being conveyed to the cities of the North, or the passage of any Northern men towards the capital."[92] The April 19 deed was not the killing of Lincoln but the murder of government troops, some unarmed. Otherwise, the plan actually implemented is identical to what Pinkerton apparently anticipated following Lincoln's assassination in Baltimore.[93]

Those empowered with great responsibility are expected in time of urgency to take great responsibility. But if Hicks was the kind of man who could timidly look the other way in April when it came time to save vital railroad bridges, was he not also the kind of man who would have looked the other way while conspirators prepared to assassinate Abraham Lincoln as he passed through Maryland in February? If he was the kind of man who would lift not a finger to ensure order in the face of clear threats of disorder in April, was he not also the kind of man who would lift not a finger to ensure Lincoln's safety in February despite clear threats—*known by Hicks to exist*—that had been made against Lincoln's life? There is further evidence of Hicks's duplicity and lack of credibility: On February 26, 1861, in response to reports that he had warned Lincoln to change his travel plans through Baltimore, Governor Hicks denied ever giving such warnings. Instead, Hicks declared that no danger threatened the president-elect in Baltimore.[94] At best, this was spin, tending to support the popular notion that Lincoln's movement was an act of cowardice. At worst, the statement that no dangers threatened Lincoln was an outright lie, and Hicks knew it. Nearly three weeks earlier, on February 7, 1861, George Stearns had sent a warning letter to Hicks that provided credible intelligence of a plot to assassinate Lincoln in or around Baltimore while passing over Felton's railroad.

Hicks's defenders would cite his early refusal to call a special section of the state legislature for a secession vote as evidence of his loyalty to the Union and therefore to Lincoln. But this is nothing more than additional evidence of an impotent leader's tendency to inaction, to let matters work themselves out by default, to claim lack of power to do anything while events gather and swirl to the point of becoming irresistible forces, at which point it becomes plausible to claim "there was nothing I could do." And, as has been previously discussed, Hicks had in fact considered the possibility of Maryland seceding and had attempted to draw strength and courage from the governors of other border slave states toward this end.

To Hicks's claim that he was a firmly pro-Union man, consider this: On April 22, 1861, after Sumter had fallen, after Virginia had seceded, after Washington had been cut off militarily by the Baltimore bridge burners and waited in anxious isolation for Union troops to come to its defense, what was Governor Hicks's solution? He not only urged Lincoln and his men against sending Union troops through Baltimore; he asked that they not even be permitted to pass through all of Maryland according to the proposed plan of bypassing Baltimore by landing a steamer in Annapolis and proceeding overland from there to Washington. Moreover, Hicks urged Lincoln to take a course of appeasement with the secessionists. Hicks felt it his duty in April 1861 to do so.

On August 23, 1866, in a letter to Lincoln's law partner William Herndon, Allan Pinkerton recalled additional evidence tending to prove Hicks's motives to side secretly with secessionist elements. Pinkerton recalled reports of Timothy Webster detailing Hicks's secessionist proclivities. "You will find much of interest in Webster's Reports," wrote Pinkerton, "showing the manner in which the first Military organization of Maryland Secessionists was formed, and the promises repeatedly made by Governor Hicks of arms being furnished to them; and, if my recollection serves me aright, of arms finally being furnished to that Company; their drilling at Belle Air, etc."[95] Unfortunately, the Webster reports Pinkerton refers to in this letter are lost to history. And by the time he wrote his August 1866 letter to Herndon, Pinkerton could no longer check his facts with either Timothy Webster or Thomas H. Hicks. Both men were already dead.

Of evidence of Hicks's true intentions, much has been made of the November 9, 1860, letter to Maryland representative Edwin H. Webster, in which Hicks writes, "Will they [the pro-slavery Maryland militia to whom arms were to be supplied] be good men to send out to kill Lincoln and his men? If not, I suppose the arms would be better sent South. How does the late election sit with you? 'Tis too bad."[96] At least one historian has derided the letter as being "of more than doubtful authenticity."[97] A close inspection of at least one version of the Hicks letter and the circumstances surrounding its publication could establish it as a forgery. Neither the letter—nor any copies of it—are to be found among the voluminous Hicks papers preserved at the Maryland Historical Society in Baltimore, despite the fact Hicks tended to maintain copies of letters he sent out on state letterhead.[98] By the time the letter was published in 1872 in Ward Hill Lamon's *Life of Abraham Lincoln*, Hicks was unable to defend himself. He had died seven years before.[99]

One version of the letter that does exist resides in the Ward Hill Lamon collection at the Henry E. Huntington Library. It is not an original document, rather, an old copy. As such, the handwriting takes on a blurred, washed-out appearance that makes comparisons with the more pristine handwriting of original Hicks letters from the same time period difficult. The signature appears similar enough to other Hicks signatures from around the same time to suggest it is a genuine copy of an original document. The handwriting also bears strong similarities to original Hicks writings, further suggesting the document's authenticity.[100]

The script in the "State of Maryland" heading is a close approximation to authentic communications from the governor, yet different enough on close inspection to suggest forgery. Moreover, the words "Executive Chamber" and "Annapolis" appear skewed to the left relative to those of original, authentic Hicks documents. Most telling, the Maryland state seal in the Hicks-to-Webster letter appears, under close scrutiny, to be a crude, hand-drawn imitation of the actual seal that appears on other official Hicks communications from the same era.[101] But as to these differences, it appears that Hicks had at least two distinct forms of letterhead, one of which was printed with the "E" in "Executive Chamber" directly under the "M" in "Maryland," and with the year printed as "186_" to permit only the last numeral to be filled in. The other version centers the "E" in "Executive Chamber" under the state seal, and has only the first two numerals for the year printed, "18_ _." This appears to be the version used in the November 9, 1860, letter.[102]

Whether the Hicks letter to E. H. Webster is authentic or a forgery may never be conclusively determined. But there are other clues that the November 9, 1860 letter, though perhaps written or copied onto nonofficial stationery, was authored by Hicks. First, the context of the letter is plausible. Written just days after the election of Lincoln, whom Hicks admittedly did not support, the letter expresses his unhappiness temporally with the event. It goes on to refer to "Harford" having "nothing to reproach herself for." This is an obvious reference, in the context of the unfortunate "late election," to Harford County, Maryland, which had cast but 81 votes for Lincoln out of a total of 3,552, or 2.3 percent.[103] The letter discusses arms shipments in the context of a prior letter from Edwin H. Webster requesting them, explaining that there were then no arms on hand to distribute in view of prior contracts for shipments to Alabama and Georgia that would need to be filled first. A forged document would not be expected to develop such a relevant, detailed, and plausible backstory.

Moreover, while some historians discredit the letter's legitimacy, others seem to accept it as authentic.[104] Hicks's biographer dismisses the letter not as a forgery, but as "an imprudent attempt at humor" that Hicks's detractors trotted out after the war began to show his duplicity, noting that "the letter was published during the year after it was written."[105] No evidence has been found that Hicks denied writing the letter in the face of such publication.

If the document, or at least the message it contains is legitimate, then in the end it is indeed Hicks's own words that convict him. But even if the Hicks letter is a forgery or had been intended as a joke, the remaining evidence against Hicks points a steady finger of accusation at him.

WITH the possible exception of Louis T. Wigfall, whose direct link to William Byrne has already been discussed, connections of the Southern leadership to the suspected Baltimore plotters are admittedly tenuous, their possible roles shadowy. Yet plausible connections do exist. It is true that no direct evidence links Vice President Breckinridge to the Baltimore Plot. But it is also true that Breckinridge was pro-secessionist, had ties to Louis T. Wigfall and William Byrne, both of whom campaigned for him, and was the reason the National Volunteers of Baltimore sprang into existence. After the election, once the National Volunteers' role allegedly changed from supporting Breckinridge's candidacy to preventing Lincoln's inauguration, it seems probable that Breckinridge would have been informed.

In February 1861, John C. Breckenridge sat a heartbeat away from the presidency. The Constitution seems to make no clear provision for what happens if, following the electoral vote count, a president-elect predeceases his inauguration. If Lincoln had died in Baltimore on February 23, 1861, Breckinridge and his supporters might have argued that Lincoln's electoral votes died with him. Then Breckinridge would have controlled a majority of the remaining electors and would have had an argument that he should have been named president.[106]

By March 1861, Breckinridge stood as an outspoken antiwar U. S. senator from his home state of Kentucky. By September 1861, having been under suspicion of treason for months, his arrest was ordered, and Breckinridge ran. Like other suspects named here, including Louis T. Wigfall and William Byrne, Breckinridge fled into the open arms of the Confederacy. He did so under cover of darkness, leaving behind his wife, children, and a state that had voted to remain loyal to the Union.[107]

Breckinridge and Missourians Waldo P. Johnson and Trusten Polk were unique among other U.S. senators who had abandoned their posts for the Confederacy—they had done so following not the tug of secession, for their home states did not secede, but following their own beliefs.[108] Such behavior is to be contrasted with that of men like Robert E. Lee, who resigned his U.S.

military commission the moment Virginia seceded. Instead, these men, Wigfall, Johnson, and Breckinridge, clung stubbornly to their U.S. Senate seats in Washington, insidiously remaining until the last possible moment, until forced to leave by expulsion, threatened capture, or both. It might be argued that they did so in hope of avoiding or shortening the war. But their subsequent behaviors belie pacifist motives.

Breckinridge entered the Confederacy as a brigadier general, rose to the rank of major general, and by January 1865 sat as the Confederate secretary of war. By April 3, 1865, he was no longer sitting as secretary of war, but running from it, as he and Jefferson Davis fled fallen Richmond for the Deep South. In a daring escape on horseback and boat, Breckinridge succeeded in navigating mosquito-infested backwaters of Florida and the Keys to sanctuary in Cuba. He paid twenty dollars in gold for the boat on which he sailed, but the transaction was hardly voluntary. The boat's owner had been forced to "sell" his craft to Breckinridge at the point of a gun.[109] Breckinridge had fallen from vice president of the United States, to shamed U.S. senator, to rebel war czar, to a fugitive desperado-pirate.

After recuperating for a month in Havana, Breckinridge sailed for England. He lived there in an elitist's exile, rubbing elbows with dignitaries, attending horse races at Ascot, and bumping into other fugitive Confederate leaders. In some ways, Breckinridge's stay was more like an extended vacation—he visited Switzerland, Constantinople, Greece, Alexandria, Jerusalem, Italy, and Cairo. He even saw the Pyramids.[110]

It might be argued that such self-imposed exile is not evidence of guilt, but only an instinctive need for self-preservation. Breckinridge's flight, it could be argued, demonstrates a rational desire to avoid languishing in federal prisons as Jefferson Davis had done, at the hands of a brutal, vengeful U. S. government. In some cases, however, Southern leaders went into exile not to merely go into hiding. Wigfall, for example, lived in exile in London after the war, where he held out hope of rebuilding the demolished Confederacy with England's aid, by provoking war between the United States and Britain.[111]

Such Confederate holdouts also had reason to flee beyond fear of indiscriminate Yankee retribution. In the summer of 1865, several of those put on trial for the Lincoln murder conspiracy would be hanged. If a man like George Atzerodt, who had abandoned his assigned role in the conspiracy—to murder Vice President Andrew Johnson—could swing for it, what about others who actively participated in the 1865 assassination conspiracy or, most relevant to this case, one fomented four years earlier? Perhaps an angry U.S. government would continue to hunt down, try, and execute suspected Lincoln assassination conspirators of whatever stripe, from whatever period of time. This too would have been a powerful motivator to leave the country and to stay away until amnesty was assured.

Breckinridge's amnesty was indeed assured in December 1868 by the general amnesty proclamation. He and his wife were then living, with other Confederate exiles, on the Canadian side of Lake Ontario. By February 1869, after an absence of nearly eight years, Breckinridge returned to Kentucky at last.[112]

It is true that Waldo Johnson's résumé prior to 1861 reveals a respectable career punctuated by military, legal, and government service. It is also true that the primary piece of evidence potentially tying Johnson to the Baltimore plotters was his excited utterance, "how the devil did he get through Baltimore?" made in response to seeing the note passed to him by James Seddon.

But there is additional evidence tending to suggest that Johnson was a duplicitous man, scheming on behalf of the Confederacy while operating as a Peace Conference delegate and then as a United States senator in the early stages of the war in 1861. Indeed, on January 10, 1862, Johnson would be ousted from the United States Senate on suspicion of disloyalty to the Union. Thereafter, he would, like other suspected traitors, fall within the warm embrace of the Confederacy, ultimately serving as a lieutenant colonel in the Fourth Missouri Infantry of the Confederate army. Like others of his stripe, Johnson would, after the war, live in exile in Canada, returning to the United States in April 1866.[113]

If Johnson was the sort of man who could, as a Peace Conference delegate and weeks later as a United States senator, scheme on behalf of the Confederacy, it is plausible that he was also scheming with Seddon and others to have Lincoln murdered in Baltimore.

The most damning testimony against James Seddon tending to show that he knew in advance of the Baltimore Plot comes from the note he passed to Waldo Johnson. As the source of this information is from Lucius Chittenden, it would be only natural that Seddon's defense would attempt to undermine Chittenden's credibility, motives, and memory. But of all the Peace Conference delegates whose speeches and utterances Chittenden recorded, it is fair to say that he was in the best position of all to accurately hear, recall, and therefore record Seddon's—Chittenden sat right beside him.[114]

But the documents that could best be able to shed light on James Seddon's involvement, if any, either in the Baltimore Plot or Lincoln's assassination four years later—Seddon's own papers—do not exist. Indeed, shortly after the end of the war, Seddon destroyed them.[115] In the law, this act is termed "spoliation of evidence." It tends to show awareness of guilt and can, in certain circumstances, result in an "adverse inference" instruction from the judge that the very act of of spoliation may be used by the jury to infer that the evidence contained in the destroyed documents would have been unfavorable to the defendant.

If Seddon were involved in the Baltimore Plot, his most likely role would have been as one of the bankrollers. Seddon was a wealthy man. The census of 1860 listed his estate as valued at nearly $400,000, likely not even including plantations he owned in the Deep South,[116] making him a multimillionaire by today's standards. He owned more than one hundred slaves, quartered in twenty-three slave houses, and lived on a Virginia plantation named "Sabot Hill." Assassins could be bought for a few hundred dollars, a few thousand at most. Seddon had yearned for the South to unite in secession since at least 1850. By 1860 he was clearly growing impatient. As the presidential election neared, Seddon feared that the election of William H. Seward "or any confessed representative of his opinions" meant that the immediate secession of the slave states was necessary. "We would be *fools* . . . if we waited till all the sanctions of legality and all powers and resources of the Government were arrayed against us," he declared.[117] Clearly, once Lincoln (a confessed representative of Seward's opinions) was elected, Seddon had motive for reversing the verdict of the ballot with that of the assassin's bullet. Indeed, there are reports of other plans to neutralize Lincoln being discussed during the height of the war at councils in which Seddon participated, along with Jefferson Davis, Judah Benjamin, and shadowy Confederate secret agents.[118]

Most compelling, there is evidence that in September 1864 Seddon, as Confederate secretary of war, was exploring the possibility of kidnapping Lincoln—at the very same time that John Wilkes Booth was contemplating doing so.[119]

CHAPTER TWENTY-TWO

THE ASSASSIN

N O TREATMENT OF CONSPIRACIES TO ASSASSINATE Abraham Lincoln would be complete without a careful inspection of John Wilkes Booth. The question is not so much if he did it, as when, where, and with whom he might have begun plotting to do it. A central premise of the case presented here is that Booth possibly conspired with those suspected of planning to assassinate Lincoln in Baltimore in February 1861. Booth was a Baltimore native. He was an ardent supporter of slavery and the Southern cause. He likely knew, indeed claimed as a friend, suspected conspirator George Proctor Kane, Baltimore's police marshal. Prior to 1861, Kane had a business interest in a Baltimore theater at which Booth played.[1] Ferrandini's hangout, Barnum's Hotel was, at least in later years, frequented by Booth; he is known to have met there with fellow Baltimoreans Samuel Arnold and Michael O'Laughlen to plot Lincoln's kidnapping in the fall of 1864.[2]

With the exception of the Pinkerton reports, firsthand accounts of the suspected Baltimore plotters, who was involved, and what was their plan, are admittedly sparse. Even the Pinkerton reports, as detailed and informative as they are, fail to mention Booth by name. About the closest they come to implicating the young tragedian is the following passage from Harry W. Davies' report of February 19, 1861, written four days before Lincoln's anticipated arrival in Baltimore: "Hillard said to me 'Give me an article of agreement that you will give my Mother Five Hundred Dollars, and I will kill Lincoln between here and Havre-de-Grace,' and then exclaimed in the language of Brutus 'Not that I love Lincoln less, but my Country more'!"[3]

It is not too difficult to imagine John Wilkes Booth uttering similar statements to incite others to act. But if he had, it would have been weeks before; on February 19, 1861, when Davies heard these words spoken, John Wilkes Booth was in Albany.

Conspiratorial assassins rarely write memoirs admitting their crime, particularly when the object of the conspiracy fails. Once again, with the exception of the Pinkerton reports, there exists precious little in the way of eyewitness testimony identifying the suspected Baltimore plotters and what role they were to play. Wigfall's testimony implicating William Byrne as leader of the assassin gang is unique in this respect.[4]

One of the ways the Baltimore Plot conspiracy and Booth's involvement in it might be established, in the absence of clear admissions of guilt, is by sewing together circumstantial evidence tending to show that the alleged plotters knew one another, held the same beliefs, worked together, lived together, and met with one another. It is no defense to say that such proofs merely establish guilt by association. By its very nature, and by definition, the unlawful act of conspiracy is a crime of association.

And it is the associations of several of the alleged conspirators, as well as their actions, both before and after the events of February 1861, that builds a plausible web of conspiracy for their possible involvement in the Baltimore Plot.

These connections, as represented in the "conspirator's web" chart, are sometimes tenuous, but often verifiable. The time periods of such connections are not in every instance contemporaneous with early 1861, but many are. Even later-developed ties between suspects, however, may point to an earlier conspiracy among them. The reason men go back to the same barber year after year is the bond of trust built up by repeated interactions. Similar bonds of familiarity can cause conspirators to seek out and enlist trusted acquaintances they have known, worked with, or conspired with, even years before.

As a general rule, evidence that a person committed a crime on a specific occasion is not admissible as evidence that the same person committed a different crime on a different occasion. There are, however, as in most rules of law, exceptions. Generally, evidence of other crimes is admissible to prove a specific crime charged when such proof tends to (1) establish motive, (2) intent, (3) the absence of mistake or accident, (4) a common scheme or plan embracing the commission of two or more crimes so related to each other that proof of one tends to establish the others, and (5) the identity of the person charged with the commission of the crime on trial.[5]

Several of those who may have been complicit in the Baltimore Plot conspiracy committed other crimes tending to show motive, intent, or a common scheme or plan. That overarching plan, broadly defined, would have been the treasonous disruption of the United States government, such as by kidnapping or killing President Buchanan or Lincoln, by blocking Lincoln's efforts to reinforce Washington with Union troops, or by conspiring to do these things.

A crime tending to show commonality with such an overarching plan includes the riotous conduct of the Baltimore mob on April 19, 1861. On that date, the mob acted in a way consistent with the suppositions played out by

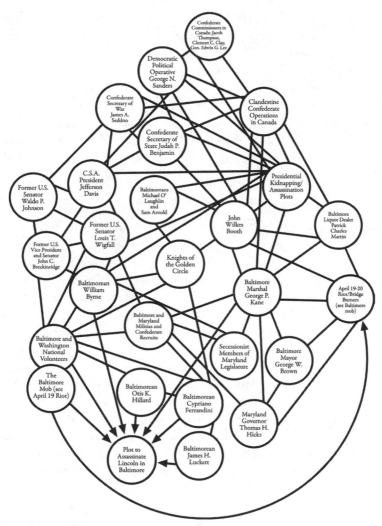

The Conspirator's Web.

Pinkerton while he met with Lincoln in Philadelphia on February 22, 1861. Pinkerton's intelligence at that time foretold that Lincoln would be assassinated in the streets of Baltimore as he traveled in an open carriage from one train depot to the other, where he would be rushed by a dense mass of roughs and shot at close range or stabbed by assassins who would then disappear in the confusion. Some of those in the crowd would stir up a row to create a police diversion. By other accounts, the mob would tear up the track to prevent Lincoln's car from being drawn through the streets and would throw concussion bombs or grenades through the car's windows to create mass confusion, as well as mass murder.[6]

Pinkerton operative Harry W. Davies witnessed such a mob, many of whom were National Volunteers, clogging Baltimore's streets the morning of Lincoln's anticipated arrival. A few weeks later, despite the efforts of Marshal Kane and his police force, the Baltimore mob halted the progress of Union troops by throwing obstacles across their path and tearing up track. They insulted, surrounded, blockaded, stoned, shot, and killed Union troops as they marched from one Baltimore train station to another.[7] The scheme that Pinkerton suspected that the mob would use against Lincoln on February 23, 1861, is virtually identical to that actually used against Union troops on April 19, 1861.

ANOTHER crime tending to show commonality with a plan to disrupt the United States government involves the treason of Mayor Brown and Marshal Kane, both of whom were indicted and imprisoned for their role in burning railroad bridges and cutting telegraph lines north of Baltimore on April 19-20, 1861. Governor Hicks, though given a pass for his involvement, nonetheless also participated in the bridge-burning conspiracy and was later ridiculed as a traitor for demanding that no more Union troops be permitted to pass through Maryland.[8]

But most intriguing is an account alleging that John Wilkes Booth may also have participated in the bridge-burning incident. Worthington G. Snethen, the same Baltimore Republican who had been providing intelligence to Lincoln during the fall and winter of 1860-61, and who had gone to Harrisburg the night of February 22 with other Baltimore Republicans to greet Lincoln, made the allegation. Snethen reported that not only was John Wilkes Booth present with those participating in the bridge-burning party under the direction of Marshal Kane on April 19-20, 1861, but that he was one of the ringleaders.[9]

In writing from Baltimore to the *Boston Commonwealth* within days of Lincoln's assassination, and while Booth was yet a fugitive, Snethen reported, "John Wilkes Booth, to whom all the evidence thus far points as the murderer, is the third son of Booth, the tragedian of years ago, and was born on High street in East Baltimore. He raised a company of desperadoes in April, 1861, and led them out to burn the bridges on the railroads running Northward. He escaped condign punishment through the mistaken leniency of the government. Wigfall is not a more desperate rebel, traitor, and secessionist, than this Booth."[10]

It is certainly possible that Booth could have been in Baltimore burning bridges on April 19-20, 1861. The previous week he had been in Portland, Maine, where he made his final appearance on April 13, 1861—coincidentally, the same day Fort Sumter surrendered. Booth left Portland in haste on

April 14, not even paying his advertisement bill. He would not return to the stage again until April 22, when he resurfaced once again in Albany.[11]

Nowhere in the country, perhaps, were events more volatile during April 1861 than in Baltimore. With all of the secessionist excitement swirling there in the wake of Fort Sumter's surrender on April 13, Lincoln's subsequent call for 75,000 troops, and Virginia's secession, it would have been in keeping with Booth's habit of putting himself where the action was to make a quick run to his hometown and participate in any pro-secession mischief then fomenting there.

Yet another Baltimorean, Patrick Charles Martin, who would, during the height of the Civil War act as a blockade runner for the Confederacy, also allegedly took part in the April 19 Baltimore uprising.[12] Martin draws interest for another reason. Martin would also serve as a clandestine link between John Wilkes Booth and Baltimore's Marshal Kane.

If John Wilkes Booth, a man known to travel extensively, even impulsively, could make a quick run to Baltimore in April 1861 between acting engagements to participate in secessionist bridge-burning schemes, could he not also have come to town during one or more of the weeks he was known to be off the stage in late 1860 or early 1861 to inspire and conspire with the Baltimore plotters? He had plenty of opportunity.

Booth visited his mother and sister in Philadelphia during the last half of December 1860. The following month, his whereabouts are not known until January 21, when he opened in Rochester. From February 3 to the 10, his whereabouts are unknown until he appears in Albany on February 11.[13] John Wilkes Booth had at least six weeks between December 1860 and early February 1861 during which he might travel to Baltimore and conspire with the plotters.

Reported loyal Baltimore Republicans to Lucius Chittenden during his secret meeting on February 17, 1861, concerning the plotters, "We know that they are not all hired assassins. There are men among them who believe they are serving their country. One of them is an actor who recites passages from the tragedy of Julius Cæsar in their conclaves."[14]

It could be argued that Chittenden's account, written many years after the actual event, might have been tainted by his knowledge of Booth's having been Lincoln's assassin. But there is more contemporaneous evidence, written years before Booth's final act, supportive of Chittenden's account. The *Albany Evening Journal* would report soon after the Baltimore Plot's exposure that "the characters and pursuits of the conspirators were various. Some of them were impelled by a fanatical zeal which they termed patriotism, and they justified their acts by the example of Brutus, in ridding the country of a tyrant. One of them was accustomed to recite passages put into the mouth of the character of Brutus, in Shakspeare's (sic) play of 'Julius Caesar.'"[15]

That description sounds an awful lot like John Wilkes Booth.

HIGHLY relevant to the Baltimore Plot is the existence of evidence of other conspiracies to either kidnap or kill Abraham Lincoln. Identifying those involved in such conspiracies might suggest their complicity in the Baltimore Plot. It is true that many of these conspiracies did not bloom until late 1864. They might thus be dismissed as too remote in time to be relevant to the Baltimore Plot, hatched as it reportedly was in late 1860 or early 1861. But recall that the motive for the suspected Baltimore plotters' efforts to assassinate Lincoln was preventing his inauguration in 1861. After Lincoln won his second term in 1864, that same motive resurfaced. Possibly the same resentments, the same apprehensions, the same objectives of some of the same plotters were aroused, now with even more fury, as four years of a bloody war under the Lincoln administration had made him a wildly unpopular president even among many Northerners.

A full exploration of all the presidential kidnapping and assassination conspiracies and those suspected of being part of them is far beyond the scope of this book. But even a high level examination of such suspected conspiracies points to the commonality of schemes and plans by at least some of those suspected of complicity in the Baltimore Plot.

One example of a presidential kidnapping plot involves none other than the Democratic Texas senator Louis T. Wigfall. Reportedly having "the eye of a man capable of anything," Wigfall allegedly attempted to enlist a gang of conspirators to kidnap President Buchanan in December 1860. According to the plan, Buchanan was to be "carried off to a secure place," paving the way for pro-slavery Vice President Breckinridge to be installed as president. With Breckinridge in power, so went the story, Wigfall believed that the South could avoid being "trapped into war."[16] How kidnapping Buchanan in December 1860 would have prevented the South from being "trapped into war" after Lincoln took office less than three months later, we are not told. But if Wigfall had a plan to kidnap Buchanan and replace him with Breckinridge, it seems that the logical endgame for such a plot would have been to find a way to maintain Breckinridge in power after March 4, 1861—perhaps by eliminating Lincoln.[17]

Wigfall allegedly went to visit Secretary of War John B. Floyd at his home on the evening of December 25, 1860, to plead his case for the Buchanan kidnapping scheme. As a member of Buchanan's cabinet, Floyd would have been a prime source of intelligence on the opportunities to seize Buchanan. As secretary of war with scores of army officers loyal to the Southern cause at his disposal, Floyd would also have been the ideal person to clear the way for Wigfall's escape from Washington as he hurried a captured Buchanan to the

The arrest of Marshal George Proctor Kane. (*Library of Congress*)

"secure place." Allegedly, this was the reason Wigfall called on Floyd—to secure his assistance with the escape. But reportedly, despite Wigfall's urging his case in the strongest terms, then losing his famous temper, Floyd refused to participate. Then, amid scandalous accusations of self-dealing, Floyd resigned as secretary of war on December 29, 1860. The Buchanan kidnapping plot never materialized.[18]

After Lincoln's first inauguration, however, and certainly by the height of the Civil War, presidential kidnapping plots began to gain traction once more. These involved, separately or in combination, efforts by James A. Seddon, Confederate secretary of war, John Wilkes Booth, likely operating as a Confederate agent, and possibly even our old friend, Baltimore police marshal George Proctor Kane.

MARSHAL KANE, it will be recalled, had conspired to destroy railroad bridges late on the evening of April 19 and early in the morning of April 20. The maneuver effectively frustrated any future attempts to send Union troops through Baltimore. The secession element there would have felt emboldened.

By June 1861, Winfield Scott was, thanks in part to intelligence from Baltimore Republican operative Worthington G. Snethen, becoming concerned over the growing strength of Baltimore secessionists, Marshal Kane chief among them. On June 24, Scott ordered Major General Nathan P. Banks to arrest Marshal Kane and four members of the Baltimore Board of Police.[19]

At 3:00 a.m. on June 27, 1861, a detachment of as many as a thousand federal troops arrived at Kane's home in Baltimore. In order to prevent any advance warning, the Baltimore police officers along the route to Kane's home were temporarily taken into custody. The Union soldiers roused Kane from his bed and removed him to Fort McHenry. These rather extreme measures demonstrate the power and sway Marshal Kane was suspected of holding in Baltimore.

Later that day, General Banks issued a proclamation justifying Kane's arrest on grounds that he had acted in concert with others to provide "hidden deposits of arms and ammunition, encourage contraband traffic with men at war with the Government and while enjoying its protection and privileges stealthily wait opportunity to combine their means and forces with those in rebellion against its authority. . . . The chief of police . . . is not only believed to be cognizant of these facts but in contravention of his duty and in violation of law he is by direction and indirection both witness and protector to the transactions and the parties engaged therein. Under such circumstances the Government cannot regard him otherwise than as the head of an armed force hostile to its authority and acting in concert with its avowed enemies."[20]

Allan Pinkerton would not have been surprised at the government's assessment of Marshal Kane. He and his operatives had reached similar conclusions months before, believing that Kane would use the privilege of his office to the advantage of the suspected Baltimore plotters by providing no escort for Lincoln and by detailing policemen at the depot who would make only a show of preserving order. Now, by putting Marshal Kane and the disloyal Baltimore police board on ice, the government had positioned itself for the speedy arrest of other prominent Baltimore secessionists and the disruption of the Maryland legislature.

By September, Allan Pinkerton was operating as "Mr. E. J. Allen," civilian chief of General George B. McClellan's secret service force. On September 11, 1861, McClellan requested that Secretary of War Simon Cameron send Pinkerton to Baltimore to take charge of arresting several prominent Baltimoreans suspected of disloyalty and to convey them to Fort Monroe.[21] Pinkerton went to Baltimore with a "sufficient number" of his detective force and early on the morning of September 13 arrested over a dozen prominent suspected Baltimore rebel sympathizers, including Baltimore mayor George W. Brown.[22]

Secretary of War Cameron, meanwhile, had directed that General Banks do everything in his power to prevent the legislature of Maryland from passing an act of secession, even if it meant arresting "all or any part of the members" of that body. "Exercise your own judgment as to the time and manner, but do your work effectively."[23]

General Banks would indeed do his work effectively. Over the next few days, Banks would arrest all of the members of the Maryland legislature who were known or suspected of disloyalty to the Union.[24]

Astonishingly, evidence exists that John Wilkes Booth himself may have been caught in the dragnet of those arrested in Baltimore during September 1861—and then let go. On October 4, 1861, a newspaper article from Baltimore reported the names of ten prisoners set free after swearing an oath of loyalty to the Union. One of those released gave his name as "John Wilkes."[25]

Booth would, on at least one subsequent occasion, swear a loyalty oath after being arrested.[26] And "John Wilkes" would have been a convenient alias for him; Booth had gone by the names "Mr. Wilkes" and "J. B. Wilkes" early in his career.[27] Even years later, his knee-high riding boot, recovered from Dr. Samuel Mudd's house on April 21, 1865, had the name "J. Wilkes" written in it.[28]

Booth very well could have been in Baltimore in September and October 1861 with plenty of time to be arrested and released; he had not performed since April 27, 1861, at the latest, in Albany, and would not perform again until October 21, 1861, in Providence, Rhode Island.[29] In May 1861, Booth was known to be in Baltimore, where he joined fellow actor William A. Howell, with whom he shared a room on High Street, in an effort to organize a company of troops and march them to Richmond. Their plans were spoiled, however, by the Union's occupation of Baltimore. Wrote Howell, "Before Wilkes Booth and myself could perfect our arrangement and organize our company and while we were waiting for instructions from Richmond, the Federal troops took possession of Baltimore and cut off all communication with the South, as well as knocked on the head our project about raising a company."[30]

In September, Allan Pinkerton had been given primary responsibility for making arrests in Baltimore of those suspected of disloyalty to the Union. Snethen reported that Booth had escaped the punishment he deserved "through the mistaken leniency of the government." Had Allan Pinkerton or the federal authorities in Baltimore, thanks to a Civil War era "catch and release" program, let John Wilkes Booth slip through their grasp?

MEANWHILE, during the summer and fall of 1861 Marshal Kane, now in custody, would be given a "guided tour" of several Union forts. From Fort McHenry, Kane was transferred in succession to Fort Lafayette, then Fort Columbus, and finally to Fort Warren in Boston.[31]

Kane naturally resented his imprisonment. He wrote embittered letters to Lincoln[32] and others complaining about the deplorable conditions of his confinement at Fort Lafayette. He demanded a trial and defiantly justified his conduct on April 19: "I glory in every act of mine connected with my administration and particularly in those connected with the occurrence at that time," wrote Kane in defense of his role in the bridge burning, "and if any portion of that conduct is treason the Government or the Know-Nothing church-burning clubs of Baltimore with their ladies and friends may convict and hang me as high as Haman before I will recant a word uttered or regret a deed done at that time."[33] Kane seems to have conveniently forgotten his "fight them and whip them or die" dispatch sent around midnight on April 19.

It is, however, neither the suspicions of a man, nor his thoughts, nor even his written words that convict him; it is his deeds. And at least while he was in prison, Marshal Kane's deeds were held in check. Other Baltimore political prisoners would be recommended for release in early 1862; Marshal Kane, however, headed a list of those whose confinement would continue, in some cases on suspicion of being "influential and dangerous" or "vindictive."[34] But on November 27, 1862, after seventeen months of incarceration, Marshal Kane's release, along with other Baltimore political prisoners, finally came.[35] He would waste no time showing where his loyalties lay.

Having missed out on nearly a year and a half of a perfectly good war, Marshal Kane had some catching up to do once freed. His first order of business upon returning to Baltimore was to publish a blistering, even threatening rebuke of Secretary Seward, whom he blamed for his incarceration. "In this imprisonment I am understood to have been the special victim of Mr. Secretary Seward, who in concert with his hired minions has omitted no occasion to heap upon me accusations which he knew to be false and therefore dared not bring to the ordeal of a public trial. To these charges the despotic censorship of the prisons in which I have been kept allowed me no reply." Kane then grew vaguely, but darkly threatening: "I can only now promise that in due time and upon a proper occasion Mr. Seward shall hear from me in a way which will procure for him if he has not already acquired it the contempt of every honest man and woman in the land."[36]

Reportedly, the obviously vindictive Marshal Kane had been released from Fort Warren with the understanding that he would go farther south.[37] Kane apparently misinterpreted this agreement, ultimately going farther *north*. Less than a year after his release, Kane had crossed through Union lines to Montreal, Canada. Here, he would participate in anti-Union plots.

Once in Montreal, Kane met up and became roommates with former Baltimore liquor dealer Patrick Charles Martin, now a Confederate blockade runner. In October or November 1863 Kane and Martin joined forces with a small group of Confederate raiders plotting to free some fifteen hundred to two thousand Confederate prisoners being held on Johnson's Island on Lake Erie, near Sandusky, Ohio. One of those prisoners included Marshal Kane's

cohort in the April 1861 bridge-burning incident Isaac Trimble, now a captured Confederate general. Kane's involvement with Patrick Charles Martin
and their efforts to implement a plot to seize Johnson's Island are summed up
in a report by Confederate Captain Robert D. Minor, CSN, to Admiral
Franklin Buchanan:

> Finding Marshal Kane and some of our friends in Montreal, we
> set to work to prepare and perfect our arrangements, the first
> object of the plan being to communicate with the prisoners on
> Johnson's Island, informing them that an attempt would be
> made to release them. This was effected through a lady from
> Baltimore, a Mrs. P. C. Martin, then residing with her husband
> and family in Montreal, and whose husband did all in his power
> to aid us in every way. She brought a letter from Baltimore,
> which General [J.J.] Archer (who, with Major-General [I. R.]
> Trimble, was a prisoner at Johnson's Island) had sent there to
> Beverly Saunders, esq., telling us to communicate with him
> through the personal columns of the *New York Herald*.[38]

As late as November 1863, Baltimore was being used as a hub for
Confederate espionage. Baltimoreans Marshal Kane, Patrick Charles Martin,
and even Martin's wife were active participants from the Confederacy's satellite office in Montreal.

Although a plan for a Confederate raid on the Great Lakes had been
hatched as early as February 1863, that plan had not been for purposes of
releasing prisoners, but, rather, to seize the USS *Michigan*. Not until August,
several months after the Union had imprisoned about two thousand
Confederate soldiers on Johnson's Island, did James A. Seddon give his blessings for a daring move to free them.[39] The strategy called for 180 raiders,
armed with navy Colt revolvers, to disguise themselves as laborers on their
way to Chicago by passenger ship. At the appropriate time, they would capture their ship, then cause it to collide "by accident" with the USS *Michigan,*
the only Union warship plying the Great Lakes. In the ensuing confusion, the
raiders would board the *Michigan,* capture the gunboat, and turn its guns on
Johnson's Island to free the prisoners.

Pursuant to General Archer's letter written to Baltimore, a personal ad was
indeed placed in the *New York Herald,* informing the prisoners that "a few
nights after the 4th of November a carriage would be at the door."[40] From this
ad, the prisoners knew when to be ready.

The Johnson's Island plot bears fingerprints of the Baltimore Plot and the
April 19th bridge-burning raid. Pinkerton's agents had reported in 1861 that
the Baltimore plotters were also staying in touch with one another through

notices published in the newspapers and had planned to arm themselves with "fine revolvers." The Baltimore plotters had planned on getting up a diversion by starting a fight. The Johnson's Island plotters also had a diversion—to ram a Union gunship with a passenger boat "by accident." By some accounts, the Baltimore plotters that had planned to halt Lincoln's train by burning bridges north of Baltimore also were to disguise themselves—not as laborers—but as African Americans, perhaps to create the ruse that the bridge burners were slaves escaping North and burning bridges behind them.[41]

Individually, these vague similarities—"blind" newspaper ads, diversions, and disguises—may do nothing more than represent various unremarkable methods of carrying out clandestine operations. But a vital common thread connects such methods with the Baltimore Plot, the bridgeburning incident, and the Johnson's Island plot. That common thread is Baltimore police marshal George P. Kane.

As the Johnson's Island raiders were assembling, preparing to board their ship at St. Catharines, Canada, on the Welland Canal between Lake Ontario and Lake Erie, they learned that Union Secretary of War Stanton had been warned of the raid. Stanton had promptly sent reinforcements to Johnson's Island. The mission was aborted.[42] Someone had betrayed the raiders.

The failure of the Johnson's Island raid would have been a demoralizing blow to the Confederacy's secret operations force. Reportedly, over $100,000 had been expended to procure the necessary equipment for the raid. Moreover, the Confederacy was running low on troops. Prisoner exchanges were a thing of the past. The Union could afford to allow its prisoners to languish in prison camp hellholes like Andersonville, because it had a seemingly limitless supply of fresh recruits. The South, on the other hand, was bleeding itself dry of young fighting men.

At some point, the balance of troops being decidedly against the South, the Wigfallian concept of kidnapping the President Lincoln fell upon the ears of the Confederate leadership. If Lincoln could be captured, and held hostage, the Confederacy might free thousands of prisoners by seizing just one man. Secretary of War Seddon and other Confederate leaders began to see the wisdom, if not necessity, of kidnapping the Union president.[43] In some ways, kidnapping was preferable to assassination. A captured Lincoln might be bargained with or bargained for—the release of sorely needed Confederate prisoners of war was the paramount objective.[44]

Captain Thomas Nelson Conrad would later take credit for initially putting the proposition of kidnapping Lincoln to Seddon. The plan involved abducting Lincoln while he rode, generally without an escort, between the Executive Mansion and Soldiers' Home during the summer and fall.[45] On

September 15, 1864, Seddon issued an order stating: "Lt. Col. Mosby and Lieutenant Cawood are hereby directed to aid and facilitate the movements of Captain Conrad." Conrad and his exploratory team left for Washington to scout the feasibility of capturing Lincoln two days later.[46]

Perhaps coincidentally, perhaps not, sometime in August or September 1864, John Wilkes Booth also hatched a nearly identical scheme to kidnap Lincoln, with two Baltimore chums, Sam Arnold and Michael O'Laughlen. Arnold and O'Laughlen had each known Booth in their youth and had each served in the same Confederate Maryland infantry regiment earlier in the war, but had never met. Over drinks and tall tales, the three Baltimoreans met at Booth's invitation at Barnum's Hotel. For all we know, while Booth conspired at Barnum's, Cypriano Ferrandini was in the building. Ferrandini would have enjoyed a certain measure of local infamy for his suspected complicity in the Baltimore Plot.

By the end of their meeting at Barnum's Hotel, Booth, Arnold, and O'Laughlen had conspired to kidnap Lincoln and had formed preliminary plans. They would overtake the president's carriage on the isolated country road between the White House and Soldiers' Home, shackle him, carry him through southern Maryland to Virginia, and thence to Richmond. Their goal was the same as Seddon's: with Lincoln as a hostage, they might secure the release of thousands of desperately needed Confederate prisoners. The basic plot agreed to, the three conspirators parted ways to await further developments.[47]

One such development would occur a few weeks later, when Booth traveled to Montreal. Here, under pretext of shipping his stage wardrobe south, he would meet with Confederate operative George N. Sanders—and seek out Marshal George P. Kane.

ONE of the most intriguing connections of all possibly tying Booth back to the Baltimore Plot and perhaps even to Cypriano Ferrandini involves the shadowy Confederate functionary and Democratic political operative George N. Sanders. A radical Kentuckian recently living in New York, Sanders had, during Buchanan's administration, been appointed in 1858 the Navy Agent for the port of New York.[48] Previously, in 1853, he had been named American Consul to London by Democratic president Franklin Pierce. While in Europe, Sanders reportedly operated in an apparent effort to divert attention from the American slave-owning democracy by pointing fingers at European monarchies, even advocating revolution there. Sanders accordingly worked his way into the inner circle of the most infamous and ardent political fanatics on the continent.[49]

On Washington's Birthday, February 22, 1854, Sanders hosted a banquet in London attended by a who's who of political radicals—Giuseppe Mazzini, Felice Orsini, Lajos Kossuth, Giuseppe Garibaldi, and Alexandre Ledru-Rollin among them.[50] Sanders soon adopted, then openly advocated Mazzini's "theory of the dagger," which holds that "tyrannicide"—assassination of an unpopular ruler—is a perfectly justifiable means of political reform. Apparently wishing to put the theory into practice, Sanders once wrote that French ruler Louis Napoleon should be killed "by any means, and by any way it could be done."[51]

Even in the United States, Sanders openly preached the merits of the guillotine and death to tyrants.[52] As an advocate of political assassination, Sanders would have found a willing acolyte in John Wilkes Booth, already predisposed to such thinking by virtue of the stage roles he played with such passion and realism and his hatred of all things abolition.

Quite possibly, Sanders had been shadowing Lincoln while he traveled from Springfield to Washington. On February 12, 1861, the *New York Times* would report that while Lincoln was at the hotel in Cincinnati, George N. Sanders was there too. "In passing to his room those that could rushed at [Mr. Lincoln], throwing their arms around him, patting him on the back, and almost wrenching his arm off. Politicians were thick; *among them George N. Sanders* and others."[53] Other, less reliable evidence, possibly places him at the Continental Hotel in Philadelphia the same week Lincoln stayed there.[54]

Sanders was also spotted lurking about Willard's Hotel around the time Lincoln was staying there. "Public Man" claimed that when he met with Lincoln on February 28, 1861, he warned the president-elect of Sanders: "I told him [Lincoln], what I believe to be perfectly true, that the worst stories about the intended incursions into Washington, and the like, all originate with men like George Saunders [*sic*], of New York . . . men who came into my mind because I had passed them in the hall of the very hotel in which we were talking, and in which they have been telling wonderful stories of conspiracy and assassination, from the hotel porches, to anybody who will listen to them for weeks past."[55]

Sanders might have found a pliant tool in Corsican immigrant Cypriano Ferrandini. And the two had a wonderful opportunity to meet at a critically important time. It will be recalled that Ferrandini was in Washington testifying before the Select Committee of Five on February 5, 1861. George N. Sanders was reportedly in Washington on February 4, 1861, monitoring the Peace Conference that had opened that day. While in Washington, Sanders was then also playing his favorite tune—loudly it seems—urging political assassinations on all who would listen.[56]

Ten days after testifying in Washington, Ferrandini told Pinkerton that, as Orsini had given his life for Italy, he was prepared to die for his country. It was commonly believed that Napoleon III stood as a barrier to Italy's political freedom. Ferrandini thus revered, and possibly even called himself, "Orsini."[57] Sanders actually knew him. On January 14, 1858, Felice Orsini and his conspirators had attempted to assassinate Napoleon III. Unlike an earlier plot involving Sanders, Orsini's almost succeeded, with the conspirators tossing percussion grenades under the emperor's carriage as he and his empress prepared to enter an opera house in Paris.[58] On March 13, 1858, Orsini was executed for his efforts. Blowing up Lincoln's railcar in 1861 with an "infernal machine" tossed into it as he rode with his family was reportedly one of the means the Baltimore plotters were considering.[59] There is thus a striking commonality of scheme between Orsini's attempted assassination of Napoleon III and the plotted assassination of Abraham Lincoln. Assassination of the despised ruler was paramount—collateral damage was of no consequence.[60]

Sanders advocated assassination of Louis Napoleon as a means of political reform "by any means, and by any way it could be done." In advocating Lincoln's assassination, Ferrandini told Pinkerton that "murder of any kind is justifiable and right to save the rights of the Southern people."[61] There is a striking similarity—a commonality of motive—in Sanders's and Ferrandini's pronouncements.[62] Might these two men, George N. Sanders and Cypriano Ferrandini, both outspoken advocates of political assassination, both present in Washington the same week in February 1861, have had an opportunity to meet, to share radical ideas, and to begin plotting a way to put them into action?

WHETHER Sanders and Ferrandini ever met is not known. What is known is that George N. Sanders did meet John Wilkes Booth. The two met in Montreal, on numerous occasions, in the fall of 1864, soon after Booth hatched his Lincoln kidnapping plot.

Termed "Little Richmond" during the war, Montreal was a sanctuary city for Confederate commissioners, secret agents, and former prisoner of war refugees. And nowhere in Montreal was Confederate activity more vibrant than at the elegant St. Lawrence Hotel on St. James Street. It was at this hotel, on October 18, 1864, that John Wilkes Booth would begin a ten-day stay, checking into room 150.[63] It was here, in Montreal, that on October 24 Booth would perform dramatic solo readings at Corby's Hall, his only performance while in town.[64] Clearly, however, a one-night performance was not the primary motivator for Booth's ten-day visit to "Little Richmond." More than likely he was in town to connect with Confederate operatives. Indeed, it was here, at Montreal's St. Lawrence Hotel, that Booth would meet George N. Sanders.

Sanders, described in 1865 as "a short-sized, low, thickset man, with grayish curly hair, a grayish moustache, and very burly form,"[65] was a man of big ideas who sought to put them into practice for personal gain. Holed up in Montreal, possibly after a trip to Richmond,[66] George N. Sanders had become an unofficial member of the Confederacy's so-called "Canadian Cabinet,"[67] having worked his way into the confidence of men like Confederate commissioner Clement C. Clay, who vouched for Sanders being "a very good man to do their dirty work."[68] From this, we can surmise that Sanders took directions and possibly money from Confederate leaders and funneled both to the hands of individuals who would actually carry out rebel clandestine operations.

What Sanders and Booth had to say to one another in October 1864 is a matter of speculation. But several eyewitnesses saw the two men talking together in the St. Lawrence Hotel that month. Testified John Deveny, a former lieutenant in Company E, Fourth Maryland Regiment, who was a witness at the assassination conspiracy trial, "I was well acquainted with John Wilkes Booth. The first time I saw him in Canada he was standing in the St. Lawrence Hotel, Montreal, talking with George N. Sanders. I believe that was in the month of October. They were talking confidentially, and drinking together. I saw them go into Dowley's and have a drink together. . . . I spoke to Booth, and asked him if he was going to play there, knowing that he was an actor. He said he was not. I then said, 'What are you to do?' He said, 'I just came here on a pleasure trip.'"[69]

Testified another witness who had resided at St. Lawrence Hall (the name by which the hotel was commonly known) between September 1864 and February 1865, "I frequently observed George N. Sanders in intimate association with Booth, and others of that class, in Montreal."[70]

Most significantly, stunning testimony exists tying Booth to Sanders and a possible plot to assassinate Lincoln at his second inaugural. In May 1865, Henry Finegas claimed that he had witnessed Sanders in Montreal on the evening of February 14 or 15, 1865, and overheard a conversation he was having with William C. Cleary[71] "in a rather low tone of voice" at St. Lawrence Hall. "I was sitting in a chair," Finegas testified, "and Sanders and Cleary walked in from the door; they stopped about ten feet from me, and I heard Cleary say, *'I suppose they are getting ready for the inauguration of Lincoln next month.'* Sanders said, *'Yes; if the boys only have luck, Lincoln won't trouble them much longer.'* Cleary asked, *'is every thing well?'* Sanders replied, *'O, yes; Booth is bossing the job.'"*[72]

From this, and other evidence gathered, it may be surmised that a plot existed to assassinate Lincoln at his second inaugural on March 4, 1865, that Booth was at the head of the enterprise in the field, and that the perennial advocate of political assassination, George N. Sanders, was operations chief for the conspiracy, perhaps the prime contractor for the job. And this leads us to the possible connection of John Wilkes Booth to two other Baltimoreans, Marshal George P. Kane and blockade-runner Patrick Charles Martin.

ADMITTEDLY, little is known of the shady Confederate operative Patrick Charles Martin, an enigma that even rebel officials termed "slippery."[73] Described as "a rather excitable, mettlesome man," Martin was a native of New York who had lived and worked in Baltimore for many years as a liquor dealer.[74] He also knew how to captain a ship; Confederate naval records refer to him as "Captain P. C. Martin." The Confederacy paid him large sums in October 1864 for smuggling provisions and ordinance stores south.[75]

There is some evidence Martin may have fled to Canada from Baltimore to avoid capture in 1861.[76] Indeed, the War Department suspected his involvement in the April 19 Baltimore uprising. At all events, Martin arrived in Montreal in late summer 1862 and reportedly began using his seafaring experience to ship contraband south.[77]

When Booth arrived in Montreal on October 18, 1864, Martin was there. Booth, however, was seeking an audience with none other than Marshal George P. Kane.[78] It will be recalled that Kane had been in Montreal the previous year, implementing his plot to free Confederate prisoners on Johnson's Island. Of all the people in the world, why would John Wilkes Booth have come all the way to Montreal to meet with Marshal Kane? It could have been to enlist Kane, another Baltimorean, in his Lincoln kidnapping plot, hatched in Baltimore just a few weeks before. Upon learning of Kane's arrest in 1861, Booth angrily claimed *"I know George P. Kane well; he is my friend."*[79] Might Booth have worked with Kane before and hoped to do so again now that Kane had been released? Had Booth learned of Kane's involvement in plotting the Johnson's Island raid, and assumed he would be in for another raiding scheme, not to rescue prisoners, but to kidnap the man whose government had imprisoned him?

We will never know for certain the answers to any of these questions. Marshal Kane was not in Montreal when Booth arrived there in October 1864. Possibly, Kane was in Richmond, where he served on General John Henry Winder's staff.[80] Winder controlled a small band of detectives who were responsible for rebel counterintelligence and spying activities, termed "Special Services."[81] In July 1863 Winder had reportedly urged Jefferson Davis to move forward with an attempt to kidnap Lincoln.[82]

Although Marshal Kane was not in Montreal to greet Booth in October 1864, Patrick Charles Martin was there, and Booth spent a fair amount of time with Martin and his family.[83] Booth ultimately asked Martin to do two favors for him. One was to ship trunks containing his theatrical wardrobe south. Booth could not both kidnap Lincoln and flee quickly if weighed down with heavy wardrobe trunks. If his plan worked, he could carry Lincoln triumphantly to Richmond, meet up with his trunks there, and get on with his acting career in the South. Perhaps he dreamed of the adulation he would receive there—slayer of Roman tyrants onstage; captor of Union tyrants off-stage.

The other favor Booth had asked of Patrick C. Martin in October was to write two letters of introduction for him; one to Dr. William Queen in Bryantown, Maryland, and the other to Marshal Kane.[84] Martin provided both letters before setting sail. While bound for Halifax, Martin's chartered schooner, the *Marie Victoria,* was shipwrecked near Bic, Quebec, after leaving Montreal on or about November 18, 1864. Patrick C. Martin and all hands were presumed lost. Although his wardrobe trunks would be recovered from the shipwreck, Booth would never receive them.[85]

The Dr. Queen letter was intended to assist Booth by enlisting support on the ground in southern Maryland for his kidnapping scheme. Booth would need such assistance as he transported a captured Lincoln through lower Maryland en route to Richmond.[86]

But the reason for the Marshal Kane letter of introduction remains a mystery. If, as Booth claimed, Marshal Kane was a friend of his, why the need for a letter of introduction? There are only two answers. Either Booth was lying when he claimed Marshal Kane for a friend and needed an introduction, or the letter Patrick C. Martin wrote for him was not merely one of introduction. Perhaps it contained instructions or certified Booth's role in their common clandestine enterprise.

That Booth sought out Patrick Charles Martin, a "slippery" character suspected of involvement in the April 19 Baltimore uprising, is significant. If Booth did not know Kane, and therefore needed a letter of introduction, such a move demonstrates that Booth knew that Kane would value Martin's judgment and that Booth had been directed to Marshal Kane by someone else, possibly the Confederate leadership. But that Patrick Martin should write such a letter on Booth's behalf demonstrates far more. Martin's endorsement of Booth also suggests that Martin had known Booth for some time, trusted him not to be a Union spy, and could testify to his dedication to the Southern cause—otherwise, how could Martin vouch for Booth in a letter of introduction with any credibility?

It might be argued that Martin's letter to Kane establishes that Booth did not know Kane. But such an argument presupposes that that Martin's letter to Kane was in fact merely one of introduction. In a time when spies were everywhere and switching sides was not uncommon, even a known friend might benefit from a letter of recommendation from another known friend. In February 1861, Kane had cast suspicion on himself, suggesting his possible complicity with the Baltimore plotters by speaking a bit too freely at Barnum's Hotel within earshot of Pinkerton. His open participation with the bridge burners had cost him seventeen months in prison. His Johnson's Island plot had been leaked to the Canadian authorities by a man Kane had trusted before it could be put into action. The leak had come from one of the plotters, a man named McCuaig, who had been introduced to Kane as a Canadian of reliable Southern sympathy.[87] No doubt Marshal Kane had learned his lesson from these experiences and was now being more cautious about those with whom he conspired.

Years later, Kane admitted receiving Patrick C. Martin's letter of introduction for Booth but claimed to have destroyed it, thus taking the letter's true contents to his grave.[88] If the letter was merely one of introduction, why destroy it? Perhaps the letter contained evidence of Booth's plans or implicated others in the kidnapping plot. Perhaps the letter was sent to remind Kane of who Booth was, of Martin's and possibly Booth's prior involvement in the April 19 Baltimore uprising; perhaps even the Baltimore Plot itself. In any event, Kane's destruction of a letter from Patrick C. Martin concerning John Wilkes Booth raises serious questions about its contents and the suspicious nature of Marshal Kane's involvement with these two men.

Kane's own account of the Martin letter, and his justification for destroying it, is illuminating. In 1876, Kane offered the following explanation during an interview published in the *New York Daily Graphic*.

> "Towards the end of the war, in March or April, I was resting, out of the way, in the Valley of Virginia. While there a letter dated the previous December was received by me from Martin, in Montreal. It said across the face, after the family and friendly matter in it was complete: 'What do you know of John Wilkes Booth? He has been here and stopped at my house. He expressed great disappointment at not finding you, and said he had expected to meet you here. What is his character? He became intimate at my house with my wife and daughter. Has he a good reputation in Baltimore?'
>
> "This part of the letter," continued Colonel Kane, "was a mystery to me. I had never known Wilkes Booth, if I had ever heard of him, and I doubt that I had ever heard of him. The host of the house where I was lodging came to me just after I received this letter and said: 'Colonel Kane, Stoneman is raiding up the valley. His scouts are close on you and you will be arrested if you stay here.' I placed the letter inside of the lining of my traveling bag, mounted a horse with the bag, and rode through the woods and broken country to Danville, where I arrived nearly dead with fever and fatigue. Just after I arrived there Mr. Davis and his party, flying from Richmond to Charlotte, came along and I rode with them in the car to Greensboro', where I had to stop off. While lying there, hardly in my senses, after some days had

elapsed, the man of the house said to me: 'Colonel Kane, we have a part of a torn New York newspaper here which contains some startling intelligence. A man named Wilkes Booth has assassinated President Lincoln.' I endeavored," said Colonel Kane, "to recall where I had heard that name. I rose up almost delirious and tapped my forehead, muttering 'Wilkes Booth. Who is he? How is he connected with me?' Then in a few minutes I cried to the man: 'Bring me that satchel!' I tore out Martin's letter and read it again. And," concluded the Colonel, "although I never knew Booth, that letter might have cost me my life if it had been found secreted in the satchel at that time."[89]

Kane's story, though entertaining, seems full of holes and flavored with fabrication. First, Martin apparently already knew Booth. Otherwise, Martin would never have written a letter of introduction on his behalf to Confederate sympathizer Dr. William Queen. Kane's claim that Martin's letter sought to gather information on Booth's reputation therefore seems implausible, and out of step with Booth's having gone to Montreal specifically to see Kane, not approval from Martin. Second, Martin's shipwreck occurred on or about November 18, 1864. With Martin presumed dead, he could not have written a letter to Kane dated December 1864. Perhaps Kane's memory of the letter's date had faded. Or perhaps the letter was not *dated* December; perhaps he had *received* the letter in December, rather than March or April as he had claimed. Third, Kane's testimony that he had never known Booth and doubted he had ever heard of him is at odds with Booth's insistence that Marshal Kane was a friend of his. Moreover, Kane's denial that he had ever heard of Booth seems improbable, given Booth's national celebrity and the fact he had acted at a theater in Baltimore in which Kane at one time held a financial interest. Fourth, by Kane's admission, he hid the letter "in the lining of my traveling bag" when confronted with the threat of capture, at a time prior to knowing of Booth's role in the Lincoln assassination. If the letter was merely one of introduction of a man he did not know, why did Kane feel the need to treat it like a state secret? That he initially hid Martin's letter rather than destroying it suggests that Kane intended to put the letter to some future use. Fifth, by 1876, the only other people in the world who could have disputed Kane's account of the letter, Patrick Charles Martin and John Wilkes Booth, were long dead. Kane could say anything he wanted about the letter's contents with no fear of being challenged. Sixth, Booth had come to Montreal, apparently without a letter of introduction, expressly to see Marshal Kane. By Kane's own recollection of the Martin letter, Booth "expressed great disappointment" at not finding Kane at Martin's house and said that "he had expected to meet" Kane there. If Booth did not need a letter of introduction to meet Marshal

Kane in Montreal, why would he have needed one to attempt meeting him in Virginia? Perhaps most telling, Kane does not specify who delivered Martin's letter to him, implying that the letter arrived in the normal course, that is, through the mail. But if Martin was writing letters of introduction for Booth, why not just give them to Booth for hand delivery to the intended recipient? Why trust the mails of Canada, the United States, and the Confederacy, or even involve a Confederate courier with such a document? Booth hand-delivered Martin's letter of introduction to Dr. Queen in Bryantown;[90] it seems plausible that he might have done the same with Martin's letter to Marshal Kane. If John Wilkes Booth had himself hand-delivered the letter of introduction from Martin to Marshal Kane in late 1864 or early 1865, a time during which Booth was traveling extensively, the question becomes, what else might the two men have said to one another? Dr. Queen was not executed for having received a letter of introduction written on behalf of John Wilkes Booth. In all likelihood, Kane would not have been either—unless that letter was something more.

Regardless of whether he knew Marshal Kane or not, that Booth was seeking an audience with him at the same time he was perfecting his plot to kidnap Lincoln suggests that Booth may have wanted Kane to assist. Indeed, it has been posited that Kane and Martin, who had conspired to organize the failed Johnson's Island raid in November 1863, may have initially hatched the Lincoln kidnapping plot in Canada in the winter of 1863-1864. This chronology makes sense. Having failed in one scheme to rescue Confederate prisoners—by springing them from Johnson's Island with a raiding party in November 1863—it seems plausible that Kane and Martin would next hit on another plan to effect the same result—kidnap Lincoln and hold him hostage to secure the Confederate prisoners' release. Given the enormous expenditure on their clandestine operations already, it is only natural they would want to attempt some other enterprise to justify the money and trust shown them.

By February 15, 1864, Kane was being serenaded in Richmond; here, he may have presented the idea.[91] If so, Kane's boss in Richmond, General Winder, likely would have approved, having reportedly urged Jefferson Davis to move forward with a Lincoln kidnapping plot as early as July 1863.[92] It has also been suggested that Kane, who allegedly knew the Booth family in Baltimore, might have recommended to Confederate authorities that Booth be recruited for the scheme to kidnap Lincoln.[93]

If the plan to kidnap Lincoln had originated with or been renewed by Marshal Kane, there exists vague, yet tantalizing evidence that by the summer of 1864, Kane's plan had reached and was being seriously considered by the highest levels of the Confederate army and government.

On June 26, 1864, Robert E. Lee wrote to Jefferson Davis concerning the possibility of rescuing Confederate prisoners from Point Lookout, near the St.

Marys River in southern Maryland. Lee suggested that the raiding party would necessarily be small, as it would need to cross over from Virginia at the Potomac near the mouth of the Chesapeake, where the river is about 6 miles wide. "I can devote to this purpose the whole of the Marylanders of this army, which would afford a sufficient number of men of excellent material and much experience, but I am at a loss where to find a proper leader," Lee wrote. Perhaps the idea of rescuing prisoners, involving Marylanders, and the need for a suitable leader, ideally one from Maryland, brought to mind the former Baltimore police marshal George P. Kane. In any case, Lee switched topics, from that involving Point Lookout to one involving Kane: "With relation to the project of Marshal Kane, if the matter can be kept secret, which I fear is impossible, should Genl Early cross the Potomac, he [Kane] might be sent to join him [Early]."[94]

It has been inferred that "the project of Marshal Kane" was the capture of Abraham Lincoln.[95] It is assumed that General Jubal Early's purpose in crossing the Potomac was to free Confederate prisoners at the weakly garrisoned Point Lookout, on the southernmost tip of Maryland.[96] Perhaps Lee's reference to Kane' joining up with Early was intended to mean that if Kane could gain possession of Lincoln, the prisoners' release might be bargained for should an attempt to release them by force fail. Or perhaps Lee considered that Kane might, with Lincoln in his custody, present his prize to Early for incarceration at a seized Point Lookout or for transportation south with the freed prisoners.

We may never know. Neither the plan to seize prisoners at Point Lookout, nor the "project of Marshal Kane," whatever it may have been, ever materialized. But the plot to kidnap Lincoln was not wholly abandoned by the Confederacy. It appears to have been handed off to John Wilkes Booth a few months after Lee's letter, in the fall of 1864.

Booth's acting engagements had tapered off drastically since May 1864, when he concluded a month-long appearance in Boston. Indeed, he would only perform twice more in 1864, on October 24 in Montreal, and on November 25 with brothers Edwin and Junius in New York. He would perform not at all in December, once in January 1865, not at all in February, and just once more, on March 18, at Ford's Theatre in Washington.[97] It would seem that Booth had all but abandoned his once successful acting career in favor of pursuing the scheme to kidnap Lincoln.[98]

After leaving Montreal, by November 1864 Booth was in Washington, as was Captain Thomas Nelson Conrad. Conrad would later claim that he had failed in an attempt in late September to kidnap Lincoln.[99] It has been suggested that Conrad may have handed off the kidnapping plan he had been scouting with James A. Seddon's blessing—and therefore Jefferson Davis's—

to Booth at this point. Both Conrad and Booth were in Washington between November 9 and 16, 1864, although there is no proof that the two men actually met while there.[100]

What is clear is that Booth was pursuing the Lincoln kidnapping plot with zeal around this time. With his letter of introduction from Patrick Charles Martin in hand, he met with Dr. William Queen in Bryantown, Maryland, about 20 miles south of Washington, on or about November 12, 1864. The next day at church, likely by prior arrangement, Dr. Queen introduced Booth to the not yet famous Dr. Samuel A. Mudd.[101] Between November 16 and December 12, Booth was in New York, where he purchased two Spencer carbines, three pistols, ammunition, daggers, and two sets of handcuffs. On his way back to Washington, Booth dropped most of these weapons with Sam Arnold in Baltimore.[102] On December 21, Booth was back in Bryantown, again meeting with Dr. Mudd. Mudd introduced him to a Confederate operative, Thomas H. Harbin, who agreed to assist in the plot to kidnap Lincoln.[103] Within a few days, a Confederate secret service courier in Maryland, John H. Surratt Jr., was also enlisted in the scheme.[104] A few weeks later, on January 14, Surratt purchased a large boat in southern Maryland that the conspirators secluded in a tributary to the Nanjemoy Creek with the intent of using to pilot a captured Lincoln across the lower Potomac.[105]

Ultimately, those joining Booth in the Lincoln kidnapping plot would include Booth, Surratt, David Edgar Herold, Lewis Thornton Powell, George Atzerodt, and Baltimoreans Michael O'Laughlen and Sam Arnold. There were undoubtedly others involved in the conspiracy; their names, however, are lost to history.[106]

Weeks and months passed. Booth traveled back and forth between Washington, New York, Philadelphia, and Baltimore, where on February 21, he stopped at Barnum's Hotel. From here, he sent a mysterious telegram to John Parker Hale Wentworth, a nephew of Senator John P. Hale, that read: "I am here. Will you keep promise to-day or tomorrow. Let me know. I cannot stay."[107] In fact, Booth did not stay in Baltimore. By February 22, he was back in Washington.[108]

And it was here, in Washington, that John Wilkes Booth's planning matured to preparation. On March 15, Booth arranged for co-conspirators John Surratt and Lewis Powell to occupy the president's box at Ford's Theatre. The two were not there to watch the play being performed that night—*The Tragedy of Jane Shore*—but to become familiar with the box's layout. Perhaps to avoid appearing suspicious, Booth had arranged for eighteen-year-old Honora Fitzpatrick and ten-year-old Mary Apollonia Dean, both tenants at Mary Surratt's H Street boardinghouse, to join Mary's son John Surratt and Lewis Powell in the box.[109] To those who didn't know them, the two conspirators might thus pass for a couple of upstanding young men, chaperoning their little sisters to a night on the town.

Later that night, over drinks, cigars, and steamed oysters at Gautier's Restaurant near Twelfth Street and Pennsylvania Avenue, Booth unveiled the details of his grand plan to his co-conspirators, Sam Arnold, Michael O'Laughlen, Lewis Powell, John Surratt, George Atzerodt, and David Herold. Lincoln was known to frequent Ford's Theatre where he always occupied the box in which Surratt and Powell had sat that night. The next time Lincoln appeared at Ford's, Sam Arnold would enter the president's box and pounce on Lincoln on Booth's cue. Booth and Atzerodt would handcuff Lincoln and lower him to the stage, where the well-built Powell would be waiting to catch him. In front of a live audience, the conspirators would carry the six-foot-four-inch president off-stage and hurry him from the theater to a carriage waiting in the alley behind Ford's Theatre. They would spirit their prize out of Washington and rendezvous with Surratt and Herold after crossing the Potomac's eastern branch.[110] Lincoln had been smuggled into Washington by his friends four years before. Now he would be smuggled out of the capital by his enemies.

So insane did this plan sound to Sam Arnold that he threatened to quit the conspiracy. "You can be the leader of the party, but not my executioner," Arnold told Booth.[111] In fact, Arnold thought the whole plan to kidnap Lincoln was now pointless. The original theory was that a captured Lincoln might be exhanged for Confederate prisoners of war. But General Grant had resumed prisoner exchanges on January 18. Within a month exchanges were occurring at a rate of three thousand per week.[112] Capturing Lincoln now would do nothing to free more Confederate soldiers; indeed, it might cause the Union to suspend the exchanges pending Lincoln's safe return.

But Booth could not be persuaded to abandon his kidnapping plans and indeed persuaded most of his conspirators not to abandon them either. Perhaps Booth felt that Lincoln's capture might induce the North to call off the war. Or perhaps kidnapping Lincoln had never really been Booth's only objective. Perhaps Booth adhered to the ominous directive Jefferson Davis had reportedly given other would-be Lincoln kidnappers in July 1863: "President Davis further said that he did not wish that the life of Lincoln should be taken unless absolutely necessary; that if he could be brought a prisoner alive it would serve the country equally as well and perhaps better than to kill him, but that if it was necessary for our own safety, or we could do no better, that we should mete out to him the deserts that the greatest tyrant the world ever saw deserves, which is death."[113]

On March 17, 1865, Booth apparently sensed that a promising opportunity to kidnap Lincoln had finally presented itself. Lincoln would not be abducted from a crowded theater, but on a lonely road. Booth reportedly learned that Lincoln would be visiting the Campbell Military Hospital, located near

Soldiers' Home, outside Washington. The president was to attend a matinee showing of *Still Waters Run Deep*. At two o'clock in the afternoon, Booth gathered his conspirators together in front of Mary Surratt's boardinghouse on H Street, and revealed the new plan. It sounded much like an old one.

The conspirators would wait for Lincoln's carriage at a remote location along Seventh Street. When his carriage returned from the hospital, they would intercept it and overpower the driver. Booth's first kidnapping plot had been to nab Lincoln while he rode between the White House and Soldiers' Home. Campbell Military Hospital was not far from Soldiers' Home. The same post-abduction plan Booth had implemented with Dr. Mudd's assistance the previous December, carrying Lincoln through lower Maryland to a boat waiting near Nanjemoy Creek for crossing the lower Potomac, could still be used.

Booth, Arnold, and O'Laughlen rode out of Washington on Seventh Street toward the hospital. But Lincoln did not appear at the play. Either Booth's intelligence was faulty, or, as has recently been suggested, Booth knew Lincoln would not be there, and the attempt was a mere charade; Booth's real motive may have been to further implicate Arnold and O'Laughlen in the conspiracy so that they would have to think twice about withdrawing from it.[114]

The next day, Booth was performing in *The Apostate* as Pescara at Ford's Theatre.[115] It was the last performance he would ever give. It was not, however, the last time he would appear at Ford's Theatre.

No golden opportunity to capture Lincoln would ever again present itself to Booth and his accomplices.[116] As March bled into April, Booth reflected on another opportunity that had been lost—not for kidnapping, but for assassinating Lincoln—one that had presented itself on inauguration day, March 4, 1865.

In addition to plotting Lincoln's kidnapping, there is evidence that John Wilkes Booth was "bossing the job" for Lincoln's assassination at his second inaugural on March 4, 1865. Whether or not this is true, one fact is undeniable: Booth stood within shooting distance of Lincoln as he was being sworn in that day.

It has been reported that on Saturday, March 4, 1865, when the presidential procession was gathering in the Senate chamber prior to the inauguration ceremonies, a man attempted to force his way through the line of Capitol police, which had formed to insure order. The police were attempting to prevent the large number of persons who had gained access to the Capitol Rotunda from joining the presidential procession or reaching the outer door. But one man persisted. He forced his way through the ranks against the diligent efforts of one of the policemen on duty, John W. Westfall, to stop him.

Westfall reportedly grabbed the man, called for backup, and ordered the door-keeper to "[s]hut that door!" The doorkeeper complied, and the procession halted until, after a struggle, the intruder was reportedly overcome. The man was placed into custody downstairs in the guardroom, and, it is reported, was released after the inauguration ceremonies were over. The intruder, allegedly, was John Wilkes Booth.[117]

But either Westfall's story was a fabrication, or the man apprehended was not Booth, or, consummate actor that he was, Booth had talked his way out of the predicament. Reportedly, Booth had previously secured through Lucy Hale, a young woman with whom he was romantically linked, and also the daughter of Senator John P. Hale, an official pass to the Capitol stands for the inauguration ceremony.[118] Possibly the curious telegram Booth had sent to John Parker Hale Wentworth less than two weeks before had been for the same purpose—Wentworth was Lucy Hale's first cousin.[119]

Regardless of how he procured the official pass, Booth once again demon-strated his ability to put himself in the right place at the right time. Perhaps Booth, a well-known actor with a senator's pass in hand, was able to fabricate a plausible explanation for his determination to get near the procession. In any event, he was not in custody in the Capitol guardroom during the inaugura-tion ceremonies. A photograph taken that day unmistakably shows the mus-tachioed John Wilkes Booth, dressed in black and wearing a stovepipe hat, standing on a railed balcony at the east front of the Capitol, overlooking Lincoln as he gives his inaugural address. Even then, Booth was within clear pistol shot of the president.[120] But if Booth intended to assassinate Lincoln at the second inaugural, for reasons that will never be known, he held his fire.

One month later, on Friday, April 7, 1865, Booth was in New York. Here, at a saloon on Houston Street known as "The House of Lords," he boasted to fellow actor and Baltimore friend Samuel Knapp Chester[121]—another man Booth had previously attempted, unsuccessfully, to enlist in his Lincoln kid-napping plot—that he had been able to get dangerously near Lincoln at the inauguration. Recalled Chester, "We had not been there long before he exclaimed, striking the table, 'What an excellent chance I had to kill the President, if I had wished, on inauguration day!' He said he was as near the President on that day as he was to me."[122]

It would, perhaps, be easy to excuse the actions of John Wilkes Booth, his co-conspirators, and the Baltimore plotters, if plotters they were. Many Baltimoreans believed fervently, as had their forefathers, in "States Rights," and saw Lincoln as a despotic threat to such perceived rights—rights they believed their forefathers had fought, bled, and died for during the American Revolution. Moreover, Baltimoreans lived in a town and lived in a time that together served as a fulcrum and a focal point for a nation poised on a delicate balance between the perpetuity of the Union and the inalienability of states' rights, including the sovereign right of self-determination. But both of those laudable objectives—perpetuity of the Union and sovereignty of the states—would eventually submit, as inanimate ideals eventually must, to the most paramount of all rights, the most perpetual of all truths of a just and free society—that all persons are created equal.

It would also be easy to blame Abraham Lincoln, the North, and the South for the bloody war that sought to determine, by the power of force, each side's vision of what it means to be a free nation. It took four years of a bloody civil war to resolve what should instead have been immediately apparent to all by the power of the pen and the force of reason—that in any serious contest between the rights of the state and the rights of the individual to life, liberty, and the pursuit of happiness, the former must yield to the latter. Were it otherwise, ours would not be a government of "We the People."

But excusing the Baltimore plotters' actions would justify "tyrannicide," a perversion in a democratic society that empowers a rebellious few to reverse the verdict of the ballot, cast by millions, with the verdict of the bullet, cast by one. And blaming those responsible for pursuing the War of the Rebellion rather than averting it through compromise, concession, or Constitutional amendment does nothing but view with the clarity of hindsight an "irrepressible conflict" that 150 years ago must, ironically, have presented itself as a much more obscure picture.

And yet, looking back with hindsight has its appeal, for it allows us to imagine, "what if?" What might have been, had Abraham Lincoln not been warned of the Baltimore Plot, or if, despite that warning, he had determined not to heed it? How might the rising tide of events that would shape the nation's future, leaving in its wake a foundational cornerstone of its past, been turned? Would justice for all persons merely have been further delayed? Or would it have been forever denied?

What might have been, had federal authorities pursued the suspected Baltimore plotters, rather than letting them go, allowing them to bleed into the Confederacy, permitting men like Louis Wigfall, like William Byrne, and ultimately men like Marshal Kane and John Breckinridge to just slip away? Might John Wilkes Booth himself have been caught in the dragnet? Would a trial of those who had allegedly conspired to assassinate Lincoln have convinced the president that he owed it to his nation, to his family, to himself, to take reasonable precautions for his personal safety? Might such a trial have convinced the president of the folly of entering a private box at Ford's Theatre without any security detail and without posting even a single guard at the door, on the evening of April 14, 1865?

Of course, none of these questions can be answered, even with the clarity of hindsight. Lincoln was warned of the Baltimore Plot. He did heed those warnings. And perhaps still regretting that move even four years later, he did enter an unguarded box at Ford's Theatre at around 8:30 on the evening of April 14, 1865.

Unlike the morning on which Lincoln had arrived, in disguise, in Washington just over four years earlier, on this night he arrived in plain view. Unlike his arrival four years earlier, tonight neither Ward Hill Lamon nor Allan Pinkerton stood by his side. Lamon, who on prior occasions was said to have watched Lincoln like a mother hen, patrolling the White House grounds at night and even sleeping on the floor outside the president's bedroom, had gone to Richmond. Pinkerton was in New Orleans on private business. How might the mighty course of history have been changed had at least one of these two stalwart protectors been here, with Lincoln, tonight?

It might also have been well for men like Elmer Ellsworth, or Pinkerton's best agent, Timothy Webster, or General Scott's handpicked bodyguard, Colonel Edwin Vose Sumner, or Captain George W. Hazzard to have been here for Lincoln this evening, as they had been while his train steamed from Springfield toward Washington in February 1861. But by April 14, 1865, all of these men were long dead. All but Sumner, who died of natural causes in March 1863, had been casualties of the war.

Hazzard died in August 1862 from injuries suffered at the battle of White Oak Swamp.

Ellsworth was cut down in May 1861 in the flower of youth while storming a rebel hotel in Alexandria, Virginia, pursuing the militarily vital objective of a Confederate flag flying from the roof. Next to the raw recruits who had died in Baltimore as a result of the April 19 riot, Ellsworth was one of the first Union soldiers killed in the war. Lincoln mourned Ellsworth's loss like that of a son.

Timothy Webster was hanged—twice—for spying, in Richmond on April 29, 1862. On the first attempt, the knot slipped, dropping Pinkerton's best operative to the ground. "I suffer a double death!" Webster was heard to cry out as he faced the noose again.[123] On the second attempt, the knot held. Timothy Webster was gone.

Tonight, Lincoln had entered Ford's Theatre with his wife and one lone soldier, more social companion than bodyguard, Major Henry R. Rathbone, and his fiancée, Miss Clara Harris. Mary Todd Lincoln had, four years earlier, joined her husband on the journey that had brought him here, resolving to see him to Washington "danger or no danger." Tonight, they sat side by side in the president's box. Lincoln held Mary's hand. Perhaps they thought of another passenger on the Lincoln Special who was no longer with them. Their darling son Willie had died within a year of arriving in Washington.

Like a perfect storm, the opportunity for the crime of the century had presented itself. Lincoln, who had regretted his secret passage through Baltimore four years earlier, had shunned bodyguards throughout his presidency, often riding unescorted and at night along the desolate stretch between the White House and Soldiers' Home. On one such ride his top hat was shot from his head.

A few minutes after 10:00 p.m., a man so well known at Ford's Theatre that he would have needed neither a ticket nor an explanation ascended the stairs and slipped into the vestibule outside the president's box.

Using techniques more like those of a spymaster than a stage actor, John Wilkes Booth barred the outer door to the vestibule with a perfectly sized plank of wood that he had likely placed there earlier that day, wedging one end against the door, the other into a carefully mortised hole in the plaster hidden behind a flap of wallpaper on the opposite wall. Next, he peered through a peephole that he likely had bored through one of the panels in the door that led to the box. The target of Booth's hatred—the gutless tyrant who had snuck through Baltimore, then strangled it with martial law, Marshal Kane's arrest, and Union occupation, and then suppressed his beloved Maryland's ability to secede with the despotic imprisonment of its legislators—was clearly visible, just four feet away. The only thing between Booth and the president was one more door.[124] Booth knew that door would be open. On a prior occasion, likely the night of the March 15 performance, Booth had noticed that the latching mechanism was in such a state of disrepair as to make the door impossible to fasten.[125]

With the silence of a cat, John Wilkes Booth gripped the porcelain knob. The door to the president's box opened, as he knew it would. Booth opened the door in the name of vengeance, in the name of self-aggrandizement, in the name of meting out retribution on a man who had liberated millions and yet was branded a tyrant. Booth stepped inside the dimly lit box. The gaslights hissed.

And then John Wilkes Booth—the same man who was at John Brown's hanging; the same man who in December 1860 had written that now was the time to crush the abolition serpent in its birth; the same man who was allegedly present at the treasonous April 19-20, 1861, bridge-burning incident north of Baltimore; the same man who had declared Baltimore's traitorous marshal George P. Kane for a friend and had sought him out in Canada; the same man who in fact had conspired with Baltimore colleagues at Barnum's Hotel in 1864 to abduct Lincoln; the same man who had rued the lost opportunity to shoot Lincoln while he stood steps away from the president at his second inauguration—prepared to close the door. He prepared to close the door on tolerance. Prepared to close the door on forgiveness. Prepared to close the door on reconciliation and on hope.

But John Wilkes Booth still had one last opportunity to change his mind. He might turn around and walk back out the door. Or he might have a change of heart, perhaps even introduce himself to the president, who had seen him on stage at least once before. Booth's performance that night, as if to insult Lincoln, had been uncharacteristically flat. But Lincoln would have remembered him and probably with kindhearted compliments.[126]

Yes, Booth might still quit the conspiracy. He might hurry from Ford's Theatre, jump on the horse he had waiting for him in the alley outside, and race to recall his co-conspirators, one of whom, George Atzerodt, he had dispatched to murder Vice President Johnson, the other, Lewis Powell, he had ordered to assassinate Secretary of State William Seward. John Wilkes Booth might go on with his promising young life and allow so many others to go on with theirs.

There was still time. Time to change his mind. Time to walk away. Time to go back out that door. Perhaps, in the anxious seconds as he stood in the dim box, John Wilkes Booth replayed in his mind the things he had written, the things he had spoken, and the things he had thought of doing before. What would he do now? What should he do now?

The war was almost over. The Union was all but restored. Slavery was all but abolished. And the architect of it all, Abraham Lincoln, was at the zenith of his presidency. No longer in the prime of his mortal life, he was by any measure at the peak of his political one. Against the odds, he had won reelection after Atlanta had fallen. Then Richmond fell. And just a few days ago, Lee had surrendered to Grant. Everything was falling into place at last.

But one man's victory is another man's loss; so too with nations at war. The country John Wilkes Booth had loved was all but defeated, its way of life all but gone. Was it mere fate that had put him in this place, at the point of the spear, in this time, with this momentous opportunity? Was it mere fate that now made it seem all too easy, almost scripted? Was it luck? Coincidence? Or was it something else? Might the golden opportunity Booth now possessed have been but the inevitable culmination of an ongoing, relentless, irrepressible series of interconnected and previously unsuccessful plots and conspiracies to kill Lincoln that had begun in Baltimore four years earlier?

Just steps away now, with his back to the door, Abraham Lincoln sat peacefully in his chair, relishing the moment, with his wife at his side, holding her hand. Clutching a Deringer pistol in one hand and a menacing bowie camp knife in the other, John Wilkes Booth of Baltimore quietly closed the door.

NOTES

CHAPTER I

1 David C. Mearns, *The Lincoln Papers* (Garden City, N.Y.: Doubleday, 1948), vol. 1, p. 304.

2 U.S. Constitution, art. 2, sect. 4.

3 See generally George William Brown, *Baltimore and the Nineteenth of April, 1861* (Baltimore: Johns Hopkins University Press, 2001; originally published, Baltimore: N. Murray, 1887); Thomas Scharf, *History of Maryland* (Hatboro, Pa.: Tradition Press, 1967; reprint of 1879 edition), vol. 3.

4 See generally Sanford H. Kadish and Monrad G. Paulsen, *Criminal Law and Its Processes*, 3rd ed. (Boston: Little, Brown, 1975), pp. 87-99.

5 Ibid.

6 Ibid., pp. 416-495; Henry Campbell Black, *Black's Law Dictionary*, 5th ed. (St. Paul: West Publishing Co., 1979), pp. 34, 280, 889.

7 *Black's Law Dictionary*, pp. 337 and 914.

8 William H. Herndon and Jesse W. Weik, *Abraham Lincoln: The True Story of a Great Life* (New York: D. Appleton, 1930), vol. 2, p. 306.

9 *American Annual Cyclopædia and Register of Important Events of the Year 1861* (New York: D. Appleton, 1870), vol. 1, p. 196.

10 Letter of Abraham Lincoln to Erastus Corning and others (Copy No. 2), June 1863, Abraham Lincoln Papers at the Library of Congress. The view that the South had been preparing for secession for thirty years was shared by others, and essentially admitted by South Carolina, in 1860-61. Maryland's Governor Hicks, for example, declared as much in response to a call from secessionist Maryland legislators for a special convention to decide whether Maryland should cast her lot with the United States or the Confederacy. In his address, Hicks railed against secession as leading inevitably to civil war. He asked, rhetorically, what good would convening the legislature do to solve such a crisis? "We are told by the leading spirits of the South Carolina Convention that neither the election of Mr. Lincoln nor the non-execution of the Fugitive Slave law, nor both combined, constitute their grievances. They declare that the real cause of their discontent dates as far back as 1833." *American Annual Cyclopædia*, vol. 1, p. 443.

11 Charles Eugene Hamlin, *The Life and Times of Hannibal Hamlin* (Cambridge, Mass.: Riverside Press, 1899), p. 376.

12 Carl Sandburg, *Abraham Lincoln: The War Years* (New York: Harcourt, Brace, 1940), vol. 1, pp. 106-107.

13 Ibid.; William C. Davis, *Brother Against Brother: The War Begins* (Alexandria, Va.: Time-Life Books, 1983), p. 78.

14 For a more detailed description of the Bleeding Kansas events, upon which this section relies heavily, see Davis, *Brother Against Brother,* pp. 70-79.

15 *The Conspiracy to Break Up the Union: The Plot and Its Development* (Washington, D.C.: Lemuel Towers, 1860), p. 2.

16 This, according to the philanthropist Dorothea Dix, who in the months leading up to the war had visited the Border States and apparently taken an informal straw poll. "I *know* that quite 2/3 of the Southern vote is for the Union" Dix wrote in January 1860. Thomas J. Brown, *Dorothea Dix, New England Reformer* (Cambridge, Mass.: Harvard University Press, 1998), p. 272.

17 See, e.g., *American Annual Cyclopædia*, vol. 1, p. 473, reporting the following argument by a Mississippi anti-secessionist: "There is no wrong if we are united that we cannot remedy under the Constitution, and no right that it cannot protect. Our safety, our existence, now depends upon the integrity of that instrument. The moment we throw off the restrains of the Constitution, surrendering to the North our rights in the territories, our interests in the public domain—in our courts, our navy and our army, and our Federal Treasury—that moment we are doomed to destruction. Secession can afford no palliation for our wrongs; it can only precipitate us into greater evils, as we must forfeit all our rights under the Constitution when we leave the Union and give to our Northern foes all they need to render their aggressive policy more effective." See also p. 337, relating to Georgia's selection of delegates for the upcoming state convention on secession, urging the people of Georgia to require every candidate to that convention to take "a distinct position against immediate State secession, at least until a proper effort of cooperation had failed."

18 Brown, *Dorothea Dix*, p. 272.

19 Evidence that Lincoln had, at the time of his election, no intention of abolishing or otherwise interfering with slavery in the South is shown in a letter he wrote on December 22, 1860, to Alexander H. Stephens of Georgia, who would later become vice president of the Confederate States: "I fully appreciate the present peril the country is in and the weight of responsibility on me. Do the people of the South really entertain fears that a Republican administration would, directly or indirectly, interfere with the slaves? If they do, I wish to assure you, as once a friend, and still, I hope, not an enemy, that there is no cause for such fears. The South would be in no more danger in this respect than it was in the days of Washington. I suppose, however, this does not meet the case. You think slavery is right and ought to be extended, while we think it is wrong and ought to be restricted. That I suppose is the rub. It certainly is the only substantial difference between us." John G. Nicolay, *A Short Life of Abraham Lincoln* (New York: Century, 1902), pp. 165-166.

20 Benjamin J. Lossing, *Pictorial Field Book of the Civil War* (Baltimore: Johns Hopkins University Press, 1997), vol. 3, p. 97.

21 Even prior to Lincoln's election, the South was itching for a fight so badly that many Southerners actually *hoped* Lincoln would win, thereby providing a pretext for secession and eventual war for which some had been plotting as long as thirty years. For example, in a passionately worded letter to New York banker, cotton and guano merchant, erstwhile slave importer, and Confederate arms shipper Gazaway Bugg Lamar, his son, Charles A. L. Lamar wrote from Savannah on November 5, 1860, the day before Lincoln's election, of his intent to organize a military company and order arms with the approval of Georgia's governor Joseph Emerson Brown: "We shall have disunion certain if Lincoln is elected. . . . I am about to organize a company—Gov. Brown approves it, & says, I can order the Arms & pay for them & he will refund the money out of the 1st appropriation for the purchase of Arms—The Legislature meets on the 7th & that will be the first thing they will do—I have ordered 100 pistols & 100 sabres this day of Saml Colt Hartford. I am going to have 4

pieces of cannon attached. . . . *I hope Lincoln may be elected. I want dissolution, & have I think contributed more than any man South for it.*" Charles A. L. Lamar to Gazaway Bugg Lamar, November 5, 1860, Microfilm Reel 400, Special Collections, Manuscript, Archives, and Rare Book Library, Emory University Woodruff Library, Atlanta (emphasis added).

22 *American Annual Cyclopædia,* vol. 1, p. 410. Lincoln received 1,866,452 popular votes out of 4,680,193 votes cast; Douglas, 1,375,157; Breckinridge, 847,953; and Bell, 590,630. Scharf, *History of Maryland,* p. 356.

23 John T. Willis, *Presidential Elections in Maryland* (Mt. Airy, Md.: Lomond Publications, 1984), p. 55; Charles L. C. Minor, *The Real Lincoln* (Gatsonia, N.C.: Atkins-Rankin, 1928), p. 145, citing Josiah Gilbert Holland, *Life of Abraham Lincoln* (Springfield, Mass.: Gurdon Bill, 1866), p. 296. In some of the seceded states, such as Alabama and Texas, Lincoln received not one vote. *American Annual Cyclopædia,* vol. 1, pp. 9 and 689. Breckinridge, the pro-slavery candidate, narrowly defeated Bell in Maryland, garnering all of her eight electoral votes. Willis, *Presidential Elections in Maryland,* p. 55.

24 Courtney B. Wilson and Shawn Cunningham, *The Baltimore Civil War Museum, President Street Station: A Visitor's Guide* (Baltimore: Baltimore Civil War Museum, President Street Station, 1997), p. 11. See also *American Annual Cyclopædia,* vol. 1, p. 445.

25 George L. P. Radcliffe, *Governor Thomas H. Hicks of Maryland and the Civil War* (Baltimore: The Lord Baltimore Press, 1901), p. 19.

26 Ibid., p. 23, citing the *Baltimore American,* December 3, 1860, and the *Baltimore Sun,* November 24, 1860.

27 Abraham Lincoln to Erastus Corning and others (Copy No. 2) June 1863.

28 Charles Winslow Elliott, *Winfield Scott: The Soldier and the Man* (New York: Macmillan, 1937), p. 690 n. 35.

29 See, e.g., Minor, *The Real Lincoln,* p. 145, citing General Butler's book at page 220, "the capture and occupation of Washington would have almost insured the Confederacy at once a place by recognition as a power among the nations of the earth." See also *Daily Pittsburgh Gazette,* January 7, 1861.

30 Radcliffe, *Governor Thomas H. Hicks of Maryland,* pp. 43-44.

31 Frederick W. Seward, *Seward at Washington, 1846-1861* (New York: Derby and Miller, 1891), p. 502.

32 Radcliffe, *Governor Thomas H. Hicks of Maryland,* p. 30.

33 Thomas H. Hicks to James L. Dorsey, March 5, 1859, Accession No. 50531, MS 1263, Maryland Historical Society, Baltimore.

34 Radcliffe, *Governor Thomas H. Hicks of Maryland,* p. 34.

35 James C. Welling to Thomas H. Hicks, December 21, 1860, Accession No. 47948, MS 1313, Maryland Historical Society, Baltimore.

36 *American Annual Cyclopædia,* vol. 1, p. 443.

37 See Radcliffe, *Governor Thomas H. Hicks of Maryland,* p. 27.

38 Ibid., p. 17, citing House Documents (Md. 1860), Document KK; Senate Documents (Md.), 1860- Document CC. Note, however, that Baltimore's Mayor Brown, in his inaugural address, declared that "The policy of Maryland is to adhere to the Union." Ibid., p. 19.

39 Ibid., pp. 19-20, 47.

40 Maryland's population in 1860 comprised 516,128 whites, 83,718 free African Americans, and 87,188 slaves. *American Annual Cyclopædia*, vol. 1, p. 442.

41 Scharf, *History of Maryland,* p. 361.

42 Mearns, *Lincoln Papers*, vol. 2, p. 588.

43 Radcliffe, *Governor Thomas H. Hicks of Maryland*, p. 34. Georgia's A. R. Wright would be the last Southern emissary to visit Hicks. Ibid., p. 49.

44 *American Annual Cyclopædia*, vol. 1, pp. 442-443.

45 George S. Bryan, *The Great American Myth* (New York: Carrick & Evans, 1940), p. 17.

46 Radcliffe, *Governor Thomas H. Hicks of Maryland, p.* 26.

47 Elliott, *Winfield Scott*, p. 690 n. 35.

48 Radcliffe, *Governor Thomas H. Hicks of Maryland*, p. 35, n.

49 Palmer would also greet Lincoln upon his arrival in Harrisburg on February 22, 1861. Bradley Hoch, *The Lincoln Trail in Pennsylvania: A History and Guide* (University Park: Pennsylvania State University Press, 2001), p. 17.

50 Letter from Alexander K. McClure to Abraham Lincoln, January 15, 1861, Abraham Lincoln Papers at the Library of Congress.

51 *Daily Pittsburgh Gazette*, January 8, 1861 (emphasis added).

52 Radcliffe, *Governor Thomas H. Hicks of Maryland*, p. 33.

53 One of these pleas to Hicks was found among the Felton Papers. On April 17, 1861, a Delaware slave owner, William H. Ross, warned Hicks of an anonymous tip from a New York merchant of Virginia birth that "the Republican party mean a cruel war with the South, for the express purpose of creating Negro insurrection and the liberation of all our slaves." The writer pleaded with Hicks to consider "little Delaware," and the fact it would, if Maryland and Virginia seceded, go out with them. He claimed to be one of the largest holders of slaves in the state, and fretted that civil war would mean his financial ruin, in part because of his investments in Virginia, Tennessee, and Missouri state bonds, which would soon be worthless. He also feared that the protection of slaves offered by the North would be "the kind of protection which the wolf gives to the lamb." Despite Ross's injunction to consider the letter in strict confidence, Hicks sent a copy of it to Samuel Morse Felton. Felton Papers (no. 1151), Box 1, Folder 4, Historical Society of Pennsylvania, 1300 Locust Street, Philadelphia.

54 Alexander K. McClure to Abraham Lincoln, January 15, 1861.

55 Ibid. Possibly referring to E. G. Kilbourn, speaker of the Maryland legislature. Radcliffe, *Governor Thomas H. Hicks of Maryland*, pp. 24-25.

56 See proclamation of Thomas H. Hicks to the people of Maryland, dated April 18, 1861: "The people of this State will, in a short time, have the opportunity afforded them in a special election for members of the Congress of the United States to express their devotion to the Union or their desire to see it broken up." *American Annual Cyclopædia*, vol. 1, p. 444.

57 Hoch, *Lincoln Trail*, p. 80.

58 See generally *American Annual Cyclopædia*, vol. 1, pp. 55, 442.

59 In the November 1860 election, Lincoln received 1,866,452 of the 4,680,193 votes cast. Because, however, he carried the most populous states, including all the Northern states

(except for splitting New Jersey with Douglas)—California, Connecticut, Illinois, Indiana, Iowa, Maine, Massachusetts, Michigan, Minnesota, New Hampshire, New Jersey (4), New York, Ohio, Oregon, Pennsylvania, Rhode Island, Vermont, and Wisconsin—he controlled 180 electoral votes to John C. Breckenridge's 72, John Bell's 39, and Stephen Douglas's 12. In contrast, Lincoln had virtually no support in the Southern states, and in several received not a single vote. In Maryland, he received only 2,294 of the total 92,441 votes cast, a paltry 2.5 percent. Scharf, *History of Maryland*, p. 356.

60 See, e.g., Timothy Webster's report, dated February 26, 1861, in Norma B. Cuthbert, ed., *Lincoln and the Baltimore Plot, 1861, from Pinkerton Records and Related Papers* (San Marino, Calif.: Huntington Library, 1949), p. 99.

61 See letter of Thomas H. Hicks to Abraham Lincoln, May 26, 1862, Maryland Historical Society, Baltimore.

62 Radcliffe, *Governor Thomas H. Hicks of Maryland*, p. 20.

63 Ibid., p. 15.

64 Facsimile in the Ward Hill Lamon Papers, Box 1, Huntington Library; Radcliffe, *Governor Thomas H. Hicks of Maryland*, p. 20. Hicks's reference to "Harford" may mean Harford County, the county of Bel Air, location of the farm of John Wilkes Booth's father. It was in this county that secessionist rangers would drill in January and February of 1861, allegedly intent on preventing Lincoln's passage through, and/or to prevent the passage of Northern troops to the South.

65 John W. Forney, *Anecdotes of Public Men* (New York: Harper & Brothers, 1873), p. 248 (emphasis added).

66 Seward, *Seward at Washington,* p. 502.

67 Mearns, *Lincoln Papers*, vol. 1, p. 296.

68 *CW,* 4:132 (emphasis added). See Searcher, *Lincoln's Journey to Greatness*, p. 9.

69 Mearns, *Lincoln Papers*, vol. 1, p. 298.

70 David Hunter to Abraham Lincoln, December 20, 1860, in Mearns, *The Lincoln Papers*, vol. 2, p. 346-347. "Wide Awakes" was a term given to the torch-lit processions of young Republicans, originally volunteer firemen, who first organized such clubs in 1860 to draw people to political rallies. "With an inexpensive but effective equipment of glazed cap and cape, and a lighted torch, they drilled and marched, executing manœuvres with military precision to the sound of martial music. It was a novelty that enlivened the tedium of speech-making, and drew crowds to attend political meetings, that otherwise would have kept aloof." Seward, *Seward at Washington*, p. 461; Donald, *Lincoln*, p. 254. The glazed caps and oilcloth capes protected the Wide Awakes from the sparks of their own torches. Burlingame, ed., *Lincoln's Journalist,* p. 346 n. 2.

71 William E. Doster, *Lincoln and Episodes of the Civil War* (New York: G. P. Putnam's Sons, 1915), p. 60.

CHAPTER 2

1 There are those, for example, who claim that the Civil War had nothing to do with slavery; it was all about "states' rights." This argument merely cloaks the real issue—slavery—in a more patriotic cloth woven of a more constitutionally defensible yarn. It also ignores voluminous contrary evidence, some of which will be presented subsequently.

2 See J. C. Furnas, *The Americans: A Social History of the United States, 1587-1914* (New York: G. P. Putnam's Sons, 1969), p. 115 n. 106.

3 Even as of the date of this writing, 2008, America had lived with slavery 244 years, compared with 143 years without it.

4 See, e.g., *American Annual Cyclopædia,* vol. 1, p. 130.

5 Sandburg, *Abraham Lincoln: The War Years,* vol. 1, p. 105.

6 Speech of A. H. Stephens, vice president of the C.S.A., given in Savannah on his return from the Confederate Convention, Horace Greeley, *The American Conflict: A History of the Great Civil War in the United States of America, 1860-1864* (London: Bacon, 1865), vol. 1, p. 417.

7 U.S. Constitution, art. 1, sect. 2, clause 3, provides: "Representatives and direct Taxes shall be apportioned among the several States which may be included within this Union, according to their respective Numbers, which shall be determined by adding to the whole Number of free Persons, including those bound to Service for a Term of Years, and excluding Indians not taxed, three fifths of all other Persons."

8 Ibid., art. 4, sect. 2, clause 3. The problem with using this clause to justify slavery is that it refers to "Persons," not "property," and would apply equally to escaped white prisoners and escaped slaves.

9 The argument falls apart with the realization that Congressional representation is not awarded for three-fifths of a plow horse or a cow.

10 U.S. Constitution, art. 5.

11 *Journal of the Convention of the State of Arkansas* (Little Rock, Ark.: Johnson & Yerkes, 1861), pp. 131-132.

12 Ibid., p. 132.

13 In 1860, the population of the states that would ultimately secede— Alabama, Arkansas, Florida, Georgia, Louisiana, Mississippi, North Carolina, South Carolina, Tennessee, Texas, and Virginia—totaled 5,450,711 whites and 3,520,902 slaves, as well as a small number of free African Americans. In Mississippi and South Carolina, slaves actually outnumbered whites; in South Carolina the ratio was a little over 4:3. *American Annual Cyclopædia,* vol. 1, p. 130. Because a slave counted only as three-fifths of a person, the 3.5 million slaves in the seceded states contributed only 2.1 million persons toward congressional representation, leaving 1.4 million uncounted for that purpose. Had these persons been free, they would have contributed to increasing the congressional representation of the seceded states by nearly twenty percent. As a practical matter, however, even a 20 percent increase in congressional representation would have made little difference—the North had far too many people, roughly 25 million to the South's 9 million.

14 Southern leaders claimed, however, that even nonslaveholders in the South supported slavery and hence secession. It was said that nonslaveholding Southerners feared the day when millions of slaves would be freed. The argument went that when that day came, wealthy Southern slave owners would flee the country, leaving the poorer nonslaveholding Southerners to fend for themselves against the retribution of millions of loosed slaves. Alvy L. King, *Louis T. Wigfall: Southern Fire-eater* (Baton Rouge: Louisiana State University Press, 1970), p. 109 n. 61.

15 Louis T. Wigfall, *Speech of Hon. Louis T. Wigfall, of Texas, in Reply to Mr. Douglas, Delivered in the Senate of The United States, December 11th and 12th, 1860* (Washington, D.C.: Lemuel Towers, 1860), p. 12.

16 Ibid., p. 13.

17 King, *Louis T. Wigfall*, p. 3.

18 Ibid., pp. 30-35.

19 Mrs. D. Girard Wright[Louise Wigfall, daughter of Senator Wigfall], *A Southern Girl in '61: The War-Time Memories of a Confederate Senator's Daughter* (New York: Doubleday, Page, 1905), p. 31.

20 See generally ibid., pp. 3-9.

21 King, p. 77.

22 Rumor is not fact, and with few exceptions is inadmissible to prove anything in court. But even rumor gives reason to suspect and to investigate further. Moreover, rumor, in the form of the defendant's reputation in the community, is sometimes admissible to rebut the claims of a defendant's "character witness" that he enjoys a good reputation, e.g., for truthfulness.

23 Floyd resigned December 29, 1860; Thompson resigned January 8, 1861; and Thomas, January 11, 1861. *American Annual Cyclopædia,* vol. 1, pp. 701-704.

24 U.S. War Department, *The War of Rebellion: A Compilation of the Official Records of the Union and Confederate Armies* (Washington, D.C.: Government Printing Office, 1880–1901) (cited hereafter as *OR* followed by series and volume number), series 1, vol. 1, p. 252.

25 Per J. G. Foster to General Totten, January 9, 1861, *OR* 1:1, p. 136.

26 *OR* 1:1, p. 253.

27 *Fort Sumter: Anvil of War*, National Park Service Handbook (Washington, D.C.: U.S. Department of the Interior), p. 21; *OR* 1:1 pp. 134-136. Ironically foreshadowing Northern military bungling during the early stages of the war, while South Carolina's Governor Pickens had gotten Wigfall's intelligence that *The Star of the West* was on its way to Fort Sumter with reinforcements, Major Anderson failed to be similarly informed by the U.S. military. Thus, when the vessel came under fire at Charleston harbor, Major Anderson was unaware of the reinforcements she had brought for him, and therefore "did not feel the force of the obligation to protect her approach as [he] would naturally have done had this information reached [him]." Ibid., p.140.

28 King, *Louis T. Wigfall*, p. 113; Roy Franklin Nichols, *The Disruption of American Democracy* (New York: Macmillan, 1948), p. 501.

29 See, e.g., William A. Tidwell, with James O. Hall and David Winfred Gaddy, *Come Retribution: The Confederate Secret Service and the Assassination of Lincoln* (Jackson: University Press of Mississippi, 1988), p. 228.

30 *New York Evening Post*, March 27, 1862. Clipping enclosed in a letter dated April 6, 1862, from Joseph Hazzard to S. M. Felton, Felton Papers (no. 1151), Box 2, Folder 1.

31 King, *Louis T. Wigfall*, p. 107 n. 55; and pp. 110-111 nn. 66 and 67.

32 Ibid., p. 100.

33 Edwin V. Sumner to Abraham Lincoln, December 17, 1860, Abraham Lincoln Papers at the Library of Congress.

34 Asia Booth Clarke, *John Wilkes Booth: A Sister's Memoir*, ed. Terry Alford, (Jackson: University Press of Mississippi, 1996), p. 82. As early as December 1860, J. Wilkes Booth predicted the dire consequences of a civil war in writing to a Northern audience a speech he would never give: "You would hate and envy the confederation of the south. You would say she is weak in numbers, we are strong. We will force her to submit and once more restore the union. The South will call in the powers of Europe. Fearce Civil War will follow. And then, what then." John Wilkes Booth, *"Right or Wrong, God Judge Me": The Writings of John Wilkes Booth*, ed. John Rhodehamel and Louise Taper (Urbana: University of Illinois Press, 1997), p. 61.

35 Abraham Lincoln to Erastus Corning and others (Copy No. 2), June 1863.

36 *American Annual Cyclopaedia*, p. 166.

37 Ibid., p. 168.

38 Wigfall, *Speech of Hon. Louis T. Wigfall*, p. 21.

39 Jefferson Davis to George Lunt, January 17, 1861, in *The Papers of Jefferson Davis*, vol. 7, p.14.

40 Even Alexander H. Stephens conceded that Thomas Jefferson and other architects of the Constitution anticipated that slavery would eventually fade away. Following his selection as vice president of the Confederacy, Stephens spoke to a Savannah crowd, saying "[slavery] was an evil they knew not well how to deal with; but the general opinion of the men of that day was, that, somehow or other, in the order of Providence, the institution would be evanescent and pass away. This idea, though not incorporated in the Constitution, was the prevailing idea at the time." Spouting racist rhetoric, Stephens concluded that such ideas were fundamentally wrong: *"They rested upon an assumption of the equality of races. This was an error."* Greeley, *The American Conflict*, p. 417.

41 Ibid., pp. 417-418.

42 Rodehamel, John, and Louie Taper, eds., *Right or Wrong, God Judge Me*, p. 64.

43 John G. Nicolay and John Hay, *Abraham Lincoln: A History* (New York: Century, 1890), vol. 3, p. 308.

44 Marquis James, *They Had Their Hour* (Indianapolis: Bobbs-Merrill, 1934), p. 144.

45 Examples include the Election Riot (1752), the Whig Club Riot (1777), Lee's Mob (1778), the Embargo Riot (1794), the Geneva Gin Riot (1808), the Mob of 1812, and the Maryland Bank Riot (1835). Frank B. Marcotte, *Six Days in April: Lincoln and the Union in Peril* (New York: Algora, 2005), p. 32; Scharf, *History of Maryland*, pp. 23-24.

46 Violence in many American cities prevailed in the mid-1800s, as handguns proliferated and populations grew; Baltimore was thus not unique in that regard. It was, however, the duration, degradation, and depravity of its violence that set Baltimore apart from other American cities.

47 Scharf, *History of Maryland*, p. 12 n. 1.

48 Ibid., p. 17 n. 1.

49 Marcotte, *Six Days in April*, pp. 31-32; Scharf, *History of Maryland*, pp. 6-17.

50 Scharf, *History of Maryland*, pp. 282-283.

51 Ibid., pp. 251-252.

52 See generally Tracy Matthew Melton, *Hanging Henry Gambrill: The Violent Career of Baltimore's Plug Uglies, 1854-1860* (Baltimore: Maryland Historical Society, 2005).

53 J. Thomas Scharf, *History of Baltimore City and County* (Baltimore: Regional, 1971), vol. 1, pp. 126-127.

54 Worthington G. Snethen to Abraham Lincoln, November 3, 1860, Abraham Lincoln Papers at the Library of Congress.

55 George S. Bryan, *The Great American Myth* (New York: Carrick & Evans, 1940) p. 41 at n. 44, citing the *New York Times*, March 5, 1857, p. 1.

56 Bryan, *The Great American Myth*, p. 41 at n. 43.

57 Noted Montgomery Blair, chairman of the first Maryland Republican State Convention in Baltimore on April 26, 1860, "The public mind in Maryland is not now ripe for emancipation, and no scheme for it has been proposed or discussed." Willis, *Presidential Elections in Maryland*, pp. 54-55.

58 Marcotte, *Six Days in April*, p. 161.

59 George W. Hazzard to Abraham Lincoln, January 1861, Abraham Lincoln Papers at the Library of Congress.

60 James, *They Had Their Hour*, p. 150; see also Bryan, *The Great American Myth*, p. 42.

61 See, e.g., Allan Pinkerton, report, February 15, 1861, in Cuthbert, *Lincoln and the Baltimore Plot*, pp. 34-35.

62 Greeley, *The American Conflict*, p. 420.

63 There exists evidence that the then embryonic Confederate leadership represented by members of states that had seceded, or soon would, including Jefferson Davis, Clement Clay, Judah P. Benjamin, and Senator Louis T. Wigfall, wanted to avoid, or at least delay, civil war if at all possible. In a January 15, 1861, letter to South Carolinian Isaac W. Hayne, these men exhorted South Carolina to tread lightly and not precipitate war, notwithstanding Major Anderson's occupation of Fort Sumter, at least until February 15, when a convention would be held in South Carolina. "We desire to see such an adjustment and to prevent War or the shedding of blood." Letter dated January 15, 1861, to Isaac W. Hayne, *Papers of Jefferson Davis*, vol. 7, pp.10-12.

64 Harold Holzer, ed., *Abraham Lincoln as I Knew Him: Gossip, Tributes and Revelations from His Best Friends and Worst Enemies* (Chapel Hill, N.C.: Algonquin, 1999), p. 110.

CHAPTER 3

1 According to one account, the Lincolns had abandoned their Springfield home the evening of February 9 and would stay at the Chenery House until Lincoln's departure February 11. Henry Villard, *Lincoln on the Eve of '61,* ed. Harold G. Villard and Oswald Garrison Villard (New York: Alfred Knopf, 1941), p. 69. By another account, the Lincolns had moved into the Chenery House on February 8. Bernhardt Wall, *Following Abraham Lincoln: 1809-1865* (New York: Wise-Parslow, 1943), p. 270.

2 Villard, *Lincoln on the Eve of '61,* pp. 70-71.

3 Herndon and Weik, *Abraham Lincoln*, vol. 2, p. 217.

4 Villard, *Lincoln on the Eve of '61*, pp. 50-51.

5 Mearns, *The Lincoln Papers,* p. 348.

6 Harold Holzer, ed., *Dear Mr. Lincoln: Letters to the President* (Reading, Mass.: Addison-Wesley, 1993), p. 340; see William Hanchett, *Out of the Wilderness: The Life of Abraham Lincoln* (Urbana: University of Illinois Press, 1994), p. 27, for a rendering of the Tinsley Building.

7 Holzer, *Dear Mr. Lincoln*, p. 342.

8 Ibid., p. 341.

9 Herndon and Weik, *Abraham Lincoln*, vol. 2, p. 195. Lincoln's friend and bodyguard, Ward Hill Lamon described it as "a gloomy day; heavy clouds floated overhead, and a cold rain was falling." Ward Hill Lamon [with Chauncey F. Black], *The Life of Abraham Lincoln: From His Birth to His Inauguration as President* (Boston: James R. Osgood, 1872), p. 505.

10 *Daily Pittsburgh Gazette*, February 12, 1861, p. 3.

11 John Hay, *Lincoln's Journalist: John Hay's Anonymous Writings for the Press, 1860-1864*, ed. Michael Burlingame (Carbondale: Southern Illinois University Press, 1998), p. 24. For a photograph of the Great Western depot and the first locomotive to pull the Lincoln Special, the *L. M. Wiley*, see Victor Searcher, *Lincoln's Journey to Greatness: A Factual Account of the Twelve-Day Inaugural Trip* (Philadelphia: John C. Winston, 1960). Nicolay and Hay referred to the depot as a "rather dingy little railroad station." *Abraham Lincoln: A History*, vol. 3, p. 290.

12 Burlingame, ed., *Lincoln's Journalist*, p. 24.

13 Villard, *Lincoln on the Eve of '61*, p. 71.

14 Nicolay and Hay, *Abraham Lincoln*, vol. 3, p. 290.

15 The engine had been built by the Hinkley Locomotive Works, Albany Street, Boston, in 1855, their 568th locomotive. Ironically, the engine had been named after L. M. Wiley, a director of the Great Western Railroad and a Charleston cotton plantation owner. The wood-burning locomotive had a huge balloon-shaped bonnet stack common during the era, and a 4-4-0 wheel arrangement—four leading wheels, four drive wheels, and no trailing wheels, then the most popular wheel arrangement for American locomotives. Searcher, *Lincoln's Journey to Greatness*, facing p. 56; John H. White Jr., *A History of the American Locomotive: Its Development: 1830-1880* (New York: Dover, 1979), pp. 33, 117.

16 See, e.g., John H. White Jr., *American Locomotives* (Baltimore: Johns Hopkins University Press, 1997), pp. 218-220.

17 Searcher, *Lincoln's Journey to Greatness*, facing p. 56.

18 See, e.g., *New York Times*, February 18, 1861, p. 8, ProQuest Historical Newspapers.

19 Villard, *Lincoln on the Eve of '61*, pp. 49-50.

20 Mearns, *The Lincoln Papers*, vol. 2, p.425.

21 Ibid., pp. 432-433.

22 Festus P. Summers, *The Baltimore and Ohio in the Civil War* (New York: G. P. Putnam's Sons, 1939), pp. 45-46. See also *Richmond Daily Enquirer*, February 28, 1860.

23 Summers, *The Baltimore and Ohio*, p. 46.

24 Horace Greeley to Abraham Lincoln, December 22, 1860, in Mearns, *The Lincoln Papers*, vol. 2, p. 349.

25 *American Annual Cyclopædia*, vol. 1, p. 750. Note that James G. Berret would arrive on

August 25, 1861, under arrest, at Fort Lafayette, where he remained until September 14. Ibid., p. 361.

26 Ibid., vol. 1, p. 750.

27 Lamon, *The Life of Abraham Lincoln*, p. 505.

28 Nicolay and Hay, *Abraham Lincoln*, vol. 3, p. 291; Villard, *Lincoln on the Eve of '61*, p. 71.

29 *Daily Pittsburgh Gazette*, February 12, 1861, p. 3.

30 Lamon, *The Life of Abraham Lincoln*, p. 506.

31 Because Lincoln made the speech without notes, the transcription of it varies. There is no definitive record of the text. The account presented here most certainly is not the exact words spoken, but draws favor for being at least partially scribbled down by Lincoln himself moments after he uttered the speech. This version of the speech was scrawled down in pencil just as the Lincoln Special pulled out. Henry Villard, who joined Lincoln on board, had found the speech "wonderfully moving," and urged Lincoln to record it, so it might be telegraphed from the next station and preserved for posterity. Lincoln complied, sitting in a coach seat with a pad of paper handed him by Nicolay. The first two lines are in a steady hand, which quickly deteriorates due to the train's jostling motion. Perhaps realizing the futility of his own shaking hand, Lincoln handed the pad back to Nicolay after the fourth sentence and dictated to him, beginning after the words "I now." The original document is in the Library of Congress. Villard's editors gave him the credit for inducing Lincoln to preserve the speech in writing while on the moving train, so that it could be telegraphed at the next stop. After the speech was recorded, Lincoln handed the manuscript to Villard, and then retreated to his private stateroom, "where he sat alone and depressed until called to address the crowds when the train stopped." Villard, *Lincoln on the Eve of '61*, p. 73; *CW,* 4:190; Searcher, *Lincoln's Journey to Greatness*, pp. 5-6.

Philadelphia Inquirer, February 12, 1861, p. 1.

32 *Daily Pittsburgh Gazette,* February 12, 1861, p. 3.

33. Ibid.

34 Burlingame, ed., *Lincoln's Journalist,* p. 24.

35 *Philadelphia Inquirer,* February 12, 1861, p. 1.

36 David Herbert Donald, *Lincoln* (London: Jonathan Cape, 1995), p. 273; *New York Times,* February 13, 1861, p. 1, ProQuest Historical Newspapers.

37 This telegram has not been found.

38 Burlingame, ed., *Lincoln's Journalist,* p. 24.

39 Jean H. Baker, *Mary Todd Lincoln* (New York: W. W. Norton, 1987), p. 164.

40 Villard, *Lincoln on the Eve of '61*, p. 53.

41 *New York Times,* February 13, 1861, p. 1, ProQuest Historical Newspapers.

42 Searcher, *Lincoln's Journey to Greatness*, p. 1; *Daily Pittsburgh Gazette,* February 12, 1861, p. 3. The Great Western timetable set 8:00 a.m. as the time for departure. Searcher, *Lincoln's Journey,* facing p. 56. Newspapers reported that the train left at 8:30 a.m. See, e.g., *Philadelphia Inquirer,* February 12, 1861, p. 1, and *New York Times,* February 12, 1861, both reporting that "The train left at precisely half past eight."

43 Herdon and Weik, *Abraham Lincoln*, vol. 2, p. 197.

44 The time card as reproduced in Searcher, *Lincoln's Journey*, facing p. 56.

45 Ibid., pp. 6-9.

46 Douglas L. Wilson and Rodney O. Davis, with Terry Wilson, *Herndon's Informants: Letters, Interviews, and Statements about Abraham Lincoln* (Urbana: University of Illinois Press, 1998), pp. 595-596; Herndon and Weik, *Abraham Lincoln*, vol. 2, p. 190.

47 See photo of Sarah Bush Lincoln in Charles Hamilton and Lloyd Ostendorf, *Lincoln in Photographs: An Album of Every Known Pose* (Norman: University of Oklahoma Press, 1963), p. 297.

48 Herndon and Weik, *Abraham Lincoln*, vol. 2, pp. 190-191.

49 Ibid., pp. 191-192.

50 Ibid., pp. 193-194.

51 Quote attributed to speech given to the Lawyers Club of Atlanta by Russell S. Bonds, author of *Stealing the General: The Great Locomotive Chase and the First Medal of Honor* (Philadelphia: Westholme Publishing, 2007).

52 Burlingame, ed., *Lincoln's Journalist*, p. 23.

53 For one of the more complete accounts of who made up the presidential suite, see ibid., pp. 352-353 n. 14.

54 The political friends are reported as: Norman B. Judd, Lincoln campaign manager and prominent Chicago attorney later to become Lincoln's minister to Prussia; David Davis, Eighth Circuit judge before whom Lincoln had appeared many times on the circuit, and whom he would later name a Supreme Court Justice; Ebenezer Peck, another Chicago attorney and campaign worker who would later be appointed to the Court of Claims; Orville H. Browning, former state senator from Quincy (after Stephen A. Douglas's untimely passing a few months later, Lincoln would recommend Browning to complete the unexpired Senate term); O. M. Hatch, Illinois secretary of state; Jesse K. Dubois, Illinois state auditor; John "Honest John" Moore, former Illinois governor; Richard Yates, incumbent Illinois governor. Searcher, *Lincoln's Journey to Greatness*, pp. 6-9.

55 The family members included, in addition to Robert, Lincoln's brother-in-law and personal physician, Dr. W. S. Wallace. Robert also brought along his Springfield chum George C. Latham. Ibid.

56 The journalists included: Henry Villard of the *New York Herald*, whose dispatches were used by the Associated Press; Henry M. Smith of the *Chicago Tribune*; and Edward L. Baker, editor of the *Illinois State Journal* (Springfield). Ibid. Joseph Howard Jr. of The *New York Times* and an anonymous embedded reporter for the *New York World* would also join the party.

57 The railroad employees on board when the train left Springfield are reported as: Lucian Tilton, Lincoln friend and president of the Great Western Railroad (Lincoln had leased him his Springfield house and sold him much of his furniture); F. W. Bowen, superintendent of the Great Western Railroad; Walter C. Whitney, conductor; Edward H. Fralick, engineer; Benjamin A. Gordon, fireman; Thomas Ross, brakeman; and Platt Williamson, baggagemaster. Searcher, *Lincoln's Journey*, pp. 6-9.

58 Francis Fisher Browne, *The Every-day Life of Abraham Lincoln* (New York: N. D. Thompson, 1887), p. 256.

59 *Philadelphia Inquirer,* February 22, 1861.

60 Ibid.

61 The opposition party members are reported as: William Butler; William H. Carlin; M. S. Cassell (or William Hassell); D. H. Gilmer; Jackson Grimshaw; J. A. (or G. A.) Hough; W. Jameson (or Jamieson); E. F. (or E. S.) Leonard. See Searcher, *Lincoln's Journey to Greatness,* pp. 6-9; See also *New York Times,* February 12, 1861, p. 1, ProQuest Historical Newspapers.

62 See, e.g., *New York Times,* February 12, 1861, p. 1, ProQuest Historical Newspapers.

63 Searcher, *Lincoln's Journey to Greatness,* pp. 6-9. There is some discrepancy as to which of the military men reported to be on board the Lincoln Special at the time of its departure were actually there. William S. Wood, superintendent of arrangements, in his circular of instructions anticipates Colonel Sumner, Major Hunter, and Captain Hazzard being on board when the Special departs. Sandburg, *Abraham Lincoln: The War Years,* vol. 1, p. 35. Herndon states that Colonel Sumner and "other army gentlemen" were also in the car. Searcher, however, reports that they would all join the train later: Sumner and Hunter at State Line (Indiana) and Pope and Hazzard at Indianapolis. Each of these four officers had volunteered their services and either obtained official leaves of absence from military service for the occasion or had other excuses for being on liberty for the trip—for example, Hazzard was on sick leave, extended. Pope was on detached service that permitted freedom of movement. Of these four, Hunter seems the most likely to have been on the train as it pulled out, as Villard's dispatch from Tolono, Illinois, indicates he was. Searcher notes, however, that Villard's dispatch is the only one to so indicate. Searcher, *Lincoln's Journey,* pp. 9–10.

64 *Philadelphia Inquirer,* February 22, 1861.

65 *American Annual Cyclopædia,* vol. 1, p. 722.

66 David Hunter to Abraham Lincoln, March 4, 1861, Abraham Lincoln Papers at the Library of Congress.

67 Colonel Sumner had earlier, possibly at Lincoln's urging, proposed to Hunter that he accompany the party on the Lincoln Special. Sumner wrote Lincoln that he and Hunter "are old officers and old friends, and if any difficulty should arise, which is barely possible, I should hope that we might be of some service to you." E. V. Sumner to Abraham Lincoln, December 17, 1860, in Mearns, *The Lincoln Papers,* vol. 2, pp. 343-344. See also letter dated December 18, 1860, from David Hunter to Abraham Lincoln, indicating that Lincoln's "kind invitation" had been "conveyed through Col. Sumner." Ibid., pp. 346-367.

68 Burlingame, ed., *Lincoln's Journalist,* p. 135.

69 *American Annual Cyclopædia,* vol. 1, p. 724.

70 *Philadelphia Inquirer,* February 22, 1861.

71 Ibid.

72 George W. Hazzard to Abraham Lincoln, November 5, 1860, Abraham Lincoln Papers at the Library of Congress; Searcher, *Lincoln's Journey to Greatness,* p. 9.

73 George W. Hazzard to Abraham Lincoln, July 11, 1860, Abraham Lincoln Papers at the Library of Congress. Note, however, that leading secessionists, such as Alabaman Yancey, allegedly wanted Lincoln to win and had set the Democratic Party up for the loss. Their supposed motive was to hurry the cotton ctates into secession under the pretext that they could not live under a government controlled by Lincoln.

74 *American Annual Cyclopædia,* vol. 1, p. 123.

75 George W. Hazzard to Abraham Lincoln, October 21, 1860, Abraham Lincoln Papers at the Library of Congress.

76 John Smith Dye, *History and the Plots and Crimes of the Great Conspiracy to Overthrow Liberty in America* (New York: Self-published, 1866), p. 110.

77 George W. Hazzard to Abraham Lincoln, October 21, 1860.

78 George W. Hazzard to John G. Nicolay, July 6, 1861, Abraham Lincoln Papers at the Library of Congress

79 George W. Hazzard to Abraham Lincoln, October 21, 1860.

80 George W. Hazzard to Abraham Lincoln, January 1861, Abraham Lincoln Papers at the Library of Congress.

81 These items are on display at Ford's Theatre National Historic Site, Washington, D.C., and were observed by the author March 1, 2007.

82 Sandburg, *Abraham Lincoln: The War Years*, vol. 1, p. 35.

83 Ellsworth's Zouaves gave an exhibition drill in Baltimore on August 1 and 2, 1860. J. Thomas Scharf, *The Chronicles of Baltimore* (Baltimore: Turnbull Brothers, 1874), p. 575. Hay described Ellsworth's dress and weaponry two months later: "Tonight Ellsworth & his stalwart troup arrived. He was dressed like his men, red cap, red shirt, grey breeches grey jacket. In his belt, a sword, a very heavy revolver, and what was still more significant of the measures necessary with the turbulent spirits under his command, an enormously large and bloodthirsty looking bowie knife, more than a foot long in the blade, and with body enough to go through a man's head from crown to chin as you would split an apple." John Hay, diary entry, May 2, 1861, *Inside Lincoln's White House: The Complete Civil War Diary of John Hay,* ed. Michael Burlingame and John Ettlinger (Carbondale: Southern Illinois University Press, 1997), pp. 16-17.

84 *American Annual Cyclopædia,* vol. 1, p. 284.

85 Ibid.

86 Donald, *Lincoln*, p. 254.

87 Villard, *Lincoln on the Eve of '61*, p. 61.

88 Not wanting to vote for himself, Lincoln cut off the top portion of the ballot. He cast his vote in support of the other Illinois Republicans running for their respective offices. Donald, *Lincoln*, p. 255.

89 Sandburg, *Abraham Lincoln: The War Years*, vol. 1, p. 35.

90 See Searcher, *Lincoln's Journey to Greatness*, facing p. 56, showing a photograph of the pass issued to George W. Hazzard.

91 *American Annual Cyclopædia,* vol. 1, p. 722. As a congressman, Lincoln had opposed the Mexican War as an act of unprovoked United States aggression. Taking an unpopular position that might have contributed to his losing re-election in 1848, Representative Lincoln argued that by invading Mexico, President Polk had exceeded his Constitutional authority. Wrote Lincoln to Herndon on the subject: "The provision of the Constitution giving the war-making power to Congress . . . was dictated, as I understand it, by the following reasons: kings had always been involving and impoverishing their people in wars, pretending generally, if not always, that the good of the people was the object. This, our convention

understood to be the most oppressive of all kingly oppressions; and they resolved to so frame the Constitution that no one man should hold the power of bringing this oppression upon us. But your view destroys the whole matter, and places our President where kings have always stood." Abraham Lincoln to William Herndon, February 15, 1848, in Herndon and Weik, *Abraham Lincoln*, vol. 1, p. 268. Herndon's "view on the matter" had been that President Polk, as commander in chief of the U.S. Army and Navy, had the power, indeed the duty, to wage war on Mexico if necessary to protect against an invasion that appeared imminent. Herndon believed that "measures otherwise unconstitutional might become lawful by becoming indispensable." Ibid., p. 266.

92 *Philadelphia Inquirer,* February 22, 1861.

93 Edwin V. Sumner to John G. Nicolay, January 7, 1861, Abraham Lincoln Papers at the Library of Congress.

94 Searcher, *Lincoln's Journey to Greatness*, p. 13.

95 H. Draper Hunt, *Hannibal Hamlin of Maine: Lincoln's First Vice President* (Syracuse, N.Y.: Syracuse Univerity Press, 1969), p. 141, citing letters from Preston King to Hannibal Hamlin, February 4 and 7, 1861, Hamlin Papers, University of Maine.

96 Charles Eugene Hamlin, *The Life and Times of Hannibal Hamlin*, p. 383. Hamlin's departure date in this account is given as February 11 rather than the 18th.

97 Ibid., p. 384.

98 Hunt, *Hannibal Hamlin*, p. 141.

99 The members of the Select Committee of Five were: William A. Howard, chairman, of Michigan, Lawrence O'Bryan Branch of North Carolina, Henry Laurens Dawes of Massachusetts, John Cochrane of New York, and John Hickman of Pennsylvania. *Reports of the Select Committee of Five*, Report No. 91, 36th Congress, 2nd Session, February 28, 1861, (cited hereafter as "Report No. 91"), p. 22. With the exception of Branch, a Southern Democrat, the other four members of the Select Committee of Five were all Northerners, and either were, or would become, Republicans. See *Biographical Directory of the United States Congress*, http://bioguide.congress.gov.

100 Report No. 91, p. 1.

101 Ibid., p. 13.

102 Ibid., p. 50.

103 Ibid., p. 51.

104 Report No. 91, p. 52.

105 Ibid., p. 54.

106 Ferrandini's first name is more frequently spelled "Cipriano." The court reporter spelled it "Cypriano" when he testified before the Select Committee of Five, and thus this spelling is used herein.

107 Allan Pinkerton report, February 15, 1861, in Cuthbert, *Lincoln and the Baltimore Plot*, pp. 36-37.

108 *Reports of the Select Committee of Five,* 36th Congress, 2nd Session (1861), Report No. 79 (cited hereafter as "Report No. 79"), p. 132.

109 Tidwell, *Come Retribution,* p. 228.

110 Cuthbert, *Lincoln and the Baltimore Plot*, pp.28-29 n. 36; Tidwell, *Come Retribution*, pp. 226-229.

111 Nicolay and Hay, *Abraham Lincoln: A History*, vol. 3, p. 306, citing Ferrandini's testimony before the Select Committee of Five, Report No. 79, pp. 133-137.

112 Nicolay and Hay, *Abraham Lincoln: A History*, vol. 3, p. 307.

113 Harry W. Davies, report, February 12, 1861, in Cuthbert, *Lincoln and the Baltimore Plot*, p. 29.

114 Cuthbert, *Lincoln and the Baltimore Plot*, p. 140 n. 45.

115 Report No. 91, p. 54.

116 Ibid., pp. 54-55.

117 Burlingame, ed., *Lincoln's Journalist*, p. 25. Sunset in Indianapolis on February 11, 1861, occurred at 6:17 p.m. See U.S. Naval Observatory Astronomical Applications Department, http://aa.usno.navy.mil/cgi-bin/aa_pap.pl.

118 Searcher, *Lincoln's Journey to Greatness*, p. 12.

119 Ibid., p. 1.

120 *Philadelphia Inquirer,* February 12, 1861, p. 1; see also Burlingame, ed., *Lincoln's Journalist*, p. 25.

121 Bernhardt Wall, *Following Abraham Lincoln* (New York: Wise Parslow, 1943), p. 273.

122 Burlingame, ed., *Lincoln's Journalist*, p. 27.

123 Greeley, *The American Conflict*, vol. 1, p. 419.

124 *Philadelphia Inquirer,* February 12, 1861, p. 1; see also, Nicolay, *A Short Life of Abraham Lincoln*, p. 171.

125 Greeley, *The American Conflict*, vol. 1, p. 419. Greeley's account of the speech is much longer than that reported in other sources.

126 Burlingame, ed., *Lincoln's Journalist*, p. 27.

127 *Philadelphia Inquirer,* February 12, 1861, p. 1.

128 Ward Hill Lamon, *Recollections of Abraham Lincoln, 1847-1865*, ed. Dorothy Lamon Teillard (Washington, D.C.: Published by the author, 1895), p. 33.

129 Doris Kearns Goodwin, *Team of Rivals* (New York: Simon & Schuster, 2005), p. 245.

130 Sandburg, *Abraham Lincoln: The War Years*, vol. 1, p. 35.

131 Searcher, *Lincoln's Journey to Greatness*, pp. 39-40; Lamon, *Recollections of Abraham Lincoln, 1847-1865*, pp. 32-33.

CHAPTER 4

1 Allan Pinkerton, *The Spy of the Rebellion* (New York: G. W. Carleton, 1884), pp. 50-51.

2 Wrote one correspondent from Baltimore on February 12: "Business remains comparatively quiet, but hopes are brightening somewhat. If political affairs become settled, we still look for a fair Spring trade. Money abundant, but only to be had on unquestionable security. Stocks are dull." See "Our Baltimore Letter," *Philadelphia Inquirer,* February 14, 1861. See also Allan Pinkerton report, February 15, 1861, in Cuthbert, *Lincoln and the Baltimore Plot*, pp. 33-35, noting businesses recently bankrupted and large numbers of unemployed workers in Baltimore.

3 James D. Horan, *The Pinkertons: The Detective Dynasty That Made History* (New York: Crown Publishers, 1967), p. 6.

4 Ibid., pp. 4-6.

5 Ibid., p. 10.

6 Ibid., pp. 15-19.

7 Ibid., p. 23.

8 Eugéne François Vidocq, Europe's famous detective, had founded his agency in 1832. Two St. Louis policemen had founded a private detective agency as early as 1846. Horan, *The Pinkertons,* p. 25.

9 Ibid., p. 26.

10 Ibid., p. 323.

11 Ibid., pp. 28-29.

12 See, e.g., October 3, 1862 photograph of Pinkerton, Lincoln, and General John McClernand standing together at Antietam, Library of Congress; Richard Wilmer Rowan, *The Pinkertons: A Detective Dynasty* (Boston: Little, Brown, 1931), p. 180; Horan, *The Pinkertons,* p. 134.

13 Allan Pinkerton, *History and Evidence of the Passage of Abraham Lincoln from Harrisburg, Pa., to Washington, D.C. on the 22d and 23d of February, 1861* (Chicago: Republican Print, 1868), pp. 8-9. Cuthbert, *Lincoln and the Baltimore Plot,* pp. 20-21. The number of operatives Pinkerton took with him on February 1, 1861 from Chicago to Philadelphia, and thence to Baltimore and other places in Maryland, varies by account, and in his *Spy of the Rebellion,* p. 47, Pinkerton puts the number of agents at four. The actual number is almost certainly five. Evidence for no more and no less than five Pinkerton operatives derives from the fact that, other than Pinkerton himself, only (1) Charles D. C. Williams, (2) Harry W. Davies (as "A.F.C."), (3) Kate Warne (as "M.B." for Mrs. Barley), (4) Timothy Webster, and (5) Hattie H. Lawton (as "H.H.L.") issued written reports from Baltimore and Maryland during February 1861. Most telling is that when Pinkerton sent his final bill to S. M. Felton for services rendered in connection with his investigation, he charged for himself from February 1 to March 1 at $10 per day and charged for only "five operatives" at $6 per day. See invoice dated March 19, 1861, from Allan Pinkerton to S. M. Felton, Felton Papers (no. 1151), Box 1, Folder 3, Historical Society of Pennsylvania. While Pinkerton deducted some of the per diem charges (i.e., those extending to March 8) for himself and the five operatives, he made no mention of any other operatives or deducting any other charges for operatives' time. Had there been more than five operatives, Pinkerton almost certainly would have either billed for their time or made mention of them to Felton as being billed "no charge."

14 Charles D. C. Williams and Harry W. Davies were aliases. Williams was likely one of three Pinkerton agents—Pryce Lewis, John Scully, or Samuel Bridgman. Cuthbert, *Lincoln and the Baltimore Plot*, p. 20.

15 George W. Walling, *Recollections of a New York Chief of Police* (New York: Caxton Book Concern, 1888; reprint, Montclair, N.J.: Patterson Smith, 1972), p. 68.

16 Ibid., p. 68.

17 Albany *Atlas and Argus,* February 11, 1861, p. 2.

18 Tidwell, *Come Retribution*, p. 255; Scharf, *The Chronicles of Baltimore*, p. 526. As ownership interest in the theater changed over the years, so did its name, which was originally the Howard Athenæum, and later became known as "Arnold's Olympic." John Wilkes Booth's sister referred to it as the "St. Charles Theater," rather than the "Charles Street Theater," by which it had more recently become known. Scharf, *Chronicles*, p. 526; Asia Booth Clarke, *John Wilkes Booth: A Sister's Memoir*, ed. Terry Alford (Jackson: University Press of Mississippi, 1996), p. 77 n.

19 Michael W. Kauffman, *American Brutus: John Wilkes Booth and the Lincoln Conspiracies* (New York: Random House, 2004), p. 421 n. 18, citing letter of Asia Booth Clarke, dated June 19, 1859, Peale Museum, Baltimore.

20 Kauffman, *American Brutus,* p. 101 n. 17.

21 Ibid., p. 109.

22 Clarke, *John Wilkes Booth*, p. 78.

23 Stanley Kimmel, *The Mad Booths of Maryland* (Indianapolis: Bobbs-Merrill, 1940), p. 158; Tidwell, *Come Retribution*, p. 257.

24 Both of Richmond's theaters fronted Broad Street, the Richmond Lyceum, or Broad Street Theater, on Broad between Sixth and Seventh Streets, and the Marshall Theatre, or Richmond, on Broad between Seventh and Eighth. See map of Richmond, Virginia, 1861-1865, in David J. Eicher, *Dixie Betrayed: How the South Really Lost the Civil War* (New York: Little, Brown, 2006), frontispiece.

25 Kauffman, *American Brutus*, p. 105.

26 Ibid., p. 112.

27 Clarke, *John Wilkes Booth*, p. 108; Tidwell, *Come Retribution,* p. 256.

28 Tidwell, *Come Retribution,* p. 256.

29 Kauffman, *American Brutus*, p. 422 n. 32; Clarke, *John Wilkes Booth*, p. 81

30 Tidwell, *Come Retribution,* p. 256.

31 Kauffman, *American Brutus*, p. 106.

32 Clarke, *John Wilkes Booth*, p. 81; Kauffman, *American Brutus*, p. 106.

33 Tidwell, *Come Retribution,* p. 256; Clarke, *John Wilkes Booth*, p. 81n.

34 J. C. Furnas, *The Americans: A Social History of the United States, 1587-1914* (New York: G. P. Putnam's Sons, 1969), p. 410. Edwin Booth verifies such accounts: "While at the farm in Maryland, he would charge on horseback through the woods, 'spouting' heroic speeches, with a lance in his hand, a relic of the Mexican War, given to father by some soldier who had served under Taylor." Asia Booth Clarke, *The Unlocked Book: A Memoir of John Wilkes Booth by his sister Asia Booth Clarke*, ed. Eleanor Farjeon (New York: G. P. Putnam's Sons, 1938), p. 202.

35 Only six, Junius Jr., Rosalie Ann, Edwin, Asia, John, and Joseph would survive to adulthood. Kauffman, *American Brutus*, p. 415 n. 4.

36 Clarke, *John Wilkes Booth*, pp. 36-38. Young Booth was playing "telegraph" with a few chums. It involved stringing a line of fireworks across the street and, presumably, setting them off to startle passersby. One such person, whose hat was knocked off by the line as he passed under it, was not amused, and had young Booth arrested by the local constable. A friend of the family, clerk of the city commissioners, Cornelius M. Cole, paid the fine and secured the boy's release. Ibid., p. 38.

37 Kauffman, *American Brutus*, p. 90.

38 Kimmel, *The Mad Booths of Maryland*, p. 186.

39 Roy Z. Chamlee, *Lincoln's Assassins: A Complete Account of Their Capture, Trial, and Punishment* (Jefferson, N.C.: McFarland, 1990), p. 15. The boys were apparently in rebellion over poor food. See Clarke, *The Unlocked Book*, p. 60.

40 Clarke, *John Wilkes Booth*, p. 35.

41 Ibid., p. 53n; Chamlee, *Lincoln's Assassins*, p. 14.

42 William Hanchett, *The Lincoln Murder Conspiracies* (Urbana: University of Illinois Press, 1983), p. 38.

43 Kimmel, *The Mad Booths of Maryland*, pp. 15-16. Junius Brutus Booth Jr. was born December 22, 1821. Kauffman, *American Brutus*, p. 415 n. 4.

44 Kimmel, *The Mad Booths of Maryland*, p. 32.

45 Rodehamel, John, and Louie Taper, eds., *Right or Wrong*, pp. 4-5.

46 Kimmel, *The Mad Booths of Maryland*, pp. 149-150; Rodehamel, John, and Louie Taper, eds., *Right or Wrong,* p. 5.

47 Rodehamel, John, and Louie Taper, eds., *Right or Wrong,* p. 46, which notes that Booth's mother wrote Junius Jr. on October 3, 1858, reporting that Wilkes was earning $11 a week. Kimmel, *The Mad Booths of Maryland*, p. 151.

48 Kimmel, *The Mad Booths of Maryland*, p. 153.

49 Tidwell, *Come Retribution*, pp. 256-257.

50 After being shot in the buttocks when his agent, Matthew Canning, accidentally discharged a pistol on October 12, 1860, in Columbus, Booth was sidelined for over a week. Attendance at the Columbus Theater fell without him. Ibid.

51 Playbill, in Gordon Samples, *Lust for Fame: The Stage Career of John Wilkes Booth* (Jefferson, N.C.: McFarland, 1982), p. 50.

52 Rodehamel, John, and Louie Taper, eds., *Right or Wrong,* p. 49.

53 Samples, *Lust for Fame*, pp. 50-51.

54 Kimmel, *The Mad Booths of Maryland*, p. 158. By other accounts, Booth had joined George W. L. Bickley's Knights of the Golden Circle in Richmond in 1858 or 1859. Tidwell, *Come Retribution*, p. 255 n. 11. Cypriano Ferrandini's commission in the Knights, dated August 8, 1859, is signed by the same man, George Bickley. Tidwell, p. 228. Even if Booth joined the Richmond order, it is possible Booth attended Baltimore conclaves of the Knights. Commerce and travel between Richmond and Baltimore was brisk. They were in many ways sister cities. Kauffman, *American Brutus*, p. 100.

55 Tidwell, *Come Retribution,* p. 228.

56 Tales of Booth's father and grandfather, most likely the more noble stories, were told by "Old Joe," an elderly slave who had known both men. Clarke, *John Wilkes Booth*, p. 60.

57 Indeed, the combined Douglas-Breckenridge tickets in 1860 resulted in forty-seven percent of the popular vote going to the Democrats, with the Republican Lincoln receiving only thirty-nine percent. Nichols, *The Disruption of American Democracy*, p. 370.

58 Booth was still recovering from the bullet wound he had received in the backside in Columbus in October. Tidwell, *Come Retribution*, pp. 256-257.

59 Clarke, *John Wilkes Booth*, p. 81.

60 Rodehamel, John, and Louie Taper, eds., *Right or Wrong,* p. 48 n. 3.

61 Excerpt from draft of speech written by J. Wilkes Booth in Philadelphia in December 1860 (hereafter Booth Manifesto), as published in *"Right or Wrong, God Judge Me": The Writings of John Wilkes Booth,* p. 57. If Booth gave the speech, no published evidence of this survives.

62 Booth initially wanted to preserve the Union, but wanted the North to accept the South's demands. See Booth Manifesto.

Chapter 5

1 Villard, *Lincoln on the Eve of '61,* p.79; Searcher, *Lincoln's Journey to Greatness*, p. 37, quoting Orville Browning's diary.

2 Burlingame, ed., *Lincoln's Journalist,* p. 23.

3 *New York Times,* February 13, 1861, p. 1, ProQuest Historical Newspapers.

4 Ibid.

5 Villard, *Lincoln on the Eve of '61,* p. 80; *New York Times,* February 13, 1861, p. 1, ProQuest Historical Newspapers.

6 Searcher, *Lincoln's Journey to Greatness,* p. 9.

7 Burlingame, ed., *Lincoln's Journalist,* p. 29.

8 Searcher, *Lincoln's Journey to Greatness*, p. 41.

9 Ibid., pp. 41-42.

10 Ibid., p. 42.

11 Ibid., p. 43.

12 *Philadelphia Inquirer,* February 13, 1861, p. 1.

13 Ibid.; *CW,* 4:197.

14 *Springfield (Ill.) Journal,* March 6, 1861, as reprinted in Cuthbert, *Lincoln and the Baltimore Plot,* p. 129.

15 *Philadelphia Inquirer,* February 22, 1861.

16 Donald, *Lincoln,* p. 244.

17 Gilbert A. Tracy, ed., *Uncollected Letters of Abraham Lincoln* (Boston: Houghton Mifflin, 1917), p. 93 n.1.

18 Donald, *Lincoln,* p. 248. Indeed, if there were any caucusing or alliance building, the seating would have permitted Lincoln's supporters to at once befriend both the New Yorkers and the Pennsylvanians, perhaps even pitting one against the other.

19 Burlingame, ed., *Lincoln's Journalist,* pp. 17-23.

20 Cuthbert, *Lincoln and the Baltimore Plot,* p. 25.

21 Nicolay and Hay, *Abraham Lincoln: A History,* vol. 3, p. 307.

22 George H. Bangs, report, February 12, 1861, in Cuthbert, *Lincoln and the Baltimore Plot,* p. 25.

23 William H. Scott, report, February 13, 1861, in ibid., p. 31.

24 Albany *Atlas and Argus,* February 12, 1861, p. 1.

25 Ibid.

26 Ibid., p. 2.

27 Searcher, *Lincoln's Journey to Greatness*, p. 48.

28 *Philadelphia Inquirer,* February 13, 1861, p. 1. See also Burlingame, ed., *Lincoln's Journalist,* p. 29.

29 *Philadelphia Inquirer,* February 13, 1861, p. 1.

30 Browne, *The Every-day Life of Abraham Lincoln*, pp. 382-383, quoting Hon. William Henry Smith, a resident of Cincinnati.

31 *New York Times,* February 18, 1861, p. 2, ProQuest Historical Newspapers.

32 *Philadelphia Inquirer,* February 13, 1861, p. 1.

33 Browne, *The Every-day Life of Abraham Lincoln*, p. 268.

34 Donald, *Lincoln,* pp. 186-187. By other accounts, Stanton referred to Lincoln as a "giraffe" and ridiculed his soiled linen duster for displaying perspiration stains on the back that resembled "a dirty map of the continent." Browne, *The Every-day Life of Abraham Lincoln*, p. 269.

35 Burlingame, ed., *Lincoln's Journalist,* p. 31.

36 *CW,* 4:200-201.

37 *CW,* 4:201.

38 Charles Williams was probably the alias for one of Pryce Lewis, John Scully, or Samuel Bridgman. Cuthbert, *Lincoln and the Baltimore Plot*, p. 20.

39 Charles D. C. Williams, report, February 12, 1861, in ibid., pp. 26-27.

40 Ibid., p. 27.

41 R. B. Coleman to Simeon Draper, January 24, 1861, Abraham Lincoln Papers at the Library of Congress.

42 Ibid.; James, *They Had Their Hour,* p. 144; see also Scharf, *History of Maryland*, vol. 3, p. 384; Burlingame, ed., *Lincoln's Journalist,* p. 42.

43 Pinkerton, *The Spy of the Rebellion,* p. 55; Cuthbert, *Lincoln and the Baltimore Plot*, p. 20.

44 Harry W. Davies, report, February 12, 1861, in Cuthbert, *Lincoln and the Baltimore Plot,* pp. 28-29.

45 Ibid., p. 30.

46 Kauffman, *American Brutus,* pp. 119-120.

47 Arthur F. Loux, *John Wilkes Booth Day by Day* (Privately published, 1990), copy in Surratt House Museum library, Clinton, Md., p. 219, citing the Albany *Atlas and Argus,* February 18, 1861.

48 Ibid., p. 219, citing the *New York Clipper,* February 23, 1861.

49 Ibid., p. 219.

50 Kauffman, *American Brutus,* p. 113; Tidwell, *Come Retribution: The Confederate Secret Service and the Assassination of Lincoln,* p. 255; Kimmel, *The Mad Booths of Maryland,* pp. 158-159.

51 Samples, *Lust for Fame,* p. 60.

52 *New York Times,* February 18, 1861, p. 2, ProQuest Historical Newspapers.

53 Sanders's presence at the hotel is recorded in The *New York Times,* February 13, 1861, p. 1, ProQuest Historical Newspapers.

54 Burlingame, ed., *Lincoln's Journalist*, p. 31.

55 Searcher, *Lincoln's Journey to Greatness*, p. 58.

CHAPTER 6

1 *New York Times*, February 14, 1861, p. 1, ProQuest Historical Newspapers.

2 "Counting the Votes," *Philadelphia Inquirer*, February 14, 1861, p. 1.

3 *New York Times*, February 14, 1861, p. 1, ProQuest Historical Newspapers; Lucius Eugene Chittenden, *Recollections of President Lincoln and His Administration* (Harper & Brothers, 1891), p. 40.

4 Chittenden, *Recollections*, p. 41.

5 Ibid., pp. 40-41. But see *Philadelphia Inquirer*, February 14, 1861, p. 1, reporting that while visitors arriving at the Capitol center doors were turned away by Capitol police, they were sent to either the House or Senate wings, "more to prevent confusion, by obstructing the passage of the Senators when they repaired to the House, than because of any danger of a disturbance." No doubt many would-be observers were turned away, however, as by 10:00 a.m., the gallery was already filled, and the doorkeeper reportedly did endeavor to exclude "outside barbarians." Ibid.

6 Frank Abial Flower, *Edwin McMasters Stanton: The Autocrat of Rebellion, Emancipation, and Reconstruction* (Akron, Ohio: Saalfield, 1905), p. 97.

7 *CW*, 4:170.

8 Chittenden, *Recollections*, p. 40.

9 During the month of January, Wigfall had been sending intelligence and treasonous orders from Washington to his Southern brethren. For example, on January 2 he sent the following dispatch (*OR* 1:1, p. 252.):

> Hon. M .L. Bonham, Charleston, S.C.:
>
> Holt succeeds Floyd. It means war. Cut off supplies from Anderson and take Sumter soon as possible.
>
> Louis T. Wigfall.

On January 8, 1861, Wigfall provided critical military intelligence to Governor Pickens of South Carolina (*OR* 1:1, p. 253):

> The *Star of the West* sailed from New York on Sunday with Government troops and provisions. It is said her destination is Charleston. If so, she may be hourly expected off the harbor of Charleston.

The *Star of the West* had, under orders of Secretary of War Holt, sailed from New York on January 5 with 250 troops to reinforce Anderson at Fort Sumter. Reaching Charleston early in the morning, she was fired upon by order of Governor Pickens, who had previously been warned of her coming by Wigfall's dispatch. Pickens was therefore prepared for the attack. The *Star of the West* was thus repelled, forced out to sea, and returned to Fort Monroe—based on military intelligence passed to seceded Governor Pickens by a sitting U.S. senator. Secretary of the Interior Jacob Thompson of Mississippi, who resigned his office that same day, January 8, 1861, also sent a dispatch warning of *The Star of the West*, his warning going to Judge Longstreet. Flower, *Edwin McMasters Stanton*, pp. 98-99. In a theme that would become fairly common, those arguably committing treasonous acts appear to have justified those acts as necessary to halt even worse consequences of Northern actions. In this case, Thompson's resignation was, he reasoned, occasioned by Secretary Holt's order to move reinforcements to Fort Sumter, thereby countermanding a promise from Buchanan that no troops would be sent to the South before the subject had been put before the cabinet. Flower, p. 98.

On February 20, 1861, Wigfall informed Pickens (*OR* 1:1, p. 257):

> Attempt to re-enforce Anderson [at Ft. Sumter] by stealth at night in small
> boats determined on.
> Answer if received.
> Louis T. Wigfall.

Wigfall continued his dispatches of intelligence and orders right up to the date of Lincoln's inauguration, again writing from Washington to Governor Pickens on March 4, 1861:

> Do not permit any attack on Sumter without authority of Government of
> Confederated States. This is all important. Inaugural means war. There is
> strong ground for belief that re-enforcements will be speedily sent. Be vig-
> ilant.
> Louis T. Wigfall.

To this dispatch, L. Q. Washington replied (*OR* 1:1, p. 261):

> I concur, and believe this Government will act promptly.
> L. Q. Washington.

10 Flower, *Edwin McMasters Stanton*, p. 97.

11 Chittenden, *Recollections,* p. 40.

12 Flower, *Edwin McMasters Stanton*, p. 97. (Note that Flower erroneously gives February 15 as the date of the count; it occurred on February 13.)

13 *CW,* 4:170.

14 Albany *Atlas and Argus,* February 14, 1861, p. 1, col. 7. *Daily Pittsburgh Gazette,* February 14, 1861, p. 3.

15 The telegram had read (Cuthbert, *Lincoln and the Baltimore Plot*, p. 26):

> W. H. Scott
> Lafayette
> Ind.
> J—says will be at Columbus Thirteenth—Pittsburgh Fourteenth—form
> your own estimate by enquiring at Indianapolis.
> G. H. Bangs.

16 William H. Scott, report, February 13, 1861, in Cuthbert, *Lincoln and the Baltimore Plot*, p. 31.

17 Ibid.

18 Ibid.

19 Norman B. Judd to Allan Pinkerton, November 3, 1867, in Pinkerton, *History and Evidence,* p. 17; see also Pinkerton, *The Spy of the Rebellion,* p. 74.

20 Pinkerton's admonition to Judd is consistent with a similar instruction he had given in January to Felton to preserve secrecy, saying "on no conditions would I consider it safe for myself or my operatives were the fact of my operating known to any Politician, no matter of what school, or what position." The breadth of this injunction thus included even Lincoln. Accordingly, Judd withheld the information from everyone else in the Lincoln party. But Pinkerton would later imply the decision to withhold had been Judd's not his. See *Spy of the Rebellion,* p. 74. "This information Mr. Judd did not divulge to anyone, fearing to occasion undue anxiety or unnecessary alarm, and knowing that I was upon the ground and could be depended upon to act at the proper time." See also Whitney, Henry C., *Lincoln the Citizen,* vol. 1 of *A Life of Lincoln,* ed. Marion Mills Miller (New York: Baker & Taylor, 1908), p. 301. Indeed, Judd claimed that he kept the information to himself "to avoid causing anxiety on the part of Mr. Lincoln, or any of the party." Norman B. Judd to Allan Pinkerton, November 3, 1867, in Pinkerton, *History and Evidence,* p. 17.

21 Report No. 91, p. 55.

22 J. Bond Chaplain to James L. Dorsey, February 13, 1861, Accession No. 50531, MS 1263, Maryland Historical Society, Baltimore.

23 Report No. 79, p. 168.

24 It would, however, later be reported that Hicks did testify to the Select Committee that a clerk in the Census Bureau named Goldsborough had told Hicks "that he was meeting nightly with a band of men who were plotting for the seizure of the Capital. It is said that Goldsborough now denies having had any authority for such a statement, and his friends say he made it to frighten Gov. Hicks into calling a State Convention." *New York Times,* February 14, 1861, p. 1, ProQuest Historical Newspapers.

25 Report No. 79, p. 174.

26 *New York Times,* February 14, 1861, p. 1, ProQuest Historical Newspapers; Albany *Atlas and Argus,* February 14, 1861, p. 1. Compare this account to the slightly different version reported in the *Daily Pittsburgh Gazette* of the same date: "his belief that a conspiracy existed in connection with the Federal Capital was, he said, superinduced by private . . . letters and newspaper articles, that such a combination did not exist in Maryland; but in other Southern States at the time his publication being in the middle of January. He was satisfied of an existing organization having in view illegal interference with the Federal authorities and the seizure of the public property, but for some time past whatever may have been the designs of any secret confederation or association, he was satisfied that such purposes have been abandoned." *Daily Pittsburgh Gazette,* February 14, 1861, p. 3.

27 Cuthbert, *Lincoln and the Baltimore Plot,* pp. 140-141 n. 46, citing Report No. 79.

28 James C. Welling to Thomas H. Hicks, December 21, 1860, Accession No. 47948, MS 1313, Maryland Historical Society, Baltimore.

29 George Stearns to Thomas Hicks, February 7, 1861, Maryland Historical Society, Baltimore. Hicks claimed that he had appeared voluntarily before the Select Committee of

Five, when in reality it was necessary for the committee to repeatedly call for him to testi-fy and at one point to attempt taking his testimony in Annapolis. The day he testified, a friend of Hicks who had accompanied him to Washington wrote James L. Dorsey concern-ing Governor Hicks's testimony in Washington:

> United States of America
> Thirty Sixth Congress
> Washington City February 13, 1861
> My Dear Dorsey.
>
> I went to Annapolis Saturday Evg, where the Governor asked me to come here with him, he intended to return yesterday evening, but has put off until tomorrow, he is doing good here and may be instructed to remain still longer, if so and I do not get back in time to make weekly reports on Friday morning, will you please get into the desk by some means, and get blanks for the reports and make them out for me—there is a key over the mantle piece that may fit—. I hope though to get back to Balte. tomorrow. Things are looking pretty well and the Gov has every hope, his presence here will greatly help the "Union."
> Truly Yrs & etc
> J. Bond Chaplain
> The Gov came here of his own accord, and was not summoned by the Committee.

J. Bond Chaplain to James L. Dorsey, February 13, 1861, Accession No. 50531, MS 1263, Maryland Historical Society, Baltimore, MD.

30 Report No. 79, p. 175, emphasis added.

31 Report No. 79, p. 175.

32 J. Bond Chaplain to James L. Dorsey, February 13, 1861.

33 Villard, *Lincoln on the Eve of '61*, pp. 80-81.

34 *Lafayette (Ind.) Journal,* February 16, 1861, as reported in "Attempts Upon Mr. Lincoln's Life," *New York Times,* February 26, 1861, p. 8, ProQuest Historical Newspapers.

35 "Attempts Upon Mr. Lincoln's Life."

36 Lamon, *The Life of Abraham Lincoln,* p. 507.

37 "Progress of the President Elect towards Washington," *New York Times,* February 14, 1861, p. 1, ProQuest Historical Newspapers.

38 Allen Thorndike Rice, *Reminiscences of Abraham Lincoln by Distinguished Men of His Time* (New York: North American Review, 1888), p. 31.

39 Chittenden, *Recollections,* p. 41.

40 Ibid., p. 42.

41 Rice, *Reminiscences of Abraham Lincoln,* pp. 31-32.

42 Chittenden, *Recollections,* p. 43; *Philadelphia Inquirer,* February 14, 1861, p. 1.

43 *New York Times,* February 14, 1861, p. 1, ProQuest Historical Newspapers.

44 Chittenden, *Recollections,* p. 43.

45 *Philadelphia Inquirer,* February 14, 1861, p. 1.

46 Chittenden, *Recollections,* p. 44; *Philadelphia Inquirer,* February 14, 1861, p. 1.

47 *Philadelphia Inquirer,* February 14, 1861, p. 1.

48 "Affairs of the Nation," *New York Times,* February 14, 1861, p. 1, ProQuest Historical Newspapers.

49 Chittenden, *Recollections,* p. 45.

50 Ibid.

51 *Philadelphia Inquirer,* February 14, 1861, p. 1; "Progress of the President Elect towards Washington," *New York Times,* February 14, 1861, p. 1, ProQuest Historical Newspapers.

52 *Philadelphia Inquirer,* February 14, 1861, p. 1.

53 *CW,* 4:205-206 (emphasis added).

54 "Progress of the President Elect towards Washington," p. 1.

55 Searcher, *Lincoln's Journey to Greatness,* p. 69; *Philadelphia Inquirer,* February 14, 1861, p. 1.

56 Chittenden, *Recollections,* p. 46.

57 *New York Times,* February 18, 1861, p. 2, ProQuest Historical Newspapers.

CHAPTER 7

1 *Philadelphia Inquirer,* February 15, 1861, p. 1; Villard, *Lincoln on the Eve of '61,* p. 83.

2 Searcher, *Lincoln's Journey to Greatness,* p. 73.

3 "Progress of the President Elect towards Washington," *New York Times,* February 14, 1861, p. 1, ProQuest Historical Newspapers.

4 Searcher, *Lincoln's Journey to Greatness,* p. 72. Villard, *Lincoln on the Eve of '61,* p. 83.

5 Another nickname given to Robert Lincoln. The Indianapolis *Daily Journal,* February 13, 1861.

6 Villard, *Lincoln on the Eve of '61,* pp. 84-85.

7 See, e.g., "Arrival and Reception at Indianapolis," *New York Times,* February 12, 1861, p. 1, ProQuest Historical Newspapers, noting that upon Lincoln's arrival in Indianapolis, "The President stood in his carriage, acknowledging the welcome of the surrounding thousands." See also the Indianapolis *Daily Journal,* February 12, 1861.

8 *New York Times,* February 15, 1861, p. 1, ProQuest Historical Newspapers; *Philadelphia Inquirer,* February 15, 1861, p. 1.

9 *CW,* 4:207.

10 *Daily Pittsburgh Gazette,* February 15, 1861.

11 *CW,* 4:207.

12 *Daily Pittsburgh Gazette,* February 15, 1861.

13 Ibid.; *Philadelphia Inquirer,* February 15, 1861, p. 1.

14 *Daily Pittsburgh Gazette,* February 13, 1861.

15 *Daily Pittsburgh Gazette,* February 15, 1861.

16 Ibid.

17 Ibid.

18 Ibid.

19 "The President Elect on His Triumphal Tour," *Philadelphia Inquirer,* February 18, 1861.

20 *CW,* 4:210-211; *Daily Pittsburgh Gazette,* February 16, 1861.

21 Ibid. (first emphasis added, second emphasis original).

22 Ibid.

23 "The President Elect on His Triumphal Tour."

24 Ibid.

25 Searcher, *Lincoln's Journey to Greatness,* p. 95.

26 *Daily Pittsburgh Gazette,* February 16, 1861.

27 Searcher, *Lincoln's Journey to Greatness,* p. 95.

28 "The President Elect on His Triumphal Tour."

29 Searcher, *Lincoln's Journey to Greatness,* p. 96; *Daily Pittsburgh Gazette,* February 16, 1861. By another account, the shattered glass incident occurred at Ravenna, where double loaded cannon gave a salute as the train departed, shattering a window in the forward car and one in the rear car by which Mrs. Lincoln sat. "The President Elect on His Triumphal Tour."

30 *CW,* 4:215.

31 Allan Pinkerton, report, February 15, 1861, in Cuthbert, *Lincoln and the Baltimore Plot,* pp. 32-34.

32 Ibid., p. 32.

33 Ibid., p. 33.

34 Ibid., p. 34.

35 Ibid., pp. 35-36.

36 The Cleveland *Plain Dealer,* February 16, 1861, p. 3.

37 *Daily Pittsburgh Gazette,* February 16, 1861; *CW,* 4:215; "The President Elect on His Triumphal Tour."

38 "The President Elect on His Triumphal Tour."

39 Ibid.

40 *Daily Pittsburgh Gazette,* February 16, 1861; *CW,* 4:215-216.

41 Nicolay and Hay, *Abraham Lincoln: A History,* vol. 3, p. 306, citing Ferrandini's testimony before the Select Committee of Five, Report No. 79, pp. 133-137. Generally, Pinkerton used the name "Hutcheson" as his alias. But frequently Pinkerton and others recalled it as "Hutchinson," particularly in later accounts. See, e.g., Pinkerton to Herndon, August 23, 1866, in Cuthbert, *Lincoln and the Baltimore Plot,* p. 5.

42 Tidwell, *Come Retribution,* p. 229; Allan Pinkerton, report, February 15, 1861, in Cuthbert, *Lincoln and the Baltimore Plot,* p. 36.

43 "Historian Attributes Lincoln 'Plot' to Private Detective's Imagination," *Baltimore Sun,* March 31, 1950.

44 Scharf, *The Chronicles of Baltimore,* p. 569; Goodwin, *Team of Rivals,* p. 226.

45 Pinkerton report, February 15, 1861, in Cuthbert, *Lincoln and the Baltimore Plot,* pp. 36-37.

46 Ibid., p. 37.

47 Report No. 79, p. 134.

48 Referring to Felice Orsini, an Italian patriot who attempted to assassinate Napoleon III, and was executed March 13, 1858. Cuthbert, *Lincoln and the Baltimore Plot*, p. 139 n. 42. See also Michael St. John Packe, *The Bombs of Orsini* (London: Secker and Warburg, 1957). Compare Chittenden's account, in which a barber named Ruscelli, who called himself "Orsini," was employed to assassinate Lincoln. Chittenden, *Recollections,* p. 61.

49 Pinkerton report, February 15, 1861, in Cuthbert, *Lincoln and the Baltimore Plot*, p. 37.

50 Ibid., p. 38.

CHAPTER 8

1 "The President Elect on His Triumphal Tour," *Philadelphia Inquirer,* February 18, 1861.

2 Burlingame, ed., *Lincoln's Journalist,* p. 31.

3 Ibid., p. 32.

4 The Cleveland *Plain Dealer,* February 14, 1861, p. 2.

5 Ibid.

6 Searcher, *Lincoln's Journey to Greatness*, pp. 113-114.

7 Burlingame, ed., *Lincoln's Journalist,* p. 32.

8 It would be reported this day that "The President elect still labored under the effect of the fatigues of the previous day, and was rather reserved. His hoarseness induced him to speak less to-day than during any of the preceding stages of the journey." *New York Times*, February 16, 1861, p. 1, ProQuest Historical Newspapers. Curiously, whether by coincidence or mental slip, Lincoln had just confused the young girl's name with an alias for one of Pinkerton's operatives. Then working in Baltimore, Kate Warne was operating under the code name "Miss Barley."

9 *CW,* 4:219.

10 By other accounts, Lincoln left the car to greet Miss Bedell. *CW,* 4:219.

11 Grace Bedell, December 14, 1866, in Herndon and Weik, *Abraham Lincoln*, vol. 2, pp. 197-198n.

12 Burlingame, ed., *Lincoln's Journalist,* p. 32.

13 Albany *Atlas and Argus,* February 18, 1861, p. 3.

14 Ibid.

15 Clarke, *The Unlocked Book*, p. 115.

16 See generally Stephen Berry, *House of Abraham: Lincoln and the Todds, a Family Divided by War* (Boston: Houghton Mifflin, 2007).

17 George Stearns to S. M. Felton, April 1, 1862, Felton Papers (#1151) Box 2, Folder 1, Historical Society of Pennsylvania, Philadelphia.

18 Cuthbert, *Lincoln and the Baltimore Plot*, p. 91.

19 Albany *Atlas and Argus,* February 18, 1861, p. 3.

20 Burlingame, ed., *Lincoln's Journalist,* p. 33.

21 Searcher, *Lincoln's Journey to Greatness*, p. 126.

22 Burlingame, ed., *Lincoln's Journalist,* p. 33.

23 Charles M. Snyder, *The Lady and the President: The Letters of Dorothea Dix & Millard Fillmore* (Lexington: University of Kentucky Press, 1975), pp. 342-343.

24 *New York Times*, February 18, 1861, p. 1, ProQuest Historical Newspapers.

25 Burlingame, ed., *Lincoln's Journalist,* at 34.

26 *Philadelphia Inquirer,* February 18, 1861, p. 1.

27 Allan Pinkerton, report, February 21, 1861, in Cuthbert, *Lincoln and the Baltimore Plot,* p. 53.

28 Ibid.

29 Burlingame, ed., *Lincoln's Journalist,* p. 34.

30 *Philadelphia Inquirer,* February 18, 1861, p. 1; Searcher, *Lincoln's Journey to Greatness,* p. 129.

31 Villard, *Lincoln on the Eve of '61,* p. 91.

32 Searcher, *Lincoln's Journey to Greatness,* p. 134.

33 Greeley, *The American Conflict,* p. 415 n. 15.

34 Chittenden, *Recollections,* p. 58.

35 Ibid., pp. 58-59.

36 Ibid., p. 59. Note that New York detectives Thomas Sampson and Eli De Voe, under assumed names "Anderson" from Augusta and "Davis" from Mobile, respectively, "stayed at the Fountain Inn and for some weeks had a good time." Walling, *Recollections,* pp. 69, 71. Sampson, De Voe, and fellow New York detective David S. Bookstaver had arrived in Baltimore on February 1. Tidwell, *Come Retribution,* p. 231. Interestingly, Maryland's governor Thomas H. Hicks would also be a guest at the Fountain Hotel on at least one occasion when he stayed in Baltimore. See, e.g., letter of Thomas H. Hicks to Mrs. James L. Dorsey, dated June 11, 1863, sent in an envelope of that hotel, indicating William H. Clabaugh as the proprietor. Accession No. 50531, MS 1263, Maryland Historical Society, Baltimore.

37 The B&O Railroad owned the route from Washington to Baltimore, and its depot in Baltimore was situated at the corner of Camden and Howard Streets.

38 The Fountain Hotel in Baltimore had been a haunt of John Wilkes Booth's in his youth. See J. Wilkes Booth to T. William O'Laughlen, November 12, 1855, in Rodehamel, John, and Louie Taper, eds., *Right or Wrong,* p. 43.

39 Chittenden, *Recollections,* p. 59.

40 Possibly H. W. Hoffman, a Baltimore official whom Chittenden would three months later describe as "an old friend of mine and a thorough Union man." Lucius E. Chittenden, *Invisible Siege: The Journal of Lucius E. Chittenden, April 15, 1861-July 14, 1861* (San Diego: Americana Exchange Press: 1969), p. 28.

41 Chittenden, *Recollections,* p. 60.

42 The little band of Baltimore Republicans had endured, during a Wide Awake procession in Baltimore the previous October, "showers of eggs, brick-bats and injurious epithets from the mob." Worthington Snethen to Abraham Lincoln, November 3, 1860, Abraham Lincoln Papers at the Library of Congress. They "had braved obloquy and persecution and risked their lives to vote for [him]." Worthington Snethen to Abraham Lincoln, February 25, 1861, Abraham Lincoln Papers at the Library of Congress.

43 The "Canton station," also known as the President Street Station, was the depot served from the north by Samuel M. Felton's Philadelphia, Wilmington, and Baltimore Railroad. If Lincoln approached Baltimore from Philadelphia, he would arrive at this station. If, on the other hand, he approached from Harrisburg, on the Northern Central Railroad, he would arrive at the Calvert Street Station.

44 Chittenden, *Recollections,* p. 60.

45 Ibid.

46 Ibid., pp. 60-61.

47 Pinkerton report, February 15, 1861, in Cuthbert, *Lincoln and the Baltimore Plot,* p. 37. Orsini was executed March 13, 1858. Cuthbert, *Lincoln and the Baltimore Plot,* p. 139 n. 42.

48 Chittenden, *Recollections,* p. 61.

49 Ibid.

50 Ibid., p. 62.

51 Ibid., pp. 61-62.

52 Ibid., p. 62.

53 Ibid.

54 Ibid.

55 See, e.g., Clarke, *The Unlocked Book,* p. 81.

56 Tidwell, *Come Retribution,* pp. 256-257.

57 Rodehamel, John, and Louie Taper, eds., *Right or Wrong,* pp. 55-64.

58 See Loux, *John Wilkes Booth Day by Day,* pp. 230-233.

59 Ibid., pp. 216-219.

60 Burlingame, ed., *Lincoln's Journalist,* p. 37. The anonymous correspondent's reference was not to the entire trip, but in particular the Monday, February 18, ride from Buffalo to Albany.

CHAPTER 9

1 Samples, *Lust for Fame,* p. 58.

2 Kauffman, *American Brutus,* p. 117; Samples, *Lust for Fame,* p. 61.

3 Samples, *Lust for Fame,* pp. 52-53.

4 Loux, *John Wilkes Booth, Day by Day,* p. 220, citing Albany *Atlas and Argus,* February 18, 1861, p. 3.

5 For example, the paper, in commenting on Lincoln's visit to Albany, said: "But lo! The wine is out, the cord severed and the cork released, and instead of sparkling champagne that bubbled over, there is a frothy rush of root-beer—yeasty foam, inspired flatulence, slops and dregs." Samples, *Lust for Fame,* p. 60.

6 See, e.g., Albany *Atlas and Argus,* February 11, 1861, p. 2.

7 Clarke, *The Unlocked Book,* p. 153.

8 Bryan, *The Great American Myth,* p. 125.

9 Letters from John F. Wright, January 24, 1861, and David Wylie, January 25, 1861, both to Abraham Lincoln. In Harold Holzer, ed., *The Lincoln Mailbag: America Writes to the President, 1861-1865* (Carbondale: Southern Illinois University Press), pp. 3, 4.

10 Edward Steers, *Blood on the Moon: The Assassination of Abraham Lincoln* (Lexington: University Press of Kentucky, 2001), p. 16; Illinois Historical Preservation Agency, Springfield.

11 Samples, *Lust for Fame,* p. 158. There is other vague evidence that Booth or his fellow conspirators had failed at least once in poisoning Lincoln. The "Charles Selby" letter, claimed to be in Booth's handwriting, was introduced at the conspirators' trial in 1865 and contains tantalizing clues: "Dear Louis: The time has at last come that we have all so wished for, and upon you everything depends. As it was decided before you left, we were to cast lots. Accordingly we did so, and you are to be the Charlotte Corday of the nineteenth century. When you remember the fearful, solemn vow that was taken by us, you will feel there is no drawback—*Abe* must *die,* and *now.* You can choose your weapons. The cup, the *knife,* the *bullet.* The cup failed us once, and might again. . . . Get introduced, congratulate him, listen to his stories—not many more will the brute tell to earthly friends." *The Assassination of President Lincoln and the Trial of the Conspirators,* comp. Benn Pitman (Cincinnati: Moore, Wilstach & Baldwin, 1865), p. 40; Louis J. Weichmann, *A True History of the Assassination of Abraham Lincoln and of the Conspiracy of 1865,* ed. Floyd E. Risvold (New York: Knopf, 1975), pp. 64-65.

12 Wrote his sister Asia Booth Clarke, after Wilkes Booth laughingly confessed to being a dealer in quinine, "The real genuine quinine was a most expensive drug; he rejoiced that he had plenty of money to buy it, but knew people who supplied him with the perfect article, there was so much paltry stuff called by the name employed in northern hospitals. Wilkes was an expert in this matter." Clarke, *John Wilkes Booth,* p. 83. See also Hanchett, *The Lincoln Murder Conspiracies,* p. 42 nn. 23, 24, noting that Confederate friends of Booth sometimes referred to him as "Doctor."

13 At the conspiracy trial, Sanford Conover testified of a proposal by a Dr. Blackburn to poison the Croton Dam reservoir with such poisons in later years. See Pitman, *Trial of the Conspirators,* p. 30.

14 See, e.g., Nichols, *The Disruption of American Democracy,* p. 441.

15 Kimmel, *The Mad Booths of Maryland,* p. 158.

16 On February 14, the Albany *Atlas and Argus* reported that the day before, in New York, three boxes of ammunition, one containing 2,000 boxes of percussion caps, and the others, 5,000 cartridges with ball attached, designed for Minnie rifles, were seized by police on board the steamer *Huntsville,* destined for Savannah. Albany *Atlas and Argus,* February 14, 1861, p. 1.

17 Chittenden, *Recollections,* p. 64.

18 Ibid.

19 Burlingame, ed., *Lincoln's Journalist,* p. 36.

20 Searcher, *Lincoln's Journey to Greatness,* p. 145.

21 Searcher, p. 149; Burlingame, ed., *Lincoln's Journalist,* p. 37.

22 Albany *Atlas and Argus,* February 20, 1861, p. 3.

23 Ibid.; "Reception and Speech at Albany," *New York Times,* February 19, 1861, p. 1, ProQuest Historical Newspapers; Searcher, *Lincoln's Journey to Greatness,* p. 153.

24 Albany *Atlas and Argus,* February 19, 1861, p. 2.

25 "The Quarrel for the Custody of the President Elect!" Albany *Atlas and Argus,* February 19, 1861, p. 2

26 Searcher, *Lincoln's Journey to Greatness*, pp. 154-155.

27 "Crowding on Lincoln's Carriage," Albany *Atlas and Argus,* February 19, 1861, p. 3.

28 "President Lincoln at Albany," Albany *Atlas and Argus,* February 19, 1861, p. 2.

29 H. P. Phelps, *Players of a Century: A Record of the Albany Stage* (Albany, N.Y.: McDonough, 1880), p. 305.

30 Phelps, *Players of a Century*, p. 326.

31 Ibid.

32 Albany *Atlas and Argus,* February 19, 1861, p. 2.

33 Ibid.

34 Ibid.; *New York Times,* February 19, 1861 p. 8, ProQuest Historical Newspapers.

35 Worthington G. Snethen to Abraham Lincoln, February 15, 1861, Abraham Lincoln Papers at the Library of Congress.

36 Mearns, *The Lincoln Papers,* vol. 2, p. 410.

37 "Committee Appointed to Meet Mr. Lincoln," *New York Times,* February 15, 1861, p. 1, ProQuest Historical Newspapers. The New York committee included General Welch, Adjutant General Reed, Inspector General Jackson, Quartermaster General Van Vechten, and Colonel Morgan, aide-de-camp. Advance official welcomes had been made by other cities and states as well. For example, on the first day of his journey, upon arriving in Indianapolis, Lincoln was met by delegations from both the Cincinnati and Columbus City Counsels and a joint committee of the Ohio Legislature. The Indianapolis *Daily Journal,* February 12, 1861.

38 Kate Warne (as M.B.), report, February 18, 1861, in Cuthbert, *Lincoln and the Baltimore Plot*, p. 40.

39 Cuthbert, *Lincoln and the Baltimore Plot*, p. 21, citing *Spy of the Rebellion* at 75.

40 Allan Pinkerton, *The Expressman and the Detective* (Chicago: Keen, Cooke, 1875), p. 94. See also Horan, *The Pinkertons.* p. 29.

41 Pinkerton, *The Expressman and the Detective*, p. 95; Horan,*The Pinkertons*, p. 29.

42 There is some question as to the exact date Pinkerton started his agency, with the years 1850 and 1852 both having been given by him. Horan, *The Pinkertons*, p. 520 n. 4. It appears that both dates are correct; in 1850, Pinkerton formed the North-Western Police Agency with Chicago attorney Edward Rucker. His partnership with Rucker dissolved within the first year, after which Pinkerton operated the agency alone. He renamed it the Pinkerton Agency in 1852. http://www.findagrave.com/cgi-bin/fg.cgi?page=gr&GRid =817.

43 Pinkerton, *The Expressman and the Detective*, p. 95; Horan, *The Pinkertons*, p. 29.

44 Pinkerton, *The Expressman and the Detective*, p. 95.

45 Ibid.

46 Ibid., p. 101.

47 Frank Morn, *The Eye That Never Sleeps* (Bloomington: Indiana University Press, 1982), pp. 36-37; Horan, *The Pinkertons*, p. 520 n. 3.

48 Morn, *The Eye That Never Sleeps*, p. 54.

49 William Stearns to Allan Pinkerton, December 4, 1867, in Pinkerton, *History and Evidence*, pp. 24-25.

50 Ibid., p. 25.

CHAPTER 10

1 *New York Times*, February 20, 1861, p. 1, ProQuest Historical Newspapers.

2 Villard, *Lincoln on the Eve of '61*, pp. 95-96.

3 *New York Times*, February 20, 1861, p. 1, ProQuest Historical Newspapers.

4 Ibid.

5 Ibid.

6 Searcher, *Lincoln's Journey to Greatness*, p. 170; *New York Times*, February 20, 1861, p. 1, ProQuest Historical Newspapers.

7 Searcher, *Lincoln's Journey to Greatness*, pp. 168-172.

8 *New York Times*, February 20, 1861, p. 1, ProQuest Historical Newspapers.

9 Ibid.; CW, 4:229.

10 The town described in Pinkerton's reports as Perrymansville is what is now Perryman, Maryland, located near the Aberdeen Proving Ground. Another similarly named town, Perryville, (formerly Perrysville) is on the northern bank of the Susquehanna across from Havre de Grace. Perryman is farther south than Perryville, on the north shore of the Bush River. Pinkerton describes Perrymansville, where he sent Webster, as "a Station about 9 miles South of Havre-de-Grace, on the P.W. and B.R.R." Cuthbert, *Lincoln and the Baltimore Plot*, p. 4. This location confirms it as what is now Perryman. See also note 18, infra.

11 William Gilmore Beymer, *On Hazardous Service* (New York: Harper & Brothers, 1912), p. 260.

12 Webster's right eye, as depicted in the only known likeness of him, bears a strong resemblance to that which would become the symbol of Pinkerton's "The Eye That Never Sleeps" logo.

13 Beymer, *On Hazardous Service*, p. 260; see also Pinkerton, *Spy of the Rebellion*, p. 56.

14 Possibly Captain Benedict H. Kean, in command of the Spesutia Rangers, arrested on May 18, 1861, but later released, after credible witnesses vouched for him as having opposed the destruction of bridges, presumably the PW&B railroad bridges destroyed the previous month. Below is a letter reporting on the arrest of Captain Kean, as found at OR 2:1, p. 573:

> Headquarters Camp Susquehanna,
>
> Perryville, Md., May 19, 1861.
>
> Maj. F. J. Porter,
>
> Assistant Adjutant-General.
>
> Major: I have the honor to report that last evening signal rockets were reported in direction of Aberdeen. I immediately proceeded to Havre de Grace (Lieutenant-Colonel Birney being absent) and finding they were not according to code agreed upon considered no re-enforcement necessary. I

proceeded to Aberdeen to ascertain why the rockets had been fired and at that post they were reported as having been seen in the direction of Perrymansville. Taking a guard to that point I found all quiet.

Information having been given in relation to Capt. Benedict H. Kean, in command of Spesutia Rangers, William B. Michael and Thomas Wilson, Captain Hofmann, of Company E, First Regiment, Philadelphia City Guards, arrested them, the first as in command of forces hostile to United States and the two latter-named gentlemen as being engaged in destruction of bridges. The arrests were made quietly and every consideration shown to the gentlemen detained. They were taken to Perryville and lodged at my quarters. From representations made by Captain Kean and by other parties the Spesutia Rangers have not been engaged or intending to engage against the Government. His action in opposing the destruction of the bridges as represented by credible parties induced his release on parole of honor to appear if wanted. The others I believe to have been engaged in destruction of bridges and that the evidence will be ample to sustain the fact. I am now detaining them until I receive instructions from headquarters.

I have the honor to be, very respectfully, your obedient servant,

Chas. P. Dare,

Commanding Post.

15 Keen, Springer, and Taylor were associated with the secessionist group known as the Perrymansville Rangers. Wilson and Davis, *Herndon's Informants*, p. 280 n. 27.

16 Cuthbert, *Lincoln and the Baltimore Plot*, p. 137. This itinerary was published in the Springfield Journal on February 13, 1861, and other contemporary newspapers, some with slight variations.

17 The Pinkerton manuscript is not clear at this point. Cuthbert indicates the word used could be "trip." Timothy Webster, report, February 19, 1861, in Cuthbert, *Lincoln and the Baltimore Plot*, p. 45.

18 Ibid. Because Webster was reporting from Perrymansville, it may be assumed that by "this Road" the man calling himself Taylor meant the Philadelphia, Wilmington, and Baltimore Railroad, and by "that Boat" he meant the steamer that ferried railcars across the Susquehanna from Perryville (not to be confused with Perrymansville, note 10 supra, a town further south in Maryland) to Havre de Grace. The town called "Perrysville," and now named "Perryville," was described thus in 1861: "PERRYSVILLE, a village in Cecil County, Maryland, is on the east or left bank of the Susquehanna River at the head of the Chesapeake Bay, and opposite Havre-de-Grace. It is 37 miles from Baltimore on the line of the Baltimore and Philadelphia Railroad. The first troops for Washington after the difficulty at Baltimore were transferred from the cars to the steamboat here and taken to Annapolis, thus avoiding Baltimore entirely." *American Annual Cyclopædia*, p. 575.

19 Timothy Webster, report, February 19, 1861, in Cuthbert, *Lincoln and the Baltimore Plot*, p. 45.

20 Allan Pinkerton, report, February 15, 1861, in Cuthbert, *Lincoln and the Baltimore Plot*, p. 36; Tidwell, *Come Retribution*, p. 229.

21 Timothy Webster, report, February 19, 1861, in Cuthbert, *Lincoln and the Baltimore Plot*, pp. 45-46.

22 Kate Warne, reports, February 18 and 19, 1861, in Cuthbert, *Lincoln and the Baltimore Plot*, pp. 40-41.

23 "Arrival and Reception in New York," *New York Times*, February 20, 1861, p. 1, ProQuest Historical Newspapers.

24 Villard, *Lincoln on the Eve of '61*, p. 97.

25 Flower, *Edwin McMasters Stanton*, p. 97.

26 "The Reception of the President Elect," *New York Times*, February 20, 1861, p. 4, ProQuest Historical Newspapers.

27 Sandburg, *Abraham Lincoln: The War Years*, vol. 1, p. 56.

28 Searcher, *Lincoln's Journey to Greatness*, pp. 182-183; "Arrival and Reception in New York."

29 "Arrival and Reception in New York."

30 Sandburg, *Abraham Lincoln: The War Years*, vol. 1, p. 58.

31 "News of the Day," *New York Times*, February 20, 1861, p. 4, ProQuest Historical Newspapers.

32 Searcher, *Lincoln's Journey to Greatness*, p. 185, quoting Genesis 15:1.

33 "Arrival and Reception in New York."

34 Searcher, *Lincoln's Journey to Greatness*, p. 184; "Arrival and Reception in New York." By some accounts, Lincoln arrived at the Astor House at 4:00 p.m. See, e.g., Warne report, February 19, 1861, in Cuthbert, *Lincoln and the Baltimore Plot*, p. 41. By other accounts, Lincoln arrived at the Astor House at 4:30. See, e.g., "Arrival and Reception in New York."

35 Sandburg, *Abraham Lincoln: The War Years*, vol. 1, p. 57; Searcher, Lincoln's Journey to Greatness, p. 186.

36 Sandburg, *Abraham Lincoln: The War Years*, vol. 1, p. 56.

37 Browne, *The Every-day Life of Abraham Lincoln*, p. 276.

38 Kate Warne, report, February 19, 1861, in Cuthbert, *Lincoln and the Baltimore Plot*, p. 41.

39 Wall, *Following Abraham Lincoln*, p. 241; Harold Holzer, "The Photograph That Made Lincoln President," *Civil War Times* (November/December 2006): 25-33.

40 See generally Holzer, "The Photograph That Made Lincoln President."

41 *CW*, 4:229-230; "Arrival and Reception in New York." p. 8.

42 "Arrival and Reception in New York."

43 Searcher, *Lincoln's Journey to Greatness*, p. 187; "Arrival and Reception in New York."

44 See, for example, Washburne's letter of January 10, 1861 to Lincoln, wherein he reports "I believe Va. and Maryland are both rotten to the core. We have had one of our friends from N.Y. (the kind I wrote about) in Baltimore, sounding matters there, and he gives most unfavorable reports." Elihu B. Washburne to Abraham Lincoln, January 10, 1861, Mearns, *The Lincoln Papers*, vol. 2, p. 398.

45 "Arrival and Reception in New York."

46 Norman B. Judd to Allan Pinkerton, November 3, 1867, in Pinkerton, *History and Evidence*, p. 17; Henry C. Whitney, *Lincoln the Citizen*, vol. 1 of *A Life of Lincoln*, ed. Marion Mills Miller (New York: Baker & Taylor, 1908), p. 301.

47 Norman B. Judd to Allan Pinkerton, November 3, 1867, in Pinkerton, *History and Evidence*, p. 17.

48 Ibid.

49 Likely one of Judd's questions was, why did this agent need to travel all the way to New York to deliver her message? He later reported that Warne advised that Pinkerton did not trust the mail for such important matters. Ibid., p. 18.

50 Ibid., p. 17.

51 Kate Warne, report, February 19, 1861, in Cuthbert, *Lincoln and the Baltimore Plot*, p. 42.

52 Ibid. Warne was one to know about the delays associated with rail travel. She had left Pinkerton in Baltimore the previous afternoon on the 5:16 train for New York and did not arrive in New York until 4:00 a.m. the next day, nearly twelve hours later. But it seems possible that if Warne had sent a telegram to Pinkerton the evening of the February 19, he would have been able to get to New York well before the Lincoln party left town at 8:00 a.m. on Thursday, February 21.

53 Allan Pinkerton to William Herndon, August 23, 1866, in Cuthbert, *Lincoln and the Baltimore Plot*, p. 9.

54 Warne report, February 19, 1861, in Cuthbert, *Lincoln and the Baltimore Plot*, p. 42; Norman B. Judd to Allan Pinkerton, November 3, 1867, in Pinkerton, *History and Evidence*, p. 18.

55 Warne report, February 19, 1861, in Cuthbert, *Lincoln and the Baltimore Plot*, pp. 43–44.

56 Ibid., p. 44.

57 Ibid.

58 Alan Hynd, *Arrival: 12:30; The Baltimore Plot Against Lincoln* (Camden, N.J.: Thomas Nelson & Sons, 1967).

59 Warne report, February 19, 1861, in Cuthbert, *Lincoln and the Baltimore Plot*, p. 44.

60 See, e.g., Allan Pinkerton to William Herndon, August 23, 1866, in Cuthbert, *Lincoln and the Baltimore Plot*, pp. 9-10.

61 Warne report, February 19, 1861, in Cuthbert, *Lincoln and the Baltimore Plot*, p. 44.

62 Harry W. Davies, report, February 19, 1861, in Cuthbert, *Abraham Lincoln and the Baltimore Plot*, p. 46. In what seems a game of cat and mouse, Hillard thus seeks a legal document from Davies, an "article of agreement" or contract that he must have known no sane person would execute, as it would have provided Hillard with a document to use against Davies, e.g., for blackmail. Alternatively, the document would have provided evidence, albeit contrived, of Davies' complicity in the plot. Perhaps Hillard wanted to judge Davies' reaction to the offer as a means of testing him.

63 Harry W. Davies, report, February 19, 1861, in Cuthbert, *Abraham Lincoln and the Baltimore Plot*, pp. 46-47. William Shakespeare, *Julius Caesar*, act 3, scene 2 (emphasis added). Hillard's tirade bears remarkable resemblance to similar utterances reportedly written by John Wilkes Booth in his letter to the National Intelligencer the day he shot

Lincoln. Then, he wrote (Rodehamel, John, and Louie Taper, eds., *Right or or Wrong*, pp. 149-150),

> When Caesar had conquered the enemies of Rome and the power that was his menaced the liberties of the people, Brutus arose and slew him. The stroke of his dagger was guided by his love of Rome. It was the spirit and ambition of Caesar that Brutus struck at.
> "Oh that we could come by Caesar's spirit,
> And not dismember Caesar!
> But alas!
> Caesar must bleed for it."
> I answer with Brutus:
> He who loves his country better than gold or life.

64 Possibly referring to a company of the National Volunteers or to Company B, Maryland Regiment, of the Knights of the Golden Circle, headed by George Bickley and of which Cypriano Ferrandini was also a member. Tidwell, *Come Retribution*, p. 228.

65 This restaurant was likely located in Mann's Hotel, on Baltimore, near North Street. Scharf, *History of Baltimore City and County*, vol. 2, p. 517.

66 Harry W. Davies, report, February 19, 1861, in Cuthbert, *Lincoln and the Baltimore Plot*, pp. 47-48.

67 Ibid. Hillard's reference to the "Committee" is to the Select Committee of Five, before whom he had testified two weeks earlier. During that testimony, he denied having been a member of any military organization and testified that he had no knowledge of any organization inimical to the government or to President-elect Lincoln. He did admit, consistent with Ferrandini's testimony, that the National Volunteers might resist the passage of troops from the North through Baltimore. He refused to answer when asked for the names of members of the National Volunteers. He was not forced to answer but was warned that he might be recalled if the committee deemed it necessary, in which case he would be compelled to answer. Cuthbert, *Lincoln and the Baltimore Plot*, pp. 140-141 n. 45, citing the Select Committee of Five's Report No. 79, pp. 144-155.

68 Cuthbert, *Lincoln and the Baltimore Plot*, pp. 139-140 n. 45.

69 Report No. 79, pp. 145-151.

70 The Committee, curiously, did not directly ask Ferrandini if he was a member of the National Volunteers. Ferrandini implied that he was only a member of the Constitutional Guards, but admitted that this company had recently adjourned to drill at the headquarters of the National Volunteers. Report No. 79, pp. 132-139.

71 Davies report, February 19, 1861, in Cuthbert, *Lincoln and the Baltimore Plot*, p. 48.

CHAPTER 11

1 This was likely the alias of one of three known Pinkerton agents: Samuel Bridgman, Pryce Lewis, or John Scully. Cuthbert, *Lincoln and the Baltimore Plot*, p. 20. Lewis and Scully would later attempt to rescue Pinkerton agent and Union spy Timothy Webster from Richmond in 1862. Edwin C. Fishel, *The Secret War for the Union* (Boston: Houghton Mifflin, 1996), pp. 148-149.

2 Allan Pinkerton (as J. H. Hutcheson) to S. M. Felton, February 25, 1861, Felton Papers (no. 1151), Box 1, Folder 3, Historical Society of Pennsylvania. Thirteen months later, John Wilkes Booth would stay at the St. Nicholas Hotel while performing in New York City. *New York Times*, March 17, 1862, p. 8. ProQuest Historical Newspapers.

3 Allan Pinkerton, report, February 21, 1861, in Cuthbert, *Lincoln and the Baltimore Plot*, p. 59.

4 See, e.g., testimony of Otis K. Hillard, *Reports of the Select Committee of Five,* Report No. 79, p. 152.

5 Report No. 79, p. 145.

6 Harry Davies, report, February 12, 1861, in Cuthbert, *Lincoln and the Baltimore Plot*, p. 29.

7 *Harper's Weekly*, March 9, 1861, p. 151.

8 Charles D. C. Williams, report, February 20, 1861, in Cuthbert, *Lincoln and the Baltimore Plot*, p. 50.

9 Ibid.

10 "Movements of the President Elect Today," *New York Times,* February 20, 1861, p. 8, ProQuest Historical Newspapers.

11 *New York Times,* February 21, 1861, p. 1, ProQuest Historical Newspapers.

12 *New York Times,* February 21, 1861, p. 1, ProQuest Historical Newspapers.

13 "The Incoming Administration," *New York Times,* February 21, 1861, p. 1, ProQuest Historical Newspapers.

14 Sandburg, *Abraham Lincoln: The War Years,* vol. 1, p. 59.

15 "The Incoming Administration," *New York Times,* February 21, 1861, p. 1.

16 *Philadelphia Inquirer,* February 21, 1861, p. 1.

17 "The Incoming Administration," *New York Times,* February 21, 1861, p. 1.

18 Browne, *The Every-day Life of Abraham Lincoln*, p. 276.

19 *New York World*, February 21, 1861, p. 8.

20 "The Incoming Administration," *New York Times,* February 21, 1861, p. 1, 8.

21 *New York World*, February 21, 1861, p. 8.

22 Hunt, *Hannibal Hamlin of Maine*, p. 143.

23 Ibid.

24 Hamlin, *The Life and Times of Hannibal Hamlin*, p. 387.

25 Ibid.

26 "News of the Day," *New York Times,* February 21, 1861, ProQuest Historical Newspapers.

27 *Philadelphia Inquirer,* February 21, 1861, p. 1.

28 Searcher, *Lincoln's Journey to Greatness*, p. 189.

29 Hamlin, *The Life and Times of Hannibal Hamlin*, p. 388.

30 Kennedy reported these facts in a narrative written years later, on August 13, 1866, to Benson J. Lossing. See Benson J. Lossing, *Pictorial History of the Civil War in the United States of America,* 3 vols. (Mansfield, Ohio: Estill, 1866), vol. 2, pp. 147-148 n. In that letter,

Kennedy sought to set the record straight. He had read an account of Lincoln's journey to Washington written by Lossing, which gave credit to Pinkerton, and found it faithful "as far as the narrative goes," but regretted that "it was not more full in showing how and to whom the country is indebted for the safety of [Lincoln's] life at that important period."

31 Lossing, *Pictorial History of the Civil War*, vol. 2, pp. 148-149n.

32 Ibid., p. 148n. Kennedy reports Stone's mistrust of the mails and yet reports that Bookstaver had posted a letter to him "briefly stating the condition of things," before going on the 4:00 a.m. train to Baltimore.

33 Report No. 79, pp. 90-91.

34 Lossing, *Pictorial History of the Civil War*, vol. 2, p. 149n. Colonel Stone's narrative as reported hereinafter derives from John A. Kennedy's letter to Benson J. Lossing written on August 13, 1866, including an extract of a letter from Stone to Kennedy.

35 Report No. 79, pp. 57-58.

36 Lossing, *Pictorial History of the Civil War*, vol. 2, p. 149n. This report, supposed to be written by Stone to Kennedy after the events took place (and included in an August 18, 1866, letter from Kennedy to Lossing), bears a striking resemblance to Pinkerton's account and his plan as implemented, suggesting either that some of Pinkerton's plan might have been obtained, e.g., from General Scott, or that Stone (or Kennedy), having learned after the fact the details of Pinkerton's plan, was simply adopting elements of it as his own. Six weeks after meeting with Bookstaver, Colonel Stone would write William Seward "on the subject of which we conversed this morning," including rumors that "Mr. Forsyth, one of Mr. Jeffn Davis' commissioners asserted on Wednesday to Dr Mackie, clerk in the State Department, that within sixty days, the Government of the Confederate States would embrace this city [Washington] and all the States north as far as New York That said States would extend their protection thus far, but would cut off those damned puritan States east, and never let them come in." Other rumors included one that Mrs. Jefferson Davis told a friend visiting Washington to tell Mrs. Davis's friends there "I shall be happy to see them in the White House in June." Yet another rumor reported by Stone was that there was a report of "a young man formerly employed by Gilman, the Druggist on Pa Avenue, [who] stated that there were thousands of young men in Virginia, here [Washington] and in Baltimore ready to rise up armed at a given signal by Mr Davis—That the attack on Fort Sumpter [*sic*] would be the Signal for action here, and plenty of men would rise to seize and hold the Capital until the Southern Army could reach here," and "that the President, Cabinet Officers and General Scott would be made prisoners at the outset." Stone's letter concludes, "It would not to me be an improbable conception, that those who now rule the southern states intend to secure to themselves the prestige of possessing this capital, and forcing a revolution here and in the middle states—." Charles P. Stone to William H. Seward, April 5, 1861, Abraham Lincoln Papers at the Library of Congress. The rumored plan to make prisoners of Lincoln and the cabinet bears a striking resemblance to John Wilkes Booth's aborted kidnapping plot and, later, his plan to kill Lincoln, Seward, and Vice President Johnson.

37 Lossing, *Pictorial History of the Civil War*, vol. 2, p. 149n.

38 By this statement, it is unclear if Seward meant by "this crisis" the assassination threat or the broader secessionist threat. If the former, perhaps Seward intended to remain in Washington in the event assassination did result, and succession planning proved necessary.

39 Washington H. Penrose Collection (no. 492), from Penrose diary, December 1859 to July 1862, entry dated February 21, 1861, Historical Society of Pennsylvania, 1300 Locust Street, Philadelphia.

40 Pinkerton, *Spy of the Rebellion*, pp. 80-81.

41 Allan Pinkerton to William Herndon, August 23, 1866, in Cuthbert, *Lincoln and the Baltimore Plot*, p. 9; Allan Pinkerton, report, February 21, 1861, in Cuthbert, *Lincoln and the Baltimore Plot*, p. 52.

42 Allan Pinkerton to William Herndon, August 23, 1866, in Cuthbert, *Lincoln and the Baltimore Plot*, p. 6.

43 See, e.g., "Samuel M. Felton's Narrative," in Forney, *Anecdotes of Public Men*, pp. 248-251. Indeed, before hiring Pinkerton, Felton had laid his suspicions before Baltimore marshal George P. Kane. After claiming to have thoroughly investigated the rumors, Kane said there was no foundation for them. After this, Felton determined to have nothing to do with Kane and hired Pinkerton. Ibid., p. 250.

44 Francis Tiffany, *Life of Dorothea Lynde Dix* (Boston: Houghton, Mifflin, 1890), p. 334. For a substantially identical but more thorough Felton account, see Forney, *Anecdotes of Public Men*.

45 Allan Pinkerton, report, February 21, 1861, in Cuthbert, *Lincoln and the Baltimore Plot*, pp. 52-53.

46 Ibid., p. 53.

47 "He [Kane] scouted the idea that there was any such thing on foot; said he had thoroughly investigated the whole matter, and there was not the slightest foundation for such rumors. I then determined to have nothing more to do with Marshal Kane." Instead, Felton turned to "a celebrated detective, who resided in the West," whom he had employed previously. The detective, of course, was Allan Pinkerton. Forney, *Anecdotes of Public Men*, pp. 250-251.

48 *American Annual Cyclopædia,* vol. 1, p. 419.

49 Ibid.

50 Pinkerton report, February 21, 1861, in Cuthbert, *Lincoln and the Baltimore Plot*, pp. 53-54.

51 Ibid. p. 54. Warne had either come directly to Philadelphia from New York, meeting Pinkerton there on the February 21, or traveled from New York to Baltimore on February 20 as planned, meeting Pinkerton there and returning with him to Philadelphia later that day. Their reports do not make this clear.

52 Scharf, *History of Maryland,* pp. 387-388 n. 2.

53 Ibid., p. 388, citing the Baltimore *American* of February 26, 1861. Ironically, the Baltimore paper credited Marshal Kane with providing the information that induced Mr. Lincoln to alter his travel plans—not out of fear for his life, but to avoid the possible breach of the peace upon the Baltimore Republican Committee. Ibid.

54 Ibid.

55 Ibid.

56 Ibid.

57 Lincoln's physical traits, including his large hands and feet, unusual height, awkwardness, odd-shaped head, sad disposition, deep-set eyes, large ears, high cheekbones, sharp chin, long, thin neck, narrow chest, and humped shoulders are all traits of Marfan syndrome, a hereditary disease of the bones, muscles, and ligaments that can also present with heart problems. Lincoln and his four sons may have had the disease. Ironically, those afflicted with the disorder also tend to benefit from extraordinary intelligence and sensitivity— "unusual qualities of mind and spirit." Arthur Whitman, "Lincoln's Strange Malady," *Pittsburgh Press,* February 10, 1963.

58 Lamon, *The Life of Abraham Lincoln,* p. 470.

59 See, e.g., *Frank Leslie's Illustrated Weekly,* July 26, 1856, illustrating a collision between passenger and excursion trains near Camp Hill Station, Pennsylvania, on July 17, 1856; August Mencken, *The Railroad Passenger Car: An Illustrated History of the First Hundred Years, With Accounts by Contemporary Passengers* (Baltimore: Johns Hopkins Press, 1957), p. 121.

60 Cuthbert, *Lincoln and the Baltimore Plot,* pp. 9, 14, 54.

61 Pinkerton report, February 21, 1861, in Cuthbert, *Lincoln and the Baltimore Plot,* pp. 55-56.

62 *New York Times,* February 22, 1861, p. 1, ProQuest Historical Newspapers.

63 *Philadelphia Daily Evening Bulletin,* February 22, 1861, p. 2.

64 See Albany *Atlas and Argus,* February 22, 1861, p. 2.

65 Rodehamel, John, and Louie Taper, eds., *Right or Wrong,* p. 64 n. 2.

66 *Philadelphia Inquirer,* December 14, 1861, p. 2; see also Rodehamel, John, and Louie Taper, eds., *Right or Wrong,* p. 64 n. 2, p. 65 nn. 7, 10.

67 Rodehamel, John, and Louie Taper, eds., *Right or Wrong,* p. 55 (strikethrough and carrots original).

68 *New York Times,* February 22, 1861, p. 1, ProQuest Historical Newspapers.

69 Burlingame, ed., *Lincoln's Journalist,* p. 41.

70 *Philadelphia Daily Evening Bulletin,* February 22, 1861, p. 2.

71 See, e.g., *Philadelphia Inquirer,* February 19, 1861, p. 8; February 20, 1861, p. 8; and February 21, 1861, p. 8.

72 *Philadelphia Inquirer,* February 19, 1861, p. 8; and February 21, 1861, p. 8.

73 See *Harper's Weekly,* vol. IX, No. 452 (August 26, 1865).

74 Pinkerton report, February 21, 1861, in Cuthbert, *Lincoln and the Baltimore Plot,* p. 56.

75 Possibly referring to Ms. Dix and the unidentified gentleman from Baltimore who had passed periodic reports of the conspiracy to Felton, first coming to the attention of the bridgekeeper at Back River Bridge (near Baltimore). See William Schouler, *A History of Massachusetts in the Civil War* (Boston: E. P. Dutton, 1868), p. 60.

76 Kate Warne, report, February 19, 1861, in Cuthbert, *Lincoln and the Baltimore Plot,* p. 44.

77 See Herndon's notes of an interview with Norman B. Judd in Cuthbert, *Lincoln and the Baltimore Plot,* p. 109. Judd apparently took a regular train from Harrisburg to Philadelphia after the Lincoln Special on the night of February 22-23. When asked what he was doing on that train, Judd reportedly indicated to Henry C. Whitney, who was riding the same

train and was surprised to see Judd on it, that he had "grown so nervous at the noise and excitement of the journey with the President that he had concluded to slip quietly away where he could get some rest and tranquillity." Whitney, *Lincoln the Citizen*, p. 300. Perhaps. But perhaps Judd wanted to avoid being on the Lincoln Special that would be leaving Harrisburg early the next morning for Baltimore, and thereby avoid any danger that might still befall it. According to Whitney, "Judd questioned me as to what I had heard about the journey so closely as to arouse my curiosity, and he whispered to me significantly, 'I'll tell you more when we get to Philadelphia.'" Ibid.

78 Pinkerton report, February 21, 1861, in Cuthbert, *Lincoln and the Baltimore Plot*, p. 57.

79 Ibid.

80 The Continental Hotel was located at 91 Chestnut Street, Philadelphia. It had a capacity of 1,300 guests and was operated by J. E. Kingsley & Company. *The Centennial Exhibition and the Pennsylvania Railroad* ([Chicago]: Rand, McNally, 1876), p. 42.

81 Letter from Norman B. Judd to Allan Pinkerton, dated November 3, 1867, in Pinkerton, *History and Evidence,* p. 18. Judd gives the place of the encounter at the corner of Broad and Chestnut. Ibid. The cavalcade, however, did not actually cross this intersection, rather it, crossed Broad on Walnut. *The Philadelphia Inquirer,* February 22, 1861, p. 8.

82 Pinkerton report, February 21, 1861, in Cuthbert, *Lincoln and the Baltimore Plot*, pp. 57-58.

83 Ibid., p. 58.

84 Pinkerton, *History and Evidence,* p. 15.

85 "Samuel M. Felton's Narrative," in Forney, *Anecdotes of Public Men*, p. 253. See also Felton's letter dated October 30, 1867, to Benson J. Lossing: "On the night of Mr. Lincoln's arrival in Philadelphia I sent by Pinkerton for Mr. Judd & met him at a Hotel in Phila[delphia] when I made known to him the plot & told him to say to Mr. Lincoln that I advised his going to Washington that night in our Sleeping Car & that he should not go to Harrisburg as he had arranged." Felton also reported in this letter that he had on this date seen an account in the *New York Times* by John A. Kennedy. Felton denied that Kennedy had any involvement in Felton's planning. Felton Papers (no. 1151), Box 2, Folder 6, Historical Society of Pennsylvania.

86 Pinkerton report, February 21, 1861, in Cuthbert, *Lincoln and the Baltimore Plot*, pp. 58-59. Judd had conversed with Pinkerton agent William H. Scott in Cincinnati—"He spoke very feelingly of A.P. [Allan Pinkerton] and said they had trained in the same school together." William H. Scott, report, February 13, 1861, in Cuthbert, *Lincoln and the Baltimore Plot*, p. 31.

87 As recounted by Felton ("Samuel M. Felton's Narrative," in Forney, *Anecdotes*, p. 251),

> There were then drilling upon the line of the railroad some three military organizations, professedly for home defense, pretending to be Union men, and, in one or two instances, tendering their services to the railroad in case of trouble. Their propositions were duly considered; but the defense of the road was never intrusted [sic] to their tender mercies. The first thing done was to enlist a volunteer [Pinkerton operative] in each of these military companies. They pretended to come from New Orleans and Mobile, and did

not appear to be wanting in sympathy for the South. They were furnished with uniforms at the expense of the road, and drilled as often as their associates in arms; became initiated into all the secrets of the organization, and reported every day or two to their chief [Pinkerton], who immediately reported to me the designs and plans of these military companies. One of these organizations was loyal, but the other two were disloyal, and fully in the plot to destroy the bridges and march to Washington to wrest it from the hands of the legally constituted authorities. Every nook and corner of the road and its vicinity was explored by the chief and his detectives, and the secret working of secession and treason laid bare and brought to light.

The two disloyal organizations were likely the Perrymansville Rangers and the Spesutia Rangers.

88 Pinkerton report, February 21, 1861, in Cuthbert, *Lincoln and the Baltimore Plot*, p. 53.

89 Ibid., pp. 59-60.

90 Ibid., p. 60.

91 See, e.g., Howard's account in the *New York Times*, February 22, 1861, p. 1, ProQuest Historical Newspapers.

92 Pinkerton report, February 21, 1861, in Cuthbert, *Lincoln and the Baltimore Plot*, p. 60.

93 Ibid., pp. 60-61.

94 Mearns, *The Lincoln Papers*, vol. 2, pp. 437-439.

95 In fairness, it does not appear that Lincoln ever answered Snethen's Albany letter. It also does not appear, however, that he ever received an invitation from Baltimore's mayor. See Snethen's February 25th letter to Lincoln, indicating that Snethen had not heard from Lincoln in reply to his Albany note and that Mayor Brown had apparently assured Snethen that "he did not believe the Council would take action, and that he [Mayor Brown] should be present in his official capacity, to receive you [Lincoln], and to accompany you alone, in a private two-seat carriage," and that "a strong force of police was to be present at the Depot upon your arrival, to prevent the pressure of the crowd around the carriages, when they should drive off under the protection of the Mayor. The disembarkation was to be effected within the enclosure of the Depot, in the presence of the Committee of 100 [Republicans] and such other citizens as chose to be present. No request was made by any of your friends for the presence of the Police." Worthington G. Snethen to Abraham Lincoln, February 25, 1861, Abraham Lincoln Papers at the Library of Congress.

96 Pinkerton report, February 21, 1861, in Cuthbert, *Lincoln and the Baltimore Plot*, p. 61.

97 See, e.g., special pass issued by W. S. Wood to Captain George W. Hazzard, granting him permission to ride on the Lincoln Special Searcher, *Lincoln's Journey to Greatness*, p. 56.

98 See, e.g., the anonymous reporter's stinging criticism of Mr. Wood for waking the party at 4:00 a.m. for an early start in leaving Buffalo. Burlingame, ed., *Lincoln's Journalist,* p. 36.

99 Whitney, *Lincoln the Citizen*, p. 301.

100 "Samuel M. Felton's Narrative," in Forney, *Anecdotes*, p. 253.

101 Allan Pinkerton to William Herndon, August 23, 1866, in Cuthbert, *Lincoln and the Baltimore Plot*, p. 10.

102 Norman B. Judd to Allan Pinkerton, November 3, 1867, in Pinkerton, *History and Evidence,* p. 18.

103 Pinkerton to Herndon, August 23, 1866, in Cuthbert, *Lincoln and the Baltimore Plot*, p. 10.

104 This may be because Judd reportedly feared that Lincoln would not consent to a change of plan unless Pinkerton, who was known to Lincoln "as an old acquaintance and friend," upon whom Lincoln had prior occasions to test his "reliability and prudence," did the urging. See Pinkerton, *Spy of the Rebellion*, p. 83. Judd later confirmed that "Lincoln liked Pinkerton—had the utmost confidence in him as a gentleman, and a man of sagacity." Herndon's notes of an interview with Norman B. Judd, in Cuthbert, *Lincoln and the Baltimore Plot*, p. 109.

105 Pinkerton report, February 21, 1861, in Cuthbert, *Lincoln and the Baltimore Plot*, p. 62

106 *Philadelphia Inquirer,* February 22, 1861.

107 Frederick W. Seward, "How Lincoln Was Warned of the Baltimore Assassination Plot," reprinted in William Hayes Ward, ed., *Abraham Lincoln: Tributes from His Associates; Reminiscences of Soldiers, Statesmen and Citizens* (New York: Thomas Y. Crowell, 1895).

108 Ibid., pp. 61-62.

109 Pinkerton report, February 21, 1861, in Cuthbert, *Lincoln and the Baltimore Plot*, p. 62.

110 Pinkerton to Herndon, August 23, 1866, in Cuthbert, *Lincoln and the Baltimore Plot*, p. 10.

111 Judd to Pinkerton, November 3, 1867, in Pinkerton, *History and Evidence,* p. 19.

112 Pinkerton report, February 21, 1861, in Cuthbert, *Lincoln and the Baltimore Plot*, pp. 62-63.

113 Judd to Pinkerton, November 3, 1867, in Pinkerton, *History and Evidence,* p. 19.

114 Henry Sanford was an employee of the Adams Express Company who would go on to become its President. See letter, Sanford to Robert Pinkerton, May 17, 1898, Box 23, Folder 4, The Pinkerton Papers at the Library of Congress.

115 See, e.g., advertisement for the Adams Express Company, in Mencken, *Railroad Passenger Car*, p. 130.

116 Pinkerton report, February 21, 1861, in Cuthbert, *Lincoln and the Baltimore Plot*, p. 63. At first, the request by Pinkerton might seem like overkill. But Pinkerton had performed service in the past for Felton and other railroads to solve train robberies. He knew how such criminals thought and how they might seize on opportunities that presented themselves. While his suggestion to the Adams Express to double its messengers might have done little to save an imperiled Lincoln, it demonstrates that Pinkerton was looking out for the welfare of his other paying clients.

117 Ibid., p. 55.

118 Ibid., p. 64.

119 This somewhat derogatory remark by Pinkerton in reference to Ellsworth suggests Pinkerton did not appreciate being shunned by the brash young colonel. All but extinct, the term "equerry" refers to a "groom" for horses, or "an officer in the service of a royal or other exalted personage, charged with the care of the horses." Also, "at the English Court,

an officer of the royal household, charged with the duty of occasional attendance on the sovereign." See *The Compact Edition of the Oxford English Dictionary*, s.v. "equerry."

120 Pinkerton report, February 21, 1861, in Cuthbert, *Lincoln and the Baltimore Plot*, p. 64.

121 Ibid.

122 Herndon's notes of an interview with Judd, in Cuthbert, *Lincoln and the Baltimore Plot*, p. 109.

CHAPTER 12

1 Allan Pinkerton, report, February 21, 1861, in Cuthbert, *Lincoln and the Baltimore Plot*, p. 64.

2 William Herndon's notes of an 1866 interview with Norman B. Judd, in Cuthbert, *Lincoln and the Baltimore Plot*, p. 109. Note, however, that it has also been reported that Lincoln suspected that Pinkerton tended to exaggerate. Morn, *The Eye That Never Sleeps*, p. 40.

3 Pinkerton report, February 21, 1861, in Cuthbert, *Lincoln and the Baltimore Plot,* p. 64.

4 At one point, Lincoln had to sue one of his railroad clients, the Illinois Central Railroad, for his $5,000 fee. With Judge David Davis presiding, he won. Donald, *Lincoln*, p. 156.

5 Morn, *The Eye That Never Sleeps*, p. 40.

6 George S. Bryan, *The Spy in America* (Philadelphia: J. B. Lippincott, 1943), p. 47.

7 By another account, it was Pinkerton who informed Lincoln of the plot. Whitney, *Lincoln the Citizen*, p. 301.

8 Pinkerton report, February 21, 1861, in Cuthbert, *Lincoln and the Baltimore Plot*, p. 64. Several years later, in December 1864, Lincoln recalled that Pinkerton informed him of the assassination plot. Lossing, *Pictorial History of the Civil War,* vol. 1, p. 279.

9 Norman B. Judd to Allan Pinkerton, November 3, 1867, in Pinkerton, *History and Evidence,* p. 19.

10 Pinkerton report, February 21, 1861, in Cuthbert, *Lincoln and the Baltimore Plot*, p. 64.

11 Ibid., p. 65. Interestingly, with the 20-20 vision of hindsight, portions of this description also aptly describe John Wilkes Booth.

12 Lincoln's account, as reported in Lossing, *Pictorial History of the Civil War,* vol. 1, p. 279; Pinkerton report February 21, 1861, in Cuthbert, *Lincoln and the Baltimore Plot*, pp. 65-66.

13 See Edward Stanley Lanis, "Allen [*sic*] Pinkerton and the Baltimore 'Assassination' Plot Against Lincoln," *Maryland Historical Magazine*, vol. 45, no. 1 (March 1950): 7.

14 Pinkerton report, February 21, 1861, in Cuthbert, *Lincoln and the Baltimore Plot*, p. 66; Judd to Pinkerton, November 3, 1867, in Pinkerton, *History and Evidence,* p. 19.

15 Pinkerton report, February 21, 1861, in Cuthbert, *Lincoln and the Baltimore Plot*, p. 66; Judd to Pinkerton, November 3, 1867, in Pinkerton, *History and Evidence,* p. 19.

16 Pinkerton report, February 21, 1861, in Cuthbert, *Lincoln and the Baltimore Plot*, p. 66. Pinkerton held secrecy most dear. "Secrecy is the one thing most necessary to the success of the detective, and when a secret is to be kept, the fewer who know of it the better." Pinkerton, *History and Evidence,* p. 6.

17 Report from Washington of embedded *New York Times* correspondent Joseph Howard Jr., who accompanied the Lincoln Special from Harrisburg to Washington on February 23,

1861; "The Incoming Administration," *New York Times,* February 26, 1861, p. 8, ProQuest Historical Newspapers. While the three supposed plans are not reported by Pinkerton himself, it is likely that he reported them to the *Times* correspondent, given the accuracy of the other details reported in the account, and its reference to confirmation by a "celebrated Western detective who had been detailed from Chicago." Ibid.

18 Indeed, Pinkerton would claim that in all subsequent meetings with Lincoln, he never saw him more "cool, collected and firm" than that night. "In fact he did not appear to me to realize the great danger which was threatening him at that moment. He said that if once he reached Washington there was no danger; Mr. Buchanan would soon vacate, and he could rely upon General Scott until that time for protection." Pinkerton to Herndon, August 23, 1866, in Cuthbert, *Lincoln and the Baltimore Plot*, p. 11.

19 Pinkerton report, February 21, 1861, in Cuthbert, *Lincoln and the Baltimore Plot*, p. 66.

20 Pinkerton to Herndon, August 23, 1866, in Cuthbert, *Lincoln and the Baltimore Plot*, p. 10.

21 Lincoln's account, in Lossing, *Pictorial History of the Civil War*, vol. 1, p. 279; Pinkerton to Herndon, August 23, 1866, in Cuthbert, *Lincoln and the Baltimore Plot*, p. 10.

22 See "Map of Philadelphia Showing Lines and Depots of the Pennsylvania Railroad Company," in *The Centennial Exhibition and the Pennsylvania Railroad* ([Chicago]: Rand, McNally., 1876).

23 Lossing, *Pictorial History of the Civil War*, vol. 1, pp. 279-280.

24 Judd to Pinkerton, November 3, 1867, in Pinkerton, *History and Evidence,* p. 19.

25 Pinkerton report, February 21, 1861, in Cuthbert, *Lincoln and the Baltimore Plot*, pp. 66-67. The version of Lincoln's reply as reported by Judd is: "I cannot go tonight. I have promised to raise the flag over Independence Hall to-morrow morning, and to visit the Legislature at Harrisburg, beyond that I have no engagements. Any plan that may be adopted that will enable me to fulfill these two promises I will carry out, and you can tell me what is concluded upon to-morrow." Judd to Pinkerton, November 3, 1867, in Pinkerton, *History and Evidence,* p. 19.

26 Lossing, *Pictorial History of the Civil War*, vol. 1, pp. 279-280.

27 Herndon's notes of an 1866 interview with Judd, in Cuthbert, *Lincoln and the Baltimore Plot*, p. 110.

28 Pinkerton to Herndon, August 23, 1866, in Cuthbert, *Lincoln and the Baltimore Plot*, p. 8; Pinkerton report, February 21, 1861, Cuthbert, *Lincoln and the Baltimore Plot*, p. 68.

29 Pinkerton report, February 21, 1861, Cuthbert, *Lincoln and the Baltimore Plot*, p. 68.

30 Ibid., p. 67.

31 Ibid., pp. 67-68.

32 Judd to Pinkerton, November 3, 1867, in Pinkerton, *History and Evidence,* p. 19.

33 Pinkerton report, February 21, 1861, in Cuthbert, *Lincoln and the Baltimore Plot*, p. 68.

34 Seward, "How Lincoln Was Warned of the Baltimore Assassination Plot," in Ward, *Abraham Lincoln*, p. 61.

35 Ibid.

36 Cuthbert, *Lincoln and the Baltimore Plot*, p. 131 n. 29; Sandburg, *Abraham Lincoln: The War Years*, vol. 1, p. 69.

37 Winfield Scott to William H. Seward, February 21, 1861, Abraham Lincoln Papers at the Library of Congress.

38 Lossing, *Pictorial History of the Civil War*, vol. 2, p. 149 n.

39 Memorandum of Charles P. Stone, February 21, 1861, Abraham Lincoln Papers at the Library of Congress. The New York detective who had been on duty in Baltimore three weeks past was David S. Bookstaver. See Lossing, *Pictorial History of the Civil War*, vol. 2, p. 149 n.

40 Seward, "How Lincoln Was Warned," pp. 62-63.

41 Statement of Abraham Lincoln in 1864 to Benson J. Lossing, in Lossing, *Pictorial History of the Civil War*, vol. 1, pp. 279-280.

42 Seward, *Seward at Washington*, pp. 508-509. See also Seward, "How Lincoln Was Warned," pp. 62-64.

43 Pinkerton report, February 21, 1861, in Cuthbert, *Lincoln and the Baltimore Plot*, pp. 66-67.

44 *American Annual Cyclopædia*, p. 419.

45 Enoch Lewis to Allan Pinkerton, November 7, 1867, in Pinkerton, *History and Evidence*, p. 31.

46 Pinkerton to Herndon, August 23, 1866, in Cuthbert, *Lincoln and the Baltimore Plot*, p. 12.

47 Pinkerton report, February 21, 1861, in Cuthbert, *Lincoln and the Baltimore Plot*, p. 68.

48 This motto and logo was first used as a trademark by Pinkerton's National Detective Agency, Inc., in 1884. See U.S. Trademark Registration No. 0539452.

49 Pinkerton report, February 22, 1861, in Cuthbert, *Lincoln and the Baltimore Plot*, p. 69.

50 This address is given as Franciscus's office address in his November 5, 1867, letter to Pinkerton. Pinkerton, *History and Evidence*, p. 29.

51 Pinkerton gives the time of his catching up with Franciscus as 3:00 a.m. on February 22. Pinkerton to Herndon, August 23, 1866, in Cuthbert, *Lincoln and the Baltimore Plot*, p. 12. Franciscus gives the time of Pinkerton's arrival as between 11:00 p.m. and midnight on February 21. G. C. Franciscus to Allan Pinkerton, November 5, 1867, in Pinkerton, *History and Evidence*, p. 29. Since Pinkerton was meeting with KateWarne at 3:00 a.m., he could not also then have been in West Philadelphia meeting with Franciscus. Warne report, February 22, 1861, in Cuthbert, *Lincoln and the Baltimore Plot*, p. 80.

52 Pinkerton to Herndon , August 23, 1866, in Cuthbert, *Lincoln and the Baltimore Plot*, p. 12.

53 Franciscus to Pinkerton, November 5, 1867, in Pinkerton, *History and Evidence*, p. 29.

54 Pinkerton report, February 22, 1861, in Cuthbert, *Lincoln and the Baltimore Plot*, p. 69; Franciscus to Pinkerton, November 5, 1867, in Pinkerton, *History and Evidence*, p. 29.

55 Pinkerton to Herndon, August 23, 1866, in Cuthbert, *Lincoln and the Baltimore Plot*, pp. 12-13.

56 Judd to Pinkerton, November 3, 1867, in Pinkerton, *History and Evidence*, p. 20.

57 William Mason's Taunton, Massachusetts, works built the *Comet* and the *Meteor,* which pulled the Lincoln Special from Pittsburgh and Wellsville, respectively. Searcher, *Lincoln's Journey to Greatness*, pp. 94-95. For a representative Mason locomotive, the *Phantom,* built

in 1857, see White, *American Locomotives,* pp. 383-389.

58 Sunset in Harrisburg, Pennsylvania, on February 22, 1861, occurred at 5:52 p.m., and twilight ended at 6:19 p.m. U.S. Naval Observatory Astronomical Applications Department data for February 22, 1861, at http://aa.usno.navy.mil/data/docs/RS_OneDay. html.

59 Enoch Lewis, general superintendent of the Pennsylvania Railroad at the time, later recalled that he met "on appointment" with Judd and Franciscus the evening of February 21, 1861. Lewis was in Philadelphia to arrange for Lincoln's special train from Philadelphia to Harrisburg the next morning; at that time, Lincoln was scheduled to proceed from Harrisburg to Baltimore on February 23 on the Northern Central Railroad. During this meeting, Enoch recalled that the plot to assassinate Mr. Lincoln and the plan to alter his route by taking a special from Harrisburg to Philadelphia that night on the Pennsylvania Railroad was revealed to him, as it would have been his job to make the necessary arrangements for a special train of the Pennsylvania Railroad. Lewis to Pinkerton, November 7, 1867, in Pinkerton, *History and Evidence,* p. 31.

60 See, e.g., Bradley R. Hoch, *The Lincoln Trail in Pennsylvania* (University Park: Pennsylvania State University Press, 2001), p. 20.

61 Judd to Pinkerton, November 3, 1867, in Pinkerton, *History and Evidence,* p. 19-20; Pinkerton report, February 22, 1861, in Cuthbert, *Lincoln and the Baltimore Plot,* p. 69; Pinkerton to Herndon, August 23, 1866, in Cuthbert, *Lincoln and the Baltimore Plot,* p. 13; Whitney, *Lincoln the Citizen,* p. 302.

62 Whitney, *Lincoln the Citizen,* p. 302.

CHAPTER 13

1 *New York Times,* February 23, 1861, p. 1, ProQuest Historical Newspapers.

2 *New York Times,* February 25, 1861, p. 8, ProQuest Historical Newspapers.

3 *Philadelphia Inquirer,* February 23, 1861, p. 2; Forney, *Anecdotes of Public Men*, pp. 244-245.

4 *Philadelphia Inquirer,* February 23, 1861, p. 1.

5 Ibid., p. 2; Forney, *Anecdotes of Public Men*, pp. 244-245.

6 *Philadelphia Inquirer,* February 23, 1861, p. 3.

7 *Philadelphia Inquirer,* December 14, 1861, pp. 2-3; See also Rodehamel, John, and Louie Taper, eds., *Right or Wrong*, pp. 55, 65, n. 7.

8 *Philadelphia Inquirer,* February 23, 1861, p. 1 (emphasis added).

9 Ibid.

10 Ibid., p. 2.

11 Ibid. (emphasis added). For slightly different versions, see *American Annual Cyclopædia,* vol. 1, pp. 417-418, and *CW,* 4:240-241.

12 Allan Pinkerton, report, February 22, 1861, in Cuthbert, *Lincoln and the Baltimore Plot,* p. 70. Sunrise in Philadelphia on February 22, 1861, occurred at 6:44 a.m. U.S. Naval Observatory Astronomical Applications Department data for February 22, 1861, at http://aa.usno.navy.mil/data/docs/RS_OneDay.html.

13 *New York Times,* February 23, 1861, p. 1, ProQuest Historical Newspapers.

14 Ida Tarbell, *The Life of Abraham Lincoln* (New York: Lincoln History Society, 1909), vol. 2, p. 215.

15 *CW*, 4:242 n. 1.

16 *American Annual Cyclopædia,* vol. 1, p. 418; *CW*, 4:241-242.

17 Searcher, *Lincoln's Journey to Greatness*, p. 152, facing photograph page; Hoch, *Lincoln Trail in Pennsylvania*, p. 8.

18 *New York Times,* February 23, 1861, p. 1, ProQuest Historical Newspapers.

19 *Philadelphia Inquirer,* February 23, 1861, p. 3.

20 *New York Times,* February 23, 1861, p. 1, ProQuest Historical Newspapers.

21 *Philadelphia Inquirer,* February 23, 1861, p. 3.

22 Pinkerton to Herndon, August 23, 1866, in Cuthbert, *Lincoln and the Baltimore Plot*, p. 14.

23 Pinkerton report, February 22, 1861, in Cuthbert, *Lincoln and the Baltimore Plot*, p. 70; George R. Dunn to Allan Pinkerton, November 7, 1867, in Pinkerton, *History and Evidence,* p. 35.

24 Harry C. Davies, report, February 19, 1861, in Cuthbert, *Lincoln and the Baltimore Plot*, p. 48.

25 Charles D. C. Williams, report, February 20, 1861, in Cuthbert, *Lincoln and the Baltimore Plot*, p. 49.

26 George R. Dunn to Ward Hill Lamon, March 27, 1888, in Cuthbert, *Lincoln and the Baltimore Plot*, pp. 143-144 n. 53.

27 Pinkerton report, February 22, 1861, in Cuthbert, *Lincoln and the Baltimore Plot*, p. 70; George R. Dunn to Allan Pinkerton, November 7, 1867, in Pinkerton, *History and Evidence,* p. 35.

28 Pinkerton report, February 22, 1861, in Cuthbert, *Lincoln and the Baltimore Plot*, p. 71.

29 Norman B. Judd to Allan Pinkerton, November 3, 1867, in Pinkerton, *History and Evidence,* pp. 20-21.

30 Ibid.

31 Pinkerton report, February 22, 1861, in Cuthbert, *Lincoln and the Baltimore Plot*, p. 71.

32 Seward, "How Lincoln Was Warned of the Baltimore Assassination Plot," p. 64.

33 Address obtained from letterhead of letter dated April 18, 1861, from H. E. Thayer to S. M. Felton, Felton Papers (no. 1151), Box 1, Folder 4, Historical Society of Pennsylvania.

34 H. E. Thayer to Allan Pinkerton, November 3, 1867, in Pinkerton, *History and Evidence,* pp. 39-40.

35 Lanis, "Allen [*sic*] Pinkerton and the Baltimore 'Assassination' Plot Against Lincoln," p. 9.

36 See Andrew Wynne's letter to Allan Pinkerton, November 3, 1867, in Pinkerton, *History and Evidence,* p. 41.

37 Ibid. Westervelt's name is spelled "Westervilt" in one of Pinkerton's reports. See Cuthbert, *Lincoln and the Baltimore Plot*, p. 74 (H. Sanford telegram reporting to Pinkerton that Westervelt will leave at noon for Harrisburg with a professional climber).

38 Thayer to Pinkerton, November 3, 1867, in Pinkerton, *History and Evidence*, p. 40.

39 Generally, Pinkerton used the name "Hutcheson" as his alias. But frequently Pinkerton and others recalled it as "Hutchinson," particularly in later accounts. See, e.g., Pinkerton to Herndon, August 23, 1866, in Cuthbert, *Lincoln and the Baltimore Plot*, p. 5.

40 *Philadelphia Inquirer,* February 23, 1861, p. 3.

41 Hoch, *Lincoln Trail*, p. 11.

42 *New York Times*, February 25, 1861 p. 8, ProQuest Historical Newspapers. It was reported that "A great crowd followed the carriages, but a powerful posse of police, under Chief Ruggles, prevented any crowding upon the party." *Philadelphia Inquirer,* February 23, 1861, p. 3.

43 *New York Times,* February 23, 1861, p. 1, ProQuest Historical Newspapers.

44 Claude R. Flory, "Garman, Black, and the Baltimore Plot," *Pennsylvania Magazine of History and Biography* (January 1970): 102.

45 Hoch, *Lincoln Trail*, p. 14; *New York Times,* February 23, 1861, p. 1, ProQuest Historical Newspapers.

46 Flory, "Garman, Black, and the Baltimore Plot," p. 102; *New York Times*, February 25, 1861 p. 8, ProQuest Historical Newspapers.

47 Pennsylvania Official Transportation and Tourism Map, Department of Transportation, Commonwealth of Pennsylvania Department of General Services (2003).

48 Hoch, *Lincoln Trail*, p. 14.

49 Ibid.

50 *New York Times,* February 23, 1861, p. 1, ProQuest Historical Newspapers. Note that on the return trip, it is reported that John Pitcairn Jr. was in charge of the telegraph instrument. Enoch Lewis to Allan Pinkerton. November 7, 1867, in Pinkerton, *History and Evidence,* p. 31.

51 Pinkerton report, February 22, 1861, in Cuthbert, *Lincoln and the Baltimore Plot*, pp. 69-70.

52 Judd to Pinkerton, November 3, 1867, in Pinkerton, *History and Evidence,* p. 20.

53 Judd to Pinkerton, November 3, 1867, in Pinkerton, *History and Evidence,* p. 21; statement of Norman B. Judd as taken down in William Herndon's notes of an 1866 interview with Judd, in Cuthbert, *Lincoln and the Baltimore Plot*, p. 112.

54 Statement of Norman B. Judd in Cuthbert, *Lincoln and the Baltimore Plot*, p. 112.

55 G. C. Franciscus to Allan Pinkerton, November 5, 1867, in Pinkerton, *History and Evidence,* p. 29.

56 *New York Times*, February 25, 1861, p. 8, ProQuest Historical Newspapers.

57 Burlingame, ed., *Lincoln's Journalist*, p. 41.

58 Ibid.

59 Hoch, *Lincoln Trail*, pp. 13-14.

60 *New York Times,* February 23, 1861, p. 1, ProQuest Historical Newspapers.

61 Summers, *The Baltimore and Ohio in the Civil War*, p. 46.

62 Summers, *The Baltimore and Ohio in the Civil War*, pp. 47-48.

63 Pinkerton report, February 22, 1861, in Cuthbert, *Lincoln and the Baltimore Plot*, p. 72.

64 Ibid.

65 George Stearns to S. M. Felton, April 1, 1862, Felton Papers (no. 1151), Historical Society of Pennsylvania.

66 See Felton's typed narrative dated January 17, 1866, Felton Papers (no. 1151), vol. 2, p. 11, Historical Society of Pennsylvania. This narrative closely follows that appearing in Lossing's work, but includes additional details, particularly of S. M. Felton's early life, Nicholas P. Trist's account, as well as an account of the Baltimore Riots of April 1861 and subsequent events. Felton's efforts to protect his road had not gone unnoticed by the suspected conspirators, who could easily have surmised the intent of whitewashing (fireproofing) the bridges and the hundreds of armed guards at the bridges. In his February 12, 1861, report, Pinkerton operative Harry W. Davies recounted a conversation he had in Baltimore with a daguerreotype artist from New Orleans named "Mr. Hughes," who, after indicating that Baltimore was about half secessionist, stated: "'I understand *that they have men watching the Rail Road Bridge between here and Philadelphia: the Rail Roads are afraid that they will be destroyed—but I do not know if it will do any good'*—winking at the same time." Davies report, February 12, 1861, in Cuthbert, *Abraham Lincoln and the Baltimore Plot,* p. 28.

67 William Stearns to Allan Pinkerton, December 4, 1867, in Pinkerton, *History and Evidence*, pp. 25-26. This curious statement of Stearns's is not explained, either in his letter or in Pinkerton's reports. Perhaps sending a dispatch from Philadelphia was deemed unsafe because the telegraph operators there were thought to be untrustworthy. Or perhaps sending the dispatch from Philadelphia would be too soon, giving anyone who intercepted it and understood its meaning an extra hour, relative to Wilmington 30 miles down the road, to plan an attack on the train.

68 Pinkerton report, February 22, 1861, in Cuthbert, *Lincoln and the Baltimore Plot*, pp. 72-73.

69 Ibid., February 25, 1861, Abraham Lincoln Papers at the Library of Congress.

70 Allan Pinkerton, report, February 21, 1861, in Cuthbert, *Lincoln and the Baltimore Plot*, p. 68.

71 Worthington G. Snethen to Abraham Lincoln, February 25, 1861, Abraham Lincoln Papers at the Library of Congress.

72 Snethen to Lincoln, February 15, 1861, Abraham Lincoln Papers at the Library of Congress.

73 Worthington G. Snethen to Abraham Lincoln, February 25, 1861, Abraham Lincoln Papers at the Library of Congress.

74 See, e.g., itinerary as reproduced in Cuthbert, *Lincoln and the Baltimore Plot,* p. 137. But at least one newspaper erroneously reported Lincoln would arrive in Harrisburg on Thursday February 21. See "Mr. Lincoln to Visit Harrisburg," *New York Times*, February 16, 1861, p. 1, ProQuest Historical Newspapers.

75 Scharf, *History of Maryland,* vol. 3, p. 384.

76 Copy of Baltimore Republican Committee minutes, February 21, 1861, Abraham Lincoln Papers at the Library of Congress.

77 Extract of Minutes, February 21, 1861, The Abraham Lincoln Papers at the Library of Congress; Scharf, *History of Maryland,* vol. 3, pp. 384-385. A month later, Snethen would recommend that Lincoln consider for public office many of the Baltimore Republicans who

had gone to Harrisburg. W. G. Snethen to Abraham Lincoln, March 25, 1861, Abraham Lincoln Papers at The Library of Congress. Snethen would also later recommend to General Winfield Scott that Palmer be named as U.S. attorney in Baltimore to replace William Addison. W. G. Snethen to Winfield Scott, June 29, 1861, Abraham Lincoln Papers at the Library of Congress.

78 Scharf, *History of Maryland,* vol. 3, p. 385, citing a correspondent for the *Baltimore Exchange* who accompanied Snethen's committee to Harrisburg.

CHAPTER 14

1 Mearns, *The Lincoln Papers*, vol. 2, p. 443.

2 Allan Pinkerton, report, February 21, 1861, in Cuthbert, *Lincoln and the Baltimore Plot*, p. 52.

3 Reported Pinkerton, "I did not believe it was possible he (Lincoln) or his personal friends could pass through Baltimore in that style alive." Ibid., p. 60.

4 It is unclear if the letter was written on February 22 or some other Friday morning in February. The date "February 22, 1861" is ascribed by Mearns. Mearns, *The Lincoln Papers*, vol. 2, p. 443. It is assumed that since the letter was written "Friday Morning" in the context of Lincoln's passage through Baltimore, it was written on Friday, February 22, 1861. Abraham Lincoln Papers of the Library of Congress.

5 Burlingame, ed., *Lincoln's Journalist*, p. 41.

6 Alexander K. McClure, *Abraham Lincoln and Men of War-Times* (Philadelphia: Times Publishing, 1892), p. 38.

7 Nicolay and Hay, *Abraham Lincoln: A History,* vol. 3, p. 308.

8 Ibid.

9 Lossing, vol. 1, pp. 279-280.

10 *Philadelphia Inquirer,* February 23, 1861, p. 1.

11 Burlingame, ed., *Lincoln's Journalist,* p. 41.

12 *CW*, 4:242.

13 *CW*, 4:243.

14 *CW*, 4:243-244.

15 Lincoln had spoken twice that morning in Philadelphia, once at Leaman Place, once in Lancaster, and now twice in Harrisburg. *CW*, 4:240-245.

16 Cuthbert, *Lincoln and the Baltimore Plot*, p. 112; Pinkerton, *History and Evidence*, p. 21.

17 *CW*, 4:245.

18 Burlingame, ed., *Lincoln's Journalist,* p. 41. Built in 1857-58 at the corner of Market Street and Market Square in Harrisburg, the Jones House had, in 1859, hosted King Edward of England, then the Prince of Wales. But even though the place was literally fit for a king, the anonymous *World*, possibly John Hay, reporter found the Jones House unsuitable, at least for a party the size of the Lincoln suite. He reported that the accommodations were "unprecedentedly bad; some of the suite and party were unaccommodated with rooms; several in one bed, and others had no rooms at all." Ibid. The *New York Herald* echoed Hay's criticism of both the Jones House and the Harrisburg crowd. Bryan, *The Great American Myth*, p. 27, citing the *New York Herald* of February 23, 1861, which reported that

"No terms are too severe to characterize the conduct of the crowd about the hotel and the arrangements there."

19 Governor Curtin to Allan Pinkerton, December 8, 1867, in Pinkerton, *History and Evidence*, p. 37.

20 Allen Thorndike Rice, ed., *Reminiscences of Abraham Lincoln by Distinguished Men of His Time* (New York: North American Review, 1888), p. 224; Whitney, *Lincoln the Citizen*, pp. 309-310; John S. Goff, *Robert Todd Lincoln: A Man in His Own Right* (Norman: University of Oklahoma Press, 1969), p. 37. See also Benjamin Perley Poore, *Perley's Reminiscences of Sixty Years in the National Metropolis* (Philadelphia: Hubbard Brothers, 1886), vol. 2., pp. 65-67. Other accounts put the incident in Indianapolis. See, e.g., Helen Nicolay, *Personal Traits of Abraham Lincoln* (New York: Century, 1913), p. 162; Helen Nicolay, *Lincoln's Secretary: A Biography of John G. Nicolay* (New York: Longmans, Green, 1949), pp. 63-64.

21 Nicolay, *Personal Traits of Abraham Lincoln*, p. 162.

22 Whitney, *Lincoln the Citizen*, p. 310.

23 Donald, *Lincoln*, p. 275. See Goff, *Robert Todd Lincoln*, pp. 36-38; Nicolay, *Personal Traits of Abraham Lincoln*, pp. 162-164.

24 Rice, *Reminiscences of Abraham Lincoln*, p. 224.

25 Lamon, *Recollections of Abraham Lincoln*, p. 36. See also Michael Burlingame, ed., *An Oral History of Abraham Lincoln: John G. Nicolay's Interviews and Essays* (Carbondale: Southern Illinois University Press, 1996) pp. 108-110 n. 47. Robert Lincoln later denied that his father scolded him over the incident. See Nicolay, *Lincoln's Secretary,* p. 65.

26 Rice, *Reminiscences*, p. 224.

27 Sandburg, *Abraham Lincoln: The War Years*, p. 75.

28 Lamon, *Recollections*, p. 35.

29 Whitney, *Lincoln the Citizen*, p. 310.

30 Abraham Lincoln to George D. Prentice, February 2, 1861, in Tracy, *Uncollected Letters of Abraham Lincoln*, pp. 175-176.

31 Albany *Atlas and Argus,* February 18, 1861, p. 2.

32 Rice, *Reminiscences of Abraham Lincoln*, p. 224.

33 Ibid.

34 Lamon, *Recollections,* p. 36.

35 Rice, *Reminiscences*, p. 224; Nicolay, *Personal Traits*, pp. 164-165; "Centurama" article, episode 16, Historical Society of Dauphin County.

36 Sandburg, *Abraham Lincoln: The War Years*, p. 75.

37 See Lamon, *Recollections,* p. 37 ("Suiting the action to the word, Mr. Lincoln took his Address from the bag and carefully placed it in the inside pocket of his vest, but held on to the satchel with as much interest as if it still contained his 'certificate of moral character.'") But see Goff, *Robert Todd Lincoln*, p. 38, recounting that after the incident, Lincoln carried the grip back to his room, handed it to Robert, told him what it contained, and ordered "Now you keep it!" See also Nicolay, *Lincoln's Secretary,* p. 65.

38 Norman B. Judd to Allan Pinkerton, November 3, 1867, in Pinkerton, *History and Evidence*, p. 21. There is some question regarding Major Hunter's presence. Hunter had seriously injured his shoulder in Buffalo. On February 21, Hunter was reported as having been

replaced by Captain J. C. Robinson. *New York Times*, February 22, 1861, p. 1, ProQuest Historical Newspapers.

39 *Philadelphia Inquirer*, February 25, 1861, p. 1.

40 Lamon, *Recollections*, p. 41. By other accounts, however, Lamon was already aware of the plot as early as Friday morning in Philadelphia. See, e.g., Seward, "How Lincoln Was Warned of the Baltimore Assassination Plot," p. 64.

41 Judd to Pinkerton, November 3, 1867, in Pinkerton, *History and Evidence*, p. 21.

42 Herndon's notes of an 1866 interview with Norman B. Judd, in Cuthbert, *Lincoln and the Baltimore Plot*, p. 112 (emphasis added).

43 Ibid.

44 Judd to Pinkerton, November 3, 1867, in Pinkerton, *History and Evidence*, p. 21.

45 From Judd's account as reported by Whitney, *Lincoln the Citizen*, p. 303; Herndon's notes, in Cuthbert, *Lincoln and the Baltimore Plot*, p. 112.

46 Donald, *Lincoln*, p. 242.

47 From Judd's account as reported by Whitney, *Lincoln the Citizen*, p. 303.

48 Ibid.

49 Burlingame, ed., *Lincoln's Journalist,* p. 42. By "ride from depot to depot" the anonymous reporter likely means in a horse-drawn carriage. Whether Lincoln took the Northern Central Railroad or the Philadelphia, Wilmington, and Baltimore road, he would be required to pass through the streets of Baltimore from one depot to another. In the case of the former route, he would arrive at Calvert Street Station and travel south to the Camden Street Station, likely by carriage. In the case of the latter route, he would arrive at the President Street Station and take Pratt Street west to the Camden Street Station. It is clear that one route by which Lincoln would not need to leave his railcar would be by taking the PW&B from Philadelphia to Baltimore's President Street Station (or Canton Depot), at which point his car could be uncoupled and pulled by horses over tracks on Pratt Street to the Camden Street Station. Lincoln could literally be taken from one Baltimore depot to the other without leaving his curtained sleeping berth.

50 George W. Hazzard to Abraham Lincoln, January 1861, Abraham Lincoln Papers at the Library of Congress; see also Mearns, *The Lincoln Papers*, vol. 2, pp. 430-433.

51 Ellsworth's Zouaves gave an exhibition drill in Baltimore on August 1 and 2, 1860. Scharf, *The Chronicles of Baltimore*, p. 575.

52 Burlingame, *Oral History of Abraham Lincoln*, p. 114 n. 48.

53 Lamon, *Recollections,* p. 42.

54 From Judd's account as reported by Whitney, *Lincoln the Citizen*, p. 304. Lamon was not the only armed man in Lincoln's party. Captain George Hazzard carried a dirk, brass knuckles, and eye shields (possibly to protect against an acid attack) while accompanying Lincoln on the trip. These items are on display at Ford's Theatre National Historic Site, Washington, D.C., and were observed by the author March 1, 2007.

55 Burlingame, *Oral History of Abraham Lincoln*, p. 113.

56 In a passage crossed out in Judd's 1866 interview, Herndon recorded Judd's possible motives for choosing Lamon: "Lamon was a fighting Cock. If I [Judd] had gone, Sumner, Pope, &c. would have got mad, but Lamon's going could insult nor wound the feelings of

any one. So it was concluded, Lincoln agreed with me, or I should have been kicked out of court." Cuthbert, *Lincoln and the Baltimore Plot*, p. 113.

57 Lossing, *Pictorial History of the Civil War*, vol. 1, p. 280.

58 Lamon, *Recollections*, p. 42.

59 From Judd's account as reported by Whitney, *Lincoln the Citizen*, p. 303.

60 Judd to Pinkerton, November 3, 1867, in Pinkerton, *History and Evidence*, p. 22.

61 Whitney, *Lincoln the Citizen*, p. 303.

62 Judd indicates that he broke from the party around 4:00 p.m. to go to the railroad station and the telegraph office, the others going to dinner. Pinkerton, *History and Evidence*, p. 22.

63 This, from the woman who knew him best, his wife: "Mr. Lincoln was mild in his manners, but he was a terribly firm man when he set his foot down. None of us, no man or woman, could rule him after he had once fully made up his mind." Herndon and Weik, *Abraham Lincoln*, vol. 2, p. 223.

64 Mary Todd had thirteen siblings, five from her mother and eight from her stepmother. Berry, *House of Abraham*, pp. vi-vii, 25.

65 Goodwin, *Team of Rivals*, p. 7.

66 Donald, *Lincoln*, pp. 107-108.

67 Ibid.

68 Burlingame, ed., *Lincoln's Journalist*, p. 24.

69 Baker, *Mary Todd Lincoln*, p. 164.

70 Villard, *Lincoln on the Eve of '61*, pp. 52-53.

71 Pinkerton report, February 21, 1861, in Cuthbert, *Lincoln and the Baltimore Plot*, p. 57.

72 *New York Times*, February 21, 1861, p. 8, ProQuest Historical Newspapers.

73 *New York World*, February 22, 1861, p. 8.

74 Charles Eugene Hamlin, *The Life and Times of Hannibal Hamlin*, p. 389.

75 *New York Times*, February 23, 1861, p. 1, ProQuest Historical Newspapers. These men reportedly included Samuel C. Fessenden, John N. Goodwin, Charles W. Walton, John H. Rice, and Frederick A. Pike of the Maine delegation to the next Congress, George Lewis of New Haven, J. W. North of Minnesota, Mark Howard of Connecticut, Colonel Allen and Linus B. Comins of Boston and Judge [Joseph M.?] Day of Massachusetts. Hamlin, *Life and Times*, p. 389; *New York World*, February 23, 1861, p. 4.

76 Hamlin, *Life and Times*, p. 389; *New York World*, February 23, 1861, p. 4.

77 *New York World*, February 23, 1861, p. 4.

78 Ibid.

79 *New York Times*, February 23, 1861, p. 1, ProQuest Historical Newspapers.

80 Hamlin, *Life and Times*, pp. 389-390.

81 McClure, *Abraham Lincoln and Men of War-Times*, pp. 44-45.

82 Villard, *Lincoln on the Eve of '61*, p. 53.

83 Mary Todd Lincoln to David Davis, January 17, 1861, in Justin G. Turner and Linda Levitt Turner, *Mary Todd Lincoln: Her Life and Letters* (New York: Knopf, 1972), p. 71.

84 Jennifer Fleischner, *Mrs. Lincoln and Mrs. Keckly* (New York: Broadway Books, 2003), p. 198.

85 McClure, *Abraham Lincoln and Men of War-Times*, p. 45. Interestingly, contemporaneous accounts of those who did not know the true story reported that Mr. and Mrs. Lincoln retired early that night on plea of fatigue. Burlingame, ed., *Lincoln's Journalist,* p. 42.

86 Sunset in Harrisburg on February 22, 1861 occurred at 5:52 p.m., and twilight ended at 6:19 p.m. U.S. Naval Observatory Astronomical Applications Department data for February 22, 1861, at http://aa.usno.navy.mil/data/docs/RS_OneDay.html.

87 McClure, *Abraham Lincoln and Men of War-Times*, p. 44.

88 Judd to Pinkerton, November 3, 1867, and Franciscus to Pinkerton, November 5, 1867, in Pinkerton, *History and Evidence,* pp. 22 and 29; William Bender Wilson, *History of the Pennsylvania Railroad Company* (Philadelphia: Henry T. Coates, 1899), p. 316.

89 Franciscus to Pinkerton, November 5, 1867, in Pinkerton, *History and Evidence,* pp. 29-30.

90 Scharf, *History of Maryland,* vol, 3, p. 384.

91 Account of Norman B. Judd of August 1866, in Cuthbert, *Lincoln and the Baltimore Plot,* p. 113; Lamon, *Life of Abraham Lincoln,* pp. 522-523.

92 Judd to Pinkerton, November 3, 1867, in Pinkerton, *History and Evidence,* p. 22; Whitney, *Lincoln the Citizen*, p. 305. Franciscus reports that Lincoln had neither a cloak nor shawl, but did have a soft wool hat that he put on as he left the hotel. Franciscus also claims that he lent Lincoln his overcoat, which he wore as the train approached Philadelphia until he was seated with Pinkerton in the carriage there. Franciscus to Pinkerton, November 5, 1867, in Pinkerton, *History and Evidence,* p. 30.

93 "Pea-jacket," per Judd as reported in Whitney, *Lincoln the Citizen*, p. 305; "Kossuth" hat as reported by George R. Dunn in letter to Allan Pinkerton, November 7, 1867, in Pinkerton, *History and Evidence,* p. 36; "felt hat as were in common use at the time" as reported by Governor Curtin to Allan Pinkerton, December 8, 1867, Pinkerton, *History and Evidence*, p. 37.

94 Lamon, *Life of Abraham Lincoln,* p. 523.

95 Whitney, p. 303.

96 See, e.g., Ward Hill Lamon Papers, Huntington Library.

97 McClure, *Abraham Lincoln and Men of War-Times*, p. 46.

98 Charles Hamilton and Lloyd Ostendorf, *Lincoln in Photographs: An Album of Every Known Pose* (Norman: University of Oklahoma Press, 1963), p. 73.

99 Judd to Pinkerton, November 3, 1867; Curtin to Pinkerton, December 8, 1867; and Franciscus to Pinkerton, November 5, 1867, all in Pinkerton, *History and Evidence,* pp. 22, 37, and 29-30.

100 Lossing, *Pictorial History of the Civil War,* vol. 1, p. 280. Early in December 1864, historian Benson J. Lossing called on President Lincoln at the White House, along with one of his closest friends, Chicago congressman Isaac N. Arnold. They met with Lincoln in the room where cabinet meetings were held, overlooking the Potomac and the Washington Monument. At Lossing's request, Lincoln recounted what he recalled of the secret passage through Baltimore.

101 See, e.g., Cleveland Moffett, "How Allan Pinkerton Thwarted the First Plot to Assassinate Lincoln," *McClure's Magazine* vol. 3 (June-November 1894), p. 526, Box 23, Folder 7, Pinkerton Papers at the Library of Congress. Moffett identifies the actual names of Pinkerton's agents, rather than the aliases generally used in their reports. These include George H. Bangs, Hiram B. Jones, William Norris, Paul H. Dennia, John Kinsella, Francis Warner, William H. Scott, and Timothy Webster. Ibid. Some later accounts, likely fiction-alized and citing no authority, report that Pinkerton had sent some of his agents to Harrisburg with Lincoln, not going himself for fear of being recognized. According to at least one such account, the unnamed Pinkerton agents observed in the lobby of the Jones House two of the suspected Baltimore conspirators. Alan Hynd, "The Case of the Plot that Failed," *True Magazine*, August 1950, p. 74.

102 McClure, *Abraham Lincoln and Men of War-Times*, p. 47.

103 *New York World*, February 25, 1861, p. 4.

104 Lamon, *Recollections*, p. 43.

105 Judd to Pinkerton, November 3, 1867, in Pinkerton, *History and Evidence*, p. 22.

106 Lamon, *Recollections*, p. 43.

107 Whitney, *Lincoln the Citizen*, p. 304.

108 Judd to Pinkerton, November 3, 1867, Pinkerton, *History and Evidence*, p. 22.

109 Wilson and Davis, *Herndon's Informants*, p. 316.

110 Curtin to Pinkerton, December 8, 1867, in Pinkerton, *History and Evidence*, pp. 37-38.

111 Wilson and Davis, *Herndon's Informants*, p. 316.

112 Telegram from Henry Sanford to Allan Pinkerton, in Cuthbert, *Lincoln and the Baltimore Plot*, p. 74.

113 Lamon, *Recollections*, p. 40. McClure reports that Pennsylvania Railroad employee Thomas A. Scott supervised the cutting of the telegraph wires and that this occurred around 7:00 p.m. McClure, *Abraham Lincoln and Men of War-Times*, p. 47.

114 Rowan, *The Pinkertons*, p. 108.

115 H. E. Thayer to Allan Pinkerton, November 3, 1867, in Pinkerton, *History and Evidence*, p. 39.

116 Andrew Wynne to Allan Pinkerton, November 3, 1867, in Pinkerton, *History and Evidence*, p. 41. Unclear is whether the operator already knew that the lines to Baltimore were cut before Wynne asked him to send this message. If so, we are left to wonder who might have been trying to send dispatches to Baltimore in the moments proximate Lincoln's departure from Harrisburg.

117 By 1860, there were approximately 9,000 locomotives in the U.S. Typical locomotives of the era were of the 4-4-0 wheel arrangement, indicating four large drive wheels under the cab and four smaller ones up front under the cylinders. Such engines, also later called the "American" type, were popular because they well served every railroad need, passenger, freight, and switching. Its four connected drive wheels gave the 4-4-0 good power. At the time Lincoln's Special ran, conversion from wood burners to coal-fired engines was increas-ing—coal burned hotter and coal-fired engines accordingly ran faster. White, *American Locomotives* pp. 46, 574-575.

118 Accounts of Daniel E. Garman and Edward R. Black, in Flory, "Garman, Black, and the 'Baltimore Plot,'" pp. 101-103; Hoch, *The Lincoln Trail in Pennsylvania*, p. 18.

119 John Pitcairn Jr. to Allan Pinkerton, November 23, 1867, in Pinkerton, *History and Evidence*, p. 33. Enoch Lewis, however, recounts that he waited at the train for Lincoln's arrival and that only Franciscus and Lamon accompanied him there. Enoch Lewis to Allan Pinkerton, November 7, 1867, Pinkerton, *History and Evidence*, p. 31.

120 Flory, "Garman, Black, and the 'Baltimore Plot,'" pp. 101–103.

121 In addition to Franciscus and Lewis, John Pitcairn, in charge of a telegraph instrument, and T. E. Garrett, general baggage agent, were also reportedly on board. Enoch Lewis to Allan Pinkerton, November 7, 1867, Pinkerton, *History and Evidence*, p. 31.

122 McClure, *Abraham Lincoln and Men of War-Times*, p. 47; Pitcairn to Pinkerton, November 23, 1867, in Pinkerton, *History and Evidence*, p. 33.

123 Flory, "Garman, Black, and the 'Baltimore Plot,'" p. 102.

124 Rice, *Reminiscences*, p. 36. This account, given by Elihu B. Washburne, erroneously gives the date as February 23. It would have been February 22.

125 Seward, *Seward at Washington*, p. 511; Glyndon Van Deusen, "Seward and Lincoln: The Washington Depot Episode," *University of Rochester Library Bulletin*, vol. 20, no. 3 (Spring 1965).

126 Rice, *Reminiscences*, p. 36.

127 Hamlin, *Life and Times*, p. 390; Searcher, *Lincoln's Journey to Greatness*, p. 220.

128 Rice, pp. 36-37.

129 Pinkerton report, February 22, 1861, in Cuthbert, *Lincoln and the Baltimore Plot*, p. 76.

130 Ibid.

CHAPTER 15

1 Account of Edward R. Black, in Flory, "Garman, Black, and the 'Baltimore Plot'" (hereinafter Black account), p. 103.

2 White, *A History of the American Locomotive*, p. 74.

3 John W. Starr Jr., *Lincoln & the Railroads* (New York: Dodd, Mead, 1927), p. 191.

4 White, *A History of the American Locomotive*, p. 215.

5 Ibid., p. 216. The Pennsylvania Railroad used box-style lamps on its engines until World War I.

6 Garman reports he lit the head light before the train started. Account of Daniel E. Garman, in Flory, "Garman, Black, and the 'Baltimore Plot'" (hereinafter Garman account), p. 101. Lamon reports that the lamps in the car were not lit. Lamon, *Recollections*, p. 37.

7 U.S. Naval Observatory Astronomical Applications Department data for February 22, 1861, at http://aa.usno.navy.mil/data/docs/RS_OneDay.html.

8 Lamon, *Recollections*, p. 43.

9 Pitcairn's account claims that neither the engineer nor the fireman knew they had Lincoln on board. John Pitcairn Jr. to Allan Pinkerton, November 23, 1867, in Pinkerton, *History and Evidence*, p. 33.

10 Likely Leaman Place, located about midway between Harrisburg and Philadelphia; see Hoch, *The Lincoln Trail in Pennsylvania*, map, p. 22. By other accounts, the train also

stopped at Downingtown to take on water. See Pitcairn to Pinkerton, November 23, 1867, Pinkerton, *History and Evidence*, p. 33. It is likely the train stopped at both places to take on water as well as one or two other places, given the rate with which the locomotive was burning coal and boiling water, thanks to Garman's efforts. Locomotives of the era typically needed to stop about every 25 miles to take on water and fuel. The tender typically held both fuel, either wood or coal, and also held water in a U-shaped tank that surrounded the fuel. White, *A History of the American Locomotive,* pp. 223–224. Leaman Place would likely have been the more secluded spot and close to the halfway point, Downingtown being on the outskirts of Philadelphia.

11 Garman account, p. 102.

12 Ibid. Black later claimed, however, that he did know what was up. In his account, he details that at about 7:00 p.m. he had received quiet orders to take car 29 and run about one mile east from Harrisburg Station, stopping near Hanna Street, and there await further orders. "I had been told quietly that Lincoln would not be allowed to pass through Baltimore alive, and we must secretly get him to Washington another way." Black account, p. 103.

13 Garman account, p. 102.

14 Black account, p. 103.

15 Pitcairn to Pinkerton, November 23, 1867, Pinkerton, *History and Evidence*, p. 33.

16 Black account, p. 103.

17 Governor Curtin to Allan Pinkerton, December 8, 1867, as reported in Pinkerton, *History and Evidence*, pp. 39–40; Hoch, *Lincoln Trail*, p. 19.

18 These men included Joseph Howard Jr. for the *Times*, Simon P. Hanscom for the *Herald*, and the anonymous "Special Correspondent" for the *World*. Searcher, *Lincoln's Journey to Greatness*, p. 263, notes that Hanscom had replaced Villard.

19 Burlingame, ed., *Lincoln's Journalist*, p. 42.

20 Simon P. Hanscom, Civil War era Washington correspondent for the *New York Herald*. See William Osborn Stoddard, *Inside the White House in War Times: Memoirs and Reports of Lincoln's Secretary*, Michael Burlingame, ed. (University of Nebraska Press, 2000), p. 245, n. 103. Hanscom's name is sometimes spelled "Hanscomb," including in Pinkerton's reports. See, e.g., Allan Pinkerton, report, February 23, 1861, in Cuthbert, *Lincoln and the Baltimore Plot*, p. 86. During his testimony before the Select Committee of Five on January 31, 1861, Charles P. Stone identified Hanscom as the source for information that the National Volunteers in Washington had "some 1,500 who could be depended upon to take this city." Report No. 79, p. 91.

21 *New York Times*, February 25, 1861, ProQuest Historical Newspapers.

22 Rowan, *The Pinkertons*, pp. 118–119. Allan Pinkerton reportedly enjoyed telling this story himself and credited the *Herald* with accurately reporting the plot but would never reveal who among the group remaining in Harrisburg had held the two reporters at bay with an unloaded pistol.

23 The *New York Times* reported that "an officer entered the room of our correspondent at the hotel and informed him of what had occurred, but would not permit him to leave the room until morning, by which time Mr. Lincoln had arrived in Washington." Bryan, *The Great American Myth*, p. 33, citing the *New York Times*, October 31, 1867, p. 2.

24 *New York Times*, February 23, 1861, p. 8, ProQuest Historical Newspapers.

25 Allan Pinkerton, report, February 22, 1861, in Cuthbert, *Lincoln and the Baltimore Plot*, p. 76. Presumably, Pinkerton was able to send a telegram to Harrisburg from Philadelphia because only the Northern Central's wires in and out of Harrisburg to and from Baltimore had been cut.

26 H. W. Thayer to Allan Pinkerton, November 3, 1867, and Andrew Wynne to Allan Pinkerton, November 3, 1867, in Pinkerton, *History and Evidence,* pp. 40, 42. Pinkerton's alias, "Hutcheson," is spelled "Hutchinson" in Thayer's November 3, 1867 letter.

27 George H. Burns was, according to Pinkerton, "an attaché of the American Telegraph Company and confidential agent of E. S. Sanford, Esq., who acted as my messenger, and who afterwards distinguished himself for his courage and daring in the rebellion." Pinkerton, *The Spy of the Rebellion,* p. 82.

28 Allan Pinkerton, report, February 22, 1861, in Cuthbert, *Lincoln and the Baltimore Plot*, p. 77.

29 Hoch, *Lincoln Trail*, p. 11. The Pennsylvania Railroad's West Philadelphia train station was located on Market Street, at approximately the same location as Amtrak's 30th Street Station is today. Ibid., p. 12.

30 Because Pinkerton had orchestrated virtually every other detail of the plan, it seems logical to assume that he had recommended and specified the disguise Lincoln wore. Not a single Pinkerton report, however, indicates who made the suggestion to Lincoln to wear a disguise. It is possible that Lincoln made the decision himself, given the disguise he chose is virtually identical to that recommended by George Hazzard in his January 1861 warning letter to Lincoln.

31 Pinkerton report, February 22, 1861, in Cuthbert, *Lincoln and the Baltimore Plot*, p. 77. Five years later, Pinkerton would recall the Kossuth hat being black rather than brown. Allan Pinkerton to William Herndon, August 23, 1866, in Cuthbert, *Lincoln and the Baltimore Plot*, p. 15.

32 Pinkerton report, February 22, 1861, in Cuthbert, *Lincoln and the Baltimore Plot*, p. 77. H. F. Kenney describes the same scene this way in a letter written years later to Pinkerton: "I proceeded to the West Philadelphia depot, and we met there at about 10 p.m. We had to wait but a short time when a special train arrived with but one passenger car attached, from which President Lincoln, with Mr. Ward H. Lamon and a few other gentlemen, officers of the Pennsylvania Railroad Company, alighted. Upon their alighting, I had the honor of being introduced by you to President Lincoln, and he, with Mr. Lamon, forthwith got into the carriage." (H. F. Kenney to Allan Pinkerton, December 23, 1867, in Pinkerton, *History and Evidence,* p. 28.)

33 Garman account, p. 102.

34 Pinkerton report, February 22, 1861, Cuthbert, *Lincoln and the Baltimore Plot*, p. 69.

35 Ibid., p. 77.

36 Pitcairn to Pinkerton, November 23, 1867, in Pinkerton, *History and Evidence,* p. 33.

37 H. F. Kenney to Allan Pinkerton, December 23, 1867, and Enoch Lewis to Allan Pinkerton, November 7, 1867, in Pinkerton, *History and Evidence,* pp. 28 and 31-32.

38 Kate Warne, report, February 22, 1861, in Cuthbert, *Lincoln and the Baltimore Plot*, p.

80; George R. Dunn to Allan Pinkerton, November 7, 1867, in Pinkerton, *History and Evidence,* pp. 35-36; George R. Dunn to Ward H. Lamon, March 27, 1888, in Cuthbert, pp. 143-144 n. 53.

39 Dunn to Pinkerton, November 7, 1867, in Pinkerton, *History and Evidence,* pp. 35-36. At this point, it is unclear whether Warne or Dunn knew that Ward Hill Lamon would also need a ticket; Dunn's letter fails to mention that he purchased a ticket for Lamon. Possibly, Pinkerton himself had not known for certain that Lamon would accompany Lincoln until the burly Virginian showed up at the West Philadelphia depot. Pinkerton reports that on February 21 while they met at the Continental Hotel, Mr. Lincoln believed Mrs. Lincoln would insist on Lamon accompanying him, and later, while they rode in the carriage the evening of February 22 from West Philadelphia, confirmed she had so insisted. Allan Pinkerton, reports, February 21 and 22, 1861, in Cuthbert, *Lincoln and the Baltimore Plot,* pp. 67 and 78. It seems reasonable to conclude, therefore, that Pinkerton was expecting Lamon or at least a fourth person to join them, given his instructions to Warne to secure four sleeping berths and given Judd's recollection that the plan adopted by Pinkerton in Philadelphia at the Continental Hotel early on the morning of February 22 involved one companion accompanying Lincoln from Harrisburg. Judd to Pinkerton, November 3, 1867, in Pinkerton, *History and Evidence,* p. 20.

40 Dunn to Lamon, March 27, 1888, in Cuthbert, *Lincoln and the Baltimore Plot*, pp. 143-144 n. 53. Dunn's expression "knowing the public feeling" possibly references the public feeling against Lincoln in Baltimore, from which Dunn had just returned after spending the day.

41 Dunn to Pinkerton, November 7, 1867, in Pinkerton, *History and Evidence*, pp. 35-36.

42 Dunn to Lamon, March 27, 1888, Cuthbert, *Lincoln and the Baltimore Plot*, pp. 143-144 n. 53; Dunn to Pinkerton, November 7, 1867, Pinkerton, *History and Evidence,* pp. 35-36.

43 Warne report, February 22, 1861, in Cuthbert, *Lincoln and the Baltimore Plot*, p. 80.

44 Pinkerton report, February 22, 1861, in Cuthbert, *Lincoln and the Baltimore Plot*, pp. 77-78.

45 Ibid., p. 78.

46 Ibid., p. 79.

47 Ibid.

48 George Stearns to S. M. Felton, April 1, 1862, Felton Papers (no. 1151), Box 2, Folder 1, Historical Society of Pennsylvania.

49 Kenney to Pinkerton, December 23, 1867, in Pinkerton, *History and Evidence,* p. 28.

50 Allan Pinkerton to William Herndon, August 23, 1866, in Cuthbert, *Lincoln and the Baltimore Plot*, pp. 15-16.

51 Schouler, *A History of Massachusetts in the Civil War*, p. 64.

52 Dunn to Pinkerton, November 7, 1867, in Pinkerton, *History and Evidence,* p. 36. Dunn was subsequently informed that the third man was "a Mr. Lamon." Ibid.

53 Dunn to Lamon, March 27, 1888, in Cuthbert, *Lincoln and the Baltimore Plot*, p. 143 n. 54; Pinkerton report, February 22, 1861, in Cuthbert, *Lincoln and the Baltimore Plot*, p. 79.

58 Pinkerton report, February 22, 1861, Cuthbert, *Lincoln and the Baltimore Plot*, p. 79; Lamon, *Life of Abraham Lincoln,* p. 524.

55 Schouler, *A History of Massachusetts in the Civil War*, p. 64.

56 Kenney to Pinkerton, December 23, 1867, in Pinkerton, *History and Evidence,* p. 27.

57 Schouler, *A History of Massachusetts in the Civil War*, p. 63.

58 Pinkerton report, February 22, 1861, in Cuthbert, *Lincoln and the Baltimore Plot*, p. 75; S. M. Felton, report, January 17, 1866, p. 13, Felton Papers (no. 1151), vol. 2, Historical Society of Pennsylvania.

59 Kenney to Pinkerton, December 23, 1867, in Pinkerton, *History and Evidence*, pp. 27-28; Pinkerton report, February 22, 1861, in Cuthbert, *Lincoln and the Baltimore Plot*, p. 79.

60 Warne report, Friday, February 22, 1861, in Cuthbert, *Lincoln and the Baltimore Plot*, pp. 80-81. There would seem to be no reason for Warne to report on Lincoln's less than attractive appearance. It is somewhat out of character for her, as one whose reports were generally strictly business. Recall, however, that Warne was writing the reports not for herself, but for her employer—Pinkerton. Is it possible she was sending him messages that she found other men unattractive? In her dispatch from New York, Warne hinted that she had refused what appeared to be an advance on behalf of Henry Sanford to come to her room. Before leaving Warne's room at the Astor House, E. S. Sanford asked Warne if he could bring Henry Sanford to her room. Warne does not directly state the purpose of this proposed introduction, leaving the reader to guess, but she handles Sanford's proposition with disarming businesslike dispatch: "I said that if it was necessary I should see Henry Sanford in regard to any business matter I would do so, but not otherwise." Kate Warne, report, February 19, 1861, in Cuthbert, *Lincoln and the Baltimore Plot*, p. 43.

61 Allan Pinkerton, report, February 23, 1861, in Cuthbert, *Lincoln and the Baltimore Plot*, p. 82.

62 Others in the Baltimore "Committee of Escort" included Judge William L. Marshall, chairman of the Committee of 100, Joseph M. Palmer, of Frederick City, Leopold Blumenberg, Captain William E. Beale, James E. Bishop, William E. Gleeson, Francis Corkran, and William E. Coale, who reportedly joined the Committee of Escort with William Gunnison upon the Committee's arrival in Harrisburg. Extract of Minutes, February 21, 1861, Abraham Lincoln Papers at the Library of Congress; Scharf, *History of Maryland*, vol. 3, pp. 384-385.

63 Snethen to Lincoln, February 25, 1861, Abraham Lincoln Papers at the Library of Congress.

64 *New York World*, February 23, 1861, p. 4; Burlingame, ed., *Lincoln's Journalist*, p. 42.

65 See *New York World*, February 25, 1861, p. 4.

66 Burlingame, ed., *Lincoln's Journalist*, p. 42. The published itinerary had the party leaving Harrisburg at 9:00 a.m., arriving in Baltimore at 12:30 p.m., and in Washington at 4:30 p.m. See Cuthbert, *Lincoln and the Baltimore Plot*, p. 137.

67 *New York World*, February 23, 1861, p. 4; Burlingame, ed., *Lincoln's Journalist*, pp. 42, 354 n. 20.

68 In fairness, Delaware had by now already resolved not to secede, even though it was a slave state. In 1860, the state had but 1,798 slaves, compared with 19,723 free African Americans. In January 1861, a commissioner from Mississippi, Henry Dickinson, addressed the Delaware legislature in Dover, urging the state to secede. The Delaware assembly's pro-Union response was swift; the House unanimously resolved and the Senate

concurred by majority the disapproval of Mississippi's proposed course of secession. *American Annual Cyclopædia*, vol. 1, p. 256.

69 Narrative of Samuel M. Felton, in Schouler, *A History of Massachusetts in the Civil War*, p. 63.

70 Schouler, *A History of Massachusetts in the Civil War*, p. 64.

71 See Pinkerton, *The Spy of the Rebellion*, pp. 77-79. See also Newspaper clipping of an article by L. A. Newcome, found in the Pinkerton Papers at the Library of Congress, Box 24, Folder 1. By other accounts, the secret conclave met on February 8. Moffett, "How Allan Pinkerton Thwarted the First Plot to Assassinate Lincoln," from the Allan Pinkerton files at the Library of Congress, Box 23, Folder 7. John Wilkes Booth's whereabouts on February 8, 1861 are not known. Loux, *John Wilkes Booth Day by Day*, p. 218.

72 For one of the accounts of eight red ballots, see Moffett, "How Allan Pinkerton Thwarted the First Plot to Assassinate Lincoln." Pinkerton's account years later also indicates the use of red ballots to determine the assassin. Pinkerton, *The Spy of the Rebellion*, pp. 69, 78.

73 Newspaper clipping of an article by L. A. Newcome, in the Pinkerton Papers at the Library of Congress, Box 24, Folder 1.

CHAPTER 16

1 Rowan, *The Pinkertons*, p. 112.

2 Pinkerton, *The Spy of the Rebellion*, p. 96.

3 Allan Pinkerton to William Herndon, August 23, 1866, in Cuthbert, *Lincoln and the Baltimore Plot*, p. 16.

4 Ibid.

5 Pinkerton, *The Spy of the Rebellion*, p. 96. Most likely, the Pinkerton operative at Havre de Grace was Timothy Webster. Webster had been stationed in Perrymansville and reported from there. See, e.g., Timothy Webster, report, February 19, 1861, in Cuthbert, *Lincoln and the Baltimore Plot*, p. 45. See also Rowan, *The Pinkertons*, p. 113.

6 Schouler, *A History of Massachusetts in the Civil War*, p. 64.

7 Allan Pinkerton, report, February 23, 1861, in Cuthbert, *Lincoln and the Baltimore Plot*, p. 81; Pinkerton, *The Spy of the Rebellion*, p. 96.

8 Pinkerton, *The Spy of the Rebellion*, p. 96.

9 Pinkerton report, February 23, 1861, in Cuthbert, *Lincoln and the Baltimore Plot*, p. 81.

10 Pinkerton to Herndon, August 23, 1866, in Cuthbert, *Lincoln and the Baltimore Plot*, p. 16.

11 See "Map Showing Route of Rail Road Through Baltimore from President Street Station to Camden Street Station," Brown, *Baltimore and the Nineteenth of April, 1861*, frontispiece. An interesting account of the right of way enjoyed by passenger cars being pulled through Baltimore when arriving from Philadelphia on their way to Washington follows from an account written of a passage in 1855: "We got to Baltimore [on the Philadelphia, Wilmington, and Baltimore Railroad] about four, where change of cars number two took place. We were conveyed through the town in cars on a railway laid in the streets. . . . I asked [the conductor] if the railway had the prior right of passing [over ordinary vehicles].

He replied, 'Well, the city gives us the right of way through the streets; and as to the right to pass first, I *take* it, and I guess that's just about how the law stands.'" William Ferguson, *America by River and Rail* (London: James Nisbet, 1856), p. 99.

12 Pinkerton, *The Spy of the Rebellion*, p. 96; Lamon, *Life of Abraham Lincoln*, p. 525.

13 McClure, *Abraham Lincoln and Men of War-Times*, pp. 47-48.

14 Ibid., p. 48.

15 *Philadelphia Daily Evening Bulletin,* February 23, 1861, p. 1; *Philadelphia Inquirer,* February 23, 1861. Van Wyck would later enter the Union Army as a colonel in the Fifty-sixth Regiment, New York Volunteers, and later be brevetted brigadier general. See Biographical Directory of the Unites States Congress, http://bioguide.congress.gov.

16 *New York World,* February 25, 1861, p. 4.

17 *Philadelphia Daily Evening Bulletin,* February 23, 1861, pp. 1, 5.

18 *Philadelphia Daily Evening Bulletin,* February 23, 1861, p. 5.

19 Rice, *Reminiscences of Abraham Lincoln*, p. 37.

20 Ibid.

21 Jo Daviess County is the rural Illinois county from which Washburne hailed, having been appointed in 1846 as the prosecuting attorney, an office he held for two years. Rice, *Reminiscences of Abraham Lincoln,* p. 613.

22 Ibid., pp. 37-38. Washburne's account that Lincoln was among the last to leave the train is at odds with Pinkerton's, which states that he and Lincoln were among the first to leave the car. Pinkerton report, February 23, 1861, in Cuthbert, *Lincoln and the Baltimore Plot*, p. 82. This can perhaps be reconciled if we assume the sleeper car would tend to be the last to empty as sleeping or groggy passengers collected their things after climbing from their berths. Lincoln may thus have been among the first to leave the sleeper car, but that car, farthest from the front of the train, may have been among the last on the train to empty its passengers into the depot.

23 Presently at this location is the southernmost bend of the Metro's Red Line and the Japanese American Memorial.

24 Pinkerton report, February 23, 1861, in Cuthbert, *Lincoln and the Baltimore Plot*, p. 81.

25 Ibid., p. 82.

26 Ibid.

27 Ibid.

28 Washburne recalled these events a bit differently from Pinkerton (Rice, *Reminiscences of Abraham Lincoln*, p. 38):

> When they were fairly on the platform and a short distance from the car, I stepped forward and accosted the President:
> "How are you Lincoln?"
> At this unexpected and rather familiar salutation the gentlemen were apparently somewhat startled, but Mr. Lincoln, who had recognized me, relieved them at once by remarking in his peculiar voice:
> "This is only Washburne!"
> Then we all exchanged congratulations and walked out to the front of the depot, where I had a carriage in waiting.

29 Unclear is whether they took the most direct route, up the wide, unpaved, tree-lined thoroughfare of Pennsylvania Avenue, or followed a more circuitous path, as Pinkerton had done the previous night while killing time in Philadelphia. Rice, *Reminiscences of Abraham Lincoln*, p. 38.

30 Pinkerton report, February 23, 1861, in Cuthbert, *Lincoln and the Baltimore Plot*, p. 82.

31 Ibid.

32 Richard Wallace Carr and Marie Pinak Carr, *The Willard Hotel: An Illustrated History* (Washington, D.C.: Dicmar, 2005), p. 27; Pinkerton report, February 23, 1861, in Cuthbert, *Lincoln and the Baltimore Plot*, p. 82.

33 As one newspaper would report, "a suite of five elegantly furnished rooms in the southwest corner of Willard's, fronting on Pennsylvania Avenue and overlooking the White House, have been set apart for President Lincoln and his family." *New York World,* February 25, 1861, p. 4.

34 Sandburg, *Abraham Lincoln: The War Years*, p. 89; Willard Hotel Museum, Washington, D. C., visited March 2, 2007. Whitney, *Lincoln the Citizen*, p. 306 (location of suite of rooms reserved for Lincoln and his family). His suite not yet being ready, Lincoln was assigned temporary quarters in a different room. Pinkerton to Herndon, August 23, 1866, in Cuthbert, *Lincoln and the Baltimore Plot*, p. 17.

35 Rice, *Reminiscences of Abraham Lincoln*, pp. 37-39.

36 Seward claimed in a letter written home that day that "The President-elect arrived *incog.* at six this morning. I met him at the depot; and after breakfast introduced him to the President and Cabinet." Seward, *Seward at Washington*, p. 511. Pinkerton's and Washburne's accounts contradict this, suggesting that Seward was not at the train station to meet Lincoln. But years later, Pinkerton recalled that Seward *was* waiting for Lincoln outside the depot in the carriage Washburne had led them to. Pinkerton, *The Spy of the Rebellion,* p. 98.

37 Rice, *Reminiscences of Abraham Lincoln*, p. 39.

38 Pinkerton report, February 23, 1861, in Cuthbert, *Lincoln and the Baltimore Plot*, p. 83.

39 Ibid.

40 Ibid.

41 Ibid.

42 Ibid., p. 81.

43 Pinkerton to Herndon, August 23, 1866, in Cuthbert, *Lincoln and the Baltimore Plot*, p. 16.

44 Pinkerton report, February 23, 1861, in Cuthbert, *Lincoln and the Baltimore Plot*, p. 84.

45 Ibid. The telegram to Bangs is, except for reference to "Barley," representative of the others, and reads:

> "G. H. Bangs
> 80 Washington Street, Chicago
> Plums has Nuts-arri'd Barley—all
> Right.
> E. J. Allen."

"Plums" was Pinkerton's code word for himself, "Nuts" meant Lincoln, and "Barley" meant Washington. The other telegrams Pinkerton reported sending went to Judd in Harrisburg,

Franciscus or Lewis, and Felton in Philadelphia, and E. S. Sanford in New York City. Cuthbert, *Lincoln and the Baltimore Plot*, pp. 84-85.

46 McClure, *Abraham Lincoln and Men of War-Times*, p. 48. Note that Pinkerton does not record having sent this telegram to Thomas A. Scott.

47 Worthington G. Snethen to Abraham Lincoln, February 25, 1861, Abraham Lincoln Papers at the Library of Congress.

48 Ibid.

49 Scharf, *History of Maryland*, vol. 3, p. 385; *New York World*, February 25, 1861, p. 5 (from the *Baltimore Patriot*).

50 Scharf, *History of Maryland*, vol. 3, p. 385.

51 *New York World*, February 25, 1861, p. 4.

52 Ibid.

53 *New York Times*, February 25, 1861, p. 1, ProQuest Historical Newspapers; *Pittsburgh Gazette*, February 25, 1861, p. 2.

54 See, e.g., Sandburg, *Abraham Lincoln: The War Years*, pp. 78, 80.

55 King, *Louis T. Wigfall*, p. 35.

CHAPTER 17

1 See Scharf, *Chronicles of Baltimore*, p. 569.

2 Lamon would indeed send a dispatch to Wilson concerning Lincoln's safe arrival in Washington. See letter from Charles Wilson to Ward Hill Lamon, February 25, 1861, in the Ward Hill Lamon Papers, Huntington Library, thanking Lamon for sending the dispatch. Lamon's brief, by-lined account would appear in the Chicago *Daily Evening Jounral* on February 23, 1861.

3 Allan Pinkerton, report, February 23, 1861, in Cuthbert, *Lincoln and the Baltimore Plot*, pp. 85-86.

4 Ibid., pp. 87-88. It is unclear how Hanscom, who had reportedly been in Harrisburg the night before, had managed to get to Washington on February 23 ahead of Mrs. Lincoln and suite, in time to be seen by Pinkerton, who would leave Washington on the 3:10 p.m. train for Baltimore, running into the suite at Annapolis Junction. Report, Allan Pinkerton, February 23, 1861, *Cuthbert, Lincoln and the Baltimore Plot*, p 88. Perhaps Hanscom had taken an earlier train that morning from Harrisburg.

5 See, e.g., letters of recommendation of E. R. Allen, W. Bushnell, and Jesse W. Fell to Abraham Lincoln, February 2, 1861, and Jesse K. DuBois, February 4, 1861, among many others. Ward Hill Lamon Papers, Box 2, Huntington Library.

6 Pinkerton had foreseen this very possibility a month earlier, when Samuel Felton had first retained him to commence investigations in Baltimore. As Pinkerton wrote to Felton at the time: "As I have before remarked Secrecy is the Lever of any success which may attend my operations and as the nature of this service may prove of a character which might to some extent be dangerous to the persons of myself, or any operatives, I should expect that the Fact of my operating should be known only to myself or such discreet persons connected with your Company as it might be absolutely necessary should we be entrusted with the same. But on no conditions would I consider it safe for myself or my operatives were the fact of my operating known to any Politician, no matter of what school, or what position."

Allan Pinkerton to S. M. Felton, January 27, 1861, in Cuthbert, *Lincoln and the Baltimore Plot*, pp. 24-25.

7 Chittenden, *Recollections*, pp. 65-66 (emphasis added).

8 See, e.g., *American Annual Cyclopædia*, vol. 1, p. 477.

9 *Biographical Directory of the United States Congress*, http://bioguide.congress.gov. See also http://stclair.mogenweb.org/StClairPeople/StClairPeopleWaldoPJohnson.htm

10 Chittenden, *A Report of the Debates and Proceedings in the Secret Sessions of the Conference Convention*, p. 207.

11 Chittenden, *Recollections*, pp. 51-52.

12 Chittenden, *Report of the Debates*, p. 145.

13 Ibid., p. 148 (emphasis added).

14 Kane made this statement to New York Police Superintendent John A. Kennedy in January 1861. See Lossing, *Pictorial History of the Civil War*, vol. 2 p. 148.

15 Chittenden, *Recollections*, p. 66.

16 O'Brien, "James A. Seddon," p. 219.

17 U.S. Constitution, art. 2, sect. 1, par. 6.

18 King, *Louis T. Wigfall,* pp. 99-100.

19 The Twelfth Amendment superseded a confusing article 2, section 1, paragraph 3, which provided:

> The Electors shall meet in their respective States, and vote by Ballot for two Persons, of whom one at least shall not be an Inhabitant of the same State with themselves. And they shall make a List of all the Persons voted for, and of the Number of Votes for each; which List they shall sign and certify, and transmit sealed to the Seat of the Government of the United States, directed to the President of the Senate. The President of the Senate shall, in the Presence of the Senate and House of Representatives, open all the Certificates, and the Votes shall be counted. The Person having the greatest Number of Votes shall be the President, if such Number be a Majority of the whole Number of Electors appointed; and if there be more than one who have such Majority, and have an equal Number of Votes, then the House of Representatives shall immediately chuse by Ballot one of them for President; and if no Person have a Majority, then from the five highest on the List the said House shall in like Manner chuse the President. But in chusing the President, the Votes shall be taken by States, the Representation from each State having one Vote; a quorum for this Purpose shall consist of a Member or Members from two thirds of the States, and a Majority of all the States shall be necessary to a Choice. In every Case, after the Choice of the President, the Person having the greater Number of Votes of the Electors shall be the Vice President. But if there should remain two or more who have equal Votes, the Senate shall chuse from them by Ballot the Vice President.

20 Chittenden, *Recollections*, p. 67.

21 Chittenden, *Report of the Debates*, p. 336.

22 Chittenden, *Recollections*, p. 67 (emphasis added).

23 *New York World,* February 25, 1861, p. 4.

24 Report from Washington of *New York Times* correspondent Joseph Howard, who accompanied the Lincoln Special from Harrisburg to Washington on February 23, 1861, as reported in the *New York Times,* February 26, 1861, p. 8, ProQuest Historical Newspapers.

25 Whitney, *Lincoln the Citizen*, p. 304.

26 *New York World,* February 25, 1861, p. 4.

27 *Philadelphia Inquirer,* February 25, 1861, p. 1.

28 Ibid.; Goff, *Robert Todd Lincoln*, p. 38; Baker, *Mary Todd Lincoln*, pp. 166-167.

29 William Schley to Abraham Lincoln, February 23, 1861, from the Abraham Lincoln Papers at the Library of Congress.

30 Ibid.

31 Harry W. Davies, report, February 23, 1861, in Cuthbert, *Lincoln and the Baltimore Plot*, p. 90.

32 Ibid., pp. 90-91.

33 See, e.g., ibid., p. 91.

34 *New York World,* February 25, 1861, pp. 4, 5.

35 *Philadelphia Inquirer,* February 25, 1861, p. 1.

36 *New York Times,* February 26, 1861, p. 8, ProQuest Historical Newspapers. Reprinted by numerous other newspapers, including the *Pittsburgh Gazette,* February 28, 1861, p. 1, cols. 4-5.

37 It is possible that either William S. Wood was the man mistaken for Lincoln (as Howard had also reported), or that it was Francis S. Corkran, one of the Baltimore Republicans. Corkran, "of Baltimore, and one of the Maryland electors, a tall 'Friend,' looked very much like Mr. Lincoln, and it was urged that he take off his white hat, turn down his coat collar, dispense with his 'thee and thou,' and we would put him off for Old Abe; he thought, however, that it would not do, as he was too well known to try it." *Philadelphia Inquirer,* February 25, 1861, p. 1.

38 Ibid.

39 Ibid.

40 Frank Moore, ed., *The Rebellion Record: A Diary of American Events* (New York: G. P. Putnam, 1861-68), vol. 1, p. 33, citing the *Baltimore American.*

41 *Philadelphia Inquirer,* February 25, 1861, p. 1.

42 Scharf, *History of Maryland,* vol. 3, p. 386. Scharf reports this intersection was at Charles and Bolton Streets. The tracks of the Susquehanna Railroad, which had merged with the Northern Central in 1854, actually crossed Charles Street at Biddle Street, not Bolton Street. Clayton Colman Hall, ed., *Baltimore: Its History and People* (New York: Lewis Historical Publishing Co., 1912), vol. 1, p. 485; S. Augustus Mitchell, Map of Baltimore (Philadelphia, 1860), http://alabamamaps.ua.edu/historicalmaps/us_states/maryland/index. html. It is likely that Mary Lincoln and her sons disembarked at this point for a short carriage ride south on Charles Street to Mount Vernon Square.

43 Reported the *Times,* after arriving at the depot, "Mrs. Lincoln and her son[s] were taken to a carriage, which they entered without attracting much attention, and were driven to the house of the President of the road." *New York Times,* February 26, 1861, p. 8, ProQuest Historical Newspapers.

44 *Philadelphia Inquirer,* February 25, 1861, p. 1. This account is in error, as Mrs. Lincoln and her family were actually driven to the Gittings home on Mount Vernon Square.

45 Moore, *Rebellion Record,* vol. 1, p. 33, citing the *Baltimore American.* It makes sense that Mary Lincoln and sons would have left the train at an earlier stop than the Calvert Street Station if they were to dine at Gittings's Mount Vernon Square mansion. The train was approaching Baltimore from the north, and Calvert Street is several blocks south of Mount Vernon Square. Thus, in getting off early, the Lincolns not only avoided the throng at Calvert Street Station, they avoided the need to backtrack.

46 Bryan, *The Spy in America,* p. 172. Lincoln would later thank Mrs. Gittings for the courtesy shown his family, when she and her husband appealed to him for clemency to save the life of three condemned Maryland spies, John H. R. Embert, Samuel B. Hearn, and Braxton Lyon. Lincoln had pardoned many condemned men during the war, saying, "You do not know how hard it is to let a human being die, when you feel that a stroke of your pen will save him." When Mrs. Gittings pleaded for the lives of the three Marylanders, Lincoln reportedly said: "Madam, I owe you a debt. You took my family into your home in the midst of a hostile mob. You gave them succor, and helped them on their way. This debt has never been paid and I am glad of the opportunity. I shall save the lives of these men." Ibid.

47 Scharf, *History of Maryland,* vol. 3, p. 386.

48 *New York World,* February 25, 1861, p. 4.

49 Ibid.

50 Pinkerton report, February 23, 1861, in Cuthbert, *Lincoln and the Baltimore Plot*, p. 88.

51 Ibid.

CHAPTER 18

1 Pinkerton report, February 23, 1861, in Cuthbert, *Lincoln and the Baltimore Plot*, p. 89.

2 Ibid.

3 *Philadelphia Inquirer,* February 25, 1861, p. 1.

4 "The Reception Mr. Lincoln Escaped in Baltimore," *New York Times,* March 11, 1861, p. 2, ProQuest Historical Newspapers.

5 Reported the *Baltimore Patriot* under the heading "Incidents at the Depot":

"Owing to discussions, some few fights occurred, but the prompt efforts of the police soon succeeded in quelling all disturbances, and the participants marched to the station house. The entire police force, under the command of Marshal Kane and Deputy Gifford, were on the ground, and preserved good order." Perhaps those who had started the fight would have fought anyway. Perhaps, however, they had merely failed to get the word that Lincoln was not among the traveling suite. Reprinted in the *New York World,* February 25, 1861, p. 5.

6 Pinkerton report, February 23, 1861, in Cuthbert, *Lincoln and the Baltimore Plot*, p. 89.

7 Allan Pinkerton, report, February 23, 1861, in Cuthbert, *Lincoln and the Baltimore Plot*, p. 90.

8 According to Pinkerton operative Harry W. Davies, he gave his report to Pinkerton at the Howard House, presumably where Pinkerton stayed while in Baltimore. Davies report, February 23, 1861, in Cuthbert, *Lincoln and the Baltimore Plot*, p. 94.

9 Pinkerton report, February 23, 1861, in Cuthbert, *Lincoln and the Baltimore Plot*, p. 90.

10 Davies report, February 23, 1861, in Cuthbert, *Lincoln and the Baltimore Plot*, p. 94.

11 Ibid., pp. 91-92.

12 Ibid, pp. 91-92.

13 Ibid, p. 92.

14 Ibid., February 23 and 24, 1861, in Cuthbert, *Lincoln and the Baltimore Plot*, pp. 92, 96-97.

15 Ibid., February 23, 1861, in Cuthbert, *Lincoln and the Baltimore Plot*, p 93.

16 Charles D. C. Williams, report, February 20, 1861, in Cuthbert, *Lincoln and the Baltimore Plot*, p. 49. Pinkerton identified Sherrington as "Captain," who had spoken of an unidentified "privateer," presumably someone interested in making money for securing Lincoln's assassination. Pinkerton report, February 21, 1861, in Cuthbert, *Lincoln and the Baltimore Plot*, pp. 59-60.

17 Davies report, February 25, 1861, in Cuthbert, *Lincoln and the Baltimore Plot*, p. 97.

18 Walling, *Recollections of a New York Chief of Police*, p. 71.

19 *Biographical Directory of the United States Congress*, http://bioguide.congress.gov.

20 As seen by the author February 10, 2007, at the Civil War exhibit at the Atlanta History Center.

21 Davies report, February 23, 1861, in Cuthbert, *Lincoln and the Baltimore Plot*, p. 93.

22 A photograph taken soon after his arrival in Washington shows a weary Lincoln apparently trying to hide his swollen, possibly slightly paralyzed right hand behind the arm of the chair in which he is seated. Kunhardt, Philip B., Jr., Kunhardt, Philip B., III, and Kunhardt, Peter W., *Lincoln: An Illustrated Biography* (New York: Knopf, 1992), pp. 24-25.

23 Chittenden, *Recollections*, pp. 68-69.

24 Ibid., p. 69.

25 Chittenden, *Recollections*, p. 71. Contemporaneous accounts reported that Senator Salmon P. Chase, former governor of Ohio, rather than Chittenden, presented the Peace Conference delegates, starting with President Tyler, to Mr. Lincoln. See, e.g., Albany *Atlas and Argus*, February 25, 1861, p. 2.

26 Chittenden, *Recollections*, p. 72.

27 Ibid., pp. 73-74.

28 Dodge need not have been concerned for his company. Phelps Dodge & Co. would go on to become one of the country's foremost mercantile and metals businesses. In 2007, Phelps Dodge became part of Freeport-McMoRan Copper & Gold Inc. See www.fcx.com/company/history.htm.

29 Chittenden, *Recollections*, p. 75 (first emphasis added, second emphasis original).

30 Chittenden, *Recollections*, p. 76.

31 Chittenden, *Recollections*, pp. 76, 78.

32 Ibid., p. 77.

33 Davies report, February 23, 1861, in Cuthbert, *Lincoln and the Baltimore Plot*, pp. 94-95.

34 Albany *Atlas and Argus*, February 18, 1861, p. 3.

35 Clarke, *The Unlocked Book,* p. 123.

36 Ibid., pp. 123-124. Perhaps in claiming the "votes were doubled to seat" Lincoln, Booth was referring to the fact the Democratic Party had split itself in two, the Breckenridge and Douglas factions, thereby, in effect, "doubling" the electoral votes, relatively speaking, for Lincoln.

37 Pinkerton, *The Spy of the Rebellion,* p. 69.

CHAPTER 19

1 Scharf, *History of Maryland,* vol. 3, pp. 387-388 n. 2. Scharf, clearly partisan in his views, pronounces that Lincoln's decision to alter his route was thus made at Marshal Kane's suggestion. In the same breath, Scharf both castigates Lincoln for allowing himself to be "weakly" led into his altered course and yet commends Kane for suggesting it. Ibid., pp. 386-387.

2 Worthington G. Snethen to Abraham Lincoln, February 25, 1861, Abraham Lincoln Papers at the Library of Congress.

3 Ibid.

4 *New York Times,* February 27, 1861, p. 4, ProQuest Historical Newspapers.

5 *New York Times,* February 26, 1861, p. 8, ProQuest Historical Newspapers.

6 *American Annual Cyclopædia*, vol. 1, p. 419.

7 As reported in the *Pittsburgh Gazette,* February 26, 1861, p. 3, col. 4.

8 Bryan, *The Great American Myth*, pp. 43-44 and n. 45, citing the *New Orleans Picayune* of March 7, 1861.

9 The Baltimore correspondent for the *New York Times* was representative of the indignity Baltimoreans felt, claiming that they and their city had been given a bad rap: "Baltimore City, some two years ago, was, and anterior to that time had been, the scene of many a cruel and wicked outrage. The Know-Nothing Party controlled the City Government, and, under its rule, lawlessless [*sic*] and violence usurped our streets, and the most public thoroughfares were disgraced by open and deliberated violations of order and decorum. Assassination and murder invaded the fireside and selected its victims from among the executive officers of the law. Men, bodly [*sic*] eminent, in talent and position, winked at and tolerated this state of affairs, through partisan motives and for party purposes." But in more recent times, the correspondent pointed out, Baltimore, through the Reformers, had instilled order and "its present most effective and valuable police system, superior for all purposes of order and protection to any elsewhere to be found in the United States." The correspondent naively argued that there were few men in Maryland who favored secession and none who would, "for a moment, have countenanced any insult or outrage to the President elect on his passage through this State to Washington. . . . All, therefore, that has been published about conspiracies and plots in Baltimore and Maryland, is absurd and false; the inventions of panic-makers, and reckless disturbers of public confidence and respect. . . . The President elect was badly advised, and the friends of the Government here regret exceedingly that such should have been the case. He would have been received by the city authorities with the honor and respect due to the Presidency, and this without regard to

party feelings or considerations of any kind whatever. Ample security had been provided for his comfort and convenience, both here and on the line of his travel through the State." "Baltimore City—No Longer Mobtown—Efficiency of Its Present Police System—Preparations for the Reception of Mr. Lincoln—Disappointment, Rumors and Libels," *New York Times,* February 28, 1861, p. 8, ProQuest Historical Newspapers.

10 Moore, *Rebellion Record,* vol. 1, p. 34, citing the *Baltimore Sun.*

11 "The Story About Baltimore," *Philadelphia Inquirer,* February 25, 1861, p. 1. This argument is a non sequitur. By definition, a conspiracy, a plot among a handful of assassins to murder Lincoln, would have been hatched in secrecy and would not, therefore, have been "known or thought of generally." Indeed, the only reason the plot was suspected at all was because men like Pinkerton, Kennedy, and Chittenden had infiltrated its inner circle. More significant, the reporter's argument converts Baltimore and Maryland's failure to make adequate security preparations for receiving the president-elect from evidence of complicity to evidence of pure intent. Remarkably, this argument relies on the failure to provide a military escort, as had every other major city on the Lincoln Special's route, as evidence that there was no Baltimore Plot. There had, for example, been no evidence of an Albany plot. Or a Philadelphia lot. Or a Harrisburg plot. And yet, military honor guards were out in force in each of these cities to escort Lincoln and assist with crowd control.

Moreover, it wasn't as if Baltimore could not have mustered out militia to provide a military escort for Lincoln, even at a moment's notice, had it desired to do so. Indeed, on the afternoon of October 17, 1859, after news of John Brown's raid had reached Baltimore, the city's militia immediately responded. Major General George H. Steuart instantly tendered the services of his division, and five companies commanded by Lieutenant Colonel Egerton quickly assembled and left by train for Harpers Ferry that same afternoon, "amid cheers of the immense crowd who had collected at the depot." Six cars were filled with militia, including the Independent Greys, Law Greys, Baltimore City Guard, and Wells and McComas Riflemen, "numbering 201 muskets." The next day, the Lafayette Guards, with Captain Ferrandini in command, turned out at the Camden Street Station "ready to proceed to the seat of war." Scharf, *Chronicles of Baltimore,* p. 569. How many of these companies had planned to tender their services for the protection of Lincoln? History records none. Baltimore's failure to provide Lincoln a military escort evidences both means and opportunity for carrying out an assassination. Whether or not he was present for John Brown's capture, George P. Kane was reportedly a member of the Independent Greys, having been commissioned an ensign. He would, during the Civil War, serve as a colonel for the Confederacy in the First Maryland Regiment of Artillery. Wilbur F. Coyle, *The Mayors of Baltimore* (Baltimore: Baltimore Municipal Journal, 1919), p. 139.

12 "The Story About Baltimore," *Philadelphia Inquirer,* February 25, 1861.

13 Ibid.

14 Radcliffe, *Governor Thomas H. Hicks,* p. 47, citing the *Baltimore American,* February 27, 1861. But as has been noted previously, Hicks had reason to believe, at least two weeks earlier, that there were indeed plots in Baltimore to murder Lincoln. See George Stearns to Thomas H. Hicks, February 7, 1861, in the Thomas H. Hicks Papers, Maryland Historical Society, Baltimore.

15 Albany *Atlas and Argus,* February 25, 1861, p. 2.

16 Ibid.

17 Albany *Atlas and Argus,* March 4, 1861, p. 2.

18 *New York World,* February 25, 1861, p. 5.

19 *New York Times,* February 26, 1861, p. 1, ProQuest Historical Newspapers.

20 William Louis Schley to Abraham Lincoln, February 23, 1861, The Abraham Lincoln Papers at the Library of Congress. William Louis Schley was a Baltimore attorney, described as one of "the most eminent and distinguished constitutional lawyers of the State [of Maryland] and the country." Schley would later represent Major General John L. Wool in a suit brought by Severn Teackle Wallis, Frank Key Howard, and Henry M. Warfield for "falsely, unlawfully and by force" imprisoning them in Fort Monroe. Schley petitioned the court to remove the case to United States Court, which petition was granted. The suit was eventually dropped. Scharf, *History of Maryland,* vol. 3, pp. 590 and 523 n. 1.

21 Bronson Murray to Ward Hill Lamon, February 27, 1861, in the Ward Hill Lamon Papers at the Huntington Library. Murray would later hint to Lamon that there might be an opportunity for both men to make profit on contracts for unspecified material to be purchased in New York, presumably for the administration. Murray to Lamon, March 7, 1861, Ward Hill Lamon Papers, Huntington Library.

22 Mary Chesnut, *Mary Chesnut's Civil War,* ed. C. Vann Woodward (New Haven, Conn.: Yale University Press, 1981), p. 13 (entry for March 1, 1861). The "Brewster" referred to is Henry Percy Brewster, a South Carolina native who, like Senator Wigfall, would move to Texas; he would become secretary of war of the Texas Republic and a prominent lawyer in Washington, D.C., and Texas. Ibid., p. 11 n. 6.

23 Ibid., p. 8 (entry for February 25, 1861).

24 Burlingame, ed., *Lincoln's Journalist,* p. 44, citing the *New York World,* February 27, 1861, p. 3. Lincoln may, in fact, have publicly put his own spin on the story through the anonymous *World* reporter. Historians generally accept that this embedded reporter, who had been traveling with the Lincoln Special since its departure, was Lincoln's personal secretary John Hay. In an article published four days after Lincoln's arrival in Washington, this anonymous *World* reporter sought to paint the president-elect as a courageous, almost unwilling participant, forced to take part in a scheme urged upon him by others. Lincoln had gone along with the ruse more to humor well-meaning yet overly protective friends, than out of any real fear of danger.

> Mr. Lincoln, . . . submitting entirely to the direction of his friends, left Harrisburg at once, and reached Washington as has been before recounted. . . . There will, of course, be future dislocations concerning the matter. Even up to this time it is impossible to form an opinion which may not be controverted by the revelations of tomorrow. I do not think, however, that the existence of an organized plot against the President's life will be established.

If the *World* report was Hay's, and if Lincoln had sanctioned the account, it therefore stands to reason that, under cloak of double anonymity, Hay was giving voice to the story of the Baltimore Plot as both he—and Lincoln—wished it to be told: The plot was a swirl of rumors, so numerous, varied, and far-fetched it was difficult to discern truth from fantasy. Lincoln had no fear of assassination, but submitted to the alarmist pleas of his friends, including Allan Pinkerton, named in the report. Lincoln came early to Washington at

General Scott and Senator Seward's insistence, the two requesting his "immediate presence," suggesting the need to attend to some urgent, but vague and presumably top-secret government business. He acted for them, not for himself. And he also acted to save the Baltimore Republicans from the insults they would have received from a city and a state that had utterly failed to extend even the simple courtesy of inviting the president-elect of the United States to lunch. In the final analysis, the *World* story blamed Pinkerton, Lincoln's friends, and Baltimore.

25 Bryan, *The Great American Myth*, p. 41 and n. 44, citing the *New York Times*, March 5, 1857 p. 1.

26 Harry W. Davies report, February 23, 1861, in Cuthbert, *Lincoln and the Baltimore Plot*, pp. 93-94.

27 Ibid., pp. 94-95.

28 Ibid., February 24, 1861, in Cuthbert, *Lincoln and the Baltimore Plot*, pp. 96-97.

29 Lossing, *Pictorial History of the Civil War*, vol. 2, p. 148n. Kennedy claimed to have "ascertained from Marshal Kane himself" the means by which Maryland would be "precipitated out of the Union." This involved waiting for Virginia to secede, then following suit. Fort McHenry, meanwhile, would be garrisoned by a single guard, and "guarded" on the outside by Baltimore police to prevent its premature capture by Baltimore roughs. It seems unlikely that Kane would have shared this intelligence with Kennedy had he known Kennedy was superintendent of New York police. This suggests Kennedy possibly met with Kane under an assumed identity. General Scott, acting quickly on Kennedy's intelligence, ordered troops from Washington to garrison Baltimore's Fort McHenry on January 9. (ibid.). On January 12, three companies of United States light artillery from Fort Leavenworth arrived in Baltimore and occupied Fort McHenry. Scharf, *History of Baltimore City and County*, vol. 1, p. 128.

30 Walling, *Recollections of a New York Chief of Police,* p. 69. A third detective, David S. Bookstaver, would arrive in Baltimore later. It would also be reported that in addition to Walling, Sampson, and De Voe, two improbably named New York City detectives, "Young" and "Elder," possibly aliases, had also been stationed in Baltimore and Washington for the past few weeks. *New York Times,* February 27, 1861, p. 4, ProQuest Historical Newspapers.

31 Walling, *Recollections of a New York Chief of Police*, p. 71. Sampson recalled that the alias he used was "Anderson," as reported in Walling's book, published in 1888. Ibid., p. 69. Pinkerton, however, believed that Sampson was calling himself "Thompson." Pinkerton report, February 25, 1861, in Cuthbert, *Lincoln and the Baltimore Plot,* p. 97. Because Pinkerton's report is more contemporaneous with the events recorded, his identification of Sampson's alias as "Thompson" is used herein. It is possible, however, that Pinkerton was incorrect in his assumption that "Thompson" was Sampson, just as he was incorrect in believing that "Davis" was Walling. Ibid. The Fountain Inn, on the northwest corner of Light and German Streets, was a favorite of Eastern Shoremen, who could walk up Light Street from their ships docked in the basin. Erected around the time of the American Revolution, George Washington actually slept there, in September of 1781, while on his way to Virginia. Scharf, *History of Baltimore City and County*, vol. 2, pp. 513-515. This is likely the "Hotel Fountain" Chittenden referenced in his account.

32 Walling, *Recollections of a New York Chief of Police,* pp. 69-71.

33 Ibid., p. 71.

34 Ibid., p. 72.

35 Ibid.

36 Allan Pinkerton, February 25, 1861, in Cuthbert, *Lincoln and the Baltimore Plot*, pp. 97-98.

37 Walling, *Recollections of a New York Chief of Police,* p. 72.

38 Ibid., pp. 73-74.

39 Ibid., p. 74.

40 Ibid., p. 75.

41 Ibid.

42 Here Wigfall refers to the Peace Conference that had assembled in Washington on February 4, and would adjourn two days later, on February 27, 1861.

43 *The Papers of Jefferson Davis*, vol. 7, p. 60.

44 Johnson's U. S. senate career began on March 18, 1861. Wigfall's ended on March 23, 1861. Biographical Directory of the Unites States Congress, http://bioguide.congress.gov. One is left to wonder if the Confederacy had passed the torch from one disloyal senator-informant to another. Johnson would remain in the U.S. senate until his expulsion for disloyalty to the Union on January 10, 1862. Ibid. It has been suggested, however, that Wigfall's reference to "Johnson" was intended to mean Joseph Eggleston Johnston. *The Papers of Jefferson Davis*, vol. 7, p. 61, n. 4.

45 Ibid. (emphasis added).

46 Chesnut, *Mary Chesnut's Civil War*, p. 12 (entry for February 28, 1861).

47 Walling, *Recollections of a New York Chief of Police,* p. 76.

48 Ibid., pp. 76-77.

49 Pinkerton report, February 26, 1861, in Cuthbert, *Lincoln and the Baltimore Plot,* pp. 98-99.

50 Timothy Webster, report, February 26, 1861, in Cuthbert, *Lincoln and the Baltimore Plot*, p. 99.

51 Ibid., p. 100.

52 Possibly referring to William Byrne, identified as president of the National Volunteers in Baltimore. Charles D. C. Williams, report, February 20, 1861, in Cuthbert, *Lincoln and the Baltimore Plot*, p. 49.

53 Harry W. Davies, report, February 26, 1861, in Cuthbert, *Lincoln and the Baltimore Plot*, pp. 102-104.

54 Loux, *John Wilkes Booth Day by Day*, p. 221, citing Albany *Atlas and Argus*, March 2, 1861.

55 Chittenden, *Recollections,* p. 82.

56 Sandburg, *Abraham Lincoln: The War Years,* vol. 1, p. 76. But note that Kennedy earlier had telegraphed William S. Wood, reporting that it would be "perfectly safe" for Lincoln to proceed down the Susquehanna Line through Maryland.

57 Pinkerton report, February 28, 1861, in Cuthbert, *Lincoln and the Baltimore Plot*, pp. 104-105.

58 Ibid., p. 105.

59 Davies report, March 1, 1861, in Cuthbert, *Lincoln and the Baltimore Plot*, p. 105.

60 Ibid., p. 106.

61 Ibid.

62 Ibid.

CHAPTER 20

1 *New York Times,* March 5, 1861, p. 1; *New York Tribune,* March 5, 1861, p. 5.

2 *New York Times,* March 4, 1861, p. 1.

3 Ibid.

4 *New York Times,* March 5, 1861, p. 1.

5 *Philadelphia Inquirer,* March 4, 1861, p. 1.

6 *New York Times,* March 4, 1861, p. 1.

7 *Philadelphia Inquirer,* March 5, 1861, p. 1.

8 Ibid.

9 *Philadelphia Inquirer,* March 4, 1861, p. 1.

10 *New York Times,* March 5, 1861, p. 8.

11 Albany *Atlas and Argus,* March 5, 1861, p. 2.

12 *New York Times,* March 5, 1861, p. 8.

13 *New York Times,* March 5, 1861, p. 1.

14 Chittenden, *Recollections,* p. 85.

15 *New York Times,* March 5, 1861, p. 1.

16 Albany *Atlas and Argus,* March 5, 1861, p. 2.

17 *Philadelphia Inquirer,* March 5, 1861, p. 1.

18 *New York Times,* March 5, 1861, p. 1; Chittenden, *Recollections,* p. 85.

19 *New York Tribune,* March 5, 1861, p. 5. By other estimates, the numbers were more modest, between 25,000 and 50,000. Ibid., p. 5.

20 Thousands of the Baltimore influx were reportedly tourists who were connecting in Baltimore en route to Washington from other cities. *Philadelphia Inquirer,* March 4, 1861, p. 4.

21 *New York Times,* March 4, 1861, p. 1. Continued the article, "It is believed that their purpose is not to make a demonstration against Mr. Lincoln, but, if anything, to create a disturbance, and plunder private persons, and commit depredations upon the citizens."

22 Burlingame, ed., *Lincoln's Journalist,* p. 50, citing the *New York World,* March 5, 1861, p. 3.

23 *Atlanta Southern Confederacy,* March 4, 1861, p. 2.

24 *New York Times,* March 5, 1861, p. 1

25 *Philadelphia Inquirer,* March 5, 1861, p. 1.

26 Ibid.; *New York Times,* March 5, 1861, p. 1.

27 *Philadelphia Inquirer,* March 5, 1861, p. 1.

28 Ibid.

29 Chesnut, *Mary Chesnut's Civil War*, p. 15.

30 Chittenden, *Recollections*, p. 86.

31 *American Annual Cyclopædia*, vol. 1, p. 751; Chittenden, *Recollections*, p. 85.

32 Bryan, *The Great American Myth*, p. 54; *Philadelphia Inquirer*, March 5, 1861, p. 1.

33 *Philadelphia Inquirer*, March 5, 1861, p. 1.

34 Ibid.

35 Sandburg, *Abraham Lincoln: The War Years*, vol. 1, p. 121.

36 *Philadelphia Inquirer*, March 5, 1861, p. 1.

37 *New York Times*, March 5, 1861, p. 1; *American Annual Cyclopædia*, vol. 1, p. 751.

38 *New York Times*, March 5, 1861, p. 1.

39 *New York Times*, March 5, 1861, p. 8. Senator Douglas reportedly held Lincoln's top hat. Bryan, *The Great American Myth*, p. 54.

40 *New York Tribune*, March 5, 1861, p. 5.

41 *New York Times*, March 5, 1861, p. 1. There is no evidence that Wigfall was armed as he stood watching Lincoln's inauguration. It was not uncommon, however, for government leaders of the era to carry firearms in Washington, as evidenced by Congressman Van Wyck's use of his weapon in fending off would-be assassins. As a sitting Senator who knew how to use a gun and had dueled and killed previously, Wigfall could easily have carried a weapon and gotten close to Lincoln on the podium.

42 Benn Pitman, comp., *The Assassination of Abraham Lincoln and the Trial of the Conspirators*, (Cincinnati: Moore, Wilstach & Baldwin, 1865), p. 45.

43 *CW*, 4:265.

44 Chittenden, *Recollections*, p. 88.

45 *Atlanta Southern Confederacy*, March 5, 1861, p. 2.

46 *New York Times*, March 5, 1861, p. 1.

47 Ibid.

48 *CW*, 4:262.

49 *CW*, 4:263.

50 *CW*, 4:264-265.

51 *CW*, 4:265.

52 *CW*, 4:265-266.

53 *OR*, series 1, vol. 1, p. 261.

54 *CW*, 4:266.

55 Ibid.

56 *CW*, 4:267.

57 *CW*, 4:268.

58 *New York Times*, February 19, 1861, p. 4, ProQuest Historical Newspapers.

59 In addition to van Buren and Lincoln, Justice Taney administered the oath to Presidents Harrison, Polk, Taylor, Pierce, and Buchanan. Judge William Cranch administered the oath to Presidents Tyler and Fillmore. Malcom Townsend, ed., *Handbook of United States Political History* (Boston: Lothrop, Lee & Shepard Co., 1905), p. 314.

60 *CW*, 4:268.

61 *CW*, 4:271.

62 Herndon and Weik, *Abraham Lincoln*, vol. 2, pp. 206-207. The authors do not report the name of this witness.

CHAPTER 21

1 See, e.g., *OR* 2:1, pp. 667-675, detailing the numerous members of the Maryland state legislature, many from Baltimore, who were arrested on suspicion of conspiring to pass an act of secession in the summer of 1861. Many were confined, in succession, to Forts McHenry, Lafayette, and Warren.

2 Indeed, it would be reported in newspapers at the time that "the names of the conspirators will not at present be divulged. But they are in possession of responsible parties, including the President." Moore's *Rebellion Record,* Documents, p. 35.

3 Ferrandini might be painted as an outspoken barber who could, under the influence of alcohol, utter some outrageous statements, but nothing more. He was still clipping hair and shaving throats in 1877 in the basement of Barnum's Hotel. Baltimore census records show that he was a married man with several sons who joined him in his trade. In 1886 a reporter for the *Baltimore Sun* found him living in retirement, a respected citizen. Tilton, Clint Clay, "First Plot Against Lincoln," *National Republic* (February 1936) p. 7. In one interview, Ferrandini claimed that he never planned to kill Mr. Lincoln. "Of course," he said, "I may have talked a lot. All of my customers were Southern sympathizers and I wanted to hold their patronage." Ibid.

4 Allan Pinkerton to William Herndon, August 5, 1866, in Cuthbert, *Lincoln and the Baltimore Plot*, p. 2. Pinkerton reminded Herndon a few weeks later to "please consider Mr. Luckett's name as confidential." Ibid., p. 18. See Herdon-Weik Collection, Library of Congress.

5 Bryan, *The Great American Myth*, pp. 57-58, citing Doster, *Lincoln and Episodes of the Civil War,* p. 29.

6 Doster, *Lincoln and Episodes of the Civil War*, p. 29.

7 Fishel, *The Secret War for the Union*, pp. 53-55; Horan, *The Pinkertons*, p. 121.

8 Bryan, *The Great American Myth,* p. 58. It seems possible that Doster's "Major Allen" was not Pinkerton, as Pinkerton was not a government employee, but rather worked as a government contractor. Fishel, *The Secret War for the Union*, p. 54.

9 By the summer of 1861, a congressional subcommittee was holding McCarthyesque hearings to determine whether any government employees held Southern sympathies. The committee received about 550 allegations and found more than 200 of them well founded. See Fishel, *The Secret War for the Union*, pp. 56-58.

10 Ibid., pp. 53-54.

11 Horan, *The Pinkertons*, p. 65.

12 U.S. Constitution, Sixth Amendment (1791).

13 Scharf, *History of Maryland,* vol. 3, p. 398.

14 Edward Bates to William Price, January 6, 1863, *OR* 2:1, p. 667.

15 U.S. Constitution, Sixth Amendment.

16 While spying under contract for the army during the early stages of the war, Pinkerton refused to identify his operatives by name even to the government, providing in his monthly invoices only their initials as a means of keeping their identities secret. Fishel, *The Secret War for the Union*, p. 54.

17 Beymer, *On Hazardous Service*, p. 267.

18 Fishel, *The Secret War for the Union*, p. 89.

19 Whether or not he was a Baltimore plotter, a contractor from Baltimore named William Campbell was, in the fall of 1861, apparently working with Webster and even provided Webster an introduction to the Confederate general John H. Winder's office. Fishel, *The Secret War for the Union*, p. 90. So complete and convincing was Webster's cover story that he was even able to procure passes from Acting Secretary of War Judah P. Benjamin. Ibid., pp. 98-99.

20 Harry W. Davies, report, February 23, 1861, in Cuthbert, *Lincoln and the Baltimore Plot*, p. 92.

21 Hillard's account in testimony before the Select Committee of Five on February 6, 1861, that there were six thousand National Volunteers in Baltimore is loosely corroborated by the testimony of Baltimore resident Joseph H. Boyd, who testified, when questioned before the Select Committee of Five on February 9, 1861, about the National Volunteers that "there are some 2,500 of them, I believe; there was some three months ago." Report No. 79, pp. 146-147, 159.

22 John A. Kennedy to George P. Kane, February 28, 1861, in Scharf, *History of Maryland*, vol. 3, pp. 392-393. Pinkerton recounted similar emigration: "Here [Maryland] as elsewhere, conspiracy had been at work for months, and many of the prominent political leaders were in full accord with the rebel government. The legislature was believed to be unreliable, and treason had obtained so firm a foothold in the populous city of Baltimore, that a secret recruiting office was sending enlisted men to Charleston." Pinkerton, *Spy of the Rebellion*, p. 103.

23 Cuthbert, *Lincoln and the Baltimore Plot*, p. 141 n. 47; testimony of Joseph H. Boyd, February 9, 1861, Report No. 79, p. 159.

24 See, e.g., Tidwell, *Come Retribution*, p. 228. Byrne was also allegedly a member of the Knights of the Golden Circle, another secret secessionist paramilitary unit.

25 Charles C. D. Williams, report, February 20, 1861, in Cuthbert, *Lincoln and the Baltimore Plot*, p. 49. It is possible Byrne was in Washington on February 26, 1861, along with other members of the National Volunteers, in advance of Lincoln's inauguration. See report of Harry W. Davies, dated February 26, 1861, in Cuthbert, *Lincoln and the Baltimore Plot*, p. 102, wherein an acquaintance of Hillard's reportedly remarked, "There stands Jim [*sic*] Burns, Commander of the National Volunteers."

26 Testimony of Joseph H. Boyd, February 9, 1861, Report No. 79, p. 158.

27 *Biographical Directory of the United States Congress*, at http://bioguide.congress.gov.

28 Wright, *A Southern Girl in '61*, pp. 36-37.

29 Ibid., pp. 41-46. See also "Fort Sumter," Official National Park Handbook (Washington: U. S. Government Printing Office, 1984) p. 29.

30 *New York Evening Post*, March 27, 1862. Clipping enclosed in a letter from Joseph

Hazzard to S. M. Felton, April 6, 1862, Felton Papers (no. 1151), Box 2, Folder 1, Historical Society of Pennsylvania, Philadelphia.

31 King, *Louis T. Wigfall,* pp. 113-114; Nichols, *The Disruption of American Democracy,* p. 501; *The Papers of Jefferson Davis,* vol. 7, pp. 51-52, n. 7.

32 Tidwell, *Come Retribution,* p. 68. These men were advised to contact Lucius Quintius Washington for advice. L. Q. Washington would later become affiliated with the Confederate State Department. Ibid., p. 275.

33 Lamon, *The Life of Abraham Lincoln,* pp. 526-527.

34 Lamon, *The Life of Abraham Lincoln,* p. 512.

35 Ibid., pp. 512-513.

36 Ibid., p. 513 (emphasis added).

37 Pinkerton wrote Lamon letters on October 31, November 24, and December 28, 1867, beseeching Lamon to back up his rebuttal of New York Police Superintendent John A. Kennedy's claim, recently published in Lossing's *Pictorial Field Book of the Civil War,* that Kennedy and his operatives deserved all the credit for uncovering the Baltimore Plot. Pinkerton had written similar letters to others that knew of his involvement, including Norman Judd and S. M. Felton, all of whom wrote back supporting Pinkerton's claim to thwarting the plot. These letters would be published in Pinkerton's *History and Evidence of the Passage of Abraham Lincoln from Harrisburg, Pa., to Washington, D.C.* in 1868. See generally Cuthbert, *Lincoln and the Baltimore Plot,* pp. 114-123.

38 Cuthbert, *Lincoln and the Baltimore Plot,* pp. 86-87. Lamon was incorrect in his timing. Pinkerton's February 23, 1861, report was written several years before the publication of Kennedy's claim. Ibid., p. 86n.

39 "It is now an acknowledged fact that there never was a moment from the day he [Lincoln] crossed the Maryland line, up to the time of his assassination, that he was not in danger of death by violence, and that his life was spared until the night of the 14th of April, 1865, only through the ceaseless and watchful care of the guards thrown around him." Lamon, *Recollections of Abraham Lincoln,* p. 47. Note, however, that in Lamon's original manuscript, he wrote, "There never was an hour from the time he entered Washington on the 23d of February, 1861, to the 15th of April, 1865, that he was not in danger of his life from violence, and beyond question, had it not been for the watchfulness of his friends by day and night, he would have been murdered long before he was." Cuthbert, *Lincoln and the Baltimore Plot,* p. 122.

40 Bryan, *The Great American Myth,* pp. 36-37.

41 Allan Pinkerton to S. M. Felton, April 13, 1861, Felton Papers (no. 1151), Box 1, Folder 4, Historical Society of Pennsylvania; Horan, *The Pinkertons,* p. 59.

42 Abraham Lincoln as recorded by Isaac N. Arnold, *The History of Abraham Lincoln and the Overthrow of Slavery* (Chicago: Clarke, 1866), p. 171; Cuthbert, *Lincoln and the Baltimore Plot,* p. xvi.

43 Lossing, *A Pictorial History of the Civil War,* vol. 1, pp. 279-280 (emphasis added).

44 "The Change in Mr. Lincoln's Route,"*New York Tribune,* February 27, 1861, p. 8.

45 Davies report, February 23, 1861, in Cuthbert, *Lincoln and the Baltimore Plot,* p. 91.

46 William J. Evitts, *A Matter of Allegiances: Maryland from 1850 to 1861* (Baltimore: Johns Hopkins University Press, 1974), p. 150.

47 Worthington G. Snethen had suggested to Lincoln that he might win Baltimore over with a well-worded speech (Worthington G. Snethen to Abraham Lincoln, February 15, 1861, Abraham Lincoln Papers at the Library of Congress):

> If you should decide to stop in Baltimore, we are of opinion, that the masses of our community will gladly avail themselves of the opportunity to testify their appreciation of your presence, and to hear from your own lips, one of those felicitous responses to their salutations, which have gone so far to win the popular heart.
>
> I have taken the liberty of handing this note to you through the hands of Governor Morgan, lest it might reach you in time thro' any other channel.
>
> Waiting your early reply.
>
> I am Faithfully Yr. Friend
>
> W. G. Snethen

48 "Mr. Lincoln, the President elect of the United States, will arrive in this city with his suite this afternoon by special train from Harrisburgh [*sic*], and will proceed, we learn, directly to Washington. *It is to be hoped that no opportunity will be afforded him—or that, if it be afforded, he will not embrace it—to repeat in our midst the sentiments which he is reported to have expressed yesterday in Philadelphia.*" *Baltimore Exchange*, February 23, 1861, quoted in Greeley, *The American Conflict*, pp. 420-421n. (emphasis added).

49 Lossing, *Pictorial History of the Civil War,* vol. 1, p. 278. Lossing also posits that in this building the Baltimore plotters held their secret meetings to plan Lincoln's assassination as well as to plan an attack on Union troops on April 19.

50 Davies report, February 23, 1861, in Cuthbert, *Lincoln and the Baltimore Plot*, p. 93. The meeting room was located on the third floor of the building.

51 Testimony of Joseph H. Boyd, February 9, 1861, Report No. 79, p. 160. Boyd was a successful Baltimore lumber merchant whose business was on South Caroline Street. Testimony of Philip P. Dawson, February 6, 1861, Report No. 79, pp. 156-157.

52 Brown, *Baltimore and the Nineteenth of April, 1861*, p. 38.

53 These pikes, or spears, became known as "Ross Winans Pikes," "Kane Pikes," and "Baltimore Pikes." Most of them, 1,500, were confiscated by federal authorities on May 21, 1861, and taken to Fort McHenry for destruction. Wilson and Cunningham, *Baltimore Civil War Museum*, p. 20. Ross Winans would later be arrested on September 11, 1861, on suspicion of being a disloyal member of the Maryland legislature. *OR* 2:1, p. 671. Nine days later, his release was ordered by William Seward on grounds that he was "an aged person and . . . rather infirm." *OR* 2:1, p. 686.

54 Brown, *Baltimore and the Nineteenth of April, 1861,* pp. 37-38.

55 Wilson and Cunningham, *Baltimore Civil War Museum*, p. 22.

56 Ibid., p. 14.

57 Ibid.

58 Ibid.

59 Ibid.

60 Account of Ernest Wardell, in Wilson and Cunningham, *Baltimore Civil War Museum*, p. 15.

61 *Daily Exchange,* April 20, 1861, in Wilson and Cunningham, *Baltimore Civil War Museum*, p. 15.

62 Recall that a man named Mr. Forward had accurately predicted almost two months earlier that Charleston would be the opening battlefield. "If Lincoln had gone through [Baltimore] when he was expected, he would have been shot, and then Baltimore would have been the battle-field, but now he thought Charleston would be." Timothy Webster, report, February 26, 1861, in Cuthbert, *Lincoln and the Baltimore Plot*, p. 99.

63 Those killed from the Massachusetts Sixth included Luther C. Ladd, Sumner H. Needham, Charles A. Taylor, and Addison O. Whitney. Those of the Pennsylvania Twenty-sixth and Twenty-seventh Regiments killed included John Greaves, George Leisenring, Peter Rogers, Albert G. Rowland, Lineous Jennings, and a German solder, name unknown. The Baltimore civilians killed included William Clark, James Clark, S. Constant, Robert W. Davis, Flannery (first name unknown), Sabastian Gees, Patrick Griffin, William Maloney, James Meyers, Philip Thomas Miles, and William Reed. Wilson and Cunningham, *Baltimore Civil War Museum*, p. 33.

64 Brown, *Baltimore and the Nineteenth of April, 1861,* p. 51.

65 Presentment and newspaper clipping from the National Archives, NARA Mid Atlantic Region (Philadelphia), ARC Identifier 278860, http://arcweb.archives.gov/arc/action/ShowFullRecord?%24submitId=1&%24showFullDescriptionTabs.selectedPaneId=digital&%24resultsDetailPageModel.pageS. See also Wilson and Cunningham, *Baltimore Civil War Museum*, p. 18.

66 Brown, *Baltimore and the Nineteenth of April, 1861,* p. 63.

67 Ibid.

68 Allan Pinkerton, reports, February 22 and 23, 1861, in Cuthbert, *Lincoln and the Baltimore Plot*, pp. 78 and 83.

69 Helen M. Linscott to Abraham Lincoln, November 14, 1864, Abraham Lincoln Papers at the Library of Congress.

70 Frank A. Bond to George P. Kane, April 24, 1861, Abraham Lincoln Papers at the Library of Congress.

71 Worthington G. Snethen to Winfield Scott, June 29, 1861, Abraham Lincoln Papers at the Library of Congress.

72 Brown, *Baltimore and the Nineteenth of April, 1861,* pp. 98-99.

73 *American Annual Cyclopaedia,* p. 361.

74 Scharf, *History of Maryland,* vol. 3, p. 395.

75 On February 15, 1861, Pinkerton was introduced by James Luckett to Ferrandini and a Captain Turner at Barr's Saloon in Baltimore. Pinkerton report, February 15, 1861, in Cuthbert, *Lincoln and the Baltimore Plot*, p. 36-37.

76 Isaac Arnold, "The Baltimore Plot to Assassinate Abraham Lincoln," *Harper's New Monthly Magazine*, June 1868, p. 125.

77 Ibid., p. 126.

78 Cuthbert, *Lincoln and the Baltimore Plot*, pp. 136-138.

79 *The New York Times,* February 26, 1861, p. 8, ProQuest Historical Newspapers. The party was apparently divided, with Mrs. Lincoln and her sons and some of the men dining at the Gittings home, while others, including the newspaper reporters, dined at the Eutaw House.

80 George P. Kane to the *Baltimore Sunday Telegram,* June 21, 1868, in Scharf, *History of Maryland,* p. vol. 3, p. 395. According to Kane, "as the train reached the crossing on Charles street, north of the monument, it was to be stopped at that point, where I was to be in readiness with carriages to receive the General and his guests, and convey them to Mount Vernon Place. The intended debarkation on North Charles street, was under no apprehension or suspicion of intended violence or insult to Mr. Lincoln if carried to the depot, but because the route along Charles street, passing the monument, and through Mount Vernon Place, afforded a view of the most beautiful part of Baltimore, and would relieve the visitors of the necessary annoyance from noise and confusion incident to a rail-road depot, and even greater than these, the annoyance of being brought into contact with the element which would be in waiting to advertise themselves for office." Kane wrote, "I had carriages in readiness to carry out my part of the arrangements, when the news reached Baltimore that Mr. Lincoln was in Washington." Mrs. Lincoln and her sons would in fact be conveyed in those carriages to the Gittings home.

81 Brown, *Baltimore and the Nineteenth of April, 1861,* pp. 11-12.

82 Another possibility is that Mayor Brown's waiting for Lincoln was a ruse to distract the Baltimore mob into believing Lincoln would arrive at the Calvert Street Station, thereby avoiding trouble, while Kane escorted Lincoln to the Gittings mansion. Neither Kane nor Brown, however, suggests that this was their intent. But Kane's plan to pull Lincoln from the train far north of the Calvert Street Station does tend to suggest that Kane thought there would be trouble waiting for Lincoln at the Calvert Street Station, his denials notwithstanding.

83 Wrote John H. Dike, Captain of Company "C," Seventh Regiment, "Mayor Brown attested to the sincerity of his desire to preserve the peace, and pass our regiment safely through the city, by marching at the head of its column, and remaining there at the risk of his life." Brown, *Baltimore and the 19th of April,1861,* p. 54.

84 Marcotte, *Six Days in April*, p. 52.

85 Radcliffe, *Governor Thomas H. Hicks,* p. 56.

86 Ibid.

87 Ibid., p. 57.

88 See Radcliffe, *Governor Thomas H. Hicks,* p. 56; see also Scharf, *History of Maryland,* vol. 3, p. 411, quoting ex-Governor Lowe as saying that Hicks "emphatically and distinctly replied in the affirmative" to Mayor Brown, who had asked if the bridges should be destroyed.

89 Brown, *Baltimore and the Nineteenth of April,* p. 58.

90 Scharf, *History of Maryland,* vol. 3, p. 413. Note, however, that Marshal Kane's indictment accuses him of participation in burning bridges and cutting telegraph lines on the Northern Central's line. Presentment dated July16, 1861, Indictment dated July 19, 1861,

National Archives, http://media.nara.gov. Future Confederate general Isaac R. Trimble reportedly carried out Hicks's orders to burn the bridges. *The Papers of Jefferson Davis*, vol. 7, p. 119, n. 4.

91 Radcliffe, *Governor Thomas H. Hicks*, p. 57.

92 Pinkerton, *Spy of the Rebellion,* p. 72.

93 In fairness, Pinkerton's account of burning bridges and cutting telegraph lines after Lincoln's assassination in Baltimore was written many years later in his somewhat fictionalized account, *Spy of the Rebellion.* This later account could have been informed by Pinkerton's knowledge of what actually occurred on April 19, 1861, rather than what his operatives had discovered in Baltimore in February of that year.

94 Radcliffe, *Governor Thomas H. Hicks*, p. 47, citing the *Baltimore American,* February 27, 1861.

95 Allan Pinkerton to William Herndon, August 23, 1866, in Cuthbert, *Lincoln and the Baltimore Plot*, p. 4.

96 Radcliffe, *Governor Thomas H. Hicks*, p. 20.

97 Bryan, *The Great American Myth*, p. 39.

98 On the other hand, the content of the letter is not of the sort Hicks would have wanted to preserve with extra copies.

99 Lamon, *Life of Abraham Lincoln*, p. 518. Governor Hicks died while serving as a United States senator for Maryland on February 14, 1865. *Biographical Directory of the United States Congress*, http://bioguide.congress.gov.

100 Compare the signature from the Hicks letter dated November 9, 1860, Ward Hill Lamon Papers, Huntington Library, with that in a letter dated April 22, 1861, from Hicks to Lincoln, Abraham Lincoln Papers at the Library of Congress, and that in the letter from Hicks to the editors of the *Baltimore Patriot*, dated May 25, 1860, available at http://memory.loc.gov/mss/mal/mal1/028/0288600/001.gif. The signature in the suspect document contains the characteristic "Tho. H. Hicks" abbreviated form, the "T" that sweeps across to form the middle initial "H," which positions the cross strike high before concluding the signature with "Hicks" and the characteristic underline flourish. Both "H's" put a little foot on the first leg of the "H" but not the second, another characteristic of a genuine Hicks signature. The handwriting style of the suspect letter generally appears quite similar to known authentic originals and includes a number of Hicks's idiosyncrasies. For example, comparing the November 9, 1860, letter with another that Hicks, rather than a secretary, appears to have written to Lincoln in 1862, we see his tendency to extend his "t" crosses well across other letters in the word and to loop the tail of "d's" at the end of words like "and" and "friend" and "head" back toward the beginning of the word. The "A" in "Alabama" from the suspect letter appears very similar to the "A" in "A. Lincoln" in the original 1862 letter. The "G" in the word "Gentleman" from the November 9, 1860, letter appears quite similar to the "G" in "Gen. Wool" from the 1862 letter. Compare also the handwriting in the Hicks November 9, 1860, letter with a letter from Thomas H. Hicks to Abraham Lincoln, October 31, 1862, Abraham Lincoln Papers at the Library of Congress.

101 See, e.g., letters of Thomas H. Hicks to the editors of the *Baltimore Patriot*, May 25, 1860, available at http://memory.loc.gov/mss/mal/mal1/028/0288600/001.gif; to William

Seward, March 28, 1861, and to Winfield Scott, April 22, 1861, both available at the Abraham Lincoln Papers at the Library of Congress.

102 Compare letter of Thomas H. Hicks to E. H. Webster, November 9, 1860, Huntington Library, with that of Hicks to Winfield Scott, January 11, 1861, Hicks Papers at the Maryland Historical Society, Baltimore. The state seal is different on these two letters, with that on the November 9 letter appearing crudely drawn.

103 Evitts, *A Matter of Allegiances*, p. 150.

104 Radcliffe, *Governor Thomas H. Hicks*, p. 20. See also Scharf, *History of Maryland*, vol. 3, p. 369, declaring in reference to Hicks's letter, "such was at this time the attitude, and such the language of Governor Thomas H. Hicks."

105 Radcliffe, *Governor Thomas H. Hicks*, p. 20n.

106 See U.S. Constitution, Twelfth Amendment.

107 Breckinridge was not officially expelled from the U.S. Senate until December 4, 1861, through a resolution charging him with supporting the rebellion. *Biographical Directory of the United States Congress*, http://bioguide.congress.gov.

108 William C. Davis, *Breckinridge: Statesman, Soldier, Symbol* (Baton Rouge: Louisiana State University Press, 1974), p. 287.

109 A. J. Hanna, *The Escape of the Confederate Secretary of War John Cabell Breckinridge, as Revealed by His Diary*, reprinted in *Register of the Kentucky State Historical Society*, October 1939, p. 10 n. 34.

110 Ibid., p. 12 n. 39.

111 King, *Louis T. Wigfall*, p. 230. When he finally did return to the United States, in 1873, Wigfall chose as his sanctuary city, of all places, Baltimore. *Biographical Directory of the United States Congress*, http://bioguide.congress.gov.

112 Hanna, *Escape of the Confederate Secretary of War*, p. 13 n. 40.

113 *Biographical Directory of the United States Congress*, http://bioguide.congress.gov. See also St. Clair County Politicians, http://rootsweb.com.

114 Seddon's biographer indicates that Chittenden was not only the official recording secretary of the Peace Conference, but also that "it is assumed that the general tenor of the transcription of his *Report* is as near an approximation of Seddon's participation as is to be had. The language recorded is in keeping with the character of the man." O'Brien, "James A. Seddon, Statesman of the Old South," p. 224 n. 2.

115 Ibid., p. ii.

116 Ibid., pp. 210-211.

117 Ibid., p. 206.

118 Ibid., p. 526 n. 2, citing *The Assassination and History of the Conspiracy* (Cincinnati: J. R. Hawley, 1865), pp. 56-60.

119 Tidwell, *Come Retribution*, p. 334.

CHAPTER 22

1 Scharf, *The Chronicles of Baltimore*, p. 526. In response to a remark by a fellow actor that Stanton should be put to death with a pistol for having Kane arrested, Booth reportedly flew into a rage and exclaimed, "Yes, sir, you are right! I know George Kane well; he is my

friend, and the man who could drag him from the bosom of his family for no crime whatever, but a mere suspicion that he may commit one some time, deserves a dog's death!" Kimmel, *The Mad Booths of Maryland*, pp. 167-168.

2 Kimmel, *The Mad Booths of Maryland*, pp. 186-187.

3 Harry W. Davies, report, February 19, 1861, in Cuthbert, *Lincoln and the Baltimore Plot*, pp. 46-47 (emphasis added).

4 The story implicating Wigfall appeared in an article published in the *New York Evening Post* with a dateline of March 27, 1862. Wigfall was in Richmond that week. "Hon. L. A. Wigfall, of Texas, was among the visitors at the Convention yesterday. His personal advantages, we may be excused for saying, are altogether above the average of the human family, and as far as his mental capacity is concerned, we are fully aware that he has made his mark at Washington. Mr. Wigfall was the recipient of a compliment in the shape of a serenade, (the First Regiment Band having been employed for the purpose,) last night, at the Spotswood Hotel." *Richmond Daily Dispatch* on March 28, 1862, p. 1.

5 See, e.g., *People v. Molineux,* 168 N.Y. 264, 61 N.E. 286, 293-294 (1901); David W. Louisell, John Kaplan, and Jon R. Waltz, *Cases and Materials on Evidence,* 4th ed. (Mineola, N.Y.: Foundation Press, 1981), p. 315.

6 Crittenden, *Recollections of President Lincoln,* pp. 61-63.

7 This act gave Baltimore the distinction of suffering the first casualties of the war from unfriendly fire. The first deaths of the war actually occurred at Fort Sumter, when two Union men died while saluting the colors as they were being lowered, as part of the terms of surrender. These deaths, however, were accidental and the result of friendly fire.

8 A particularly edifying account of Hicks's consent to the bridge burning holds that Hicks said "it seems to be necessary," or words to that effect, in the presence of several witnesses, including E. Louis Lowe, Marshal George P. Kane, Mayor George Brown, and the mayor's brother John Cumming Brown. Hicks repeated his consent to burning bridges soon thereafter, reportedly in the presence of his brother. Report of George William Brown, May 9, 1861, *OR* 2:1, pp. 569-570.

9 Bryan, *The Great American Myth,* p. 75 n. 1. Snethen made his allegations in the *Boston Commonwealth* on April 22, 1865, p. 2.

10 *Boston Commonwealth,* April 22, 1865.

11 Loux, *John Wilkes Booth Day by Day,* pp. 227-229.

12 Patrick Charles Martin was a native of New York, but he had reportedly been a liquor dealer in Baltimore for many years before the war. A letter in the Union War Department files referred to him as "an uncompromising rebel of the 19th of April notoriety." Tidwell, *Come Retribution,* pp. 329-330.

13 Loux, *John Wilkes Booth Day by Day,* pp. 210-219.

14 Chittenden, *Recollections of President Lincoln,* p. 63 (emphasis added).

15 Moore, *Rebellion Record,* vol. 1, p. 35 ("Brutus" emphasis original; other emphasis added).

16 *Diary of a Public Man,* pp. 38-39.

17 As has been previously set forth, if Lincoln was unavailable for the inauguration on March 4, 1861, there exists at least an argument that Breckinridge would have had a claim to the presidency, as he would have controlled the majority of remaining electoral votes

from the November election. There is also an argument, however, that Vice President-elect Hamlin would have been inaugurated as vice president and then immediately would have taken the oath of office as president. Another possibility would have been that the House of Representatives would have chosen the president from among the remaining candidates—Breckinridge, Douglas, and Bell. U.S. Constitution, Twelfth Amendment. Most interesting is that if the question needed to be resolved in the courts, the all-Democrat, pro-slavery U.S. Supreme Court would have made the decision.

18 *Diary of a Public Man,* pp. 38-39.

19 These included Charles Howard, William H. Gatchell, Charles D. Hinks and John W. Davis, whose arrest was reported in a proclamation on July 1, 1861 by General Banks. *OR* 2:1, p. 625.

20 *OR* 2:1, pp. 624-625. A few days later, Banks would report to the citizens of Baltimore that "the police headquarters under charge of the board when abandoned by their officers resembled in some respects a concealed arsenal." Announcement to the people of the city of Baltimore, July 1, 1861, *OR* 2:1, p. 625.

21 Simon Cameron to Major General John A. Dix, September 11, 1861, in *OR* :1, p. 678. Those Pinkerton was to arrest and take to Fort Monroe, "in order to get them away from Baltimore as quietly as possible," included T. Parkin Scott, S. Teackle Wallis, Henry M. Warfield, F. Key Howard, Thomas W. Hall Jr., and Henry May. See also letter from Major General George B. McClellan to Simon Cameron, September 11, 1861, in ibid., p. 678.

22 Those Pinkerton arrested included William G. Harrison, Lawrence Sangston, Ross Winans, J. Hanson Thomas, Andrew A. Lynch, C. H. Pitts, Leonard G. Quinlan, Robert M. Denison, T. Parkin Scott, S. Teackle Wallis, Francis Key Howard, Thomas W. Hall, Henry May, and Henry M. Warfield. Allan Pinkerton to William Seward, September 23, 1861, in *OR* 2:1, pp. 688, 692.

23 Cameron to Banks, *OR* 2:1,pp. 678-679.

24 Nathan P. Banks to Col. R. B. Marcy, September 20, 1861, in *OR* 2:1, pp. 684-685.

25 Hanchett, *The Lincoln Murder Conspiracies*, p. 41 n. 21, citing an unidentified clipping dated October 4, 1861, found in the investigation and trial papers relating to the assassination of President Lincoln, microcopy 599, roll 3, frame 0123, National Archives.

26 While others arrested by the Lincoln administration would often not swear a loyalty oath, Booth, the consummate Thespian, could perhaps justify his actions as one playing the role of a Confederate spy. It appears he may have acted consistently in this regard on at least one other occasion, securing his release after being arrested for uttering anti-Union sentiments in St. Louis in 1862 by paying a fine and swearing an oath of loyalty to the Union. Samples, *Lust for Fame,* p. 138.

27 See, e.g., Samples, *Lust for Fame,* pp. 39, 41.

28 Testimony of Lieutenant Alexander Lovett, May 16, 1865, in Pitman, *Trial of the Conspirators*, p. 87.

29 Loux, *John Wilkes Booth Day by Day,* pp. 229-255.

30 Ibid., p. 232.

31 *OR* 2:1, pp. 619-620, 622.

32 See, e.g., George P. Kane to Abraham Lincoln, September 30, 1861, *OR* 2:1, p 648.

33 George P. Kane to George W. Porter, September 25, 1861, *OR* 2:1, pp. 644-645; see also George P. Kane to General James M. Anderson, September 25, 1861, *OR* 2:1, pp. 646-647. For Marshal Kane's side of the story detailing his courageous conduct in protecting the Union troops during the Baltimore riot on April 19, followed by his meeting that night with Governor Hicks, during which "the governor deemed it proper and agreed with Mayor Brown and myself that the bridges on the roads by which troops would likely come should be destroyed as the only means of impeding them and avoiding the threatened conflict," see letter from George P. Kane to Charles Howard, May 3, 1861, *OR* 2:1, pp. 628-630.

34 See Major General John Dix to Secretary of War Edwin M. Stanton, February 20, 1862, *OR* 2:1, pp. 738-739. Mayor Brown, though being given letters of commendation for his gallant efforts to prevent the Baltimore mob from injuring Union soldiers on April 19, would nonetheless continue to be held in custody until a new Baltimore mayor was elected.

35 Other Baltimore or Maryland political prisoners released that date included Mayor George W. Brown, Charles Howard, Frank K. Howard (Francis Key Howard), Henry M. Warfield, William G. Harrison, Robert Hull, S. Teackle Wallis, Dr. Charles Macgill (of Hagerstown, MD), William H. Gatchell, Thomas W. Hall, and T. Parkin Scott. Col. J. Dimick to General L. Thomas, November 27, 1862, *OR* 2:1, p. 748; Scharf, *History of Maryland,* vol. 3, p 524. Charles Howard and William H. Gatchell had been members of the Baltimore Board of Police, who along with fellow board members Charles D. Hinks and John W. Davis had been arrested July 1, 1861 by General Banks. *OR* 2:1, p. 625.

36 George P. Kane to "My Fellow Citizens of the State of Maryland," November 29, 1862, *OR* 2:1, p. 666.

37 Coyle, *The Mayors of Baltimore,* p. 141; Scharf, *History of Maryland,* vol. 3, pp. 523-524. By other accounts, the release of the Maryland prisoners, including Kane, Mayor Brown, Charles Howard, and William H. Gatchell, Baltimore police commissioners, Severn Teackle Wallis, Henry M. Warfield, William G. Harrison, and T. Parkin Scott, ex-members of the Maryland legislature from Baltimore, Frank Key Howard, Thomas W. Hall Jr., Robert Hull, and Dr. Charles Macgill, was "without imposing any condition upon them whatsoever." Scharf, *History of Maryland,* vol. 3, p. 523.

38 Captain Robert D. Minor, CSN, to Admiral Franklin Buchanan, CSN, in *Official Records of the Union and Confederate Navies* (Washington, D.C.: U.S. Government Printing Office, 1880-1891) (hereafter cited as *ORN*), series 1, vol. 2, pp. 822-828; Tidwell, *Come Retribution,* p. 330.

39 The original plan ran into a snag because Jefferson Davis feared a Confederate raid in the Great Lakes, launched from Canada, might create an international incident with Great Britain, thereby threatening the construction in Britain of ironclad steamers for the C.S.A. These were likely the same steamers George N. Sanders, discussed below, had contracted for. Captain Robert D. Minor to Admiral Franklin Buchanan, February 2, 1864, *ORN,* series 1, vol. 2, p. 823.

40 Tidwell, *Come Retribution,* pp. 180-181, 330

41 George Stearns to S. M. Felton, April 1, 1862, Felton Papers (no. 1151), Box 2, Folder 1, Historical Society of Pennsylvania.

42 Tidwell, *Come Retribution,* pp. 178-181.

43 By one account, early in the war, Seddon seems not to have been interested in partici-pating in Lincoln's kidnapping. "The laws of war and morality, as well as Christian princi-ples and sound policy forbid the use of such means," Seddon allegedly said early on. Donald, *Lincoln*, p. 549.

44 Ibid., p. 549.

45 Tidwell, *Come Retribution*, p. 283.

46 Ibid., p. 285.

47 Kauffman, *American Brutus*, pp. 133-134; Kimmel, *The Mad Booths of Maryland*, pp. 186-187.

48 "Monthly Summary of Events," Frank Leslie's New Family Magazine, in *The United States Democratic Review*, vol. 42:1 (New York: Langley, July 1858) p. 84.

49 Tidwell reports that Sanders had been a political operative for the Southern faction of the Democratic Party for many years prior to 1862. Tidwell, *Come Retribution*, p. 175.

50 Michael St. John Packe, *The Bombs of Orsini* (London: Secker and Warburg, 1957), pp. 140-141.

51 Tidwell, *Come Retribution*, p. 331.

52 Ibid., pp. 331-332. Sanders spoke at a meeting in New York on September 22, 1855, celebrating the French Republic of 1792. He was quoted in the *New York Herald* the next day.

53 *New York Times*, February 13, 1861, p. 1, ProQuest Historical Newspapers (emphasis added).

54 *Philadelphia Inquirer*, February 19, 1861, p. 8; and February 21, 1861, p. 8.

55 Lincoln reportedly reacted to the warnings of "Public Man" by showing him a caution-ary note from Senator Sumner. "He [Lincoln] listened to me very attentively, and, sudden-ly stretching out his hand, picked up and handed me a note to look at. I recognized Senator Sumner's handwriting as I took it, and was not, therefore, particularly surprised to find it alarmish and mysterious in tone, bidding Mr. Lincoln, for particular reasons, to be very careful how he went out alone at night." *Diary of a Public Man*, p. 62.

56 Tidwell, *Come Retribution*, p. 332.

57 Reported Chittenden concerning his clandestine meeting with a suspected plotter arranged by loyal Baltimore Republicans, "They had employed Ruscelli to do the job; Ruscelli was a barber who called himself Orsini since he escaped from Italy, where he was in trouble for killing some men who failed to pay their ransom." Chittenden, *Recollections*, p. 61.

58 Packe, *The Bombs of Orsini*, pp. 258-264.

59 Chittenden, *Recollections*, p. 62. The embedded *New York Times* reporter, Joseph Howard Jr., detailed as one of three options for murdering Lincoln that "it was determined, by means of an infernal machine, to blow up the car in which Mr. Lincoln was to ride. The objection to this was, that the infernal machine might perhaps work both ways, or fail to accomplish the desired end." *New York Times*, February 26, 1861, p. 8. By working "both ways," the plotters likely meant that the bomb might kill or injure them as well Lincoln. This is in fact what happened to Felice Orsini, who was injured on the right temple by a fragment from the third hand grenade tossed under Napoleon III's carriage—an attempt

that likewise failed in its objective to assassinate the French ruler. Orsini was executed by guillotine on March 13, 1858. Packe, *The Bombs of Orsini*, pp. 261-262, 281. Rumors of a live hand grenade being found on Lincoln's train in Cincinnati occurred at the same time George N. Sanders was in town. "Attempts on Lincoln's Life." *New York Times*, February 26, 1861, p. 8; *New York Times*, February 13, 1861, p. 1, ProQuest Historical Newspapers.

60 Both Napoleon III and Empress Eugènie were slightly injured in the attack and proceeded to the opera. But the grenade attack had been deadly, wounding 156 and killing eight. Packe, *The Bombs of Orsini*, p. 261.

61 Allan Pinkerton, report, February 15, 1861, in Cuthbert, *Lincoln and the Baltimore Plot*, p. 37.

62 Jacob Thompson allegedly repeated similar themes. During the conspiracy trial one witness testified that Thompson had told him that "the killing of a tyrant was no murder." Testimony of Sanford Conover, May 20, 1865, in Pitman, *Trial of the Conspirators*, p. 29. Conover's testimony is generally discredited.

63 Tidwell, *Come Retribution*, p. 328; Kauffman, *American Brutus*, p. 140.

64 Samples, *Lust for Fame*, p. 223.

65 Cross-examination of Henry Finegas, May 26, 1865, in Pitman, *Trial of the Conspirators*, p. 39.

66 Tidwell, *Come Retribution*, p. 288.

67 Kauffman, *American Brutus*, pp. 342-343.

68 Testimony of Richard Montgomery, May 12, 1865, in Pitman, *Trial of the Conspirators*, p. 25.

69 Testimony of John Deveny, May 12, 1865, in Pitman, *Trial of the Conspirators*, pp. 38-39.

70 Testimony of Hosea B. Carter, May 29, 1865, in Pitman, *Trial of the Conspirators*, p. 38. By "others of that class," Carter was undoubtedly referring to "the clique of men who were known there [the St. Lawrence Hotel] as Confederates." These Southerners, twenty or thirty in number, boarded at the hotel. They included, in addition to Sanders and Booth, former Alabama senator Clement C. Clay, William C. Cleary, and Beverly Tucker, among others. See also testimony of Deveny, May 12, 1865, pp. 38-39, and Henry Finegas, May 26, 1865, p. 39. In addition to these men, the government sought to arrest Jefferson Davis and Jacob Thompson in connection with Lincoln's assassination and offered rewards for their capture. In response, Thompson and Tucker vehemently denied any involvement with Booth. See Kauffman, *American Brutus*, p. 336.

71 William C. Cleary was "a sort of confidential secretary to Jacob Thompson." Testimony of Richard Montgomery, May 12, 1865, Pitman, *Trial of the Conspirators*, p. 25.

72 Testimony of Henry Finegas, May 26, 1865, Pitman, *Trial of the Conspirators*, p. 39 (emphasis added).

73 Kauffman, *American Brutus*, p. 141.

74 *New York Daily Graphic*, March 22, 1876. Interestingly, on February 23, 1861, Otis K. Hillard remarked to Pinkerton operative Harry W. Davies that "Charles Meyers, a liquor dealer in Baltimore, had today given Five thousand dollars to the National Volunteers." Davies report, February 23, 1861, in Cuthbert, *Lincoln and the Baltimore Plot*, p. 95. Might

"Charles Meyers" have been an alias for Baltimore liquor dealer Patrick Charles Martin?

75 Tidwell, *Come Retribution,* pp. 329-330, citing *ORN,* series 2, vol. 2, pp. 714, 728, 735. The Confederate Navy Department had ordered $27,358.32 worth of provisions and clothing, and $4,149.65 in ordinance from Martin. *ORN,* series 2, vol. 2, p. 714.

76 By one account, Martin was one of the party of rebels who along with Commodore Hollins and Zarvona Thomas, alias the "French Lady," captured the steamer *St. Nicholas* at Point Lookout on June 28, 1861, took it to Cone Point, Virginia, and transformed it into a bay privateer for the Confederacy. Many of the rebel party were captured ten days later and confined to Fort McHenry. Martin, however, escaped to Canada. *New York Daily Graphic,* March 22, 1876.

77 Tidwell, *Come Retribution,* pp. 173, 330.

78 Kauffman, *American Brutus,* p. 141.

79 During rehearsals for *The Robbers* one morning in New York in March 1862, a member of Booth's company read aloud a report of the Baltimore police marshal's arrest and his imprisonment in Fort McHenry by order of Secretary Stanton. Marshal Kane, it will be recalled, had been arrested for treason the previous June on suspicion of burning railroad bridges outside of Baltimore in April 1861. The cast debated over what should be done, some arguing that Stanton should be shot. Booth had listened attentively, but without comment, all week as the company debated politics. Upon learning of Kane's imprisonment, however, and in reaction to the suggestion that Stanton should be shot for ordering Kane's arrest, an incensed Booth shouted from backstage, "Yes, sir, you are right! I know George P. Kane well; he is my friend, and the man who could drag him from the bosom of his family for no crime whatever, but a mere suspicion that he *may* commit one sometime, deserves a dog's death!" Kimmel, *The Mad Booths of Maryland,* pp. 167-168; Kauffman, *American Brutus,* p. 124; Samples, *Lust for Fame,* p. 170. A witness to Booth's tirade was more amazed by the manner in which he had delivered his opinion than the words that carried it. "It was not the matter of what was said; it was the manner and general appearance of the speaker, that awed us. It would remind you of Lucifer's defiance at the council. He stood there the embodiment of evil. But it was for a moment only, for in the next breath with a sharp, ringing voice, he exclaimed, 'Go on with the rehearsal!' . . . I could never forget the scene; the statuesque figure of the young man uttering those few words in the centre of the old stage of Wallack's can never be forgotten." Samples, *Lust for Fame,* p. 170, citing John Joseph Jennings, *Theatrical and Circus Life* (1882). For details of Kane's arrest, see *Baltimore Sun,* June 28, 1861, and *OR,* 2:1, pp. 620-630. One historian has noted that Booth exaggerated his friendship with Kane, having never actually known him, but it is possible that his father did. Kane, along with William Key Howard, William R. Travers, William Sperry, and others, was, through the Kemble Company of Baltimore, a joint owner of Baltimore's Howard Athenaeum and Gallery of Arts, in which Booth's father had played, thus likely making Kane an acquaintance of Booth's father and possibly John Wilkes Booth himself. Kauffman, *American Brutus,* pp. 124, 426 n. 41. See also Clarke, *Unlocked Book,* p. 118.

80 Tidwell, *Come Retribution,* pp. 61, 126-127.

81 Ibid., pp. 125-127.

82 Testimony of John H. Patten, February 24, 1866, *OR* 2:8, p. 884.

83 Kauffman, *American Brutus,* p. 141.

84 Kauffman, *American Brutus,* p. 141.

85 Tidwell, *Come Retribution,* p. 331. The trunks containing Booth's wardrobe, as well as other personal effects, were later salvaged and purchased by Edwin Booth through an intermediary, before being lost in a fire at the Winter Garden Theater in 1867. Kauffman, *American Brutus,* pp. 377-378; see p. 472 n. 4 for government archival resources detailing correspondence relating to Booth's trunks and an inventory of items contained therein. By one account, Martin's shipwreck was an act of sabotage perpetrated by one Alexander H. Keith Jr., alias "Thomassen." In an interview in 1876, Kane reported that Keith had induced Martin to sail against the advice of his friends. Keith, an alleged explosives expert, reportedly had planted a time bomb on Martin's ship, which caused an explosion and a total loss of the ship. Keith, who had taken out an insurance policy on the ship, allegedly collected roughly $100,000 in insurance proceeds. *New York Daily Graphic,* March 22, 1876.

86 Tidwell, *Come Retribution,* p. 331.

87 Captain Robert D. Minor to Admiral Franklin Buchanan, February 2, 1864, *ORN,* series 1, vol. 2, pp. 825-826.

88 Kauffman, *American Brutus,* pp. 140-141, 430 n. 25. Kane reportedly admitted to George Alfred Townsend in an interview that he destroyed the Booth letter. Ibid., citing the *New York Daily Graphic,* March 22, 1876, and the *Cincinnati Enquirer,* April 18, 1892.

89 *New York Daily Graphic,* March 22, 1876.

90 Testimony of John C. Thompson, son-in-law of Dr. William Queen, *New York Daily Graphic,* March 22, 1876.

91 Tidwell, *Come Retribution,* p. 187 n. 43 and p. 275.

92 Testimony of John H. Patten, February 24, 1866, *OR* 2:8, p. 884.

93 William A. Tidwell, *April '65: Confederate Covert Action in the American Civil War* (Kent, Ohio: Kent State University Press, 1995), pp. 138-139.

94 *The Wartime Papers of R. E. Lee,* ed. Clifford Dowdey (Boston: Little, Brown, 1961), p. 808; Tidwell, *Come Retribution,* pp. 145-146, 275.

95 Tidwell, *Come Retribution,* p. 275.

96 See, e.g., Tidwell, *Come Retribution,* pp. 145-147. As another possibility, Early may have intended to capture Washington and Lincoln both. Ibid., p. 19. Under this scenario, Lee's reference to Kane joining Early may have meant to join him in Washington as part of a Lincoln kidnapping plot.

97 Samples, *Lust for Fame,* pp. 223-224.

98 Around this time, Booth was also suffering from bronchitis, which at times made him unable to speak above a whisper. Kimmel, *The Mad Booths of Maryland,* p. 187.

99 By Thomas Conrad's uncorroborated account, in late September 1864, he attempted to capture Lincoln while he rode in a carriage on his way to Soldiers' Home. The attempt was reportedly abandoned, however, when Lincoln appeared with a cavalry escort. Tidwell, *Come Retribution,* pp. 291-292.

100 Ibid., pp. 19-21; p. 334.

101 Ibid., pp. 334-335.

102 Ibid., pp. 336-337.

103 Ibid., p. 337.

104 Ibid., p. 338.

105 Ibid., p. 339.

106 Ibid., p. 341.

107 Ibid., p. 408.

108 Ibid., p. 409.

109 Kauffman, *American Brutus,* p. 179.

110 Ibid., pp. 179-181; Tidwell, *Come Retribution,* p. 413.

111 Kauffman, *American Brutus,* p. 181.

112 Ibid., pp. 181, 438 n. 11.

113 Testimony of John H. Patten, February 24, 1866, *OR* 2:8, pp. 883-884.

114 Kauffman, *American Brutus,* pp. 184-186. In addition, Booth needed Arnold and O'Laughlen to return the weapons and other kidnapping paraphernalia that he had entrusted to the two men two weeks earlier.

115 Samples, *Lust for Fame,* p. 224.

116 By one account, perhaps a revised version of the plot earlier discussed, Booth had proposed a preposterous plan of abducting Lincoln from Ford's Theatre, suggesting that the powerfully built Powell seize him, then lower him from the president's box to Sam Arnold waiting on stage. Kimmel, *The Mad Booths of Maryland,* pp. 202-203.

117 Osborn H. Oldroyd, *The Assassination of Abraham Lincoln* (Washington, D.C.: O. H. Oldroyd, 1901), p. 216. Tidwell notes that Westfall's story is not terribly convincing. Tidwell, *Come Retribution,* p. 408.

118 Tidwell, *Come Retribution,* p. 408.

119 Ibid., p. 408.

120 Hamilton and Ostendorf, *Lincoln in Photographs*, p. 209.

121 Samuel Knapp Chester, whose real name was Sam Knapp, also known as S. C. Knapp, had made his stage debut in Baltimore on November 12, 1856. Scharf, *Chronicles of Baltimore,* p. 443; Kauffman, *American Brutus,* p. 95.

122 Testimony of Samuel Knapp Chester, May 12, 1865, in Pitman, *Trial of the Conspirators,* pp. 44-45; Tidwell, *Come Retribution,* p. 408, citing statement of Samuel K. Chester, M-599, reel 4, frames 0142-70, National Archives.

123 Fishel, *The Secret War for the Union,* p. 149. Webster was discovered through the efforts of General Winder, to whom Marshal Kane reported while in Richmond. Tidwell, *Come Retribution,* pp. 61, 126.

124 See generally testimony of Henry R. Rathbone, May 15, 1865, in Pitman, *Trial of the Conspirators,* pp. 78-79. See also James L. Swanson, *Manhunt: The 12-Day Chase for Lincoln's Killer* (New York: HarperCollins, 2006), pp. 35-43.

125 Kimmel, *The Mad Booths of Maryland,* p. 202.

126 It seems likely that Lincoln saw Booth perform on more than one occasion. Hay notes in his diary entry for November 9, 1863, "Spent the evening at the theatre with the President Mrs Lincoln, Mrs Hunter Cameron and Nicolay J Wilkes Booth was doing the 'Marble Heart.' Rather tame than otherwise." By several accounts, Lincoln was impressed

with Booth's performance, applauded him "rapturously," and even sent word backstage that he wished to make the actor's acquaintance. Booth reportedly evaded the requested interview. Hay, *Inside Lincoln's White House*, pp. 110, 325 n. 271. In addition to the *Marble Heart* performance, Lincoln reportedly saw Booth play Richard III and Hamlet. Ibid., p. 326 n. 271. By at least one account, Lincoln was also present for Booth's final performance, when he played Pescara in *The Apostate* at Ford's Theatre on March 18, 1865. Allegedly, Booth, in uttering threats as part of the play, on three occasions "came very near and put his finger close to Mr. Lincoln's face." See Samples, *Lust for Fame,* pp. 176-177. Booth may have been especially frustrated on this occasion, having reportedly failed in an attempt to abduct Lincoln the previous day.

BIBLIOGRAPHY

Manuscript Collections

The Abraham Lincoln Papers at the Library of Congress

The Felton Papers at the Pennsylvania Historical Society

The Hicks Papers at the Maryland Historical Society

The Pinkerton Papers at the Library of Congress

The Ward Hill Lamon Papers at the Huntington Library

Congressional Reports

Reports of the Select Committee of Five, 36th Congress, 2d Session, Report No. 79 (Washington: Government Printing Office, 1861).

Reports of the Select Committee of Five, 36th Congress, 2d Session, Report No. 91 (Washington: Government Printing Office, 1861).

Books and Pamphlets

Address and Resolutions Adopted at the Meeting of the Southern Rights Convention of Maryland, (Baltimore: J. B. Rose & Co. 1861).

American Annual Cyclopædia and Register of Important Events of the Year 1861, The (New York: D. Appleton & Co., 1870).

Anonymous, *Diary of a Public Man,* Bullard, Lauriston F., ed., (New Brunswick: Rutgers University Press, 1946).

Arnold, Isaac N., *The History of Abraham Lincoln and the Overthrow of Slavery* (Chicago: Clarke, 1866).

Baker, Jean H., *Mary Todd Lincoln, A Biography* (New York, London: W.W. Norton & Company, 1987).

Basler, Roy P., ed., *Collected Works of Abraham Lincoln,* (New Brunswick, N.J.: Rutgers University Press, 1953-55).

Berry, Stephen W., *House of Abraham: Lincoln and the Todds, a Family Divided by War,* (Boston: Houghton Mifflin, 2007).

Beymer, William Gilmore, *On Hazardous Service: Scouts and Spies of the North and South* (New York-London: Harper & Bros., 1912).

Brown, George William, *Baltimore and the Nineteenth of April, 1861* (Baltimore: Johns Hopkins University, 1887).

Brown, Thomas J., *Dorothea Dix, New England Reformer* (Cambridge-London: Harvard University Press, 1998).

Browne, Robert H., M.D., *Abraham Lincoln and the Men of His Time* (New York: Eaton & Main, 1901).

Browne, Francis Fisher, *The Every-day Life of Abraham Lincoln* (Chicago: Browne & Howell Co., 1913).

Brumbaugh, Martin G., Walton, Joseph Solomon, *Stories of Pennsylvania or School Readings from Pennsylvania History* (New York: American Book Company, 1897).

Bryan, George S., *The Great American Myth* (New York: Carrick & Evans, Inc., 1940).

Bryan, George S., *The Spy in America* (Philadelphia: J.B. Lippincott Company, 1943).

Burgess, George H. and Miles C. Kennedy, *Centennial History of the Pennsylvania Railroad Company, 1846–1946* (Philadephia: Pennsylvania Railroad Co., 1949).

Burlingame, Michael, ed., *An Oral History of Abraham Lincoln: John G. Nicolay's Interviews and Essays* (Carbondale-Edwardsville: Southern Illinois University Press, 1996).

Burlingame, Michael ed., *Lincoln's Journalist: John Hay's Anonymous Writings for the Press* (Carbondale, Illinois: Southern Illinois University Press, 1998).

Burlingame, Michael and Ettlinger, John R. Turner, eds., *Inside Lincoln's White House, The Complete Civil War Diary of John Hay* (Carbondale, Illinois: Southern Illinois University Press, 1997).

Carr, Richard Wallace and Carr, Marie Pinak, *The Willard Hotel: An Illustrated History* (Washington, D.C.: Dicmar Publishing, 2005).

The Centennial Exhibition and the Pennsylvania Railroad (Philadelphia: Rand, McNally & Co. 1876).

Chamlee, Roy Z., *Lincoln's Assassins: A Complete Account of Their Capture, Trial, and Punishment* (Jefferson, N.C.: McFarland & Company, Inc., 1990).

Chesnut, Mary, *Mary Chesnut's Civil War*, Woodward, C. Vann, ed. (New Haven, Connecticutt: Yale University Press, 1981).

Chittenden, Lucius Eugene, *A Report of the Debates and Proceedings in the Secret Sessions of the Conference Convention, for Proposing Amendments to the Constitution of the United States* (New York: D. Appleton & Co., 1864).

Chittenden, Lucius Eugene, *Recollections of Abraham Lincoln and his Administration* (Harper & Brothers, 1891).

Chittenden, Lucius E., *Invisible Siege: The Journal of Lucius E. Chittenden, April 15, 1861-July 14, 1861* (San Diego: Americana Exchange Press, 1969).

Clarke, Asia Booth, *The Unlocked Book: A Memoir of John Wilkes Booth by his sister Asia Booth Clarke*, Farjeon, Eleanor, ed. (New York: G. P. Putnam's Sons, 1938).

Clarke, Asia Booth, *John Wilkes Booth: A Sister's Memoir by Asia Booth Clarke*, Alford, Terry, ed. (Jackson: University of Mississippi Press, 1996).

The Conspiracy to Break up the Union. The Plot and Its Development (Washington City, D.C.: Lemuel Towers 1860).

Crist, Lynda Lasswell and Dix, Mary Seaton, eds., *The Papers of Jefferson Davis,* 7 vols. (Baton Rouge: Louisiana State University Press, 1992).

Cuthbert, Norma B., *Lincoln and the Baltimore Plot, 1861, from Pinkerton Records and Related Papers* (San Marino, California: Huntington Library, 1949).

Davis, Jefferson, *The Papers of Jefferson Davis, Volume VII* (Baton Rouge: Louisiana State University Press, 1991).

Davis, William C., *The Civil War: Brother Against Brother, The War Begins* (Alexandria, Virginia: Time Warner Books, 1983).

Davis, William C., *Breckinridge: Statesman, Soldier, Symbol* (Baton Rouge: Louisiana State University Press, 1974).

Donald, David Herbert, *Lincoln* (London: Jonathan Cape, 1995).

Doster, William E., *Lincoln and Episodes of the Civil War* (New York: G. P. Putnam's Sons, 1915).

Dye, John Smith, *History and the Plots and Crimes of the Great Conspiracy to Overthrow Liberty in America* (New York: Privately Published, 1866).

Eicher, David J., *Dixie Betrayed: How the South Really Lost the Civil War* (Boston: Little, Brown and Company, 2006).

Elliot, Charles Winslow, *Winfield Scott: The Soldier and the Man* (New York: The MacMillan Co., 1937).

Evitts, William J., *A Matter of Allegiances: Maryland from 1850 to 1861* (Baltimore: Johns Hopkins University Press, 1974).

Ferguson, Andrew, *Land of Lincoln* (New York: Atlantic Monthly Press, 2007).

Fishel, Edwin C., *The Secret War for the Union: The Untold Story of Military Intelligence in the Civil War* (New York: Houghton Mifflin,1998).

Fleischner, Jennifer, *Mrs. Lincoln and Mrs. Keckly* (New York: Random House, 2003).

Flower, Frank Abial, *Edwin McMasters Stanton: The Autocrat of Rebellion, Emancipation and Reconstruction* (New York: The Saalfield Publishing Co.,1905).

Forney, John W., *Anecdotes of Public Men* (New York: Harper & Brothers, 1873).

Furnas, J. C., *The Americans: A Social History of the United States 1587-1914* (New York: G. P. Putnam's Sons, 1969).

George, Joseph, Jr., "Philadelphians Greet Their President Elect -1861," *Pennsylvania History*, XXIX, No. 4, October, 1962.

Greeley, Horace, *The American Conflict: A History of the Great Civil War in the United States of America, 1860-1864* (London: O.D. Case & Company, 1865).

Goldsborough, WilliamWorthington, *The Maryland Line in the Confederate Army, 1861-1865* Vol. 1 (Baltimore: Guggenheimer, Weil & Co., 1900).

Goff, John S., *Robert Todd Lincoln: A Man in His Own Right* (Norman: University of Oklahoma Press, 1969).

Goodwin, Doris Kearns, *Team of Rivals* (New York: Simon & Schuster, 2005).

Hall, Clayton Colman, ed., *Baltimore: Its History and People* (New York: Lewis Historical Publishing Co., 1912).

Hamilton, Charles, and Ostendorf, Lloyd, *Lincoln in Photographs: An Album of Every Known Pose* (Norman, Oklahoma: University of Oklahoma Press, 1963).

Hamlin, Charles Eugene, *The Life and Times of Hannibal Hamlin* (Cambridge: Riverside Press, 1899).

Hanchett, William, *The Lincoln Murder Conspiracies* (Urbana: University of Illinois Press, 1983).

Hanchett, William, *Out of the Wilderness: The Life of Abraham Lincoln* (Urbana: University of Illinois Press, 1994).

Harper, Robert S., *Lincoln and the Press* (New York: McGraw-Hill Book Company, Inc., 1951).

Hay, Clara S., *The Life and Letters of John Hay* (Harper & Brothers, 1915).

Herbert, Capt. George B., *The Popular History of the Civil War in America* (New York: F. M. Lupton, 1884).

Herndon, William H. and Weik, Jesse W., *Abraham Lincoln: The True Story of a Great Life,* 2 vols. (New York: D. Appleton and Company, 1930).

Herndon, William H. and Welk, Jesse, *Herndon's Life of Lincoln* (Cleveland: World Pub. Co., 1942).

Hoch, Bradley, *The Lincoln Trail in Pennsylvania: A History and Guide* (University Park: Pennsylvania State University Press, 2001).

Holland, Josiah Gilbert, *The Life of Abraham Lincoln* (Springfield, Mass.: Gurdon Bill, 1866).

Holzer, Harold, ed., *Dear Mr. Lincoln: Letters to the President* (Reading, Mass.: Addison-Wesley Publishing Company, 1993).

Holzer, Harold, ed., *The Lincoln Mailbag: America Writes to the President 1861-1865* (Carbondale, Illinois: Southern Illinois University Press, 1998).

Holzer, Harold, ed., *Abraham Lincoln as I Knew Him: Gossip, Tributes and Revelations from His Best Friends and Worst Enemies* (Chapel Hill, N.C.: Algonquin, 1999).

Horan, James David and Swiggett, Howard, *The Pinkerton Story* (New York: Putnam, 1951).

Horan, James D. *The Pinkertons: The Detective Dynasty that Made History* (New York: Crown Publishers, Inc., 1967).

Howard, George Washington, *The Monumental City, Its Past History and Recent Resources* (Baltimore: J.D. Ehlers & Co., Engravers and Steam Book Printers, 1873-1876).

Hungerford, Edward, *The Story of the Baltimore & Ohio Railroad* (New York: The Knickerbocker Press, G.P. Putnam and Sons, 1928).

Hunt, H. Draper, *Hannibal Hamlin of Maine: Lincoln's First Vice-President* (Syracuse: Syracuse University Press, 1969).

Hynd, Alan, *Arrival: 12:30: The Baltimore Plot Against Lincoln* (Camden, N.J.: Nelson, 1967).

James, Marquis, *They Had Their Hour* (Indianapolis: The Bobbs-Merrill Company, 1934).

Jeffreys-Jones, Rhodri, *Cloak and Dollar-A History of American Secret Intelligence* (New Haven: Yale University Press, 2002).

Jones, Thomas D., *Memories of Lincoln* (New York: Press of the Pioneers, 1934).

Journal of the Convention of the State of Arkansas (Little Rock, Ark.: Johnson & Yerkes, 1861),

Kadish, Sanford H. and Paulsen, Monrad G., *Criminal Law and its Processes,* 3rd Ed. (Boston: Little, Brown & Co., 1975).

Kauffman, Michael W., *American Brutus: John Wilkes Booth and the Lincoln Conspiracies* (New York: Random House, 2004).

Kimmel, Stanley, *The Mad Booths of Maryland* (Indianapolis: The Bobbs-Merrill Company, 1940).

King, Alvy L., *Louis T. Wigfall: Southern Fire-eater* (Baton Rouge: Louisiana State University Press, 1970).

Kunhardt, Philip B., Jr., Kunhardt, Philip B., III, and Kunhardt, Peter W., *Lincoln: An Illustrated Biography* (New York: Knopf, 1992).

Lamon, Ward Hill and Black, Chauncy F., *The Life of Abraham Lincoln: From His Birth to His Inauguration as President* (Boston: James R. Osgood and Company, 1872).

Lamon, Ward Hill, *Recollections of Abraham Lincoln 1847-1865*, Dorothy Lamon Teillard, ed. (Washington, D.C.: Privately Published, 1911).

Lee, Robert E., *The Wartime Papers of R.E. Lee*, Clifford Dowdey and Louis H. Manarin, eds. (New York: Bramhall House, 1961).

Leech, Margaret, *Reveille in Washington* (New York: Time Inc., 1962, Reprint).

Lloyd, Mark, *The Guinness Book of Espionage* (Da Capo Press, 1994).

Logan, John Alexander, *The Great Conspiracy Its Origin and History* (Freeport, N.Y.: Books for Libraries Press, 1971, Reprint).

Lossing, Benson J., *Pictorial History of the Civil War in the United States of America,* vols. 1 and 2 (Philadelphia: G. W. Childs, 1866-1868).

Lossing, Benson J., *Pictorial Field Book of the Civil War,* vol. 3 (Baltimore: Johns Hopkins University Press, 1997; reprint of original published in 1874 by T. Belknap).

Lossing, Benson J., *A History of the United States* (New York: James Sheehy, Publisher, 1881).

Louisell, David W., Kaplan, John, and Waltz, Jon R., *Cases and Materials on Evidence,* 4th Ed. (Mineola, N.Y.: The Foundation Press, Inc., 1981).

Loux, Arthur F., *John Wilkes Booth, Day by Day* (Privately Published, 1990).

Mansch, Larry D., *Abraham Lincoln, President-Elect: The Four Critical Months from Election to Inauguration* (Jefferson, N.C.: McFarland & Co., 2005).

Mansfield, Edward Deering, *Life and Services of General Winfield Scott* (Auburn: Derby & Miller, 1852).

MacKay, James, *Allan Pinkerton: The Eye Who Never Slept* (Edinburgh: Mainstream Publishing, 1996).

Marcotte, Frank, *Six Days in April: Lincoln and the Union in Peril* (New York: Algora Publishing, 2005).

Markle, Donald E., *Spies and Spymasters of the Civil War* (Hypocrene Books: New York, 2004).

Marquis, James, *They Had Their Hour* (Indianapolis: Bobbs-Merrill, 1934).

McClellan, George Brinton, *Report on the Organization and Campaigns of the Army of the Potomac* (Sheldon & Co. Pub., 1864).

McClure, Alexander K., *Abraham Lincoln and Men of War-Times* (Philadelphia: The Times Publishing Company, 1892).

Mearns, David C. ed., *The Lincoln Papers,* 2 vols. (New York: Doubleday, 1948).

Melanson, Philip, *The Secret Service: The Hidden History of an Enigmatic Agency* (New York: Caroll & Graf Publishers, 2002).

Mencken, August, *Railroad Passenger Car: An Illustrated History of the First Hundred Years, With Accounts by Contemporary Passengers* (Baltimore: Johns Hopkins Press, 1957).

Melton, Tracy Matthew, *Hanging Henry Gambrill: The Violent Career of Baltimore's Plug Uglies, 1854-1860* (Baltimore: Maryland Historical Society, 2005).

Minor, Charles C., *The Real Lincoln: From the Testimony of His Contemporaries* (Gastonia, North Carolina: Atkins-Rankin Company, 1928).

Monaghan, Jay, *Abraham Lincoln Deals with Foreign Affairs: A Diplomat in Carpet Slippers* (Lincoln: University of Nebraska Press, 1997).

Moore, Frank, ed., *The Rebellion Record: A Diary of American Events,* 7 Vols., (New York: G. P. Putnam, 1861-68).

Morse, John Torrey, *Abraham Lincoln* (Boston : Houghton Mifflin, 1893).

Neu, Irene D., *Erastus Corning: Merchant and Financier, 1794-1872* (Ithaca, New York: Cornell University Press, 1960).

Nichols, Roy Franklin, *The Disruption of American Democracy* (New York: The MacMillan Company, 1948).

Nicolay, Helen, *Personal Traits of Abraham Lincoln* (New York: Century, 1913).

Nicolay, Helen, *Lincoln's Secretary: A Biography of John G. Nicolay* (New York: Longmans, Green, 1949).

Nicolay, John G., Hay, John, *Abraham Lincoln, A History* (New York: The Century Co., 1890).

Nicolay, John G., *A Short Life of Abraham Lincoln* (New York: The Century Co., 1902).

Oates, Stephen B., *The Approaching Fury: Voices of the Storm, 1820-1861* (New York: Harper Collins Publishers, 1997).

Oates, Stephen B, *With Malice Toward None: The Life of Abraham Lincoln* (New York: Harper & Row, 1977).

O'Brien, Gerard Francis John, *James A. Seddon, Statesman of the Old South,* Ph.D. Thesis, (University of Maryland, 1963).

Official Records of the Union and Confederate Armies in the War of the Rebellion, 128 vols., (Washington: Government Printing Office, 1880-1891).

Official Records of the Union and Confederate Navies in the War of the Rebellion, 30 vols., (Washington: Government Printing Office, 1894-1922).

Oldroyd, Osborn H., *The Assassination of Abraham Lincoln Flight, Pursuit, Capture, and Punishment of the Conspirators* (Washington, D.C.: Privately Published, 1901; Reprint, Bowie, MD: Heritage Books, Inc., 1990).

Phelps, Henry Pitt, *Players of a Century: A Record of the Albany Stage* (Albany: McDonough Co., 1880).

Pinkerton, Allan, *The Expressman and the Detective* (Chicago: Keen, Cooke & Co., 1875).

Pinkerton, Allan, *History and Evidence of the Passage of Abraham Lincoln from Harrisburg, Pa., to Washington, D.C. on the 22d and 23d of February, 1861* (Chicago: Republican Print, 1868).

Pinkerton, Allan, *The Spy of the Rebellion* (New York: G. W. Carlton & Company, 1884).

Pitman, Benn, ed., *The Assassination of President Lincoln and the Trial of the Conspirators* (Cincinnati-New York: Moore, Wilstach & Baldwin, 1865).

Poore, Benjamin Perley, *Perley's Reminiscences of Sixty Years in the National Metropolis* (Philadelphia: Hubbard Brothers, 1886).

Radcliffe, George L. P., *Governor Thomas H. Hicks of Maryland and the Civil War,* Ph. D. Dissertation (Baltimore: The Lord Baltimore Press, 1901).

Rice, Allen Thorndike Rice, *Reminiscences of Abraham Lincoln by Distinguished Men of His Time* (New York: The North American Review, 1888).

Riddle, Albert G., *Recollections of War Times: Reminiscences of Men and Events in Washington, 1860-1865* (New York: Putnam, 1895).

Rhodehamel, John, and Taper, Louis, eds., *"Right or Wrong, God Judge Me": The Writings of John Wilkes Booth* (Urbana, IL: University of Illinois Press, 1997).

Roscoe, Theodore, *The Web of Conspiracy: The Complete Story of the Men Who Murdered Abraham Lincoln* (Englewood Cliffs, N.J.: Prentice-Hall, Inc., 1959).

Rowan, Richard Wilmer, *The Pinkertons: A Detective Dynasty* (Boston: Little, Brown, and Company, 1931).

Samples, Gordon, *Lust for Fame: The Stage Career of John Wilkes Booth* (Jefferson, N.C.: McFarland & Company, 1982).

Sanders, Gerald, *Abraham Lincoln Fact Book & Teacher's Guide* (New York: Eastern Acorn Press; Eastern National Park & Monuments Association, 1982).

Sandburg, Carl, *Abraham Lincoln: The War Years,* vol. 1 (New York: Harcourt, Brace & Company, 1939).

Scharf, J. Thomas, *History of Baltimore City and County,* 2 vols. (Baltimore: Regional Publishing Co., 1971).

Scharf, J. Thomas, *History of Maryland,* 3 vols. (Hatboro: Tradition Press, 1967 reprint of 1879 edition).

Scharf, J. Thomas, *The Chronicles of Baltimore,* vol. 2 (Baltimore: Turnbull Brothers, 1874).

Schouler, William, *A History of Massachusetts in the Civil War* (Boston: E.P. Dutton & Co., 1868).

Searcher, Victor, *Lincoln's Journey to Greatness: A Factual Account of the Twelve-Day Inaugural Trip* (Philadelphia: John C. Winston Co., 1960).

Seward, Frederick W., "How Lincoln Was Warned of the Baltimore Assassination Plot," in Ward, William Hayes, *Reminiscences of Soldiers, Statesmen and Citizens* (T. Y. Crowell & Company, 1895).

Seward, Frederick W., *Seward at Washington, 1846-1861* (New York: Derby and Miller, 1891).

Smith, Steven L., *John Wilkes Booth Day by Day* (Surratt House Museum, Clinton, MD: Privately Published, 1998).

Snyder, Charles M., *The Lady and the President, The Letters of Dorothea Dix & Millard Fillmore* (Lexington: The University of Kentucky Press, 1975).

St. John Packe, Michael, *The Bombs of Orsini* (London: Secker and Warburg, 1957).

Starr, John W. Jr., *Lincoln & the Railroads* (New York: Dodd, Mead & Company, 1927).

Steers, Edward, *Blood on the Moon: The Assassination of Abraham Lincoln* (Lexington: The University Press of Kentucky, 2001).

Stoddard, William Osborn, *Inside the White House in War Times: Memoirs and Reports of Lincoln's Secretary,* Michael Burlingame, ed. (Lincoln: University of Nebraska Press, 2000).

Stover, John F., *History of the Baltimore and Ohio Railroad* (West Lafayette: Purdue University Press, 1987).

Summers, Festus P., *The Baltimore and Ohio in the Civil War* (New York: G. P. Putnam's Sons, 1939).

Swanberg, W. A., *First Blood: The Story of Fort Sumter* (New York: Charles Scribner's Sons, 1957).

Swanson, James L., *Manhunt: The Twelve Day Chase for Lincoln's Killer* (New York: William Morrow, 2006).

Swett, Leonard, "Conspiracies of the Rebellion," *North American Review* (1887) CXLIV.

Tarbell, Ida M., *The Life of Abraham Lincoln* (New York: Lincoln History Society, 1909).

Taylor, John M., *William Henry Seward* (New York: HarperCollins, 1991).

Taylor, Frank H., *Philadelphia in the Civil War 1861-1865* (Philadelphia: The City, 1913).

Tidwell, William A., *April '65: Confederate Covert Action in the American Civil War* (Kent, OH: The Kent State University Press, 1995).

Tidwell, William A., Hall, James O., and Gaddy, Winfred, *Come Retribution: The Confederate Secret Service and the Assassination of Lincoln* (Jackson, MS: University Press of Mississippi, 1988).

Tiffany, Francis, *Life of Dorothea Lynde Dix* (Boston-New York, Houghton Mifflin Company, 1890).

Townsend, Maclom, ed., *Handbook of United States Political History* (Boston: Lothrop, Lee & Shepard Co., 1905).

Tracy, Gilbert A., ed., *Uncollected Letters of Abraham Lincoln* (Boston-New York: Houghton Mifflin, 1917).

Treese, Loretta, *Railroads of Pennsylvania: Fragments of the Past in the Keystone Landscape* (Mechanicsburg, PA: Stackpole Books, 2003).

Turner, George Edgar, *Victory Road the Rails; The Strategic Place of the Railroads in the Civil War* (Indianapolis: Bobbs-Merrill, 1953).

Turner, Justine G. and Turner, Linda Levitt, *Mary Todd Lincoln: Her Life in Letters* (New York: Kopf, 1972).

U.S. Department of the Interior, *Fort Sumter: Anvil of War, National Park Service Handbook* (Washington, D.C.: Government Printing Office).

U.S. War Department, *The War of Rebellion: A Compilation of the Official Records of the Union and Confederate Armies* (Washington, D.C.: Government Printing Office, 1880–1901).

Villard, Henry, *Lincoln on the Eve of '61*, ed. Harold G. Villard and Oswald Garrison Villard (New York: Alfred Knopf, 1941).

Wall, Bernhardt, *Following Abraham Lincoln, 1809-1865* (New York: The Wise-Parslow Company, 1943).

Walling, George W., *Recollections of a New York City Chief of Police* (Montclair, N.J.: Patterson Smith, 1972; reprint of 1888 printing, New York: Caxton Book Concern, Ltd.).

Wallis, Severn Teackle, *Correspondence Between S. Teackle Wallis, Esq., of Baltimore, and the Hon. John Sherman, of the U.S. Senate, Concerning the Arrest of Members of the Maryland Legislature, and the Mayor and Police Commissioners of Baltimore, in 1861* (Baltimore, 1863).

Washington, John E., *They Knew Lincoln* (New York: E. P. Dutton & Co., 1942).

Weichmann, Louis J., *A True History of the Assassination of Abraham Lincoln and of the Conspiracy of 1865*, ed. Floyd E. Risvold (New York: Knopf, 1975).

White, John H., Jr., *A History of the American Locomotive: Its Development: 1830-1880* (New York: Dover, 1979).

White, John H., Jr., *American Locomotives* (Baltimore: Johns Hopkins University Press, 1997).

Whitney, Henry Clay, *Lincoln the Citizen, Volume One of a Life of Lincoln,* Miller, Marion Mills, ed., (New York: The Baker & Taylor Co., 1908).

Wigfall, Louis T., *Speech of Hon. Louis T. Wigfall, of Texas, in Reply to Mr. Douglas, Delivered in the Senate of The United States, December 11th and 12th, 1860* (Washington: Lemuel Towers, 1860).

Willis, John T., *Presidential Elections in Maryland* (Mt. Airy: Lomond Publications, Inc., 1984).

Wilmer, L. Allison, Jarrett, J.H., Vernon, George W.F., *History and Roster of Maryland Volunteers, War of 1861-5,* Vol. 1 (Baltimore: Guggenheimer, Weil & Co., 1898).

Wilson, Courtney B., and Cunningham, Shawn, *The Baltimore Civil War Museum, President Street Station: A Visitor's Guide* (Baltimore: The Baltimore Civil War Museum – President Street Station Inc., 1997).

Wilson, Douglas, I., Wilson, Terry, eds., *Herndon's Informants: Letters, Interviews, and Statements about Abraham Lincoln* (Urbana, IL, University of Illinois Press, 1998).

Wilson, Rufus Rockwell, *Lincoln in Caricature* (New York: Horizon Press, 1953).

Wilson, William Bender, *History of the Pennsylvania Railroad Company* (Philadelphia: Henry T. Coates & Company, 1899).

Wright, D. Girard, *Address of Mrs. D. Girard Wright, President of the Maryland Division, United Daughters of the Confederacy to the State Convention* (Baltimore, December 7, 1903).

Wright, Mrs. D. Girard, *A Southern Girl in '61: The War-Time Memories of a Confederate Senator's Daughter* (New York: Doubleday, Page & Company, 1905).

Young, Robin, *For Love & Liberty: The Untold Civil War Story of Major Sullivan Ballou & His Famous Love Letter* (New York: Thunder's Mouth Press, 2006).

ARTICLES

Arnold, Isaac Newton, "The Baltimore Plot to Assassinate Abraham Lincoln," *Harper's New Monthly Magazine*, vol. XXXVII (New York: Harper & Brothers, Publishers, June-November 1868).

Flory, Claude R. "Garman, Black, and the "Baltimore Plot," *Pennsylvania Magazine of History and Biography* (January 1970).

Harper's Weekly, March 9, 1861.

Hall and Mione, "John Wilkes Booth: The Money Trail," *Lincoln Herald*, Vol. 105 No. 1 (Spring 2003).

Hall, James O. "The First War Department Telegram about Lincoln's Assassination," *Surratt Courier* 22 No. 1 (January 1997).

Hanna, A. J., "The Escape of Confederate Secretary of War John Cabell Breckinridge, As Revealed by His Diary," *Register of the Kentucky State Historical Society,* Volume 37, Number 121 (October, 1939, Reprint).

Holzer, Harold, "The Photograph that Made Lincoln President," *Civil War Times* (Nov/Dec 2006).

Hynd, Alan, "The Case of the Plot that Failed," *True Magazine* (August 1950).

Lanis, Edward Stanley, "Allen [sic] Pinkerton and the Baltimore 'Assassination' Plot Against Lincoln," *Maryland Historical Magazine*, Vol. XLV, No. 1 (March 1950).

Moffett, Cleveland, "How Allan Pinkerton Thwarted the First Plot to Assassinate Lincoln," *McClure's Magazine* (November 1894).

"Monthly Summary of Events," Frank Leslie's New Family Magazine, in *The United States Democratic Review,* vol. 42:1 (New York: Langley, July 1858).

Stone, Charles P. (Gen.), "Washington on the Eve of War, Battles and Leaders of the Civil War," *Century Magazine*, vol. I, p. 24 (July 1883).

Tilton, Clint Clay, "First Plot Against Lincoln," *National Republic* (February 1936).

Van Deusen, Glyndon, "Seward and Lincoln: The Washington Depot Episode," *University of Rochester Library Bulletin,* vol. 20, no. 3 (Spring 1965).

Washburn, Elihu B., "Abraham Lincoln in Illinois," *North American Review* 141 (1885).

NEWSPAPERS AND JOURNALS

The Atlas & Argus (Albany)

The Atlanta Southern Confederacy

The Boston Commonwealth

The Baltimore Sun
The Charleston Daily Courier
The Cleveland Plain Dealer
Daily Evening Journal (Chicago)
The Indianapolis Daily Journal
Journal of the Convention of the State of Arkansas
The New York Daily Graphic
The New York Herald
The New York Times
The New York Tribune
The New York World
The Philadelphia Evening Daily Bulletin
The Philadelphia Inquirer
The Pittsburgh Daily Gazette
The Richmond Daily Dispatch

LIBRARIES, MUSEUMS, AND HISTORICAL SOCIETIES

Atlanta History Center
Baltimore Civil War Museum – President Street Station, Baltimore, MD
B & O Railroad Museum, Baltimore, MD
Cobb County Public Library
Dauphin County Historical Society
Emory University Robert W. Woodruff Library
Emory University Law Library
Ford's Theatre Museum
Fulton County Public Library
Historical Society of Pennsylvania
Hunt Library, Carnegie Mellon University
Huntington Library
Library of Congress
Maryland Historical Society
National Archives
Senator John Heinz Pittsburgh Regional History Center
Willard Hotel Museum

INDEX

abolition, abolitionism, 3, 6, 12, 75–77, 129, 202, 380, 395

abolitionists, 6, 72, 73, 76, 113, 178

act of secession, 24, 91, 335, 337, 374, 474

Adams Express Company, 145, 187, 188, 440

Alabama, 6, 10, 12, 26, 52, 75, 122, 145, 165, 281, 362, 399, 402, 480, 486

Albany, New York, 33, 40, 71, 72, 81, 82, 88, 117, 118, 129–141, 143, 147, 157, 184, 290, 304, 309, 320, 330, 367, 370, 371, 375, 406, 413, 416, 417, 419, 420, 424, 426–428, 437, 439, 449, 466, 467, 468, 469, 471, 472

Alexander, William, 166, 321

Allegheny City, Pennsylvania, 106, 107

Allen, E. J., (alias of Allan Pinkerton), 251, 268, 275, 288, 338, 374, 461

Alliance, Ohio, 108

American Revolution, 21, 74, 392, 470

American Telegraph Company, 144, 158, 159, 181, 182, 207, 208, 210, 228, 234, 260, 311, 456

Annapolis, Maryland, 61, 62, 95, 97, 143, 173, 341, 353, 361, 362, 421, 430

Appleby farm, 11, 143

Arizona, 53

armed guards, 99, 249, 447

Arnold, Sam, 74, 379, 389, 390, 489

assassinate, assassination, 1–3, 14, 16, 18, 25, 35, 37–39, 56, 70, 88, 89, 93, 95–97, 118, 123–125, 128, 135, 146, 157, 164, 171–175, 179, 180, 183, 190, 191, 195, 219, 220, 249, 258, 261, 262, 270, 271, 277, 278, 280, 291–293, 295, 297, 303, 304, 309, 310, 313, 329, 337, 340, 342, 344–346, 354, 356, 360, 364, 365, 367, 370, 372, 378, 380–382, 386, 391–393, 396, 403, 417, 424, 427, 434, 440–442, 444, 445, 450, 452, 459, 466, 468, 473, 476–478, 480, 481, 483, 486, 489

assassination plots, 172, 180, 278, 313, 440–442, 445, 450

assassins, 2, 3, 29, 31, 35, 45, 65, 128, 129, 147, 150, 190, 210, 228, 236, 240, 249, 255, 256, 262, 265, 266, 277, 284, 293, 297, 299, 327, 328, 344, 366, 367, 369, 371, 415, 468, 473

Astor House, New York, 151, 153–157, 160, 168, 180, 431, 458

Atzerodt, George, 364, 389, 390, 396

Baltimore, Maryland, passage through, 15, 25, 28, 31, 32, 35, 41, 59, 61, 110, 138, 143, 163, 176, 177, 180, 182, 183, 185, 189, 190, 192, 193, 196, 197, 206, 207, 211, 219, 220, 224, 225, 227–231, 238, 249, 253, 259, 260, 269, 272, 277, 278, 284, 288, 290, 291, 302, 304–306, 309–311, 313, 317, 319, 336–338, 341, 346, 347, 349, 352, 357, 359–361, 365, 373, 395, 433, 448, 452, 455, 459

Baltimore and Ohio Railroad, 15, 41–43, 128, 183, 213–214, 254, 260, 264, 267, 325, 357, 425

Baltimore City Council, 29, 214

Baltimore mob, 30, 121, 174, 230, 336, 347, 348, 349, 350, 356, 368, 369, 479, 484

Baltimore Plot leadership, 256

ACKNOWLEDGMENTS

So many people contributed to this book that it is difficult to know where to begin. On the other hand, it is quite easy. My parents, George and Judith Kline, taught me early in life the merits of persistence and hard work, diligent study, the power of words, and the beauty of reading. Through no fault of theirs, these lessons sunk in fairly late in the game. To them I dedicate this book.

To my great friend, teacher, coworker, and running pal Russell S. Bonds, author of the magnificent *Stealing the General,* who fired the engine for this work and helped keep it going, meticulously reviewing early drafts and offering valuable suggestions for much needed improvement. Russ tirelessly answered my numerous questions about conducting historical research in general, and the War of the Rebellion in particular. On many occasions he appeared at my door, smile on his face, holding in his hands a book or document or website that would be key to my research.

Thanks to Lisa Lazar, Reference Librarian at the Senator John Heinz Pittsburgh Regional History Center, who provided great assistance in researching *The Daily Pittsburgh Gazette,* and located photographs of the Monongahela House. To Jennifer Bator, and Lauren Paige Zabelsky, Photographic Service Coordinator, also of the Pittsburgh Regional History Center; Jennifer, for valuable research and reproduction guidance and introducing me to the Pittsburgh Historical Magazine, and Lauren, for assisting greatly with photographic reproductions of *The Daily Pittsburgh Gazette,* which enabled me to enlarge and read the fine print, always essential for a fastidious lawyer. Jack Gumbrecht, of the Historical Society of Pennsylvania, conducted research relating to Lincoln's stay in Philadelphia, the hotels there, Samuel Felton, and assisted greatly in gathering and working with the Felton Papers. Lorette Treese, author of *Railroads of Pennsylvania* and Archivist at Bryn Mawr College, provided difficult to find information and the key reference concerning the Edwin Black and Daniel Garman accounts. The professional staff at the Huntington Library, including Juan Gomez, Catherine Wehrey, Meredith Berbée, Bert Rinderle, and Laura Stalker, assisted me with the Ward Hill Lamon Papers. Special thanks to Karen Lightner, Curator, Print & Picture Collection at the Free Library of Philadelphia, who sent useful information concerning the photographs of Lincoln taken at the flag raising ceremony in Philadelphia. To the staff of the Emory University Woodruff Library Manuscript, Archives, and Rare Book Library, for being patient, helpful, and demonstrating the utmost respect for the historical treasures they gave me the privilege to inspect. Ms. Evelyn L. James, of the Historical Society of Dauphin County, Harrisburg, PA, provided the image and historical information concerning the Jones House and Mr. Lincoln's brief visit to Harrisburg. David Angerhofer, Archivist at the Maryland Historical Society in Baltimore, gave kind assistance with the Thomas H. Hicks collection. Lia Apodaca, Manuscript Reference Librarian at the Library of Congress, Washington, D.C., helped greatly with making use of the Pinkerton collection. Ms. Gloria E. Henning, Periodicals Specialist at the Hunt Library, Carnegie Mellon University, provided invaluable assistance in conducting online research of the *New York Times* using the ProQuest database. Ms. Joan L. Chaconas, at the Surratt House Museum, James O. Hall Research Center, sent portions of Arthur F. Loux's privately published *John Wilkes Booth Day by Day.* Ms. Ann K. Sindelar, Reference Supervisor, Western Reserve Historical Society, went beyond the call of duty to locate and provide a photo of the *Dean Richmond.* Sincere thanks to Mr. Jeff Korman, Manager of the Maryland Department at the Enoch Pratt Free Library in Baltimore for his assistance in securing the permissions and a high resolution image of the beautiful Cator Print of Baltimore for the back jacket. Thanks to all the helpful library assistants at the Merchant's Walk Branch of the Cobb County Library, for all their help in solving the mysteries of the WorldCat library system and obtaining numerous obscure references through interlibrary loan. Special thanks to Ms. Lajoie Y. Madison, Library Assistant in the Georgia Room at the Cobb County Library Main Branch, for her patient assistance in helping me use those infernal microfilm readers.

Thanks, too, to those associated with Westholme Publishing, including Mr. Tracy Dungan, for preparing the wonderful maps, and patiently and good-naturedly dealing with my requests for revisions throughout the production process, Jennifer Shenk, my editor extraordinaire, for catching innumerable mistakes on top of her terrific copy editing, Trudi Gershenov for her wonderful book jacket, and my publisher, Bruce Franklin, who wore many hats throughout the process—agent, mentor, coach, editor, counselor, and most of all, friend.

My wife Denise and my children Elizabeth and Kevin were forced to endure countless hours, then weeks, then months, then years of my inattention as I sat cloistered in my study while researching, then writing, then rewriting this book. Their patience and understanding put me forever in their debt. I owe you the most valuable thing a husband and father can give to his family other than more of his unconditional love—more of his undivided time.